Chester Morris

Chester Morris
His Life and Career

SCOTT ALLEN NOLLEN *with*
YUYUN YUNINGSIH NOLLEN

McFarland & Company, Inc., Publishers
Jefferson, North Carolina

ALSO BY SCOTT ALLEN NOLLEN AND FROM MCFARLAND

Takashi Shimura: Chameleon of Japanese Cinema (2019), *Abbott and Costello on the Home Front: A Critical Study of the Wartime Films* (2009; paperback 2019), *The Making and Influence of* I Am a Fugitive from a Chain Gang (2016), *Three Bad Men: John Ford, John Wayne, Ward Bond* (2013), *Robert Louis Stevenson: Life, Literature and the Silver Screen* (1994; paperback 2012), *Louis Armstrong: The Life, Music and Screen Career* (2004; paperback 2010), *Paul Robeson: Film Pioneer* (2010), *Robin Hood: A Cinematic History of the English Outlaw and His Scottish Counterparts* (1999; paperback 2008), *Boris Karloff: A Critical Account of His Screen, Stage, Radio, Television and Recording Work* (1991; paperback 2008), *Warners Wiseguys: All 112 Films That Robinson, Cagney and Bogart Made for the Studio* (2008), *Sir Arthur Conan Doyle at the Cinema: A Critical Study of the Film Adaptations* (1996; paperback 2005), *Jethro Tull: A History of the Band, 1968–2001* (2002), *The Boys: The Cinematic World of Laurel and Hardy* (1989; paperback 2001)

Frontispiece: Chester Morris in his Beverly Hills home (early 1930s).

LIBRARY OF CONGRESS CATALOGUING-IN-PUBLICATION DATA

Names: Nollen, Scott Allen, author. |
Nollen, Yuyun Yuningsih, 1979– author.
Title: Chester Morris : his life and career /
Scott Allen Nollen with Yuyun Yuningsih Nollen.
Description: Jefferson, North Carolina : McFarland & Company, Inc.,
Publishers, 2020 | Includes bibliographical references and index.
Identifiers: LCCN 2019049228 | ISBN 9781476677293 (paperback : acid free paper) ∞
ISBN 9781476638393 (ebook)
Subjects: LCSH: Morris, Chester. | Actors—United States—Biography. |
Magicians—United States—Biography. | Labor movement—
United States—History—20th century.
Classification: LCC PN2287.M69985 N65 2020 | DDC 792.02/8092 [B]—dc23
LC record available at https://lccn.loc.gov/2019049228

BRITISH LIBRARY CATALOGUING DATA ARE AVAILABLE

**ISBN (print) 978-1-4766-7729-3
ISBN (ebook) 978-1-4766-3839-3**

© 2020 Scott Allen Nollen with Yuyun Yuningsih Nollen.
All rights reserved

*No part of this book may be reproduced or transmitted in any form
or by any means, electronic or mechanical, including photocopying
or recording, or by any information storage and retrieval system,
without permission in writing from the publisher.*

Front cover: Chester Morris in a publicity still
for the 1936 film *They Met in a Taxi*

Printed in the United States of America

*McFarland & Company, Inc., Publishers
Box 611, Jefferson, North Carolina 28640
www.mcfarlandpub.com*

For Ariskia and Julio

Table of Contents

Preface by Yuyun Yuningsih Nollen — 1
Introduction by Scott Allen Nollen — 3

1. Magic Lad of the Morris Family — 7
2. A Dignified Life in Hollywood? — 17
3. *The Big House* — 35
4. *King for a Night* — 69
5. *Public Hero Number 1* — 97
6. *Flight from Glory* — 124
7. *Meet Boston Blackie* — 152
8. *Aerial Gunner* — 173
9. Boston Blackie Leaves Hollywood — 214
10. *Unchained* — 224
11. Double-Breasted Suits to *Blue Denim* — 236
12. From *Naked City* to *Route 66* — 243
13. The Last Day of the Play — 255
14. Requiem for a Working Actor — 265

Appendix A: Chester Morris Filmography — 267
Appendix B: Television Programs — 285
Appendix C: Radio Programs — 298
Appendix D: Stage Performances — 303
Appendix E: Films Announced for Chester Morris but Produced with Another Actor — 308
Chapter Notes — 310
Sources and Bibliography — 315
Index — 319

Preface
by Yuyun Yuningsih Nollen

This book about Chester Morris was truly unexpected. I hadn't considered being involved in contributing to a book until after I married a writer.

In the past, having always lived on Java, I was really interested in the outside world of other people's habits, languages, music and films, but I never had much knowledge of the older films.

Learning about the classic films has been, as Chester would say, "wonderful." Being introduced to so many great films has made me fascinated, especially in the performers, one of the most appealing being Chester Morris.

The first of his films I saw, *King for a Night* (1933), became one of my favorites. His character, a young son and brother who loves his family enough to sacrifice himself for the younger sister, is remarkable. I also enjoy this film because of the small role played by the always entertaining Warren Hymer, one of the first classic actors with whom I became familiar.

Chester's "Boston Blackie" film series followed. His former thief turned private detective always is accused of committing crimes by Inspector Farraday, but equally adored by his funny little friend, "The Runt," who tells him, "I love you more than anything in this world." Blackie and Runt always solve mysteries, making Farraday regret his accusations.

As I became interested in Chester Morris, my many questions prompted my husband to reply, "We may as well write a book about this underrated actor and fascinating man. No one ever has, and it is much needed." He asked me to be his collaborator, especially his research associate, which helped complete this book in record time.

Chester's physical presence (especially his sharp eyes) impressed me immediately, but being involved in the research and watching the films made me astonished at the range of this multi-talented actor, who had many qualities of which few people are aware. He was very versatile, capable of playing "good," "bad" and, particularly, the shades of gray—even two characters in the same film.

The character I really admire, in *I Promise to Pay* (1937), is a husband and father who loves his wife and child to the point of having to deal with criminal moneylenders. This unusual character, unlike others we often encounter in films, helps solve a problem without resorting to force or violence.

In the course of researching and writing the book, we both learned that Chester Morris truly was a loving husband and father. He was visited on film sets by his family, and, when not shooting, always spent his time with them, often taking them on vacation. He publicly praised and demonstrated affection for his wife, even in the presence of other women, which is something most husbands (in my experience) don't usually do.

Besides stage, film, radio and television work, Chester also was skilled at magic, which he often demonstrated in live shows, including several years of volunteer performances for the U.S. armed forces. He also was a skilled pianist, and his characters play the violin and accordion, respectively, in *Sky Giant* (1938) and *No Hands on the Clock* (1941).

Another of Chester's favorite hobbies was making amateur films, short "documentaries" about the activities of family and friends, and even one silent comedy production of which he was particularly proud. Dropping his usual humble persona on this one occasion, he was pleased to credit himself as player, writer, producer and director!

Introduction
by Scott Allen Nollen

Prior to this volume, nothing book-length had been published on the fascinating life and 53-year stage, film, radio, television and magic career of Chester Morris, scion of a prominent theatrical family and one of the pioneer actors of the Hollywood "talkie revolution." His story, researched entirely from previously untapped primary sources, provides a look, not only at the achievements of an individual artist, but also the innovative cultural context in which he worked and, to a certain extent, helped to develop. The writing of this book commemorates the centennial of Morris' first professional acting role on Broadway in 1918.

To reconstruct the life and career of an individual, framed within its historical context, the biographer hopes to discover as many primary sources as possible. Fortunately, many have become available in electronic form during recent years. Whenever possible, Chester's story is told in his own words, gleaned from contemporary interviews and features published in newspapers and the many trade and fan publications that were ubiquitous during cinema's "golden age." Excerpts from contemporary reviews also provide a look at how his work was received during his career. Therefore, this only book on Chester Morris, a chronological documentary history, is a wholly original work.

It also is a necessary work about a lifelong, dedicated and versatile actor, once under contract to the great Broadway impresario, playwright and composer George M. Cohan, who stood at the forefront of the talkie revolution with an Academy Award nomination in *Alibi* (1929), his Hollywood debut, and later became a household name as one of the most popular film series characters, Boston Blackie, during the early 1940s. During this period, he also was recognized for "doing his part" by performing as a magician in nearly 400 USO-Camp Shows for military personnel throughout the nation, participating in War Bond sales drives and starring in heroic roles reflecting the home-front mandate of President Franklin D. Roosevelt's Office of War Information (OWI).

Due to the lack of serious evaluation of Chester's career, some film buffs have assumed that he "never quite hit the big time." This is only one of several incorrect assumptions that have proliferated for decades. The fact that, at the dawn of his film career, he played the male lead to such top female stars as Loretta Young, Dolores Costello, Norma Shearer, Sylvia Sidney, Carole Lombard, Joan Blondell, Jean Harlow and Jean Arthur is solid proof that he probably had nowhere to go but *down* as he continued working in Tinseltown.

Because of his decision to forgo big-screen roles following the low-budget science-fiction/horror thriller *The She-Creature* (1956), and not appearing in another until his final, posthumously released film, *The Great White Hope* (1970), in favor of returning to his first love, the stage, and exploring a wider range of roles on television, Chester has been written off as "washed up" by the mid–1950s. (At least one Hollywood journalist tried to declare his career moribund as early as mid–1930.) Nothing could be further from the truth, as is the widely believed myth that he committed suicide when he took an overdose of barbiturate sleeping pills in September 1970, when he was continuing tirelessly to work as a professional performer every day.

The life and career of Chester Morris make for an *interesting* story about succeeding in the competitive, cutthroat culture of Hollywood and functioning as a dedicated professional in a precarious occupation providing very little security, a subject he often addressed in interviews. At one point, he was one of the biggest, most admired and likable stars, whose good friends made up a veritable "who's who" of Hollywood.

He was a versatile actor playing a wide array of characters in every possible medium: stage, film, radio and television, all of which require a different style. His live performances also encompassed one-man personal appearances and hundreds of shows as the most celebrated amateur magician in the film industry. In 1966, a journalist at the *Spokane Daily Chronicle* called him "one of the most continuously successful actors of them all."[1]

Cognizant that he never attained "job security," Chester worked from February 1918 until his final day in September 1970, taking every possible avenue: stage (Broadway, local and touring companies); film (silent features, sound features and shorts); radio (roles and as himself); television (roles and as himself; including numerous game-shows and the very first "reality show") and personal appearances (both amateur and professional, including an English music hall tour).

During his Hollywood film career, one aspect of his versatility was the duality he brought to many of his characterizations. Some characters are morally ambiguous, others use an outward persona to mask their true identities; and, in one film, he plays twin brothers, one "good" and the other "evil." During the 1930s, duality was a popular cinematic element. "Jekyll and Hyde" characters were effectively played by, most obviously, Fredric March (in his Academy Award-winning performance) and Boris Karloff, who also was one of the talented actors who successfully played twin or related characters (in a group including Edward G. Robinson, Stan Laurel and Oliver Hardy, Ronald Colman and Louis Hayward).

One lengthy retrospective on Chester's career, by screenwriter DeWitt Bodeen (*Cat People* [1942], *I Remember Mama* [1948], *Billy Budd* [1962]), was published by *Films in Review* in 1980. Displaying the same intelligence that permeates his film scripts, Bodeen opens his article with "Hollywood will never again see an actor who so consistently behaved with the professionalism that ruled Chester Morris."[2]

Beyond his professional achievements as an artist and entertainer, Chester made significant contributions affecting many people, including his family and friends, countless colleagues who benefited from his labor activism (especially during the early years of the Screen Actors Guild), and thousands, both civilian and military, whom he touched with his wide-ranging volunteer activities, on- and off-stage. The facts reveal that the world was improved by his presence.

One person can make a difference, and he was one of many from his generation *who did*. Anyone can benefit from his example. Chester was not an obvious promoter, but one with a light touch. More than any other factor, his innate humility is responsible for his relative obscurity.

Chester led a primarily "clean-cut," respectable existence. Save for his professional association with the often less-than-laudable producer-director Roland West, and the grounds on which Suzanne Kilborn Morris' divorce was granted in November 1939, there is no remotely sensationalistic, scandalous or salacious, "Hollywood Babylon"-style material in his history.

Hopefully this unique volume will stand as an indispensable reference on Chester's life and multifaceted career. Readers should come away, not only with a clear understanding of his abilities as an actor, but also as an erudite and well-informed individual who combined natural talent and early exposure to an artistic, professional environment with an insatiable curiosity leading to a lifelong self-education of considerable scope. Like many autodidacts, Chester left school to learn his craft through hard-won experience, both from his colleagues and, as he emphasized, "getting out there and playing the game."

Integral to the story are the lives and careers of Chester's parents, actor-producer William and actress Etta Hawkins Morris; his brothers, writer Gordon and actor Adrian; sister, actor Wilhelmina; and wives, actress Suzanne Kilborn Morris and model Lillian Kenton Morris. Excerpts from contemporary reviews help fill in gaps left by the dozen Chester Morris films that either are "lost" or not available for viewing. Synopses of the films are necessarily included only to the extent required to provide context for analyses of his performances, and especially for the titles that cannot be viewed.

The appendices include the most complete lists of Chester Morris' film and television credits ever assembled. Each title includes basic production personnel and primary cast members. (Seven to eight decades after they were released, one feature and three short films are now included for the first time, as are several television programs in which he was previously unidentified.) Also featured are first-ever comprehensive listings of his radio and stage appearances, which have never been published in either written or electronic form, plus a listing of film roles announced for him that ultimately were played by other actors.

Like filmmaking, this book is the result of necessary collaboration. My wife and collaborator, Yuyun Yuningsih Nollen, and I extend a grateful thank you to Sarah Berry, a world-class Chester Morris admirer, collector and researcher, who kindly provided us with many of his films that previously had been lost from my once-mighty archives during a very difficult relocation to the other side of the globe. Sarah also contributed many excellent research materials and scans of original studio still photographs (several of which are reproduced here) from her private collection.

At age 99, character actor extraordinaire Nehemiah Persoff, still actively writing and painting watercolor landscapes, recalled working with Chester in the 1961 *Naked City* episode "Make-Believe Man." A veteran of both the New York Dramatic Workshop and the Actor's Studio, he once served an as intern to Stella Adler. His recollection of shooting a scene for "Make-Believe Man" suggests that Chester, a professional actor before "The Method" became influential in the United States, used a similar psychological strategy of being "in character," combining internal thoughts and emotions with experiences from external environmental factors.

Yuyun and I also would like to thank the following individuals, who contributed or expressed their interest and support for this project: Pete Arroyo, John F. Colaresi, Robert Cremer, Thomas Kessel, Dorothy Kosich, Kris Marentette, Rose Minenna, Shirley A. Nollen, Vincent Paterno, Gaya Tinmahan, David C. Tucker, Robert Tuttle, Rocco Verdico, Alfredo Martin Villanueva and my longtime friend, Valerie Yaros, archivist at the Screen Actors Guild.

1

Magic Lad of the Morris Family

William Henry Morris was born on New Year's Day 1861 at 5 Barton Street in Boston, Massachusetts. His father, Henry Morris (born 1835), and mother, Maria Lloyd Morris (born 1833), both hailed from Ireland (County Kildare and County Kerry, respectively). Of his siblings, three sisters, Elouisa, Mary Esther and Ellen Maria, died in infancy. A fourth sister, Sarah, was born in Massachusetts in January 1863 and died in Manhattan on January 17, 1901.

Barely a teenager, William began his professional acting career in an adaptation of Victorien Sardou's French play *Ferréol* on the stage of the Boston Museum in 1876. Later in his life, Chester remarked,

> My dad … played with Edwin Booth in the Boston Museum famous stock company. Dad was in the resident company, started there when he was a kid. And Mr. Booth and Mr. [Lawrence] Barrett, they would join and play a week with the resident company. The business had all been set … for *Hamlet*. And they knew where Mr. Booth was going to be, and he never even rehearsed with them.
>
> Dad [recalled] watching him one night, and he had two friends backstage with him, and he was telling them some off-color story … and the stage manager said, "Mr. Booth, Mr. Booth—*cue!*"
>
> And he was charming enough to say, "Excuse me," and he went on the stage and did the soliloquy, and he came off and he said, "And then, so and so" … and he picked the story up right from where he'd left off.[1]

On October 21, 1890, William opened in the original run of David Belasco and Henry C. DeMille's *Men and Women* at Proctor's Theatre on Broadway. As William Prescott, he supported Maude Adams, Emmett Corrigan and Etta Hawkins.

In 1891, William, introduced by Belasco, married Etta, born Henrietta Luna Hawkins in Aurora, Illinois, to Swiss immigrant Anna Gutherza and Illinois native William Delos Hawkins, on August 21, 1865. Earlier, Etta had appeared in the original productions of Belasco's *May Blossom* (1884) and Henry C. DeMille and Charles Barnard's *The Main Line; or, Rawson's Y* (1886), directed by Belasco, on Broadway. For a time, Anna and William Hawkins took care of Henry C. and Beatrice DeMille's young sons, William C. and Cecil B., while their parents were away on tour in the Bronson Howard play *The Young Mrs. Winthrop*, in which Etta played the ingenue.

William and Etta's first child, Lloyd Gutherz Morris, was born in Manhattan on October 29, 1892. Six years later, a second boy, Gordon, was born on November 6, 1898. Little more than 15 months passed before John Chester Brooks Morris arrived on February 26, 1901. Following the tragic death of Lloyd at age nine on January 26, 1902, a daughter, Wilhelmina, was born (nearly nine months later, to the day) on October 22, 1902. A fourth son, Adrian, was born on January 12, 1907, at the new family home at 63 Elm Avenue in Mount Vernon, Westchester County, New York.

During Chester's childhood, William continued his Broadway career, playing a major role in the National Theatre Company's production of Shakespeare's *Much Ado About Nothing* (1904) at the Princess Theatre. He followed the Bard with roles in the original runs of Rupert Hughes' melodrama *The Triangle* (1906) at the Manhattan Theatre, William J. Hurlbut's drama *The Writing on the Wall* (1909) at the Savoy Theatre, and David Belasco's production of Leo Ditrichstein's comedy *Is Matrimony a Failure?* (1909–1910) at the Belasco Theatre.

On May 11, 1907, Etta and two other women were arrested at a "bucket shop" where illegal stock-market business allegedly was being transacted at 1 Newark Street in Hoboken, New Jersey. The establishment was well furnished, with an outside office used by men, while a similarly posh "parlor" was reserved for the women.

G.L. White, reputed proprietor of the establishment, Henry Marshall, a telegraph operator, Etta, and her female cohorts, Mary Jones and Anna Sellars, were among the 11 "prisoners ... locked up in default of bail" at Hoboken Police Headquarters. While Jones and Sellars revealed their Manhattan addresses, Etta refused, "hint[ing] that she was highly connected." All three women were reported being "handsomely dressed, and all had small rolls of money."[2]

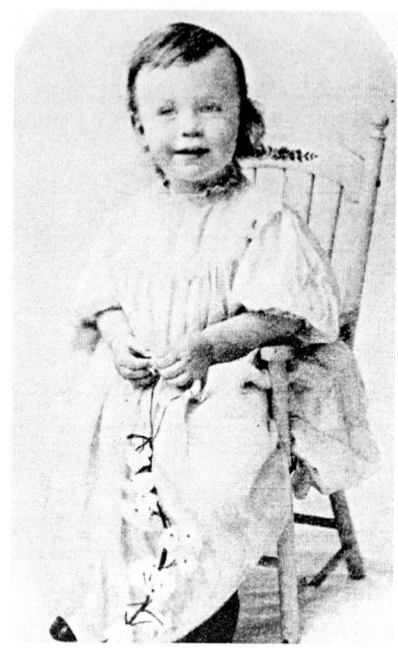

John Chester Brooks Morris, New York City (1902).

In 1910, the Morrises' maid, 23-year-old Katie King, who had immigrated at age seven with her parents from Ireland to New York, was living with the family in Mount Vernon. During this time, Chester, who always had displayed artistic ability, took piano lessons for six months on the baby grand in the front room. He especially demonstrated aptitude for sonatas, including those of Ludwig van Beethoven and Frédéric Chopin, which, according to Adrian, he played "better than his teacher."[3]

On Chester's 10th birthday, his father was playing Dr. Dallas in David Belasco's original production of Hermann Bahr and Leo Ditrichstein's *The Concert* (1910–1911) at the Belasco Theatre. For the remainder of the decade, William kept busy in a dozen more Broadway plays. William A. Brady's production of writer-director Philip Bartholomae's comedy *Little Miss Brown* (1912) was followed by his own production of Cosmo Hamilton's *The Blindness of Virtue* (1912), Brady's production of Owen Davis' *The Family Cupboard* (1913–1915), Byron Ongley and Emil Nyitray's *He Comes Up Smiling* (1914), Avery Hopwood's *Sadie Love* (1915–1916), the first production of Max Marcin's *Cheating Cheaters* (1916–1917), Belasco's production of John Meehan's *The Very Minute* (1917), Michael Morton's *On with the Dance* (1917), Valverde Musical Enterprises' revue *The Land of Joy* (1917–1918), Jack Larric and Gustav Blun's *A Sleepless Night* (1919) and Edward Locke's comedy *The Dancer* (1919).

William appeared in his first motion picture, the Victor Film Company's short *The Heart of the Night Wind*, distributed by the Universal Film Manufacturing Company on November 27, 1914. Directed by Walter Edwin, the film also featured Charles Ogle, who eventually appeared in over 300 films but is best remembered as the first screen actor to play Mary Shelley's Monster, in the Edison Manufacturing Company's 16-minute "adaptation" of *Frankenstein* (1910).

William received top billing for playing the title character in Thanhouser-Mutual's four-reeler *Monsieur Lecoq* (1915), based on the novel by Èmile Gaboriau. In the Quality-Metro Pictures production of Shakespeare's *Romeo and Juliet* (1916), for which the 33-year-old Francis X. Bushman doubled as director and Romeo, William played Abraham in a cast also including Fritz Leiber and Helen Dunbar. Solax Film Company's four-reel comedy *The Ocean Waif* (1916), directed by Alice Guy-Blanché and costarring Carlyle Blackwell, Doris Kenyon and Edgar Norton, marked his final film appearance until 1930.

Chester's interest in playing the piano waned, and his first great ambition was to become a magician. One day, his mother allowed him to skip a session at Mount Vernon's Lincoln Elementary school to see his idol Harry Houdini perform in New York. Fifty years later, he vividly remembered,

> He was playing at the Bronx Opera House.... I never met Houdini, but later I became quite good friends with Bess, his wife, on the [West] Coast. And I was telling her about this incident, and she laughed.... The afternoon that I saw Houdini, he had accepted a challenge from the Ebling Brewing Company in the Bronx, to get out of a hogshead of beer. So, the barrel had been brought on the stage. And, of course, for every challenge that he accepted, it was stipulated that he must have either a barrel or a case—or whatever he was to get out of—he must have that in his dressing room 24 hours before the actual performance. So, nobody knew what he did do, how it was gimmicked.
>
> But … the audience came to see him get out of this thing, and they had all the people from the Ebling Brewing Company, and they stood there with the big cans of beer, and they filled the hogshead. And Houdini came out in his funny little Keystone Cop bathing suit … and he got in the barrel, and they clamped the top on and they locked it, and they put the cabinet around. And he had a man there with a watch. If he wasn't out in four minutes, he was to break through … the fellow with the axe. And the music playing *forte*, and plenty of brass.
>
> What he used to do … his own apparatus, he was out in half a second, and he used to read a book in the cabinet. And he'd let this tension build and build, until he thought the audience couldn't stand any more, and then he'd come through, all out of breath.
>
> On this special day, Bessie told me that he had never accepted a beer challenge before. And Houdini was a very fastidious man, kept himself in great trim, didn't smoke, never drank. And the minute he got in the hogshead of beer, he absorbed all this alcohol through the pores. He got out all right, but he was *stinking drunk*! And he was reeling, and I remember, I told her the effort it must have taken to get out of that barrel, because he reeled all over the stage. She said, "He certainly did, Chester. He tried hot coffee and Worchestershire Sauce, and everything else, to sober him up."[4]

On February 16, 1913, Chester's 12th birthday, he received the tools necessary for an aspiring prestidigitator. He recalled,

> My dad gave me one of those little Mysto Magic sets that A.C. Gilbert used to make in Bridgeport. They were pretty cheap things, but that led to a larger set the next Christmas, and finally I was up to the $50 set. And then it became a real hobby.[5]

Armed with his gear and billing himself as "The Mysterious Morris," he began staging shows for friends in the family home. Adrian served as his assistant, until a grave error led to his "contract" being "terminated." Little brother later admitted, "in the middle of the 'egg in the hat' trick, the egg broke, on my head. The audience laughed, the spell had broken. Mysterious Morris was mysterious no longer."[6] Chester said,

> Dad sneaked into the basement and I didn't see him. After it was all over he informed me that if I ever did any of that Mysterious Morris stuff again he'd disown me. I must have been pretty terrible. The kids guessed what I was going to do before I did it and told me immediately afterwards just how I'd done it.[7]

Chester and Adrian attended the same dancing school. While the former was assigned to the Saturday night junior class, little brother was relegated to the "Master and Misses" group held earlier in the afternoon. Adrian later remembered,

> I shall never forget the reception when I took a particular little lady to my class in the afternoon, and he took the same little woman to his class at night. He told me afterwards that he rather thought I had the advantage that day, because the girl was so tired by evening she couldn't dance.[8]

The brothers were not hampered by the sibling rivalry affecting so many families. Adrian said, "Chester and I unfortunately always fell in love with the same girl. But unlike most kids that age, we never quarreled about it—never permitted petty jealousies to mar our friendship."[9]

On February 7, 1917, 18-year-old Gordon Morris made his Broadway debut as an architect in a revival of William Vaughn Moody's drama *The Great Divide*, which ran for 53 performances at the Lyceum Theatre, where it closed the following month. Between October 1917 and May 1918, he would appear in two original Broadway productions, Monckton Hoffe's *Anthony in Wonderland*, which closed at the Criterion Theatre after just seven performances, and Hubert Osborne's *April*, playing 31 times at the Punch and Judy Theatre.

When the United States entered World War I in 1917, Chester, only 16 years old, visited Mount Vernon Mayor Edwin M. Fisk, to see if there was any way he could join the American Expeditionary Forces. As his Honor had done for other local underage boys, he appointed Chester a sergeant in the Mount Vernon homeguard. A Democrat, Fisk was defeated by Republican Edward F. Brush later that year. Both men ran for the office on several occasions.

Chester had performed on stage with Mount Vernon's Westchester Players, but William tried to discourage him from following in the family footsteps, insisting that a college education would point toward a career suited to his real strengths. Chester was too restless to commit to four years of formal academic study, but his interest in painting and drawing led to the New York School of Fine and Applied Arts. He particularly enjoyed creating landscapes, calmly turning over to Adrian canvases that occasionally required weeks to complete.

He often spent more time attending plays at a local theater than in class, where he was supposed to be developing his skill for magazine illustration. At 16, after about one month at the school, he began acting professionally, in the seriocomic feature *An Amateur Orphan*, directed by Van Dyke Brooke at the New Rochelle, New York, studio of the Thanhouser Film Corporation and released by the Pathé Exchange on June 3, 1917. Thanhouser was paying $50 per week, a sum that induced Chester to seek more work in lieu of his art studies. He failed to tell his parents about the decision, and when the manager of the Mount Vernon theater ran the film, billing him as "Local Boy Makes Good," William again protested his hasty judgment. "I guess I was pretty bad," he later admitted.[10]

Chester then was cast (in the small role of Dan) by Fort Lee, New Jersey's Goldwyn Pictures Corporation in director William Worthington's *The Beloved Traitor*, released during February 1918. Frank L. Packard's novel, adapted by George Loane Tucker and Kenneth Macgowan, was brought to life by a fine cast of film pioneers, including Mae Marsh, E.K. Lincoln, Hedda Hopper and George Fawcett, produced by Samuel Goldwyn and photographed by George W. Hill.

Eight days before his 17th birthday, on February 18, 1918, Chester, quite handsome with black hair, green eyes, and standing 5'9" (the summit of his height), opened (as Sam

Carter), in support of Lionel Barrymore and Evelyn Archer, in John D. Williams' production of Augustus Thomas' drama *The Copperhead* at the Shubert Theatre. The four-act play, adapted from a story by Frederick Landis, also featuring Doris Rankin and 15-year-old Raymond Hackett, ran for 120 performances, closing that June. The Civil War plot about Milt Shanks (Barrymore), a purported Northern traitor who had worked undercover for the late President Abraham Lincoln to learn the secrets of the pacifistic "Copperheads," was considered by the reviewer for *The New York Times* as "more faithful to the history than to the drama."[11]

The Beloved Traitor (1918): Chester Morris, in his second film, with Mae Murray. Shot by cinematographer George W. Hill, who later directed him in *The Big House* (1930).

Chester later recalled,

> I was 16 years old, and that was the play that made [Lionel] a star. He was great, and we became very close through the years, and I knew Jack [Barrymore] very well. I saw a performance of *Hamlet* of Jack's in New York. And one evening … Doug Fairbanks and Mary Pickford were sitting in the box, and right in the middle of the *Hamlet* soliloquy, Jack said, "And how are things in Pickfair?" and went right on with it.[12]

Hoping for another Broadway assignment, Chester joined a road company performing the Winchell Smith–John E. Hazzard play *Turn to the Right*, for which he confidently billed himself as "The Youngest Leading Man on the American Stage." He next played Sam Disbrow in Peg Franklin's comedy *Thunder*, produced by John Golden at the Criterion Theatre for just 33 performances, opening on September 22, 1919, and closing the following month. Another Broadway comedy, Charles L. Wagner's production of Clare Kummer's *The Mountain Man*, running for 163 performances from December 12, 1921, through April 1922, featured him as Carey, a distant relative of the title character, Aaron Winterfield (Sidney Blackmer).

The Morris household now was being managed by Agnes Jarvis, an Austrian immigrant who had joined them in 1920. But Chester was hardly ever there. In fact, he proved so effective in light fare that the comedy roles continued: Lexington Dalrymple in Martin Brown's *The Exciters* (September 22–October 1922), in which he shared the Times Square Theatre stage with Tallulah Bankhead, Alan Dinehart, Frederick Kerr and Aline MacMahon; and Wallace King in Jack Alicoate's *Extra* (January 23–February 1923) at the Longacre Theatre. For a time, he played the youthful Yank in a touring production of Arthur Goodrich's *So This is London*, but his asking price of $350 per week to appear in the London edition was turned down by George M. Cohan.

In between stage appearances, Chester played Tom O'Hara in Postman Pictures' dramatic feature *Loyal Lives* (1923), distributed by Brooklyn's Vitagraph Company of America, just a short time before the studio was bought by Warner Bros. Mary Carr and William Collier, Jr., also costarred in this Whitman Bennett production directed by Charles Giblyn.

He then teamed up with his family to perform William's original sketch called *All the Horrors of Home*, first at the Palace Theatre and then on the vaudeville circuit. He remembered that the concept resulted from a domestic situation, following a visit from a young neighbor who soon would begin a successful career as a story editor and producer in Hollywood:

> The Morrises were all starving in New York ... and I had a job for the fall, but it was only June. And no one was working. Dad wasn't working, and my brother and sister weren't working. We were paying $400 a month for the apartment. It was pretty dull.
>
> David Selznick, who lived down on the corner, was selling radio. He and his mother and Myron living in this little apartment, and they were broke ... *really* broke. David and my sister, Willy, used to go out a bit, and he was a wonderful guy.... He came in one day, and mother had been playing cards. I was reading a fan magazine, and my kid brother was playing the piano. Nobody was talking to anybody.
>
> The doorbell rang, and we went to the door, and it was Dave Selznick. He had a box of candy that I'm sure he'd picked up off a counter someplace. He presented it to my sister, and mother put the

The Morris Family: From left, Etta Hawkins, Adrian, William, Wilhelmina and Chester, at home in New York City (1924).

cards away, and I put the fan magazine away, and the kid stopped playing the piano. We sat and talked to Dave for about three-quarters of an hour, and Dad sat over in the corner, listening to all this....

Finally, Dave left, and Dad said, "You know, that just bears out a contention of mine that a family never feels the necessity of entertaining themselves." He said, "Now ... I took a play into Lee Shubert to find out if he'd like to do it, and I come home, and no one asked me what Lee Shubert said. And I've sat over here in the corner. Mother was playing cards, you were reading, your brother playing the piano.... But the moment the doorbell rang, and the stranger came in, the cards were put aside, the magazines were dropped, and all activities that had *started*. You were all very interested to know what David Selznick had been doing. I've never seen the family so charming, but not to me."

Well, I started to think about this, and I said, "Dad, we've either got a good three-act play here, or a vaudeville sketch." So, we started to kick this around, and Dad went in his room and he wrote all night. The next morning, he came out at 10 o'clock, and we all gathered, and he read the sketch, which he had titled, "All the Horrors of Home." And he called Mr. [Edward] Albee, who was the head of the Keith-Orpheum circuit, at the Palace Theatre. They were old friends, and he said, "Ed, I've got something I want to read to you."

So, I went with him. We went to Albee's office, and Dad read him the sketch. And Albee said—this was on a Thursday—he said, "Could you open, Will, in Greenpoint, Monday night? Let me see it. But I will only book this sketch with the proviso that your family plays it. Your wife plays the mother, and your daughter and your son." And he said, "I think a thing like this would be good for vaudeville, to have a family do it."

So, we all got up in the parts, and we opened Monday night, and we played that sketch for two and a-half years. It was a comedy ... with a serious undertone. Every father in the audience understood it.[13]

The family hit some historic venues on the Keith-Orpheum circuit, splitting $1,750 per week, during the lengthy *Horrors* tour. "It was so wonderful," Chester admitted. "We played the old Palace twice in its heyday, and that was an event."[14]

In 1925, the tour reached Los Angeles, where the family played two daily shows at the

The William Morris and Family Players: Etta, Wilhelmina, William, Chester and Adrian (1924).

Orpheum. During a second stopover, they performed three times daily at the Hillstreet Theatre. Now hailed as the most commercially successful Hollywood filmmaker of the 1920s, Cecil B. DeMille was reunited with the Morris clan, who decided to forego the remainder of the tour to allow Chester to accept the director's offer to move him into feature films. At the family's own expense, he then spent the next four months on various studio sets, heeding DeMille's suggestion to "observe, study and learn."[15]

Finally, Chester, believing he would be playing a supporting role, instead was cast in the uncredited bit part of a party guest in DeMille's historical fantasy-drama *The Road to Yesterday*, produced by DeMille Pictures Corporation and released by Producers Distributing Corporation in the United States (1925) and Great Britain (1926). Hedging his pitch to William Morris about "putting your boy in pictures," the director characteristically gathered an all-star cast, including Joseph Schildkraut, Jetta Goudal, William Boyd, Vera Reynolds and Trixie Friganza.

Chester is clearly identifiable in two group shots, the first at the 16:30 mark, dressed in tie and tails and smiling, as his character and other revelers at the Paulton home observe the arrival of Kenneth (Schildkraut) and Malena (Goudal). He is on screen for five seconds. Other uncredited roles are played by future Laurel-and-Hardy foil Walter Long and Sally Rand (as another party guest). Portions of the $500,000 production were shot on location at the Grand Canyon.

After completing *The Road to Yesterday*, DeMille happily sailed the high seas during a two-month cruise aboard his yacht. William, realizing that they had been conveniently forgotten, used the paltry remains of the family finances to pay for their travel back to Philadelphia, where the *All the Horrors of Home* tour resumed.

Meanwhile, Gordon Morris, who had left acting behind in favor of playwriting, remained in New York to see his comedy *Jack in the Pulpit* receive the Broadway treatment at the Princess Theatre. Featuring Robert Ames, Helen Carrington and Edna West, the play opened on January 6, 1925, but unfortunately closed after only seven performances.

Chester next hit the road with George M. Cohan, playing Waly Calhoon in the 1926 Chicago run of the impresario's *The Home Towners*. Retained for the Broadway version, produced from August 23 through October 1926 at the Hudson Theatre, he appeared with Welsh actress Peg Entwistle who, in 1932, would tragically jump to her death from the "Hollywoodland" sign in Los Angeles, aged just 24. (Her only film, MGM's *Thirteen Women* [1932], costarring Myrna Loy and Irene Dunne, was released posthumously.)

Before *The Home Towners* closed, Chester, now under contract to Cohan, saw his career suddenly shift from comedy to melodrama when he was recast as Val Parker in Margaret Vernon's *Yellow*. Costarring Hale Hamilton, Selena Royle, Marjorie Wood and Spencer Tracy, the original National Theatre production ran for 135 performances from September 21, 1926, through January 1927.

During the run of the drama, Chester dined out with Cohan. In a feature story about his career prior to accepting the Parker role, *The New York Times* waggishly reported,

> In his eight years on the stage Morris had invariably been cast in heroic parts. So ethically correct, in fact, had been his greasepaint deportment that his repertoire of abstemious young gentlemen comprised every known paragon of virtues, vegetarians included. Hither and thither he went, from one engagement to another, approved by middle-aged ladies who imagined that sex appeal was an outdoor sport practiced by the Boy Scouts of America.
>
> Such was Chester Morris two months ago, fresh from the Chicago run of Cohan's other play, "The Home Towners," and at that time in the throes of rehearsals for the New York opening at the Hud-

1. Magic Lad of the Morris Family

son. The manager meanwhile had placed in rehearsal the melodrama "Yellow," but for want of a suitable actor in the many "sided" part of its central character....

All the horrible details of "Val" Parker's unmoral character put a lump in young Morris' throat. Mentally he saw his past ideals laid on a pyre of brimstone and smolder away in a cloud of profane and unholy smoke. Mr. Cohan noticed his silence and asked the reason, which, it may be stated, is a manager's prerogative.

"It's the part," Morris explained. "You see, this Parker's such a no good guy. I've never played anything like him before. I honestly don't think I can do it." But Mr. Cohan is not the least convincing of mortals, and a few minutes later Morris left for his own apartment with the manuscript of "Yellow" in his pocket and in his heart a conviction that if Cohan were at the helm he could play Iago before an audience of nuns and get applause.[16]

Cohan once told Chester, "Boy, if you'd never done a thing in this world to be proud of, I'd love you because you love your father and mother."[17]

Fellow Manhattan native Suzanne Reddeman Kilborn (born in 1908), who had been acting in stock productions for Paramount, met Chester during a dress rehearsal. Following

Whispering Friends (1928): Broadway poster from George M. Cohan's comedy produced at the Hudson Theatre, featuring Chester Morris as Al Wheeler.

a courtship alternated with stage work, Chester proposed one Saturday evening after a mutual performance. On November 8, 1926, they were married in Rye, New York, and, when word of the marriage became public, Paramount cancelled her contract. On the morning after the wedding, they returned to the theater, only to discover that the show soon would be closing.

As Rocky Morse in *Crime*, by Samuel Shipman and John B. Hymer (father of actor Warren Hymer), Chester shared the stage with Kay Johnson, Jack LaRue, Douglass Montgomery, Sylvia Sidney and future Hollywood director Irving Rapper. Directed by A.H. Van Buren at the Eltinge 42nd Street Theatre, this first run of *Crime* proved a hit, playing for 186 performances from February 22 through August 1927. Chester then joined a road company to perform the play at Chicago's Adelphi Theatre, where he experienced another lengthy run in the Rocky role.

Between melodramas, Chester played Al Wheeler in the original 112-performance run of Cohan's farce *Whispering Friends* (February 20–May 1928) at the Hudson Theatre. William Harrigan, Edith Gresham and Elsie Lawson also costarred under the direction of Sam Forrest.

Chester became a father on June 28, 1928, when Suzanne delivered a healthy baby boy, John Brooks Morris, in New York City. Around this time, film pioneer D.W. Griffith, who had seen Chester on the stage, requested that he appear in a sound screen test. He agreed but never saw the result nor heard from the director again.

For the time being, Chester left thoughts of a film career behind, preferring the steady work and good salaries afforded by the stage. However, closing after only 21 performances, Samuel Shipman and John B. Hymer's *Fast Life*, directed by A.H. Van Buren from September 26 through October 1928 at the Ambassador Theatre, soon would be adapted for the screen. It proved to be Chester's last Broadway play for nearly 30 years, for he answered the call of a Hollywood film offer. Producer Roland West had seen the Griffith sound test and wanted him for the lead in an upcoming important feature.

The stage version of *Fast Life*, produced by A.H. Woods, proved memorable to the Morris family as the only Broadway collaboration between father and sons. While Chester played the aptly named Chester Palmer, William portrayed his old man, Richard Palmer. Adrian appeared, too, as Press Carroll. The impressive cast also included Claudette Colbert, Donald Dillaway and Crane Wilbur.

William's other work on the Great White Way during the 1920s included David Belasco's original production of Jean Archibald's comedy *Call the Doctor* (1920) at the Empire Theatre, his own original production of Graham Moffat's Scottish comedy *Don't Tell* (1920) at the Nora Bayes Theatre, Charles Dillingham's first-run production of William Le Baron's farce comedy *The Scarlet Man* (1921) at Henry Miller's Theatre, and Charles Frohman's first-run production of William (*Sherlock Holmes*) Gillette's melodrama *The Dream Maker* (1921–1922) at the Empire Theatre.

William A. Brady produced and directed the original 125-performance run of Jules Eckert Goodman's drama *Chains* (1923–1924) at the Playhouse Theatre, also featuring Katherine Alexander, Gilbert Emery, Helen Gahagan and Paul Kelly. William costarred with Spencer Tracy, Barlowe Borland, Grant Mitchell, Natalie Moorhead and Nan Sunderland in another farce written and produced by George M. Cohan, *Baby Cyclone*, which ran for 184 performances from September 12, 1927, through February 1928, at Henry Miller's Theatre, just before he joined his sons for the *Fast Life* dates.

2

A Dignified Life in Hollywood?

An adaptation of *Crime*, which had been a hit in New York and Chicago, was considered as Chester's inaugural Hollywood project; but when it was cancelled, he accepted the male lead in Roland West's screen version of the Broadway play *Nightstick*. Written by John Griffith Wray, J.C. Nugent, Elliott Nugent and Elaine Stern Carrington, the original stage production opened at the Selwyn Theatre on November 11, 1927, and ran for 84 performances, closing in January 1928. On April 26, Roland West had announced that he would direct the film, with Camilla Horn and William Boyd in the lead roles.

In July 1928, West, aided by D.W. Griffith, made a distribution deal with United Artists, with a projected release date in December. *Nightstick* was planned as one of United Artists' first "all-talkie" features; and, although the company was rebuilding its stages to be equipped for sound, the film would be distributed in both silent and sound versions.

Considering Chester the "ideal type for the role of the gunman," Chick Williams, West dropped Boyd from the cast, and replaced Horn with Eleanor Griffith.[1] Chester initially resisted a move to Hollywood, but United Artists head Joseph M. Schenck made a deal with Broadway producer A.H. Woods, who released him from the run of *Fast Life*. He recalled how the mask of Tinseltown had to be worn as soon as he arrived in November 1928:

> When I went ... my little boy was four months old. We had a little West Indian nurse for him, and I was advised by the publicity department of United Artists ... that when *The Chief*, the train, arrived in Pasadena, we were to be met, and that Mrs. Morris and the nurse and the baby were to leave the train at the last car. They would have a car to meet them there, but they were not to get off where I was to get off. I came to Hollywood *unmarried*. Nobody could be married in 1928.[2]

Principal photography, with synchronized camerawork and voice recording, was slated to begin on November 15 at United Artists Studios, with rehearsals to start two weeks earlier. Literally learning on his feet, Chester benefited from the tutelage of Australian-born Mae Busch (1891–1946), who had been in films since 1915, playing female leads to Erich von Stroheim, Lon Chaney, Sr., and Stan Laurel and Oliver Hardy, with whom she eventually would appear in 13 shorts and features. Chester said, "Mae Busch worked with me ... [and] gave me many good pointers on screen technique—was glad to do it."[3]

During the early talkie period, when a scene required a character to be fired upon within the camera frame, live bullets still were used to achieve the effect of a surface near the actor being hit. During a scene in which Chick Williams hides in a closet, Chester told West "it would be all right to pepper" the door with lead while he flattened his body on the opposite side of the enclosure. After finishing the scene, he witnessed the "sharpshooter" straining to read the print in a newspaper, and "the fellow couldn't see further than this nose!"[4]

On January 29, 1929, with shooting of the all-talkie version completed, the title was changed to *Alibi*. In March, *Motion Picture* magazine, displaying a strong territorial, sentimental attitude, reported,

> Every stage player has had to learn how to talk. But every screen aspirant cannot learn how to photograph well. Millions are being spent in a frantic building of soundproof stages in Hollywood at this moment. It would cost comparatively little to give the present players a few lessons in voice handling, inflection and tone control. Will they be willing to learn these things? They must, or fall by the wayside. Very few of the younger screen favorites have had stage experience: Anita Page, Alice White, Buddy Rogers, Janet Gaynor, Charlie Farrell, Dolores Costello, Sue Carol. They have come to the screen from college classrooms and debutante parties. Their success is very precious to them. They will work, study, practice scales, do anything to keep their places in the Kleigs. Give them a chance and see.
>
> We protest. This morning we received notice that Vilma Banky has as her new leading man, Robert Montgomery, chosen from fifty New York stage stars instead of from a hundred Hollywood possibilities. Eleanor Griffith, Broadway favorite, arrives to play the leading feminine role in United Artist's "Nightstick." Opposite her is Chester Morris, another importation from the footlights. Two more stage newcomers are in the cast, Regis Toomey and Harry Stubbs....
>
> We protest. Not because we wish to seem inhospitable to these visitors from the footlights; not because we are afraid that they might not succeed on the screen; but because we feel that we have enough talent within the industry now to fill the needs of the talkies, because we know that the fans do not want to lose their film friends, who are our friends, too.
>
> These newcomers are probably nice boys and girls, but they're not home folks. We don't know their fine qualities and failings; we haven't watched them grow from gawky youngsters into famous stars, we don't know any interesting gossip about them; they haven't confided their private joys and griefs to us, shown us their new cars and Italian villas and babies, clasped our hands and wept on our shoulder. They're not our own. And we should be a poor friend if we wouldn't stand up for our own.[5]

Following the *Alibi* wrap, Chester admitted,

> [I]f it hadn't been for Mr. West, and Mae Busch and Pat O'Malley ... I don't know what I would have done. I've been on the stage for ten years. George Cohan turned me from a nice boy into a stage criminal when he gave me the lead in *Yellow*. But stage experience doesn't mean I know anything about pictures....
>
> When I went out on the United Artists' lot ... I was more frightened than I had ever been at any Broadway first night. Up to this time I had heard that all you need to make a good talking picture was a cast of fine actors from the legitimate stage.... You can get the finest actor on Broadway but if he doesn't have that intangible screen personality, he's a flop. Nobody can describe that intangible quality, and nobody knows if he has it until the camera focuses on him.[6]

A March 12 trade preview of *Alibi* at Grauman's Chinese Theatre culminated with Chester and Sue escaping by running down an aisle to an exit behind the screen. He claimed his acting was terrible, that he "never went through such an ordeal," and already had packed his bags to head back to New York aboard the *Chief*. Roland West called the following morning, insisting that he "gave one of the finest performances Hollywood has seen for a long time." As predicted by *The Film Daily* that same day, United Artists responded by offering him a contract..[7]

The New York City premiere was held at the 44th Street Theatre on April 8, when a repeat of the Hollywood "riot" occurred. Adrian, who joined Chester at the screening, recalled,

> I sat with him ... and when it was over most of the audience rushed down to where we were to sing his praises. He just stood there like a great big kid with tears in his eyes. Success—after all his years

Above: Alibi (1929): Chester Morris (left), in his "talkie" debut, as gangster Chick Williams, with Eleanor Griffith and Harry Stubbs [original lobby card]. *Right: Alibi* (1929): Harry Stubbs (left) and Chester Morris (in his Academy Award–nominated performance).

of playing the "sticks"—four-a-day in vaudeville, and every other hardship a struggling actor has to contend with—had fallen on him like a meteor. It was too much for one evening. He went home and cried like a baby.[8]

In his April 10 *Variety* review, "Land" praised Chester's vivid performance:

> From the human interest standpoint, picture belongs to Chester Morris, virile stage juvenile. He comes as a welcome variance from the pretty boys. And he can troupe like the old days. In this picture he is a cruel, cold-blooded gangster, quick to let 'em have the works. When he starts to play more sympathetic roles he should develop as a general fav.... Morris impersonates a clever young rodent with the instincts of a Chinese

brigand. Quick to shoot when his adversary's back is turned, he is a sniveling, groveling coward when cornered himself.[9]

Four days later, *The Film Daily* reported that Chester had agreed to star in a second feature for West.[10] The respected industry publication's review, published on April 14, referred to his performance as "stirring" and the film being "in big money class ... gripping underworld drama with strong opening and closing ... sympathy for the crook is artfully played up in the first half and later swings the other way after you've really begun to root for him."[11] Several reviewers agreed that the film version was a distinct improvement on a "second-rate" play.[12]

Gene Cohn, a writer for the Newspaper Enterprise Association (NEA) Service, was quite enthusiastic:

> The most important event, in my opinion, since the movies learned to talk is Chester Morris.
> Chester Morris was, until a few months ago, a young juvenile of the Broadway stage who could have compiled a volume on the general subject of "bad breaks" and tough luck. His name had never flared in the big lights, nor was he pursued about by managers. The last three plays he had appeared in now rest peacefully in Cain's warehouse.
> Then came one of those accidents of movie discovery ... "Alibi" ... revives hopes in the future of sound pictures and establishes Chet Morris as the find of the year. Oddly enough, it is in certain silent sequences that Morris does his best performing—a fact that gives new zest to the argument that Broadway has a very fair chance of battling Hollywood for supremacy. Certainly in "Alibi," the actors picked from the stage act rings around the recruits lifted by Hollywood from cafeteria counters and photographs.[13]

On Sunday, April 21, a radio adaptation of *Alibi*, directed by West (who also took over Pat O'Malley's role) and starring Chester and Eleanor Griffith, was aired nationwide on 47 stations as an episode of Columbia Broadcasting's *Majestic Theatre of the Air*. The live performance, arranged by United Artist's Warren Nolan, began in New York at 9 p.m. Early on the morning of Tuesday, April 23, Chester, Sue and West headed back to Hollywood.

Three months after expressing resistance toward welcoming stage actors into the movies, *Motion Picture* magazine highly praised *Alibi* and its makers, including the new leading man from Broadway:

> For out and out bang-up entertainment, this screen translation tops 'em all to date.... Director-producer Roland West has contributed several of the most sensationally stirring sequences yet seen in the cinema. It is a very distinct triumph, too, for every member of the cast. Most of these are stage folk especially imported for the film. At least two of these vault in a single bound to front-row spots in the film firmament. Chester Morris, in his first movie [sic], renders a simply superb, subtly shaded characterization which is always thoroughly convincing. To him go premier honors. Next is Regis ("Pat") Toomey in a portrayal of a "smiling cop" which may well set a new style in heroes.[14]

Arguably, it may be best that Toomey's interpretation of undercover cop Danny McGann didn't become a genre archetype. His mannered histrionics, particularly the overplayed slurring of his "drunk" act intended to deceive the gang of veteran criminals, doesn't fool anyone, on or off screen. McGann is at the center of the taskforce to bring down Chick Williams, who, just released from prison, commits a robbery during which a police officer is killed, and then uses his marriage to Joan (Griffith), daughter of Sergeant Pete Manning (Purnell Pratt), as his alibi.

West's method of using the sound format to prolong the histrionics of his actors is prominent during Toomey's death scene, when McGann whines his way through an excruciating close-up as the cop, felled by Williams' bullet, expires on the floor. "I never give a copper an even break!" the gangster announces just before he fires and then flees the scene. Fighting with the other cops in the dark, he rushes onto the roof and jumps to the adjacent building but loses his footing, plummeting spectacularly to his death.

West's visual style, realized by cinematographer Ray June (who faced new technical challenges created by the Movietone optical sound-on-film method) and editor Hal C. Kern, is a cut above that of many talkies released in 1929, and the pre–Warner Bros. gangster elements are at the forefront of the sound crime genre, but much of the acting creates a stilted atmosphere common to the era. Despite some overemphasis on his eyes in close-ups, Chester's believable performance is an impressive starring debut.

West's use of a tracking camera energizes the opening scene, during which Williams is released from prison. This mobility (which would become a visual trademark in his work), coupled with a continual variety of shots and creative angles, sets *Alibi* apart from many early talkies, which, often sacrificing cinematic style for a concentration on *talk*, are little more than filmed plays. A touch of realism is achieved by using only on-screen sources for musical accompaniment, especially in the scenes set in the atmospheric nightclub that serves as Williams' front.

More than three decades after the success of the film, Chester recalled the groundbreaking nature of his character:

> In *Alibi*, he was a very charming, put-upon fellow who'd done a stretch in prison, and *shouldn't have*. He'd been framed, ostensibly ... and I played him as ... very charming.... And it wasn't until the middle of the picture that you realized what a so-and-so this guy was....[15]

At the second Academy Awards held at the Cocoanut Grove of the Ambassador Hotel, on Thursday, April 3, 1930, *Alibi* competed for Outstanding Picture, Best Actor (Chester) and Best Art Direction (William Cameron Menzies). The long-established Warner Baxter won the Best Actor Award for his portrayal of the Cisco Kid in Fox's *In Old Arizona* (1929). MGM landed the awards for Outstanding Picture (*The Broadway Melody* [1929]) and Art Direction (Cedric Gibbons, *The Bridge of San Luis Rey* [1929]).

The success of *Alibi* immediately gained Chester several major studio offers and increased attention from the Hollywood movie magazines. He and Sue invited *Screenland*'s "party reporter" Grace Kingsley over to their new hillside California Spanish–style home, featuring an open fire in the living room and small balconies overhead, to enjoy pepper-and-garlic seasoned steaks barbecued in the patio's charcoal-heated brick oven. Chester had spent some of his hard-earned pay on "spiritualist medium props" in the hope of attracting "quality ghosts," a new expansion of his interest in magic. The dinner of steaks was to be followed by a buffet for more guests, including Robert Montgomery, Neil Hamilton and Harry Stubbs, intending to witness the host's live performance.

Kingsley, calling Chester one of "the stage stars [who] add zest to the social life of the picture colony," reported,

> Chester ... led us out to see the barbecue process. He wouldn't leave it to a servant for anything, but himself places the steaks between the big pieces of rock salt and, when they are done, brushes them off with a soft little brush, and there they are, wonderful and juicy and ready to serve....
>
> "The steaks came awfully late," said Mrs. Morris, "and we thought we might have to barbecue the baby. Couldn't disappoint guests, you know."[16]

Unfortunately, Chester's practicing had damaged some of his props, so he and Stubbs collaborated on some reliable slight-of-hand routines featuring cards and one in which three aluminum cups "disappeared." Director Lewis Milestone, who soon would begin production on Universal's *All Quiet on the Western Front* (1930), portrait painter Roy Atkinson, Jason Robards, Sr., Edward Nugent, Helen Twelvetrees, Natalie Moorehead and, briefly, James and Lucile Gleason were also on hand for the fun and games. Sue and Atkinson, both capable musicians, took turns playing the piano, before little Brooks put in a late appearance to close out the night.

In the July 1929 *Screenland* feature article "The New Technique of the Talkies," headlined, "The Brains of Stage and Screen Unite in Creating Talkies. Chester Morris from Broadway is the Hit of 'Alibi,'" Rosa Reilly praised,

> "Alibi" is perhaps the best crook film ever made. And its excellence is due, in great part, to two people: Roland West, the director, and Chester Morris, who plays the part of Chick Williams, the killer. Why, that boy Morris can express more sex appeal simply by bending his head in a girl's direction, as he does in the theater scene in "Alibi," than most heroes can in a hundred feet of amorous contortions.
>
> This picture has speed and the sinister, staccato sound quality of a machine gun. Every sequence is staccato. Morris and West suggest rather than work out long involved situations ... [they] have taken sound and so dramatized it that an almost perfect talking picture has resulted.[17]

Reilly immediately was impressed by Chester, dressed in a gray suit, white shirt and wine-colored tie, with brown shoes, a plaited gold bracelet and jade pinkie ring (his longtime favorite piece of jewelry). She advised her readers that they soon would be hanging his photograph alongside those of John Gilbert and Ronald Colman, but that he was refreshingly "regular, simple, unassuming ... [and] downright likable."[18]

By the time *Alibi* proved a hit, Chester had developed an understanding of the basics of early sound filmmaking, something that very few actors (or directors) had in the beginning:

> West has injected talking into the picture without lowering the action one jot. That's a terribly hard thing to do. And something that a lot of directors fall down on.
>
> When talkies first began, the directors tried to take a stage play and transfer it whole-hog to the screen. But that didn't work out.... On the stage you can watch two or three people talking quietly around a table for fifteen or twenty minutes without feeling any sense of slow tempo. But that won't go over in a talking picture. We are accustomed to lots of action in our movies. And if we don't have it, the picture falls flat.... [I]t seems to me that a perfect motion picture is like playing a chromatic scale on the saxophone. Each note rises a half-tone higher than the preceding one. So in a movie, each scene must rise higher than the one preceding it. And in a talkie when all you hear is a knot of people sitting in the same place talking ... the picture is apt to be a flop.
>
> But never for a second does Roland West let this happen in "Alibi".... He keeps his characters constantly moving. One bit of action rises hard and fast on the last bit of action, increasing the whole in tone and tempo until he reaches his climax.[19]

He also clearly understood the essential difference between stage and film acting, and the equally important distinction separating silent technique from that requiring dialogue:

> [In a silent film] if you want to get over [the] simple phrase, "You are a lovely girl," long before you say it, you must strike an elaborate pose to intimate what is coming and then say the words. That striking of the elaborate pose and then saying the words was what made talking pictures drag.
>
> Roland West overcame that in "Alibi" by making the words and the pose simultaneous. That's what gave it that staccato quality. There's no long dragging wait for the actor to gear himself up and express in pantomime what he is going to say later in words.... One of the first necessities ... in making a successful talking picture is in finding the best dialogue writers you can get. Words that sound fine on the stage sometimes seem positively silly in a talkie. Then, too, the novelty merely of hearing words issue from a screen character's mouth is no longer sufficient. The audience must be amused, stimulated, entertained. The dialogue must sparkle.

West … doesn't blueprint everything for you. He just suggests and lets the brain of the audience do the rest. He has pared his dialogue down to the bone, leaving a lot to the imagination. His characters express more by what they don't say than by what they do.[20]

In the July 1929 issue of *Photoplay* magazine, Leonard Hall, referring to the new Hollywood sensation as "Young King Leer," headlined his feature article, "How Chester Morris Snarled Himself to Fame in the Talkies" and claimed, "Mr. Morris' sudden success is one of these overnight miracles produced by the over-a-couple-of-nights talkies. They make and break fast in these pinwheel days, and Mr. Morris was one of the fastest hits on record…."[21]

On July 26, 1929, Warner Bros. ran advertisements in the major trade publications, announcing that their 1930 season would feature only "35 of the finest pictures ever delivered by one company" and promising, "THERE WILL BE NO PROGRAM PICTURES." The studio's stars, comprising "the greatest roster of talent ever assembled by one company," were headed by the illuminated brilliance of Al Jolson, John Barrymore and Dolores Costello; and included Edward Everett Horton, George Arliss, H.B. Warner, Myrna Loy, Chester and Rin Tin Tin, the German Shepherd who saved the studio from bankruptcy and established the production career of screenwriter Darryl F. Zanuck!

Chester now was being paid $2,500 per week (but, as he would reveal several years later, only a percentage of this amount reached his bank account). He had been offered long-term contracts by several major studios but remained signed to Roland West and United Artists. On loan out to Warner Bros.-First National, he appeared in John F. Goodrich's faithful adaptation of *Fast Life* (1929), directed by John Francis Dillon, which premiered in New York City on August 15, 1929. The next day, *The Film Daily* reported,

> Starting out on a tempo of jazz, made exceedingly natural and true to life by intelligent direction, the drama veers sharply toward one tragedy, almost embraces another and carries on to its conclusion on a well-sustained level of suspense. It sounds like a picture of merit and it is.[22]

Billed below leads Douglas Fairbanks, Jr., and Loretta Young, Chester reprised his Broadway role, here named Paul (rather than Chester) Palmer. *The Film Daily* added,

> Loretta Young … is splendid and most emphatically a star of tomorrow. Doug Fairbanks, Jr., does nice work when called upon … which isn't often. Chester Morris, who did such fine trouping in "Alibi," is third lead in a role to which he imparts dramatic power that practically makes the picture his.[23]

The secretly married Douglas Stratton (Fairbanks) and Patricia Mason (Young) are ready to turn in for the night when spurned would-be suitor Rodney Hall (Ray Hallor) enters through a window. In the ensuing struggle, Hall is killed, and Douglas subsequently is sentenced to be executed in the electric chair. Though Hall was murdered by Paul Palmer, he is encouraged by his uncle, the prison warden (Frank Sheridan), to remain silent, in hope of furthering the political career of his father (William Holden), the governor (and marry the grieving widow to boot). With time running out, the warden reveals the truth, prompting Paul to commit suicide.

Photoplay magazine published a negative view of *Fast Life*: "One of the sadder failures of the summer melodramas, due to extreme pokiness in direction, and an unbelievable story. Even Chester Morris … is so dragged by the pace that his face-making looks like an old-time slow-motion film."[24] *Picture Play*, though recommending it "with reservations," also had an overall disapproving view of the film, pointing out flaws inherent in many early sound productions: "A hollow story, top-heavy with theatrics and bombastic talking."[25]

Chester, unhappy with his own performance, and describing the basic difference between stage and sound-film acting technique, humbly explained,

> It wasn't the director's fault that I acted so badly. We were working from a poor script, to begin with. As I had played the part on the stage in New York, he let me do it just as I had there, and he gave his attention to the other members of the cast. He thought I could take care of myself, but I failed to take into consideration the fact that screen photography magnified my size twenty times, and that the camera was almost on my nose in other shots. My work would have been all right on the stage, where a distance separates the actor from the audience, but on the screen it was terrible.[26]

Chester's own honest assessment was reflected by that of *Variety*'s "Waly," who had seen the stage production prior to reviewing the film:

> First National brings the stage play practically line for line and set for set to the talker screen. Picture version is better played, but the average audience will rebel against over-mugging, during which long chunks of dialog, that drag to the point of fan restlessness, are released.
>
> Hysteria is much better for live reproduction if it is to be carried to extent it exists in this picture.... Chester Morris is a little out of cast in the role of the Governor's weak-kneed son. Morris' performance is good, but he is directorially driven to too much wailing and feature clinching.
>
> The last few sequences, dealing with the innocent man in the death house and the warden wondering how he will break it to his brother that the official son is the murderer, are attention getters. Some excellent prison interiors....[27]

(No prints of *Fast Life* have ever been found, although discs featuring the soundtrack recording have survived.)

William A. Wellman directed *Woman Trap* at Paramount during the spring of 1929. The screenplay by Bartlett Cormack and Louise Long was adapted from Edwin Burke's one-act vaudeville play *Brothers*. While shooting a scene late one afternoon, Chester, playing criminal Ray Malone, was visibly nervous, prompting Wellman to ask, "What's the matter with you?"

"It's this way, Mr. Wellman," Chester replied. "My wife's at a bridge party and I promised her positively I would go home at five-thirty to feed the baby."[28]

Much to the regret of Mrs. Malone (Effie Ellsler), her two sons, Dan (Hal Skelly), a by-the-book police officer, and Ray, a young hooligan, become seriously estranged. (Two years later, Wellman would direct another crime drama about opposing brothers, Warner Bros.' *The Public Enemy* [1931], starring James Cagney and Donald Cook.)

The film opens with the brothers living in the family apartment with their mother. Dan, attempting to teach no-good Ray a lesson, lifts him out of bed, carries him into the bathroom, throws him into the tub, and spanks his bum. The cinematic life of crime established in *Alibi* continues for Chester, as Ray loses a monogrammed cufflink during a fight with a "federal dick" who is killed. Meanwhile, Dan is promoted to a captaincy on the police force, and their mother tragically loses her sight.

When Ray faces capture, he is aided by Kitty (Evelyn Brent), sister of Eddie Evans (Leslie Fenton), Dan's ex-partner, who was convicted of murder partly on the latter's testimony. After temporarily hiding out in an Oregon lumber camp, Ray returns to the city to visit his mother. During a speakeasy fight, he accidentally kills another federal dick. Facing arrest by his own brother, he kills himself.

Playing another unlikable character (and his second in a row to commit suicide), Chester gives a predominantly nonverbal performance, offsetting Ray's negative traits with thespian skill. *Photoplay* named *Woman Trap*, released on September 28, 1929, one of the best pictures of the following month, also including Chester in its list of best performers with Richard Arlen, Evelyn Brent, Ina Claire, Gary Cooper, Edmund Lowe, Victor McLaglen, Basil Rathbone, Norma Shearer and Anna May Wong. *Picture Play* magazine proved lukewarm, but singled out Chester as the film's highlight:

> Curiously "Woman Trap" fails in effectiveness, though it has much at the outset to insure a successful picture. For one thing, such players as Evelyn Brent, Chester Morris and Hal Skelly ... must rank among your favorites. Yet even he is not altogether at his best, though Mr. Morris approaches his performance in "Alibi."[29]

Screenland editor Delight Evans wrote,

> Here's an out-and-out melodrama, one of the grim-and-gripping kind. If you like that sort of thing, you'll fall right into the "Woman Trap." It has Chester Morris in one of his now famous bad boy roles, and Chester is enough for me. I could watch him indefinitely—that graceful panther-like tread, that sudden brave turn of his sleek head, that—here, here! Chester is running right away with me, and I can't let *that* happen, fun or no fun. Mr. Morris is one of the three stars of this film; Hal Skelly and Evelyn Brent are the others.... This is no part for the subtle Miss Brent. She is wasted on a regular-girl role; she should always be cast as a suave and silken siren. It's Chester's show as far as I'm concerned.[30]

In December 1929, *Talking Picture Magazine* published the article "I Know Chester Morris" by his younger brother, using the pseudonym "Adrian O'Hara," in which he went to great lengths ballyhooing his now-famous sibling, whom he portrayed as a true Renaissance Man, excelling in music, painting and acting:

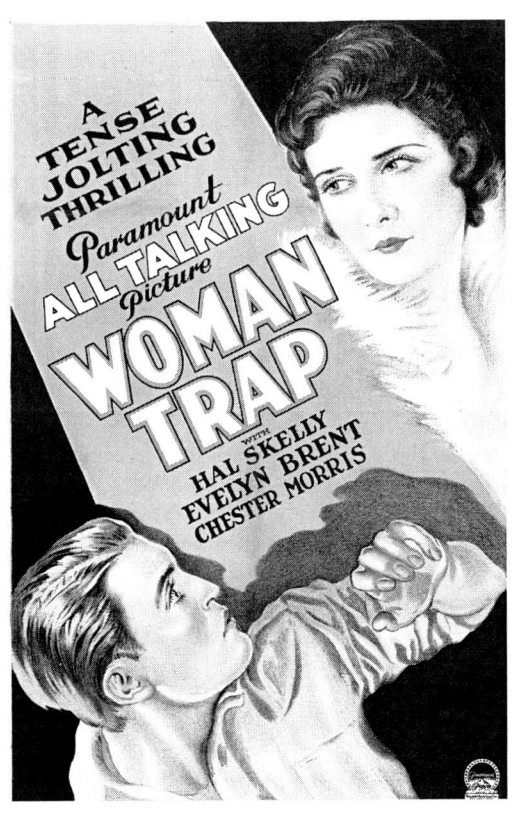

> Chester was a funny sort of kid. He dabbled in most everything, yet there was nothing he really couldn't do.... It would be unfair to say that Chester had missed his vocation. But had he cared to, he would surely have been one of our great painters.... He never seemed to realize what a God-given talent he possessed in this direction. I don't believe the boy even knows what a wonderfully fine actor he is, and what splendid things the future holds in store for him.... [S]uccess would change a lot of people—not Chester Morris. All the success in this world couldn't possibly take away that terrific amount of truth, soul and sincerity in that boy's make-up. It's firmly imbedded. I speak from practical experience, not from interviews. I love the kid to death, and why not—I'm his little brother.[31]

Chester appeared in two skits for Darryl F. Zanuck's all-star Warner Bros. revue *The Show of Shows*, directed by John G. Adolfi and released nationwide on December 28, 1929. Above the Winter Garden Theatre, Warners constructed an enormous lighted sign trumpeting 40 stars featured in the film, including John Barrymore, Richard Barthelmess, Alice White, Dolores Costello, Loretta Young, Ben Turpin, Betty Compson, Douglas Fairbanks,

Woman Trap (1929): Chester Morris and Evelyn Brent featured in the poster art for this early sound crime drama directed by William A. Wellman [original one-sheet poster].

Jr., Myrna Loy, Marion Nixon, Sally O'Neil, Noah Beery, H.B. Warner, William Collier and Chester.

In this two-hour variety parade of music, comic and dramatic acts (Barrymore portrays Richard III in a scene from Shakespeare's *Henry VI, Part 3*), Chester first appears at the 15:30 mark, remaining on screen for a brief 1:30. As master of ceremonies Frank Fay attempts to perform, Chester emerges from behind the stage curtain, accompanied by Jack Mulhall and Sôjin (Kamiyama, born in Japan in 1884 and later to appear in Akira Kurosawa's *Seven Samurai* [1954]). Chester, in sarcastic mode, scoffs at Fay's "singing," and the host counters by disparaging his "kind of actor." He participates in two additional sequences, one involving the 1892 British song "Daisy Bell (Bicycle Built for Two)." This overlong Warners promotion for its current "talkie" performers may have been difficult even for contemporary audiences to watch in its entirety.

Still on loan to Warner Bros., Chester played his sophomore role for the studio in the aptly titled *Second Choice* (1930), directed by Howard Bretherton. Joseph Jackson adapted the screenplay from an Elizabeth Alexander novel originally serialized in *The Saturday Evening Post*. Again alternating a melodramatic, soap-opera character in between his gangsters, he is Don Warren, a penniless and boozing young man involved in a love triangle with Vallery Grove (Dolores Costello) and Owen Mallory (Jack Mulhall), with whom she experiences a rocky but ultimately successful marriage. The screenplay offered little opportunity for the trio, all of whom were soundly criticized by *The New York Times*:

> The director holds the attention of the spectator with such devices as a party in a house that is being moved through the streets, racy foreign cars that dash over the landscape, settings that look improbable, and the scowling of Chester Morris who, since "Alibi," has apparently continued playing similar roles. Mulhall is miscast as Mallory and gives a halting performance. Miss Costello moves slowly and speaks the pseudo-smart lines with uncertainty.[32]

The *Hollywood Filmograph* offered a split decision:

> Chester Morris gave a very splendid, honest portrayal of the "first choice" of Dolores Costello and his was the outstanding character. Miss Costello was beautiful in the leading feminine role, but there seemed to be an unnaturalness about her characterization. Jack Mulhall, as the other half of the "second choice" gave his usual satisfactory and natural performance.[33]

The Film Daily noted that the "dialogue is considerably stilted," but added, "Chester Morris scores as the unfortunate youth."[34] In his *Variety* review, "Waly," pointing out that the "characterizations … are frequently unnatural," also suggested that Chester had yet to tone down his theatrical histrionics for the camera: "Morris shows a tendency toward stage hysterics when he flashes a gun on the heroine in a final effort to get her to leave her husband."[35]

Chester's next assignment at Warner Bros. was the male lead, gangster Nickey Solomon, opposite Alice White, as stenographer Sheba Miller, in *Playing Around* (1930), which Mervyn LeRoy directed from September 9 through mid–October 1929. After shooting wrapped at the First National studio, where films were made into the wee hours, Chester, with his penchant for witty exaggeration, revealed,

> We began every evening at seven and worked all night. As I can't sleep in the daytime, it was a rather terrible experience for me. By the time we were finished, I was almost ready for a sanitarium. After I had slept for a week or so, my wife and I and another couple went on a yachting trip.[36]

Jack (William Bakewell), a soda jerk, is in love with Sheba, who lives with her father (Richard Carlyle), but cannot keep up with her preference for the swinging nightlife. The film opens with an elaborate production number at the Pirate's Den nightclub, where Solomon is selected to judge the prettiest pair of legs during the "Pageant of the Knees." As a string of young women parade behind the stage curtain, Solomon quickly chooses the shapely stems of Sheba. As she exits the club with Jack, the egotistical gangster informs his companions, "I want to enter her life well-recommended, so I'll introduce myself."

As their date ends, Sheba tells Jack, "I don't want to get married yet."

"I know," he replies. "You want to be playing around all the time."

Smooth operator Solomon is interested in pursuing Sheba; but, for the time being, she prefers going to the movies to see Warner Bros.' top attraction, Al Jolson, in an "all-talking, all-singing, all-weeping" production. With *Playing Around*, the Brothers Warner offered Chester a character a bit more developed than those he had portrayed previously. The female screenwriting team of Adele Comandini and Frances Nordstrom provided a pair of gossiping ethnic neighbor ladies, Mrs. Fenerbeck (Ann Brody) and Mrs. Lippincott (Nellie V. Nichols), whose voyeurism (including binoculars) sparks plenty of pseudo-Shakespearean commentary helping to propel the major plot of the ill-fated romance between Sheba and Solomon.

Now engaged to Sheba, Solomon holds up her father at his tobacco shop, gunning him down when the old man reaches for a pistol stashed on a shelf behind the cash register. As with Chester's other early screen criminals, Solomon winds up in a bad way; although, unlike Chick Williams and Ray Malone, he survives smugly to walk away under arrest at

Playing Around (1930): Chester Morris as gangster Nickey Solomon.

the film's end. Tricked into thinking the old man has died, Solomon is played for a sucker by the intrepid soda jerk, and Jack rides off with Sheba at the wheel of Nicky's expensive automobile. When a cop mentions Solomon's conman abilities, she paraphrases his remark: "You mean he *was* a pretty smooth young fellow."

Playing Around was released on January 19, 1930, just two weeks after *Second Choice*. In March, *The New Movie Magazine* reported, "Morris is the best of the cast,"[37] while *Talking Screen* considered the actors, and a non-thespian attribute of White's, the primary drawing cards:

> If you're an Alice White fan, you won't mind the flimsy plot in this one. It smacks very much of "Broadway Babies," but is a better show for the money....
>
> Alice shows a neat pair of legs again. Carolyn Snowden, the dusky dancer, leads a peppy revue, while Helen Wherle is excellent. William Bakewell is the drug clerk, and Chester Morris is the fascinating villain.[38]

The following month, Chester's fourth Warner Bros. assignment, *She Couldn't Say No* (1930), directed by Lloyd Bacon, was released. Top-billed Winnie Lightner plays Winnie Harper, torch singer at a nightclub run by racketeer "Big John" (Tully Marshall), whose associate, Jerry Casey (Chester), attempting to go straight, becomes her manager. Winnie is disappointed by Jerry's romantic involvement with society girl Iris (Sally Eilers) but bails him out of jail after he is arrested while operating with Big John's gang. Jerry, unable to shake the criminal life, is gunned down during an altercation with the mob. Before Jerry expires in her arms, Winnie, realizing that he has backed her current musical revue, vows to move on.

Tom Lewis, in his *Hollywood Filmograph* review, gushed over the film:

> Winnie Lightner, the stage's greatest contribution to the screen since the advent of Al Jolson, will win millions of new fans with her picture, "She Couldn't Say No"....
>
> Chester Morris is personable and smooth. He fights hopelessly against a resistless force. Psychologically, the emotional conflict is true to life—and, as such, is understandable to all. We sympathize with him. When he dies we feel a distinct loss. And how artistically Lloyd Bacon handled that death scene! It is all-powerful—the very essence of art.... Camerawork by James Crees is beautiful. Miss Lightner and the whole organization rate congratulations. The picture is a winner.[39]

Variety's "Char" concurred:

> Title for draw and Winnie Lightner, with Chester Morris ably assisting, sends "She Couldn't Say No" through value as a programmer ... it's Miss Lightner who supplies the entertainment here....
>
> Another story of racketeers behind that saucy title. And with Chester Morris picked to play the tough gunman aspiring to more elite embraces than his cabaret singer sweetheart can offer, there's a fine actor in the cast to lend Miss Lightner support....
>
> Sally Eilers and Tully Marshall turn in fine accounts of themselves.... Photography and recording an asset.[40]

(*She Couldn't Say No* is another film for which no prints are known to exist.)

On November 6, 1929, RKO Radio's intention to star Chester as the title character in director Herbert Brenon's *The Case of Sergeant Grischa* (1930) was announced. Five days later, with rehearsals underway, Radio Pictures' president Joseph I. Schnitzer selected the project as a "roadshow attraction," greenlighting the shoot to begin at RKO Studios on November 18. In a cast including Betty Compson, Alec B. Francis, Gustav von Seyffertitz, Jean Hersholt, Paul McAllister and Rudolph Schildkraut, Chester "picked what [was] regarded as one of the film plums of the year."[41]

2. A Dignified Life in Hollywood?   29

Elizabeth Meehan based her screenplay on the 1927 novel by Prussian-born Jewish World War I veteran and anti-war activist Arnold Zweig (1887–1968). The publication of *Der Streit um den Sergeanten Grischa* [*The Case of Sergeant Grischa*], the first part of the epic six-cycle *Der große Krieg der weißen Männer* [*The Great War of the White Men*] (1927–1957), brought him international acclaim.

At the time *Grischa* was published, Zweig initiated a 12-year correspondence with Sigmund Freud that lasted until the psychoanalyst's death in 1939. He began writing for the anti–Nazi newspaper *Die Weitbühne* [*World Stage*] in 1929. When Adolf Hitler became Chancellor of Germany in 1933, he went into voluntary exile in Czechoslovakia, then moved on to Switzerland and France. He returned to his homeland in 1948, was involved with the Soviet occupation zone in East Germany, became a member of parliament and the World Peace Council, was awarded the 1958 Lenin Peace Prize by the USSR, and earned seven separate nominations for the Nobel Prize in Literature.

A reviewer wrote of the novel, "'Grischa' is of heroic stature, with its head in the clouds of human destiny, with the mysterious richness and texture of life itself, a tremendous parable of the clash between right and wrong, a true catharsis of pity and terror, noble, original and a war-scarred masterpiece."[42]

In the film, Russian Army Sergeant Grischa Prapotkin [alias "Ilja Pavlovitsch Bjuscheff"] escapes from a German prison camp in Poland during the winter of 1917. He is briefly reunited with his wife, Babka (Compson), and baby, but he cannot shake his intention to return to Russia. Captured and sentenced to death as a spy by the Germans, he meets his end after appeals fail, and a telegram containing an order to halt the execution is lost in a storm.

Scenes set in a prison camp and snow-covered forest through which Grischa escapes were shot at the RKO Ranch, a newly acquired 100-acre tract in the San Fernando Valley 40 miles outside Hollywood. Foliage expert Juro ["Joe Evergreen"] Hirai supplied over 1,600 trees for the location. Art director Max Rée designed a group of buildings and a cathedral to be used in several sequences. An enormous silver balloon was sent aloft to warn aircraft that a sound picture was being filmed on the ground below.

Austro-Hungarian actor Hans Joby, who attained the rank of major with the 1st Bavarian Infantry, 3rd battalion, fighting on five fronts during World War I, served as technical adviser on the film. Chester, with his head shaved, was described as having "that Barrymore look" by *Screenland* reporter Helen Ludlam, for whom he recalled his interviews with Herbert Brenon:

> I just hated to go. I had heard how hard Herbert was to get along with—how exacting—how temperamental and given to brain storms. When I got to the studio and we had talked for awhile he told me he had "Alibi" in his mind and couldn't get it out. He didn't see how the man who played "Alibi" could play *Grischa* and asked me whether I could say or do anything that would get the type out of his mind. "No," I said, "I don't think I can." Herbert looked at me and thought a minute. "Shaving your head might make the difference," he decided.
>
> So for no reason that I can figure out unless it was my subconscious mind directing me, I went over to the barber shop on the lot and had my head shaved as clean as a whistle. Sue met me in the studio commissary for lunch and when I told her what I was going to do she begged me to forget it. My negative state of mind had communicated itself to her and she was sure the part wasn't for me and that I would be unhappy in the engagement.
>
> I felt the same way, but in spite of it I went right over to the barber and off came the hair. Funny the way things happen.
>
> The lady who was working on the screen story was present during my next interview with

Herbert. After taking one look at me her nose went a mile in the air. I could see that I was "out" as a type for *Grischa* as far as she was concerned. All I wanted to do was romp home and end the interview. If there is anything I cannot stand it is to be some place where I am not wanted. But Herbert was pacing up and down by that time and then he began telling the story to me and characterizing *Grischa*. Before he was half through, I was crazy to do the part. Of course, Herbert is wonderful. He'd put enthusiasm into a puppet because he is a dynamo himself. "Mr. Brenon," I said, "you've got to let me play *Grischa* because—and then I paced around in my turn telling him just what I thought *Grischa* ought to do here and there and what have you. We ended with an enthusiastic handshake and a pair of grins recorded by a still camera."[43]

The Case of Sergeant Grischa (1930): Chester Morris had his head shaved to win the titular role of the doomed Russian soldier in director Herbert Brenon's screen adaptation of Arnold Zweig's anti-war novel *Der Streit um den Sergeanten Grischa*.

Brenon wrote an article, "Great Opportunities Offered for Strong Dramatic Talking Pictures," for the December 29, 1929, issue of *Hollywood Daily Screen World*, revealing a director's view of what types of feature films might dominate the sound era:

> Personally, I am of the opinion that a good story well told will always meet with popular reception by American audiences. The type of story is not as important as the story itself.
>
> I believe the greatest opportunity lies in the production of strong, dramatic plays as talking pictures....
>
> Pictures like "The Case of Sergeant Grischa," which I have just finished directing for Radio Pictures, have a market virtually without competition because so few of their type are made. "Grischa" is a powerful human drama. It has the pulse of life running through it; the spectator can feel it; the characters are genuine; the tinsel has been stripped off and we see and hear real human beings. Such pictures are founded on character rather than on plot and situation.
>
> "The Case of Sergeant Grischa" was written as a novel by Arnold Zweig. It was a bestseller both here and throughout Europe. It deals with the fate of a simple Russian peasant-soldier, Grischa (played by Chester Morris in the picture), who is caught in the machinations of the German military machine during the war.[44]

In a review titled, "Elements of Greatness," *Motion Picture* magazine noted,

If this were a foreign film, we would call it Art. Audiences fed on movie formula will be bewildered by the way the characters meet the different situations in the story, and possibly indignant at finding that they are asked to think.... Sergeant Grischa, a tiny, unimportant human atom caught in the machinery of War for a moment, threatens to stop the machinery itself. Nations are involved in the question of the justice of his fate, armies hesitate and—but the ending is as different as the rest.

In this jagged scrap torn from life, Chester Morris gives a rather terribly poignant study as the bewildered, childlike Grischa....[45]

Photoplay concurred:

In a season of musical fluff and drawing room persiflage, "The Case of Sergeant Grischa" stands out like a lighthouse. It is one of the important productions of the new year—stark, compelling drama marching relentlessly to a tragic close, almost unrelieved by humor. Too drab and wordy to have a widespread appeal, it is nevertheless another directorial achievement for Herbert Brenon.

It is another war story, but there are no trench scenes. The action is laid on the Eastern front of the German Army. The tragic death of the escaped Russian soldier by a German firing squad is brilliantly handled, almost unbearable in its intensity. Chester Morris is superb as the human, lovable Grischa.[46]

The Film Daily called the secondary love theme "unimportant" with respect to "the story which resembles a preachment against the injustices of war," but joined the other publications in acclaiming that "Chester Morris is aces as the condemned prisoner."[47] *Variety*'s "Sime," however, was blunt in pointing out the film's shortcomings:

There is no entertainment in "Grischa." ... After watching this blundering lout with his Park Ave. dialog for about two reels, about the only regret [is that] he was not shot earlier and the picture made into a short. To give a peasant who confesses he can neither read nor write, dialog that would fit a Belasco society drama was giving this picture a kick in the slats before the rest of the works are thrown into it....

Neither Grischa nor anyone else in this film draws an iota of sympathy. That makes it doubly hard. Grischa is often cringing, and the girl episode doesn't harmonize so well either for him. As the player of the role, Chester Morris does real well, technically, but the role is against him and also the picture's prospects.[48]

The Case of Sergeant Grischa, made on a budget of $467,000, proved too grim for audiences. Losing $170,000 at the box office, Paramount did not reissue what is now considered another "lost" film. (No negative or print footage has ever been found.)

As 1929 came to a close, *The Film Daily* published a front-page article by Jack Alicoate, in which the journalist named his dozen most "compelling impressions of the past twelve months." Number three on his list was "The performance of Chester Morris in 'Alibi.'"[49]

Metro-Goldwyn-Mayer acquired the screen rights to Katherine Ursula Parrott's novel *Ex-Wife* on October 10, 1929, considering Greta Garbo or Claudette Colbert for the title role. Universal, attempting to cash in on the novel's success, was making plans for a film called "Ex-Husband," starring Joseph Schildkraut.

In November 1929, MGM announced that John Meehan and Nick Grinde would be co-directing "Ex-Wife," but two months later, the feature was dropped from the studio's production schedule. However, on January 28, 1930, *The Film Daily* reported that Robert Z. Leonard would direct *The Divorcée*, starring Norma Shearer, for MGM. The following day, *Variety* objected to the "whitewashing" of Parrott's original title.

Production on *The Divorcée* began on February 1, 1930, with *Exhibitors Herald-World* claiming it would feature the first "all stage" supporting cast in motion pictures. Four years would pass before Chester revealed the difficulties he faced on the set, in general and during his love scenes with Norma Shearer, due to problems created by his inadequate wardrobe.

The plot of *The Divorcée* is simple, one of mutual adultery committed by a couple, Ted (Chester), a "poor newspaperman," and Jerry (Norma Shearer), celebrating their third wedding anniversary. Though Jerry had agreed to maintain a "liberal" attitude about marriage, she immediately embarks on a vengeful affair with her husband's friend, Don (Robert

The Case of Sergeant Grischa (1930): Chester Morris and Betty Compson in the lavish poster art [original six-sheet poster].

Montgomery), after Ted comes clean about a "meaningless" drunken one-night stand just before he leaves on a business trip. Upon his return, Jerry is frank about her behavior, which Ted cannot accept.

Jerry obtains a divorce, maintaining a path of numerous love affairs. When Paul (Conrad Nagel) confesses his undying love for her, Jerry plans to marry him. But Paul's current wife, Helen (Florence Eldridge), disfigured in an auto accident caused by his drunk driving, makes an impassioned plea for him to remain faithful. Jerry and Ted, now in Paris, meet again on New Year's Eve, realizing they still love each other. Their dance-floor embrace closes the film.

Though he later claimed being uncomfortable while shooting the love scenes, Chester and Norma Shearer share many effective moments. He gives a solid, believable performance, ranging from quiet indignation and sorrow to powerful drunken melodrama at a private party during which Ted shoves a large cake off a table and fights with other guests. But *The Divorcée* is Norma Shearer's vehicle, and her overshadowing of Chester is directly proportional to the difference in the size of their billing in the film's credits and original advertising.

2. A Dignified Life in Hollywood? 33

The Divorcée (1930): Chester Morris and Norma Shearer in the MGM screen adaptation of Katherine Ursula Parrott's novel *Ex-Wife* [original lobby card].

Jerry and Ted are a memorable couple. Some of the dialogue by John Meehan is exemplary of the content that led to the "self-regulation" of the Production Code four years later. Their initial scene opens romantically, with them kissing on the bank of a picturesque stream.

>TED: "When I've saved enough money, we're going to be married."
>JERRY: "It sounds as though you're proposing to my grandmother. What am I going to be doing while you're saving the first million?"
>TED: "*Waiting* for me."
>JERRY: "Waiting isn't my idea of the King of Indoor Sports. I've no intention of waiting around for three or four years while you harvest an additional crop of wild oats."
>TED: "Oh, now, *see here*, darling. I'm not as bad as all that."
>JERRY: "No, but you're no Saint Anthony. You're just human. S*o am I*. That's why I don't want to wait."
>TED: "Jerry, you certainly say it straight."
>JERRY: "*Sure*, isn't that the way we were going to be? Straight from the shoulder? Open, above board?"
>TED: "Oh, you're a great girl. You know, you've got a *man's point of view*."
>JERRY: "That's why we're going to make a go of it—*everything equal*."
>TED: "You bet."
>JERRY: "Seventy-five, twenty-five."

Following the announcement of their engagement to family and friends, they spoof, in full view of the gathering, Shakespeare's famous *Romeo and Juliet* balcony scene as Ted climbs up the balustrade of a staircase to kiss Jerry between the posts. On their third anniversary, before Ted is forced to reveal the truth about his extramarital dalliance, he embraces Jerry, admitting, "I like to make love to you when you *scream for help*." Placing her hand to her throat, she makes a gesture of silence, adding, "Can't *scream*."

In his first of two back-to-back collaborations with Robert Montgomery, Chester plays a character at odds with that of the actor destined to become one of his closest longtime friends in the film capital. Best man at Ted's wedding, Don then takes advantage of Jerry's initial wanton binge. Later, when meeting Ted, divorced, unemployed and hungover, in a diner, Don is frightened off when his former pal admits he might "kill" the man who dallied with his ex-wife.

While making *The Divorcée*, Chester also solidified his friendship with Florence Eldridge (who shared the same city and date of birth, as well as the date of her stage debut) and her husband, Fredric March (to whom she was married from 1927 until his death in 1975). The powerhouse theatrical couple often joined Chester and Sue at their home and for leisurely events on the town. (Like Chester, Eldridge, after the 1940s, would focus primarily on stage and television roles.)

Photoplay was effusive in its praise for *The Divorcée*:

> [W]hereas the book, although it sold hugely, was not what you might call a classic, the picture is.
> This has turned out to be a problem piece, as neat an essay on marital unfaithfulness as has been made in Hollywood. It sets Norma Shearer at the very top of the acting class. It gives Chester Morris a chance for another swell performance. The direction is as subtle as the scent of orchids and the clothes are gorgeous.
> You won't forget this picture and you'll undoubtedly go home and have a good long talk with your spouse. But more important, you'll be amused and held spellbound until the last reel. Don't miss it.[50]

The Film Daily appreciated the "top-notch" quality in every department, being particularly impressed with "some of the best acting that has come from Norma Shearer and Chester Morris," making "it sure to click in a big way."[51] *Broadway and Hollywood "Movies"* magazine, which chose *The Divorcée* as its "Picture of the Month," reported, "The sweet, refined beauty that Norma Shearer possesses is well set off by the stern, vigorous, almost-hard lines of Chester Morris' physiognomy."[52]

Shearer received an Academy Award nomination for her performances in this film and MGM's *Their Own Desire* (1929), also costarring Robert Montgomery. But when she won Best Actress in a Leading Role at the 4th annual ceremony on November 10, 1931, only *The Divorcée* was acknowledged.

On March 26, 1930, *Variety* reported that Joseph M. Schenck of United Artists had purchased the film rights to the play *La Morte in vacanza* by Italian World War I veteran Alberto Casella, which was translated by Walter Ferris into the English *Death Takes a Holiday*. Schenck intended the property to be produced by Roland West and star Chester as "Prince Sirki" (The Grim Reaper). Samuel Goldwyn previously had considered buying the play for Ronald Colman. (The material remained undeveloped until Maxwell Anderson and Gladys Lehman wrote a screenplay for director Mitchell Leisen, who made a film version, starring Fredric March, at Paramount in 1934.)

3

The Big House

Model, actress, artist, war correspondent and author Frances Marion (1888–1973), born Marion Benson Owens in San Francisco, has been called the greatest female screenwriter of the 20th century. She enjoyed fruitful filmmaking associations with director Lois Weber and actress-producer Mary Pickford, and for 22 months was married to director George W. Hill, who had risen to prominence as a cinematographer during the early silent period. (In 1918, he filmed Chester in *The Beloved Traitor* at New York's Goldwyn Pictures.) Beginning in the mid–1920s, he directed and produced several top titles at MGM starring such heavyweights as Lon Chaney, Sr., and Wallace Beery.

Hill and Marion had followed news coverage of several prison riots and a resulting federal investigation during 1929, believing that a properly researched story on the subject could make for a powerful feature film. Hill wrote a 27-page treatment, "The Reign of Terror: A Story of Crime and Punishment," which he submitted to MGM's Irving Thalberg, who assigned the screenplay to Marion.

Allowed access to prison personnel and inmates at several major correctional facilities, including San Quentin in California's Marin County just north of her stomping grounds, Marion used material from in-depth interviews to write the script for *The Big House*, with additional dialogue contributed by Joe Farnham and Martin Flavin (whose play *The Criminal Code* was produced on Broadway in 1929). Pleased with Chester and Robert Montgomery's performances in *The Divorceé*, Thalberg and Hill cast them as two of the trio of prisoners whose entanglements comprise the plot of the film. To play hardened murderer "Machine Gun" Butch Schmidt, they wanted Chaney, but his serious illness (soon to end with his death on August 26, 1930, at age 47) prevented him from accepting such an intense, taxing role.

Marion, while in the studio commissary one day, observed Wallace Beery, whose successful silent career had stalled with the coming of talkies, attacking a plate of spaghetti, and was reminded of an inmate she had seen at San Quentin. Beery was recruited, and the eager actor relished working on the MGM prestige film.

Chester, receiving top billing, was pleased to accept the part of John Morgan, incarcerated for robbery but, wishing to "go straight," working toward an early parole for good behavior. On the flip side, Montgomery was playing Kent Marlowe, convicted of manslaughter for killing a man while driving drunk, and driven by fear to protect his own skin at any cost, even stooping to violate the "convicts' code" by becoming a stool pigeon and backstabber. Marion's innovative script would provide an archetype for the popular prison subgenre.

Hill's directorial approach mirrored the "documentary" effort Marion put into the

The Big House (1930): From left, Chester Morris, Harold Wenstrom and Reggie Lanning shoot a close-up of convict John Morgan after his 30 days in the "dungeon."

screenplay. Forbidding the lead actors to wear conventional makeup, he also warned them that any evidence of "acting" would result in their walking papers.

Photoplay reporter Sara Hamilton, who visited the set during Hill's shooting of the violent jailbreak scene (in which World War I tanks from the U.S. Army's 40th Infantry Division were used), was startled by the rapid fire of machine guns. She arrived just in time to witness Montgomery being shot down. Later, his friend and costar took her on a tour of the prison block: "Chester Morris show[ed] us the dark damp cell where he is kept in solitary confinement, and the prison hospital with the long rows of white iron beds. It's the most depressing place I've ever been in."[1]

An MGM "casting call" was made for a dozen cockroaches to be used in the big prison race scene involving Chester, Beery and Montgomery. The insects, much loved by the cinematic inmates, were purchased from small boys who happily rounded them up in exchange for a fee and visit to the studio.

Wisely, Thalberg decided to preview the film. The screenplay originally depicted the character of Anne (Leila Hyams) as the wife of "Dean" Marlowe, but many (particularly female) viewers, disliked the "adulterous" affair that developed between the lonely wife and John Morgan. Several scenes were reshot, with Hyams' character reworked as the sister of Kent Marlowe, and this relationship provides Morgan with his believable redemption at the film's end.

3. The Big House

The massive concrete edifice of the Big House looms over a paddy wagon moving through the prisoners' entrance, carrying Marlowe to incarceration for manslaughter. Warden James Adams (Lewis Stone, an actor Chester greatly admired), a fair-minded and compassionate professional, laments that he must house Marlowe in a cell with Schmidt, a cold-hearted killer, and Morgan, "the slickest crook we ever had here," a primarily self-interested man but regretting his past acts and hoping to be paroled. (Marion incorporated actual comments by the San Quentin warden into Adams' scripted dialogue.) On the other hand, Schmidt has committed three murders for the paltry sum of $500, and even "sometimes" regrets poisoning his lover.

The illiterate Schmidt listens as Morgan reads his letters to him, remarking to his fellow inmates that one of them "is too juicy for you guys." Morgan also offers some help to Marlowe, but the spineless young man accustomed to privilege turns on him after Oliver (Fletcher Norton), snitch of the yard, suggests that informing may shorten his sentence. Schmidt incites a disturbance over the appalling food in the prisoners' mess, and Marlowe, handed the killer's knife beneath the table, plants in in Morgan's jacket. Schmidt is escorted to solitary confinement; and Morgan, instead of being paroled a year early for good behavior, also is tossed into a cell in "the dungeon."

Following a month in the damp dark and filth, the seriously ill Morgan, feigning unconsciousness, is taken to the hospital ward. During the night, he hides in the morgue wagon, successfully achieving the first escape from the prison in five years. In the city, he walks to a bookstore owned by Marlowe's sister, Anne, whom he had seen during her recent visit to the prison. Intending to seek retribution against Marlowe, Morgan instead becomes interested in Anne and her kind family after she lies to Sgt. Donlin (Robert Emmett O'Connor) about his identity.

The cop has recognized the convict, however, and eventually arrests him at the Marlowe home. Back in stir, he is advised by Schmidt, "Don't let the gang know that you're going straight. They used to have a lot of respect for you."

Refusing to join the prison break planned by Schmidt, Marlowe and others, Morgan does not reveal any information to Wallace (De Witt Jennings), head of the guards, but, believed complicit by Butch, risks his life to help save the officers during the ensuing violent stand-off. Tear gas canisters explode, a tank rolls in, and Marlowe is killed. Schmidt intends to shoot Morgan but, learning the truth about Marlowe, customarily admits he was "just kidding."

Morgan, praised as a hero for stopping the "orgy of murder," is pardoned by the governor. Chester's top cinematic character to date, Morgan, planning to settle on government land in "the islands," exits the prison into Anne's waiting arms.

Released on June 24, 1930, in New York, *The Big House* was a smash hit, becoming the first film to win Academy Awards for Best Screenplay (by a female in a non-acting capacity) and Best Sound (by Douglas Shearer, Norma Shearer's brother and Irving Thalberg's brother-in-law; one of his 14 career nominations and seven wins). Nominated for Best Picture, it lost to Lewis Milestone's superb adaptation of Erich Maria Remarque's anti-war masterpiece *All Quiet on the Western Front*. Wallace Beery also was nominated, but the Best Actor award went to George Arliss (as *Disraeli* [1929]), whose histrionics remained much admired during the early talkie era.

Norbert Lusk, in his *Picture Play* review, wrote,

> Whether "The Big House" has the elements of great popularity, time alone will tell. But whether it has or hasn't, it is a magnificently savage picture of life behind prison walls. Devoid of prettiness or

The Big House (1930): Chester Morris (left) and Wallace Beery in MGM's groundbreaking prison drama [original lobby card].

romanticizing, it may not please the larger public, although a love story has been pressed into service to supply this need....

Wallace Beery is sly, cruel, the experienced criminal, but withal a likable fellow. His performance is beyond superlatives. It is great acting and surpasses any of his efforts in silence. Chester Morris is ideally cast as Morgan, the slick forger, though enough of a fighter to hold his own among the prisoners and sufficiently ingratiating to win the sister of one of the men.... Equal in every respect to his fellows is Robert Montgomery, as the freshman among the convicts. Last seen as the flippant philanderer in "The Divorcée," his new role offers as great a contrast as could be imagined. The breaking down of his morale until he turns "yellow" is superbly delineated....

So powerful is the acting ... that the spectator shares their prison sentence with them.[2]

During the early sound period, major films also were shot in alternate non–English-language versions. MGM accompanied its English release with European editions in Spanish (*El presidio*, directed by Edgar Neville and Ward Wing, with José Crespo as Morgan), German (*Menschen hinter Gittern*, directed by Pál Fejös, with Gustav Diessl as "Morris") and French (*Révolte dans la prison*, directed by Fejös and Hill, with Charles Boyer as "Fred" Morgan).

The Big House, depicting the idea that the U.S. prison system often helps develop hardened criminals rather than "rehabilitating" them, remains a relevant film nine decades later.

The three leading performances and groundbreaking screenplay are well supported by the imposing, often expressionistic visual style created by Hill, cinematographer Harold Wenstrom and art director Cedric Gibbons. Many scenes, involving innovative moving camera, stark compositions and lighting techniques, stand out in this early talkie: the towering, imposing walls of the prison; powerful long shots of inmates parading through the yard; Marlowe, stripped, shown from behind while measured by prison guards; Morgan being led into the deep, dark dungeon; Schmidt leading the violent, tragic riot; and Morgan framed from behind in long shot as he walks out to meet Anne at the end.

The use of sound is also quite innovative. The dungeon sequence, during which Morgan suffers in his filthy cell, features a lengthy static shot of the shadowy uninhabited corridor, its eerie silence finally broken by Schmidt's agonized shout for his fellow inmate. During an era when the incidental musical score had yet to be developed, this stark use of offscreen dialogue, a technique made possible by the sound format, had a powerful dramatic effect on audiences. Many of the trademark elements of the prison subgenre, including the sounds of iron cell doors clanging closed, tin plates and cups being banged on mess tables, hundreds of feet stomping on concrete, and the cascade of machine-gun bullets, began in *The Big House*.

The film inspired Chester's finest characterization to date. In 1946, when asked by *Life* magazine to write a brief article on his favorite cinematic role, he chose John Morgan.

Following Chester's move to Los Angeles, William Morris began to alternate stage roles on Broadway with film appearances for Hollywood companies. At Jolson's 59th Street Theatre in New York, he produced a nine-performance original run of the vaudeville revue *Sir Harry Lauder* (April 21–26, 1930), starring the famous music-hall entertainer from Edinburgh, Scotland, supported by the Arnaut Brothers, the Eno Troupe of Japanese Jugglers, Fitzgerald and Hoag, Don Julian and Stella Powers. Following the close of this production, he returned to California to visit his son and accept more film work.

Chester admitted,

> It took more than a year and a half of high-powering on my part to get Dad out to Hollywood and into pictures. You see, Dad has been on the stage more than forty years—and veterans of the stage get funny that way. Think it cheapens their art to do their stuff before the camera.
>
> Reminds me of the time when he was asked if he'd play a role in a stage play wherein I was the lead. "Would you mind supporting your son?" the producer wired him. "Why not?" he wired back, "I've been doing it all his life!"[3]

Adrian Morris also followed his brother to Tinseltown, where he made his initial silver-screen appearance (an uncredited role as one of the crew of the airship *Los Angeles*) in Frank Capra's aviation epic *Dirigible*, released on April 4, 1930, by Columbia. The production's $1-million budget, a considerable sum for frugal studio boss Harry Cohn, was not wasted on such fine talent as cinematographer Joseph Walker (and seven additional cameramen, some of whom shot impressive aerial footage at the U.S. Naval Air Station at Lakehurst, New Jersey, and "South Pole" scenes in California's San Gabriel Valley), and the powerhouse cast headed by Jack Holt, Ralph Graves, Fay Wray, Hobart Bosworth, Roscoe Karns, Harold Goodwin and Clarence Muse.

Meanwhile, William's reputation was landing him somewhat larger Hollywood roles. Released in both silent and sound versions during August 1930, *The Convict's Code* was directed by Harry J. Revier for Trem Carr Pictures, just one year before the Poverty Row producer established Monogram Pictures. Billed third, William plays Theodore Perry, in support of Cullen Landis and Eloise Taylor.

At Columbia, William costarred with Bert Lytell, Dorothy Sebastian, Richard Tucker, Claire McDowall, Howard C. Hickman and Francis McDonald in the crime drama *Brothers* (1930), directed by Walter Lang. Joseph L. Mankiewicz wrote the screenplay for Paramount's crime spoof *The Gang Buster* (1931), directed by A. Edward Sutherland and featuring William with Jack Oakie, Jean Arthur, William ["Stage"] Boyd, Wynne Gibson, Francis McDonald and Tom Kennedy.

Initial evidence of Roland West's main interest in Chester, using him, not as an artistic asset, but a purely financial one, appeared in the July 16, 1930, issue of *Variety*:

> Through loans to five different companies over a period of a year, Roland West has garnered a reported $460,000 on Chester Morris, taken from the legit for "Alibi" which West made for UA release. Since that picture Morris, who is under a personal five-year contract to West, has been loaned to MGM, Radio, WB, FN and Paramount, with West reported figuring this a wise move in an effort to build up his protégé through roles opposite such stars as Norma Shearer, Dolores Costello, Leila Hyams, Winnie Lightner, Evelyn Brent and Betty Compson.
>
> Morris' second for UA release, with West producing, will be "The Bat Whispers," just placed in production with Morris given the star rating. Between "Alibi" (UA) and this, Morris has been loaned for nine different pictures.[4]

On August 31, 1930, *The Film Daily* reported that West was considering Chester to reinterpret the much-loved roles played by Rudolph Valentino in sound remakes of *The Sheik* (1921) and *The Son of the Sheik* (1926). Nothing transpired, however, and one year later, Chester laughed off such suggestions, with *Silver Screen* magazine reporting that

(From left) Writer Charles Walt, producer-director Roland West and Chester Morris discuss a potential film project (1930).

Romanian-born actor Georges Metaxa, who had costarred with Claudette Colbert in Paramount's *Secrets of a Secretary* (1931), was hoping to follow in Valentino's sandy footsteps.

Chester's second project with West, *The Bat Whispers* (originally titled "Whispers"), a remake of the director's own 1926 silent adaptation of the 1920 Mary Roberts Rinehart and Avery Hopwood play *The Bat* (based on Rinehart's bestselling 1908 novel *The Circular Staircase*), was completed in late summer 1930. Receiving top billing, Chester, whose role was enlarged from the earlier film version portrayed by Eddie Gribbon, also was the sole actor named on the posters. After finishing his scenes, he and Sue left for New York, where they arrived during the first week of October.

The production, released by United Artists on November 29, 1930, was shot in three versions: a widescreen (2:1 ratio) edition, in a 65mm process called "Magnifilm"; and two standard (1.33:1 ratio) 35mm negatives (from which domestic and foreign prints were struck). Two other features, Fox's *The Big Trail*, directed by Raoul Walsh and starring John Wayne, and *Billy the Kid*, directed by King Vidor and costarring Johnny Mack Brown and Wallace Beery, were released in widescreen editions during 1930 (but the expense required by their exhibition soon waylaid such wide-format theatrical films until the rise of television two decades later).

The plot of *The Bat Whispers* is simple, although the execution often results in narrative chaos mixing villainous mayhem with (sometimes unintentional) humor. Master criminal "The Bat," whose megalomania leads him to scoff at any efforts made by the police to stop him, robs a socialite's safe and a bank vault in the town of Oakdale on his way to a country mansion leased by Mrs. Cornelia Van Gorder (Grayce Hampton), where he terrorizes the occupants. The loot from the bank robbery, supposedly stolen by a teller, has reportedly been stashed there.

Lieutenant Detective Anderson of the City Police (Chester) arrives to question Cornelia, while her niece, Dale (Una Merkel), requests Richard Fleming (Hugh Huntley), nephew of the Oakdale bank president, but he is shot dead shortly after his arrival. Cornelia then sends for a private detective (Charles Dow Clark). The inebriated, quivering caretaker (Spencer Charters) is accosted by the Bat, who orders everyone to leave. Subsequently the lights flicker on and off, and the villain's shadow is seen by the occupants in various parts of the mansion.

Anderson claims that Mr. Fleming robbed his own bank and accuses Dr. Venrees (Gustav von Seyffertitz) of collusion in the crime. The loot is discovered in a "hidden" room, where Fleming is found dead behind a wall. As flames are seen exploding in the garage, the Bat appears, is apprehended, and then escapes in the dark, only to be caught in an enormous bear trap set by Lizzie Allen (Maude Eburne), the terrified maid.

The Bat is unmasked, proving to be the man impersonating Anderson, whom he earlier had knocked unconscious. "I've got the greatest brain that ever existed," he boasts, claiming that his escape is imminent, for "no jail can hold" him.

A curtain then closes, and the audience is transported from the cinema to a stage play. Chester emerges from behind the curtain to inform everyone that they will remain safe from the Bat only if they do not "divulge his identity to anyone" after leaving the theater.

Considered "old-fashioned" at the time, the film was made marketable by West's (pre–William Castle) gimmicky technical style, including innovative mobile camera, with cinematographers Robert H. Planck (65mm) and Ray June (35mm) implementing a variety of odd lighting set-ups, camera angles and tracking effects (achieved with a special dolly designed by technician Charles Cline) to make the most of art director Paul Roe Crawley's

The Bat Whispers (1930): From left, Una Merkel, Chester Morris, Charles Dow Clark, Maude Eburne and Spencer Charters in the poster art for Roland West's second screen adaptation of the Mary Roberts Rinehart and Avery Hopwood play *The Bat* [original half-sheet poster].

innovative "dark house" set designs and convincing miniatures. When shooting in the standard ratio, June necessarily employed framing techniques, especially more close-ups, differing from those emphasized by Planck, who had a larger visual canvas.

This technical rationale prevented the film from looking like a filmed play but did little to alleviate the histrionics. West carried over the expressionism into the characterizations, many of which are wildly overplayed. *Motion Picture* magazine reported, "Chester Morris, in a high collar, a mustache and a pallid makeup romps in and out of scenes in a role much different from any he has had. You probably won't like him as well here."[5] *Silver Screen*, however, issuing its "great" rating, enthused, "Oh, what a thriller ... simply elegant direction by Roland West, beautiful settings, a great cast headed by the immaculate Chester Morris and fair Una Merkel ... one of the most exciting movies in many a month."[6]

Chester, made up with graying temples, and delivering a stylized, theatrical, at times grimacing performance, is nearly unrecognizable at times. (West's tight, low-key closeups make him appear positively ghoulish.) This role propelled him even further into the Hollywood stratosphere. On New Years' Eve, United Artists officially announced that he had "been promoted to the rank of star."[7]

Mordaunt Hall, in his *New York Times* review, wrote,

3. The Big House   43

The Bat Whispers (1930): From left, Gustav von Seyffertitz, Grayce Hampton and Chester Morris.

[In] "The Bat Whispers" there is Chester Morris, who stepped a great many rungs up the ladder of film fame through his work in Mr. West's previous production. Mr. Morris, however, does not run away with this screen offering, for the palm for acting is easily won by Grayce Hampton, who gives an extraordinarily facile interpretation of the determined Mrs. Cornelia Van Gorder, who is not going to be bluffed out of a house she has rented by any phantoms.... It is a well-directed film, but it seems rather a waste of time for Mr. West, for there is nothing new even in this bigger and better "Bat."[8]

The characterization that tests the nerves of the stoutest viewers is Maude Eburne's Lizzie, whose paranoiac, over-the-top, whiny eccentricity builds to a fever pitch. It is the shrieking maid, however, whose ridiculous behavior aids in the apprehension of the Bat.

Norbert Lusk, writing in *Picture Play*, perhaps offered the most "forward-looking" contemporary review, titled "The Bat Flaps":

"The Bat Whispers" comes to the talkies minus most of the suspense which characterized the silent version....
  A series of early robberies by "The Bat" detract from, rather than heighten, the suspense.
  Chester Morris wears a mask during most of the picture, thank Heaven, for when he isn't masked, he mugs as even he has never been known to do before....

The picture itself is tedious and might much better have been left wherever it has lain during these past ten [sic] years.⁹

Though the dated, often confusing *The Bat Whispers* was not a commercial success, it proved a solid stepping stone in the "dark house" subgenre of the thriller film, following *The Bat* and Universal's *The Cat and the Canary* (1927), directed by Paul Leni from a script adapted from the 1922 John Willard play (heavily influenced by the 1920 stage version of *The Bat*). Nearly two years after *The Bat Whispers* was released, James Whale's darkly comic *The Old Dark House* (1932), featuring Boris Karloff, Melvyn Douglas, Charles Laughton, Ernest Thesiger and Raymond Massey, arguably marked the apex of the subgenre. Whale identified *The Cat and the Canary* as being a major influence on the direction of his four Universal horror classics: *Frankenstein* (1931), *The Old Dark House*, *The Invisible Man* (1933) and *Bride of Frankenstein* (1935). And Maude Eburne's intermittently ear-splitting histrionics can be considered a forerunner to the behavior of Whale's female eccentrics, particularly those played by Una O'Connor (albeit with a wee bit more restraint) in *The Invisible Man* and *Bride of Frankenstein*.

Comic book writer and artist Bob Kane, when creating his famous superhero "the Bat-Man" in 1939, reportedly was inspired by Douglas Fairbanks, Sr.'s, portrayal of the titular character in *The Mark of Zorro* (1920), the huge bat-like "ornithopter" flying machine diagrammed by Leonardo da Vinci in the 15th century, and the shadowy, caped-and-hooded character in *The Bat* and *The Bat Whispers*. The "whispering" of the character in the sound version is also recalled in the performances of Michael Keaton in Tim Burton's *Batman* (1989) and Christian Bale, whose malevolent underplaying of Kane's character occasionally renders his dialogue unintelligible, in Christopher Nolan's immensely successful trilogy *Batman Begins* (2005), *The Dark Knight* (2008) and *The Dark Knight Rises* (2012).

Prior to the release of *The Bat Whispers*, Chester's name was mentioned during casting discussions for Universal's *Dracula* (1931), directed by Tod Browning. The studio initially had considered Lon Chaney, Sr., for the titular role, but his death resulted in the consideration of many other actors, including Arthur Edmund Carewe, John Carradine, William Courtenay, Ian Keith, Paul Muni, Joseph Schildkraut, Conrad Veidt and John Wray before production began on September 29, 1930. Bela Lugosi, who had played the vampire count in the original Broadway production at the Fulton Theatre during 1927–1928, campaigned successfully for the role after a national touring version of the play reached Los Angeles.

Chester, Sue and one-year-old Brooks now were living at 6662 Whitley Terrace in Los Angeles. A daughter, brown-haired, blue-eyed Cynthia Suzanne, was born there on October 16, 1930. Also sharing their residence were Ebon, the family dog, and Alice Foote Mac-Dougall, the cat.

On the "Bests of 1930" list published in *The 1931 Film Daily Yearbook of Motion Pictures*, Chester (for *The Case of Sergeant Grischa* and *The Big House*) was named as one of the "Players mentioned most often, during 1930, in Photoplay Magazine's 'Best Performances of the Month' Section." Ruth Chatterton and John Barrymore (mentioned four times each) were at the pinnacle of the group, followed by Gary Cooper, Edmund Lowe, Ramon Novarro, Jack Oakie and William Powell (three times) and 24 others (twice), including Richard Arlen, Lew Ayres, Warner Baxter, Ronald Colman, Joan Crawford, Greta Garbo, John Gilbert, O.P. Heggie, Buster Keaton, Fredric March, and Chester's costars Robert Montgomery and Norma Shearer. *The Big House* also was voted one of the "Ten Best Pictures of 1930" in the *Film Daily* Nationwide Poll.

In early 1931, Chester bought a 16mm camera and began experimenting with his own home-movie productions. He also developed a strong interest in still photography, often challenging Robert Montgomery to out-do his own work. The two friends used the same photo processing lab, where Leslie Howard also dropped off his negatives, and they all prevailed upon the technician to supply them with the best printing supplies. On February 16, Chester and Sue, accompanied by Mr. and Mrs. Roland West, left, via the Panama Canal, on a lengthy cruise and European vacation.

In April 1931, *Picture Play* magazine published a feature, "The Crowded Hour," by Samuel Richard Mook, chronicling the work of actors who left the New York stage for Hollywood, some of whom "achieved a spot in the sun," while others "ignominiously returned to Broadway":

> With the coming of talkies there was the now well-known influx of stage talent which completely merged the stars and featured players whose names formerly graced the billboards. A native film player was harder to find in the cast—almost—than the proverbial needle in the haystack.
>
> When the smoke of battle cleared away and it was possible to sift the wheat from the chaff, the performances turned in by, and the impressions made by, the stage players make interesting reading....
>
> Ruth Chatterton has scored the biggest individual success. About washed up on the legitimate stage ... she was among the first signed up....
>
> At the moment there is more fan interest in Robert Montgomery than any other actor—star or otherwise. His films have been one long string of successes....
>
> Chester Morris probably scored the most sensational success of them all when the talkies first came in. His performance in "Alibi" was an outstanding triumph for him and for a time he was the most sought man in pictures.... His career ... suffered a letdown just before "The Big House," and his following deserted him to an extent. His latest, after a long absence from the screen, is "The Bat Whispers." A few more like it and it will be "Chester breathes his last."
>
> The surprising part of these successes is that, with the exception of Chatterton, not one of them was a star or even a featured player on the stage.[10]

Chester *had* been a featured player on Broadway and the road; and his "long absence from the screen" lasted less than five months (the time lapse between the respective releases of *The Big House* and *The Bat Whispers*). But, in the cutthroat, competitive culture of Hollywood, where a "star" is just as easily buried as elevated "overnight," having one's career prematurely pronounced D.O.A. may happen at any time.

On April 21, Chester and Sue arrived back in Los Angeles following their two-month vacation to Europe. (Chester later would reveal the unsatisfactory nature of much of the trip.) His third collaboration with Roland West, the Prohibition maritime adventure *Corsair*, soon went into production, with a location shoot scheduled at Catalina Island.

As John Hawks, who "progresses" from college football star to Wall Street pawn and hooch hijacker, Chester costars with Thelma Todd, making her debut in a dramatic role under the pseudonym "Alison Loyd." Adapted by West and Josephine Lovett from a fact-based novel by former prohibition agent Walton Green, the film wastes both Chester, whose adequate performance cannot compensate for a poorly developed character, and Todd/Loyd, who, as Alison Corning, primarily sits around in lovely attire, reciting stiff dialogue.

The unconvincing romantic relationship between Hawks and Alison is well-represented when she tells him, "I should thank you for not making love to me," and he replies, "Why, I never thought of such a thing." Nonetheless, after Hawks is fired by her father, Wall Street "baron" Stephen Corning (Emmett Corrigan), and retaliates by taking to the sea aboard the rum-runner *Corsair*, pirating the shady old man's bootleg booze, he and Alison become engaged by the film's end.

Hawks' refusal to persuade an old woman to exchange her valuable bonds for the "worthless stock" peddled by Corning and Company provides an ironic parallel to a real-life stock market incident. Twenty-four years earlier, Chester's mother was arrested for being in a Hoboken "bucket shop" with a small roll of cash.

United Artists released *Corsair* on November 28, 1931, to meager box office returns. In the review "Old-Fashioned Villainy Running Wild," *Motion Picture* magazine claimed,

> It's no place for a chap like Chester Morris. Not that Chester isn't as villainous as the rest. [He] does well enough with his assignment, and Thelma Todd ... is, likewise, unfortunately cast. There are the expected heavies led by Fred Kohler, and the usual drunken comics headed by Frank McHugh. Altogether "Corsair" should not be taken seriously.[11]

Variety's "Sid" elaborated on these aspects:

Corsair (1931): At eventide off Catalina Island, Chester Morris stands atop the gunwale of the schooner used during location shooting.

> West hasn't done so well with this gat opera. It's really rather old fashioned at this time, with neither the playing, dialog or action unfolding other than much worn material. And none of the characters make a pertinent bid for audience sympathy....
>
> Film will hardly provide Chester Morris with a popularity spurt after a somewhat lengthy absence from theatre projection. An odd billing sidelight, both on the screen and in publicity matter, is that West's name is above the title, with Morris beneath, but preceded by the term "starring"....
>
> Morris' performance is an in-and-out affair always handicapped by the hokum of the writing. A good actor who is not at his best here.[12]

The November 22, 1931, issue of *The Film Daily* was generally unenthusiastic: "Entertaining but farfetched melodrama ... photography is highlight.... Action is quite plentiful and interest holds up generally, but the dialogue is rather bad."[13] One week later, the same publication featured a paid promotion for *Corsair* on its cover, including positive review excerpts from several major publications selected by West. This did little to bolster attendance, and *Corsair* proved to be West's final film.

Though *Alibi* is the only West production that provided Chester with a full-blooded characterization, all three, often visually impressive, films offered dissimilar roles that made the work interesting for him. Following *Corsair*, Thelma Todd returned to more successful comedy films, and Chester moved on to several top roles at the major Hollywood studios; but, as he would reveal later, escaping from West was far more problematic.

3. The Big House

West, attempting to counter the lackluster reviews of *Corsair*, acted like a carnival barker in the print medium, running a full-page advertisement announcing, "WIN $2,500.00—We Want Publicity and We'll Give $5,975.00 to Get It!":

> As a means for introducing this amazing distribution of $5,975.00 in prizes to the public, we offer a special test in the seventeen pictures of Chester Morris shown here. Chester Morris, you know, is the United Artists' star, who is now appearing in the great new movie, "Corsair." "Corsair" is a picture everyone will enjoy. By all means, plan to see it if you love romance, adventure and genuine thrills.
>
> And if you would like to win $2,500.00 easily and quickly as I will tell you, read the instructions below and send your answer ... quick!

Entries were to be mailed to a "prize director" at an office on North Dearborn Street in Chicago.

In June 1931, *Motion Picture* magazine published an interview with "America's Sherlock Holmes," William J. Burns, founder of the Burns International Detective Agency and former director of the Bureau of Investigation (BOI), the forerunner of the FBI, from 1921 to 1924. During a discussion about the possible infiltration of Hollywood by organized crime, when asked who in motion pictures best represented the real-life gangster, Burns replied,

> Chester Morris. In his picture "Alibi," he was the modern crook to perfection. Polished, pleasant, mild-mannered, without a single earmark of the crook; but deadly and fast in action when cornered. Real gangsters who have drifted out here to work in the gang and prison pictures were turned down by casting directors because they were better drawing-room types than anything else.[14]

On July 10, 1931, Chester was the featured performer in the syndicated comic strip "Star Dust" by Westphal. The strip used the standard publicity practice of listing his birthday as February 26, *1902*, and mentioned his early stage work, films for Warner Bros.-First National, role in *The Case of Sergeant Grischa* and leisure activities of golf and tennis.

The colorfully titled Howard Hughes project *Cock of the Air*, yet another of the self-indulgent millionaire's aviation pictures, went into production during mid–September 1931. An early version of the screenplay, submitted to Hughes in July by Lewis Milestone, had been judged as possibly reaching "beyond the limits of good taste" by Colonel Jason Joy of the American Motion Picture Pilots (AMPP) association. The title character, aviator Lieutenant Roger Craig (assigned to Chester), engaged in entirely too much "suggestive" behavior, including keeping a black book noting all his female conquests. Particularly objectionable was a scene in which he was to go after armor-clad cabaret performer Lilli de Rousseau (Billie Dove) with a can opener. These perverse elements, so typical of Hughes (who consistently would heap them upon his sexpot actresses, from Jean Harlow to Jane Russell and Janet Leigh), had to be altered or eliminated altogether. Silent star Dove previously had headlined Hughes' *The Age for Love* (1931), directed by Frank Lloyd, and featuring Adrian Morris in a supporting role.

Very much a hands-on producer, Hughes (who credited himself as director on *Hell's Angels* [1930], with James Whale listed as dialogue director) insisted that Chester spank Billie Dove so hard that the sound of his palm connecting with her rear end would dominate the scene. Though he followed the order, relayed by director Thomas Buckingham, to the point that the actress developed a posterior bruise, the effect ultimately was erased from the soundtrack.[15]

Buckingham wrapped production in early October, and Colonel Joy screened the edited film the following month. In a letter to Hughes, he wrote,

I have come away greatly disappointed that all of the suggestions made by us at the time we read the script have been ignored. Our first and most serious objection is to the fact that, beginning with the conversation between the two officers at the banquet in Italy until the scene in the dressing room where Roger asks Lilli to marry him, the principal theme is of maneuvering of a lecherous young man in his attempt to carry out one more seduction.[16]

In a reference touching on Hughes' lifelong obsession with breasts (which would be given ultimate on-screen representation with the special brassieres he designed for Russell in *The Outlaw* [1943] and Leigh in *Jet Pilot* [1957]), Joy added that Dove's pair were "overexposed in almost all of her costumes." Concluding that the AMPP would not approve the film unless several changes were made, he also arranged an additional screening for Italian representatives who might object to the blatantly ridiculous depiction of wartime conditions in their nation. However, Vice Consul of Italy R. Dalla Rosa had no objections to the film, and a second observer, Baron Valentin Mandelstamm, failed to provide any specific details about his "mild" concerns.

Hughes, in a repeat of his actions with another of his controversial features, *Scarface* (1932), attempted to distribute the film without the approval of the Motion Picture Producers and Distributors of America (MPPDA), but was ordered to cut specific material deemed "immoral" under the current Production Code. Lewis Milestone re-edited the entire film

Cock of the Air (1932): Chester Morris and Billie Dove in one of the film's controversial scenes [original lobby card].

(removing a total of 1,800 feet), with the stipulation that his name not be included in the credits or exploitation. (However, Milestone appears in an uncredited bit role, as a pipe-smoking man standing in a doorway, in the finished film.) The altered version, passed by the MPPDA, was released by United Artists on January 23, 1932.

Whereas *Hell's Angels* includes serious scenes of aerial warfare, *Cock of the Air* is primarily a 74-minute party, with one lengthy, exciting sequence featuring authentic airborne footage typical of the producer. The film opens and closes with the woman-chasing Roger Craig, initially behind a closed door with a sexy female during a wild soirée in Italy, and ultimately embracing Lilli de Rousseau, who accepts his marriage proposal, at a Paris theater where she performs as Joan of Arc. After using Roger, who goes AWOL to fly her to Paris during the war, she realizes that the former "Don Juan" truly loves her.

World War I is only a backdrop for the sex comedy. Charles Lederer's "romantic" dialogue is delivered remarkably well by Chester, who also consistently displays his talent for Stan Laurel–style nonverbal expression and gestures. Throughout his career, he would incorporate this visual technique with his well-enunciated diction, blending them into a primarily naturalistic style.

When first squiring Lilli in Italy, where the authorities are uncomfortable about her presence, Roger calls her, "Signorina Whatever—Whatever Happens Is Not My Fault."

During a scene in which Roger lodges in Paris, Chester plays it nearly nude, wearing only a small towel around his waist. Earlier, after spanking Lilli, Roger sits down, facing the back of the chair. Holding a bottle of champagne between his legs, he opens it, propelling the cork toward her face. This unsubtle "innuendo" is indicative of the film's general content.

Cinematographer Lucien Andriot keeps the film moving with countless tracking shots (forward, reverse and left to right) and striking compositions that make the most of Richard Day's lavish art direction. Billie Dove (who would appear in only one more film before retiring) is equally accomplished and alluring, and Matt Moore, as Craig's orderly, Terry, who keeps a log of his amorous activities, contributes substantially to the well-played humor.

Hughes typically promoted the aviation aspects of the picture. Arrangements were made with the Curtis-Wright Flying Service, "the nation's most powerful aviation organization," to provide participating exhibitors with gratis material, including color posters, for lobby displays. Curtis-Wright also suggested that prizes for contest winners be in the form of scholarships for ground courses, full flying courses and mechanics instruction courses, all offered at special lower fees. Additionally, each exhibitor was encouraged to declare a community "Aviation Week," during which heavy exploitation of *Cock of the Air* would "pack them into your theatre!"[17]

Roland West's idea of casting Chester in former Valentino roles was still the stuff of industry propaganda. Drawing attention to his versatility, especially his talent for comedy and romance, the pressbook suggested that *Cock of the Air* presented a "new Chester Morris" to filmgoers.

In his *New York Times* review, Mordaunt Hall wrote facetiously,

> Miss Dove does extremely well. She out-Eugénies anyone in the line of hats and in a closing scene she dons a suit of shining armor. Mr. Morris is alert and reckless as the ace of lovers and the devil among flyers. Another player who seizes all the opportunities offered in this nightmare is Mr. Moore. Whatever has been deleted by the censor does not seem to have made any difference to the story, for it is not one of those sensitive works that could be any the worse or any less coherent for a generous pruning.[18]

In her article "Even Heroes Are Getting Human," published in the October 1931 issue of *Silver Screen* magazine, Laura Benham focused on Chester's professional virtues:

> Another actor who is liked more for his weakness than his strength is Chester Morris, for with few exceptions, his roles have been unflattering. As the ex-husband in "The Divorcée," he was anything but an admirable individual—but who could blame Norma Shearer for returning to him? And in "The Big House," though he finished in a blaze of glory, he certainly got off to a bad start. Yet Leila Hyams forgave and forgot all his sins—and didn't we all? For there's something about Chester Morris that "gets under your skin."
>
> His appeal is not that of a boy but of the man. He personifies the underdog—the man who does wrong, not because he likes it, but because he cannot help himself. He is the man that any one of us might be but for the grace of God.
>
> And because you recognize that quality and are so aware of Morris' very human frailty, you cannot find it in your heart to blame him.[19]

Chester's interest in magic also began to attract the press. On October 12, *Variety* included him in a list of Hollywood actors who were beginning to outnumber the professional prestidigitators at meetings of the local branch of the Society of Magicians. While Neil Hamilton and Harold Lloyd were identified as possessing "the most pretentious equipment" ($10,000 or more) and performing at a major venue like the Shrine Auditorium, Chester, Charles Chaplin, Glen Tryon, Buster Collier, Douglas Fairbanks, Buster Keaton and James Hall were more likely to demonstrate their sleight-of-hand talents at their own private shows.[20]

In early December 1931, Chester, on loan to Paramount, began playing San Francisco confidence man John "Doc" Madison in *The Miracle Man*, billed behind female lead Sylvia Sidney as his accomplice, Helen Smith. (Gary Cooper had been considered for the Madison role, but his traveling and living in Europe and Africa during 1931–1932 temporarily put his Hollywood career on hold.) For a Chinatown parade scene filmed on First National's "Oriental set" and involving Chester, Sidney, John Wray and Ned Sparks, 200 Chinese actors and actresses were hired to provide authentic background atmosphere.

Fleeing the city after nearly killing Nikko (Boris Karloff), owner of a Chinatown bazaar, Madison becomes involved with "The Patriarch" (Hobart Bosworth, who replaced the recently deceased Tyrone Power, Sr.), a "faith healer" in Meadville, California. Madison's female cohort, Helen Smith, poses as Helen Vail, the Patriarch's grandniece, aided by the contortionist criminal "The Frog" (Wray) and pickpocket Harry Evans (Sparks). Madison enlists "The Frog" to perform a phony "transformation" during one of the Patriarch's "miracle" sessions, but the true healing of two disabled people, Bobbie Holmes (Robert Coogan, younger brother of Jackie, Chaplin's *The Kid*) and Margaret Thornton (Virginia Bruce), sets all of Meadville flocking to the scene.

Madison, in Helen's name, collects thousands of dollars in donations, supposedly to build a chapel where more miracles may be performed, from the local believers. When Margaret's wealthy brother, Robert Thornton (Lloyd Hughes), falls in love with Helen, and the three accomplices no longer wish to extort the seriously ailing Patriarch, Madison plans to flee with the cash. He has a change of heart, however, after Robert admits that Helen turned down a proposal of marriage because of her love for him. Madison returns and reunites with Helen as the Patriarch dies.

The novel by Robert Hobart Davis and Frank L. Packard first was published in the February 1914 issue of *Munsey's Magazine*. On September 21, 1914, George M. Cohan's stage adaptation opened at the Astor Theatre on Broadway and ran for 97 performances, closing in December. The Mayflower Photoplay Company, under the direction of George Loane Tucker on the Universal lot, shot the first screen adaptation distributed by Famous Players-Lasky Corporation and Paramount-Artcraft on August 26, 1919. Thomas Meighan and Betty Compson played the leads, supported by Lon Chaney, Sr., as the Frog and Joseph J. Dowling as the Patriarch.

During production, Chester, acting in a film based on a play by his former manager, told a reporter for the *Los Angeles Times*, "One must feel modest trying to duplicate the former work of an actor like Meighan. If I do as well as he, I shall be grateful."[21]

Interestingly, Chester's John Madison uses the alias "John Morgan," his character name in *The Big House*, in this film. Along with the principal actors, the supporting cast also is top-notch, particularly Irving Pichel as Henry Holmes, the atheist father of little Bobbie, who experiences an epiphany after his boy is cured by the Patriarch, and Boris Karloff, who worked in this film between the shooting and release of James Whale's *Frankenstein*, which would help propel him to major stardom during 1932. Karloff only appears in two brief scenes early in *The Miracle Man*, but his talent for playing oily, reptilian lechers is fully on display, behavior that sends Nikko, at the hands of Madison, hurtling over a staircase railing to a near-fatal crash on the apartment-house floor far below.

The faith-healing scene is well acted, directed (by Norman Z. McLeod) and edited (by an uncredited technician), with the musical score (an uncommon element in a film made in late 1931) also providing dramatic emphasis. Unlike many dramas about strong religious faith, *The Miracle Man* features a healer who is not a preacher, but a pray-er, providing redemption by example of his own conviction.

The June 1932 issue of *The New Movie Magazine* praised *The Miracle Man* as "a picture with splendid inspirational and spiritual value."[22] Rita C. McGoldrick of *Motion Picture Herald* rated the film "excellent ... with a strong cast giving a dramatically fine performance."[23] Issuing its "good" rating, *Silver Screen* magazine considered the overall effect of the film inferior to the original silent adaptation, but praised several of the performers:

> [The characters'] gradual reformation is still a beautiful thing and so is the miracle of the little crippled boy, played excellently by Bobby Coogan. Sylvia Sidney, as the girl in the gang, is miscast and Chester Morris is not as convincing as was Thomas Meighan. John Wray does splendidly by the Lon Chaney role, and Ned Sparks, as the fourth crook who specializes in watches, gives plenty of laughs to the first part of the picture. Hobart Bosworth, as the saintly patriarch, and Irving Pichel, as the scoffing, blasphemous father of crippled Bobby Coogan, are excellent.[24]

The Miracle Man (1932): Sylvia Sidney and Chester Morris in the poster art for the film, which briefly teamed him with his friend Boris Karloff for the first time [original window card].

Chester's family members continued landing supporting roles in major studio productions. RKO Radio's romantic drama *Behind Office Doors* (1931), directed by Melville H. Brown, costars Mary Astor, Robert Ames and Ricardo Cortez, supported by Catherine Dale Owen, Edna Murphy, Charles Sellon and William Morris (as Banker Charles H. Robinson).

Remaining at RKO, William played Frederick Weston in Victor Schertzinger's drama *The Woman Between* (1931), supporting a top cast including Lili Damita, Lester Vail, O.P. Heggie, Miriam Seeger, Anita Louise, Blanche Friderici and Halliwell Hobbes. Filmgoers familiar with Chester's performances could witness that William's distinctive speech patterns, pronunciation and enunciation had been passed on to his most famous son.

Two more uncredited roles at Columbia followed for Adrian Morris, the Officer in *Arizona* (1931), starring John Wayne in an early role, and Snooper the Henchman in *Pagan Lady* (1931), starring Evelyn Brent, Conrad Nagel and Charles Bickford, before other companies began to award him more visible parts with screen billing. Howard Hughes hired him for *The Age for Love* (1931), released by United Artists, costarring Billie Dove, Charles Starrett and Lois Wilson. He then was cast as Allen by Raoul Walsh for Fox's romantic comedy-drama *Me and My Gal* (1932) with Spencer Tracy, Joan Bennett, J. Farrell MacDonald and pioneering film actor Henry B. Walthall.

Wilhelmina ("Willette") Morris, now 28, trod the stage boards during 1931, costarring with Harry Green in *The Ambulance Chaser* at the Hollywood Playhouse. At Chester's behest, she also tried her luck at the film studios but was rejected because her face was too asymmetrical. Worse yet, she had no interest in playing the stereotypical roles usually offered to young actresses. She said,

> I like drama—rough and ready drama like Chester portrays. If anything is terrible, it is being "just the type" for an ingenue....
>
> I never wanted to go on the stage. All the rest of the family seemed to take it as a matter of course, but it always scared me to death. Whenever they gave plays at school, they would try to enlist me, just because my family was a theatrical one. Whenever I'd feel a play in the air, I would always get an attack of laryngitis or, simpler yet, go into hiding.[25]

On February 26, 1932, Adrian married stage actress Eva Virginia Shipley in Beverly Hills. Just as his film roles began to improve, those of father Morris moved in the opposite direction. In J. Walter Reuben's *The Roadhouse Murder* (1932), based on a novel by Maurice Level, William played the Judge, supporting Dorothy Jordan, Eric Linden, Purnell Pratt, Roscoe Ates, David Landau, Bruce Cabot, Phyllis Clare, Gustav von Seyffertitz and Roscoe Karns. Produced for RKO by Willis Goldbeck and the Morrises' former New York neighbor David O. Selznick, this atmospheric thriller was shot by cinematographer J. Roy Hunt, who worked on many of the studio's best films of the early 1930s.

William briefly took a step up to MGM for *The Washington Masquerade* (1932), directed by Charles Brabin and featuring Chester's original Broadway mentor, Lionel Barrymore, as well as Karen Morley, Nils Asther, William Collier, Sr., Rafaela Ottiano, C. Henry Gordon, Berton Churchill and Henry Kolker. This tale of political opportunism, in which Barrymore's Senator Jefferson Keane falls victim to young Consuela Fairbanks (Morley), who uses her relationship with him to aid a lobbyist, provided William with one of his best Hollywood credits. At MGM, he also played the uncredited role of Hamilton in Edgar Selwyn's *Skyscraper Souls* (1932), costarring Warren William, Maureen O'Sullivan, Anita Page and Norman Foster.

Following another uncredited part (as the Medicine Man) in Fox Film Corporation's

The Golden West (1932), directed by David Howard and featuring George O'Brien, Janet Chandler and Onslow Stevens, William realized that his brief career in Hollywood was nearing its end. Instead of languishing in more unnoticeable roles, he appeared in a San Francisco stage production of *The Vinegar Tree* and returned to New York to resume treading the boards of Broadway.

Paramount next cast Chester opposite Carole Lombard in "The Beachcomber," initially under the direction of William C. DeMille, who walked off the project after only two weeks of shooting. The original schedule was expanded from four to eight weeks; and, although David Burton and William Schorr were considered as replacements for DeMille, Alexander Hall eventually completed the production, which included rewrites and reshooting much of the original footage.

The finished film was released as *Sinners in the Sun* on May 13, 1932, after which Paramount announced that Chester, "who is really popular on the lot," would costar with Richard Arlen in *Come On, Marines!* and Regis Toomey in *The Glass Key*. (The studio did make both films, in 1934 and 1935, respectively, but Chester did not work on either of them.)[26] Neither "The Beachcomber" (the title of Mildred Cram's original story) nor *Sinners in the Sun* accurately represents the content of the film.

New York model Doris Blake (Lombard), who unhappily still lives in an apartment

Sinners in the Sun (1932): Chester Morris and Carole Lombard in their first of two romantic screen pairings.

with her disagreeable family, rebuffs her boyfriend, auto mechanic Jimmie Martin (Chester), choosing not to wed until they can afford it. Hired as a chauffeur by wealthy Claire Kinkaid (Adrienne Ames), Jimmie eventually is persuaded to get married, although he still loves Doris. Meanwhile, Doris has been staying out late at night with millionaire Eric Nelson (Walter Byron), who has promised to divorce his wife. After a series of unfortunate events, Doris refuses to marry Eric, and reunites with Jimmie after Claire amicably agrees to end their marriage.

Chester believably portrays the likable, somewhat naïve, working-class man who sleeps with his dog, becoming entangled with women with different incomes but also sincerely looking to add affection to their empty personal lives. Lombard and Ames, ideally cast in their roles, are well-supported by Alison Skipworth as Doris' mother and Cary Grant (in his second screen role) as Ridgeway, a pretty playboy. Ridgeway's caddish ways contribute to the depressive behavior of Doris' friend, Lil (Rita La Roy), who kills herself during a high-society soirée.

Hall's admirable pacing of the familiar plot is aided by the ace cinematography of Ray June. One montage sequence depicts Chester relying entirely on his nonverbal acting skills as Jimmie enjoys wild times with Claire. *Sinners in the Sun* is loaded with illicit drinking, gambling, and a parade of scantily clad young models, just the combination of elements that would help establish enforcement of the Production Code two years later.

In April 1932, *Motion Picture* magazine published a letter attributed to Laurence Elliston Smith of Cincinnati, Ohio, titled, "More of Chester Morris," in which this reader assigned social significance to his acting:

> There are actors and actors, but only one Chester Morris. Swaggering, devil-may-care, serious and concerned, villain or hero—he lives the part. I actually admired his dirty work in "Alibi." He was so bad that he was good. His remarkable change from the suave, dangerous criminal to the craven coward placed him at the head of my list of "who's who in filmland." It is not the parts he plays but how he plays them that has earned my admiration. He more than justified the faith the public placed in him when "The Big House" came to set the town a-talkin'. Give us more of this master of situations that we may secure material for conversation other than the Sino-Japanese affair and the depression.[27]

On April 3, 1932, the *Los Angeles Times*, prompted by the recent abduction of the Lindbergh baby and a threat against the small daughter of actress Ann Harding, ran the feature story "Hollywood Protects Itself Against Kidnappers: Precautions Taken in the Movie Colony." The safeguards taken for the children of directors Charles Chaplin and John Ford, and actors George Bancroft, Richard Barthelmess, Joan Bennett, Charles Bickford, John Boles, Clive Brook, Eddie Cantor, Harry Carey, Jack Holt, Buster Keaton, Victor McLaglen, Conrad Nagel and Spencer Tracy were described, as well as some apparent plots directed toward top stars Joan Crawford, Gary Cooper and Mary Pickford.

Referring to three-year-old Brooks, Chester, "refus[ing] to be alarmed at the infectious fear … agitating parents all over the country," offered, "I put him out on the front lawn, all alone, with a sign on him, and nobody will take him."[28]

MGM director Jack Conway began shooting *Red-Headed Woman*, pairing Chester with 21-year-old Jean Harlow, on April 28, 1932. Harlow was cast in the title role, her first to require talent beyond stereotypical "vamping," by Irving Thalberg, who had ordered the screen test. Wynne Gibson, Dixie Lee, Lillian Roth and Alice White auditioned but were turned down. Prior to Harlow winning the role, MGM had requested Nancy Carroll (refused by Paramount) and Helen Twelvetrees (refused by RKO), and considered Greta Garbo, Lillian Roth, Jeanette MacDonald and Peggy Shannon. Clara Bow and Colleen Moore turned down the "trashy" part outright.

F. Scott Fitzgerald initially was announced to adapt the script from the bestselling novel by Katherine Bush, but pioneer screenwriter Anita Loos eventually was hired. Marcel De Sano was set to direct the film but was replaced before shooting began. Twenty-five years later, Chester claimed that, after "Jean Harlow's director" wasted an entire morning composing and lighting a tight close-up on her lips, a new filmmaker was assigned two days later. His witty explanation: "He lost so much saliva drooling over Jean he collapsed, and they had to hire another one."[29]

Harlow's inexperience resulted in one office sequence being consigned to the cutting-room floor. As Chester (playing businessman William Legendre, Jr.) and Leila Hyams (his wife, Irene) were having a conversation, Jean (stenographer Lil ["Red"] Andrews) was instructed to keep typing, then look up after they had passed her desk. Following several unsuccessful takes, much to Conway's aggravation, she could not properly time her reaction. Distracted, Jean then became convinced that Leila was enjoying her struggle. When the director finally wrapped for the day, Jean stormed angrily from the studio.[30]

During production, Chester was visited in his dressing room by fellow MGM players Lionel Barrymore, William Collier, Sr., and his father, all of whom were appearing in *Washington Masquerade*. Their recollections of shared acting experiences, both serious and humorous, proved quite enlightening.

In Renwood, the small company town of *Red-Headed Woman*, Lil Andrews is a bad girl. The film opens with a series of shots (added after a sneak preview) depicting her various attractions: red hair, shapely figure and especially her legs, one sporting a garter in which she places a small portrait of William Legendre, Jr., her married boss whom she long has planned to seduce. She lingers at Bill's home while working late one night, but leaves after his wife, Irene, returns. Bill, who told her, "You're too pretty and I don't trust myself," insists that the incident is meaningless. His father, William Sr. (Lewis Stone), attempts to transfer her to a new job in Cleveland the following day.

At the Log Cabin nightclub, where Bill and Irene are enjoying themselves, Red follows him into a private phone booth and kisses him. "This is insane!" Bill exclaims.

Harlow excels in bad behavior throughout the film, but her talent was transformed by this role; and Red's pathological persistence, though narcissistic, is also intriguing. A subsequent scene involves Red drunkenly stomping, and then kissing, a framed portrait of Bill as a record of the murder-inspired song "Frankie and Johnny" plays in her room. She eventually gets her wish and marries Bill after Irene divorces him. Soon she begins working her wiles on another man, older Legendre business associate Charles B. Gaerste (Henry Stephenson), who plans to marry her, but simultaneous dalliances with Albert (Charles Boyer), his French chauffeur, derail this objective.

Red's "three-timing" involving Bill, Charles and Albert inevitably leads to tragedy. After Bill moves into his father's home and begins reconciling with Irene, she shoots him as he attempts to drive away with his former wife. He recovers and declines to press charges against her. In Paris two years later, the remarried Bill and Irene see Red, now the mistress of an aging, bearded French millionaire, being chauffeured away from the horse races by none other than Albert!

The conniving, gold-digging tramp character, one of Harlow's early specialties, is played to perfection in *Red-Headed Woman*. Red's accusation that William Legendre, Sr., who hands her a $500 check to leave town, is a "dirty, gumshoeing, hypocritical sneak" is

Red-Headed Woman (1932): Jean Harlow and Chester Morris in one of the film's most volatile moments [original lobby card].

an example of Anita Loos' wicked "pre–Code" dialogue, particularly effective when aimed at an honorable actor like Lewis Stone. Chester also excels in his characterization, which he was careful to make quite different than Ted in *The Divorcée* and Jimmie in *Sinners in the Sun*.

Jack Conway's tasteful direction includes just enough allure and a hint of violence to engage audience interest: Harold Rosson tilting the camera, showing Harlow's legs as Red drops her skirt or Una Merkel's shoulders as Sally, her roommate, gets ready for bed; and editor Blanche Sewell cutting to a shot outside Red's apartment as Bill knocks her down during his attempt to leave the locked room. "Do it again! I like it!" she masochistically shouts after he slaps her the first time.

Thalberg and coproducer Albert Lewin's casting of Chester's *Big House* costars Hyams and Stone is also effective, as is the presence of Boyer (who plays Chester's character in the French version of the prison film), who began acting in Hollywood the previous year, and May Robson as Bill's Aunt Jane.

Even in a film released prior to enforcement of the Production Code, the dénouement of *Red-Headed Woman* is unorthodox, one that must have surprised filmgoers who would expect a self-absorbed, greedy and vindictive character like Lil Andrews to receive her comeuppance by the film's end. A commercial success, it grossed $750,000 on a $400,000 budget, leading to Harlow's subsequent casting by MGM in *Red Dust* (1932) with Clark Gable. *Screenland* editor Delight Evans wrote,

> "Red-Headed Woman" ... presents Jean Harlow, for the first time, as an actress. She *is* a surprise! All the platinum and other blondes will go red-head now. Not a family picture, children, so try to keep your parents at home.... See this for sheer amusement. Jean plays a mean part so cleverly that you can't help liking this wild red-headed woman.[31]

Herbert Brenon originally had planned to direct a film adaptation of the controversial *The Bitter Tea of General Yen* for Columbia while on loan from RKO Radio, but both studios became fed up with his unprofessional behavior, resulting in his leaving Hollywood for Britain, where he owned property. His intention to feature Chester as the titular character ended with his departure, and the film, with Frank Capra as director, began shooting on July 7, 1932. Nils Asther played Yen, with Barbara Stanwyck cast as the female lead.

In early August 1932, the independent company Ben Verschleiser Productions signed Chester for the top-billed role in *Breach of Promise*, directed by Paul L. Stein. Verschleiser adapted Rupert Hughes' story "Obscurity" for the screenplay, with additions by John Goodrich, Anthony Veiller and Art Miller. Produced by prominent Chickasaw actor-director Edwin Carewe, the project was wrapped in late August and released by World Wide Pictures on October 23.

James Pomeroy (Chester), a young politician, is victimized by a $50,000 breach of promise suit after innocently becoming involved with Hattie (Mae Clarke), the adopted daughter of farm couple Joe and Cora Pugmire (Charles Middleton and Elizabeth Patterson). His reputation in the gutter, James joins it there by copiously applying alcohol to the situation, until Hattie confesses the truth to the district attorney (Theodore von Eltz). Convicted of perjury, she is sentenced to one year in prison, but a grateful James promises to await her release.

The Film Daily praised the picture's innovative elements:

> [L]ittle surprise twists and unexpected developments ... keep building the suspense to an unusual ending. The obvious seldom happens in this film, but always the unlooked for, which makes it very refreshing and intelligent entertainment. Chester Morris gives a convincing and stirring performance as the candidate for Senator who is almost ruined socially, politically and financially by the breach of promise suit instituted by Mae Clarke. Miss Clarke plays her role with fine repression and understanding. Worthy of special commendation is Charles Middleton for his part of a hard, narrowminded foster father, which conveys a sense of gripping power. The girl's final atonement for the wrong she has done the man she loves is cleverly handled in a succession of very moving scenes.[32]

In his review for *Hollywood Filmograph*, Lou Jacobs praised the entire cast, particularly the leads: "Chester Morris gives a sterling portrayal of the senator and Mae Clarke is delightful as the girl. A remarkably well drawn character part was portrayed by Charles Middleton as the cruel guardian."[33] (*Breach of Promise* is another film believed to be "lost.")

In the August 1932 issue of *Broadway and Hollywood "Movies"* magazine, Harry Carey served as guest editor of "The Month's Mail." The first letter he included in the section, titled, "Takes Tobin to Task," was submitted by a reader identified only as "M.T.K.":

> I cannot agree with Genevieve Tobin who, in your July issue, defined her ideal man as a combination of James Cagney, Leslie Howard and Clive Brook. I wouldn't select any Englishman for my list, which is as follows:
> Charles "Buddy" Rogers for virility; Chester Morris for "guts," as Miss Tobin called it; Fredric March for brains; and Paul Lukas for dignity.[34]

Breach of Promise (1932): From left, Charles Middleton, Mae Clarke and Chester Morris in a tense scene [original photo from the personal collection of Mae Clarke].

Not confining herself strictly to actors hailing from the United States, however, M.T.K. did include the Budapest-born Lukas.

In October 1932, Herbert Wilcox, productions director of British and Dominions, Ltd., published an opinion piece in the London tabloid *Daily Mail*, stating,

> Britain has no leading man with the standard of virility which cinema audiences of today demand of their film heroes.... At the present time I cannot name one straight actor in Britain with a fraction of the popular appeal commanded by such men as Clark Gable, Robert Montgomery, Gary Cooper, Richard Arlen, Chester Morris, Fredric March or Warren William.[35]

As a reply to Wilcox, Bernard Charman, London Correspondent for *Motion Picture Herald*, wrote,

> Ask any average English filmgoer to name half a dozen British screen stars without stopping to think, and he will give you—Tom Walls, Ralph Lynn, Jack Hulbert, Leslie Fuller, Jack Buchanan, Gordon Harker (perhaps) and no more.
> There is certainly not a Gable in that crowd. In considered argument one constantly is hearing such names as John Stuart, Colin Clive, Garry Marsh, Harold Huth, Henry Kendall ... but, painful as it may be to confess, there is not one of them to be compared with ... Robert Montgomery or ... Gary Cooper. Their respective merits as actors do not enter into the question, for several of the

British players mentioned have been known to put over first rate performances of a type (while the careers of the Hollywood players have not all been without blemish). But none of them has ... given us a virile performance to compare, for example, with that of Warren William in "The Mouthpiece." Unless ... the Captain Stanhope of Colin Clive in "Journey's End" can be excepted.

That again, switches the argument to another track—is it the material we lack or the knowledge of how to develop it?[36]

As a member of the Academy of Motion Picture Arts and Sciences (AMPAS), Chester was elected, with Reginald Barlow, Warner Baxter, Hedda Hopper and Edward G. Robinson, to the executive committee of the Actors' Branch, who met to choose their chairman at an annual banquet on November 18, 1932. The other branches consisted of directors (including Cecil B. De Mille, Alfred E. Green, Robert Z. Leonard, Rouben Mamoulian and Fred Niblo), producers (Louis B. Mayer, Bud P. Schulberg, David O. Selznick, Winfield Sheehan and Jack L. Warner), assistant directors, technicians and writers.

In November 1932, Ray Enright began directing *Blondie Johnson* at Warner Bros. for $151,000 on a 25-day shooting schedule which wrapped in early December. On the following February 25, the film became the first 1933 release to feature Chester, who plays the type of role in which the studio usually cast James Cagney, who would star in five Warner Bros. productions that year: *Hard to Handle*, *Picture Snatcher*, *The Mayor of Hell*, *Footlight Parade* and *Lady Killer*, the last being the only title involving a gang story. At this point, due to public pressure, the studio known for its gritty Great Depression crime stories was beginning to ease off the serious gangster elements in favor of parody, with former thug boss *Little Caesar* Edward G. Robinson becoming bootlegger-cum-social climber *The Little Giant* in early 1933.

Screenwriter Earl Baldwin had provided the dialogue for *The Widow from Chicago* (1930), Robinson's first Warner Bros. gangster drama, and *The Mouthpiece* (1932), the studio's adaptation of Frank J. Collins' play about a prosecutor (Warren William) who turns to defending guilty clients after convicting an innocent man subsequently sent to the electric chair. Adding another fresh twist to keep Warners' gangster genre afloat, Baldwin wrote the original story and screenplay for *Blondie Johnson*, a young woman determined to succeed as a con artist after grinding Depression poverty hastens her mother's death and she is denied government relief.

Informed that there are two ways to make money, she replies, "The hard way and the easy way," choosing the latter alternative, first scamming city dwellers with the aid of taxi driver Red Charley (Sterling Holloway) and then Danny Jones (Chester), one of her marks with whom she then collaborates in bigger criminal "insurance" schemes. A major component of Baldwin's innovative concept was having the female operator achieve success in a nonromantic, intelligent manner, rather than using the common, simple expedient of sex.

With Joan Blondell cast in the titular role, the studio needed an actor with a solid background in cinematic crime. Its principal star, Cagney, demanded top billing (along with many other conditions), and the role of Danny Jones, right-hand man to Max Wagner (Arthur Vinton), the city's big rackets boss, though the male lead, also would serve as sidekick to the female mob leader. Chester had no qualms accepting a role that expanded his repertoire, even though Danny (like his other Warner Bros. characters) is set squarely within the conventions of the popular crime genre.

Unlike many stars of "golden age" Hollywood, Chester proved that he was, not a screen personality, but an *actor*, consistently developing character differences that ideally set each

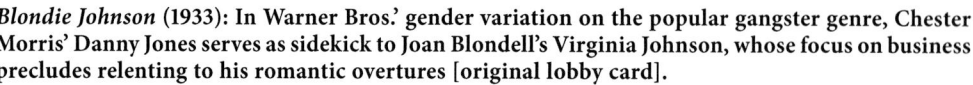

Blondie Johnson (1933): In Warner Bros.' gender variation on the popular gangster genre, Chester Morris' Danny Jones serves as sidekick to Joan Blondell's Virginia Johnson, whose focus on business precludes relenting to his romantic overtures [original lobby card].

subsequent role apart from the last. From the time he signed with Warner Bros. in 1930 until his first project of 1933, James Cagney had made 11 films for a single studio; while Chester made 18, for United Artists, Paramount, Warner Bros., MGM and World Wide Pictures. Prior to *Blondie Johnson*, he had played criminal roles in half his films, but for the new assignment, he was careful to blend the Warner Bros. "type" with aspects of his own style. Arguably, very few actors could chew gum, smoke and clearly enunciate dialogue simultaneously, and Chester does so convincingly throughout the film.

Some viewers may think of Danny Jones as a Cagney role, but James (or "Jim," not "Jimmy," a nickname used by strangers) could not have played it as filmed. Cagney, a non-smoker, begrudgingly handled a cigarette very few times in his career, and, as capable and magnetic as he was, would not have cared for this role (perhaps inciting another of his legendary bouts with Jack Warner [or "The Shvontz," as Jim called him]). Like Cagney, Chester does smack Blondell in the mug in one scene, although the "punch" comes from off camera, and they undeniably have ample chemistry throughout the film. Virginia Johnson is just too interested in business to relent to Danny's continual overtures for pleasure.

In an early role, Allen Jenkins already had supported Warners' stars Paul Muni (*I Am a Fugitive from a Chain Gang* [1932]) and Cagney (*Hard to Handle*), and soon would become one of the most memorable, frequent comic-criminal sidekicks (to Edward G. Robinson, Humphrey Bogart, Errol Flynn, George Sanders and others) in Hollywood history. At this point, he had played somewhat more serious, rough characters in Warners' *Three on a Match* (1932) and *Lawyer Man* (1932), both with Joan Blondell, following them up with his role as gang member Louie in *Blondie Johnson*. The cast also includes two frequent Laurel and Hardy colleagues, Walter Long (in the uncredited role of Artie, one of Wagner's associates) and Mae Busch (as Mae, a moll), Chester's former "acting coach" during the production of *Alibi*.

The consistent acting is supported by snappy dialogue. When Danny tells Blondie that he's interested in having a conversation, she counters, "But you do all your talking with your hands." Baldwin's writing is solid, with the Depression poverty aspect falling in line with Warners' gritty, powerful features *I Am a Fugitive from a Chain Gang*, *Heroes for Sale* and *Wild Boys of the Road* all being produced during 1932 and 1933.

As in many early 1930s crime films, isolated acts of violence are primarily suggested, occurring off-screen, although a little "blood" appears on the hand of Max, who is whacked in an innovative, unforgettable scene rivaling earlier moments in the Warner Bros. gangster genre, particularly during the conclusions of *Little Caesar* and *The Public Enemy* (1931). As he enjoys a drink in an apartment, Wagner is machine-gunned by a shooter hidden behind a revolving bookcase bar.

The production benefits from the work of cinematographer Tony Gaudio, who already had shot *Little Caesar* and *Tiger Shark* (1932) for Warners, where he would go on to serve as director of photography on *The Story of Louis Pasteur* (1936), *Anthony Adverse* (1936), for which he won an Academy Award, *The Life of Emile Zola* (1937), *The Adventures of Robin Hood* (1938), *High Sierra* (1941) and many other first-rate features. In a banquet scene, during which Danny speaks about his successful scheme to get Louie acquitted at a murder trial, Gaudio repeats a memorable camera setup he had used to frame Robinson at a party in *Little Caesar*.

The Film Daily praised Baldwin's innovative depiction of gender as realized by Blondell: "A fresh twist is given here to the gangster melodrama by having a girl as the brain behind the works. Miss Blondell does some of her best work and shows dramatic ability in some of the scenes."[37] Chester, too, gives one of his best performances since *The Big House*, playing a primarily nonviolent criminal who is more complex and likable than his earlier gangsters for Warner Bros. and other studios.

In October 1932, *Motion Picture* magazine ran a feature on the attitudes of Hollywood film-industry professionals toward Prohibition. Of the 312 individuals interviewed, 286 (nearly 92 percent) favored repeal. Chester, who always voiced a high respect for legitimate law and order, said, "Didn't we take on a greater evil than the saloon when the Eighteenth Amendment brought the speakeasy into such abundant being? Repeal is the only cure for the speakeasy, which is reason enough to vote for repeal."[38]

The presidential election of Franklin D. Roosevelt one month later soon brought an end to Prohibition. In February 1933, the U.S. Congress adopted a resolution proposing the 21st Amendment, which would repeal the 18th and initially modify the Volstead Act to permit the sale of beer (and eventually restore control of alcohol to the states), which was ratified 10 months later. On December 5, Utah, the 36th state to approve the measure, provided the necessary majority.

Following passage of the 21st Amendment, *Motion Picture* published a follow-up to its earlier article, announcing, "The stars didn't go wild on Repeal Night. They stayed right

The Infernal Machine (1933): Genevieve Tobin and Chester Morris in the poster art for director Marcel Varnel's screwball comedy about an anarchists' timebomb scare aboard an ocean liner [original insert poster].

at home—in their own swelegant barrooms." Indeed, Chester had "one of the best" custom bars installed in the Morris home: Similar to the cinematic version on the set of *Blondie Johnson*, it was "concealed behind a sliding bookcase in his library."[39]

Chester began working with director Marcel Varnel to shoot *The Infernal Machine* at Fox Studios on December 3, 1932. Adapted from Karl Sloboda's novel by Arthur Kober, this screwball comedy about an anarchists' timebomb scare aboard an ocean liner costars Chester as Robert Holden, a stowaway, and Genevieve Tobin as Elinor Green, a fellow American who had accidentally met him in Paris. Varnel completed the shoot in early January 1933.

The solid supporting cast of Victor Jory, Elizabeth Patterson, Edward Van Sloan, James Bell and Arthur Hohl could not overcome what exhibitors and audiences considered laggard direction and befuddled dialogue, and the picture did poor box office nationwide. *The Film Daily* called it "mild entertainment ... lack[ing] definite punch ... pretty loose and unconvincing."[40] *Variety*'s "Abel" liked it even less:

"Infernal Machine" is a bushleague title for a major company production.... Starts off interestingly, but then becomes placid despite the intended hecticism of discovering the titular infernal machine which threatens to blow up the transatlantic liner enroute from Paris to New York.... Chester Morris is the stowaway who manages to be very natty throughout after an adventurous meeting on the Paris boulevards.[41]

In early 1933, the effects of the Great Depression hit the film industry particularly hard. Placed in receivership, the Paramount-Publix theater chain petitioned for voluntary bankruptcy in March. As a result, an industry-wide resolution required its "high-salaried" employees either to accept an eight-week salary reduction or work four weeks without pay. An "emergency committee" headed by actor Lawrence Grant was attended by a large group of performers, including Chester,

Ralph Bellamy, Charles Bickford, Mary Brian, Clive Brook, James Cagney, June Collyer, Neil Hamilton, Jack Holt, Hedda Hopper, Myrna Loy, David Manners, Conrad Nagel, Edgar Norton, Pat O'Brien, Elizabeth Patterson, Dick Powell, Purnell Pratt, Lewis Stone, Thelma Todd and Regis Toomey. Later that month, six actors (Berton Churchill, Alden Gay, Charles Miller, Grant Mitchell, Ralph Morgan and Kenneth Thomson) gathered to establish the Screen Actors Guild.

In mid–January 1933, Jesse L. Lasky reportedly was interested in casting Chester as Theseus in *The Warrior's Husband*, to be released by Fox.[42] By the time director Walter Lang began shooting the film in early February, David Manners had been cast opposite leading lady Elissa Landi.

In March 1933, Ray Enright directed the Jefferson Pictures Corporation production "The Black Ace" (also titled "Black Flash" and "Design for Murder" at various points) costarring Chester and Vivienne Osborne, supported by Frank McHugh, Allen Jenkins, Henry Stephenson, Grant Mitchell and Charles Middleton. Writer Ralph Spence crafted the screenplay in the style of a traditional mystery play.

Chester was in familiar company while shooting "The Black Ace," having worked with Enright and Jenkins on *Blondie Johnson*, Middleton on *Breach of Promise*, Stephenson on *Red-Headed Woman* and McHugh on *Corsair*. Neil Broderick (Chester) is a self-confessed author of "rubbish" crime novels who meets Martha Winters (Osbourne) on a train bound for the estate of Thornton Duke (Stephenson), a close friend of Marsden (Oscar Apfel), the latest victim of "The Black Ace," a mysterious killer who murders at an appointed time, leaving an ace of spades behind on the body.

Martha is the daughter of Austin Winters (Mitchell), Drake's secretary, who pieces together a jigsaw puzzle on the boss' desk, indicating that the Black Ace next will strike "at seven tomorrow night." The following day, Drake and Winters, accompanied by Broderick and Martha, take a flight to stay at his plantation in Louisiana, where a pair of obtuse Chicago detectives, Clancy (McHugh) and Dugan (Jenkins), also arrive. During a blackout, Winters is murdered. Broderick discovers a letter on the body, in which Winters claims to know the identity of the killer; but before Drake can read it aloud, the lights again go out. Only blank paper and an ace of spades are discovered.

The pilot is murdered, Simons (Middleton), the "coroner," is revealed as a federal agent, and Broderick, long suspected by the detectives, accuses Drake of being the Black Ace. Broderick, who earlier vented his frustration by threatening to "wrap a table around [Dugan's] head," engages in a furious brawl with Drake, who is dispatched after Pompey (Gus Robinson), the faithful butler, accidentally skewers him with his own cane, armed with a retractable spike.

Produced on a limited budget, the film, released as *Tomorrow at Seven* by RKO Radio on June 2, 1933, benefits from an effective visual style created by Edward Jewell's art direction, Charles Schoenbaum's camerawork (including some interesting subjective tracking shots) and Enright's direction. The serious actors in the cast often are upstaged by McHugh and Jenkins, who naturally pours forth a torrent of jargon unintelligible to the others. *The Modern Screen* magazine, particularly appreciating the humor, proclaimed the film "swell": "Here's a super-creepy mystery opus with gobs of thrills and hysterical giggles.... Chester Morris scores heavily but those two hick cops, Allen Jenkins and Frank McHugh, are so dumb they practically steal the show. Kids will like it."[43]

On March 10, 1933, an earthquake hit Los Angeles. Chester first had experienced a major tremor seven years earlier, and readily admitted to having a "definite phobia [of]

Tomorrow at Seven (1933): Chester Morris, Henry Stephenson, Grant Mitchell and Vivienne Osborne in the poster art for director Ray Enright's murder mystery released by RKO Radio [original one-sheet poster].

earthquakes," one shared by Robert Montgomery.[44] Each time he was threatened by such an event, feeling completely helpless, he became pale and nauseated. When he and Sue bought their new home, they had it "quake-proofed" and took out an ample insurance policy.

Following the terror of the March quake, Chester and Bob were attending a meeting at the Writers' Club when a tremor shook the building. The two macho actors quickly headed for the nearest exit, but the doors were locked. They pivoted around, embarrassed to find the rest of the 200-strong gathering, wide-eyed and silent, staring at them. Finally, actress Mae Murray spoke up. "Come children," she told them, "sit down like good little boys."[45]

Following his small part as the Medicine Man in *The Golden West*, Chester's father had not worked in nine months. In Los Angeles on May 3, 1933, William and Etta both filed voluntary bankruptcy petitions in U.S. District Court, listing liabilities of $3,853 and assets of $455. Most of the debts were owed to stores in New York.

Chester had undergone financial difficulties of his own. On May 11, he ran a full-page advertisement in *The Hollywood Reporter*, stating, "Chester Morris wishes to announce the termination of his five-year contract with Roland West." At the bottom of the page, he included, "Address all communications to Room 200, Hollywood Professional Building, Phone Hillside 1141." Signing on for new management with the Rebecca and Silton agency, he was working on a freelance basis, and would wait a year before revealing the details of his decision to break with West.

Around this time, Chester and Sue took Brooks, now five years old, and Cynthia, three, to a movie theater to catch a first glimpse of their thespian father. He explained,

> Cynthia could still be kept from the movies, but Brooks was crazy about them and wanted to see me. So I thought I might as well get it over with. But let me tell you, I went into a cold sweat when I realized that they might be still too young to understand it was only play-acting. And just suppose Cynthia, wide-eyed and trusting, should put her little hand in mine and inquire, "Why do you play bad men, Daddy?" What could I honestly answer, except, "The producers seem to think Daddy's just the type, darling."[46]

On December 9, 1932, *The Film Daily* reported that Sue (billed as Suzanne Kilborn) had signed to appear in the Warner Bros. film *She Had to Say Yes*, to be codirected by Busby Berkeley and George Amy. A slight play on the title of Chester's 1930 Warners film *She Couldn't Say No*, the debut of Mrs. Morris was released on July 15, 1933.

As Birdie Reynolds, one of the stenographers at the clothing business of Sol Glass (Ferdinand Gottshalk), Sue inspires her coworkers to charm customers in the hope of increasing sales during the depths of the Great Depression. Eventually Birdie becomes involved in a romantic triangle with Florence Denny (Loretta Young) and Daniel Drew (Lyle Talbot). Becoming the fifth member of the Morris family to try film acting, Sue both made her debut *and* her last bow with this film. Perhaps, following this experience, *she had to say no*.

Brooks initially attended the private elementary Carl Curtis School in Los Angeles, but his comments upon returning home one afternoon prompted Chester to make a quick change of venue.

"I don't want to ride on the bus anymore, Daddy," Brooks informed him.

"What's wrong with the bus?" asked Chester.

"Nothing," the boy answered, "but I want to ride up with a chauffeur like the rest of the kids."

Pleased that Brooks had been honest, Chester enrolled him at a public school where he soon became friends with children of non–film stars from all walks of life.

By August 1933, the Screen Actors Guild had attracted 48 members, several who left the Academy of Motion Picture Arts and Sciences (AMPAS) to support the new organization. At an August 24 membership meeting, several top actors became candidates in SAG elections: Fredric March, Adolphe Menjou and Robert Montgomery for the Board of Governors; and Chester, Ralph Bellamy, Robert Montgomery, Edward G. Robinson and Spencer Tracy for the Actors Branch Executive Committee.

Earlier that month, while still on the AMPAS actors executive committee, Chester, Reginald Barlow, Warner Baxter, Hedda Hopper and Adolphe Menjou all signed a telegram to his *Miracle Man* costar, Sylvia Sidney, asking her to reconsider a decision not to complete work on the Paramount picture *The Way to Love* (1933), for which director Norman Taurog reportedly had completed two-thirds of the production phase. Following a month of acting with leading man Maurice Chevalier, Sidney had undergone a throat operation, after which her physician advised her to convalesce for an extended period. Rather than return to the studio, she boarded a flight to New York, where she planned to leave for Europe with producer Bud P. Schulberg.

Paramount vice-president Emanuel Cohen had written to Sidney, asking her to return to work only when fully recovered, with the request that she not leave Los Angeles. Nonetheless, she ignored Cohen's missive, leading to a $100,000 budget increase on the film and the establishment of what the studio deemed "a highly dangerous precedent in the acting profession."

The wire sent by Chester and his cohorts read, in part:

> It has come to our attention that you have left the cast of your picture and contemplate an extended trip to Europe. If it is humanly possible to regain sufficient strength to return to work and complete your engagement, we earnestly beseech you to do so.
>
> No leading player has ever been known in the history of the stage or screen ever to violate the ethics of our profession. We beg you to consider, and do not by any action place everlasting stigma upon your fellow players. We know that as the good trouper that you are will come through and let the show go on.

Replying that she was "annoyed" by the allegations, Sidney denied that she had "walked out," claiming that the picture was "only in third day of filming" and that "the scenes in which she had appeared were minor ones that could be refilmed with little expense." As reported in *Motion Picture Herald*, "She agreed that studio physicians had examined her and pronounced her fit to work, but she said, 'they treated me like a nobody' and did not make a thorough investigation of her condition."[47] When she refused to complete the picture, Paramount assigned her role to Carole Lombard, who turned it down. Eventually Ann Dvorak was cast, and Taurog reshot all the scenes in which Sidney had appeared.

Chester appeared in one of producer-director Louis Lewyn's *Hollywood on Parade* one-reel shorts, released by Paramount in mid–September 1933. Introducing the English songwriting duo of Mack Gordon and Harry Revel to Hollywood audiences, the 10-minute film also featured impresario Sid Grauman and several other stars, including Max Baer, Maurice Chevalier, Lew Cody, Joan Crawford, Cary Grant, Marie Dressler, Jimmy Durante, Jean Harlow, Mary Pickford, George Raft, Johnny Weissmuller and Ed Wynn. One sequence featured Raft hoofing it to Gordon and Revel's performance of their number "Underneath the Harlem Moon."

Paramount released *Golden Harvest,* its dramatic film about farmers during the height of the Great Depression, on September 22, 1933. Recent protests and strikes by farmers in the Midwest and California made the topic ripe for the original story by Nina Wilcox Putnam, who recently had cowritten (with Richard Schayer) a quite different tale for Universal's macabre supernatural thriller *The Mummy* (1932), starring Boris Karloff. To bring realism to Casey Robinson's screenplay, headlined by Chester and Richard Arlen as brothers raised on their father's wheat farm, producer Charles R. Rogers sent assistant director Raoul Pagel and recording engineer Joseph Kane to the Windy City, where footage of the "wheat pit" at the Chicago Board of Trade and events at the World's Fair were filmed on location.

Director Ralph Murphy and production manager Val Paul took the primary cast and 45 crew members to Pendleton, Oregon, for a location shoot lasting three weeks, the most extensive trip organized by Paramount since the dawn of talkies. The area was chosen for the large-scale wheat harvest carried out by a diverse cross section of workers. The studio hired five actors from a Portland stock company, who flew down to Pendleton for their scenes, three others for bit roles and several hundred local extras. A 25-car freight train was chartered for use during a farm riot sequence. Richard Arlen's farming scenes required that he learn to drive a tractor, operate a harrow, and pilot a combine during the harvest.

The costars made a personal appearance at the local theater, where they attended films on many evenings. Sue accompanied Chester, and during a break from shooting, they traveled with Arlen and his wife, actress Jobyna Ralston, to Walla Walla, Washington, where they spent two days relaxing and sightseeing.

Rogers and Murphy's casting choices proved ideal: from Arlen's young man of the soil, Walt Martin, and Chester's college-educated, world-savvy marketer, Chris Martin, to Berton Churchill (in one of his most convincing performances) as the patriarch, Eben Martin, and a fine supporting cast. Julie Haydon as Ellen Goodhue, the farm girl originally engaged to Chris but who marries Walt, and Genevieve Tobin as city "society" woman Cynthia Flint, who becomes Chris' wife just as he pushes himself toward hard times, provide a believable contrast. They are depicted with a rare, admirable depth that graces Putnam and Robinson's characterizations in general.

Chester builds his characterization steadily, taking Chris from confident enthusiasm with his new career at the Chicago Board of Trade to desperate intensity, sticking with the plan to aid his brother and fellow striking farmers although it leads to insolvency. Arlen, too, demonstrates a commendable arc as Walt evolves from quiet farmer to devoted striker and agrarian representative in Washington, D.C., successfully speaking to a government committee about raising prices in the wake of his brother's financial ruin.

Several unforgettable moments distinguish the film's nimble 72 minutes. The film's lack of heavy-handedness is well-represented by a charming romantic scene involving Chris showing his childhood swimming hole to Cynthia, with whom he is visiting the farm to attend the wedding of longtime family helpers, Louis ["Loopy Lou"] Jenkins (Roscoe Ates, in an atypical non-stuttering performance) and Lydia (Elizabeth Patterson). A shot of Chris wading into the moonlit water while carrying Cynthia is stunningly rendered by cinematographer Milton Krasner.

Preceding this quiet moment is a scene, directed with an estimable level of humor by Murphy, in which the guests noisily roust the newlywed couple from their honeymoon bed. Robinson's dialogue is also consistently memorable. To boost wheat prices in Chicago, Chris predicts, "The Boston Tea Party will seem tame compared to the rumpus we're about to start." Following his failed last stand in the "wheat pit," Cynthia assures him, "I always thought I married a gentleman. I married something far better—a *man*."

Richard Arlen, who worked as a newspaper reporter in St. Paul and Duluth, Minnesota, prior to his film career, wrote a feature article, titled, "An Actor Reverts to Type," for the November 1933 issue of *Broadway and Hollywood "Movies"* magazine. Recalling details of the location shoot, he included a practical joke involving Chester:

Golden Harvest (1933): Chester Morris and Genevieve Tobin in the film's most romantic scene [original lobby card].

> Gags were flying back and forth at odd moments throughout the trip, but the best was framed by Roscoe Ates on Chester Morris. Chet arrived two days after the rest of us. Ates hired a group of boys to meet him at the station. Each was given a sign to carry which read, "Welcome Chester Conklin."[48]

The film received favorable press from reviewers impressed by its topicality and tactful dramatization. *Motion Picture Herald*'s "McCarthy" wrote, "Although there have been other farm pictures recently, 'Golden Harvest' seems to have caught the spirit of the premise more effectively. It always seems close and real."[49]

Motion Picture magazine called it a "Fine Picture with Real Drama":

> Giving more coherence to the problems of the farmers than the farmers themselves have succeeded in doing, "Golden Harvest" does not allow its serious theme to interfere with its value as entertainment. Treating of national emergencies on the screen frequently results in heavy preachments. Not so in this picture. It is pure drama, relieved by natural comedy presented with sympathetic understanding, sincerity and intelligence. Even the hardened city dweller cannot fail to be affected by this simple, fine story of the soil.
>
> Chester Morris and Richard Arlen are brothers.... Between them the brothers attempt to stave off disaster for the wheat growers by a gigantic coup. The acting is irreproachable.[50]

4

King for a Night

During a Screen Actors Guild meeting at Frank Morgan's home on October 4, 1933, applications for 21 new members were accepted. New board members also were chosen, including Chester, Ralph Bellamy, Eddie Cantor, Ann Harding, Fredric March, Groucho Marx, Adolphe Menjou, Robert Montgomery, Frank Morgan and Spencer Tracy. In absentia, Cantor, a good friend of President Franklin D. Roosevelt, was elected president of the Guild.

Menjou and March, formerly the first and second vice-presidents of AMPAS, were chosen to fill the same roles in the Guild, and Harding became third vice-president. A new membership committee, chaired by Chester, also elected James Cagney and Frank Morgan.

The October 5 *Los Angeles Examiner* reported,

> That group of prominent screen players who Monday resigned from the Academy of Motion Picture Arts and Sciences because of their opposition to the provision for a "salary control board" in the picture industries NRA [National Recovery Administration] code last night welded themselves into a new organization. They reorganized the Screen Actors Guild at a meeting at the home of Frank Morgan....[1]

Chester was mentioned in the article, as were his friends Boris Karloff and Robert Montgomery.

Following William Morris' return to the Big Apple, his first Broadway role came in an important play, Max Gordon's original production of Sinclair Lewis' *Dodsworth*, dramatized by Sidney Howard. Costarring Walter Huston and Fay Bainter, the show ran 147 performances, from February 24 to June 30, 1934, at the Shubert Theatre. William, as the Traveling Gentleman, joined the supporting cast including Hal K. Dawson, Charles Halton, Beatrice Maude, Nan Sunderland and Frederic Worlock.

Fourteen months passed before William landed another small Broadway part, the First Man, in Lew Cantor's original production of Judith Kandel's comedy *Play, Genius, Play!* Unfortunately, the play ran for just five performances, from October 30 into early November 1935, at the St. James Theatre. After returning to Los Angeles, William died there of a heart attack on January 11, 1936, just 10 days after his 75th birthday. *Photoplay* magazine subsequently acknowledged Chester's personal loss:

> Hollywood sympathizes deeply with Chester Morris. Last month his dad, William Morris, died. They were very close—the Morris family. All five of them used to act together, in the old days.
>
> Chester was mighty proud of his father, who in his day was one of best-known actors in New York. Chester's kids adored their grandfather. He made them toys and played with them. Everyone will miss William Morris.[2]

Chester in the den of the Morrises' Beverly Hills home (1933).

Adrian continued working relatively nonstop, playing uncredited or supporting parts in such major 1933 films as Warner Bros.' *The Little Giant*, with Edward G. Robinson, *The Mayor of Hell*, with James Cagney, *Bureau of Missing Persons*, with Bette Davis, Pat O'Brien and Glenda Farrell, and the powerful Depression drama *Wild Boys of the Road*, with Frankie Darro.

That year, he also played the uncredited role of a crap shooter in Universal's hard-hitting blend of domestic drama, boxing, crime and punishment, *King for a Night*, directed by Kurt Neumann and starring his brother in the lead role. Prior to signing Chester, now free from Roland West, to a two-picture contract and casting him in "Kid Gloves" (the working title of *King for Night*), producer Carl Laemmle, Jr., had asked him to play the role of Dr. Kemp in James Whale's *The Invisible Man* (1933), based on the 1897 novel by H.G. Wells.

On June 1, 1933, *The Hollywood Reporter* published the article, "Chester Morris Top in 'Invisible Man,'" which was echoed on June 10 by *Motion Picture Herald*, suggesting that Chester had signed to play the titular role of Dr. Jack Griffin, for which Whale already had passed on Boris Karloff.[3] This confusion was alleviated, however, by the June 10 publication in *Universal Weekly* of the article "Chester Morris Signed for 'The Invisible Man'":

> Universal is making extraordinary preparations for "The Invisible Man," now that it has a script with which it is perfectly satisfied. This famous novel by H.G. Wells has been in the scenario department for over a year. Finally, James Whale, the director, and Carl Laemmle, Jr., induced R.C. Sherriff to adapt it and write a screenplay from it....
>
> The first player chosen is Chester Morris for the romantic lead. This role will be far more important to the picture than the title role, as the Invisible Man is merely a voice after the second or third reel.[4]

On June 19, Chester still was listed in the preproduction credits, which included Whale, Sherriff, and English actors Dudley Digges, Henry Travers and Billy Bevan. These personnel would all remain on the project, except Chester, who would be replaced by William Harrigan in the Kemp role.[5] (Paul Lukas and Colin Clive also were considered for the role of Griffin. Whale's choice, Claude Rains, who made his sound feature debut in the film, soon became successful as a top Hollywood character star.)

On June 10, *Universal Weekly* also included the article "'Counsellor at Law' Waits on Big Casting Problem," suggesting that the studio considered Chester its most important new star:

> Who will have the big role of the year? That is a question which Hollywood is asking. Universal has not been making a great deal of noise about the Elmer Rice play, "Counsellor at Law," because of its anxiety to have the leading role properly cast. A long series of negotiations with Paul Muni failed to click, for a variety of reasons. But that has only increased the possibilities. Every leading man in Hollywood is trying to figure some way whereby this fat part will drop in his lap. Universal's contract with Chester Morris, who will play in "Invisible Man," rather inclines critical Hollywood opinion toward him.[6]

(John Barrymore and Melvyn Douglas eventually were cast in *Counsellor-at-Law* [1933], directed by William Wyler.)

Chester's decision to drop out of *The Invisible Man* was prompted by his dissatisfaction with the contract offered by Universal. According to *Variety*, he also "objected to being costarred with Claude Rains."[7] But, by July 4, Universal announced that he was ready for Carl Laemmle, Jr.'s production of "Dangerous to Women" [aka "Kid Gloves"].

In the finished film, Chester first appears as Bud Williams shooting a pair of dice at the illegal crap game, where he knocks out fighter "One Punch" Hogan (Adrian) with a single right sock to the jaw. Delivering an in-joke directed at his own brother, Chester-as-Bud suggests, "Maybe I ought to hit him again, just to change his name."

In the town of Masonville, Bud and his siblings, Lillian (Helen Twelvetrees) and John (George Meeker), still live with their father, the Rev. John Williams (Grant Mitchell). Bud's tendency to get into fights worries John, Sr., who hopes he will settle into a steady job, rather than seek bouts in the boxing ring. In New York, he attempts to establish a career as middleweight pugilist "Kid" Williams, but temporarily makes ends meet working as a "drugstore cowboy" at a soda counter, the same job at which he had failed in Masonville.

Bud falls for chorus girl Evelyn Harrington (Alice White), who introduces him to unscrupulous fight promoter Walter Douglas (John Miljan). Unknown to Bud, after Lillian arrives in the city, she strikes a bargain with the womanizing Douglas in exchange for sponsorship in the ring. Bud wins a string of bouts and, on the day of the middleweight championship, he finds Evelyn two-timing him with Douglas' married assistant, Nick Merkle (Harland Tucker). Evelyn counters by telling him about Lillian's relationship with Douglas.

Lillian has become a virtual prisoner of the promoter. When he pretends to call Bud to reveal details of their affair, she pulls a small-caliber pistol from a drawer and shoots him in the back. Bud arrives, discovers the body and gun, and orders Lillian to keep quiet about the incident. Leaving his own fingerprints on the piece, he plans to take the rap, giving her a chance at happiness with hometown sweetheart Dick Morris (Frank Albertson).

Just before he delivers a knockout blow to win the championship bout, the arena is flooded with police officers who arrest him for first-degree murder. Lillian's last-minute attempt to secure a pardon from the governor (Frederick Burton) is denied, and the Reverend, having recently suffered a stroke, arrives at the prison to be with his son, who must pay the ultimate price in order to protect his family.

The screenplay by William Anthony McGuire, Scott Pembroke and Jack O'Donnell provided a unique blend of story elements and moods for Neumann to craft an entertaining drama interspersed with humor ultimately transitioning into tragedy. The impeccable performances are capped by Chester as a likable young man trying to excel in the only profession suited to his quick temperament. The loyalty and love he feels for his family, particularly his sister and father, leads him to an act of profound self-sacrifice.

Inspired by the powerful material, Chester was able to develop an impressive range for Bud Williams, one of his finest film characterizations. Displaying an almost childlike demeanor when around his father, Bud delivers the right amount of cockiness during his fight appearances, and is passionately committed when forced into difficult situations, especially during flashes of intense anger (when delivering a sock during various altercations, including one with Evelyn) and when strongly advising his sister after she kills her abusive lover.

If she refuses to accept his plan to confess to the murder, he vows, "I'll lay you out right beside him, and *I mean it!*" In this scene, Chester is electric yet in complete control, creating a standout moment in a powerful film.

Grant Mitchell, following his somewhat sinister characterization opposite Chester in *Tomorrow at Seven*, is a calming, believably serene presence as the father wishing only the best for his son, who admits, "I've been in jams all my life." When he mentions faith in a higher power, Bud answers, "I can't believe in something I can't see."

King for a Night (1933): Chester Morris poses as Bud ("Kid") Williams in this Universal publicity still. His younger brother, Adrian Morris, briefly appears with him, playing fellow boxer "One Punch" Hogan, in one scene.

4. King for a Night 73

The scene during which he visits Bud in the prison cell, just before "the last mile," is powerful and poignant, though never sentimental nor overwrought. Although included in a "pre–Code" 1933 film, this denouement is surprising, even shocking, as a trustworthy, *innocent* man is about to pay with his life. Warner Bros. had sent Spencer Tracy to the electric chair for a murder committed by a woman (Bette Davis) in the Michael Curtiz–directed *20,000 Years in Sing Sing* (1932), released 10 months before *King for a Night*, but his character, Tommy Connors, is a hardened criminal, albeit with redeeming features.

Asked if he will say a prayer before the end, Bud tells his father, "In another minute, I'll know more about it than you do." Informed by the warden (Frank Sheridan) that he did not pray, the Reverend replies, "Thank God, he was sincere." A brief, single-shot scene, showing John, Sr., tending to a bed of chrysanthemums surrounding Bud's headstone, engraved "Champion of the World," closes the film.

The supporting cast includes comic specialist Warren Hymer (the son of playwright John B. Hymer, coauthor of *Crime* and *Fast Life*), who had played one of the convicts in *20,000 Years in Sing Sing*. As "Goofy," a punch-drunk former champion, Hymer begins swinging like a simian every time he hears a bell. Also prominent are diminutive George E. Stone as "Hymie," a boxing tout, in his first of 15 screen appearances with Chester, and boxer-actor Max ["Slapsie Maxie"] Rosenbloom in his second film. Uncredited, Walter Brennan (who had played a farmhand in *Golden Harvest*) appears in one scene as a soda jerk, and Fred ["Snowflake"] Toones plays "Othello," a masseur at the gymnasium.

Born in Nuremburg, Bavaria, Kurt Neumann had directed Universal's "dark castle" murder mystery *Secret of the Blue Room* (1933), with Lionel Atwill, Gloria Stuart and Paul Lukas, and again would work with Chester on *Let's Talk It Over* (1934), their next mutual project for the studio. In late 1933, Universal also slated Neumann to direct "The Return of Frankenstein," to costar Boris Karloff (as the Monster) and Bela Lugosi (as the scientist), after James Whale refused to make a sequel to his original *Frankenstein*. However, the studio decided to produce *The Black Cat* (1934), directed by Edgar G. Ulmer, as the first Karloff-Lugosi collaboration, and Whale relented, arguably creating his masterpiece with *Bride of Frankenstein* (1935).

Hungarian-born cinematographer Charles J. Stumar, who had filmed Universal's atmospheric Karloff thriller *The Mummy* for director Karl Freund, would shoot *Let's Talk It Over* and another of Chester's studio projects, *Embarrassing Moments* (1934). His use of odd camera setups, mobile shots and a fast-paced montage of boxing scenes (created with editor Philip Cahn), combined with the art direction of Charles D. Hall (who designed the fantastic expressionist sets for Universal's *Dracula* [1931], *Frankenstein*, *Murders in the Rue Morgue* [1932], *The Invisible Man*, *The Black Cat* and *Bride of Frankenstein*), help give Neumann's direction a very solid "Universal feel."

In the November 18, 1933, issue of *Universal Weekly*, the studio president, in his feature "Straight-from-the-Shoulder Talk by Carl Laemmle," personally promoted the film to exhibitors:

> In case you have not thought it over, let me remind you that the screen nowadays is giving you gems of acting which if done on the stage would send critics into raptures of praise.
>
> I ask you to make it a special point to see the work of Chester Morris and Grant Mitchell in Universal's excellent picture "King for a Night."
>
> Throughout this unusual effort, but especially in the [first] two reels, you will see a genuine revelation.
>
> You will witness the magnificence of two rare artists....

The story of "King for a Night" is the straightforward and logical recitation of a human interest affair which marks a fine forward step in motion pictures....

If you are afraid of a new twist in your movie entertainment, you had better not run this picture.

But if you are a showman, if you have a desire to lift your show above the commonplace, if you care to have your name associated with an outstanding piece of work—then you will book "King for a Night" and you will dignify it with the forceful advertising it deserves.

Two incomparable roles are played before your eyes—two which will linger in your memory and make you grateful that Universal had the courage to do the different thing in the way of showmanship.

—Carl Laemmle[8]

King for a Night premiered at the Mayfair Theatre in New York City on the evening of December 8, 1933. Universal's promotion mirrored campaigns for its horror films. *The New York Times* reported,

> A hooded figure swings inertly from an improvised gibbet on each side of the Mayfair box office. You may not think it relates too carefully to the prizefight melodrama "King for a Night," which is revealed inside, but it does. For the new film, after forty minutes of the routine pleasantries that accompany a young man on his way to the middleweight championship takes an unexpectedly grim turn. It places the hero in a death cell for a murder he did not commit; it permits his broken father to rise from a paralytic's bed to read the service for the dead with his boy; and, finally, the young man goes gravely and deliberately to the electric chair while the audience waits to hear of the Governor's pardon that never arrives. It is a shocking and somewhat effective conclusion for an amiable little film....[9]

Hollywood magazine was enthusiastic: "Chester Morris at last comes into his own in *King for a Night* which is without doubt his best performance since *Alibi*.... There is a powerful climax."[10] The review in *Motion Picture* pointed out that the film and acting "Packs Realism and Punch":

> Few pictures in recent years have had the courage to present as strong a dramatic climax as is contained here. It becomes more powerful because it is totally unexpected ... the story moves fearlessly to its strong climax.
>
> The ending may be a bit morbid for the average taste. Yet its power is undeniable. Chester Morris lends authority to the fighter and Grant Mitchell makes a splendid father. Helen Twelvetrees plays well.[11]

The Film Daily also was in its corner: "Very fine work by an able cast, in a story of human qualities that builds up to a real punch climax, makes this picture that should prove quite satisfying to almost any audience. This is in spite of a sad ending."[12]

Motion Picture Daily, praising the entire cast, weighed in, "Chester Morris sincerely portrays the role of a small-town fighter with the championship as his goal in a drama which will appeal generally.... Story should go over big with fight fans."[13] On November 22, 1933, the same publication also reported that Universal, worried at the initial reactions of audiences, had shot an alternate ending, offering it to exhibitors who "object to the present one." When booking the picture, they could choose either climax: the downbeat (which stands in the surviving version) or, presumably, happier resolution.[14]

The hard-hitting ending, however, reportedly affected the making of at least one other Hollywood feature. On February 20, 1934, *Motion Picture Daily* announced, "Following the stand taken by Universal in 'King for a Night,' MGM has remade the ending of 'Laughing Boy' and now has the heroine die as the picture closes."[15] *Laughing Boy* (1934), a feature about an ill-fated romance on a Navaho reservation, directed by W.S. Van Dyke, stars Ramon Novarro as the titular character and Lupe Velez as his wife, "Slim Girl."

Warner Bros. released several "post–Code" films involving capital punishment, notably two additional Michael Curtiz classics, *The Walking Dead* (1936) and *Angels with Dirty Faces* (1938), but their characters, too, differ from *King for a Night*'s Bud Williams in significant ways. In the former, Boris Karloff portrays John Elman, a Depression down-and-outer, framed by a shyster for the murder of a judge, who is revived from the dead to commit divinely ordained revenge. The latter stars the magnetic James Cagney, in one of his greatest performances, as William ["Rocky"] Sullivan, a career criminal who "cowardly" walks the last mile to provide redemption for a group of New York youths (The "Dead End" Kids).

Between *King for a Night* and the Warners films, MGM released *Manhattan Melodrama* (1934), in which Edward J. ["Blackie"] Gallagher (Clark Gable), who kills a bitter former associate (Thomas E. Jackson) threatening to derail the New York gubernatorial career of his friend, District Attorney Jim Wade (William Powell), refuses a pardon before dying in the electric chair. Prizing ethics over political ambition, Wade, admitting to the New York Legislature that murder helped him win the election, resigns in favor of making a fresh start with his wife, Eleanor (Myrna Loy).

In the June 1933 issue of *The New Movie Magazine*, society reporter Grace Kingsley again described Chester and Sue's input at a major Hollywood get-together, this time at the home of director Harry Lachman, where Elizabeth Allen, June Collyer, Stuart Erwin, Mr. and Mrs. Jean Hersholt, Mr. and Mrs. Frank Morgan, Mr. and Mrs. Eric von Stroheim, Genevieve Tobin, Spencer Tracy and Anna May Wong had gathered. Following dinner, Chester took to the piano, inspiring the gang to sing several popular songs.

On November 1, 1933, Chester and Sue hosted a Screen Actors Guild membership committee meeting at their home, attended by James Cagney, James Dunn, Lucile Gleason, Ann Harding, Jean Hersholt, Miriam Hopkins, Boris Karloff, Claude King, Frank Morgan, Eddie Nugent, Dick Powell, Warren William and Lois Wilson. The total number of members had reached 1,080. Chester's reputation as one of Tinseltown's premier party organizers was reflected at another meeting that month, at which he, Eddie Cantor and Groucho Marx were appointed to head a committee for the Guild's First Annual Ball.

Chester and Robert Montgomery both were interviewed for a November 26, 1933, *Los Angeles Times* article exploring if movie stars are "entitled to a private life," the consensus concluding that they are *not*. Montgomery replied,

> I hold no brief for those few who live in a vacuum as far as publicity is concerned, those who pretend to resent seeing their name in print. The public creates stars and to that public the stars should be grateful and should supply any reasonable information they wish.

Chester agreed, "want[ing] the world to know about him and ask about him. He is proud of the fact that he has two youngsters. He likes publicity about his children, and his home life."[16]

In late November, Chester signed another agreement with Universal, extending his contract to a three-year period. On December 6, the Screen Actors Guild determined "that a committee be appointed to confer with the Writers' Committee on collective bargaining and working conditions, said committee to consist of ... Robert Montgomery, Ivan Simpson, Claude King and Chester Morris."[17] To celebrate the holidays, while so many other Hollywood folk took holidays at the beach or skiing in the mountains, Chester and Sue stayed at home with Brooks and Cynthia.

On Tuesday, January 9, 1934, armed with baseball bats, the members of the Screen

Actors Guild committee for the gala ball (Chester, Mary Astor, James Cagney, Boris Karloff and Robert Montgomery) scheduled for the upcoming Saturday evening at the Biltmore Hotel's sumptuous Sala d'Oro ballroom, invaded the lunch rooms of the major studios, poised to beat their fellow actors into buying tickets.[18] That evening, the "gang" continued on to the Colony and Clover clubs, where they experienced similar success in "strong arming" the patrons.[19]

Five days after the festivities, on Thursday, January 18, *The Hollywood Reporter*, in an article titled, "Morris Hit by 'Flu,'" revealed that Chester was "in bed with the flu that laid him low following his appearance at the Screen Actors' Guild ball last Saturday night."[20] He remained out of commission for nearly another week, finally emerging from his sickbed on Wednesday, January 24, to begin planning a trip to New York, scheduled for the following Tuesday.[21] Loaned out by Universal to William Saal Productions, he was set to costar with Helen Morgan in the independent film *Frankie and Johnnie*.

On January 27, *Universal Weekly* reported additional details:

> Chester Morris ... is confined to his home with influenza and a heavy chest cold.... Morris is under the care of Dr. William E. Branch.
> It is expected that Morris will be confined to his home for at least a week, providing complications do not develop. He hopes to be recovered in time to play the leading role in "Frankie and Johnnie"....[22]

That month, Chester's revelations about his past treatment in Hollywood finally were reported in the press. The biggest bombshell was his admission that his "ex-friend" Roland West had bound him to a strict contract tantamount to "slavery." *Hollywood* magazine reported that he finally had been "freed" by West, who had retired from directing after the release of *Corsair* more than two years earlier. For five years, Chester had been under the complete control of West, who chose his roles and, even after focusing on running a mob-infiltrated bar and café with girlfriend Thelma Todd on the beach in Santa Monica, "farmed him out" to producers of his own choosing. Chester told *Hollywood*'s J. Eugene Crisman,

> Not once during the past five years was I ever permitted to see a script before going into the cast. A man named Jack Codd, an accountant in Sam Goldwyn's office, read scripts submitted. If he liked them, he reported to West. All I ever got was instructions to show up on the set.[23]

He also explained the reasoning behind his decision to sign with West:

> West paid me a handsome salary each week, out of his own pocket. That meant I ate whether I worked or not and I had no financial worries. At first, when other offers began to come in, I was bitter toward West. Then I began to think it over. I liked the picture game and wanted to stay. I realized that my contract bound West, just as it did me and that he was taking a big gamble on an unknown. I decided that since I was in it, I'd take it on the chin and settle down to make the best of it.[24]

However, after a few more months passed, Chester, in an interview with Mary Sharon of *The Modern Screen*, was less positive while elaborating on the terms of the deal:

> I didn't even read the contract, but merely asked [West] to give me the details.... I gave him the right to control my salary and invest it without consulting me ... if I was rented out at a larger figure than the one named in the contract, we were to split fifty-fifty on the amount received. Also, and this is the most important part, he stipulated that I was to receive only a small weekly wage. Less than most "bit" players receive. He had absolute right to handle and control every bit of money I earned above this small allowance.
> I found West a slave-driver. He loaned me out indiscriminately, at a good figure, but he never loosened up on my allowance. The first rub came when I asked for enough money to bring my fam-

ily out ... expenses were far less in Hollywood than in New York and naturally I wanted them to be with me. So, I asked for an advance on my drawing account. He refused.... He told me with finality that, if they came, they would have to come on my allowance.[25]

Chester's embarrassment at having to wear old stage clothes in *The Divorcée* was alleviated somewhat by his close friendship with Robert Montgomery, who agreed to walk in front of him while shooting certain scenes. He explained,

Some of [Bob's] fans wrote to him later and accused him of "mugging," but he was really doing me a kindness. When our close-ups were shot, he stood so that only my head and shoulders showed.

Then we had a sequence that required riding breeches.... I could not rake up enough cash to get some breeches tailored to measure. All of the fellows were going to a man named Took, an expert tailor. I begged West to let me have some money, so I could have him make me some breeches, as a great deal depended upon the impression I made in this picture, but he was adamant. He told me to go back to MGM and ask the wardrobe department to outfit me.

I told them I didn't have any breeches. They said they didn't have any either. When I insisted upon being given a pair, they finally told me, "Pardon us, Mr. Morris, but anyone who is playing leading man for Norma Shearer ought to be able to save enough to purchase riding breeches."

I explained the situation and they finally found a pair of Ramon Novarro's old breeches that he had discarded. I was doubtful about them, because Ramon's anatomy and mine have little in common, but the wardrobe fellow thought if I pinned them up in the back I might get by. So, I took them, but they didn't work. That is, not in the right way.

As to his love scenes with Shearer, he admitted,

Every time I bent over to take Norma in my arms, I'll be hanged if those darned safety pins didn't come loose with a terrific snap. You know the mike picks up funny little noises like that. They sounded just like somebody getting slapped in the face.

Finally, the sound engineer blew up and the director called it a day. I think everybody from Irving Thalberg down to the office boy stormed Roland West's office and demanded some new clothes for me. He was just as positive with them as he had been with me, but they finally made an issue of it and told him they would not consider me for future roles unless I were given a suitable wardrobe. So, he was overruled.[26]

Now, being greenlit on purchasing new clothes, Chester outfitted himself respectably. Fortunately, his subsequent roles, including John Morgan in *The Big House*, required no formal clothes, so he managed to keep his quality suits at home, saving them for special occasions rather than wearing them out while working at the studios.

Chester also described the personal friendship that he and Sue had with West and his then-wife, actress Jewel Carmen, including the European vacation on which they mutually had traveled three years earlier:

We spent every weekend with them at their beach home.... They always came to dinner at our home then. One evening, I mentioned that I would like to go to Europe. West decided that it would be nice for all of us to go together. We went via a tramp steamer. Talk about stretching money.[27]

In London, West registered at a cheap hotel that Chester described as "putrid." Since one of his major films was playing in the city at the time, he, fearing he would be recognized, left by the side entrance any time they went out.

Despite West's selfishness, Chester attempted to salvage their friendship, but the situation became so strained that he asked to be released from the contract. A period of unemployment followed, one that had a lasting impact on his career, sometimes resulting in less important films at minor studios.

Fortunately, his free agency began to attract many good offers, and his versatility allowed him to make a transition into more character-oriented roles as he grew older. Following the split with West, Sue began to handle his business affairs.

Chester's leadership in several areas of the Screen Actors Guild increased even more because of his experiences with West. On February 19, 1934, when nominees were considered for the NRA/Motion Picture Code Committee, Chester, Mary Astor, James Cagney, Ann Harding, Claude King, Robert Montgomery, Ralph Morgan, Paul Muni, Pat O'Brien, Kenneth Thomson and Richard Tucker were named to the Actor-Producer slate. (Sol Rosenblatt of the NRA eventually selected King, Montgomery, Morgan, Thomson and Tucker, with Astor, Harding, Muni, O'Brien and Chester named as alternates.)

Chester had left Los Angeles for New York on January 30. Paired with Helen Morgan on February 14, he began shooting *Frankie and Johnnie* with director Chester Erskine at the old Biograph Studios on 174th Street in the South Bronx. The facilities recently had been completely renovated for sound production, and *Frankie and Johnnie*, set in 1849 St. Louis, became the pilot project.

A favorite publicity portrait (1934) inscribed and signed to a fan by Chester Morris and later featured on the cover of *Genii* **magazine (January 1938).**

Following his arrival, he attended a supper and dance in the Terrace Room of the Hotel New Yorker, where a "caravan" touring nationwide to promote the new 20th Century–United Artists picture *Moulin Rouge* (1934) was formally presented to the local press. John Hundley was master of ceremonies, and the group of Hollywood visitors included Roscoe Ates, Mary Carlisle, Antonio Moreno, Jack Mulhall and Ben Turpin. Among those "taking a bow" were Helen Westley and Chester, who "was finally compelled to make a speech."[28]

He also participated in the inaugural broadcast of radio station WNEW on the evening of February 14, joining *Frankie and Johnnie* colleague Lilyan Tashman, Clark Gable, Edmund Lowe, Walter P. Chrysler, Mr. and Mrs. Marshall Field, and British consul general Gerald Campbell in supporting the U.S. premiere of London Films' epic *Catherine the Great* (1934), directed by Josef von Sternberg and starring Marlene Dietrich, at the Astor Theatre on Broadway.

On Friday, March 2, Mary Pickford, at the invitation of producer William Saal, arrived on the *Frankie and Johnnie* set to "christen" the remodeled studio. Pickford, who began her career with D.W. Griffith at Biograph in 1909, had retired from films three years earlier.

Frankie and Johnnie: From left, William Harrigan, Walter Kingsford, Percy Helton, supporting player, Helen Morgan, Mary Pickford, Chester Morris and supporting player, on the set at Biograph Studios, South Bronx, New York, on March 2, 1934 (the film was released by Republic Pictures in 1936) [original photo from the personal collection of Mary Pickford].

While Chester and Helen Morgan were shooting a scene, she "officially ... turned a camera crank."[29]

During production, Chester made several suggestions to Erskine that were incorporated into the script. He also told Regina Cannon of *The Modern Screen* magazine that, though he was pleased to see his home again, he missed his wife and children, whom he had called long-distance the previous evening:

> Sue put each of the youngsters on the wire, and I heard her say, "Say, 'Hello, Daddy. I love you and miss you.' Gee, I'm glad they do, but the slow dialogue, promptings and pauses was sure helping to take the telephone company out of the red."

Cannon wrote, "After this [film], Chester goes to Universal for 'Life of a Sailor,' where we trust he will get the break he deserves, for this gentleman is one of the few really capable actors on the screen."[30]

Chester enjoyed being reunited with African American dresser Victor Lloyd, with whom he previously had worked on Broadway and on tour. During production of *Frankie and Johnnie*, Lloyd recalled their past relationship, including Chester's fondness for relaxing with magic tricks between takes, for journalist Julia Gwin:

I've seen him do that before. I used to be with Mr. Morris when he was playing in "Crime" ... in New York and on the road. I certainly was glad to see him when he came back this time. I think he's about the grandest thing in the world and I've worked for a lot of them.... Jack Haley, Jack Whiting, Ralph Bellamy are a few ... but none of them like Mr. Morris. He's the kind of employer who makes you want to do your very best all the time.[31]

A sad casualty of the picture was popular, fashionable actress Lilyan Tashman, who had been married to Edmund Lowe since 1925. During 1932, she had undergone an operation in a New York hospital that was reported as an "appendectomy" at the time, but later revealed to be a procedure for abdominal cancer. Though weak and frail, she continued to act in films, but her roles were increasingly subjected to significant downsizing. She joined Chester and Helen Morgan on the *Frankie and Johnnie* set but spent far more time attempting to rest in Connecticut under the care of Lowe. She completed her scenes on March 8, 1934, but just 13 days later, died at Doctor's Hospital in New York at the age of 37.

While in New York, Chester also appeared with about 40 other film actors at an all-night party thrown by the Independent Theater Owners. Tallulah Bankhead, Wallace Beery, Clark Gable, Dorothy and Lillian Gish, Al Jolson, Edmund Lowe, Ramon Novarro and Sophie Tucker were among those who took to the stage, along with dancers from the Ziegfeld Follies and nightclub musicians ranging from Greenwich Village to Harlem. From the *Frankie and Johnnie* cast, Chester was accompanied by Morgan, and even the ailing Tashman managed to make an appearance.

After shooting wrapped on March 10, Chester boarded the *Century* for his return trip to Los Angeles. Tashman's funeral, attended by Jack Benny, Fanny Brice, Mary Pickford, Sophie Tucker and other celebrities, was held at the Temple Enamu-El synagogue on March 21. By the time the film was released, her role had been radically edited.

Hollywood magazine feature writer Harry N. Lair had visited the set, where Chester remarked that she was giving "a fine performance" and "what a joy it was to work with her."[32] However, the publication also included comments by several colleagues who, not knowing the facts about Tashman's actual illness, blamed her death on the industry's insistence that she remain slim for the cameras.

From the outset, the script by Moss Hart, based on Jack Kirkland's story inspired by the traditional 19th-century song, faced an uphill censorship battle. All motion pictures completed on or after July 1, 1934, had to receive a "certificate of approval" from the Production Code Administration prior to release. Considered of a "questionable nature," *Frankie and Johnnie* was rejected by the PCA as a "sordid sex drama," with administration director Joseph I. Breen ordering that all inclusions of the song be eliminated.

For a time, the film remained shelved, with William Saal believing he would have to produce an entirely new, whitewashed version. Lou Goldberg wrote a revised script, which was approved by the PCA in mid–February 1935, and Saal traveled to Miami to speak with Helen Morgan about appearing in the new production. Negotiations were also underway with Chester about returning to New York.

Ultimately, new scenes, depicting Johnnie's relationship with Frankie as "sinful," then were directed by John H. Auer in March 1935. (Saal and United Artists approached Paramount, RKO Radio and Mascot Pictures before a deal finally was made with Republic, who distributed the film in May 1936.)[33]

The review in *Motion Picture Daily* reflects the overall uncertainty that plagued the production:

For the most part, the film lacks the pace it might have been expected to possess, moving at a laggard rate, only gaining a bit of speed as it nears the conclusion, when Frankie, finally convinced against her will of the duplicity of her man, finds a gun and goes in search of Johnnie. Miss Morgan, it would seem, has not been given sufficient opportunity to exercise the talent for a special style of singing which she unquestionably possesses, and in some fashion her voice throughout registers poorly.[34]

The substandard quality of the sound recording is one of several defects in the finished film, but it is better than its reputation would suggest. Though hamstrung by PCA provisions, the writers were able creatively to work in a few elements that temper the overall romanticized atmosphere. Contrary to contemporary reviews, composer Victor Young did incorporate a variation on the melody of the familiar song, during the scene in which Frankie searches the saloon for Johnnie, who has promised to take her on the riverboat from St. Louis to New Orleans that evening. (Young and members of his orchestra appear in the scene.)

Chester, in duality mode, delivers a believably two-faced performance as Johnnie Drew, dividing the character between a naïve hick facade and his actual selfish con man identity. Though Johnnie marries the faithful, goodhearted Frankie, he wishes to run off with Nellie Bly (Tashman), who only is interested in the $13,000 he hustled from a pack of riverboat gamblers.

In her penultimate film performance, Helen Morgan is a highly sympathetic Frankie. The rags-to-riches torch singer who studied at New York's Metropolitan Opera and played vaudeville houses and mob-supported Chicago nightclubs lived the sad songs she sang, and that quality makes her character both likable and tragic. After *Frankie and Johnnie*, she would play her most famous character, Julie LaVerne, one last time, in Universal's *Show Boat* (1936), directed by James Whale, before returning to Chicago, where she died of cirrhosis of the liver at age 41 just five years later.

Philadelphia-born Florence Reed is a standout as Lou, the saloon owner, who uses her handkerchief to signal the bartenders to draw their pistols on an unwanted interloper. Joseph Ruttenberg and editor William P. Thompson aided Erskine in creating an impressive visual style, including an innovative use of slow motion in shots twice featuring Lou's handkerchief floating down from her watchful perch as gunfire rings out: the first time as the vengeful gamblers pursuing Johnnie are cut down in the saloon; and second, when Frankie, small pistol drawn, confronts the two-timing Johnnie outside Nellie's room, but is gunned down by Lou's right-hand man, Timothy (Walter Kingsford). This stylized demise for Johnnie culminates with a series of tracking shots dynamically capturing the reactions of several eyewitnesses. The film concludes with Curley (William Harrigan), the man who really loves Frankie, stopping her from attending Johnnie's funeral to put her on the riverboat to New Orleans.

Julia Gwin's feature article, "Frankie and Johnnie: He Was Her Man but He Done Her Wrong," was published in *Broadway and Hollywood "Movies"* magazine nearly two years before the film was released by Republic. After spending some time watching Chester on the set, she provided a keen assessment of his acting:

> The unusual thing is that, even when Chet has made us believe most in these characterizations of his, he has somehow managed to retain our sympathy, a pull on the heartstrings. He is so genuinely in earnest about what he does that he makes us believe, even against our better judgment, that for him at least these things are right—it all seems a difference of viewpoint, and that's what makes it life.

I don't feel inclined to dramatize Chester Morris—he doesn't lend himself to eulogy somehow—he is too downright honest and straightforward, but I'd be willing to wager my next year's income tax that when he makes friends they stay made. My private bet would be that you'd never come out a cropper if you placed odds on Chet, because he'd never let you down even if doing so would be a gain for him. In an emergency he would be right there, not with a lot of cheap words but with real understanding and friendship.

The same thing is true about his work. I've never seen Chester give a bad performance. I've seen him with parts that were suited to him so little that it was funny the producer was willing to gamble on him, yet he made those parts living, breathing characters.... One reason is that he doesn't impose his own personality upon the one he is playing. He lets the new personality absorb him and dominate the situation. It is the tradition of blood asserting itself again. He doesn't act—he simply is. If this were not a substantial fact, he would have been ruined by the inane judgment of men who should have known better—of producers who could have made him a box-office asset second to none if they had handled him correctly.[35]

Following the release of the film, "Nonnie" wrote in *Film Bulletin*,

"Frankie and Johnnie" was made about two years ago, just before the Legion of Decency commenced its cleanup drive. Although the story had little of the ribaldness suggested by the title of the well-known ballad, RKO, for whose release it was scheduled, thought it best to pass it up. Now, it comes through Republic, clean, sentimentally romantic and a bit dramatic.... Chester Morris turns in a fine performance as the lovin', two-timin' Johnnie.... Florence Reed is also good as Lou, the dance hall proprietress.[36]

In March 1934, Universal's Stanley Bergerman, set to produce an adaptation of the Edith Wharton story "Bread Upon the Waters," intended Chester to play the lead role of Jimmy King, a young American who marries Nadja, a Russian refugee, only to discover he is expected to support her entire family. Adapted by Gladys Unger, James Mulhauser and Barry Trivers as *Strange Wives* (1934), the finished film, featuring Roger Pryor as Jimmy and June Clayworth as Nadja, was directed by Richard Thorpe.

Back in Hollywood on March 16, Chester began acting in "Practical Joker" at Universal with director Edward Laemmle (nephew of studio head Carl Laemmle, who continuously had much of his "faemmle" on the payroll). During production, Chester sought more guidance from Laemmle, whom he believed wasn't providing enough direction for the actors, who were hampered further by new pages of rewritten dialogue handed to them on the set. The original screenplay had been adapted by Charles Logue from a William Anthony McGuire story.

While performing in a scene involving a chest of drawers and a framed picture, Chester stopped to inform the director, "I wish that there could be some reason for me to come over to this chest. If I just happened to glance up and saw the painting, and then talked to it, it would be a lot more logical than for a sane man to deliberately walk up to a picture and start gibbering to it." Laemmle finally suggested the simple expedient of having him place his handkerchief in one of the drawers, thus giving his character a reason to walk over to the chest.

Carl Laemmle, Jr., impressed with the clever work of Henry Armetta, ordered that additional footage featuring the character actor be added to his scenes. The primary cast was recalled for an extra week of shooting, a decision that proved quite dangerous for Chester and fellow actor Pat Flaherty. While filming a scene set in the cockpit of an airplane suspended 40 feet above the soundstage, both Chester and Flaherty, playing the pilot, fell all the way to the floor, with three large studio lights crashing down on them. Chester, a sleeve slashed from his coat, a shoe cut from his left foot, and suffering "severe injuries to his left hip" and pain from "crushed muscles," and Flaherty, inflicted with several body bruises, were rushed to the studio hospital for treatment. Universal reported that they both "escaped death by a miracle."[37]

Chester plays Jerry Randolph, junior member of a New York architectural firm, who constantly plays practical jokes on his friends and colleagues. After the tables are turned, he believes he is wanted for the "murder" of his best friend, Paul Doreen (Walter Wolff King). While on the lam, he becomes involved with counterfeiters who take him to Mexico. Learning that Paul is alive, he returns to New York and discovers that his "late" pal is involved with Jane (Marian Nixon), his girlfriend. When he leaves the apartment, they hear a gunshot in the hallway, and Jane runs out to reveal her true love for him. He who laughs last, laughs best, for Jerry then sits up, unharmed.

Following the wrap on April 2, Chester and Sue left for a much-needed vacation in Palm Springs. On April 21, *Universal Weekly* magazine featured him and the film, retitled *Embarrassing Moments*, on the cover. The studio released the film on July 9, just eight days after the Production Code went into effect. *The Film Daily* was not impressed with the final cut:

Universal Weekly magazine (April 21, 1934) showing Chester Morris in *Embarrassing Moments* (1934).

> Thin story material provides little for cast or director and results in mild entertainment.
>
> The trouble with this one is that a two-reel comedy idea was stretched out to make a feature, consequently it is rather feeble most of the way.... The story creates little interest or sympathy in the characters, and even the cast seems to have a hard time taking the thing seriously.[38]

Motion Picture Daily, however, was impressed by Chester's alternately comic and dramatic work:

> Chester Morris in the role of a practical joker can be funny and serious as the occasion requires. In one particular sequence—the duel in a Mexican café with Henry Armetta—Morris is exceedingly funny. After the second reel, Morris drops his air of levity and goes dramatic until the last flash when he pulls one of his practical jokes, the first to work to his advantage.
>
> Produced by Stanley Bergerman and directed by Edward Laemmle, the picture will entertain.[39]

The Hollywood Reporter review, headlined, "Morris Is Well, Direction Capital," was the most enthusiastic, especially in its advice for exhibitors:

> A dandy little comedy guaranteed to hold its own on any program. Laughs and thrills are deftly intermingled for the type of entertainment we used to have before pictures began talking so much....
>
> Chester Morris ... plays with fine authority a role that can only be described as exacting because it combines so many conflicting moods....
>
> Get behind Morris in your campaign, not so much because of this release as because of what his name will mean to you in subsequent films. This trouper is headed right for the top.[40]

Kurt Neumann again directed Chester, having just returned from Palm Springs, at Universal, in "Loves of Sailor" (aka "Love Life of a Sailor") from April 17 to May 7, 1934. While shooting the film, Chester spoke to journalist Hal Hall about the subject of naturally growing older on the screen:

> I had never given much thought to what type roles I would play in future years until my thirtieth birthday. I didn't feel a day over twenty-five on that thirtieth birthday. I guess it was just the psychological effect of passing from the twenties into the thirties that started me thinking. Ever since that birthday I have been thinking more and more about the future, and I definitely have made up my mind that there must come a time when I will no longer be youthful enough to do the roles I am playing now.
>
> The problem is to know just when to quit trying to be young. I think the only way to do the trick is to do it gradually. Sort of slide gracefully into other roles without anyone's suspecting what is happening. Thank God for one thing. I do not have the handicap that some men in pictures have. I have never been a "pretty boy" type. So, the change will be much easier for me.
>
> I have always been a great admirer of Lewis Stone, and I hope that I shall be able to follow his lead. He slipped so gracefully and gradually from the young man to early middle age, and then to a dignified and entrancing middle age, that one never realized when the change came. Today he can give a lot of young fellows lessons in how to portray a tenderness and virility in love making that makes some young lovers look like rank amateurs.
>
> When I am forty, I hope I shall have been able to keep the virility and romantic spirit of the twenties, but I do not expect to take the role of the young son of a wealthy dad and dash madly about in a topless roadster that is dolled up in college-boy fashion. That is out of the question.
>
> Fortunately, I am already playing, and always have played parts that verge on the heavy, and it will only be a step to get into roles that will fit. It will probably be some years before I do get into roles that are decidedly different from those I do now, but when I reach them I hope you will never notice the transition.... I plan to work gradually into heavy roles, and then into character parts without that awful flop which takes place when a man is suddenly called into the front office and is told he doesn't look young enough for the part.
>
> It is a pity that actors as a whole do not plan their careers beyond the good-looking, youthful stage, for I believe that the finest acting comes from the men and women who have devoted years to the gaining of experience; the finest pictures are those built around a player who portrays the roles of a man or a woman who has passed middle life. Look at George Arliss, Lionel Barrymore, Will Rogers, May Robson or Marie Dressler. They put us youngsters to shame. But they have given a lifetime to their work, and their ability has ripened along with age.[41]

Mae Clarke was cast as "Pat" Rockland in "Loves of a Sailor" after Alice White turned down the role as "not suitable to the kind of new buildup she [was] carefully maneuvering."[42] Following a title change to "Funny Thing Called Love," the new Neumann project was released by Universal as *Let's Talk It Over* on June 11, 1934.

Chester plays Mike McGann, a sailor on shore leave in New York, where he appears to "rescue" Pat, a deed reported in the local newspapers. Discovering that she possesses a $20-million fortune, Mike informs his shipmates, Gravel (Andy Devine) and Bill (Russ Brown), that he has a date with Pat. At the family mansion in Newport, Rhode Island, he attends her birthday party, encountering trouble from her boyfriend, Alex Winters (John Warburton). When Mike informs Pat that he is leaving the U.S. Navy to become a businessman, she bets with Alex that she can "make" him successful. He begins working for her father (Frank Craven), and soon offers unwanted advice, which angers her enough to abandon him. Learning about the wager, he gets drunk and drives to a mountain lodge, where he confronts Pat and Alex, who have decided to get married. After knocking Alex cold, Mike crashes his car into a tree. Realizing that she loves him, Pat weds Mike instead.

Photoplay magazine praised the acting:

Let's Talk It Over (1934): Mae Clarke (second from left) and Chester Morris (second from right), who drew praise for his believable portrayal of "gob" Mike McGann [original lobby card].

Because he makes the gob Mike McGann a believable and interesting person, Chester Morris breathes a strong life into the old tale of how a sailor falls for an heiress, shows her the futility of her useless existence, finally makes something of himself and wins her heart. Mae Clarke splendid as the girl. Frank Craven shines, as do Irene Ware, Andy Devine, John Warburton. For both young and old.[43]

The Hollywood Reporter, titling its review, "Chester Morris Does Extraordinary Job," again waxed enthusiastic, nigh hyperbolic:

Chester Morris gives one of the finest performances of his career as the gob, Mike McGann…. His keen sense of dramatic value, his timing, his simplicity and utter honesty to type, his superb sincerity—these all make his characterization a miracle of emotional lights and shadows. His Mike McGann is an extremely interesting human being.
  Direction is strong and vivid, and the writing is exceptionally smooth. With bouquets going to all departments. "Let's Talk It Over" is one of Universal's best….
  One of the beauties of Morris' characterization is that he never quite gets over being the gob. The polish is there, but his essential SELF remains the same.[44]

On May 21, 1934, Universal ran a two-page advertisement in *The Hollywood Reporter* devoted to Chester, reprinting in full the paper's glowing reviews of both *Embarrassing Moments* and *Let's Talk It Over*. "The Phantom Regiment" also was promoted as being "in preparation," but became another title on the list of unrealized Chester projects.

MGM, on May 25, announced that its forthcoming production of "Four Walls," based on the 1928 Dana Burnet-George Abbott play featuring Muni Weisenfreund [Paul Muni] and the silent film adaptation starring John Gilbert, would be delayed for three months. Considering Muni, Edward G. Robinson, Ricardo Cortez and Chester for the role of ex-convict Benny Horowitz, producer Lucien Hubbard now set his sights on Clark Gable, who was unavailable. When the film finally was directed by Paul H. Sloane as *Straight Is the Way* (1935), Franchot Tone had landed the part, opposite leading lady Karen Morley (who replaced Mae Clarke).

The Screen Actors Guild held its first annual Film Stars' Frolic at Los Angeles' newly constructed Gilmore Stadium from May 18 to 20, 1934. The event, hosted by Mary Astor, James Cagney, Eddie Cantor, Ann Harding, Boris Karloff and Dick Powell, also was attended by Chester, Ralph Bellamy, Jimmy Durante, Alice Faye, Gary Cooper, Wallace Ford, Cary Grant, William S. Hart, Bela Lugosi, Fredric March, Robert Montgomery, Edward G. Robinson, May Robson, Kenneth Thomson, Thelma Todd, Bert Wheeler and Robert Woolsey, and Alice White. Chester enjoyed palling around with Cagney and Robinson, especially as all three rode a ferris wheel together. However, only 150 of the Guild's 3,000 members made an appearance, and the union's funds were drained.

To replenish the treasury, Chester, Cagney, Harding, March, Montgomery, Dudley Digges and Leon Errol secretly loaned thousands from their personal accounts.[45] A one-reel short documenting the parade, narrated by Walter Winchell and featuring many of the performers, including Chester, was produced by Educational Films and released by Fox as *The Hollywood Gad-About* five months later.

In June 1934, Chester, Douglass Montgomery, Margaret Sullivan and Walter Woolf King all promoted their current film projects over the airwaves on the syndicated program *Hollywood Radio Previews*. Meanwhile, Universal chose the great cinematographer Karl Freund, who had directed *The Mummy*, to helm *Gift of Gab* (1934), a minor musical comedy about arrogant broadcaster Phillip ["Gift of Gab"] Gabney (Edmund Lowe) and his brief stardom at a local radio station. The studio loaded the film with current top players Gloria Stuart, Phil Baker, Victor Moore and Alice White, character favorites Henry Armetta and Sterling Holloway, and musical stars Gene Austin, the Beale Street Boys, the Downey Sisters, Ruth Etting and Ethel Waters. Freund began rolling the cameras on Monday, July 2.

For one brief scene in which they portray actors performing a radio vignette, Chester, Boris Karloff and Bela Lugosi (reteamed following their collaboration on the creepy Universal feature *The Black Cat*, directed by Edgar G. Ulmer), Paul Lukas, Roger Pryor and Binnie Barnes were added to draw a larger audience to this filmed variety review. As an "Apache dancer," Lugosi delivers one line, while, as "The Phantom," Karloff manages two plus an over-the-top laugh, and Chester, as "Doyle," basks in the luxury of about five. Lukas plays a corpse!

Motion Picture Daily was impressed by the film's "series of clever blackouts":

> This is another hilarious travesty on radio broadcasting, designed to extract a consistent flow of laughter from any audience, no matter how cynical ... orchids must go to Rian James, for his treatment, the trick photography of John P. Fulton and the intelligent execution of Karl Freund, the director.
>
> A picture of this kind should appeal to all classes, especially the radio listeners, who hear but never see their favorites.[46]

The Hollywood Reporter was quite enthusiastic:

Gift of Gab (1934): From left, Universal players Bela Lugosi, Chester Morris, Boris Karloff, Douglass Montgomery, Roger Pryor, Paul Lukas, Alice White and Binnie Barnes teamed for one brief scene, portraying actors performing a radio vignette [original lobby card].

> Good music; swell dialogue; insanely amusing sequences; an appealing, if not original, story, and grand performances throughout make this picture one of the big bets of the season.
> Edmund Lowe and Gloria Stuart carry the bulk of the plot, but it isn't as important, from an entertainment standpoint, as the gags, music and comedy scenes.... [T]he trimmings are something grand. Songs by Ethel Waters and Ruth Etting and the Downey Sisters and the Beale Street Boys ... one of the funniest farce scenes ever seen with Paul Lukas, Karloff, Roger Pryor and Chester Morris ... and very, very swell performances all around....
> The picture is a lot of fun, and with such a cast, with the music and its good direction, it's a cinch....[47]

Universal had planned to cast Chester as Charlie Denton opposite Heather Angel in the musical *Romance in the Rain* (1934), directed by Stuart Walker, but producer Stanley Bergerman, realizing that *Let's Talk It Over*, *Embarrassing Moments* and *Gift of Gab* all were slated for release within a three-month period, decided that he might suffer from a case of public overexposure. Again replacing Chester with Roger Pryor, Bergerman approved two months of vacation time and began scouting for another property for his next major picture. On July 19, 1934, Chester left Los Angeles for another round of personal appearances on the East Coast.

Chester and Sue, managing his money wisely, chose to spend any "surplus" on their home and family. Their major purchase for 1934 involved having a swimming pool installed, especially for use by Brooks and Cynthia, whom Chester believed was old enough to take lessons.

On September 10, Chester and Sue, accompanied by Robert and Betty Montgomery, "justified a childhood ambition" by appearing incognito during a lavish Los Angeles street parade organized by the Ringling Brothers-Barnum and Bailey Circus. Opening the current Hollywood dates for the circus, the parade helped publicize a matinee performance.

"Costumed as Arabs," Chester and Bob "didn't have to sign any autographs or take any bows," capping off their fun by riding horses around the circus arena. Meanwhile, the ladies graced a chariot festooned with "dusty ribbons and dim spangles."[48]

After signing Chester, Universal anxiously announced him for many film roles in which he never was cast. Another in the long list of possibilities appeared in the September 18, 1934, issue of *Variety*, when the studio, planning the next Karloff and Lugosi thriller, *The Raven* (1935), as a "special" attraction, mentioned Chester in its tendency to go "overboard on names."[49]

Produced by John W. Considine, Jr., and adapted by Bella and Samuel Spewack from a Charles Francis Coe story published in *The Saturday Evening Post*, MGM's "Repeal" was initially planned as a vehicle for Jean Harlow. Clark Gable, Lyle Talbot, Ricardo Cortez, Russell Hardie and Richard Arlen all were considered for the part of Jimmie ["Office Boy"] Burnham before Chester was cast. Considering the witty nature of the dialogue, and the sharp repartee engaged in by Chester and Carole Lombard throughout the film, Gable is arguably the only other actor on this list who could have succeeded as well in the Office Boy role.

Jack Conway began directing "Repeal" on September 20, 1934. Following the trend established at Warner Bros. moving the gangster genre toward parody and satire, MGM's entertaining contribution concerns Mary (Lombard), a chorus girl who gold-digs her way through a bootlegging gang initially led by William T. ["Shoots"] Magiz (Nat Pendleton), whom she marries for money. Unfortunately, Magiz is killed while deeply in debt.

Office Boy works as bodyguard to Magiz solely to collect $500 in weekly pay, remaining out of all racketeering activities, hoping to save enough dough to open his own auto garage. Eventually, following Mary's involvement with Magiz and criminal cohorts Daniel J. Dingle (Sam Hardy) and John Mickapopolis, aka "Mickey the Greek" (Leo Carrillo, repeatedly bragging, "I've got *braims*"), he and Mary fall in love.

Late in the film, Office Boy's actual name, James Burnham, finally is revealed: the forename first, written in the address on a postcard; and the surname later, when he lets it slip to a patron at his auto garage. Until then, even Mary calls him "Office Boy." In the process, Chester delivers some choice lines to Lombard, as both display impeccable comic timing throughout the film.

While Office Boy irons his trousers prior to Mary's wedding to Magiz, he is interrupted when she enters the room. Clad in shirt, necktie and boxer shorts, he suggests, "Next time, knock. Sometimes I take a bath, too."

When she reminds him of his responsibilities as best man at the ceremony, he points out, "Well, around here, the best is *none too good*."

After Magiz is blown up in his "bulletproof" car, Mary attempts to praise his virtues. Office Boy counters, "He would have croaked his own grandmother if she didn't sell his liquor."

Finally, fed up with the organization of assassination, Office Boy announces, "Holdups are out of my line. So are shakedowns. I'm resigning." When he suspects Mary of trying to extend her gold-digging to their relationship, he tells her, "I'm trust-fund proof. All my dough goes in the Jersey garage." But after she kisses him, he goes for another, admitting, "Now what? I must be even dumber than you."

Though the film was released after enforcement of the Production Code, the "racy" content includes a hilarious scene in which Mary's attorney (Walter Walker), his secretary (Isabelle Keith) and other gang members are present in the wedding-night bedroom, as well as two moments of homoeroticism played for humor. Out of the mob, and working at his garage, Office Boy gratefully kisses his male assistant, who quizzically mutters, "*Mr. Burnham?*" That evening, with Mary ensconced in his bedroom, he crawls into bed with the unsuspecting assistant, who, with even greater emphasis, says, "*Well, Mr. Burnham!*"

The supporting cast also features Zasu Pitts as Mirabelle, Mary's faithful sidekick, a role originally assigned to Una Merkel. Pitts participates in a funny "redistribution of wealth" scene, during which "Merry Widow" Mary hands out purloined $100 bills to grateful bystanders on a busy street, and Mirabelle stuffs handfuls of them into her blouse, just before landing a man of her own (Francis X. Bushman, Jr.). Gene Lockhart and familiar African American character actors Fred ["Snowflake"] Toones (who previously joined Chester in *King for a Night*) and Eddie ["Rochester"] Anderson also make brief appearances.

Wrapped after a month-long shoot, "Repeal" was retitled "East River," changed to "The Bride and the Best Man" for a preview showing, and finally released as *The Gay Bride* on December 14, 1934. *The New Movie Magazine* reported, "Gangster and underworld dramas will be conspicuous by their absence, except in cases where the subject is made farcical as in 'The Gay Bride.'"[50] During the week before the film opened, the Loew's State Theatre in New Orleans distributed "Chiseler's Club Cards" to patrons, informing them of honorary membership in the group, in which Carole Lombard was secretary and Chester, of course, "office boy." (The film includes a scene in which Office Boy presents a wrapped chisel to Mary as a wedding gift.) Criminally underrated, *The Gay Bride* unfortunately suffers from being produced during the transitional period when Hollywood filmmakers were forced to adapt screenplays to adhere to the strict provisions of the Production Code.

While Chester was shooting retakes for the film, Sue was interviewed by Ruth Corbin of *Silver Screen* magazine. She described their domestic relationship, admitting that her initial attempts at cooking for Chester met with limited success, but also expressed great satisfaction with their lifestyle:

> I can't tell you about all the little, absurd things that happened in those first few years of our married life. It isn't the easiest thing in the world to step off the stage and into the kitchen and be able to make the wheels go 'round without any friction. Chet and I managed to do it, because I was so anxious to be a success as a housewife and he understood and applauded my efforts.
>
> In the beginning I was quite nonchalant. I thought running a house was easy. I wouldn't even allow Chet to hire a cook. I insisted that I could do it. Armed with a good cook book I started out.... Eventually I succeeded. But it took time and patience and perseverance.
>
> I have never regretted giving up my career though. We are happy here in Hollywood. We have our own home and a nice circle of friends. Many of them were friends of ours when we were in New York.[51]

That same month, *Screenland* ran a feature, "Escape from the Work Habit!" in which Rose Tilton described the newly discovered leisure activities of Hollywood stars who pre-

The Gay Bride (1934): From left, Nat Pendleton, Sam Hardy, Chester Morris, Carole Lombard and Zasu Pitts in MGM's underrated gangster spoof released shortly after enforcement of the Production Code [original lobby card].

viously had known only nonstop work, sometimes resulting in exhaustion and major health problems. Chester's wakeup call came when Roland West controlled his career, often keeping him off the screen for prolonged periods. In response, Chester focused on improving the grounds of the Morris home, having the swimming pool installed, planting a garden, and overhauling automobiles in the garage. "I think it's fun to do something useful," he said. "Any fellow can find something to do if he casts an eye in the right direction."[52]

On the heels of *The Gay Bride*, Chester went straight to work on his next Universal project, *I've Been Around*, directed by Philip Cahn from October 29 to November 24, 1934. Screenwriter John Meehan, Jr., had begun adapting Gerald Beaumont's original story in early August, under the watchful eye of producer B.F. Ziedman, who had just signed a new contract with production head Carl Laemmle, Jr. John J. Mescall, who had shot Universal's *By Candlelight* (1933) and *One More River* (1934) for James Whale, lent his stunning cinematographic talent to *I've Been Around*, which he completed just in time to aid Whale in creating one of Hollywood's most striking black-and-white films, *Bride of Frankenstein*.

Motion Picture Daily praised Mescall's "beautiful photography" in *I've Been Around*, adding, "It all works out well after tense dramatic situations capably handled by Phil Cahn

"I'VE BEEN AROUND" — A Universal Production

I've Been Around (1935): From left, G. P. Huntley, Isabell Jewel, Phyllis Brooks and Chester Morris in Universal's melodrama, combining elements of *The Divorcée* and *Sinners in the Sun*, for which no prints are known to exist.

... who, with the aid of good acting of the entire cast, makes the best of weak material from an original by John Meehan, Jr."[53] *The Film Daily*, however, delivered a crushing blow:

> Though dressed up in stylish clothes and attractive backgrounds from the standpoint of entertainment this is a feeble and useless effort. Almost futile from its conception, neither cast nor director could save it. Story is about the marriage of Rochelle Hudson on the rebound to Chester Morris, an earlier sweetheart.... It's all pretty hard to take.[54]

Combining elements of *The Divorcée* and *Sinners in the Sun*, *I've Been Around*, even at a mere 63 minutes, overstayed its welcome by focusing solely on the up-and-down romance peppered with familiar acts of unfaithfulness, drunkenness and attempted suicide. Mescall's cinematography added some luster, but the capable supporting cast of G.P. Huntley, Phyllis Brooks, Gene Lockhart, Isabell Jewell, Ralph Morgan and Henry Armetta had few opportunities to improve the tired material. (*I've Been Around* is yet another title for which no prints have been located.)

George B. Seitz began directing the hospital drama "Ambulance Call" at MGM on November 26, 1934. Chester was cast as Dr. Bill Morgan, a role originally intended for Clark Gable, who recently had played an idealistic physician in the studio's *Men in White*

(1934). Making his starring debut (as Dr. Tommy Ellis), Robert Taylor was faced with having his role trimmed to give Chester more screen time. Reporter Mary Sharon wrote,

> Actors like to work with Chester because he is good luck for them.... I don't think it is entirely a matter of luck, but rather that he likes to help beginners get a good start.
> He helped Robert Taylor, at his own expense ... because he liked Robert and believed he had personality and ability and needed only a chance to prove it. When he accepted the story, the studio offered to cut the dialogue and scenes in which Robert appeared, but Chester would not hear of it.[55]

The film begins kinetically, with an ambulance racing through the streets toward Metropolitan Hospital. Seitz and cinematographer Lester White employ a highly mobile camera to help drive the rapid action during the opening scene. Interns Bill Morgan (Chester) and Tommy Ellis (Taylor) both appear shirtless while scrubbing up following surgery. A brilliant surgeon who values ethics and patient care over hospital politics and personal greed, Morgan immediately courts trouble by performing a life-saving appendectomy on young Frank Snowden (William Henry), against the wishes of his wealthy, influential father, Harris (Robert McWade). He then exacerbates the situation by standing up to "society doctor" Harvey (Henry Kolker) and superintendent Dr. Waverly (Raymond Walburn). "Blue blood isn't immune to gangrene," Morgan informs his boss.

Waverly fires Morgan, but he is reinstated following the personal intercession of the wealthy Mrs. Crane (Billie Burke), a hospital benefactor who offers to set up Morgan in private practice and provide plenty of "society" patients. Meanwhile, nurse Madge Wilson (Virginia Bruce), in love with Morgan, who prefers to focus on his career, eventually accepts a marriage proposal from Ellis.

Temporarily released from prison to "visit his hospitalized mother" (actually an accomplice), gangster Butch McCarthy (Johnny Hines), grabs a smuggled gun and attempts to murder Harrigan (Addison Richards), a police officer he previously wounded. Morgan tries to stop Butch, who shoots him in the abdomen. Having discovered her husband's police revolver, Mrs. Harrigan (Dorothy Peterson) guns down the gangster.

Using his knowledge of a modern surgical technique unknown to his "superiors" who have ignored it, Morgan, after being administered spinal anesthesia, guides Ellis in performing surgery on his damaged intestinal tract. Seitz and White's use of a series of close-ups, featuring mirrored reflections of the profusely sweating Morgan painfully issuing instructions to Ellis, is highly effective. Making a recovery, Morgan is "ordered" by Ellis to propose to Madge, who accepts.

Dr. Thomas M. MacLaughlin of London's St. Bartholomew's Hospital was hired as technical adviser by producer Lucien Hubbard: a fortunate move, since the film depicts its staff in spotless white and freely socializing, playfully stealing a patient's food from the kitchen and lighting matches on a "no smoking" sign. Chester benefited from the tutelage of the experienced staff physician, who helped him develop one of his most challenging film characters. Virginia Bruce replaced Fay Wray after the latter had been cast but suddenly decided not to play the female lead.

The completed film was reviewed under the title "Only Eight Hours" and eventually released as *Society Doctor* on January 25, 1935. *The Film Daily* considered it "good general appeal entertainment with excellent script, standout performances and direction that clicks."[56] *Motion Picture Daily* praised the concept and execution:

> Dramatizing the conflict of a young intern (Chester Morris) against hospital red tape and visualizing his rocky romance with Virginia Bruce and with intern Robert Taylor his rival, George Seitz has

Society Doctor (1935): From left, Chester Morris, Virginia Bruce and Billie Burke in MGM's follow-up to the earlier hospital drama *Men in White* (1934) [original title lobby card].

> directed a whipcracking picture, which, in exposing institutional shams, hands out a good, pungent show.
> Built smartly from human materials with a distinctive, central idea, the film contains comedy, pathos, suspense, melodrama, tragedy and action, building to a tense scene with Morris, under a local anesthesia, directing his own operation being performed by friendly enemy Taylor while Miss Bruce attends.
> Morris adds to his laurels by an exciting, nonchalant performance. Taylor's scenes drew applause.[57]

Variety's "Chic," calling the film "implausible" and "not consistently good entertainment," praised two of the actors:

> Morris plays the prodigy surgeon to the hilt and carries practically all of the play, getting little or no help from Miss Bruce. Miss Burke, while unimportant to the story, troupes it for second place. Robert Taylor does what he can, and the remainder are generally good without getting much chance.[58]

From 1934 through the end of 1939, Adrian Morris appeared in a total of 45 major studio features, many of them top commercial and artistic successes made by the industry's greatest directors. At Warner Bros., he supported James Cagney and Ann Dvorak in *"G" Men* (1935), Paul Muni and Ann Dvorak in *Dr. Socrates* (1935), Bette Davis, Leslie Howard and Humphrey Bogart in *The Petrified Forest* (1936), and James Cagney, Pat O'Brien and Humphrey Bogart in *Angels with Dirty Faces*.

Paramount cast him with W.C. Fields and Rochelle Hudson in *Poppy* (1936), Mae West, Edmund Lowe and Louis Armstrong in *Every Day's a Holiday* (1937), Sylvia Sidney and George Raft in *You and Me* (1938), Ronald Colman and Basil Rathbone in *If I Were King* (1938), and Barbara Stanwyck and Joel McCrea in *Union Pacific* (1939).

At MGM, he appeared as support to Wallace Beery and Robert Young in *West Point of the Air*, Paul Lukas and Madge Evans in *Age of Indiscretion*, Robert Young and Madge Evans in *Calm Yourself* (all 1935), and Walter Pidgeon and Rita Johnson in *6,000 Enemies* (1939). Columbia cast him (in the obviously complimentary role of Pigface) in *I'll Love You Always* (1935) with Nancy Carroll and George Murphy, *Coast Guard* (1939) with Randolph Scott, Ralph Bellamy and Warren Hymer, and (as a carpetbagger) in *Gone with the Wind* (1939).

RKO Radio cast him with Harry Carey and Hoot Gibson in *Powdersmoke Range* (1935), Paul Muni and Miriam Hopkins in *The Woman I Love* (1937), and Ann Sothern and Burgess Meredith in *There Goes the Groom* (1937). At 20th Century–Fox, he played a policeman in *Mr. Moto's Gamble* (1938), an entry in the Japanese detective series with a tumultuous production history and an excellent cast, including Peter Lorre, Keye Luke, Lynn Bari, Harold Huber, George E. Stone, Ward Bond and Lon Chaney, Jr. He also appeared with Warner Baxter and Lynn Bari in *The Return of the Cisco Kid*, Tyrone Power, Alice Faye and Al Jolson in *Rose of Washington Square*, and Cesar Romero and Marjorie Weaver in *The Cisco Kid and the Lady* (all 1939) at Fox.

For Nat Levine's low-budget Mascot Pictures, Adrian played somewhat more prominent roles, Deputy Abner in the comic mystery *One Frightened Night* and Sgt. Jack McGowan in the serial *The Fighting Marines* (both 1935). In Republic's *Wall Street Cowboy* (1939), he appeared as Big Joe Gillespie opposite B-Western favorites Roy Rogers, George ["Gabby"] Hayes and Raymond Hatton.

For Christmas 1934, Chester bought Brooks an electric train, which of course delighted the six-year-old boy. However, by the time he and Robert Montgomery had too much of their own fun playing with the locomotive, the motor had stopped running. Before the son could discover the damage, father rushed out to replace the entire set.

To celebrate New Year's 1935, Chester and Sue treated the children to dinner at the Brown Derby. In the January 1 issue of *Hollywood Low Down* magazine, he ran a quarter-page announcement, reading simply, "Holiday Greetings, Chester Morris."

Immediately after the holiday, Chester went back to work, costarring with Jean Parker in *Princess O'Hara*, directed by David Burton at Universal from January 2 to February 11, 1935. Damon Runyon's short story, published in *Collier's* magazine, was adapted by Harry Clork and Doris Malloy, with additional material contributed by Nat Ferber, Robert C. Rothafel and associate producer Leonard Spigelglass.

New York man about town Vic Toledo (Chester) is the sharp-dressed owner of a major taxicab company, the fashionable Shim Sham nightclub and a mighty racehorse named "Hozanna." During a "taxi war," King O'Hara (Ralph Remley), the driver of a horsedrawn hack, is accidentally killed by one of the Toledo cabbies. Vic attempts to help King's daughter, Kitty ["Princess"] O'Hara (Parker), who had been a performer at his club, but she repeatedly rebuffs his efforts.

Ordered to procure an equine replacement when the O'Hara horse, Goldberg, is stricken with pneumonia, Vic's mugs, "Last Card" Louie (Leon Errol) and Montague ["Fingers"] Spackwart (Vince Barnett), steal the prize racehorse "Gallant Godfrey" from its owner, Alberta Whitley (Verna Hillie), whom Vic has been squiring around town. Louie and Fingers coerce veterinarian Henry Spidoni (Henry Armetta) into presenting the horse, which has been disguised with paint, to Kitty, who is arrested for the theft.

Alberta agrees to drop the charges against Kitty only if "her horse" wins a race against Hozanna, on which the mob has placed all its dough. Vic tries to fix the contest but secretly resorts to signing over ownership of Hozanna to Alberta, who must honor her promise not to prosecute when the horse triumphs by one length.

The horseracing scenes were filmed on location at the Santa Anita Park racetrack in Arcadia, California, which had just opened one week before Burton began shooting *Princess O'Hara*. (The mountains in the background belie the New York setting.) Jean Parker, then 19 years old, had made her film debut three years earlier, and received top billing as the titular character. Adept at singing, dancing and gymnastics, she combined naturalism with precise enunciation in her acting technique, often playing instantly likable characters like Kitty O'Hara. She was experienced as the innocent young Damon Runyon lass, having played the daughter of "Apple Annie" (May Robson) in Columbia's *Lady for a Day* (1933), directed by Frank Capra. *Princess O'Hara* was the first of four films in which she would costar with Chester.

Each role in *Princess O'Hara* is well cast, from Chester as Vic Toledo to the many supporting players, including Leon Errol as a gruffer, tougher version of his familiar comic character, Vince Barnett and Henry Armetta in trademark roles, and Raymond Hatton, who makes an uncredited appearance as "Frying Pan," the hearing-impaired horse thief. Pioneering character actress Clara Blandick, as Miss Van Cortland, who assumes responsibility for Kitty following her arrest, delivers a choice line to the judge conducting her hearing: "Don't be legal—be *human*, for once."

Motion Picture Daily reported, This picture will delightfully surprise Damon Runyon, who may recognize but little of his original story but who will find exciting, well-made entertainment that is certain to please.

Princess O'Hara (1935): Ralph Remley (top left), Chester Morris and Jean Parker in the poster art for Universal's horseracing comedy-drama adapted from the Damon Runyon story [original one-sheet poster].

Producer Leonard Spigelglass, throwing away Runyon's script, has made fast moving race track story as his first production effort that clicks speedily.... The players carry their parts in keeping with the nature of the story and the direction of David Burton never lets things lapse.[59]

Variety's "Chic," however, thought the actors were let down by the script:

Material for a story existed in Damon Runyon's yarn if material is added in consonance with the author's style, but here the determination to be funny or dramatic—mostly funny—at all hazards spoils the chance of both the director and the players.... Dialog is a weaker point than the construction. Authors seem to hurry through the drama moments in an effort to reach the next comedy spot, and when they reach it they gag the stuff too much....

Jean Parker ... makes what sympathy she can for herself in the overstressed archness and vindictiveness, but she gets no real chance to impress her personality because she has to stand back for the laughs. Chester Morris has a walkthrough. There had to be a lead, but he is given no opportunity and it's to his credit that he makes his assignment as natural as he does.[60]

Following the wrap of *Princess O'Hara*, Chester was scheduled to visit New York for several weeks, but Universal forced him temporarily to cancel his plans by rushing him into another picture, *Storm Over the Andes*.[61] His replacement by Jack Holt in May 1935 was only one change made during the production. On June 29, while aerially inspecting sets built at the Russell Ranch in Triunfo, California, near the Pacific Ocean, director of photography Charles J. Stumar (who shot *King for a Night*, *Let's Talk It Over* and *Embarrassing Moments*) and art director G. Harrison Wiley (a veteran of *I've Been Around*) both were horrifically crushed to death by the engine of Stumar's Stinson monoplane after the left wing hit a large oak tree, causing the aircraft to plummet 600 feet and overturn near an emergency landing field. Director Christy Cabanne, who had begun 10 days before the crash, completed the shoot with cinematographer Harry Forbes on July 19.

5

Public Hero Number 1

In early 1935, the Screen Actors Guild held its Second Annual Ball, attended by more than 1,000 guests, at the Sala d'Oro of the Biltmore Hotel in Los Angeles. Guild president Kenneth Thomson gave the opening welcome and Lyle Talbot served as master of ceremonies. A fine orchestra was enjoyed by many stars and their spouses, and famed screen hoofer James Cagney had a blast continually cutting in on Chester and Robert Montgomery to whisk away Sue and Betty, respectively. Cagney got carried away at times, going so far as to steal Joan Crawford from the terpsichorean embrace of husband Franchot Tone. Soon, Chester got even, cutting in on Jim to carry away Francis Cagney during several numbers.

Chester also continued to develop his amateur magic act, including building his own sleight-of-hand devices. His latest invention was "a trick in which a rod passes through seemingly solid glass."[1]

The March 1935 issue of *Screenland* suggested, "A medal to Chester Morris because although he isn't the spectacular figure he was when the talkies first came in, he is slowly but surely fighting his way to prominence after a long siege of mismanagement and bad stories."[2]

Warner Bros. shot the film "The Farrell Case," directed by William Keighley and starring James Cagney as federal agent James ["Brick"] Davis, from February 20 to April 1, 1935. Less than three weeks after production began, on March 18, director J. Walter Ruben began shooting "B.I.D.J," another film about gangster-fighting agents of the Department of Justice, at MGM. Ruben completed production on April 19, a little more than two weeks before Warners released its feature, retitled *"G" Men*, on May 4.

As undercover Department of Justice agent Jeff Crane, Chester was joined by an ace cast, including Lionel Barrymore (top billed in a colorful supporting role), Jean Arthur and Joseph Calleia, reportedly making his screen debut (although he had played small parts in three previous films). During a visit from a reporter friend, Chester took a break while the crew were filming a long shot; and, just as he really began a rattling discussion, the assistant sound recordist approached him. "Mr. Morris," he said, "you're standing practically under the microphone so when they make another take will you keep quiet? Your conversation is coming through the mike."

"Well, fancy that," Chester replied. "You mean you could hear our conversation?"

"Yes, sir," the crew member affirmed.

Chester, his sense of humor never flagging, turned to his companion. "Isn't that wonderful?" he asked rhetorically. "Was it good conversation?" he wanted to know. "Was the dialogue snappy?"[3]

Both *"G" Men* and "B.I.D.J," retitled *Public Hero Number 1*, were released at a time

Chester poses with his new Cadillac in the driveway of the Morrises' Beverly Hills home (1935).

when the Federal Bureau of Investigation (FBI) became an independent service with the U.S. Department of Justice. Initially established on July 26, 1908, as the Bureau of Investigation (BOI), it was renamed the Bureau of Prohibition and the Division of Investigation (DOI) before the official reorganization in 1935.

"The Purple Gang" consisted of bootleggers and hijackers who began operating out of Detroit, Michigan, in the wake of Prohibition during the 1920s, eventually controlling the city's vice, gambling, liquor and drug rackets. Their methods were ruthless, incorporating arson, bombings and murder, and they muscled into labor unions and organized crime activities in other cities, reputedly including Chicago's St. Valentine's Day Massacre in 1929. By the early 1930s, gang members began to overextend themselves, with several arrests and convictions leading to the downfall of the outfit.

Wells Root's *Public Hero Number 1* screenplay, based on a story he cowrote with Ruben, combines the background of the Purple Gang with specific aspects of the violent crime and jail-break spree of John Dillinger from Indiana in May 1933 until his death at the hands of police and Division of Investigation agents in Chicago on June 22, 1934. During this time, he participated in 12 successful bank robberies with the "Dillinger Gang," which also included George ["Baby Face"] Nelson.

Public Hero Number 1 opens with Crane, in a deep undercover assignment, loudly tangling with prison guards as he bulls his way into the office of the warden (Lewis Stone, in a brief reprise of his role in *The Big House*). To gain the trust of incarcerated Purple Gang boss Sonny Black (Calleia), Crane attempts to reign supreme in their shared cell, until the stone-cold killer knocks him out with a blow to the head.

Like Wallace Beery in *The Big House*, Chester raves up a riot as Crane protests about the "stinkin' slop" served in the mess hall. In a distinctly *déjà vu* sequence, he then is consigned to the hole for 21 days, emerging to continue his rebellious ways, which culminate with an escape, during which he and Black hold up the prison board and hijack a member's car. A high-speed chase climaxes with Black being wounded by an officer's bullet.

While Sonny recuperates, Crane drives through a severe rainstorm to pick up Dr. Josiah Glass (Barrymore), a physician whose nine years of treating members of the Purple Gang led to his refuge in the bottle. Following an accident, in which Jeff unintentionally runs a bus off the road, he meets Maria

Public Hero Number 1 (1935): Chester Morris and Jean Arthur in the poster art for this exciting drama focusing on a U.S. Department of Justice investigation combining the background of the Purple Gang with events in the violent crime career of John Dillinger [original one-sheet poster].

Theresa O'Reilly (Arthur), whom he doesn't know is Black's estranged sister. Unbeknownst to Black, she wants him to sign papers from their uncle for the inheritance of a family farm.

Crane meets with his superior officer, James Duff (Paul Kelly), who advises him not to jeopardize their lengthy and dangerous investigation in Wisconsin by pursuing his personal interest in Theresa. Ordered to stay the course until locating the Purple Gang's secret hideout, he falls short when he witnesses Theresa being slapped by Black, who ejects him from the outfit after receiving a right cross to the jaw. He also loses his commission card and gun when Duff fires him from the Department of Justice.

Crane then tricks Dr. Glass into leading him to the hideout, the Little Paree roadhouse, where he pulls a Tommy gun on the inebriated physician and phones Duff. Before the agents arrive, Crane loses consciousness when Black hits him with the gang's car, and a furious shootout ensues. Many of the gangsters, including Butch (George E. Stone), are gunned down, but Sonny escapes.

Reinstated, Crane is ordered to question Theresa about her brother's whereabouts, but she refuses after learning that her former sweetheart is a "G" Man. Crane and Duff resort to running a classified, advising Sonny to accept some money from her at the Madison vaudeville theater where she is employed. When he takes the bait, the agents close in.

Public Hero Number 1 (1935): From left, Chester Morris, Jean Arthur and Joseph Calleia in one of the film's key scenes [original lobby card].

Warned by Theresa, he shoots it out with Crane while trying to escape. Wounded by one of Black's bullets, Crane finishes him off with several rapidly fired shots from his own gun. Named "Public Hero Number One," he then rushes aboard a train to prevent Theresa from leaving town.

Public Hero Number 1 is a tough, gritty feds-versus-gangsters film benefiting from the topnotch direction of J. Walter Ruben, typically stunning cinematography of Gregg Toland (whose next project was *Mad Love* [1935] with director Karl Freund at MGM) and sharp montage editing of Frank Sullivan (who also cut *The Gay Bride* and *Three Godfathers* [1936] with Chester). Enjoying the most screen time, Chester displays a wide-ranging characterization, with Barrymore well-cast in an atypical role (Dr. Glass is shot dead while having his final drink). Arthur demonstrates the unique resilience and chemistry she developed with leading men throughout her career, and Calleia, in his first featured role, succeeds as one of Hollywood's most believably icy villains.

The shootout at the Little Paree roadhouse was based on the April 22, 1934, raid by Melvin Purvis and the Division of Investigation on the Dillinger Gang at the Little Bohemia Lodge in Manitowish Waters, Wisconsin. After federal agents killed one gang member and wounded several others, Dillinger and three cohorts escaped through a back door, making their way northward through the woods until they were able to hijack a car and driver.

On Sunday, July 22, 1934, Dillinger was staked out by DOI agents at the Biograph Theater on North Lincoln Avenue in Chicago, where he had gone to watch his favorite actress, Myrna Loy, in *Manhattan Melodrama*. The theater manager, assuming that the feds were criminals planning a holdup, phoned the city police, who were ordered to stand down by the DOI. After *Manhattan Melodrama* ended, in an alley outside the theater, Dillinger, choosing to shoot it out, was hit by the bullets of three agents and fell face forward to the pavement. In the film, Black, "Public Enemy Number One," is felled by fire solely from Crane, "Public Hero Number One," and drops flat on his back, as his eyes stare blankly into the night sky.

MGM's coming-attractions trailer for the film opens with behind-the-scenes footage of Chester walking with Ruben down a street on the studio lot as they discuss the role to be played by Calleia. "I remember him, Jake," Chester tells the director. "We did a play together."

Calleia joins them, is introduced to Ruben, and they all enter a projection room to watch *The Big House*. As "The End" flashes on the screen, Ruben announces, "I think that the story of *Public Hero Number 1* is just as daring, just as timely and just as dynamic as *The Big House*."

Chester attended the May 16, 1935, premiere at the Loew's State theater in St. Louis, Missouri. The city police chief, who claimed never to have seen "a talking motion picture," joined Chester at the screening and supplied manager Chick Evens "for lobby display a lot of guns and other weapons used by former St. Louis gangsters." Local newspapers heavily publicized Chester's participation, which included a shopping tour of the area and an autograph session in the theater lobby. The president of an insurance company also attended, personally issuing "accident … policies to all patrons."[4]

Following the St. Louis opening, Chester was scheduled for a repeat performance at the Capitol Theatre in New York. MGM, however, sent a wire, ordering him to cancel the engagement and immediately report back to Los Angeles. He still owed one more film to Universal, and attorneys were waiting to hash over which studio would first nab his further services. In lieu of his personal appearance, the Capitol ran a local newspaper campaign offering a reward to the first person who brought to the theater "any of the ransom bills involved in the recent Weyerhaeuser kidnapping," an alarming case in which nine-year-old George Weyerhaeuser of the Tacoma, Washington, lumber dynasty had been abducted on his way to school just weeks earlier.[5]

Hollywood magazine noted,

> Although just another version of the Dillinger cleanup by federal agents, this picture will click everywhere. Lionel Barrymore wins honors with his characterization of a broken-down doctor.... The role of a Dillinger brings Joseph Calleia very much in prominence. Machine guns and purple gangs are everywhere, but the bad men are portrayed accurately as a bunch of heels who deserve no sympathy.... Chester Morris scores heavily in this picture.[6]

The Hollywood Reporter offered specific praise to "Chester Morris as the hero, Jeff Crane ... the best role that he's had in months and months, and he is once more the boy who sprang to fame in 'Alibi.'"[7] *Variety* agreed: "Chester Morris capably fulfils the requirements of the effacing, duty driven hero.... He plays with conviction and handles the roman[ce] nicely."[8]

The name of Calleia's character later would apply in real and "reel" life: Dominick Napolitano (1930–1981), aka "Sonny Black," a Mafia capo in the Bonanno crime family, unknowingly allowed undercover FBI agent Joseph D. Pistone, aka "Donnie Brasco," to join his crew, a move that led to his execution by a Bonanno associate in Brooklyn. Pistone's 1988 book about the case later was adapted by Paul Attanasio for the film *Donnie Brasco* (1997), costarring Al Pacino, Johnny Depp and Michael Madsen as Sonny Black (so named because of the dye Napolitano used to hide his white hair).

From May 29 to November 11, 1935, the first phase of the California Pacific International Exposition was held at Balboa Park in San Diego. Intended to boost the local economy during the Great Depression, this trade fair, the first organized since 1915, featured hundreds of exhibits, including those on the arts, ethnic cultures, history, horticulture, industry and science.

On May 17, the Screen Actors Guild named Lucile Gleason chairman of the committee in charge of the Motion Picture Hall of Fame, which would maintain a constant presence throughout the fair. Committee members included many women, including Joan Bennett, Mary Brian, Claudette Colbert, Joan Crawford, Marion Davies, Bette Davis, Dolores del Rio, Sally Eilers, Kay Francis, Ann Harding, Miriam Hopkins, Jeanette MacDonald, Helen Mack, Genevieve Tobin and Thelma Todd. The male contingent included Chester, Edward Arnold, Warner Baxter, Joe E. Brown, James Cagney, Eddie Cantor, Leon Errol, Clark Gable, James Gleason, Boris Karloff, Fredric March, Robert Montgomery, Lyle Talbot, Kenneth Thomson, Richard Tucker and Warren William.

At the event, Chester and Sue joined Ralph Bellamy, Johnny Mack Brown and their wives; and, when not sitting down to sign autographs for film fans, they toured the "Indian village" to take part in a tribal ceremony. Chief Thunder Cloud (a mysterious character actor whose real name was Victor Daniels) made a "brother" of Bellamy, who was given the honorary Native American moniker "Chenowah."

On June 5, 1935, Universal announced that Chester and Dorothy Page would costar in the dramatic musical *King Solomon of Broadway*, to be directed by Alan Crosland. However, on June 25, "by mutual consent," Universal executives and Chester, who had been dissatisfied since the problems with *Storm Over the Andes*, dissolved his contract, on which he had completed just three of six proposed features. Offered a long-term contract by

MGM, Chester shifted his work location from Hollywood to Beverly Hills, and Universal replaced him with Edmund Lowe in the titular role of Solomon McGuire. Crosland shot the picture, also featuring Pinky Tomlin (as himself), Louise Henry, Edward Pawley and Charley Grapewin, during the month of July.[9] Chester agreed to return to Universal for one more picture during the coming year, if a suitable property was found.

The Screen Actors Guild held its Annual Meeting at the Writers' Club in Hollywood on July 28, 1935. Robert Montgomery was elected to succeed president Eddie Cantor, while the vice-president positions went to James Cagney (first), Ann Harding (second) and Chester (third). Other offices were filled by Kenneth Thomson (secretary), Boris Karloff (assistant secretary), Warren William (treasurer) and Noel Madison (assistant treasurer).

Chester later recalled,

> I was one of the organizers of the Screen Actors Guild. I was vice-president when Bob Montgomery was president…. [The actors] had to have it…. I remember that Warner Bros. were doing a fight scene in the stadium … that they had built on the backlot, and they employed 200 extras. And the extras were told to bring an additional hat and coat, and so they all arrived on the backlot. Warner Bros. had put two extras, and a *dummy* between each extra. Now the extra not only had to have the dummy next to him, but he had to *clothe* him with his own coat and his own hat. And when they swayed and applauded, the dummy moved with them; and, instead of 200 extras, they had *400*…. They would do anything or everything to save money…. They wouldn't even outfit the dummy, which was amazing. They sort of linked arms with the dummy, which was wonderful.[10]

During the summer, Chester and James Cagney were at it again, this time during a party at the home of Elissa Landi. She recently had added a tennis court to her property, and the two "tough-guy" actors waged quite a spirited contest for Edward Everett Horton, Jean Muir, Merle Oberon, Gertrude Michael and Paul Cavanagh, with Chester emerging triumphant.

Following the abduction and murder of the 20-month-old son of Charles Lindbergh by Bruno Hauptmann during the spring of 1932, the 72nd United States Congress enacted the Federal Kidnapping Act, popularly called the "Little Lindbergh Law" on June 22 of that year. The senseless cruelty and brutality of the crime helped prove the necessity of allowing federal law enforcement agents to pursue kidnappers across state lines. Previously, state, county and local authorities had been unable to accomplish this task.

In MGM's *Pursuit* (1935), directed by Edwin L. Marin from Wells Root's screenplay based on the story "Gallant Highway" by Lawrence G. Blochman, Chester plays "Mitch" Mitchell, a pilot who agrees to transport little Donald McCoy ["Donny"] Smith (Scotty Beckett), the subject of a guardianship dispute, to Mexico. South of the border, he will meet back up with his mother (Dorothy Peterson), who is attempting to keep him away from her late husband's sister. After his airplane is wrecked during an accident caused by Donny, Mitch, accompanied by Maxine Rush (Sally Eilers), secretary for a private-detective agency hired to care for the boy, must drive to the destination.

Though a $20,000 reward has been offered to whomever finds the child, Mitch honors his promise to deliver Donny to Mrs. Smith for only $4,000. On the way, he unintentionally burns the farm truck used to hide their getaway car, twice risks his life to save the boy, and poses as Maxine's newlywed husband after she fools a country cop (Erville Alderson). They continually elude two ineffectual stooges (Harold Huber, Dewey Robinson) and a determined but equally inept vagabond, Thomas ["Tom"] Reynolds (Henry Travers), who stays hot on their trail.

Pursuit combines the topical subject of kidnapping with a level of humor that builds throughout the film's brisk 60 minutes, smoothly aided by Chester's talent for well-played light seriocomedy. The highpoint of the chase shenanigans occurs when Mitch and Tom wrestle inside a large kennel full of dogs at an animal hospital. In a sign of the "politically incorrect" times, Mitch, Maxine and Donny finally cross the border into Mexico wearing blackface, after trading their car for an old, run-down jalopy driven by a group of African American camp followers (headed by John Larkin). Fortunately, the scene is played with some subtlety, and the usual stereotypical mugging associated with such a scene is avoided by Marin, a versatile director who made several fine films (including *A Christmas Carol* [1938]) for MGM.

Motion Picture Daily declared *Pursuit* a solid hit:

> This is just one hilarious, breathtaking chase from start to finish through unexpected situations with no letdowns except for plenty of laughs....
>
> Young Beckett ranks among the best child actors with this performance and Henry Travers gets howls of delight as a dimwit hick who steals the child. Miss Eilers and Morris give good accounts.... Marin directed for speed and thrills ... excellent screenplay by Wells Root from the story by Lawrence Blochman.[11]

Chester's costar in *Sinners in the Sun* and *The Gay Bride*, Carole Lombard, threw a major wingding in Venice, California, during the summer, renting the House of Fun for an entire evening. The guests comprised the very firmament of Hollywood stars: Richard Arlen, Richard Barthelmess, Warner Baxter, Claudette Colbert, Marlene Dietrich, Sally Eilers, Henry Fonda, Cary Grant, Jean Harlow, Josephine Hutchinson, William Powell, Randolph Scott, many of whom were bruised and battered by the collapsing barrel and giant slide attractions. George Cukor, Wesley Ruggles, David O. Selznick, Walter Wanger and other filmmakers even dropped in. Chester was up to his usual quota of celebratory mischief, filling *Screenland* reporter Elizabeth Wilson's plate with a veritable smorgasbord as she attempted to eat a steak.[12]

On September 3, 1935, the board of directors of the Screen Actors Guild met to discuss following the recommendations of a special committee on a plan to secure producer recognition for collective bargaining under provisions of the National Labor Relations [Wagner] Act, which had become effective on July 6. Guild leaders were committed to an aggressive campaign, but the committee, consisting of Chester, Boris Karloff, Edward G. Robinson and Robert Young, intended "to conduct negotiations on a friendly basis" and were "not keen to precipitate an open battle

Pursuit (1935): From left, Sally Eilers, Chester Morris and Scotty Beckett featured on the cover of MGM's official pressbook for the film.

unless forced to do so."[13] Heeding the advice of the committee, the directors drafted a letter formally requesting a meeting to discuss recognition of the Guild under the Wagner Act.

The October 1935 issue of *The Modern Screen* published excerpts from an interview with Chester, in which he described his views on various aspects of married behavior:

> Consideration: [T]he greatest thing any man can give his wife. And it's especially important for an actor, because you know how unbearable an actor can be … after a disappointment—not getting the role I wanted—I sometimes go for hours without saying a word, sulking, because I feel sorry for myself.… It's an actor's greatest failing.… This is an awful strain on Susie and I usually try to clear out until the mood is over.
>
> I like to humor her, too. If Susie likes to have breakfast in bed, she never hears me complaining about having to eat downstairs alone.… Every husband should make it a point to indulge his wife's whims now and then—and also to go out of his way to do little favors for her. Always be considerate of her strength. And don't be backward about showing your affection for her in front of other women. A woman likes that, though she may pretend not to!
>
> Children: I never let my affection for them come before my love for Susie. When a father (or a mother) allows his children to claim first place in his interest, he weakens the close bond between himself and his wife. It's bound to happen. And it's so foolish, for children always run out on their parents when they grow up.
>
> Honesty: [T]elling the truth is one of the surest ways to preserve happiness. Even about little things. Even when Susie doesn't ask me about something, I tell her every little thing I do all day long.… It saves a lot of misunderstandings later. Her confidence in me is terribly important to her and to me, too.
>
> Humor: [H]ave a lot of laughs! A lot of them. They've got what it takes to stay married![14]

During the autumn of 1935, Chester and Robert Montgomery took a deep-sea fishing voyage along the Mexican coast, bringing back a fresh haul to Los Angeles. More maritime leisure followed on November 21, when MGM released Lewis Lewyn's musical comedy short "Pirate Party on Catalina Isle," directed by Gene Burdette and shot in Technicolor by Ray Rennahan with "A Galaxy of Screen Stars" who were enjoying a weekend at Avalon.

The Al Jolson, Buddy DeSylva and Vincent Rose song "Avalon" opens a lavish production number as a ship enters the harbor, its deck populated by a host of dancers and sword-wielding pirates. Scantily clad waterskiing females add visual splendor to the Technicolor scene. A low voice pipes, "All for Chester Morris!" and he emerges from the ship's cabin, dressed as a pirate captain, happily hamming it up. Issuing orders, he insists, "Stop firing those little shots. All the *big shots* are here!" Explaining that notorious, ship-scuttling pirates of the previous century have been replaced by "Hollywood friends, who scuttle over here in their yachts, to enjoy a little up-to-date buccaneering," he narrates shots of Cary Grant and Randolph Scott, Errol Flynn and Lili Damita, Mickey Rooney, Marion Davies and Virginia Bruce, and several musical and terpsichorean performers.

Charles ["Buddy"] Rogers and His California Cavaliers perform, swinging their opening number while wearing masks of Charles Chaplin, Stan Laurel, Oliver Hardy, Louis Armstrong and others. When Chester encounters shipboard trouble with an "inebriated" Leon Errol, he recommends an "ocean voyage with Commodore Johnny Downs and Betty Burgess," during which they sing "Smooth Sailing." Sid Silvers and Lee Tracy appear as pirates in another sequence featuring the 1933 number "The Gold-Diggers' Song (We're in the Money)." Other actors in the 19-minute film include Robert Armstrong, Lynn Bari, Vince Barnett, Jack Duffy, Irene Hervey, Blanche Mehaffey and Dick Wessel.

Motion Picture Daily reported,

Time and money were lavished on this outdoor short in Technicolor with results that are eye and ear-filling. The buccaneer costumes, a bevy of good-looking girls and a collection of singers, with outdoor action shots to lend variety make up a satisfying whole.... It's a grand short.[15]

Chester was pleased to be MGM's choice as host of the enjoyable film. That month, when the Social Security Act began, he also was content to be issued number 564-12-0920.

Chester reunited with his *Big House* costar Wallace Beery for the November 9, 1935, broadcast of the NBC radio program *Shell Chateau*, during which they performed in Howard Emmet Rogers' drama "Two Men Met at the Vail." Beery also hosted the show, featuring Helen Broderick, Lester Crawford, and Harriet Hilliard singing with Victor Young and His Orchestra.

Peter B. Kyne's novel *Three Godfathers*, based on his earlier 1910 short story "Broncho Billy and the Baby," was published in *The Saturday Evening Post* on November 23, 1912. The first film adaptation, *The Three Godfathers* (1916), directed by Edward J. LeSaint and starring Harey Carey as Bob Sangster, was followed by John Ford's *Marked Men* (1919), also featuring Carey (as Cheyenne Harry, a recurring role in his Westerns), and *Action* (1921), starring Hoot Gibson (as Sandy Brouke), although contemporary sources named J. Allan Dunn's novel *The Mascotte of the Three Star* as the source material. All three were released by Universal, with both Ford films now considered "lost."

William Wyler directed the first sound version, *Hell's Heroes* (1929), starring Charles Bickford, Raymond Hatton and Fred Kohler, for Universal. Also released in a silent edition, the film benefits from sequences of grueling realism shot at four California locations: Mohave Desert; Panamint Valley; Red Rock Canyon State Park; and the town of Bodie, used to represent New Jerusalem, where the main street and bank were featured. This gritty, unsentimental, often dark adaptation remains faithful to Kyne's story, driven by Bickford's mercenary, selfish outlaw whose moments of decency are motivated by his two companions, who take an instant liking to the newborn baby they must save from a dusty death in the desert.

Including only a modicum of the religious references and symbolism featured in later adaptations (especially Ford's 1948 Technicolor epic), this version of Kyne's Western "Christmas story" features all three godfathers deliberately committing suicide. Sangster, after briefly abandoning the baby in the desert, where a gila monster is slowly slithering across the sand, ultimately downs a bellyful of "arsenic water" to gain enough strength to reach New Jerusalem, where he dies on the floor of the church during the Yuletide service. Produced during the transitional year of 1929, *Hell's Heroes* does not waste one moment of its 68 minutes, and is arguably one of the most realistic, hard-hitting features of the early sound era.

On November 27, 1935, Richard Boleslawski (born Boleslaw Ryszard Srzednicki in Poland and trained at the Moscow Art Theatre) began directing Edward E. Paramore, Jr., and Manuel Seff's new screenplay, *Three Godfathers*, at MGM. Producer Joseph L. Mankiewicz assembled a fine cast, including Chester as Bob Sangster, Lewis Stone as James ["Doc"] Underwood and Walter Brennan as Sam ["Gus"] Bartow, and crew, headed by ace cinematographer Joseph Ruttenberg. Like its predecessor, the film includes scenes filmed in the Mohave Desert and at Red Rock Canyon State Park.

Prior to working on this film, Chester had ridden only polo ponies, including one that had been given to him by Robert Montgomery. He did not want to use a double in the action scenes, so, while on location, he took early morning rides across the desert. He learned not only how properly to handle his horse, but also discovered that he enjoyed "becoming one"

Three Godfathers (1936): Chester Morris as the outlaw Bob Sangster, arguably one of his finest film characterizations, for which he prepared extensively prior to production [original lobby card].

with the powerful animal. A creature he did *not* commune with, however, was a temporary visitor to his "portable dressing room": a rattlesnake curled up in the middle of the floor.¹⁶ At one point, Sue and the children traveled to Mohave to spend some time at the location.

Paramore and Seff incorporated the same basic story elements for *Three Godfathers* as did Tom Reed for *Hell's Heroes*, with 12 minutes of additional scenes, primarily included at the beginning, that offer greater development of the main characters and introductions to several inhabitants of New Jerusalem. Bob's former girlfriend, Molly (Irene Hervey), now engaged to Frank Benson (Robert Livingston), the town banker, provides insight into his motivation. Cynicism, deceit and selfishness has led to Bob's estrangement from the community, to which he has returned with three companions, "Doc," a tubercular cowpoke with a PhD, "Gus," an illiterate drifter, and Pedro (Joseph Marievsky), a Mexican troubadour. A master con artist, Bob is described as a "lowdown, no-account skunk" who would "kill anything from a baby to an old woman."

As in *Hell's Heroes*, the Mexican hombre stands watch in the street as the others hold up the bank. After a hearse passes behind Pedro, tensions rise during the heist, and Bob guns down Benson (who, ironically, is dressed in a Saint Nicholas suit). "There ain't no Santa Claus," he proclaims. Pedro is killed by Professor Snape (Sidney Toler) and Doc is shot in the left shoulder as the outlaws flee down main street on their horses.

This time, in the desert, Bob discovers the body of a dead man by the poisoned water hole, and a dying woman, Mrs. George Marshall (Helen Brown), with her infant son (played by eight-month-old twin girls, Jean and Judith Kircher), lying in an abandoned covered wagon. Like Charles Bickford, Chester plays Bob as a selfish mercenary who wants to drink the baby's milk, here relinquishing "his" can only when offered Doc's $5,000 bag of bank loot in exchange.

As the three (never actually called the baby's "godfathers" in this version), having lost their horses to the poison water, head on foot across the desert, Doc chooses to carry the child first, but soon succumbs to his weakened condition. Shaking hands with their compadre, Bob and Gus, carrying the baby, continue, leaving the learned Doc behind to deliver the "Tomorrow, and tomorrow, and tomorrow" soliloquy from Shakespeare's *MacBeth* and shoot himself as a large Joshua tree (as in *Hell's Heroes*) looms, like a cross, over him.

The scenes of Bob and the baby in the desert are more disturbing that their counterparts in *Hell's Heroes*. The earlier film is raw and visceral, but the newborn baby remains unrealistically quiet. For this version, Boleslawski made sure to have the Kircher twins cry throughout their effective "performances," which are believable and remarkable. When Bob abandons the child and walks away, then turns to *shoot*, killing a rattlesnake (which, unlike the gila monster in the 1929 film, is shown in the *same* shot with the baby), his motives are briefly open to question. "Now look what you've done," he says to the child. "You made me kill that poor little rattlesnake."

At times, Chester's characterization of Bob makes him even less likable than Bickford's often loathsome version. He doesn't drink as much of the poison water, and is not made up to look as ravaged as the dying Bickford; but the inclusion of Molly, to whom Bob presents the baby before dying on the floor of the church, provides a satisfying redemption both for the character and the film's dramatic arc. In the second of the film's two examples of overt Christian symbolism, after handing the child to Molly, Bob painfully straightens his back against a pillar, on which a small wreath of holiday garland hangs above his head. Thus "crucified," as Molly looks reverently on, he dies.

Silver Screen magazine praised this adaptation of a now-familiar story: "The performances of the three godfathers are outstanding, and ... Boleslawski's direction of the baby, Jean Kircher, is really something."[17] *Motion Picture Daily* elaborated,

> This tale of the three outlaws develops as an interesting character study motivated by a heart gripping theme after starting as an average action picture....
> Richard Boleslawski's direction captures the full power of the struggle of the three with their emotions and with the elements of nature.... The Joseph L. Mankiewicz production is class and the photography of Joseph Ruttenberg does the desert backgrounds full justice. All the parts are trouped splendidly.
> The picture can best be sold from the heart angle.[18]

Variety's "Wear," in his primarily positive review, pointed out an essential aspect of the casting:

> Despite minor flaws in direction and story adaptation ... "Three Godfathers" seems destined to get its share of the grosses ... a strong film [which] should prove big enough to stand alone if only because of Lewis Stone and Chester Morris.... Appears to be Metro's first earnest attempt to enter Western lists, and as such it is a commendable effort. Judged from his portrayal in this outdoor opus, it's a sad commentary that no picture company previously uncovered Chester Morris for Western roles. He is as much at home in this atmosphere as he ever was in gangster parts....
> Stone again contributes one of his grand character portrayals as the most sentimental of the three

Three Godfathers (1936): Bad Men and a Baby, (from left) Chester Morris, Walter Brennan, Jean/Judith Kircher and Lewis Stone.

outlaws. Brennan's work adds distinctive strength to film's entirety whether in humorous mood or in critical scenes near the end of the trail. That Chester Morris holds his own against such sparkling portrayals indicates the calibre of his performance.[19]

The casting of *Three Godfathers* is solid across the board. Brennan is outstanding in one of his earliest major supporting roles, and Stone offers a unique variation as the well-read, philosophical Westerner from Vermont. As "Wear's" comments suggest, those who write about Western films should not be as discriminatory as the hardy pioneers who traveled westward, displacing, through any means, including murder, the original inhabitants of the West. Many pioneers hailed from the East Coast and even farther east, across the wild Atlantic. Chester's birth in New York City made him no more "miscast" than that alpha Western star, Harry Carey, who was born in the Bronx. James Cagney, the tough guy from Hell's Kitchen, originally wanted to be a farmer, but class discrimination prevented him from attending agricultural school. He eventually proved quite versatile, especially as a dancer, starred in three Westerns, and enjoyed a lengthy, successful second career as a farmer and rancher.

Chester's interpretation of Bob Sangster is one of his finest film characters, one for which he prepared extensively before production began. The scene in which Bob, believing he will not survive to deliver the child to New Jerusalem, attempts to pray but cannot, is the emotional highpoint of the film, and is played, in close-up, with admirable restraint and for the right amount of screen time. Joseph Ruttenberg's cinematography here, and in the entire film, employs interesting compositions capturing the life-threatening environment in which the characters struggle.

Hell's Heroes and *Three Godfathers* are both devoid of the broad humor and sentimentality of John Ford's religious-allegory adaptation, *3 Godfathers* (1948), written by Laurence Stallings and Frank S. Nugent, a film the director called a personal favorite in his *oeuvre*. Harry Carey's namesake son, nicknamed "Dobe" for the shade of his trademark red hair, plays William Kearney, aka "The Abilene Kid," in this stunning Technicolor version, filmed by Winton C. Hoch at several California locations: Mohave Desert, Death Valley, Lone Pine, Owens Valley, Keeler and the RKO Encino Ranch. Transformed by Ford's extensive personal touches, this feature became the third faithful sound adaptation of Kyne's story to be produced in 18 years, a rare achievement for films based on a specific work of literature. Each title in this trio, standing on its own individual merits, is worthy of viewing.

Ford's cinematic homage to Harry Carey, Sr. (who died on September 21, 1947), *3 Godfathers* casts the son of the "bright star of the early western sky" (as he is elegized in the opening credits) as a member of the bank-robbing trinity led by Robert Marmaduke Hightower (John Wayne) and his right-hand man, Pedro ["Pete"] Roca Fuerte (Pedro Armendariz), who wage an Olympian struggle with death to save a newborn infant while fleeing from Sheriff Perley ["Buck"] Sweet (Ward Bond) and his posse through the Mohave Desert. Ford's depiction of the three "good bad men" is a fully realized expansion of his earlier silent versions; but here, in a sound film, he continually demonstrates the depth of their relationships visually. The tough, rugged outlaws don't need to verbalize their feelings. Simple gestures are combined with sensitive actions, such as the reverent behavior toward the pregnant woman (Mildred Natwick) by Pedro, the only one of the three who knows anything about childbirth.

On the cold morning of December 16, 1935, Thelma Todd was found dead in her Lincoln Phaeton convertible, which was parked inside the garage at the Pacific Palisades home of Roland West's ex-wife, Jewel Carmen. Only 29 years old, she apparently had been beaten prior to succumbing to carbon monoxide asphyxiation. The L.A. District Attorney's decision to rule the death a suicide fueled rumors that her refusal, supported by West, to cave in to gangsters who wanted to convert a portion of Thelma Todd's Sidewalk Café into a gambling casino, had directly led to her murder.

No one who knew Todd admitted ever to seeing her depressed or suicidal, and West revealed that he had locked her out of their house the previous evening, resulting in her attempt to keep warm in the car. The LAPD then concluded that the death was accidental, and a subsequent grand jury probe led to the Homicide Bureau closing the case, listing her demise as "accidental with possible suicide tendencies," although no note nor motive for taking her own life was discovered.

Todd biographer Andy Edmonds wrote that the LAPD's decision led to "a succession of confessions by strangers and friends, and lurid details of [her] private life—a life that skirted death in the fringes of the underworld. Those who were suspected had plenty of reason to kill the woman known as 'Hot Toddy.'"[20]

Following Roland West's passing on March 31, 1952, a rumor that Chester was at his deathbed, and claimed that the director had confessed to murdering her (a version of the event supported by a theory that he killed her on his yacht, *Joyita*, and then planted her body in the garage) was not substantiated. No evidence against West was ever discovered.

The truth is that Chester had ended his association with West nearly two decades earlier, and he always remained clear about the director's notorious treatment of him. In a May 1957 discussion with journalist Erskine Johnson, he said,

> I never had a chance to throw money around like everyone else in those days. That film mogul threw it around for me. When I was making $20,000 a week, he got $10,000. There was a trust fund gimmick in the contract I'm now thankful for. But when I was making my biggest films, I saw only $286 a week in cash.[21]

Robert Montgomery and Elizabeth Allen ("Betty") celebrated the birth of their son, Robert, Jr., on January 6, 1936, proudly adding the baby to their family which also included two-year-old Elizabeth. Though Mrs. Montgomery reportedly had "selected a typically fluffy ruffled cradle," Chester devotedly had set to work building his own custom crib for the new small fry.

George Cukor directed Irving Thalberg's "prestige" MGM production of Shakespeare's *Romeo and Juliet*, "arranged for the screen" by Talbot Jennings, from December 26, 1935, to mid–April 1936. Featuring a star-studded cast including Leslie Howard and Norma Shearer (at 42 and 33 years old, respectively, playing the teenage couple), John Barrymore, Edna May Oliver, Basil Rathbone, C. Aubrey Smith, Ralph Forbes, Reginald Denny and Violet Kemble Cooper, the film also employed dozens of character actors and many uncredited, $5-per-day extras, including Chester, who was working on the lot in *Moonlight Murder*, directed by Edwin L. Marin from February 10–28, 1936.[22]

A hybrid of opera and mystery that 20th Century–Fox would echo with *Charlie Chan at the Opera*, filmed later in the year with Warner Oland and Chester's friend, Boris Karloff, *Moonlight Murder* opens with a dress rehearsal of Guiseppe Verdi's *Il trovatore* at the Hollywood Bowl, at which tenor Gino D'Acosta (Leo Carrillo) is warned by a swami (Pedro de Corboda) that he will die while performing the following day. Gino is then attacked by Bejac (J. Carrol Naish), a crazed composer who is carted off to an "insane asylum."

Red herrings abound as the case is investigated by Detective Steve Farrell (Chester), sent by the continually exasperated Police Chief Quinlan (Robert McWade). Steve immediately falls for Toni (Madge Evans), the niece of Dr. Adams (Grant Mitchell), Gino's best friend, who examines his "superficial" wound. However, Gino dies from inhaling poison gas while singing an aria the next evening. After Diana (Benita Hume), Gino's lover, also succumbs to the gas, her boyfriend, Pedro (Duncan Renaldo), is arrested for the crime.

Toni analyzes the contents of a test tube discovered at the Hollywood Bowl by Steve, concluding that her uncle had filled it with the gas. Adams confesses that he committed a mercy killing by exposing Gino, who was suffering from a painful terminal throat disease, to the poison, but that Diana accidentally succumbed after opening a backup container. Bejac, who had escaped on the way to the asylum, attempts to kill the doctor but is gunned down by police. Steve supports Quinlan's belief that Bejac was the murderer, but Adams comes clean.

Chester's fast-talking comic cop, called a "bonehead" by the Chief, who temporarily busts him down to walking a beat, provided quite a dramatic descent from his previous MGM role in *Three Godfathers*, but he delivers an entertaining performance, smoking a pipe and again integrating nonverbal techniques reminiscent of Stan Laurel. Grant Mitchell, in his third film with Chester in as many years, turns in another quiet, controlled characterization, differing greatly from his roles in *Tomorrow at Seven* and *King for a Night*. Another *Tomorrow* alumnus, Frank McHugh, also plays a supporting role.

Motion Picture Daily appreciated the film's departure from the traditional mystery genre formula:

> This is something new in the line of multiple-suspect murder-mystery drama.... It is smartly directed and convincingly acted by all, with the thread of suspense adding to the pre-planned baffling complication in which tenor Leo Carrillo is warned he will be killed if he sings.... The progress of Morris' sleuthing, adding to the dramatic mystery and comedy of the show, builds to a surprise climax.... The operatic sequence by Wilhelm von Wymetal is a feature that should thrill audiences.[23]

During the production of *Moonlight Murder*, MGM announced that Chester and Madge Evans would costar in a second film, *Speed* (1936), also to feature Roland Young and Ted Healy. Before Edwin L. Marin directed the project from March 20 to April 9, 1936, only Ted Healy remained in the cast, with James Stewart, Wendy Barrie and Ralph Morgan in the roles originally intended for Chester, Evans and Young.

At a March 2, 1936, Screen Actors Guild board meeting, a letter was presented from Frank McHugh regarding the upcoming Academy Awards Dinner, to be held three days later at the Biltmore Hotel. Several members of the board had been invited, and a resolution was passed unanimously, by Chester, Robert Armstrong, Edward Arnold, James Cagney, Lucile Gleason, Claude King, Noel Madison, Fredric March, Robert Montgomery, Ralph Morgan, Edward G. Robinson, Kenneth Thomson and Donald Woods, to send a telegram to all senior Guild members, reading,

Moonlight Murder (1936): Madge Evans and Chester Morris in a posed MGM publicity portrait.

> You have probably been asked by your producer to go to the Academy dinner. We find that this is a concerted move to make people think that Guild members are supporting the Academy. The Board feels that since the Academy is definitely inimical to the best interests of the Guild, you should not attend.[24]

On March 5, the union boycotted the Academy Awards, hosted by Frank Capra at the Biltmore Bowl. Guild member Dudley Nichols won the Best Writing, Screenplay award for *The Informer* (1935), but did not attend nor accept the Oscar (the first time in Academy history that this occurred). The film also won for Best Director (John Ford), Best Actor in a Leading Role (Victor McLaglen) and Best Music, Score (Max Steiner).

After *Three Godfathers* was released by MGM on March 6, 1936, Chester dropped off Brooks and Cynthia at a local theater early one afternoon to see "their favorite actor," but when he went back to collect them at 4 p.m., they failed to reemerge. Two more hours passed, and still no children. Fearing the worst, Chester spoke with the theater's on-site nurse, who explained that they already had watched the film three times, so he finally made his way through the audience to retrieve them.

Producer Bud P. Schulberg had great difficulty making "Queer Money," which Erle C. Kenton began shooting at Columbia on March 18, 1936. The Production Code Administration recently had declared a moratorium on films depicting the activities of "gangsters" and "G-Men," and criminals were no longer to be shown engaged in armed conflict with law enforcement. Schulberg wrote to PCA director Joseph I. Breen, explaining, "We do not deal with 'gangsters and cops' but with a smart international counterfeiting ring, who are pursued by and finally defeated by the 'T men' themselves without the aid of cops or resorting to the usual gangster film gun battles."[25]

Kenton, who began his Hollywood career as one of Mack Sennett's original Keystone Cops in 1915, was a versatile director, making his first film in 1919 and consistently moving from one genre to another. Prior to "Queer Money," his top films included *The Last Parade* (Columbia, 1931), *Island of Lost Souls* (Paramount, 1933), *The Public Menace* (Columbia, 1935) and *The Devil's Squadron* (Columbia, 1936).

Several censorial changes were made to William Rankin and Bruce Manning's "Queer Money" screenplay, including the deletion of scenes depicting photography of United States currency and the counterfeiters possessing a weapons arsenal. During a time in which major "mob" actors like Edward G. Robinson and James Cagney were now playing characters on the "right" side of the law and spoofing their former public enemies, Chester, on loan to Columbia from MGM, said,

> I'm glad producers have quit casting me in gangster roles. Crime has never appealed to me. It always has seemed such a dumb thing for anybody to be at odds with organized society. Nobody can get away with it for long. I hope I'll get more roles like this one.[26]

Former bootlegging boss Capper Stevens (Lloyd Nolan), now running a St. Louis counterfeiting operation, uses his girlfriend, Aimee Maxwell (Margot Grahame), to aid in the kidnapping of U.S. Treasury master engraver Tom Perkins (Claude Gillingwater). Trailed by undercover federal agent John Joseph Madden (Chester), who cleverly appears cold-bloodedly to murder his way into the gang, they are foiled in their grand "queer money" scheme. When Aimee attempts to stop Stevens from shooting her sister, Verna (Marian Marsh), she pays with her life, and Perkins lives to engrave the invitations to the young woman's wedding to Madden.

As in several earlier films, Chester projects a strong duality in his characterization. While undercover, Madden (differing markedly from his earlier "G" Man, Jeff Crane, in *Public Hero Number 1*) is a fast-talking, gum-chewing tough guy who punches and shoots his way onto the counterfeiting gang; but, after the criminals are in custody, he reveals his true nature as a likable, standup guy with a sense of humor.

Kenton's solid pace benefits from the camerawork of John Stumar (whose late brother, Charles, had shot three of Chester's Universal films) and editing of Richard Cahoon. Though subjected to the Production Code, the film offers one conspicuously bold moment: Conman Angel White (George McKay), demonstrating to Stevens a con he pulls by taping back the middle finger of one of his hands, flamboyantly "flips him the bird." (The "finger" gesture, which originated in Ancient Greece, began to proliferate in the United States during the 1890s.)

Counterfeit (1936): From left, Marian Marsh, Margot Grahame, Lloyd Nolan, Chester Morris and Gene Morgan in a showdown between "T" Man and "queer money" ring.

Motion Picture Daily praised the film, released as *Counterfeit* on May 25, 1936:

> Tapping a subject which has had but little picture attention, this unreels as an interesting melodrama with authentic flavor....
> Erle C. Kenton's direction builds constant excitement and has the audience frequently worried over the safety of Morris. The cast members give excellent portrayals, with George McKay and John Gallaudet the best in support. The William Rankin story with the screenplay by Rankin and Bruce Manning is an education in the working of Government departments and seems accurately drawn. The Schulberg production is class and the photography by John Stumar is effective.
> As an unusual action entertainment, the offering should give general satisfaction.[27]

Playing a G-Man in two films had quite an effect on Chester, who added a new hobby to his leisure hours: collecting, not the autographs, but the fingerprints, of his friends. After having each set photographically enlarged, he strung them around the walls of the "playroom" in the Beverly Hills home.

During spring 1936, a series of health problems beset the Morris family. Sue underwent a "minor surgical procedure," Brooks and Cynthia both came down with measles, and Chester, taking a two-week break from work, had one of his wisdom teeth pulled. "Might as well get in on the family agony," he jokingly told a reporter. "Hate to be left out of anything."²⁸ After Brooks recovered, Chester prepared to send him on a campout; but, forgetting to buy a sleeping bag and a mess kit, lost so much time in traffic that the boy nearly missed the outing.

On May 15, 1936, the magazine *The Motion Picture and the Family* published a bizarre article titled, "Chester Morris Runs Restaurant for Dogs," claiming,

> Chester Morris is interested in one of the strangest businesses on record—a restaurant for dogs! Owners of pets may bring their animals to the restaurant for meals, or have the food delivered by the "canine caterer."
> This is one of the many novel hobbies pursued by well known film figures in Hollywood.²⁹

As he had done at Universal, Chester grew tired of his contract with MGM, again negotiating to end a legal agreement early. "Dissatisfied with assignments on [the] Culver City lot," he was released "by mutual consent," on condition that he would be available for one picture each year through 1938, the fulfillment date of his original contract.³⁰

From June 10 to July 8, 1936, Chester, beginning a three-year agreement with Columbia, and Fay Wray costarred in "There Goes the Bride," directed by Alfred E. Green. While shooting a scene with Henry Mollison, who plays thief Arnold Stewart, Chester failed to pull a punch and split his lip. Mollison's bad luck on the set continued: As he was carried into a room, he badly twisted his foot and then dislocated his shoulder when flopping onto a sofa.³¹

Outside the home of New York City socialite Edna Fletcher, the taxi of former boxer turned driver Jimmy ["Iron Jaw"] Donlin (Chester) is invaded by a fleeing woman (Wray) wearing a wedding dress. Jimmy agrees to help but adds that he cannot make her his "career." He puts her up in his apartment but, discovering that the real Edna (Martha Merrill) is being wed to Count Petoski (Rafael Storm), speeds back to discover that his guest is Mary Trenton, a dress model accused of stealing a valuable pearl necklace from the bride. The necklace then falls out of the dress, and Jimmy asks his fellow cabbie and sometime pickpocket, "Fingers" Garrison (Lionel Stander), to sneak it back into the Fletcher home. The necklace is proved a fake; and, aided by society newspaper editor Roger Clifton (Raymond Walburn), Jimmy, Mary and Fingers track down the real thief (Mollison) and string of

They Met in a Taxi (1936): Chester Morris poses for a Columbia publicity still.

pearls. The case solved (with Ward Bond making a brief appearance as a policeman), the happy couple embrace as the film fades to black.

Columbia released the film as *They Met in a Taxi* on September 1, 1936. Exhibitors were encouraged to play up the "runaway bride" angle made popular in the studio's multiple Academy Award-winner *It Happened One Night* (1934). Particularly adept at light romantic comedy, with a few rough character qualities thrown in, Chester is well-cast as the fast-talking, good-natured Jimmy. Under Green's admirable pacing, Wray, Stander and Walburn provide solid support; and the screenplay by Howard J. Green (who specialized in mysteries and gritty crime films, including Warner Bros.' *I am a Fugitive from a Chain Gang*, which he cowrote) features some choice dialogue. Having discovered that his guest is an imposter, Jimmy declares, "If you're Edna Fletcher, I'm *Mahatma Gandhi!*" Later, after Jimmy knocks out Arnold Stewart in the street, Fingers complains, "No necklace and this *mummy* on our hands!"

Motion Picture Daily judged it "better than average entertainment":

> Well directed, nicely produced and acted with enthusiasm by feature and supporting players, the film has a popular appeal that presages mass appreciation. Moving to the tune of light comedy, romance, mystery, drama, intrigue and suspense, the surprise dialogue tells the story, although there is sufficient action to hold attention.[32]

"McCarthy" of *Motion Picture Herald* added,

> Wisely the producer invested the story with a lot of hokum.... In that atmosphere, the picture is played with spirited enthusiasm. The work of Chester Morris and Fay Wray is consistently good. They together provide lots of laughs, but the character most likely to have audiences up on chair edges is Lionel Stander, whose dialogue and actions are amusing.[33]

In September 1936, *Screenland* magazine reported that Chester would join May Robson on a trip across the Atlantic to costar in a British feature adaptation of Jules Verne's celebrated 1876 novel *Michel Strogoff* [*Michael Strogoff: Courier of the Czar*]. Though Chester did not appear in such a project, director Jacques de Baroncelli, assisted by Richard Eichberg, made the French film *Michel Strogoff* (1936), starring Adolf Wohlbrück, which was followed by a German version, *Der Kurier des Zaren* [*The Czar's Courier*] (1936), also directed by Eichberg and featuring Wohlbrück in the title role. The following year, RKO Radio producer Pandro S. Berman imported the actor, altering his name to Anton Walbrook, for a U.S. version, *The Soldier and the Lady*, directed by George Nicholls, Jr.

On September 7, 1936, the Screen Actors Guild had "every nationality working in films" participate in the Labor Day Parade, which ran for two miles, from Broadway at 16th Street to Los Angeles City Hall.[34] "A gang of Keystone Cops chasing a scab actor [was] used as a running gag" as "the Guild's unit in a procession of 50,000 trade unionists was one of the most colorful and highly publicized features of the parade."[35] The senior Guild section consisted of Chester, Edward Arnold, James Cagney, Boots Mallory, Jean Muir, Pat O'Brien, Kenneth Thomson and Richard Tucker.

The following morning, Erle C. Kenton began shooting the U.S. Navy comedy-drama "The Depths Below," a remake of the popular Jack Holt films *Submarine* (1928), directed by Frank Capra, and *Fifty Fathoms Deep* (1931), directed by Roy William Neill, at Columbia. Billed third, Chester supports Richard Dix and Dolores del Rio in the story of two officer-pals who experience a falling out due to the selfish actions of Carmen, a nickel-a-dance girl. Though she marries Jack Dorgan (Dix), who has decided to settle down by buying a comfortable home in San Diego, she falls in love with Robert Mason (Chester), resulting in near tragedy for both men. Kenton wrapped the shoot in early November.

The rationale for producing the remake (*the* Hollywood reason for continuously making more of the same) was explained by legendarily tightfisted Columbia mogul Harry Cohn:

> I made this picture once for $40,000 and it cleaned up. So, I made it again [*Submarine*] for $100,000 and it still made money. I'm going to spend a quarter of a million on it this time, and if it still makes money, I'll know I have nothing to worry about. I can just go right on remaking this picture as long as pictures are made, and it will always make money.[36]

Three outstanding writers, Jerome Chodorov, Liam O'Flaherty (author of the original story from which Dudley Nichols adapted his script for John Ford's *The Informer*) and Dalton Trumbo, contributed to the screenplay. Ace cinematographer Lucien Ballard shot the film, featuring a capable supporting cast including John Gallaudet, Ward Bond and Francis MacDonald (who also played John Wilkes Booth in Ford's *The Prisoner of Shark Island* in 1936).

Released as *Devil's Playground* on January 24, 1937, the film opens in Manila, where Dorgan and Mason are engaging in the traditional antics of sailors on leave. Mason, disappointed that Dorgan has decided to put down more sedate roots ashore, leaves on his next duty assignment. Dorgan buys a house and expensive furniture, then meets Carmen at a dance joint, and she quickly accepts his marriage proposal. When Dorgan must return to duty, Carmen heads back to the dance hall, where she makes her trademark moves on Mason, who knows nothing about her relationship with his best friend.

Later, when Dorgan takes him home "to meet the wife," Mason attempts to leave, but Carmen acts as if he is attacking her, sending her wronged husband into a rage.

The Devil's Playground (1937): Richard Dix (left) and Chester Morris as fellow U.S. Navy submariners.

Dorgan assumes his friendship with Mason is over but must help him and his fellow sailors after they become trapped on the ocean floor, their submarine having crashed into a derelict ship they had been assigned to inspect. The film ends with the freed Dorgan again living the sailor's life with his pal.

Chester, Dix, who again demonstrates his admirable range (an outward likeability often masking a darker psychology), and del Rio all deliver fine performances. Kenton's admirable pace, concluding at 74 minutes, moves the story along briskly. The light comedy of the opening and closing scenes provides the right bookends for the military drama and romantic melodrama in between.

Film Bulletin's "Hanna" appreciated the acting:

> Dix is sincere and convincing in every scene. Morris turns in a neat performance and handles the emotional scenes in the doomed sub strongly. In the unsympathetic role of the unfaithful hussy, del Rio gets the most out of her lines. The direction is fair, and the production far better than such a story deserves.[37]

Kenton's later directorial efforts include several genre favorites for Universal: three classic horror films, *The Ghost of Frankenstein* (1942), *House of Frankenstein* (1944) and *House of Dracula* (1945); and three early Abbott and Costello comedies, *Pardon My Sarong* (1942), *Who Done It?* (1942) and *It Ain't Hay* (1943), a musical remake of *Princess O'Hara*. From 1952 to 1960, he kept busy directing dramas for television.

MGM head of production Irving Thalberg died of pneumonia on September 14, 1936. The former "Boy Wonder," who had suffered from illness since age 17, was only 37. Two days later, the studio shut down to honor his memory, and the funeral service was held at the Wilshire Boulevard Temple. All other Hollywood studios observed five minutes of silence, and tributes arrived from individuals industry-wide. Contributing to the profusion of remarks already offered, Chester said simply, "Irving Thalberg's work was not confined to any one studio. His interest embraced the entire industry."[38]

Chester's social life in the film capital continued unabated. In October 1936, *Modern Screen* magazine ran a feature on James Cagney, in which he named his closest Hollywood pals as Robert Montgomery, Pat O'Brien, Frank McHugh and Chester. Topping out at 5'6", Cagney appeared diminutive alongside Chester, who towered an entire 2.5 inches over the Warner Bros. dynamo. That same month, *Photoplay* published a feature on Montgomery, providing extensive coverage on his longtime, close relationship with Chester:

> [Bob's] close friends are the friends he made ... six years ago when he left a New York stage for Hollywood.... Chester Morris and Sue lived up the street a few doors. The years have only molded their acquaintance into a deep and abiding friendship.
> He doesn't ask or demand of his friends that they think as he does, believe as he does or even share his fondest passions, dreams and hobbies....
> He clutters up the Morris household like a pair of old shoes. Chet is just as liable to walk in his front door around noon and there, in solitary grandeur on the back patio, is Bob Montgomery, eating his lunch. "Stay for lunch," Bob will urge him. "Nice place here. Food's good, too. Sue, bring on another salad. That funny man's here again."
> "A man in his own home," Chet pretends to grumble, "can't have a salad alone. Moochers all over the place," and the repartee of cracks and sallies between the two fairly shrivels the afternoon sunshine.
> Let Chester date himself for an interview at home and there's Montgomery cramping his style, offering mortifying tidbits that leave both Chester and the interviewer limp.[39]

Montgomery served as President of the Screen Actors Guild from 1935 to 1938. Chester recalled,

> I've seen him just before he attended a Guild board meeting, and he'd be like a kid acting up all over the place. Two minutes later he sat there as president of that board, serious, firm jawed, determined that the little fellow, the less successful actor, should have his just deserts.
> Montgomery didn't need that Guild. He was on top. But the little fellows did, and he was there to see they got theirs.[40]

On the evening of November 8, 1936, Chester and Sue celebrated their 10th wedding anniversary in grand style by "taking over" the Tropics restaurant at 421 North Rodeo Drive in Beverly Hills. This "Pre-Polynesian Pop" venue catering to the Hollywood crowd had been opened earlier in the year by Harry "Sugie" Sugarman. Among the attendees was journalist Marshall Kester, who described the lavish layout:

The new tropical dining room, Hawaiian in motif and ceilinged with glass to enable guests to enjoy the illusion of heavy rain storms and thunder-and-lightning effects, was the scene of the Morrises' conviviality. A long buffet was laden at one end and the thirst-quenching counter was operated at the other end of the room. Hawaiian music and entertainment abetted the enjoyable event and more atmosphere was added with all the guests being furnished with beautiful tuberoselets.[41]

Among those joining Chester, Sue, Etta, Adrian and "Willy" were James and Frances Cagney, Robert and Betty Montgomery and other Hollywood notables, including Jean Arthur, Ralph Bellamy, Richard Boleslawski, Harry Cohn, Walter Connelly, Lloyd Corrigan, John Cromwell, Clark Gable, James Gleason, Jack Holt, Edward Everett Horton, Harry Lachman, Walter Lang, Carole Lombard, Fredric March, Edwin L. Marin, Frank Morgan, Pat O'Brien, Walter Pidgeon, Hal Roach, Rosalind Russell, David O. Selznick, Myron Selznick, Henry Stephenson, Lewis Stone, Gloria Swanson, Robert Young, and Mr. and Mrs. Darryl F. Zanuck. They all had received personal invitations containing the poetry of Chester B. Morris Himself.

"Tahitian" dancers performed "practically two floor shows ... quite a record for a private affair." Reporter Tip Poff added,

The program was repeated by popular demand and the agile ... dancers, with their own version of the hula, as well as a mystifying magician who performed prodigious feats like reducing the size of cards to the vanishing point and weaving huge brass rings together in the air, left spectators dizzy but delighted.[42]

More than 300 revelers came and went throughout the evening, some of them continuing at a second gathering held at the Morris home. On the set of Columbia's "Loan Shark" the next day, Chester, with his famously dry wit, claimed, "About half of them are still there."[43]

While shooting a scene with director D. Ross Lederman (who had begun his career as an extra in Mack Sennett's silent Keystone Cops shorts) and costar Helen Mack, Chester took matters in hand when five-year-old Patsy O'Connor was unable to relax. After several unsuccessful takes were shot, Patsy was persuaded to play "horsey" with Chester, who then resorted to a little "hypnotism" to ease her inhibitions.

The screenplay was written by Mary McCall and Lionel Houser, whose background as a New York newspaper man added verisimilitude to the story and dialogue. After seven years of marriage, clerk Edward Lang (Chester), who earns $27.50 per week, wants to treat his wife, Mary (Mack), daughter, Judy (O'Connor), and baby son, Bill, to a vacation. Denied an advance on his yearly bonus (which never arrives) by company boss B.G. Wilson (Wallis Clark), he resorts to borrowing $50 (with unspecified interest) at a local cigar counter, later learning that loan shark Richard Farra (Leo Carrillo), using the Aloha Social Club as a front, runs the racket. Farra's loyal thugs, including "Whitehat" (Marc Lawrence) and "Fancyface" (Henry Brandon), provide muscle when necessary.

Eddie's attempts to repay the money turn desperate: He steals $10 from the office petty cash fund, but when returning the money, is fired by Wilson. As he digs himself deeper into chaos, he is brutally beaten by the thugs and literally left for dead in a hole at a Works Progress Administration (WPA) site. In the hospital, he decides to cooperate with District Attorney J.E. Curtis (Thomas Mitchell) but, before he can testify, is gunned down on the steps of the Hall of Justice. His sacrifice inspires other racket victims to testify, and Farra and his mob are arrested. Eddie survives to rejoin his family and accept a job in the D.A.'s office.

During production, Columbia retitled the picture *I Promise to Pay*. While editor James

Sweeney was working in the cutting room, *Motion Picture Herald* reported on November 21,

> Three qualities, story content, cast strength and topical production details are being counted upon by the producers to make this picture a subject of more than usual interest. In plot it is a racket exposure, this time of the unscrupulous and terroristic activities of the salary loan business. A problem that regularly makes front page headlines in almost every city and town in the country, it is one in which the public should be more than ordinarily interested.[44]

Prior to the premiere on April 21, 1937, *Photoplay* magazine noted,

> Inevitably, any racket picture these days starts out as a B picture—something for the double bills. Unexpectedly, "I Promise to Pay" has become an A picture in the course of production at Columbia. Chester Morris and Helen Mack are that real, as a young tenement couple victimized by loan sharks.[45]

The Film Daily agreed:

> The subject is one that hits close to home with everyone, and therefore should be of great interest to regular audiences. D. Ross Lederman has directed the piece in a highly suspenseful manner and geared it so that it moves quickly.... The entire cast, which includes Leo Carrillo, Chester Morris, Helen Mack and Thomas Mitchell, is excellent.[46]

Lederman, working with cinematographer Lucien Ballard and editor Sweeney, crafted a 68-minute picture that moves elegantly from start to finish, consistently striking a balance between fluid camerawork and dynamic montage. Every directorial choice appears to have been made, as John Ford often said, "for a reason."

The character of a husband and father, struggling financially and emotionally to support his family, allowed Chester to move away from the "types" he often had been playing in films. He displays an impressive range in *I Promise to Pay*, eschewing familiar mannerisms for distinctly poignant expressions and even a unique gait for Eddie Lang. The realism of the scenes set in the hot, crowded street, where he approaches the cigar counter to deal with his loan problems, include his breaking into a profuse sweat. (In one shot, a poster advertising *Counterfeit* at a local movie theater can be seen in the background.) The chemistry between Chester and Patsy O'Connor is tangible, a quality emanating naturally from his own experience as a father who spent a lot of time with his children. The depth of his nuanced portrayal is evidenced by many subtle actions: At one point, he conveys, almost imperceptibly, Eddie's nervousness and fear for the safety of his family by bumping into a chair as he gets up to look out the apartment window.

Leo Carrillo gives a convincing performance as a thoroughly unlikable character, as do Lawrence and Brandon as his sleazy minions, the latter being as characteristically attractive as the former is obnoxious. Thomas Mitchell is perfectly cast as the district attorney. When Eddie, as the first victim to stand up to the gangsters, tells him, "I want to do everything I can to put them out of business," Curtis responds, "I've been around a long time. I've been a criminal lawyer and a politician. I don't rate my fellow citizens very high. There are some days when I'd give you the whole human race for a dime. Yes, and give you *nine cents* in change."

The reviewer for *The New York Times* concluded,

> It is the most acceptable Chester Morris in ever so long, and the part of the Caligulian head of the usury ring is remarkably played by Leo Carrillo. The workings of the racket as revealed by the disclosures of its New York extension in the last year or so are faithfully recorded in the film, 1,000 per-

I Promise to Pay (1937): Chester Morris (as Edward Lang) and Patsy O'Connor (as his daughter, Judy). The character of a husband and father, struggling financially and emotionally to support his family, allowed Chester briefly to move away from the "types" he often had been playing in films.

cent interest, strong-arm dunning and all. Grand jury members ought to see this picture, if only to get a glimpse of the grand jury room of the future.[47]

Wolfe-Smith, in *Film Bulletin*, provided suggestions for exhibitors on the East Coast:

The title and the words "loan shark racket" just about give you the size of this yarn, but lay your eyes to these facts. It was written by a New York reporter, who knows his rackets and who covered a loan shark racket exposé in his town for a daily sheet. It has, as its topnotch names, Chester Morris and Leo Carrillo. They may mean a lot in some places, but names don't mean a thing to a story like this one.

Your dear public on the whole is pretty much familiar with the type of louse this film exposes … this yarn touches home with plenty of your customers and your job is only to get across to them the fact that "I Promise" takes a healthy sock at the strong-arm loan sharks they should avoid. Roll up your sleeves, take out the lead and go to work on this one.[48]

At home, Chester expanded production of his 16mm "amateur pictures," which became the subject of a December 1936 feature for *Screenland*. He told journalist Ruth Tildesley that he would "almost as soon part with the family dog" than with his camera, with which he had been developing his filmmaking craft for six years, hoping to capture some realistic moments. As to his children, he explained,

> It was all very simple when they were babies, but much more complicated now. Movie actors' kids are camera-conscious, I think. They have a sort of sixth sense that knows the minute a camera begins grinding. They begin to pose and show off and aren't a bit cute. Brooks at eight is awful. He gets the finger into his mouth and giggles and struts—not amusing anybody, unless it might be himself by the time he's thirty.
>
> Frank Buck of "Bring 'Em Back Alive" has nothing on me when I'm shooting the children. I hide behind hedges, lie under clumps of shrubbery, lean from balconies or windows, or the branches of tall trees, anywhere at all so the camera won't be noticed. Then they're perfectly natural. They don't know what's going on.
>
> I think the best shots you can get are those you make when your victims don't know you're shooting, whether they are five or fifty; but it's not always practicable.[49]

Chester's favorite independent work was a silent comedy film that he produced, directed, wrote, edited and acted in with Sue, Adrian and his wife, Eva, all of whom he paid 25 cents per day, "whether on location or at home." Incorporating slow-motion, he achieved a slapstick effect in a scene involving his character digging up a huge diamond (a doorknob) in the Hollywood Hills, then running up and down slopes, and through the streets, on the way home to show his wife. Sue went so far as to shave off her eyebrows, replacing them with painted, exaggerated artwork that ran up into her hair. A shot of her knitting baby socks was juxtaposed with a title card, reading, "Ann, a one-man woman—and darn sick of it!"

By the time he finished shooting several angles of each scene, most of which wound up on his cutting-room (den) floor, Chester had spent $500 on the film, necessitating the following opening credits:

> Producer: Chester Morris
> Director: Chester Morris
> Writer: Chester Morris
> Editor: Chester Morris
> Star: Chester Morris

Chester and Sue used the film as a highlight of their parties, sending their guests into fits of laughter. "Frank Morgan was over last night," he said, "and practically rolled on the floor when he saw it."[50]

Chester also began using his amateur filmmaking skills to develop characterizations for professional assignments:

> Many Hollywood players use their home movies to give themselves tests for parts they are to play or hope to obtain....
>
> For my ... roles in "The Depths Below" and "They Met in a Taxi," my home movie tests showed me some effective things to do to differentiate the characters.... You can see yourself as others see you ... you can test yourself for grooming, dress or mannerisms. Most of us don't know we have mannerisms until we see them on the screen.[51]

Additionally, he used his home movie outfit to prove a point to his young son:

> Most people want to act. Most people are sure they *can* act, so they are usually happy to have the chance when you get out that little black box.
>
> Brooks suddenly decided he wanted to act when I was on my latest picture. I had been telling him about Scotty [Beckett], the kid who played in it, and he was sure he could do Scotty's part....
>
> "You go out of the room," I directed, "and when I give you the signal, come in, cross the room to me, hold out your hand and say, 'Hello, Dad!'"
>
> He went out, importantly. I signaled and he came in....

"You don't come into a room like that, do you?" I demanded. Then Brooks giggles. Cynthia, who had been observing the scene, offered to repeat it and did it beautifully.

Brooks may improve when he's older, but I hope he won't be a movie actor and have to earn his living by painting his face. I hope he'll be a supervisor, if he goes into the movie business.

But it's stupid for parents to try to plan their children's lives. "My boy is going to be a lawyer"—or "My son is to enter the ministry" or be a writer or whatever it is, is just hot air. He will decide for himself, or life will decide it for him.

I was to be an artist. I was taking lessons at art school when I made up my mind to act. The family knew nothing about it until they noticed in the evening paper that my film was playing at a local theater. The picture was pretty bad, but it settled my career. Acting, not drawing![52]

Chester joined host Jackie Cooper on the Monday, December 14, 1936, evening installment of the *Lessons in Hollywood* biweekly radio program, broadcast by New York's WOR from 8:00 to 8:15 p.m. (EST). Italian actress and novelist Elissa Landi was scheduled for the Wednesday, December 16, installment.

Chester and Sue, ever the amiable hosts, carried on their signature hospitality through the 1936 holidays. One of Chester's most popular concoctions, his "Holiday Special" eggnog, was the subject of a feature in *Movie Classic* magazine. As a testament to the singular popularity of this unique recipe, he and Sue received a wire from friends who recently had relocated to New York but were planning to return at Yuletide:

> Will sleep under your hospitable roof Christmas Eve. Held out against your pleas to make a flying trip west for twelve months, but thoughts of your inimitable eggnog were our downfall. Anxious to see you, Suzanne, and the youngsters, but if you are not planning to brew up a batch of your Christmas Cheer, wire immediately and we will postpone trip until next December.[53]

Chester revealed "the cherished recipe" that made "the Morris home resemble the Grand Central Station at Christmas":

> HOLIDAY SPECIAL
>
> 1 dozen fresh eggs
> 3 quarts milk
> 1 quart cream
> 1 cup sugar
> 1 quart mellowed brandy
> 1 pint Jamaica rum
> 1 teaspoon fresh grated nutmeg
>
> Beat egg whites and yolks separately. To the yolks add sugar and beat until light and creamy, then add brandy, rum and nutmeg. Blend well and add milk and cream. Cover punch bowl with stiffly beaten whites of eggs. Serve cold if preferred, but in cold weather it is delicious if warm.

As a favor to Columbia mogul Harry Cohn, Chester joined a group of studio stars attending the San Francisco premiere of *Lost Horizon* on March 2, 1937. Sue chose to stay at home when he was selected to escort Margot Grahame to the banquet honoring the "prestige" picture directed by Frank Capra and costarring Ronald Colman and Jane Wyatt. John Winburn reported in *Photoplay*,

> This bothered Chester considerably, and ... he was on pins and needles. Margot, a great tease, showed up in a ravishing gown that gave Chester the jitters. From one who was there I learned that Chester worried so over her décolleté that he even hunted up a safety pin so she'd be more conservative!
>
> As far as Sue is concerned, she need not worry about Chester; but it is an aggravation to have to put up with the Hollywood custom which ruthlessly thrusts the wife to one side.[54]

6

Flight from Glory

In April 1937, threats of mass support for a film-industry strike began to be voiced. On April 30, member unions (including painters, plasterers and plumbers) of the Federated Motion Picture Crafts (FMPC) went on strike, demanding recognition from the producers. That evening, a meeting at Screen Actors Guild headquarters was attended by two-thirds of its 33 directors, including Chester, Edward Arnold, Humphrey Bogart, Joseph Cawthorn, Joan Crawford, Lucile Gleason, Paul Harvey, Boris Karloff, Claude King, Murray Kinnell, Francis Lederer, Fredric March, Frank and Ralph Morgan, Robert Montgomery, Alan Mowbray, Elizabeth Risdon, Kenneth Thomson, Franchot Tone, Donald Woods and Robert Young. Guild business representative Aubrey Blair called for a membership meeting to be held at the Hollywood Legion Stadium.

On May 1, 3,000 technicians and workers picketed the major studios. Ninety-six percent of the major stars and contract players were ready to strike. Among those who ignored the militancy and crossed the picket lines were Clark Gable, Greta Garbo, Jean Harlow, Jeanette MacDonald and William Powell, all complaining because they had received no breakfast from chefs who had walked out. Managing to eat their early morning meal elsewhere, Jean Arthur, Jack Benny, Bing Crosby, Irene Dunne, Martha Raye and Randolph Scott also disregarded the stand of their fellow performers.

The next day, the Guild held a special board of directors meeting, at which Lionel Stander proposed that, as members of a trade union, actors not pass through picket lines, and that the organization assume financial responsibility for all legal trouble resulting from contract people refusing to cross the lines. At 8 p.m., the mass meeting began at Hollywood Legion Stadium, and the decision whether or not to cross the picket lines was afforded to each member. Resolutions were passed that any non–Guild member who accepted a job as a makeup artist, painter or in any other craft currently on strike would be refused future membership, and that charges would be filed against any Guild member who worked in any of these crafts while the strike was in progress. Joining Chester at the meeting were Edward Arnold, Ralph Bellamy, Joan Blondell and Dick Powell, James Cagney, Joan Crawford and Franchot Tone, Richard Dix, Glenda Farrell, Cary Grant, Hedda Hopper, Rochelle Hudson, Allen Jenkins, Francis Lederer, Edmund Lowe, Frank McHugh, Robert Montgomery, Paul Muni, Edna May Oliver, Bill Robinson, Lee Tracy and Robert Young.

At 10:30 p.m. on Wednesday, May 5, a special board meeting was hosted by Chester and Sue at the Morris home. A resolution was passed that, if negotiations were not considered satisfactory before a May 9 membership meeting, telegrams would be sent to all senior members, advising that a strike vote would be taken. Board member Francis Lederer resigned after his proposal that members be warned explicitly about the dangers of a strike, especially potential legal difficulties, was voted down. The following evening, two meetings, one for select members and a second for the board, were held at the home of James Cagney.

At 11 p.m. on Friday, May 7, another special board meeting was held, this time at Frank Morgan's home in Beverly Hills. Lederer's letter of resignation was read aloud by Robert Montgomery, and the board accepted it "with regrets."[1] Morgan also hosted two special meetings the next evening: one for new members and another for the board of directors. New applications from Phoebe Brand, Morris Carnovsky, Greta Garbo, and George Burns and Gracie Allen were accepted.

At a May 9 special board of directors meeting at the home of Fredric March, Robert Montgomery read a letter to the Guild's negotiating committee signed by producers Samuel J. Briskin, Eddie Mannix, Hal Wallis and Joseph M. Schenck, who had been authorized by representatives of Columbia, MGM, Paramount, First National and Warner Bros., Universal, Hal Roach and 20th Century–Fox, to approve a list of points in their proposed contract. Nine new members also were accepted, including Jean Harlow (who tragically would die less than one month later, on June 7, 1937).

At 8 p.m. on May 9, the large group assembled at Hollywood Legion Stadium for the annual membership meeting cheered loudly when Kenneth Thomson read the following handwritten letter of Guild recognition by Louis B. Mayer, Vice-President in Charge of Production for MGM, and Joseph M. Schenck, Chairman of the Board at 20th Century–Fox:

> After a number of conferences with the committee appointed by you and with Mr. Bioff, personal representative of the President of I.A.T.S.E. [International Alliance of Theatrical Stage Employees], we wish to express ourselves in favor of Guild Shop. We have also conferred with Mr. Briskin of R.K.O., Mr. Zukor of Paramount and Mr. Harry Cohn of Columbia to assure you that they are in entire agreement. We have not, as yet, had the opportunity of contacting the heads of the other companies involved.
>
> We will without delay or procrastination confer with the representatives of the other studios and bring them to our point of view, to accept Guild Shop for their studios as well.
>
> We expect to have contracts drawn between the Screen Actors Guild and the studios before the expiration of this week.[2]

The contract for actors working in feature films included a closed shop, minimum wage rates, a 10-percent pay increase for extras and a 12-hour rest period between calls. On May 15, the new agreement, signed by 13 producers, went into effect. Two weeks later, Chester began his third one-year term as the Guild's third vice-president, alongside president Robert Montgomery and fellow vice-presidents James Cagney and Joan Crawford.

More Morris social hospitality took place at their home on June 6, 1937, when Chester prepared his signature steaks on the wood-fired patio grill. Assisted by Brooks, he also performed his magic act for Robert Montgomery, Joan Crawford and Franchot Tone, Whitney DeRahm, Mr. and Mrs. Douglas Fairbanks, Jr., Dr. Bert Frohman, Fredric March and Florence Eldridge, and Elliott Nugent.

On loan-out to RKO Radio, Chester played Paul Smith, a pilot whose license was revoked after he unknowingly transported an embezzler to Mexico, in *Flight from Glory* (1937). Adapted from a Robert Hardy Andrews story by David Silverstein and John Twist, the screenplay focuses on a group of disgraced flyers operating the Trans-Andian Air Service out of a remote mountain valley into Delgado, Brazil. Directed from late June to early July 1937 by low-budget specialist Lew Landers, the film features an excellent supporting cast, including Whitney Bourne, Onslow Stevens, Van Heflin (giving a strong performance in his third film), Richard Lane (who later would play Inspector Farraday opposite Chester in Columbia's "Boston Blackie" series), Paul Guilfoyle, Solly Ward, Douglas Walton, Walter Miller and Rita La Roy.

Stevens plays hardnosed, coldhearted Ellis, the "blacksheep" outfit's boss, who will sacrifice any of his men to save a dollar. When Ellis hires George Wilson (Heflin) to replace a pilot killed in a crash, the new man, without notifying the airfield, brings along his wife

Flight from Glory (1937): From left, Chester Morris, Whitney Bourne and Van Heflin in the poster art for RKO Radio's aviation drama about a group of disgraced flyers with the Trans-Andean Air Service near Delgado, Brazil [original one-sheet poster].

(Bourne). The cynical Smith attempts to help her leave several times, but she refuses to go. Drinking heavily while on duty, Wilson eventually ignores a fellow flyer, Hanson (Lane), as he crashes; and, when too drunk to fly himself, indirectly causes the death of Hilton (Walton), who had taken his place.

After taking Ellis, who never pilots one of the "flying coffins" himself, high over the mountains, Wilson bails out without a parachute. As he lies dead below, Ellis, unable to save himself, joins Wilson in oblivion. In love with Mrs. Wilson, Smith leaves with her on a flight back to the States.

Chester gives a naturalistic, convincing performance as the railroaded, level-headed, decent pilot with a cynical exterior, and is matched by the intense Heflin and sympathetic Ward, as chief mechanic and former Russian officer "Mousey" Mousailovitch, who takes over the operation, promising new, safe aircraft for his flyers.

Flight from Glory was praised as a pioneering airline drama upon its release and became the second of nine films featuring aviation plots to star Chester. During his career, Landers also directed the same number of aerially inclined pictures. Following the August 9, 1937, premiere, *Motion Picture Daily* was impressed by the economy of the filmmakers:

> In "Flight from Glory," turned out in record time by producer Robert Sisk and director Lew Landers, RKO has commendable sustaining attraction. Presented in two sets, an interior and an exterior, the picture is grim personal drama and differently conceived romance contrasted by sequences of sensational aerial acrobatics. Though occasionally wordy, the film primarily is exciting melodrama that won the respect of the preview audience.
>
> Played by a capable cast ... giving performances not ordinarily expected in low-budgeted and quickly produced pictures, the show is a noticeable departure from formula aviation films....
>
> In the main the story is told with deft, sure and impressive strokes. That it will go over with the masses is hardly to be questioned.[3]

Variety's "Flin" was even more enthusiastic:

> Possessing distinctive entertainment features, such as an unusual scene for its action ... and a group of characters seldom encountered in motion pictures or fiction, "Flight from Glory" rates way above the average of program releases.... Whitney Bourne, young actress from Broadway ... is a new personality worth watching.
>
> Chester Morris heads the cast and the company of aviators in the spot of chief pilot. He gives a strong performance and sets the general tone of fatalism which pervades the group....
>
> Direction by Lew Landers is terse and straightforward. His scenes have movement and snap. Trick air shots and crashes are deftly illusionary. Bob Sisk's handling of the production, which reflects a modest budget, is showmanlike.[4]

On August 15, 1937, Walter Abel (filling in for Chester), Whitney Bourne and Onslow Stevens performed scenes from the film on *The Magic Key of RCA* radio program, broadcast live from Hollywood over the NBC Blue Network. Hosted by Milton Cross and Ben Grauer, the variety program, which NBC touted as one of radio's cultural contributions to the nation, featured a house orchestra directed by Frank Black (who, in 1938, passed the baton to Nathaniel Shilkret). Vocalists Doris Weston and Frank Forrest also performed on the installment featuring *Flight from Glory*. Usually originating from New York City, the broadcast was described by *Variety* as featuring "picture personalities, nearly all newcomers to radio listeners," and the movie segment "distinctly not up to the caliber of remainder of program."[5]

The August 1937 issue of *Motion Picture* magazine singled out Chester in its "spotlight": "There are actors who pick out spotlights—and spotlights that pick out ACTORS. Chester

Morris is one who is spotlighted because of one fine performance after another. And the spot shines on him anew in *Depths Below*."[6]

Four months later, *Picture Play* reported news of a more political nature, specifically "Anti-Fascist Sentiment," referring to supporters of the Second Spanish Republic against the rightwing Nationalist faction in the Spanish Civil War (1936–1939):

> The Spanish loyalist cause received its due recently ... when two ambulances were sent across country to collect funds for medical aid of the sufferers belonging to this party. The ambulances were liberally autographed with the signatures of such players as Franchot Tone, Robert Montgomery, Chester Morris, Nancy Carroll and Florence Eldridge (Mrs. Fredric March), proving perhaps that there is an active anti-imperialist party in movieland.[7]

In January 1938, Chester received the distinct honor of having his portrait featured on the cover of *Genii* magazine, the official organ of the Pacific Coast Association of Magicians, which would become the world's largest selling publication devoted to magic. The closeup, chiaroscuro image, with Chester making the most of his piercing eyes, irresistibly prompted readers to shell out their 25 cents. (Chester also autographed 8 × 10 prints of the image, shot in 1934, for select recipients. He usually sent out signed, doubleweight 5 × 7 publicity photographs to his fans.) Hailed as "Filmland's Most Accomplished Magician," he was the first Southern Californian to be awarded the Page Wright Memorial Trophy by the Pacific Coast Association.

On February 1, 1938, Chester made a guest appearance in "The History of Dallas Egan," an episode of the CBS Pacific network radio show *Calling All Cars*, hosted by James E. Davis, Chief of the Los Angeles Police Department. Nine-year-old Brooks, dismayed with the type of radio work his father had been accepting, had asked him to pursue a spot on the crime show. When the producers were unable to pay the $2,000 fee that Chester earned per radio appearance, he instead accepted a recording of the show for Brooks' collection.

On February 6, plans were announced for a "Tri-Guild Dinner Dance" to be held for members of the Screen Actors, Screen Writers and Screen Directors Guilds on April 21. The original arrangements committee included Chester and James Cagney (SAG) and Charles Brackett and John Grey (SWG). They later were joined by Frank Capra and Lewis Milestone (SDG), who also skillfully blended "social activity [with] labor organizational work."[8]

Remaining at RKO, Chester again worked with Lew Landers on the tentatively titled "Crime," an interesting variation on the gangster genre, in which he plays Gene Fillmore, a respected gentleman who doubles as a mob boss who dislikes guns and violence. Production began under the working title "See No Evil" in late February 1938, with Bert Granet and Edmund L. Hartmann providing a screenplay updated from the Samuel Shipman-John B. Hymer Broadway play *Crime* in which Chester had appeared in 1927. The studio again changed the title, to *Law of the Underworld*, before the film's release on May 8, 1938.

Walter Abel portrays Warren Rogers, who asks Fillmore to join a crime commission but then must press him for the truth about a jewel heist and resulting murder that have been pinned on an innocent young couple, Annabelle Porter (Anne Shirley) and Tommy Brown (Richard Bond), who were booked on circumstantial evidence. Double-crossed by the unscrupulous members of his gang, particularly Rocky (nasty criminal specialist Eduardo Ciannelli), his "girl," Dorothy Palmer (Lee Patrick) and Johnny (Jack Carson, in an early role), Fillmore stops their illegal activities and eventually confesses to his masterminding the original robbery, sacrificing himself to save the engaged couple from the elec-

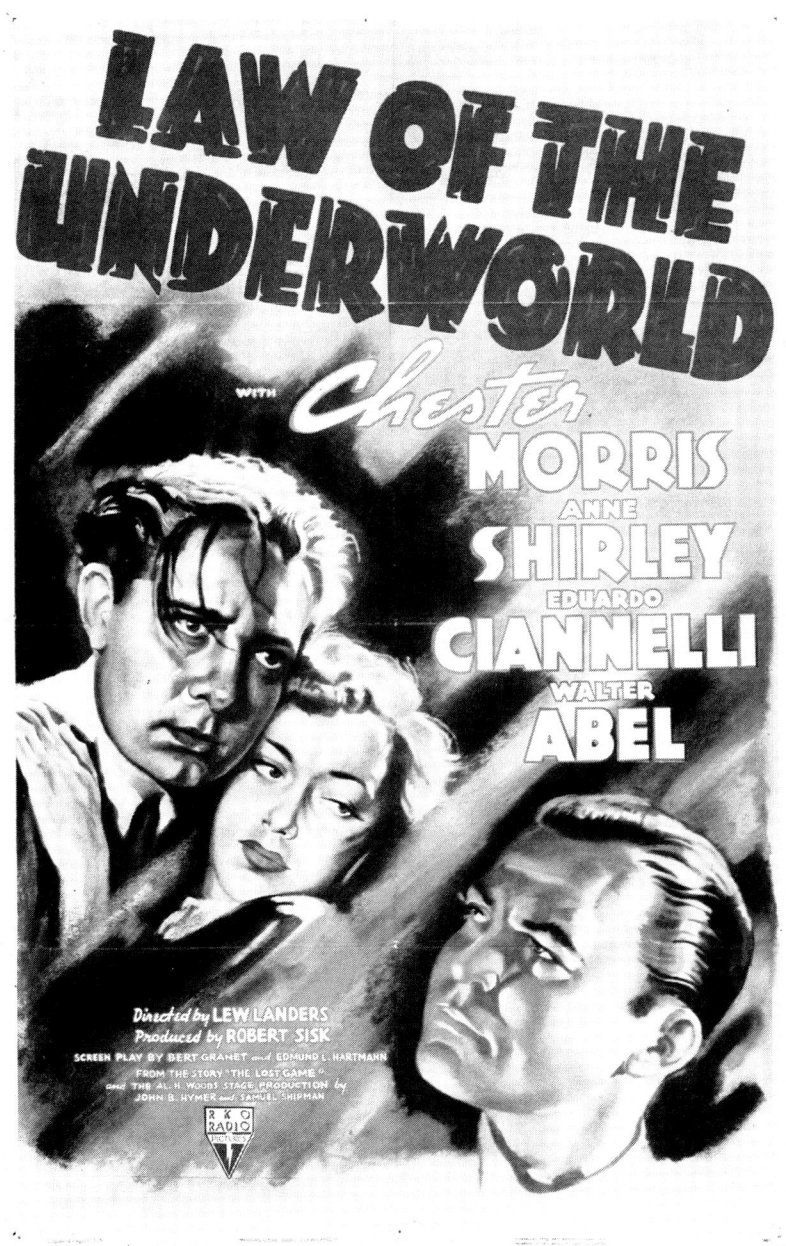

Law of the Underworld (1938): Richard Bond, Anne Shirley and Chester Morris in the poster art for RKO Radio's well-acted crime melodrama directed by Lew Landers [original one-sheet poster].

tric chair. His stated intention to head "a well-regulated business organization," not "a gang of thugs," hadn't been shared by his self-interested underlings. Chester again gives a largely quiet, understated performance.

The film faced one hurdle from the Production Code Administration. In a scene set in Fillmore's apartment, the censors insisted that Lee Patrick not remove her hat, an action that assured a proper "moral attitude" for Dorothy Palmer.[9] Although described as "an afterthought of the gangster picture cycle" by *Motion Picture Daily*, the publication considered the film a worthy addition:

> It will provide plenty of entertainment for those who like their melodrama in the raw.... The cast is topped by Chester Morris, Anne Shirley, Eduardo Ciannelli, Walter Abel, Richard Bond, Lee Patrick, Paul Guilfoyle and Eddie Acuff, all of whom deliver well-seasoned performances.... A polished directorial job has been done by Lew Landers....[10]

Following the *Law of the Underworld* shoot, Chester left Los Angeles to headline an April 1938 stage program at the State-Lake Theater in Chicago. Located on North State Street across from the Chicago Theatre, the facility opened as an Orpheum Circuit vaudeville house in 1919 and later became the major Windy City venue for the RKO theater chain.

Performing his act in two sections, he began the first by informing the audience that, in the future, film stars would be booked, not by theaters, but directly into private homes for personal appearances. This way, actors could visit people directly, rather than requiring them to go out to a theater. Using an imaginary booking into the Follansbee home in Peoria, Illinois, he performed a monologue involving a discussion with the woman of the house, playing with the baby, tangling with the dog, and listening to family members rave about their Hollywood favorites. When he heard the name "Robert Taylor," he explained that he had been sent to fill in for the heartthrob. This clever opening was followed by a selection of magic tricks. *Variety* reported,

> Surefire personal appearance for entertainment in practically any theatre anywhere. Picture name who gets friendly with an audience and then comes through with good value....
> Second half of the act Morris devotes to magic which consists of taking various items, mostly squares of silk, out of a Chinese box. It's okay stuff and handled in professional manner.
> In Morris the theatres can find a Coast name who comes to vaude prepared to do a variety act and to entertain the audience.[11]

Making several more personal appearances along the way, he arrived in New York on April 28. After a restful weekend, he returned to Los Angeles on May 1.

On April 21, while Chester was in Chicago, Francis ["Frankie"] Baker, often identified as the titular woman of the song "Frankie and Johnny," filed a suit in St. Louis, Missouri, district court, seeking $200,000 in damages from Republic Pictures Corporation, Republic Midwest Film Distributors, Inc., Select Pictures, Chester Erskine, Jack Kirkland, Helen Morgan, Chester Morris and Lilyan Tashman (although she had been deceased for more than four years), alleging that the film *Frankie and Johnnie* "defamed her character and invaded her privacy."[12]

On October 15, 1899, Baker, then 22 years old, had shot down her 17-year-old lover, ragtime pianist Allen ["Albert"] Britt, after he had returned home from a cake-walk dancing contest, where he had participated with Alice Pryor. Reportedly, Britt also had been pimping for Baker, who worked as a prostitute. Four days later, Britt, who had named Frankie as the shooter, died at St. Louis City Hospital.

At the trial the following month, Baker, claiming Britt had beaten her before pulling a knife, pleaded self-defense. Judge Willis Henry Clark, considering the account feasible, declared her not guilty. In 1901, attempting to escape equally from fame and infamy, she relocated, first to Omaha, Nebraska, and then Portland, Oregon.

According to eyewitnesses, balladeer Bill Dooley was performing the song "Frankie Killed Allen" in St. Louis just weeks after the killing. In 1904, composer Hughie Cannon

("Won't You Come Home, Bill Bailey") published the song "He Done Me Wrong" (subtitled "Death of Bill Bailey"), featuring the same melody with different lyrics. Eight years later, songwriters Frank and Bert Leighton published the same song as "Frankie and Johnny," altering Allen to "Johnny" and Alice Pryor to "Nellie Bly," the name of a New York journalist, because it was "eas[ier] to rhyme."[13]

The *Frankie and Johnnie* suit was not the first time Baker initiated legal action against a motion picture company. In 1933, she unsuccessfully sued Paramount Pictures for Mae West's performance of the song in *She Done Him Wrong*. The 1938 suit, prepared by the law firm of McLemore, Witherspoon and Lucas, contended "the circumstances were fairly portrayed in the film story," but that "Miss Baker shot in self defense and was acquitted by a coroner's jury."[14] This second statement reflects nothing in the film, which culminates with Johnnie being shot, not by Frankie, but by Timothy (Walter Kingsford).

Baker finally appeared in St. Louis to provide testimony during the autumn of 1939. The defense team retained by Republic Pictures, et al., paid $2,000 for testimony from music historian Sigmund Spaeth, who had written about the song's linkage to the 1899 killing, but afterward had traced the origin of the song back to the 1860s. The jury, unconvinced that the song and film were about Baker, found in favor of the defendants. Almost 40 years to the day of the original murder trial, Baker returned to Portland, where she died in a mental institution in 1952. Chester, involved in a personal legal situation of his own, was freed from this frivolous litigation.

In June 1938, Lew Landers teamed Chester with old colleague Richard Dix for "Ground Crew" (aka "Northern Flight"), an RKO Radio aviation drama inspired in part by Howard Hughes' upcoming trans-world flight that would begin in New York City on July 14 and continue through Paris, Moscow, Omsk, Yakutsk, Fairbanks and Minneapolis before landing back in the Big Apple in less than four days. Previously avoiding flying at all costs, due to his barely missing a flight that crashed, killing all aboard, Chester made the professional decision to gain actual experience in the air for his new role as Ken Stockton, the "wild" son of Colonel Cornelius Stockton (Harry Carey), currently stationed at the Trans-World Air Line School of Aeronautics at Grand Central Airport in Glendale, California, where many of the film's scenes were shot on location.

On the set, Chester told a reporter, "It was either fly or not play in this picture. While I have a phobia against flying, I've even a greater phobia against unemployment!"[15]

The shooting of one scene proved indicative of what Hollywood often was like for actors working under tight shooting schedules. After Landers and cinematographer Nicholas Musuraca filmed a scene in which W.R. ["Stag"] Cahill (Dix) and Meg Lawrence (Joan Fontaine) are married, Dix asked Chester to introduce him to the actress whose character he had just pretended to marry. Chester did his best but then revealed to Dix that he, too, required an actual introduction to the young lady! RKO released the film as *Sky Giant* on July 22, 1938.

Dedicated to "the unceasing work of the great air lines to pioneer new routes and to insure passenger safety," the film opens with Colonel Stockton transferred to special duty at the Trans-World Air Line School, where he arranges for "Stag" Cahill to serve as his reluctant assistant. When Ken enrolls at the school, the Colonel assumes the grueling training schedule will disqualify him, but he soon develops, not only a professional rivalry with Stag, but also a competitiveness for the attention of Meg Lawrence.

Prizing professional dedication above all else, even sleep, the Colonel pushes Ken, following a late night out with Meg, to join Stag on a high-altitude test flight, during which

Sky Giant (1938): From left, Chester Morris, Joan Fontaine and Richard Dix in RKO Radio's aviation drama inspired in part by Howard Hughes' historic trans-world flight in July of that year [original title lobby card].

he passes out. Stag completes the flight, but is reprimanded for protecting Ken, whom his father deems a "coward." Stag defends Ken and informs the Colonel that his unyielding attitude is endangering all the men, resulting in both pilots being sacked for insubordination. After two other aviators die during a test flight, Stag and Ken are rehired. Meg, realizing that Ken will only be married to aviation, accepts a proposal from Stag.

During an arctic mapping flight, Ken becomes jealous after Stag tells him about the marriage, and their colleague, "Fergie" Ferguson (Paul Guilfoyle), is injured when their plane crashes in the ice-covered mountains. Stag and Ken carry him through a blizzard; but, after a few days, bereft of feeling in his legs, he crawls off into the freezing snow to spare them further trouble. Temporarily abandoning an exhausted Stag, Ken returns, and they soon reach a village. Back in Glendale, they are honored by the head of the Bureau of Air Commerce, and Meg agrees with Stag's request to have the marriage annulled, understanding that she can wed Ken, who will "keep flying."

Chester and Richad Dix, placed in a love triangle like that depicted in *Devil's Playground*, fashioned quite different characters for this film. There is a rivalry, both professional and personal, between them, but it does not reach the level of animosity depicted in the earlier picture. Ken briefly abandons Stag to the arctic cold; but, realizing that his actions are driven by stress and lack of sleep, returns to save his life. At no time do Ken and Stag become overly emotional, always maintaining the cool nerves necessary for pilots. The "underplayed" performances of the primary actors (very much in the trademark style of Dix) bring believability to Lionel Houser's screenplay.

Ken Stockton was Chester's first character to have musical aspirations, as he briefly practices the violin after arriving at the aviation school. Ken's playing the instrument also provides a look at Chester's ambidexterity. As in many other films, he demonstrates equal physical ability with both hands, here bowing the violin with his right hand in one scene, and later throwing darts with his left during a contest with Stag. (Primarily "left-handed," his development of ability in both hands aided him greatly as a magician.)

Chester and Lew Landers continued their string of modestly budgeted RKO dramas with "The Cleanup," which began production as *Smashing the Rackets* shortly after the wrap of *Sky Giant*. This time the screenplay, adapted from a Forrest Davis story by Lionel Houser, places its star squarely on the side of stand-up law enforcement. Chester's Jim ["Socker," aka "Sock"] Conway, an FBI agent who regrets accepting a puppet political position as a New York A.D.A. until he boldly takes over a case involving a syndicate-run slot machine gang, was based on New York County D.A. Thomas Dewey (1902–1971), who had accepted that position on January 1, 1938. As New York City prosecutor and district attorney, Dewey was unrelenting in his determination to fight organized crime, particularly in bringing down Charles ["Lucky"] Luciano and Irving Wexler [aka "Waxey Gordon"], and his pursuit of Arthur Flegenheimer [aka "Dutch Schultz"], prior to the mob's own assassination of the gang boss in 1935.

Landers wrapped production during the first week of July 1938, when *Motion Picture Herald* reported,

> "Smashing the Rackets" will feature Chester Morris who, from "The Big House," has progressed through a series of gangster-racketeer films such as "Law of the Underworld," "Counterfeit" and "I Promise to Pay" as well as other melodramatic films to his present position as one of the screen's foremost interpreters of thrill action stories....[16]

When Chin Martin (stone-cold Edward Pawley), Whitey Clark (Ben Welden), Joe (Eddie Acuff) and Maxie (Paul Fix), brutal thugs enforcing the slot-machine racket, pistol whip a small boy (Scotty Beckett, Chester's child costar in *Pursuit*) to death, Conway becomes committed to destroying their operation. Determined to practice law, his mantra is "I always like to bring 'em back alive," and he even fakes a third-degree grilling of Joe to induce Maxie's confession about the murder of the innocent child.

Another case that the new Special Prosecutor clears is the mob infiltration of the Harlem numbers racket, one of many operations organized by crooked mouthpiece Steve Lawrence (Bruce Cabot), whose foot soldiers are a large group of women (including Libby Taylor, representing the many African American females involved in the real-life setup at that time, and Rita La Roy).

When the women, who have been brought in to serve as potential witnesses, express their equal fear of mob reprisals *and* police brutality, Conway assures them, "You're all going to be treated decently. I'll fire the first man who thinks his badge gives him the right to shove you around."

Ultimately, Lawrence double-crosses Martin, but is saved by his girlfriend, Letty Lane (Rita Johnson), who shoots the thug down. Stopping at nothing to save his own skin, Lawrence tries to pin the entire rap on Letty, but winds up with a 20-year prison sentence,

Smashing the Rackets (1938): Frances Mercer and Chester Morris in RKO Radio's crime drama based on the gang-busting activities of New York County District Attorney Thomas Dewey [original half-sheet poster].

and Conway opens his own law practice, right after marrying Letty's sister, Susan (Frances Mercer). The film ends with the couple embracing on the floor of Conway's new office.

Chester is convincing as the Dewey-inspired "Socker," combining just enough of his hard-edged toughness with the congeniality and charisma which had made him a favorite of filmgoers for nearly a decade. Bruce Cabot contributes another of the corrupt backstabbers that populated much of his career, and Edward Pawley, as he had so often demonstrated at Warner Bros., again proves that he arguably was the single most steely-eyed bastard with no redeeming features in the history of classic crime films.

RKO released *Smashing the Rackets* on August 19, 1938. The reviewer for *The New York Times* focused on the similarities between "Socker" and Dewey, and how Chester was ideally suited to the cinematic version:

> Although the gentleman himself is said to have forbidden the exploitation of his name and fame in films, there can be no doubt that "Smashing the Rackets" ... is inspired by the lively and dramatic career of District Attorney Th-m-s E. D-w-y.... The only striking conflict between fact and cinematic fiction involves a question of poetic license. Whereas Mr. D-w-y undoubtedly ran into many snags and dead ends in his sensational investigations, RKO's Chester Morris breezes though an entire maze of metropolitan rackets with the directness and miraculous deductive powers for which

Cynthia and Brooks, "costarring" in one of Chester's 16mm home movies, shot by the swimming pool of the Morrises' Beverly Hills home (1938).

only Mr. Morris is famous. In the space of a cinematic hour he assumes an investigation of a big city's crime, traces its involutions right down to one "big shot," sends the felon to the jug and picks up a wife in the bargain. But, of course, Mr. Morris is always the man who can do it. Capably performed by a large cast ... "Smashing the Rackets" rates as a better-than-average gangbuster melodrama. The most extraordinary thing about it is that Mr. Morris is going straight for a welcome change.[17]

On the leisure side, Chester indulged his interest in pugilism, attending bouts at the Hollywood Legion Stadium. One evening, he and Sue joined a host of film notables, including Joe E. Brown, Ann Dvorak and Leslie Fenton, Clark Gable, Pat O'Brien, Charles Ruggles, Bert Wheeler and George Raft, with whom he was photographed, enthusiastically hand in hand.

Chester and Sue, described in the press as "one of the film colony's most popular couples," began to experience marital problems during 1938, something they were unable to keep secret from the numerous movie fan magazines.[18] For a time, they were able to settle their differences, going so far as to take a second honeymoon, for a month in Honolulu.

Chester's standard method of dealing with domestic or professional tension was heading back East for a time, usually to make a series of personal appearances. Under the management of the Simon Agency's Charles Yates, he opened his magic show in Flint, Michigan, on August 26, 1938, followed by dates in Kansas City, Chicago, Washington, D.C., Philadelphia, Baltimore, Pittsburgh and Cleveland, where he played the RKO Palace with Bert Wheeler. In early October, he joined Johnny Messner and his band on stage at Manhattan's Strand Theatre, where Warner Bros.' *Secrets of an Actress* (1938), costarring Kay Francis and George Brent, was in its opening week.

On October 12, he performed an original sketch by Jerry Devine on New York's WABC-CBS radio, in which he played a champion boxer who shirks training for socializing, only to return to his senses after being brushed off by a high-society sweetheart. *Variety* reported, "Morris' ... stage turn consists of a skit and a bit of magic, but television hasn't arrived yet and radio can't project rabbit producing bits into the parlor.... Skit was light but well handled by Morris.... Well done."[19] The following day, he was the guest on CBS radio's *Kate Smith Hour*.

Back in Hollywood on October 17, Chester reported to RKO for yet another picture with Lew Landers, *Pacific Liner*, co-starring Victor McLaglen and Wendy Barrie. He worked with the same production team (Landers, producer Robert Sisk and cinematographer Nicholas Musuraca) from *Sky Giant*, this time substituting the more flamboyant McLaglen for the reserved Richard Dix in the top-billed role.

The film opens on July 2, 1932, in the port of Shanghai, China, where Captain Mathews (Halliwell Hobbess) of the SS *Arcturus* is prepared to take his passengers on a cruise to San Francisco. Again, Chester is involved in a love triangle: As Doctor Tony Craig, a specialist in tropical medicine, he signs on to the ship, ostensibly to be near his former girlfriend, Ann Grayson (Barrie), with whom engineer "Crusher" McKay (McLaglen) also is smitten.

At sea, a Chinese stowaway (Miki Morita) dies after contracting Asiatic cholera. Attempting to prevent the spread of the highly contagious disease, Crusher bolts the doors leading to the upper decks and Doc Craig experiments with ways to treat those who become infected. Crusher does his best to keep the crew working, but more deaths result in his own effort to stoke the coal boilers. He eventually is leveled by a combination of exhaustion and cholera, but rallies after the remaining crewmen, led by the paranoid "Deadeyes" (Cy Kendall), mutiny against Doc and Ann. With five crewmen dead, their corpses cremated in one of the boilers, *The Arcturus* reaches San Francisco without the passengers ever knowing about the cholera outbreak.

John Twist's screenplay, based on a story by Anthony Coldeway and Henry Robert Symonds, admirably focuses entirely on the engineer, doctor, nurse and crew, with occasional input from the captain, rather than offering any distractions from the passengers, who continue to enjoy the luxuries of the ocean liner. The valiant actions of the officers and sailors, all braving endless heat, filth and disease below, ultimately stave off any harm to those in the sun and sea air on the decks above.

Again portraying a character whose devotion to his profession outweighs personal concerns, Chester delivers a performance equal parts hardboiled and evenhanded. Released during a period when most Hollywood films reinforced the basest stereotypes of African Americans, RKO's *Pacific Liner* depicts its Black Stoker (Ernest Whitman, memorable as the servant and friend of Dr. Samuel Mudd [Warner Baxter] in John Ford's *The Prisoner of Shark Island* [1936]), in the eyes of Craig (though, in period parlance, called "the colored boy"), on the same level as the other sailors.

"It's funny," remarks the stoker as he lies in sick bay. "You're trying to help me just as much as the rest of them."

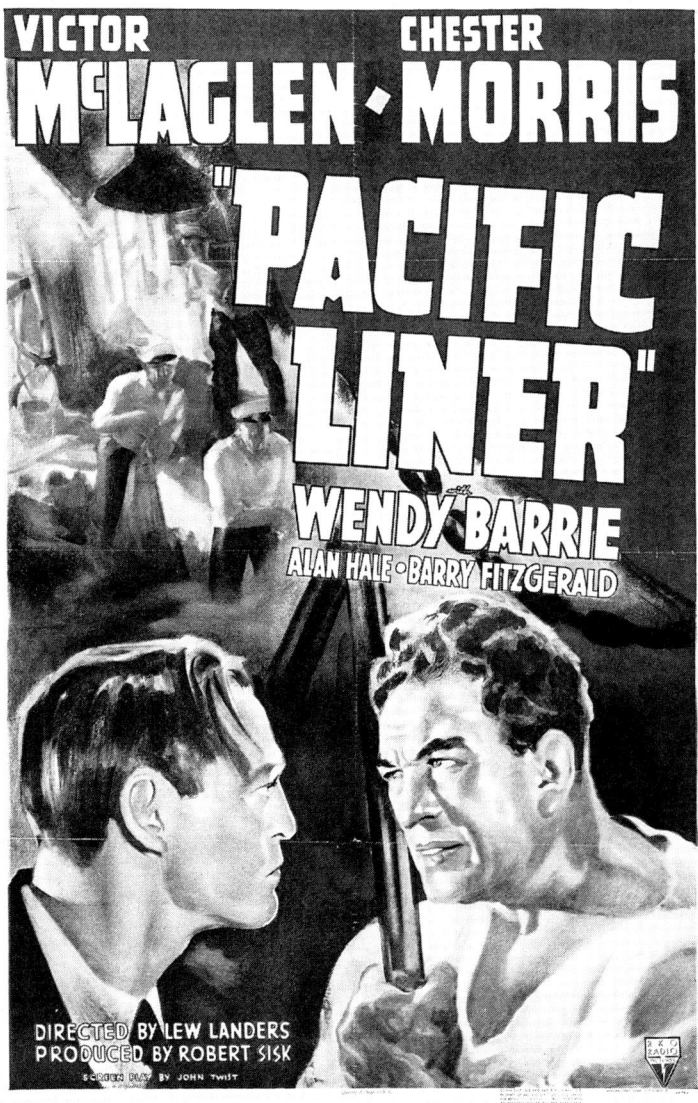

Pacific Liner (1939): Chester Morris (left) and Victor McLaglen in the poster art for RKO Radio's maritime melodrama depicting a doctor and engineer's attempts to prevent an epidemic of Asiatic cholera from spreading to the ship's passengers [original one-sheet poster].

"Well, there's nothing very funny about it," replies Craig. "You boys better start showing improvement pretty soon, or you're going to make an awful sucker out of me." The other crewmen (all called "boys" by Craig) are played by an excellent group of supporting actors, including Alan Hale, Barry Fitzgerald, Allan ["Rocky"] Lane and Paul Guilfoyle (as selfish here as he is self-sacrificing in *Sky Giant*).

Attempting a trial separation in December 1938, Chester embarked on another personal appearance tour while Sue traveled to Chicago. On the road, he continued to pursue his home-movie hobby. While performing on the East Coast, he surprised a New York audience by filming them with his 16mm camera after the theater manager turned down the house lights. Unable to return to his hotel during a taxi drivers' strike in Philadelphia, he resorted to sleeping in a dressing room, but, described in *Boxoffice* as "a vacation fugitive from Hollywood," broke the theater's summer attendance record over the course of a week.[20] He and Sue reunited for a two-week stay at the Waldorf Astoria before visiting relatives in Albany and returning to Beverly Hills for the holidays.

During this period of personal turmoil, he resigned from the board of the Screen Actors Guild, shortly after *Variety* reported that he might be under consideration for an even higher position in the union:

> Robert Montgomery, who has served as president for three years, has announced that he will not stand for reelection. James Cagney, vice-president, dislikes to preside at a meeting, and is certain to turn thumbs down on any suggestion that he move up. Joan Crawford is second v.p., but is said to share the feeling of the general membership that a man should be selected as president.
>
> Chester Morris, third v.p., has a large following in the Senior Guild and may be the nominee to receive the administration support. He would make a strong candidate if he decides to permit his name to be placed in nomination.[21]

Ralph Morgan, who had served as the Guild's first president, resumed the position when the general election of officers occurred on September 16, 1938. Chester left the board in May 1939, but remained active in other Guild activities.

Though Chester and Sue had attempted to reconcile in New York, their relationship continued to worsen after the return to California. On January 17, 1939, Chester moved from the Beverly Hills house into an apartment. The next day, the *Los Angeles Times* announced this official "split," stating that "neither would ascribe a cause, but it was indicated a divorce action is probable."[22]

While out on the town, Chester couldn't escape from photographers who snapped shots of him nightclubbing with actresses, including former star Mary Brian, who had turned to the stage during a period of film-industry disinterest, and Muriel Campbell, who played a supporting role in only one film, *She Married a Cop* (1939), released by Republic Pictures.

On January 28, 1939, *Film Bulletin* reported that Hal Roach Studios, during the pre-production phase of Lewis Milestone's *Of Mice and Men*, to be adapted by Rowland Brown from the John Steinback novel and play, was intended for Guinn ["Big Boy"] Williams (as Lennie) and Chester (as George). Both Chester and Brown were dropped, with Eugene Solow eventually writing the screenplay. Williams remained on the casting list, with both James Cagney and Humphrey Bogart considered for the George role; but, when negotiations with Warner Bros. were abandoned, Roach, at Milestone's request, cast Burgess Meredith, who previously had appeared in five feature films. Milestone also preferred Broderick Crawford as Lennie, but Lon Chaney, Jr., who had played the part in the Los Angeles stage production (with Wallace Ford as George), requested a screen test that won over the director.

Charles Vidor began directing the Columbia crime drama *Blind Alley* on February 15, 1939. The original Broadway play, by James Warwick, opened at the Booth Theatre on September 24, 1935, and ran for 119 performances, closing in January 1936. Produced by James R. Ullman and directed by C. Worthington Miner, it starred Roy Hargrave as escaped killer Hal Wilson, the role Chester plays in the film. The screenplay was adapted by Philip MacDonald (John Ford's *The Lost Patrol* [1934], Alfred Hitchcock's *Rebecca* [1940], Robert Wise's *The Body Snatcher* [1945]), Michael Blankfort and Albert Duffy.

The play and film broke new ground in the depiction of a hardened criminal whose motives have been shaped by childhood psychological trauma. As Wilson, his girlfriend, Mary (Ann Dvorak), and associates, Buck (Marc Lawrence) and Nick (Milburn Stone), hide out in the home of Dr. Shelby (Ralph Bellamy), a noted psychiatrist, the professor begins delving into his troubled past, including the abusive behavior of a father whom he had helped lead to a violent demise in a bar room shootout.

The film, to which the Production Code Administration objected on several counts, including its "sympathetic" depiction of a killer (Wilson shoots down four victims: two prison guards, the unarmed warden [John Hamilton] and a similarly weaponless friend of the Shelby family), eventually was approved by the censors. The cinematography of Lucien Ballard, featuring two expressionistic dream sequences, is a highlight. The content proved a direct influence on future films in the "home invasion" subgenre, including a remake, *The Dark Past* (1948), starring William Holden, with the screenplay adapted from the Mac-Donald, Blankfort and Duffy original, and *The Desperate Hours* (1955), costarring Humphrey Bogart and Fredric March, adapted from the play by Joseph Hayes.

In an underrated, atypical film performance, Chester (spurred by current personal conflicts to draw, Method-like, on internal psychology) is intense yet controlled as the disturbed Wilson. He describes his father as an "all-time heel," admitting that he "hated the sight of" his mother. "The old man came home and started using me as a punching bag," he tells the doctor.

Shelby's intellectual approach to stopping a killer is rebuffed repeatedly by Wilson's claim that other people are "screwballs" who use "screwball talk."

"Not screwball talk," Shelby points out, "just different." At one point, he informs Wilson that his neurotic actions stem from "a constant fear of madness." Shelby's Freudian reading of Wilson's recurrent nightmare includes his identification of bars as "cops' legs," an umbrella as "a table" and water as "blood." "You murdered your own father," he informs the guilt-ridden criminal.

"I wasn't knocked around no more," Wilson replies.

"Anyone who opposes you becomes your father," Shelby continues. "Every time you kill a man, you're killing your father over again."

Overcome by this realization, Wilson walks out the front door, pretends to ready his rifle, and is gunned down by the police. Forbidden by the Production Code to depict a character taking his own life, Wilson instead commits "suicide by cop."

Chester never displays his familiar smile in *Blind Alley*, incorporating a unique rhythm in both his phrasing of dialogue and his movements, including a distinctive gate as Wilson nervously paces about the Shelby living room (something Bogart, one of his closest friends, later used for Glenn Griffin in *The Desperate Hours*). He is well supported by Dvorak (though her role is somewhat underdeveloped), Lawrence and Stone (who plays one of the few unlikable villains of his career).

Columbia released the film on May 11, 1939. *Photoplay* considered Chester's performance a cut-above the overall production:

> Here's an out-and-out cop and robber drama with the black business of murder as its motivating theme, and the psychological exposé of a criminal's mind as its climactic aim. Frankly, the whole grim affair is far from our idea of screen entertainment, but we must give praise where praise is due and declare Chester Morris one of the best portrayers of cowardly killers on the screen. His work as an escaped convict, who takes refuge in the home of a professor of psychology, is far superior to the story material provided. Ralph Bellamy, as the calm professor who holds the criminal until the police arrive, furnishes splendid contrast to Morris' more emotional characterization.[23]

Blind Alley (1939): From left, Ann Dvorak, Chester Morris and Ralph Bellamy in Columbia's innovative psychological crime thriller based on the Broadway play by James Warwick [original lobby card].

Motion Picture Herald's William R. Weaver concurred: "'Blind Alley' is a most unusual type of melodrama. It presents Chester Morris at his deadliest best as an escaped convict and Ralph Bellamy in fine fettle as a psychiatrist who psychoanalyses the desperado while held prisoner by him. Both give excellent performances."[24]

In *Hollywood Spectator*, Bert Harlen pointed out the depth of the writing and acting:

> Chester Morris gives a vital portrayal of the killer. It is a finely thought out, excellently accented and shaded performance, one of the best I have seen this season....
>
> The psychoanalysis tenets have been set forth with admirable clarity by the script. In fact, the picture constitutes a good exposition of the basic principles of science.... The important thing is that the theories are wholly acceptable during the unfoldment of the drama, which is doubtless due in large part to the craftsmanship in the screenplay and to Bellamy's sincere playing.[25]

In 1962, Chester recalled, "*Blind Alley* was the forerunner of [the psychological gangster film]. That was *way ahead* of its time. I did [the film] with Ralph Bellamy ... my dearest friend in the theater."[26]

On February 25, 1940, *The Screen Guild Theatre* broadcast a radio version of the play, costarring Edward G. Robinson and Joseph Calleia. The success of the film also led to a Broadway revival of the play, which ran for 66 performances at the Windsor Theatre from

October 15 to December 7, 1940. Roy Hargrave returned as Wilson, as did Jay Adler as Buck.

Just as Chester's demanding role in *Blind Alley* may have provided him with a real-life catharsis, such intensity on the set also required some serious after-hours relaxation. One of his favorite activities was participating in a game popularly referred to as "Hollywood's Newest Party Rage." First introduced at the Beverly Hills home of Warner Bros. actress Anita Louise, "The Signal Game" could be played with any number of people, with one designated as "It" and another as "Signal Man." While the former left the room, the rest of the players huddled together, hatching a plot which then had to be discovered by It, assisted only by the Signal Man, who tapped out clues with a spoon. Chester participated in this hilarious madness with Louise, Buddy Adler, Lee Bowman, Gertrude Durkin, James Ellison, Glenda Farrell, Joy Hodges and Penny Singleton.[27]

He also enjoyed sitting ringside at a surprise magician's party thrown at the Cocoanut Grove, where Russ Swann was performing his professional prestidigitation. During a trick involving Swann's "transformation" of a china egg into a real one, Chester offered to help, instead pulling a fast one on the "magicker" by substituting a hardboiled egg which prevented its being broken into a glass. Quick on his feet, Swann peeled, salted and ate it before "pulling a fresh egg out of Morris' ear" to break over the practical joker's head.[28]

Chester and Glenda Farrell guest starred in Paul Franklin's "The Man from Medicine Bow," the April 9, 1939, broadcast of the CBS radio program *The Silver Theatre*. Narrated by True Boardman, the show included music by Felix Mills.

From March 30 to late April 1939, Chester costarred with Lucille Ball in the aviation disaster thriller *Five Came Back* at RKO, directed by John Farrow and featuring an impressive supporting cast: Wendy Barrie, John Carradine, Allen Jenkins, Joseph Calleia, C. Aubrey Smith, Kent Taylor, Patric Knowles and Elisabeth Risdon. Having worked to overcome his fear of flying, Chester played a pilot for the third time in as many years, this time Bill, the resilient skipper of the Panama City-bound Capelis XC-12 *The Silver Queen*, who must take charge of nine people with disparate attitudes in a life-and-death situation.

RKO purchased the original story by Richard Carroll in April 1938, intending the production as an A feature for Cary Grant. The screenplay was adapted by three writers, Jerome ["Jerry"] Cady, Dalton Trumbo and Nathanael West. Producer Robert Sisk and Farrow eventually made the film on a B budget of $225,000. Victor McLaglen and Charles Coburn were announced as costars at one point, but neither appear in the finished film. Ann Sothern was asked to play Peggy Nolan, but when she proved unavailable, the part went to Ball.

Farrow shot the film on the RKO backlot and a soundstage, on which he had art director Van Nest Polglase and his assistant, Albert S. D'Agostino, create a realistic jungle set including many imported trees. The director's perfectionism resulted in a tense set, made worse by problems experienced by Ball, who had to contend, not only with spiders that descended from one of the trees, but also with "unwanted attention" from Chester.[29] The situation is the exact opposite in the film (the aloof, all-business Bill initially is uninterested in Peggy); but, off-camera, Chester uncharacteristically was acting out on his current personal circumstances. The stress created for Ball by this, as well as several arguments with Farrow, helped her create a solid performance that would lead to many more roles at RKO (including another opposite Chester the following year).

Forced by a violent storm to land in an Amazon rainforest, Bill and his copilot, Joe Brooks (Taylor), attempt to keep the nine passengers from panicking while making necessary repairs to the plane. While in the air, their steward, Larry (Dick Hogan), during a rescue of Tommy Mulvaney (Casey Johnson), the young son of a gangster traveling with his father's associate, Pete (Jenkins), had fallen out an open door to his death.

Crimp (Carradine), a detective seeking $5,000 for returning Vasquez (Calleia), an anarchist who murdered a politician, to a South American capital, is the most selfish of the group. Hard on his venal heels is wealthy drunk Judson Ellis (Knowles), eloping with Alice Melhorne (Barrie) against his parents' wishes. Though Martha Spengler (Risdon) initially considers herself "above" stooping to manual labor, she eventually joins her husband, Professor Henry Spengler (Smith), in aiding the group. Peggy Nolan is a former "woman of the streets" seeking escape from conventional society. Following three weeks in the jungle, Crimp wanders off, and Tommy discovers his body, impaled with a large poison dart, presumably fired by one of the "head hunters" described by the professor. Pete also falls to one of the natives' darts.

After an oil leak foils a take-off, the plane is judged capable of carrying only four adults and young Tommy. Vasquez, who has proved the most helpful during their ordeal, brandishes a pistol, insisting that he decide which members of the group will be allowed on the flight. He is doomed in any event, whereas the Spenglers realize they have lived full lives, and Ellis cares only about himself.

When Vasquez announces that the pilots and young women will join Tommy aboard the plane, Ellis attacks him and is shot down. After Bill takes off, the natives begin to approach the campsite, and Vasquez, having only two bullets left in the gun, shoots the Spenglers, leaving only himself to be tortured and killed.

All the actors are well cast in their roles, with Chester playing Bill as a serious, rather detached pilot whose leadership skills help maintain order in the erratic group. Calleia gives another excellent performance, here ostensibly as a criminal able to demonstrate his true nature when faced with dire circumstances. Ball, Knowles and Jenkins (in a rare dramatic role) also proved memorable under Farrow's iron-fisted direction.

Farrow maintains a brisk pace and solid level of suspense, greatly facilitated by cinematographer Nicholas Musuraca, whose fluid camerawork adds excitement to the scenes set aboard the plane and in the jungle. The June 23, 1939, premiere earned the studio another recommendation from *Motion Picture Daily*:

> RKO during the last six months has brought forth several pictures which have surpassed expectations as to their appeal. "Five Came Back" perhaps will meet with the same response. It is a melodrama of occurrences which follow the crash of a plane.... It is simply and forcibly told, ably enacted and full of thrills and suspense....
>
> The screenplay by Jerry Cady, Dalton Trumbo and Nathanael West ... wastes little time in opening the story and continues to deliver fully throughout. John Farrow's direction of this Robert Sisk production is punctilious.[30]

In 1956, Farrow directed a $1.5-million widescreen remake, *Back to Eternity*, for RKO. Adapted from the Richard Carroll story by Jonathan Latimer, it stars Robert Ryan in the role played by Chester, supported by Anita Ekberg, Rod Steiger, Phyllis York, Keith Andes, Gene Barry, Fred Clark, Beulah Bondi and Cameron Prud'Homme.

Filling in for an ailing Franchot Tone, Chester reteamed with his *Big House* costar Wallace Beery for MGM's World War I submarine drama *Thunder Afloat*, directed on a $1-million budget by George B. Seitz from May 21 through July 1939. Location work was completed at the U.S. Naval Academy in Annapolis, Maryland, around the Coronado Islands off San Diego, and at San Pedro, California. Producer J. Walter Ruben had wanted Barbara Stanwyck to play the female lead, Susan, daughter of unruly tugboat skipper John Thorson

(Beery), but when she proved unavailable, the role went to Virginia Grey. Chester temporarily was laid low by illness, but reported back to MGM during the second week of July.

Wells Root and Commander Harvey S. Haislip, a retired U.S. Navy officer, based their screenplay on a Haislip and Ralph Wheelwright story inspired by the sinking of the barge *Perth Amboy* by a German U-boat during World War I. To add combat realism to certain scenes, Ruben persuaded the Navy to allow cinematographer John F. Seitz to shoot footage utilizing period subchasers being hit with exploding depth charges.

Thunder Afloat (1939): From left, Chester Morris, Virginia Grey and Wallace Beery in MGM's World War I submarine drama directed by George B. Seitz [original midget window card].

Released on September 15, 1939, two weeks after Hitler's Nazi army invaded Poland, *Thunder Afloat* became the first war film in which Chester appeared. Beery dominates with his familiar bluster as Thorson, but Chester proves a solid match as he transforms Richard ["Rocky"] Blake from an angry wharf brawler to a tough Navy officer ordered to hunt down German U-boats preying on U.S. cargo ships along the New England coast. Though he also enlists in the Navy, Thorson refuses to bow to military discipline, is court-martialed for insubordination and restricted to land duty. Just as he is about to desert, Blake conscripts him aboard a schooner used as a decoy against the German submarines. Spotting the commander who earlier sank his tugboat, Thorson attempts to ram the U-boat and is captured, but manages to signal Blake and is rescued. Decorated for heroism and reinstated as an ensign, he joins Blake on the fleet bound for France.

The Film Daily praised the film's "gripping, stirring story" and acting: "Wallace Beery gives a grand performance as the captain of a tugboat.... Chester Morris is splendid as Beery's shipping rival.... Virginia Grey has her best role to date and delivers solidly."[31]

On June 1, 1939, Chester was elected West Coast Regional Vice-President of the Society of American Magicians, the world's oldest fraternal magic organization, which had been founded in the back room of Martinka's magic shop in New York City on May 10, 1902. From 1917 to 1926, Chester's idol Harry Houdini, while serving as National President, greatly expanded the organization to include a unified network of professional and amateur magicians throughout the United States. (The August 1938 issue of *The Sphinx: An Independent Magazine for Magicians*, the "Official Organ" of S.A.M., featured Chester, performing his act, on the cover.)

In mid–June 1939, RKO Radio announced that Chester would costar with Richard Dix in *Men Against the Sky,* to be produced by Howard Benedict and directed by Leslie Goodwins. By the time the picture was shot in May and June 1940, Kent Taylor had been cast as aviation engineer Martin Ames, and the female lead, originally considered for Lucille Ball, had been awarded to Wendy Barrie.

On August 8, 1939, Chester continued his participation in Screen Actors Guild activities by joining president Ralph Morgan, council chairman Larry Steers, and fellow council members Edward

Magician Chester Morris, on the cover of *The Sphinx* magazine (August 1938).

Arnold, Lucile Gleason, Henry Hull, Jean Muir and Kenneth Thomson on a trip to New York. Three days later, the delegation met with the American Federation of Labor (AFL) executive council to discuss "the invasion of the actor ranks" by the International Alliance of Theatrical Stage Employees under the influence of racketeer William Morris ["Willie"] Bioff, referred to as the "personal representative" of IATSE president George Browne, who eventually extorted millions from the major film studios.

In September 1939, Dick Mook of *Silver Screen* magazine reported that Chester and Sue had "reconciled," but this rumor proved quite premature.[32] Indeed, Chester had met "socialite" Lillian Kenton Barker, daughter of New York publicity director Edwin C. Kenton, at a party, later admitting that their mutual attraction was "love at first sight."[33] She previously had been employed as a "Chesterfield Girl" in advertisements for the popular brand of cigarettes.

Chester continued to treat personal problems with the best medicine: work. Back on the road, performing his act during "vaudfilm matinees," he was headlining a show with the "Star Lane" revue from Chicago's Bon Air club, opening for a week's run on Friday, September 29, at the Orpheum Theatre in Minneapolis. This combination of singing, dancing, comedy and "Morris' magic" was reported by *Variety* as "agreeable entertainment in every respect."[34]

Comedian Eddie Garr, who introduced the performers with a "barrage of merriment-provoking" gags, stories and impressions, was followed by Chester, who again divided his time between the "private home personal appearance" sketch and magic act. *Variety*'s "Rees" added,

> Morris loses no time in getting friendly with the customers, being pleasant and personable. A monolog anent a screen player's new type of personal—in his fan's homes—is only mildly amusing, but Morris sells his magic skillfully, extracting all manner of articles from a seemingly empty Chinese tea cabinet. It's an unpretentious turn, but more than passes muster.[35]

Chester was followed by a lineup of musical and terpsichorean acts, including the solo tap routines of Alice Cavane, swing song stylings of lovely Toni Lane, song, dance and impressions of Jackie Green, and several flashy production numbers featuring a chorus line of 20 young ladies.

As part of a divorce agreement, Chester initially had planned to take custody of Brooks, while Sue would retain that of Cynthia, and pay $500 in monthly child support. However, on November 6, 1939, he entered an official denial of a "cruelty petition" filed on Sue's behalf by her attorney, Max Gifford.

To be granted a "fault divorce" due to "cruelty" on Chester's part, the following conditions had to be met:

> The filing spouse must prove that the cruelty had made marriage intolerable for them. The cruelty must have been deliberate and calculated and must not have been provoked by the filing spouse. Acts such as physical attacks, repeated displays involving screaming and violent behavior, as well as continuous false accusations, such as adultery and publicly berating and insulting a spouse or flaunting an affair with another person are some grounds of cruelty. The cruelty must have been recurrent. Single acts of cruelty in a marriage are usually not considered grounds for divorce.[36]

On November 10, Los Angeles Superior Court Judge Thomas C. Gould granted Sue a divorce, on grounds of Chester's "violent displays of temper." Newspapers reported that she "alleged her husband would … use abusive language toward her."[37] The court approved a final settlement arranged by Gifford requiring the couple to divide $200,000 in community property. Chester also agreed to establish a $100,000 trust fund for the children, whose custody was awarded to her. While Cynthia remained with Sue, Brooks often stayed with Chester in a rented house at 1211 Horn Road in Beverly Hills. Father and son were tended to by Jesse Casas, a 33-year-old Filipino cook who also lodged at the residence.

Photoplay reported, "No two people in all Hollywood tried to work out their marital troubles more earnestly than Chester Morris and his wife, Sue. After several reconciliations it ended, at last, in divorce."[38]

On the evening prior to the decree, Chester took a much-needed break by performing his magic act on NBC's *Kraft Music Hall* for Bing Crosby, who hosted the popular radio program from January 2, 1936, to May 9, 1946. As "Mysterious Morris the Mad Magician," he joined linguist Lou Holtz and longtime Crosby orchestra arranger and conductor John Scott Trotter. Daily newspapers reported, "Morris has found time between movies to achieve considerable fame as an amateur magician and is a continual cause of amazement to Bing, who knows a few tricks himself."[39]

In early November 1939, RKO had announced that Chester, Richard Dix and Lucille Ball would be cast with Hungarian actress Steffi Duna in *The Girl and the Gambler*, to be directed by Lew Landers. However, when Leo Carrillo, Tim Holt and Esther Muir replaced them, the studio reunited Chester with Dix in *The Marines Fly High*, which began shooting in late October.

In a tragic twist of fate, director George Nicholls, Jr., had informed Chester and Dix that he would not fly during the shooting of the aerial sequences. "I'm going to stay on the ground, where I'll be *safe!*" he insisted. However, on November 13, the 42-year-old Nicholls was killed instantly while driving to one of the film's locations, when his car left the road and plummeted 700 feet into Coldwater Canyon. His sister-in-law, Acta Barnett, who also was in the car, crawled more than a mile for help and was hospitalized with minor injuries.[40] RKO producer Robert Sisk then had the sad task of hiring Benjamin Stoloff to complete directing the film.

The Film Daily recommended the military reteaming of Dix and Morris, this time as leathernecks: "Story is cut from a familiar pattern, but the players are engaging, the settings are interesting and the plot is plausible. Richard Dix and Chester Morris ably portray a couple of Marines, and Lucille Ball attractively supplies the female interest."[41]

Steffi Duna also appears in the film, as Teresa, an old flame of Lieutenant Danny Darrick (Dix), complicating his current romantic intentions with Joan Grant (Ball), who needs U.S. Marine protection when her Central American cocoa plantation is raided by a revolutionary band led by John Henderson (John Eldredge), her foreman, masquerading as the bandit "El Vengador." Many elements are "cut from a familiar pattern": Danny and his pal, Lieutenant Jim Malone (Chester), are pilots competing for the attention of the same woman; the script poses no new challenges for the lead actors; and Chester's character, for the sixth time, is called "Jim" or "Jimmy."

Danny and Jimmy locate the revolutionaries' hideout and parachute to safety after their plane is shot down. While escorting Joan back to her plantation to collect the contents of a safe, they discover her neighbor murdered in his burning house. Danny and Joan are attacked at the plantation, after which El Vengador kidnaps her and sets a trap for the Marines. Danny is confined to bed, and Jimmy leads a column of Marines directly into the ambush, but his pal, disobeying orders, "borrows" a plane to fly to the rescue.

In *The New York Times*, Frank S. Nugent reviewed the premiere of the film in his familiar sarcastic style:

In a conveniently anonymous Central American republic, roughly divided into United States Marines, bandits and Lucille Ball, RKO's Bob Sisk is deploying a comfortably agile adventure known to the Rialto as "The Marines Fly High." What terror and surprises it may have for the uniniated this department knoweth not, due largely to the presence in the row right behind of a communicative gentleman who either had seen the show three times or was Jerry Cady, its author. Thus we learned, as least five machine-gun bursts in advance, that the guerrilla leader known as El Vengador really was Miss Ball's foreman, a harmless-looking chap as John Eldredge plays him; thus we were apprised in time that when Chester Morris drew a gun on Richard Dix he wasn't going to shoot Mr. Dix but the bushmaster slithering beside him. Happily "The Marines Fly High" isn't the sort of picture likely to be affected much by audience commentary—or by critic's commentary either. It doesn't stand still long enough for accurate firing, and no professional or amateur heckler has much chance against a soundtrack throbbing with airplane motors, the whine and spat of rifle fire, the stuttering thunder of machine guns. It hardly seems any time at all, the way the boys are telling it, before the marines have the situation well in hand....[42]

Chester and his costars deliver convincing performances free of surprises, and Stoloff's direction keeps all 68 minutes running at a brisk pace. Incidents such as Danny and Jimmy casually using handheld machine guns to fire from midair on ground targets seem far-fetched, but the participation of Lieutenant Commander A.J. Bolton in writing the screenplay lends the film an air of plausibility. A highlight of the supporting cast is character actor Horace McMahon (who later would appear with Chester on television) as Sergeant Monk O'Hara.

Following the divorce and completion of the *Marines Fly High* shoot, Chester again left Hollywood for an extended period, performing a solo act during a personal appearance tour of theaters across the nation. He was warmly received in Wisconsin, where one journalist wrote, "Stage stars are welcome in Milwaukee. Particularly pleasant chaps like Chester Morris. His act is amusing and soundly entertaining. It is a monolog, and it is original, dramatic, funny."[43]

Host Ken Murray welcomed Chester, Kenny Baker, Margo and vocalist Frances Langford to the February 7, 1940, broadcast of *The Texaco Star Theatre* on CBS radio. Major talent on the program included actor, playwright and screenwriter Willard Mack, who wrote the script, and composer and conductor David Broekman, who had contributed music to many early sound films, including *All Quiet on the Western Front*, *Frankenstein* and *The Old Dark House* at Universal.

The Associated Actors and Artistes of America (AAAA) held its Grand Ball at Manhattan's Waldorf Astoria on April 21, 1940, when an "estimated array of 1,000 prominent stars of screen, stage, radio, concert and variety fields" hosted lavish entertainment supporting the federation of trade unions for performing artists in the United States. Lawrence Tibbett was the current honorary chairman headquartered in the Actors Equity Building on West 47th Street.

Heavy hitters comprising the Hollywood contingent included Chester, Walter Abel, Edward Arnold, Humphrey Bogart, James Cagney, Joan Crawford, Melvyn Douglas, Lucile Gleason, Hugh Herbert, Jean Hersholt, Boris Karloff, Robert Montgomery, Frank and Ralph Morgan, Edward G. Robinson, and Kenneth Thomson, four of whom were original board members and an additional five (including Chester) early supporters of the Screen Actors Guild.

At Republic Studios, Chester's frequent colleague Lew Landers directed his next picture, *Wagons Westward*, in which he plays two opposed characters in a cast including his friend, Anita Louise, Buck Jones, Ona Munson and George ["Gabby"] Hayes. Presented with one of the biggest acting challenges of his film career, Chester was following in the footsteps of a long line of leading men throughout the history of Hollywood cinema. Those who previously had played physically identical characters (usually relatives) with opposing personalities included one of his favorites, Lewis Stone, in *The Prisoner of Zenda* (1922), William Bakewell in *The Iron Mask* (1929), Edward G. Robinson in *The Whole Town's Talking* (1935), Boris Karloff in *The Black Room* (1935), Ronald Colman in *The Prisoner of Zenda* (1937) and Louis Hayward in *The Man in the Iron Mask* (1939). While Chester was under contract at Universal, cowboy star Ken Maynard played twin brothers in the studio's B Western *Honor of the Range* (1934).

One of Republic's more ambitious Westerns, *Wagons Westward* was originally slated to star contract player John Wayne, but associate producer Armand Schaefer and Landers, who already had directed Chester in five films, realized that Wayne did not possess the range to play both characters convincingly. Like Karloff in *The Black Room*, Chester had to interpret twin brothers, one kind and fair-minded, the other a cold-hearted sadist, and then combine the traits of both as one impersonates the other. But, whereas Karloff's "evil" character kills the "good," and then attempts to pull off a masquerade for purely selfish reasons, Chester's lawman, David Cook, has his brother, Thomas, arrested and then, in his guise, ends the depredations of outlaw gangs led by Jake Hardman (Guinn ["Big Boy"] Williams) and Bill Marsden (Douglas Fowley).

Chester enjoyed the shoot, set in 1869 Mesa, Arizona, but filmed at three California locations: the Iverson Ranch at Chatworth, Alabama Hills at Lone Pine, and Burro Flats at Simi Hills. He even managed to work a card trick into a scene in which David-as-Tom enters the Bonanza Dance Hall.

While shooting a scene in which Tom accuses his girl of two-timing him with David, Anita Louise (as Phyllis Conover) responded, "Tom, I've been true to you. I've never, never loved another man!"

Breaking character, Chester snarled, "Yeah? How about *Buddy Adler*?" (The actress soon would marry Adler on May 17, 1940, one month before *Wagons Westward* was released.)

Landers and the crew were racked with laughter, and several minutes passed before shooting could be resumed. Ernest Miller's camera kept rolling, capturing all the mirth; and, after the outtake was printed, the film, with soundtrack, became one of Louise's wedding gifts to Adler.[44]

Rather than recycling the worn premise of two friends competing for the same woman, the Joseph Moncure March-Harrison Jacobs screenplay presents two Chester Morris characters involved with the same woman, Phyllis, and concluding with one of them, David, marrying her older sister, Julie (Ona Munson). Gabby Hayes, as Uncle "Hardtack," who does his best to raise Tom and then aids David, provides some classic sidekick humor. Particularly funny are scenes involving his attempts to use a set of new false teeth (first having them pried out of his mouth, and finally being "bitten" in the bum when they are in the pocket of his "Sunday Go-to-Meeting" pants at the wedding of David and Julie). Hardtack also serves a strong dramatic purpose in his loyalty to the Cook family, ultimately firing the second bullet that kills Tom, who has been shot once by the wounded David during their climactic gunfight. Having murdered Phyllis in cold blood, Tom is described by Hardtack as "hav[ing] rattlesnake blood in him."

Chester exhibits a wide array of well-controlled emotions, as his two characters (both of whom appear on screen together in a few scenes) perform activities ranging from treachery, cruelty and murder to devotion, compassion and heroism. While Tom, even as a boy, revels in shooting down wounded Native Americans, David refuses to, as stated by Tom's "Indian" servant, Pima (Charles Stevens), "hit [him] with whip." "That's how I know you not Mr. Tom," Pima explains. Just before David discovers Phyllis' body and confronts his brother in the saloon showdown, he, Pima and a band of Native Americans stop the outlaws' attack on the wagon train heading westward through Black Canyon. Like Karloff before him, Chester admirably displays separate characteristics for each brother, and skillfully shifts between them when David impersonates Tom, particularly during his scenes with Hayes.

As in *The Black Room*, a pet dog plays a role in recognizing the identity switch: whereas "Wolfram" knows that the Karloff he sees is *not* his beloved master, the dog in *Wagons Westward*, who never liked Tom, warms up to David-as-Tom, necessitating a quick explanation to keep his identity a secret.

After the June 19, 1940, premiere, *The Film Daily* reported,

> Grade "A" Western.... Audiences generally should be well pleased with this film. Using a considerable amount of imagination, a plausible story has been concocted with plenty of action and punch, and an extremely able cast has been gathered together to put the picture over. Director Lew Landers keeps the film moving rapidly....

Wagons Westward (1940): From left, Guinn ("Big Boy") Williams, Anita Louise, Chester Morris and Buck Jones in Republic's ambitious Western featuring Chester in a dual role as physically identical but morally opposed twins, David and Tom Cook [original lobby card].

Chester Morris does a nice job in a dual role. Ona Munson and Anita Louise ably fill two strong female roles, and Buck Jones heads a redoubtable gang of film bad men....[45]

Sadly, Gordon Morris, who had been ill for six months, died in Los Angeles at age 41 on April 7, 1940. Survived by his widow, he was interred next to William in the family plot of the Garden of Eternal Love section at Hollywood Memorial Cemetery (later Hollywood Forever Cemetery). Following his brief Broadway acting and writing career in 1917–1925, his contributions to cinema consisted of his play *Jack in the Pulpit* and four original stories adapted into feature films. His final screen credit came in *Under the Pampas Moon*, starring Warner Baxter, released by Fox on June 1, 1935.

On May 17, 1940, Anita Louise and Buddy Adler's wedding day, Chester, Charles Bickford and Jane Wyatt began working on *Girl from God's Country*, which director Sidney Salkow wrapped on June 8. This "far north" adventure focuses on the challenges faced by Jim Holden (Chester), a young physician in Alaska, whose nurses all have abandoned him after just a few weeks in the harsh living conditions. His latest assistant, Anne Webster (Wyatt, in her first screen role since *Lost Horizon* [1937]), plans to leave after just one day, but is impressed when Jim and his Innuit assistant, Joe (Mala), go to extraordinary lengths while delivering a baby via Caesarian section. She also witnesses Jim refuse payment from a miner, whose dying partner put an end to his own slow death from gangrene poisoning with an overdose of a painkiller provided by the doctor.

Still intending to leave, Anne is interrupted by Bill Bogler (Bickford), a U.S. Marshal who arrives with Ninimook (John Bleifer), an Innuit he has arrested for theft of valuable furs. In the process, Bogler fractured the man's skull, and Anne assists Jim as he performs delicate brain surgery.

Anne leaves, while Jim is forced to watch over the convalescing Ninimook. During a discussion of Jim's skills, Bogler mentions Dr. Gary Currier, a brilliant surgeon who had abandoned a thriving practice in Seattle after being arrested for euthanizing his terminally ill father, also a renowned physician. While visiting his neighbors, Jim discovers that Anne has remained to tend to the newborn baby. They return to his house, where Bogler arrests him. Placing Anne in charge of his patients until another doctor can arrive, he then leaves with Bogler.

Girl from God's Country (1940): Jane Wyatt and Chester Morris in Republic's "far north" adventure depicting the harsh challenges faced by a young physician in Alaska.

Anne and Joe follow, helping Jim to escape with his lead sled dog. While hiding, Jim explains that, after his father committed suicide, he took the blame to protect the old man's reputation. Bogler goes snowblind while relentlessly pursuing him through a blizzard, but Jim takes great risks to restore his enemy's eyesight. The grateful marshal releases him from custody, and he celebrates with Anne, Joe and Joe's wife, Koda (Kate Drain Lawson).

Released on July 30, 1940, *Girl from God's Country* was hailed by *Motion Picture Daily* as "one of the better pictures to come from Republic":

> Expensively mounted and showing much of Alaska's beautiful scenery, Republic's "Girl from God's Country" is the first film to make use of euthanasia as part of a screen plot....
>
> Chester Morris, as the doctor, plays one of his best roles.... Sidney Salkow, in directing the screenplay by Elizabeth Meehan and Robert Lee Johnson, imparted a well-rounded tone of entertainment to the offering....[46]

The film was also touted by *The Film Daily* as

> one of the best Republic releases of the year, [which] should prove manna from heaven to exhibitors who are looking for strong summer fare for their patrons. Filled with action and snow and ice scenes so starkly real that customers will stay two shows just to keep cool, it is not only good entertainment but timely for those Eastern hot spells.
>
> "Girl from God's Country" is a well-balanced, well-produced and well-directed film. Sidney Salkow, one of the studio's top pilots, has extracted every possibility from a good script. His direction is intelligent. Important credit for the film should go to Armand Schaefer who acted as associate producer. Chester Morris and Jane Wyatt handle their roles well.[47]

Girl from God's Country, seldom seen since its initial release, provided Chester with one of his most challenging roles. Though not the first film to incorporate the euthanasia issue (Chester's earlier feature, *Moonlight Murder*, already had done that, as a lesser plot element), the content still was unusual in 1940.

7

Meet Boston Blackie

In early November 1940, Chester took a restful sightseeing trip to San Francisco before solidifying a major life commitment. On November 20, the announcement of his impending marriage to Lillian appeared in *The Film Daily*. On Saturday the 30th, just four days after the divorce from Suzanne was finalized, their ceremony was held at the home of Frank Morgan. The road to the altar was not without a hurdle, however. After making wedding plans, Chester discovered that Sue had failed to apply for the final decree, which was required to supplement the interlocutory judgment of the previous year. Informed by his attorney about a law allowing a husband to make the application, Chester was aided further by Judge Gould, who signed the judgment.

Twice divorced at age 29, Lillian most recently had been married to Dr. Michael Barker. Dr. Sheldon Shepherd presided over the ceremony. The happy couple were prepared well in advance, having applied for their license on November 18.[1] James and Frances Cagney, and Ralph and Catherine Bellamy, just returned from a trip to Venezuela, were among the 75 guests. Plans had been made for them to leave on their honeymoon in January, soon after Chester completed work on his next Columbia assignment.

Subsequently, *Modern Screen* magazine ran a humorous article on what qualities hardened convicts supposedly preferred in their "tough-guy" movie stars, including Chester and his pal Cagney:

> Years ago, when the boys from Sing Sing to San Quentin learned that their idol, Eddie "Little Caesar" Robinson, collected *objects d'art* in his spare time, they snarled with contempt and switched to slugger Jimmie [sic] Cagney. At this writing, they're thinking of making another switch. Word has somehow leaked into the citizens of the cells that Jimmie wedding-gifted that other two-fisted toughie, Chester Morris, not with a gat or a blackjack, but with the most delicate, impractical, thin-stemmed glassware he could find on the Pacific Coast! The boys are pretty disgusted and, though they're giving Jimmie one more chance, they're quietly lining up Humphrey Bogart as a possible successor. Probably because they never heard of Bogie's flower garden![2]

The day of Chester and Lillian's wedding also marked what would become another longterm commitment for him, this one of a professional nature. Columbia announced that he was "set for the title role in the 'Boston Blackie' series, initialer [which] will roll early in December with Robert Florey directing."[3]

Chicago newspaper reporter Jack Boyle (1881–1928) created the character of reformed jewel thief and safecracker turned detective Horatio ["Boston Blackie"] Black after being sentenced to San Quentin for bad check writing and robbery resulting from an addiction to opium. In 1914, the first four short stories, "The Price of Principle," "The Story About Dad Morgan," "Death Cell Visions" and "A Thief's Daughter," were published under his *nom de plume* "No. 6066" in *The American Magazine*. In 1917, more tales, beginning with "Boston Blackie's Mary" and "The Woman Called Rita," appeared in *The Red Book*, where an additional eight were published the following year. During 1918–1919, three additional stories were published in London's *The Strand Magazine*, the longtime home of Sir Arthur Conan Doyle's Sherlock Holmes, and eight appeared in *Cosmopolitan*.

The first film adaptation, *Boston Blackie's Little Pal*, a five-reeler starring Bert Lytell, was released by Metro Pictures Corporation in 1918. Future Laurel and Hardy nemesis Walter Long played Blackie in the William S. Hart five-reeler *The Poppy Girl's Husband* (1919), codirected by Hart and Lambert Hillyer for Paramount. Lytell returned for one more film, *Blackie's Redemption* (1919); and, thereafter, the character was played by a different actor in each film: Sam De Grasse in *The Silk Lined Burglar* (1919), David Powell in *Missing Millions* (1922), Lionel Barrymore in *The Face in the Fog* (1922), William Russell in *Boston Blackie* (1923), Thomas Carrigan in *Crooked Alley* (1923), Forrest Stanley in *Through the Dark* (1924) and Raymond Glenn in *The Return of Boston Blackie* (1927). Following Boyle's death in October 1928, no more films were produced.

Chester Morris and Lillian Kenton Barker cutting their wedding cake at the home of Frank Morgan, November 30, 1940.

From December 6–27, 1940, Robert Florey directed "The Return of Boston Blackie," from an original story and screenplay by Jay Dratler, at Columbia. Chester was cast as Blackie, Richard Lane (with whom he'd worked in RKO's *Flight from Glory*) as Inspector Faraday, Rochelle Hudson as Cecelia Bradley, and George E. Stone as "The Runt," although Charles Wagenheim replaced him before shooting began.

Released as *Meet Boston Blackie* on February 20, 1941, this modestly budgeted 61-minute feature opens in New York Harbor, where Blackie, returning from Europe, aids Marilyn Howard (Constance Worth), who is being menaced by a mysterious man. Now aboard, Inspector Faraday accuses him of stealing the Mansfield pearls and confiscates his landing pass. In his stateroom, Blackie finds the body of Martin Vestrick (Nestor Paiva) and, knowing that Faraday will also pin the murder on him, takes the dead man's pass and, accompanied by the Runt, flees the ship.

After the Runt leaves for Blackie's apartment to summon Faraday, Blackie meets with Marilyn in the tunnel of love at Coney Island, where she admits to killing Vestrick in self-defense but is fatally knifed in the back before she can reveal further details. Blackie also

Meet Boston Blackie (1941): From left, in larger shot, Chester Morris, Richard Lane and Walter Sande in the first of Columbia's crime films based on the popular safecracker-turned-detective character created by Jack Boyle [original lobby card].

is blamed for this nefarious crime and, while pursued by the real killers, commandeers a car driven by lovely young Cecilia Bradley. A highlight of the film is a scene in which Blackie and Cecilia hide the car in a moving freight train.

More than a decade after beginning his film career as a leading man and top-billed star, Chester combined his natural charm, good looks (especially the trademark smile), athleticism (though he didn't like performing stunts) and talent for light tongue-in-cheek sarcasm into creating a new individual persona for the Boston Blackie character. When Blackie refers to the possibility of leaving his fingerprints behind, Chester proves he was born to deliver such lines as "Do I look like the sort who would autograph a safe?" Blackie also informs the Runt that Faraday "may convict us of a murder we didn't commit. Electrocution is so *permanent*." And when Cecelia begins to annoy him, Blackie admits, "I've never committed a crime of violence but I'm beginning to feel the urge."

Continuing to investigate the sinister events occurring at the Coney Island carnival (a classic movie setting for criminal activities), Blackie and Cecelia eventually expose an international spy ring intent on stealing a U.S. Navy bombsight, and the Runt is discovered inside the coffin-like wooden box used by illusionists when "sawing people in half." "Pull yourself together!" suggests Blackie when freeing his friend who, throughout the film, has been characteristically worried about the safety of his "boss."

Just before the final fadeout, as the Runt sits behind the wheel of their car, Blackie leans out the passenger-side window to kiss Cecelia. "Come on, come on—pull yourselves apart!" the little man commands.

The Film Daily was impressed:

> There is plenty of action in this new Columbia meller, with murder, espionage and skullduggery in wholesale lots before an exciting climax is reached. The cast is capable, the story moves along briskly, the direction is good, and for a program offering the film has more than an adequate production value....
>
> Chester Morris capably heads the cast as the suave rascal who uses extremely unethical methods to achieve his own ends.... Florey paces the action well and builds the suspense nicely.[4]

The well-balanced blend of intrigue and comedy that distinguishes the fast-paced *Meet Boston Blackie* set the stage for Columbia's forthcoming series. Richard Lane would remain to support Chester in subsequent films, and many other familiar character actors would become regulars. George E. Stone would take over as the Runt in the second film, making the character far more colorful (and lovable) than Charles Wagenheim, who had limited opportunities to create an impression.

Chester returned to NBC's *Kraft Music Hall* on June 12, 1941, to play Boston Blackie on radio for the first time, joined by Bob Burns and Donald Crisp. The impressive musical lineup featured performances by Bing Crosby, Connie Boswell and Ethel Waters (who recently starred in the original Broadway run of *Cabin in the Sky*) with John Scott Trotter and His Orchestra. While plugging *Meet Boston Blackie*, Bing began a skit with Chester, admitting, "Why, I'll never forget the first time that the mob and I met up with 'Boston.' We was on the lam, hiding out in a culvert, just outside Culvert City … playing bridge under the bridge."

Donald Crisp, currently shooting his scenes as Mr. Gwilym Morgan in John Ford's *How Green Was My Valley* (1941), played Chester's father in a promotion for U.S. Treasury Defense Savings Bonds, an "investment in democracy." "After 25 years of supporting Chester," Crisp was pleased that his son finally had landed his own job!

In early August 1941, Columbia picked up Chester's option for two more films. That month, William C. Thomas and William H. Pine of the Picture Corporation of America signed a contract with Paramount, agreeing to supply six new features per year. Three of the titles for the initial year would star Chester, and the other three would star Richard Arlen.

On August 15, Frank McDonald began directing *No Hands on the Clock* at Paramount, wrapping production just two weeks later. Assigned by his boss, Oscar Flack (George Watts), to locate Louise (Jean Parker) for her father, private detective Humphrey Campbell (Chester) marries her before they head off to Reno for a honeymoon. Flack finds them, promising Louise a fur coat if she will persuade Humphrey to track down the missing Hal Benedict, son of Nevada rancher Warren Benedict, whom the FBI also is seeking. Humphrey locks Louise in the bathroom at the hotel before beginning his investigation, which leads him to the discovery of dead redhead Irene Donovan, clutching a silver dollar in her hand. He also finds Hal's fiancée, Rose Madden (Billie Seward), in the house, but she insists that Irene was dead when she arrived.

Humphrey is joined by local investigator Clyde Copley (Lorin Raker), whose office overlooks the Darwin Mortuary, featuring a clock without hands bearing the slogan "Death is timeless." Humphrey and Louise, suspected of murdering Irene, also are pursued by Red Harris (Dick Purcell) and his stooges, Alex (John Gallaudet) and Jake, whom they had witnessed robbing a bank. Humphrey recalls that a silver dollar is Red's trademark.

Benedict receives a ransom note demanding that his ranch foreman, Harry Belding (Grant Withers), deliver $50,000 in exchange for Hal. Questioned by FBI agents, due to his resemblance to a notorious bank robber, Humphrey realizes that Red believes he is a former partner in crime. The plot becomes even more convoluted, with Keye Luke making a brief appearance as a houseboy revealing secrets about Benedict, Hal and Rose. Belding is bumped off. Humphrey colludes with Red, who has been framed for Irene's murder but is shot before he can identify the real killer. An embalmed corpse from the mortuary is used to throw suspicion onto Hal, who was murdered by Copley and Irene. Knowing too much, Irene is also murdered. Flack then collects the reward for capturing Red, as Humphrey and Louise continue their honeymoon.

No Hands on the Clock has a frequently confusing parade of twists packed into its 76

No Hands on the Clock (1941): Chester Morris and Jean Parker in their first film for independent producers William H. Pine and William C. Thomas.

minutes. The acting is first-rate, with the chemistry between Chester and Jean Parker, particularly their comic timing, again a highlight of their teaming. When Louise sees Humphrey, who is attempting to hide during his investigation, kissing a strange woman in the back of a taxi, he tells Rose Madden, "That was no lady. That was *my wife*." Back at their hotel room, trying to make up with Louise, Humphrey crosses one of the two beds and then tackles her between them. During a long single take, he pins her to the floor, showing her the newspaper and describing the murder of Irene. Later, trying to duck from the police, Humphrey drags the fully clothed Louise into the shower, where they both become drenched.

Chester also shares some memorable comic moments with George Watts, including a reference to magic that he added to the hectic proceedings. When Flack observes a man fashioning a figure from a piece of cloth, Humphrey complains, "Oh, Oscar, for the love of Pete. I'll show you how to make rabbits … using a white handkerchief." *No Hands on the Clock* also marked the second time one of Chester's characters plays a musical instrument, this time accordion. In an early scene, Humphrey briefly keys the melody from Louis Alter and Frank Loesser's song "Dolores," first recorded by Frank Sinatra with the Tommy Dorsey Orchestra for Paramount's *Las Vegas Nights*, released on March 28, 1941. The pianist in the hotel bar also plays the tune during a later scene.

The sharp dialogue by Maxwell Shane, an action and *film noir* specialist who would contribute to the scripts for seven more of Chester's Pine-Thomas films, is perfectly suited to Frank McDonald's fast-paced directorial style. The production team assembled a top supporting cast, with Purcell, Gallaudet, Withers and Luke also joined by Rose Hobart, Astrid Allwyn, Rod Cameron, James Kirkwood, Ralph Sanford and Milburn Stone.

The Film Daily declared *No Hands on the Clock* a "well-handled melodrama with enough excitement and suspense to make substantial program pic.":

> Another entry into the field of film heroes of the private detective category with the wife a necessary adjunct to the proceedings. The line this morning on Chester Morris, in the role of a private investigator, and his bride of a few hours, Jean Parker, is a favorable one.
>
> Pair make a good team and carry on with a jaunty air. It is familiar stuff but handled in a breezy style so that there are numerous chuckles spotted between the suspenseful moments….
>
> Character created by Morris is a likable one and Miss Parker is an ideal partner who likes to share her husband's adventures.[5]

William R. Weaver, in his *Motion Picture Herald* review, was suitably impressed: "This first of three melodramas to be produced by William H. Pine and William C. Thomas and to star Chester Morris is of a class and caliber to suggest extension of present planning to include a good many more."[6]

Edward Dmytryk began shooting a *Meet Boston Blackie* sequel, "The Secret of Boston Blackie," at Columbia on September 10, 1941. Jay Dratler again wrote the original story, collaborating with Paul Yawitz, who completed the final screenplay. Dmytryk, currently cutting his teeth on well-made, entertaining B features at Columbia, recently had worked with Boris Karloff on the eerie science-fiction thriller *The Devil Commands* (1941) and proved an ideal choice for the new Boston Blackie installment.

Chester liked the director, whose pacing created a sequel that arguably improves upon the original release, with Blackie and the Runt (now George E. Stone, in a delightfully endearing comic performance) mixed up with antiques thieves, led by Calder (Kenneth MacDonald, Sheriff Ed Willis in *The Devil Commands*), who blunder their way into a murder during an auction.

Stone was born Gershon Lichtenstein in Łódz, Poland (then part of the Russian Empire) on May 18, 1903. The diminutive (5'3") actor mastered English at a young age, worked in vaudeville and (billed as Georgie Stone) on Broadway before landing a supporting role as "Sewer Rat" in Frank Borzage's silent classic *7th Heaven* (1927) starring Janet Gaynor and Charles Farrell. He carved out quite a career playing street-wise sidekicks with colorful monikers like Velvet Smith, "Flash" Hoxy, Sparrow, Slinkey, Blackie, Shorty, Dippy, Johnnie the Shiek, Skeets and Boots Burnett.

Stone's performance as Otero, the faithful little pal of Cesar Enrico Bandello (Edward G. Robinson), in Warner Bros.' *Little Caesar* brought him acclaim, and he gave one of his most moving performances as Dinky, Peter Lorre's right-hand man, in Columbia's wronged-immigrant, gangster-horror melodrama *The Face Behind the Mask* (1941) shortly before the studio cast him as the Runt. Robert Florey, the French cinema critic and filmmaker who became a prolific Hollywood director of features and classic television episodes, completed *The Face Behind the Mask* just before beginning work on *Meet Boston Blackie*.

For the new film, Lloyd Corrigan joined the cast as Blackie's wealthy, eccentric benefactor Arthur Manleder, making an effective comic duo with Stone, whose version of the Runt (aided by Yawitz's script) provides an actual characterization rather than the mere sidekick sounding board of Charles Wagenheim. Likewise, Walter Sande signed on as Detective Mathews, the obtuse associate of Inspector Farraday (Richard Lane, whose character name is spelled with a double "r" in this and all subsequent series entries). Two fetching females, Diane Parrish and Mona, are played by Harriet Hilliard (later the wife of Ozzie Nelson) and Joan Woodbury, respectively.

The script again features some entertaining dialogue. Early in the film, Farraday, who naturally arrests Blackie for the murder at the antiques auction, provides some commentary on his character: "Sarcasm isn't new to you, but I thought killing was out of your line."

Later, when Manleder is accosted on a sidewalk while following Blackie, a pushy police officer elicits the response, "You've got a little Gestapo in you." Although the principal shooting wrapped on September 24, the film was released as *Confessions of Boston Blackie* on January 6, 1942, less than a month after the United States entered World War II.

This second film, including a scene in which Blackie impersonates a doctor at a hospital where Diane is recuperating from a superficial bullet wound, marked the first to feature Chester appropriating a disguise as his character pulls a fast one on Farraday. He substitutes a uniform stolen from an ice-cream man for that of the physician but is quickly unmasked by Diane. In an earlier scene, a similar ice-cream seller (future "East Side Kid" William ["Billy"] Benedict), loses his uniform in the police precinct locker room to Blackie, who then strolls directly past the Inspector. Later, the hapless hawker is deposited into the freezer of his ice-cream truck, from which he then emerges in a completely frozen state.

Confessions of Boston Blackie is a consistently entertaining 60-minute episode, aided considerably by the well-integrated humor. During the following decade, both Kenneth MacDonald (as a judge in 32 episodes, 1957–1966) and George E. Stone (as a court reporter or bartender in 46 episodes) appeared in the popular television series *Perry Mason*. By the 1950s, Stone had begun to lose his eyesight, and star Raymond Burr, whose Paisano Productions co-produced the show for CBS, personally saw to it that his friend was cast in a recurring capacity.

Variety's "Mori" wrote,

> This is a compact, deftly paced murder meller, embellished with light comedy touches, which fulfills its purpose adequately on the lower end of dual bills for which it is intended.... With Chester Morris

Confessions of Boston Blackie (1941): Chester Morris, Harriet Hilliard and Kenneth MacDonald in the Edward Dmytryk-directed follow-up to Columbia's *Meet Boston Blackie* [original one-sheet poster].

in the title role it represents the type of celluloid thriller which finds a ready audience in subsequent situations....

Blackie's continual brushes with the law, his easy escapes from the hoosegow and friendly feuding with the inspector while solving the crime provide effective comedy touches. Chester Morris is excellent in the lead, with George E. Stone filling the bill nicely as his comic sidekick.[7]

To acknowledge both New Orleans and Memphis as being the possible geographical origin of a uniquely American form of music, Paramount held simultaneous premieres of the Bing Crosby-Mary Martin musical *Birth of the Blues* in both cities on Friday, October 31, 1941. As part of his promotional work for the studio, Chester was happy to join Basil Rathbone, Charles Ruggles, Patricia Morison, Dona Drake, Ellen Drew, Phil Regan and

Jean Wallace for the screening at the Saenger Theatre in the Big Easy. Following a flight from Hollywood, the merry band boarded a river yacht for a sightseeing tour before riding down Canal Street in horsedrawn carriages to the St. Charles Hotel, where they all lodged during their visit.

Each of Chester's brothers sadly passed away at a young age. On November 30, 1941, Adrian, scheduled to begin playing a gangster in Chester's film "I'll Be Back in a Flash" the next morning, died suddenly of a brain hemorrhage, just six weeks shy of his 35th birthday. Survived by his widow, Eva, and son, William Michael Morris, he also was interred, alongside William and Gordon, in the Garden of Eternal Love at Hollywood Memorial Cemetery. Now Chester was the last of William's sons remaining.

Chester's second Pine-Thomas Productions picture for release through Paramount, "I'll Be Back in a Flash" was shot on the studio lot by director Sam White during late November and early December, just before the United States became actively involved in World War II. No references to the conflict invade this story about Jeff Morrell (Chester), a radio commentator whose only objective is getting a scoop, regardless of any ethical concerns. He is fired after broadcasting a phony boxing report, and then his zeal to land a London assignment leads to him setting up suspected murderer Eddie Nelson (Edward Norris) for arrest. Eddie is convicted and sentenced to death for the murder of his former boss, Wingy Keefe (Edwin Maxwell), but Inspector Conlon (Joe Cunningham) suggests that he may be innocent. Jeff, hoping to get back into the good graces of his mother (Elizabeth Risdon) and Susan Richards (Jean Parker), Eddie's sister, investigates the case. Jeff's assistant, Angie Moss (Ralph Sanford), tells him that his wearing of "blinders" makes him "superficial," unable to see "the human elements."

Jeff's friend and fellow reporter Norm Thompson (Dick Purcell) reveals that Keefe, doublecrossed by gambler Joey Farr (Douglas Fowley), had intended to testify to a grand jury. Jeff questions the incarcerated Eddie and delivers the new information to District Attorney E.G. Lambert (Edward Keane), who secretly is colluding with Farr. Jeff, accompanied by Conlon, who has been suspicious of Lambert, follows Farr to Pennsylvania, first to a billiard hall and then into an abandoned mine. Using tear gas, police are unable to drive him out, so Jeff, broadcasting live, secretly airs his confession during an interview. Farr ignites some dynamite, killing himself. Eddie is cleared of the murder charge, Lambert is indicted, and Jeff survives to marry Susan, broadcasting their wedding in the process.

The screenplay by Lewis R. Foster, Richard Murphy and Maxwell Shane is well-directed by White. Foster was a prolific writer who also directed scores of films, including six Laurel and Hardy shorts for Hal Roach Studios during 1929, the comedy team's first year of sound production. Cinematographer Fred Jackman, Jr., who would shoot all eight of the Pine-Thomas productions starring Chester, was the son of cinematographer-director-special effects artist Fred Jackman and nephew of cinematographer Floyd Jackman, who served as cameraman on many Roach shorts, including three featuring Laurel and Hardy during 1928–1929. One additional Laurel and Hardy veteran, Charlotte Henry, who plays Bo Peep in *Babes in Toyland* [aka *March of the Wooden Soldiers*] (1934), appears in "I'll Be Back in a Flash," as a nurse.

Paired with Jean Parker for the third time, Chester again enjoyed the duality offered by his character, displaying a marked difference between Jeff Morrell's delivery when attempting to pull off a bogus broadcast and, later, when sincerely reporting the facts of a serious, real-life event. *Showmen's Trade Review* was suitably impressed with the final cut, released as *I Live on Danger* on June 16, 1942:

I Live on Danger (1942): Chester Morris and Jean Parker in a publicity portrait for the Pine-Thomas production about Jeff Morrell, a radio commentator whose only objective is getting a scoop, regardless of any ethical concerns.

Gangland, crooked politics and radio all mixed up with romance in this one, but director White has managed to keep his story twisting and turning to cover the wide area of backgrounds in an admirable manner. Chester Morris, as the hard-hearted announcer who sees only the story and never senses the effect of his success on those who make the headlines, does an excellent job, and Jean Parker, as the sister of the convicted criminal, works with just the right amount of reserve to make her part convincing.... The camera department has been well handled and the sequences dealing with the people rescued from a burning liner strewn like debris on the beach and the capture of the murderer in the abandoned mine rate excellent.[8]

The New York Times' resident elitist curmudgeon, Bosley Crowther, who frequently was concerned with displaying his own cute cleverness rather than providing a substantive review, decided to attack the star head-on:

> It is a matter of public record—well, cinematic record, anyhow—that Chester Morris walks into and out of jeopardy like most people go around in revolving doors. Mr. Morris wouldn't feel at ease in a picture unless he were up to his eyelashes in peril, and his audience—of which there are several—wouldn't tolerate him if he weren't. So, Paramount is telling us nothing about Chet the Square-Shooter that we don't know in the title of "I Live on Danger," which came to the Rialto yesterday. And the picture is showing us very little that we haven't already seen. This time Mr. Morris is playing his familiar game of tag with Fate as a special-events broadcaster who, apparently, never takes off his hat.... Needless to say, "I Live on Danger" is an action melodrama of the low variety and Mr. Morris, Jean Parker and a slight cast play it with melodramatics that are equally low. But, somehow, a lot of movie people manage to live on this type of film.[9]

William Pine's son, Howard, who worked as assistant director on this and two subsequent Pine-Thomas productions starring Chester, and such varied features as *Danger Street* (1947), *Albuquerque* (1948) and *Manhandled* (1949), later became a production manager on the major hits *Funny Lady* (1975), *A Star Is Born* (1976) and *The Karate Kid* (1992).

On December 8, 1941, when President Franklin D. Roosevelt referred to the previous day, on which forces of the Imperial Japanese Navy Air Service attacked the United States naval base at Pearl Harbor, as "a date that will live in infamy," calling for a formal declaration of war against the Empire of Japan, pledges of immediate support were made by two film-industry leaders. In a telegram to FDR, Will Hayes, president of the Motion Picture Producers and Distributors of America, wrote,

> The [MPPDA] hereby pledge our service and support to the President of the Nation and reiterate our resolve to maintain the continued flow of wholesome entertainment as an essential contribution to military and civilian morale and to the national spirit.[10]

George Schaefer, chairman of the Motion Picture Committee Co-Operating for National Defense, followed suit:

> The [MPCCND], representing more than 12,000 theater operators and the artists, producers, distributors, newsreels and trade press, reaffirms pledge of all possible service to you, the National Government and the people of the United States in this emergency.[11]

That same day, *The Film Daily* reported that Columbia had cast Chester, John Hubbard, Harriet Hilliard (fresh from *Confessions of Boston Blackie*) and Forrest Tucker in *Canal Zone*. Production began just two days later and was wrapped by Lew Landers on December 27. The cast also includes Lloyd Bridges and Larry Parks, both of whom would rejoin Chester in Columbia's *Alias Boston Blackie* (1942). (Parks also would play a supporting role in *The Boogie Man Will Get You* [1942], costarring Boris Karloff and Peter Lorre, directed by Landers.)

On a day off from the breakneck shooting schedule, Chester reported to Paramount nonetheless, exclusively to entertain his colleagues during breaks on the set. Honing the magic act he soon would be using to divert members of the U.S. Armed Forces during nearly 400 United Service Organizations (USO) shows, he was allowed to set up on one of the soundstages, where "everything he made disappear he also made reappear." But the joke ultimately was on Chester: When he left the studio to return to his car, his overcoat had "disappeared." Try as he may, "The Mysterious Morris" could not magically wrest it back from the thief.[12]

The film opens with a written dedication:

To those valiant men who fly through endless nights of storm and fog—To those unsung heroes who deliver air power to the lines of battle—To those ferry pilots who make possible the defense of all freedoms—This picture is respectfully dedicated.

On the edge of the Panama Canal zone, U.S. Army bombers are being flown to Africa over the Matto Grosso Mountains from the Ginger Bar, a converted banana shipping station. Commander Merrill (Stanley Andrews), a former military flier, is now developing civilian pilots to handle "Flying Fortresses," aided by "Hardtack" Hamilton (Chester), a no-nonsense, by-the-book training officer.

Based on Blaine and Jean DuPont Miller's story "Heroes Come High," Robert Lee Johnson's derivative screenplay also features Harley Ames (Hubbard), an irresponsible "society playboy" (in the tradition of characters played by Lee Bowman and Dick Foran, respectively, in Universal's military preparedness pictures *Buck Privates* and *Keep 'Em Flying* [both 1941], starring Bud Abbott and Lou Costello) and Susan Merrill (Hilliard), the commander's daughter, who is unwilling to compete with aviation for Hamilton's affections.

After accidentally killing Kincaid (Parks), an Alabama recruit, during a training exercise, Ames, who was suffering from a hangover, redeems himself by rescuing Hamilton, who has crashed his plane into a dense jungle area. Hamilton is reunited with Susan in the Canal Zone, where Ames takes off with the squadron on its mission to Africa.

Canal Zone (1942): Harriett Hilliard and Chester Morris in Columbia's early contribution to Hollywood's support for the war effort, directed by Lew Landers [original half-sheet poster].

Columbia released the film on March 19, 1942, the day on which FDR (whose portrait hangs on the wall of the Ginger Bar command post) ordered male citizens of the United States, aged 45 to 64, to register for non-military duty. On March 20, General Douglas MacArthur, soon to become Supreme Commander, Southwest Pacific Area, delivered a speech in South Australia, during which, referring to the Philippines, he made his famous remark, "I came through and I shall return" (a promise he eventually kept).

Though the script is a predictable affair, the contributions of cinematographer Franz Planer and editors Art Bell and James Sweeney smoothly combine fluid camerawork and authentic aerial sequences with convincing miniature shots of the transports flying from the Canal Zone. Hilliard is not as comfortable here as in her "Boston Blackie" role, but the remainder of the cast is uniformly convincing, with Chester in fine form as the resolute military airman.

Paul C. Mooney, Jr., in *Motion Picture Herald*, praised the overall energy of the film:

> Eliminating the war angle, the plot is one that has been used time and time again. This picture, however, has literally been lifted out of its class rating by as effective a piece of directing as one will find.
> The directorial accomplishment has transmitted itself to the actors and without exception, they do a bang-up job. Chester Morris plays the rough, tough training officer with conviction, without heroics, and with a feeling for the job entrusted to him. John Hubbard's society playboy aviator, who is only concerned with personal excitement, is a made-to-order job....
> When the camera isn't focusing on the drama going on in the relay station, it is focusing on another drama, that of bombers being flown from the Canal Zone to Africa over the dangerous and scenic grandeur of the Matto Grosso in Brazil. The combination of photography and the drama going on in the bombers is of the sort to keep the audience on the edge of their seats.[13]

Following a break for the Yuletide holidays, Chester was back at Columbia on January 6, 1942, to shoot the third entry in his popular detective series, *Alias Boston Blackie*, again featuring a screenplay by Paul Yawitz, with Lew Landers back in the director's chair. Incorporating Christmas into a further development of the "domestic" relationship between Blackie and the Runt (George E. Stone), the film is an exceptional series episode, with crackling dialogue, charming humor, an interesting plot and a nearly flawless pace achieved by the reliable Landers. The regular supporting cast of Richard Lane, Lloyd Corrigan and Walter Sande is augmented by Larry Parks and Lloyd Bridges, both of whom recently had appeared in *Canal Zone* and the studio's *North of the Rockies* (1942).

Alias Boston Blackie, wrapped by Landers on January 22 and released on April 2, 1942, opens warmly with Blackie and the Runt trimming their tree. Reminiscing about his former safecracking career, Runt tells Blackie about the love of his life, a "big beautiful blonde": "I did time in eight penitentiaries, just so she could be the best-dressed Christmas tree in the underworld."

Blackie, continually insisting that the faltering Runt not fall asleep, gives his all to bring Christmas Eve cheer to the inmates at his "alma mater," the state prison, where Joe Trilby (Parks), brother of his friend, dancer Eve Sands (Adele Mara), is being held on a 15-year frameup. Behind the walls, Blackie admits that he was part of the "Class of '30" and graduated "Phi Beta Kappa from the sawmill."

"I kind of get a yen for this old joint," adds the Runt.

Speaking about Joe, who has been brewing thoughts of revenge on the two thugs who framed him, Blackie observes, "Your arithmetic gets pretty screwy when you're using a cell wall as a slate."

During the benefit show hosted by Blackie, Joe binds and gags Roggi McKay (George

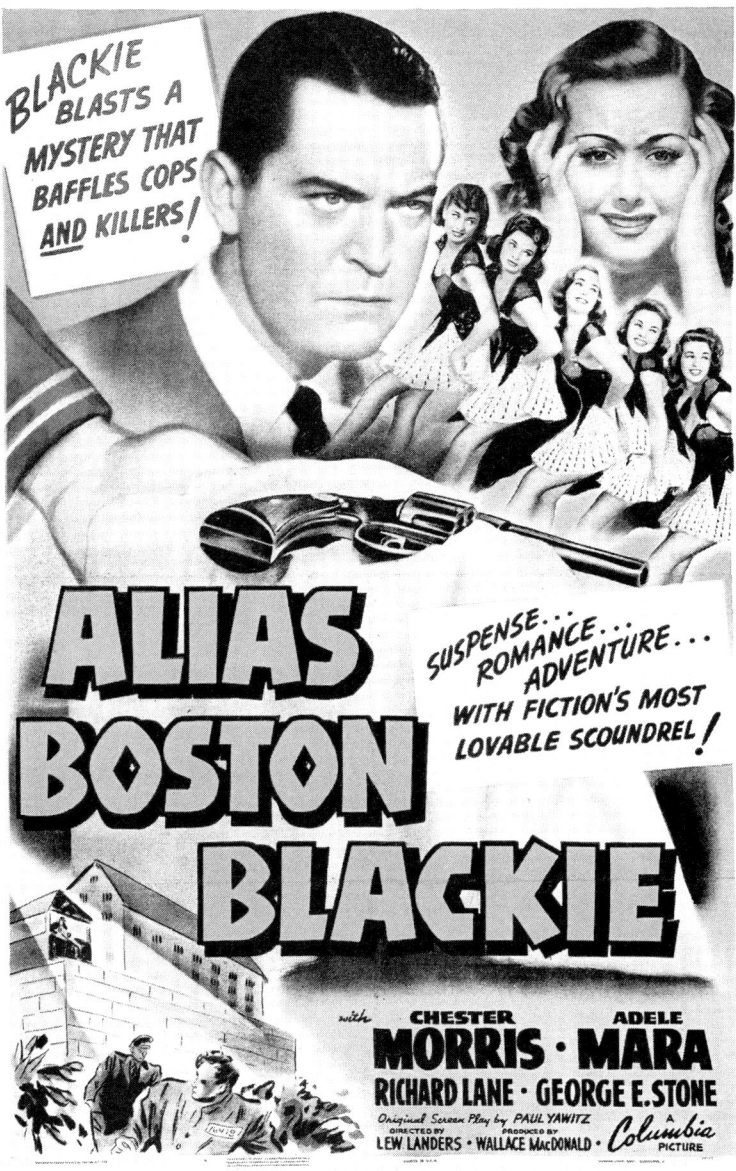

Alias Boston Blackie (1942): Chester Morris and Adele Mara in the poster art for one of the top entries in the popular crime series [original one-sheet poster].

McKay), a well-known vaudeville clown, and escapes with the rest of the troupe, Farraday (Lane) and Mathews (Sande) on the bus headed back to the city. The disguises come and go regularly throughout the film, with Joe fighting and stealing the clothes from a knocked-out Blackie, who then must don the clown's rags to get back to his apartment. "Hey, Blackie," the Runt asks, "You haven't been drinkin', have you?"

In a hilarious scene, Blackie binds Mathews, wrapping a cloth around his head, in the familiar precinct locker room, dresses in the sergeant's police uniform and then commandeers a motorcycle-with-sidecar from a group of men he has hired to deliver a singing telegram to Farraday. A furious chase ensues, with Blackie, Runt and Eve all aboard the speeding cycle, driving onto a sidewalk and crashing through fruit crates, as a police cruiser pursues from behind.

Duke Banton, one of the two men who framed Joe, is found dead, murdered by his partner, Steve Caveroni (Paul Fix). Blackie tracks down the desperate killer and, during the tense apprehension, Farraday saves his life. The closing scene shows the happy crime-fighting couple back at their holiday tree, this time celebrating the occasion with Eve, Joe, Farraday, Mathews and Manleder. "A very Merry Christmas and Happy New Year to all of us," toasts Blackie, wrapping up a very pleasant, entertaining 67-minute package.

By the time he delivered this third performance as the charismatic character, Chester had become completely comfortable in his skin, displaying that smiling-while-speaking ability that a true classic movie star possessed, along with a naturalistic and convincing acting style. The rest of the cast, including familiar heavy Cy Kendall in a brief role as friendly fence Jumbo Madigan, is equally adept, stylistically served up by Landers, the camerawork of Philip Tannura and editing of Richard Fantl.

Following the wrap of *Alias Boston Blackie*, Chester hit the road on February 23, 1942, for a two-week tour with USO–Camp Shows, Inc. The following evening, while he was away from home, U.S. naval intelligence issued a warning that an attack by Japanese forces could be expected along the coast. After flares and blinking lights were spotted near defense plants, an alert was called but lifted three hours later. Early the next morning, the city experienced an event, later named the "Battle of Los Angeles," involving air-raid sirens, a total blackout, fire from .50-caliber machine guns, and volleys of 12.8-pound anti-aircraft shells aimed at a supposed enemy force. Buildings were damaged, three people were killed in auto accidents, with two more succumbing to stress-induced heart attacks.

Shortly after the air raid subsided, Secretary of the Navy Frank Knox held a press conference, at which he claimed that "war nerves" had caused a "false alarm." (Speculation about the incident was rampant. In 1983, the U.S. Office of Air Force History finally confirmed earlier findings of the United States Coast Artillery Association that a meteorological balloon had triggered the military response, exacerbated by flares and shells from adjoining batteries.)

Chester, not having a clear understanding of what had occurred over Beverly Hills, soldiered on with his own military-oriented activities. At a time when a "number of changes [were] made ... in the regular units providing soldier entertainment," he performed at several U.S. Army camps in the Western states.[14] Praised in the press as "one of the best amateur magicians in America" (although he had been performing his act professionally for several years), he enjoyed every show on the 12-camp "Broadway Breveties" tour, which wrapped up on March 5.

At one location, he was delightfully surprised by a "tall, broad-shouldered soldier" who approached him, asking, "Do you remember a little boy named Willie who used to live next door to you in New York?"

"Certainly," Chester replied. "We were school chums. Why do you ask?"

"Well," the "large fellow" answered. "I'm little Willie."[15]

One major show, organized by Basil Rathbone's wife, Ouida, at March Field, "home of the flying fortresses," near Riverside, California, was performed for men of the U.S. Army Air Corps by Chester, Edgar Bergen, Alan Curtis and Ilona Massey, Reginald Gardiner, Betty Grable, Rita Hayworth, George Murphy and Rudy Vallee.

Chester's nonstop performances as "The Mysterious Morris" led to his election as honorary president of the Society of American Magicians during spring 1942. On April 1, *Variety* included the article "Morris Touring Camps with Amateur Magis" on its "War Activities" page:

> For years he was the life of the party, doing card tricks and what-not at school gatherings. Now Chester Morris is organizing a troupe of amateur magicians for a tour of the sticks before he starts his new three-picture contract with Bill Pine-Bill Thomas productions unit for Paramount release.
>
> In addition to his company of amateur magickers, Morris will be assisted by his wife, Lil Kenton, also an adept at the-hand-is-quicker-than-the-eye miracles.[16]

That month, USO–Camp Shows, Inc., reported that, of the organization's "approximately 25 screen names who have toured Army camps and Navy bases … since January," Al Jolson, Harpo Marx and Mickey Rooney scored as the top three. Jolson, who experienced a resurgence in popularity during the war years, played to 60,000 troops in just 10 days, while Marx entertained 57,000 in 16. Rooney exhibited his well-known energy by attracting 50,000 in only three. The size of each camp was a major factor in the magnitude of its audience. Performers who racked up large numbers were those featured at outdoor performances, while actors and singers doing their acts at small War Department theaters were far more limited. On the list, also including Jackie Cooper, Deanna Durbin, Martha Raye, Reginald Gardiner, Ann Rutherford, Judy Garland, the Ritz Bros., Ann Miller, Hugh Herbert, Rosalind Russell, Mitzi Green and Charles Butterworth, Chester checked in with a total audience of 4,870 at 11 shows.

Frank McDonald began shooting the Pine-Thomas production *Wrecking Crew* on April 6, 1942. This quickly produced film, adapted by Maxwell Shane and Richard Murphy from the original story "Alley Cat" by Robert T. Shannon and Mauri Grashin, reunited Chester with his former he-man costar Richard Arlen. On April 8, *Variety* reported, "Pine and Thomas have won the monikers 'The Dollar Bills' in Hollywood, due to the money-making records of their action films."[17]

Wrecking Crew opens with the written prologue "This is the story of the wreckers…. They tear down that others may build—Their lives are dedicated to the proposition that whatever goes up must come down, and the bigger they are … the harder they fall." Duke Mason (Chester), a risk-taking "cannonballer" for the O'Glendy Wrecking Company, is considered a "jinx" by his coworkers, but proves his mettle by saving the life of his foreman, Matt Carney (Arlen), while working atop the watertower of a hotel they are demolishing. Soon after, however, another worker, Joe Polska (Alexander Granach), falls to his death while helping Duke work on an unstable wall.

The depressed Duke then wanders the streets, where he prevents Peggy Starr (Jean Parker) from drowning herself in the river. Matt also falls for the lovely young woman, who is hired as a secretary by Mike O'Glendy (Esther Dale). To speed up demolition, Matt promotes Duke to night foreman. After tearing down a wall, Duke discovers a large sum of hidden money, which he distributes to his coworker, former baseball pitcher, Freddy Bunce (Joe Sawyer), who needs surgery on his arm, and Joe's widow, Martha Polska (Evelyn Brent), telling them it is a donation from the night crew.

Following Peggy's rejection of his marriage proposal, Matt orders Duke to stop showing off with a wrecking ball, which is then secured. The drunken Tom Kemp (Billy Nelson), a former coworker who had fought with Duke, then releases the ball, which seriously injures Emil (Fred Sherman) and damages the building, which must be reinforced prior to further demolition. Duke is blamed, and after being rejected by Peggy, fights with Matt, causing a wall to collapse.

The recovering Emil eventually identifies Kemp as the culprit. Duke, who had quit, returns to find Matt again in a life-threatening situation; but, while attempting another rescue, also becomes trapped under a collapsing wall. Nearly plummeting to their deaths, both Duke and Matt are saved by Freddy, who rallies his pitching arm to toss them a rope.

Wrecking Crew (1942): From left, Richard Arlen, Jean Parker and Chester Morris in the poster art for the Pine-Thomas production about workers whose "lives are dedicated to the proposition that whatever goes up must come down, and the bigger they are ... the harder they fall" [original one-sheet poster].

Another Pine-Thomas production released during World War II but containing no war-related content, *Wrecking Crew* nonetheless depicts a group of hard-working men necessarily pulling together to accomplish a common goal. Including the moth-eaten premise of the two male leads competing for the same female, the film features good performances from Richard Arlen and Chester, who comfortably falls into his rough-edged but good-hearted working-man persona. As in *No Hands on the Clock*, Maxwell Shane worked in some morbid foreshadowing by including a large mortuary sign in the background of an early scene, offering a "complete funeral for $125," during which members of the wrecking crew toil high atop a building. Frank McDonald ably incorporated some good stunt work and special effects by Alex Widlicska.

In his *Showmen's Trade Review* column, "Wandering Around Hollywood," Avie Mack reported,

> With so many actors, all of whom claim they "bring down the house" every time they get a part, wandering loose, it seems funny that Bill Pine and Bill Thomas had to go out and hire a professional building wrecker to technically advise on "Wrecking Crew." But they did, and a man named James Stafford, who according to reports has demolished more buildings than the RAF bombers, will show Chester Morris, et al, how to knock things flatter than the bride's biscuits.[18]

During production, Pine and Thomas signed Chester to another three-picture contract, to begin immediately after McDonald wrapped the current project. Following the film's general release on November 7, 1942, *Showmen's Trade Review* added, "Looks like the best thing Richard Arlen and Chester Morris have done and Jean Parker is splendid as the sweetheart of both."[19] "Denley," in *Film Bulletin*, called it

> One of the best of the Pine-Thomas series for Paramount ... a fast-moving film with a novel action background.... Richard Arlen, as the dependable foreman, and Chester Morris, as the happy-go-lucky gambling crew man, are nicely contrasted types and well-matched in the fistic sequences.[20]

On May 6, 1942, the day that U.S. and Filipino forces surrendered unconditionally to the Japanese Imperial Army on Corregidor, the War Productions Board aired, over New York's WJZ-Blue radio network, episode three of the program *Three Thirds of a Nation*. Originating from Hollywood, this series about "learning to do without things" emphasized conservation of the country's vital resources. The first installment, about sugar, was followed one week later by a similar plea for limited civilian uses of rubber. Written by Dorothea Lewis and narrated by Conrad Nagel, the third episode costarred Chester and Rosemary DeCamp, with music by the Leith Stevens Orchestra.[21]

From 12:05 to 12:55 a.m. (EST) on Sunday, May 31, the NBC Red network, with the cooperation of the Hollywood Victory Committee, broadcast a live all-star radio show to help raise $32 million for continued USO entertainment and recreational programs. Chester joined many fellow screen, stage and radio luminaries, including Fanny Brice, Joe E. Brown, Charles Butterworth, Linda Darnell, Deanna Durbin, Judy Garland, John Garfield, Hugh Herbert, Stan Laurel and Oliver Hardy, Mary Martin, Chico and Harpo Marx, the Ritz Brothers, Mickey Rooney, Rosalind Russell and Red Skelton. Meredith Willson conducted the orchestra. The following week, Chester left for Fort Worth, Texas, where he attended the convention of the Brotherhood of Magicians.

At Columbia, from June 18 to July 3, 1942, Michael Gordon directed *Boston Blackie Goes Hollywood*, featuring the fourth screenplay by Paul Yawitz. More simplistic than its three predecessors, and relying heavily on humor, the film features George E. Stone, Lloyd Corrigan, Richard Lane and Walter Sande supporting Chester, with Forrest Tucker (who had appeared in *Canal Zone*) appearing as "Whipper," a thug in the employ of ex-con Slick Barton (William Wright).

Instructed to hand carry $60,000 from New York to Los Angeles by Arthur Manleder (Corrigan), Blackie and the Runt, disguising themselves as "Professor Stratton" and his child-genius nephew, "Junior" (the 39-year-old Stone in schoolboy clothes), dump the contents of a souvenir ant colony onto Farraday (Lane) and Mathews (Sande) while aboard a six-hour crosscountry flight. Most of the film's 68 minutes blend comic situations with the basic plot of Manleder needing the money to buy back the stolen Monterey Diamond from Barton, and the two New York cops' intentions to solve the robbery case.

Boston Blackie Goes Hollywood (1942): Chester Morris, in his fourth outing as Jack Boyle's reformed safecracker, travels to Los Angeles to recover the stolen Monterey Diamond [original one-sheet poster].

Though the structure of the screenplay pales in comparison to Yawitz's earlier series efforts, *Boston Blackie Goes Hollywood* (the title of which is a bit misleading, since the movie capital never really becomes a feature of the story) includes the writer's usual snappy dialogue. While in the backseat of a taxi with Farraday, Blackie, admitting that he doesn't mind missing a planned vacation in Florida, informs him, "You're so bright I can get my sun tan sitting next to you."

Unlike many films (notably MGM titles and entries in Universal's horror and Sherlock Holmes series) released by the Hollywood industry during 1942, current wartime events again are alluded to only indirectly in a Blackie episode. When the Inspector bursts into Manleder's residence unannounced, Blackie asks, "Have you been taking lessons from the Gestapo, Farraday? Entering an apartment without a search warrant."

The relationship between Blackie and the Runt again is featured, with the former slapping the latter in front of the Inspector at one point. "Take it easy, Blackie," warns Farraday.

"I'll get the truth out of this little rat," Blackie growls, "if I have to break every bone in his head."

Dragged into the next room, Runt is relieved, admitting, "Oh, Blackie, I hoped you didn't mean it."

Columbia released *Boston Blackie Goes Hollywood* on November 5, 1942. *Harrison's Reports* considered it "a fair program entertainment":

> Following a pattern familiar to the other pictures in the series ... the story is, of course, far-fetched, and the melodramatics are of the sort that strain the imagination, but there is plenty of exciting action, and for that reason it should easily satisfy the action enthusiasts who care little about the plausibility of a plot. There is quite a bit of comedy, but no romantic interest.... There are no objectionable situations.[22]

On August 11, 1942, the Hollywood Victory Committee, at its Tinseltown office, unveiled a War Record Board honoring the "Gold Stars" who had toured military camps on a purely voluntary basis during their off-work time. The 36 performers included Chester, Jean Arthur, Joe E. Brown, Linda Darnell, Marlene Dietrich, Carole Landis, Stan Laurel and Oliver Hardy, Chico and Harpo Marx, Ann Miller, Jeanette MacDonald, Frank McHugh, Martha Raye, the Ritz Bros., Mickey Rooney, Rosalind Russell, Ann Rutherford, Maxie Rosenbloom and Ann Sheridan. The Committee also recognized 723 film players who made a total of 3,198 personal appearances, contributions to 422 radio shows for the armed forces, sold bonds and participated in other "patriotic activities."[23]

Frank McDonald began directing the Pine-Thomas production "You Can't Live Forever," costarring Chester, Jean Parker and Barry Sullivan, on August 19. For the screenplay, Maxwell Shane and Howard J. Green, working from an original story by Joseph Hoffman, recycled several elements from previous Pine-Thomas films.

Chester plays Washington, D.C., midget-car driver "Buzz" Mitchell, who wins a race and then fights with a competitor who nearly triggered a serious crash. Mike Douglas (Sullivan), a former partner seeking to fulfill a government contract, offers Mitchell an opportunity farther west, to drive for his nitroglycerine manufacturing and shipping company, but is turned down flat. When Mitchell is banned from racing due to an accident, he asks for a job but withholds the reason from Douglas.

Familiar plot complications arise when Douglas' secretary, Connie Baker (Parker), falls for Mitchell, but loses interest after realizing that he haphazardly handles the nitro

High Explosive (1943): From left, Chester Morris, Jean Parker and Barry Sullivan in the Pine-Thomas production focusing on the adventures of midget-car driver "Buzz" Mitchell, who self-sacrificingly meets an incendiary end [original lobby card].

while working with her brother, Jimmy (Rand Brooks). Mitchell then vengefully takes Jimmy's fiancée, Doris Lynch (Barbara Lynn), up in an airplane. Forced to take over Mitchell's work shift, Jimmy dies in an explosion after the brakes on the delivery truck fail.

An oil-refinery tank erupts, threatening a nearby munitions factory, so Douglas and Mitchell fly to collect enough nitro to extinguish the fire. Fog impedes their return, and as the plane runs low on fuel, Mitchell tricks Douglas into bailing out before sending a radio message to Connie and self-sacrificingly extinguishing the flaming tank.

Retitled *High Explosive*, the film was released by Paramount in March 1943. Reflecting a period in which the personality of a movie star often was more important than the ability of an *actor* (especially to exhibitors who preferred a similar characterization in every film), *Showman's Trade Review* noted,

> "High Explosive" is designed solely for the action fans, and they'll like it except for one thing: the hero's sacrifice at the end. It's a logical ending, to be sure, but such logic should be reserved for those dramas which cater to intellectual audiences. The average action fan expects his hero to emerge triumphant from any hazardous venture and to win the girl at the fadeout. Chester Morris, whose early career was studded with serious dramatic characterizations, has most recently portrayed a brash, cocksure individual in the Pine-Thomas action films, the group into which this picture falls. It's a portrayal that seems out of key with this actor's true character, but so long as the audience to whom this type of film is intended accepts it, one can hardly blame Morris for doing his best to essay it.[24]

8

Aerial Gunner

In September 1942, *Photoplay* ran the feature "Bogie on the Spot (Things I Don't Like About Myself)," in which the hardboiled Warner Bros. star, whose latest film was the John Huston-directed *Across the Pacific*, said,

> Maybe I should hate myself for not making a lot of friends, eh? What do you think? Friendship to me isn't just meeting and knowing a lot of people. It goes deeper than that. So I skip the mob. Louis Bromfield is one of my best friends. A friend on every occasion. So is Chester Morris.[1]

That month, the U.S. Treasury Department announced its official quota of $775 million in War Bonds sales, adding that the film industry "might reach its [own] optimistic quota of $1 billion."[2] The Hollywood Victory Committee announced assignments for the "Second Star Group," which, on September 10, would hit the road to sell bonds. Paired with 20th Century–Fox leading lady Gene Tierney, Chester was scheduled to visit Madison, Wisconsin; Fort Madison, Iowa; Rockford, Peoria, Springfield and Decatur, Illinois; the territory from Danville, Illinois, to Terre Haute, Indiana; and the territory from Paducah to Hopkinsville, Kentucky.

In Madison, a special Victory Stage was set up in the middle of State Street between the Capitol and Orpheum theaters. Chester and Gene were hosted during their personal appearance by Capitol manager Marlowe Conner, whose own "bond premiere" of Paramount's *Wake Island* (1942), directed by John Farrow, resulted in $290,000 in bond sales. The drive resulted in Dane County selling more bonds than any other in Wisconsin, exceeding its quota by 25 percent.

The relentless push during the "Salute to Our Heroes" tour proved quite exhausting for many volunteers, including Tierney, who fell asleep on Chester while traveling in a car to Rockford. At the destination, police sirens finally woke her just in time for the show. At the Decatur show, they sold a total of $308,700 in bonds, while at Fort Madison, although hampered by a rainstorm, $200,000 were sold.[3] By the end of their tour, Chester and Gene had racked up a total of $3,732,728 in sales.[4]

In mid–October 1942, Paramount announced that location sequences for the next Pine-Thomas production, *Aerial Gunner*, costarring Chester and Richard Arlen, would be shot with the full cooperation of personnel at the U.S. Army Aerial Gunnery School at Harlingen, Texas. For their 1942–1943 production season, the team's rationale for incorporating wartime elements into their proven action formula remained simple, as explained by *Variety*'s Whitney Williams:

> [The] producers, with a war raging, decided to bring in the war, but not in such a way that their pictures would be straight war melodramas, which they felt were on the wane. They hit upon a happy

medium—using some part of the service to background their plots but with the action always taking place on the training end, before the war was brought in.... Producers never plan too far ahead on this type of feature, frequently selecting their next picture from some story which appears in newspapers.[5]

William H. Pine, who also directed the film, had secured the cooperation of Jack F. Dailey, a former writer in Paramount's publicity department currently serving as Public Relations Officer at the gunnery school, as technical adviser. Production began on October 21 and wrapped in mid–November 1942. Amelita Ward, who made her debut in this film (and later married "*Dead End* Kid" Leo Gorcey), was "discovered" in Harlingen. Appearing in his third film, Robert Mitchum briefly plays the uncredited role of Sergeant Benson.

Aerial Gunner (1943): Chester Morris, Jimmy Lydon, Amelita Ward and Richard Arlen in the poster art for the Pine-Thomas production made in cooperation with the U.S. Army Aerial Gunnery School at Harlingen, Texas [original one-sheet poster].

8. Aerial Gunner

Aerial Gunner is the only Arlen-Morris film in which Chester receives first billing. A written prologue states, "This is the story of the aerial gunner … trigger man on whose sighting eye and steady finger depends the life or death of the bomber. To him—to Tail-End Charlie—this picture is dedicated."

From his hospital bed, Lieutenant Jonathan ["Jon"] Davis (Arlen) informs his commanding officer that he and mechanic Private Lancelot ["Gadget"] Blaine (Dick Purcell) are the only men from his flight unit to survive a bombing mission over Japanese territory. In a series of flashbacks, he recalls his East Coast experiences with Sergeant "Foxy" Pattis (Chester), a "typical slum kid, kicked around from the start" who "had a chip on his shoulder against the whole world." Pattis' father "was in the pen most of the time," while Davis' was a school principal.

While serving as a district attorney, Davis questioned the elder Pattis, who then committed suicide. At a Coney Island shooting gallery, Davis attempts to apologize to Pattis, who claims, "Every time the old man would get a job, you'd show up and they'd bounce him. You never let him forget for a minute that he was an ex-con. You hounded him to death!" Pointing a rifle at Davis, he adds, "Someday I'm going to get you, just the way you got my old man."

"The Japs might beat you to it," Davis, who has just enlisted in the U.S. Army, responds. To Pattis, "any guy who'd enlist would be a sucker." Davis completes flight training at Kelly Field and is assigned to the Harlingen Gunnery School, where he is stunned to learn that the "aviation weapons instructor" is none other than Foxy Pattis. While on 24-hour leave at the family ranch of recruit Sanford ["Sandy"] Lunt (Jimmy Lydon), the two men naturally vie for the affection of Sandy's sister, Peggy ("Lita" Ward).

During final testing for the gunners, Pattis rigs a moving target, hoping that Davis will fail, but is knocked unconscious on top of the speeding vehicle. Davis heroically saves Pattis, and they proceed to the airborne gunnery trials, during which Sandy, whose father died at Pearl Harbor, is fatally injured. Unaware that her trepidatious brother, refusing the instructor's advice to seek a "more appropriate" Army job, had given their father's military medal to him just before dying, Peggy blames Pattis, breaking off their engagement.

Davis is assigned to the South Pacific, where Pattis becomes the tail-gunner in his crew. Shunned by the other men, who also believe he was responsible for Sandy's death, Pattis gives Davis a letter from Peggy revealing the truth about the accident before ultimately saving his life (and that of Blaine) by singlehandedly fighting off a Japanese attack until they can get their downed plane back into the air. Hit by a grenade blast, Pattis dies clutching the medal given to him

Aerial Gunner (1943): Paramount publicity portrait of Chester Morris as Sergeant "Foxy" Pattis.

by the dying recruit. "So long, sucker," he says as Davis hits the blue. "How we doing, Sandy?"

During a major gas shortage in November 1942, Chester joined a group of fellow actors in his neighborhood to form the Brentwood Service Players, Inc. Donating their own money to rent a small theater in a Hollywood suburb, they began developing adaptations of popular plays as a "means of neighborly entertainment." Executive secretary Laraine Day welcomed the participation of an impressive lineup, including Binnie Barnes, Lee Bowman, Phyllis Brooks, Billie Burke, Eduardo Ciannelli, Philip Dorn, James Ellison, Cary Grant, Irene Hervey, Ruth Hussey, Allan Jones, Otto Kruger and Richard Whorf, who agreed to rotate as stars, bit players, stagehands, ushers and ticket sellers.[6]

Columbia hired a new writer, Howard J. Green, who worked from an original story by Aubrey Wisberg, to create the screenplay for the next "Blackie" series entry, tentatively given the unimaginative title "Boston Blackie in Trouble," directed by Lew Landers from November 13 to December 12, 1942. Less comical and shorn of the witty dialogue of the Yawitz efforts, this is a somewhat darker film, with two on-screen murders and more references to the World War II home front (though, as in the previous Blackie films, the Axis powers are not mentioned by name). The "usual suspects" in the cast are joined by (former Jumbo Madigan) Cy Kendall, as thoroughly unpleasant jewel thief and killer Joe Herschel, and Ann Savage (two years prior to her *femme fatale* role in Edgar G. Ulmer's *Detour* [1945]) as Betty Barnaby, daughter of "Diamond Ed" (Walter Baldwin), who, just sprung from prison, plans to give to her his hidden stash of ice.

"Blackie ... he's a great guy," says Barnaby to the State Prison warden (Robert F. Hill), discussing how the former inmate kindly donated a "raft" of uniforms to the baseball team behind the walls.

Retitled *After Midnight with Boston Blackie*, it became the first Columbia film in which Blackie is referred to as Horatio Black, when a train porter (Sam McDaniel, brother of Hattie) attempts to deliver a telegram from Betty Barnaby, asking him to meet her upon his arrival back in the city. Farraday and Mathews are also on board and naturally stick in their copper noses. "Ain't heard anybody call you Horatio in years," observes the Runt.

Green's screenplay includes considerable material on the Blackie-Runt relationship, highlighted by several attempts by the little man to marry Dixie Rose Blossom (Jan Buckingham), a dancing girl a head taller than he, who winds up arrested for bigamy by Farraday. Earlier, complaining that he is supposed to be saying his vows, Dixie asks Runt, "Who's the boss here: Blackie or me?"

About to leave Manleder's apartment with his *boss*, Runt counters, "Where Blackie goes, I gotta go."

Green's criminal material, particularly the murders committed by Herschel (one involving his shooting Diamond Ed in the back), lends the film a decidedly different mood than the previous series entry. The wartime elements add not only a more topical tone, but also provide content for comedy (the burning of blackout curtains in Farraday's office) and an action-packed dramatic escape by Blackie during an actual blackout, when the resourceful detective subdues the three criminals.

One scene harks back to the conclusion of MGM's *Pursuit* (1935) when Chester enacts a sign-of-the-times maneuver in which Blackie applies blackface (carbon from a car's exhaust pipe) and grabs the instrument of a bass player (Dudley Dickerson) to elude Farraday's net and sneak into the stage door of a club. Inside, he ducks into a dressing room, where an African American singer (Marguerite Whitten) inquires whether he is "putting

After Midnight with Boston Blackie (1943): As Horatio Black, Chester Morris dukes it out in the original poster art [original 30 × 40 poster].

on makeup or taking it off?" As in the earlier film, Chester doesn't belabor the now-politically incorrect business. (The previous year, even Bing Crosby, whose championing of his friend, Louis Armstrong, led to the latter's casting in Paramount's *Pennies from Heaven* [1936], had worn blackface in *Holiday Inn* [1942], directed by Mark Sandrich.)

This fast-moving, well-balanced feature culminates with Farraday's apprehension of the bigamist, who has at least two husbands in different cities. Referring to Runt, she confesses, "Whatever happens to me now, it'll be better than being married to that miniature screwball." Admitting that Farraday has saved him on this occasion, Runt again is pleased to be back with Blackie.

On November 28, 1942, Chester's *Wagons Westward* costar Buck Jones, who had been in Boston during a War Bonds sales campaign, became trapped in a raging fire at the Cocoanut Grove nightclub. He was enjoying dinner with his manager, Monogram Pictures Vice President Scott R. Dunlap, local industry executives and exhibitors when an artificial palm tree burst into flames. Attempts to extinguish it failed, and soon a large fireball and cloud of toxic gas exploded across the room. The capacity crowd panicked, resulting in 492 total casualties, including most of the two-dozen people in Jones' party. Dunlap was reported "near death" but ultimately survived, while Jones, suffering severe smoke inhalation, scorched lungs, and third- and second-degree burns to his face and neck, died two days later at Massachusetts General Hospital. He was 50 years old.

Ten months earlier, on January 16, 1942, another of Chester's costars, Carole Lombard, just 33, also had been killed while in home-front service. After traveling home to Indiana for a War Bond rally, she was anxious to return to Los Angeles. Rather than take the scheduled train, she persuaded her mother and Otto Winkler, her husband, Clark Gable's, press agent, to join her aboard a Douglas Sleeper Transport plane. Following a refueling stop at Las Vegas, the pilot, unable to navigate properly due to wartime blackout precautions, crashed into Potosi Mountain three miles outside the city, killing all 22 people aboard, including 15 U.S. Army personnel.

On December 14, 1942, Paramount announced that Chester would appear in the Pine-Thomas production *Alaska Highway* (1943), to be directed by Frank McDonald. When the film was shot at the studio the following month, Chester had been dropped from the cast, headed by Richard Arlen, Jean Parker and Ralph Sanford.

Chester and Lillian both signed on to perform in the USO-Camp Shows musical review "Show Time at the Roxy," which played Army camps throughout North and South Carolina from January 5 to 21, 1943. Near the end of the show's run, Chester responded to an article in *Variety*, in which his letter to the editor was published on January 27:

> In last week's issue you devoted quite a bit of space to the Empire theatre's 50th anniversary. It was nice. It was nostalgic—but it was cruel, for you mentioned most of the actors in the original bill, "The Girl I Left Behind Me," except the leading man! And he scored a great personal hit in the play. And wherever he is now, bless him, I'm sure he's sore as hell at your omitting his name. And so, I'm really writing this for *him*. He was my Dad—William Morris.
>
> *Chester Morris.*[7]

Chester then was scheduled to begin another tour of California camps, opening at Gardner Field in the San Joaquin Valley on Wednesday, February 23. The final performance closed the run at Fort Baker in Marin County on Thursday, March 5.

Between tours, he and Lillian joined in the elaborate celebration of President Franklin D. Roosevelt's 61st birthday on Saturday, January 30, with included events held across both Washington, D.C., and New York City from Friday morning through Sunday. In Washington, Al Jolson served as master of ceremonies and sang several signature numbers during a lavish $10 banquet at the Mayflower Hotel, where James Cagney, Sir Cedric and Lady Hardwicke, Anita Louise, Roddy McDowall, Roy Rogers, Loretta Young and Robert Young were among those creating a "riot of applause." Cagney also delivered a three-minute tribute to his fellow actors who had devoted so much time to entertaining the troops. During an informal tour of Walter Reed Hospital the previous afternoon, Cagney had become overwhelmed while visiting a paraplegic soldier wounded at Guadalcanal, and had to recover outdoors.

Other functions included a White House luncheon, attended by Bud Abbott and Lou Costello, who also appeared at every hotel, the Stage Door Canteen, and during a special program for soldiers at Fort Washington; a USO dance and reception at the Willard Hotel; and performances by the bands of Count Basie, Xavier Cugat and Fred Waring. Even inclement weather and a wartime ban on the "use of motor cars for pleasure," a restriction intended to conserve fuel, did not adversely affect public attendance.

First Lady Eleanor Roosevelt filled in for the absentee President, who would return Stateside on Saturday evening. It was later revealed that, on his birthday, he was aboard the Boeing aircraft *Dixie Clipper*, flying from Trinidad to Miami, Florida, after attending the Casablanca Conference with British Prime Minister Winston Churchill and Free French Generals Charles de Gaulle and Henri Giraud in Morocco. At the Willard USO reception, Mrs. Roosevelt was "aided" by Charlie McCarthy while cutting the birthday cake.

The New York affairs included a $35,000-per-ticket President's Birthday Ball held in the main ballroom at the Waldorf Astoria, where a "mammoth show" featured 300 Hollywood players, comics, dance teams, a 125-strong youth choir, and the orchestras of Carmen Cavallero, Sammy Kaye, Johnny Long, Charlie Spivak and Teddy Wilson. Simultaneous shows were staged in three other rooms: the Latin-American, Lower Basin Street, and the Army and Navy Canteen, featuring Billie Holiday. Top Big Apple performers Oscar Levant, Zero Mostel, Hazel Scott and Gladys Swarthout were supplemented by a Hollywood contingent led by Chester and his good pals, Ralph Bellamy and Humphrey Bogart, Jeanne Cagney, Lili Damita and Jack Oakie. At the Roxy, Guy Lombardo's band backed stunning vocalist Nan Wynn.[8]

Before returning to Los Angeles, Chester costarred with Donna Keath on the Saturday afternoon radio program *Armstrong's Theatre of Today*. The 30-minute program, combining news reported by George Bryan with original romantic dramas performed by Hollywood actors, was broadcast by CBS from 1941 to 1954.

Sharing the airwaves with Charles Laughton and Brian Donlevy, Chester played Lieutenant Masterman in Bill Henry's adaptation of the naval war drama "Stand by for Action" on CBS radio's March 8, 1943, broadcast of *The Lady Esther Screen Guild Theatre*. Laughton and Donlevy reprised their roles from MGM's film version of the previous year, in which Chester's *Society Doctor* colleague Robert Taylor plays Masterman.

Released by Paramount on March 20, *Aerial Gunner* marked an impressive directorial debut for William Pine. He and cinematographer Fred Jackman, Jr., made excellent use of the Harlingen locations and aerial footage for the combat scenes set in the South Pacific. The footage was matched up expertly by editor William H. Ziegler. The technical achievements, necessary to depicting the realistic military milieu, marked a great improvement over the miniatures and back-screen projection used in *Wrecking Crew*.

Motion Picture Daily was impressed by the film's improvement on current military-based offerings:

> With Chester Morris, Richard Arlen, Jimmy Lydon and Dick Purcell portraying members of a bomber crew, and with the resources of the Army's aerial gunnery training division at disposal and generously utilized, this William Pine-William Thomas production is a natural for single bill territory. It represents an advance for the producing twosome whose melodramas have elevated par for that field of entertainment, and it does everything with planes that the super-specials have done,

plus a good many things with the matter of military training methods which they have not.... It is a balanced narrative ... and different enough from the pattern worn thin by overuse for service pictures.

Pine directed the picture, as well as co-producing it with Thomas, and set something of a record for first endeavors in that department of production by turning out a job that would reflect credit upon a veteran.[9]

Film Bulletin's "Denley" called the film a "compact, timely and action-packed programmer ... the best of the Pine-Thomas series to date.... Richard Arlen and Chester Morris give their customary two-fisted portrayals with the latter having a slight edge in the acting division."[10]

The Allied forces had brought the lengthy Guadalcanal Campaign against the Japanese to a successful conclusion in February 1943. Able to establish major ports and air bases on Guadalcanal, they proceeded to the other Solomon Islands, gaining a strategic advantage they held for the remainder of the war. In May, Canadian and U.S. forces were ordered to defeat the Japanese in the Aleutian Islands, where invasions of Attu and Kiska had been used as diversions during the June 1942 Battle of Midway.

A special showing of *Aerial Gunner* was held at the Arcadia Theatre in Harlingen, Texas, on May 8, 1943, capping off a weeklong drive to sell War Bonds. This "celebration encompassing the entire Rio Grande Valley" attracted Pine and Thomas, Chester, Marjorie Reynolds, Barbara Britton, Johnnie Johnson and Gil Lamb from Paramount to make personal appearances at the screening.

Also attending were Texas Governor Coke R. Stevenson, General Gerald C. Brant, head of the Gulf Coast Air Training Center, and his chief of staff, General O.C. Carter. A contingent from Mexico included Governor Magdelino Aguilar of Tamaulipas, Governor Benecio Lopez Padilla of Coahuilla, Governor Eulogio Ortiz, chief of the Northern Mexico military section, and Governor General Bonifacio Salinas Leal of Neuvo Leon.

Seats were reserved for patrons who purchased bonds during the drive and a "souvenir ticket at regular admission prices."[11] The event, lasting two days, included breakfast for visiting members of the press; full-dress military review commanded by Colonel J.R. Morgan; luncheon at the Gunnery School Officers Club; parade featuring defense guards, motor corps and 26-piece military band; plane tours; international reception and street dance with music provided by a Mexican group; and a broadcast of Interstate Theatres' *Showtime* program on KGBS radio.

To officially commemorate the May 8 premiere, the Rio Grande Valley newspaper *Morning Star* published a special 32-page *Aerial Gunner* edition. Chester and Marjorie Reynolds rode together in an open convertible during the parade and teamed up for the 60-minute War Bond rally. The premiere seating alone (1,800 tickets) brought $50,000 in bond sales.

Prior to two screenings of the film, the first of which began at 7:30 p.m., a reception for all the guests was hosted by the Harlingen Chamber of Commerce at the Madison Hotel. The dance, illuminated by anti-aircraft searchlights, was held in front of the Arcadia Theatre until 10 p.m. The 30-minute *Showtime* program, featuring all the stars, was broadcast at 3:30 p.m. on Sunday, followed by a wild-game dinner at Matamoras, Mexico. Over the weekend, several thousand visitors joined the 16,000 residents of the town.

The "western premiere" of the film, attended by Colonel Martinus Stenseth, his officers and enlisted men, was held at the Las Vegas Army Gunnery School on Tuesday, May 18. That evening, the nationwide radio program *Johnny Presents Ginny Simms*, starring the popular singer-actress, was broadcast from the military post. Chester, William Thomas, Richard Arlen, Amelita Ward, Jimmy Lydon, Dick Purcell, Billy Benedict and Ralph Sanford all joined Simms for a special show staged for Gunnery School personnel.

From March 25 through early April 1943, Chester costarred with Nancy Kelly (who replaced Sylvia Sidney) and William Henry in Pine and Thomas' "Black Tornado," directed by William Berke from yet another Maxwell Shane screenplay. Prior to production, the producers reportedly "borrowed practically every wind machine" in Los Angeles to use during the shooting of the storm scenes.[12]

A ferocious tornado strikes the coalmining town of Linden, Illinois, on July 6, 1939, wiping out the new home of mine owner Pete Ramsey (Chester), who recounts events from the previous year. Footage from a 1939 Texas tornado, plus special-effects footage shot at the Fine Arts Studio in Hollywood, were incorporated into the storm sequences.

Ramsey, like the men in his employ, began his career working in the Linden mine. At the local tavern, he fell in love with social-climbing singer Victory Kane (Kelly). When Sally Vlochek (Gwen Kenyon) was blinded after being brought into the mine by Bob (Henry), Ramsey's younger brother, he was threatened by her father, Big Joe (Nestor Paiva). Ramsey's response during the accidental explosion earned him a promotion.

Victory agreed to marry Ramsey, encouraging him to become a "coal baron." His ambition was met with antagonism from both Linden and his fellow workers. After Charlie Boswell (Joe Sawyer), disabled by the explosion, was demoted by Ramsey, he committed suicide. Victory was bequeathed Charlie's property, on which Ramsey discovered enough coal to open his own mine.

Convinced by Gary Linden (Morgan Conway) that Ramsey was responsible for blinding Sally, Big Joe agreed to dynamite his mine. Many relationship complications, including an affair between Victory and Gary, set in, resulting in a massive explosion trapping Pete, Bob and Big Joe in the Ramsey mine. After being freed, Ramsey returned home to find Victory with Gary, whom he tossed out. The tornado hit, destroying the house and killing the adulterous couple. Ramsey, ending his flashback recollections, then begins a new life with Sally.

The dramatic relationship twists in Shane's screenplay are an improvement over the three previous Pine-Thomas offerings. As Pete Ramsey, Chester demonstrates some emotional range; and, in one scene, he shows his skills as an illustrator when Pete sketches Victory at the tavern. The supporting cast, including the ubiquitous Joe Sawyer, is solid, with Kelly also performing two original songs, "I'm Afraid of You" and "There Goes My Dream," by composer Frederick Hollander and lyricists Ralph Freed and Frank Loesser (respectively).

For the film's August 1943 release, Paramount shortened the title to *Tornado*. *Variety*'s "Walt" noted the greater development in the writing department:

> *Tornado* is a well-told and neatly paced melodrama that will catch plenty of datings as a strong dual supporter.... Maxwell Shane has devised an interesting script, which is unfolded at a fast and consistent pace by director William Berke. Morris capably handles the lead spot, with Miss Kelly okay as the scheming and opportunist wife....[13]

In late June 1943, Paramount announced another contract with Pine-Thomas, this time requiring a year's commitment of eight features, including three pairing Chester with Russell Hayden. On June 28, Chester supported Barbara Stanwyck in a reprise of her Hannah Sempler Hoyt role in the Paramount film *The Great Man's Lady* (1942), broadcast on

Tornado (1943): From left, bottom shot, Chester Morris, Nancy Kelly and Bill Henry in the poster art for the Pine-Thomas production depicting events before and after a ferocious twister strikes the coal mining town of Linden, Illinois, on July 6, 1939 [original one-sheet poster].

the CBS program *The Lux Radio Theatre*. Directed by Sanford Barnett from a George Wells adaptation of W.L. River's screenplay, the show, hosted by Cecil B. DeMille, also featured Joseph Cotten and Ruby Dandridge.

At the Los Angeles Wilshire Ebell Theater on July 16, Chester joined other members of the Pacific Coast Association of Magicians to perform a full evening's program. The *Los Angeles Times* singled out the Mysterious Morris:

> Movie glamour added to magic certainly adds up to something. So, it isn't surprising that a huge crowd attended the show....

And the movie folk who took part didn't trade on their film glamour, either, but produced one of the best magic shows the old town has seen.

Chester Morris naturally was one of the particular drawing cards and proved himself an excellent showman. His humor helped a lot, too, what with his burlesque trick bits and his gentle kidding of the audience.[14]

Columbia relied on Paul Yawitz to contribute another detective series script for "The Gamble of Boston Blackie," which began shooting on July 26, 1943. Making his directorial debut, William Castle assembled the usual suspects (Chester, George E. Stone, Lloyd Corrigan, Richard Lane, Walter Sande; and back as "Jumbo Madigan" after playing the killer in the previous entry, Cy Kendall) for a plot involving Blackie's selfless effort to obtain paroles for convicts who can be put to better use producing war-related materiel at Arthur Manleder's Tool and Machine Company.

Yawitz again integrated effective comedy into his depiction of a serious subject (the first in the series directly tied to the war effort), with Blackie and the Runt having a field day donning several disguises (including those of carpet movers, police officers and old scrubwomen) to elude Inspector Farraday and Sergeant Mathews and retrieve $60,000 that two criminals, "Red" Taggart (John Harmon) and "Nails" Blanton (Douglas Fowley), are attempting to grab from Dooley Watson (Erik Rolf), their former accomplice and one of the parolees whose actions could doom the noble home-front experiment, "the advance guard that the whole nation will be watching." During a scuffle, Taggart is killed by his own gun, and Blackie gallantly takes the rap to save the project.

Yawitz's script again features some memorable dialogue. At one point, Blanton, with his extortion scheme about to fall apart, accuses, "You've been seeing too many *bad movies*, Blackie."

Supported by Manleder and their group of parolees, the intrepid duo wrings a confession out of Blanton regarding Watson's accidental shooting of Taggart. Praised by Farraday, they are awarded with a second group of convicts released to aid the war effort.

Also appearing in the cast are Jeanne Bates (in her film debut, as Watson's wife, Mary) and future Western regulars Arthur Hunnicutt (as convict Elwood ["Tex"] Stewart) and Ray Teal (as Policeman Joe). Wrapped on August 9, the film was released as *The Chance of a Lifetime* on October 26, 1943. *Variety*'s "Donn" appreciated the performances:

> Morris does a good job and carries the action throughout. George E. Stone works in some comedy as Morris' right-hand man, and laughs also come through in the work of Lane as the inspector.... Lloyd Corrigan as the harassed plant manager delivers well in a natural comedy role....
> Rolf, as the unjustly accused ex-con, rounds out a well-balanced and capable cast.[15]

On August 25, 1943, *Variety* announced that British comic Sid Field had signed Chester to play the Hippodrome in London, to be followed by a four-week magic tour of the provinces. The possibility of shooting a "Boston Blackie" film set in England also was mentioned.[16] With the war raging, neither of these proposed efforts were realized, but Chester did not rule out playing English music halls at a later date.

On Sunday, September 19, 1943, Chester guested with Stuart Erwin on CBS radio's *Coronet Little Show*. The following evening, he returned to *The Lux Radio Theatre*, to support Rosalind Russell in reprising her RKO film role of Tonie Carter, loosely based on pioneer aviator Amelia Earheart, in "Flight for Freedom." Directed by Sanford Barnett and adapted by George Wells from the Oliver H.P. Garrett–S.K. Lauren screenplay, the program, hosted by Cecil B. DeMille, also included George Brent (in the role originally played by Fred MacMurray).

The Chance of a Lifetime (1943): Chester Morris in the poster art for this Columbia series entry involving the selfless efforts of Horatio ("Boston Blackie") Black to obtain paroles for convicts who can contribute to the war effort [original one-sheet poster].

In October, Pine-Thomas and Paramount announced that Chester would be starring in the upcoming features "Hell's Afloat" and "Tenderloin." The producers still were scouting for a third title to complete their Morris quota in the yearly contract with the studio.

In November 1943, Barbara Barker of Hollywood won a $1 prize for her sarcastic letter, "Well, Why?" submitted to *Photoplay*, in which she asked,

> Why waste ...
> ... Robert Preston in those crummy things with Ellen Drew in them? Is De Mille the only one in Hollywood that recognizes real talent?
> ... perfectly good music on Betty Grable?
> ... sarongs on Maria Montez? On her they look like gunny sacks.

... Chester Morris in "B's"? He ought to get an Oscar for the patience of Job.

... Dana Andrews in second leads? He is certainly better than Henry Hayseed Fonda, but still he plays second fiddle! I don't get it.

... Deanna Durbin in these "I'm twenty-one now" pictures. We believe her. Anyway, she should sing "Begin the Beguine" more often and leave the classics to the prima donnas.

... time? Universal seem to have hit another jackpot in Donald O'Connor. We want to see more of him! Well? What are you waiting for?[17]

The Hollywood Victory Committee announced on November 17 that a drive had begun for "100 star volunteers" to visit every training camp and military hospital in the United States during the Christmas–New Year's week, to entertain the 78 percent of servicemen who would not be issued holiday leave. The first group to volunteer consisted of Chester, Robert Benchley, William Bendix, Kay Francis, Veronica Lake, Fred MacMurray, Harpo Marx, Dick Powell, George Raft, Martha Raye, Dinah Shore and Franchot Tone.[18]

CBS welcomed Chester back for another broadcast of *The Lux Radio Theatre* on November 29. Hosted by Cecil B. DeMille, "The Navy Comes Through," starring Pat O'Brien in a reprise of his Chief Michael Mallory role from the 1942 RKO film version, was directed by Sanford Barnett from an Aeneas MacKenzie and Roy Chanslor script.

On December 3, Chester was the guest of Freeman Gosden and Charles Correll on *The Amos 'n' Andy Show*, broadcast by NBC radio. Frank McDonald began shooting "Tenderloin," set primarily in New York City during 1911, at Paramount on December 10. In writing their "original" story, Howard Emmett Rogers and James Edward Grant borrowed liberally from *Manhattan Melodrama* and *Angels with Dirty Faces* in devising the plot involving three childhood friends who court trouble, again becoming involved in the Tenderloin District as adults.

In 1896, Ross Hadley, Michael McGlennon and Mary Hayes are entertaining some locals by singing "East Side, West Side, all around the town" when Ross lifts a wallet from the pocket of a wealthy resident. He is sent to reform school, Mike's policeman father assumes responsibility for his son, and Mary's father, Ulysses Sylvester Rogers (Lloyd Corrigan), promises to take her west with him.

Fifteen years later, Ross, while working as croupier at the gambling establishment of Chappie Wilson (Sheldon Leonard), persuades Faye Lawrence (Lee Patrick), a former bookie's wife, to bankroll his own club. Mike has followed the family tradition of becoming a cop, and Mary, using the stage name Vi Parker, "The Garter Girl," is singing while seated on a suspended crescent moon at Chappie's joint. With Mike's unsolicited help, Ross steals Mary away from Chappie and installs her as singer at his new nightspot.

Ross makes a series of financial and political moves, including paying off Faye, double-crossing "Honest" John McGrady (Charles Arnt), a corrupt alderman, and wangling Mike's promotion to Captain of the Tenderloin District, a position he accepts only on condition that there are "no strings attached." Faye pays Chappie to have Ross murdered, but a police officer is fatally shot during the hit. Mike then raids every gambling joint in the district. Ross, assuming he is immune, is surprised when his club is invaded, and he and his cohorts are hauled off in a paddy wagon.

Ross has Mike busted down to beat cop status, but he soon accepts the position of special investigator for the Citizen's Anti-Crime Committee from prosecutor Thomas J. Dennis (Robert Middlemass). Chappie engineers an elaborate frame of Mike, who is photographed while being set up with a "$10,000 bribe." Ross, who had planned to sail for Florida with Mary, is wounded in a shootout while stealing evidence from the office of

Chappie, whom he guns down. Mike intends to arrest Ross, who turns over the evidence to Mary before toppling from her apartment steps into the street, where he dies, stating that he has disproved his father's prediction that he would end up "in the electric chair."

The electric chair reference is one of many *Manhattan Melodrama* and *Angels with Dirty Faces* elements, which include the relationship between the trio of lead characters (incorporating the obligatory Pine-Thomas "love triangle"), the use of the 1894 song "The Sidewalks of New York," Mike's crusade against Ross, which (like Pat O'Brien's against Cagney in *Angels*) is depicted during a montage of newspaper headlines, and the Ross-Chappie office shootout (clearly modeled on the *Angels* showdown between Cagney and Bogart, incidentally two of Chester's best friends). Screenwriters Maxwell Shane and Irving Reis also paraphrased the final line from Warner Bros.' *The Roaring Twenties* (1939), which features another Cagney-Bogart shootout, concluding with Panama Smith (Gladys George) telling a cop that bootlegger Eddie Bartlett, who now lies dead on the steps of a church, "used to be a big shot." In *Gambler's Choice* (the film's release title), Ross makes the dying declaration that he was about to catch "the Tenderloin by the tail."

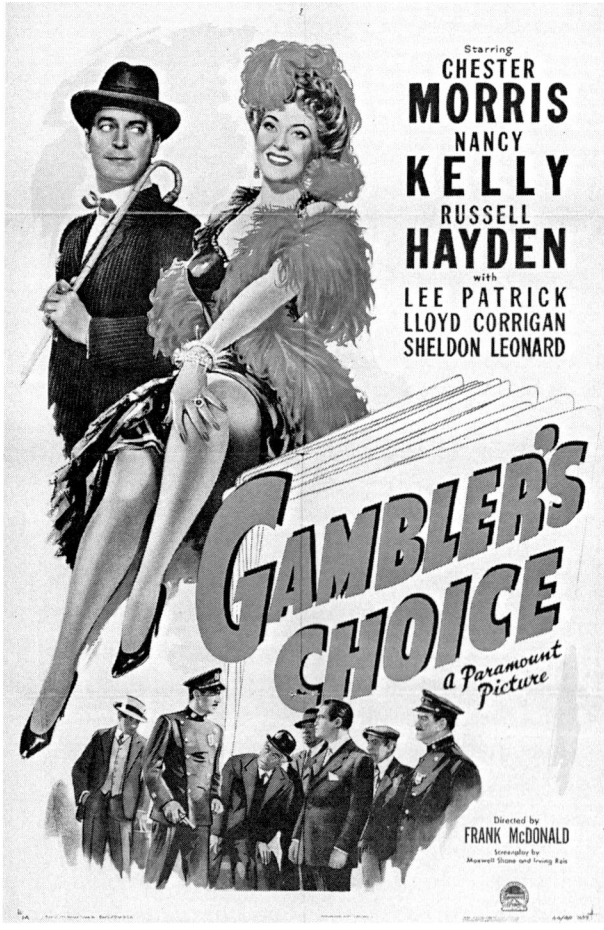

Gambler's Choice (1944): Chester Morris and Nancy Kelly in the poster art for the Pine-Thomas production set in New York's Tenderloin district, borrowing liberally from *Manhattan Melodrama* (1934) and *Angels with Dirty Faces* (1938) [original one-sheet poster].

8. Aerial Gunner

The cast members are convincing in their derivative roles, with Lloyd Corrigan making a non–"Blackie" appearance alongside Chester, who plays Ross Hadley with customary energy. Paramount's April 27, 1944, release received a positive notice from *Showmen's Trade Review*:

> The Pine-Thomas team has drawn a big hand here and the profits that accrue will pass to the exhibitors. Though the story is not new ... the formula has been dressed up to kill and the result has a fillip that makes it a moneymaker. It is striking and entertaining film fare and everyone will enjoy seeing it. The handicaps are the shortness of the film and the lack of big marquee names. Heading the cast, Chester Morris as the tough guy gambler who will do anything to succeed is extremely effective, even to the end where he gives his life for the friends he loves. Nancy Kelly ... does a fine acting job and puts over the songs delightfully.[19]

In January 1944, Pine-Thomas Productions announced that Chester would star in "Thunder Mountain," which eventually was cast with Robert Lowery in the lead role of Forest Service ranger Don Bradley. Released by Paramount as *Dark Mountain*, the film also features Chester's *Alibi* costar Regis Toomey. Dick Purcell, who recently had acted in four films with Chester, also had been announced for the project but died of a heart attack three days before director William Berke began shooting on April 13, 1944.

Representing Terneen Productions, producer Phil L. Ryan, partnered with executive producer Pat O'Brien, hired A. Edward ["Eddie"] Sutherland to direct a wartime project alternately called "Pilebuck" and "By Secret Command" from January 17 to March 8, 1944. Adapted by Roy Chanslor from the John and Ward Hawkins story "The Saboteurs" published in *The Saturday Evening Post*, the production included location work at the California Shipbuilding Corporation ["Calship"] shipyards on Terminal Island, located between San Pedro and Long Beach in Los Angeles County. In May 1941, Calship had been created specifically to build "Liberty Ships," cargo vessels for the U.S. fleet and lend-lease deliveries of war materiel to Great Britain and the USSR.

Costarring O'Brien as Sam Gallagher, foreign correspondent turned undercover agent for U.S. Naval Intelligence, and Carole Landis as Jill McCann, an FBI agent posing as his wife, the film also features Chester in a supporting role as Gallagher's alienated brother, Jeff, who hires him as a pilebuck at the shipyards. An introductory voiceover states,

> Here is a drama of the home front, about the men and women who are building America's Victory Fleet. Ships for guns, tanks and planes. Ships for food and medicine. Ships to bridge the world. Sturdy ships, honest ships, built for America's own fighting forces, to carry them to battle, and to bring them back, victorious.

James Thane (Charles D. Brown) has assigned Sam to investigate potential sabotage at the shipyard, where he ultimately foils a gang of German operatives, led by Colonel Hugo Von Braun, aka "Brownell" (Tom Tully), who are planning to detonate the facilities, including a docked aircraft carrier. In the process, Jeff is seriously injured while trying to repair a sabotaged set of steel beams, and the territorial though loyal pilebuck "Red" Kelly (Barton MacLane), mistaken for Sam, is murdered by one of the Nazi spies. Recovering, Jeff reconciles with Sam and marries Lea Damaron (Ruth Warrick), a woman both brothers had loved. Reassigned to Combat Intelligence, Sam, planning to adopt two "cover children," Paul (Richard Lyon) and Joan (Carol Nugent), proposes to Jill, who accepts.

The entire cast gives restrained, believable performances in *Secret Command*, the title under which Columbia released the film on July 30, 1944. Chester's screen time pales to that of "star producer" O'Brien, but his laconic characterization is quite different than those of Boston Blackie and the two-fisted working men of the Pine-Thomas films. The tension between the brothers, due to Jeff's assumption that Sam neglected their mother during her fatal illness, is palpable.

MacLane and Wallace Ford, as Miller, a fellow agent assigned to the shipyard, both provide strong support. Appearing in her 52nd Hollywood film, 25-year-old Carole Landis delivers a strong, mature performance opposite the earnest O'Brien, who was 44 at the time. A stunning beauty whose talent was overshadowed by her physical appearance, she led an unhappy existence wracked by poor health, financial problems and failed romances, ending tragically just four years later when she took an overdose of Seconal at her Brentwood home.

Secret Command, a serious dramatic depiction of a small group of agents battling wartime espionage, features humor only during brief scenes in which O'Brien interacts with the two child actors. The scenes set at the shipyard, particularly the visceral fight sequences, are well-directed by Sutherland, with sharp editing contributed by Viola Lawrence. The technical team of David Allen, Ray Cory, Robert Wright, Russell Malmgreen and Harry Kusnick received an Academy Award nomination for Best Special Effects.

In an advance review, *The Hollywood Reporter* was enthusiastic about the box-office possibilities:

> Gripping, suspenseful action picture which registers solidly as real entertainment of the kind which should go big with today's audiences. Extemely well directed, produced, played and written. With its all-around quality and its name draw, it has every prospect of doing notably well for itself.[20]

Showmen's Trade Review was particularly positive about the cast:

> There is pace to this that builds suspense like a mystery thriller; and it is that pacing, with a tight, fast-moving story, that makes it a fine bet for the top spot in most situations.... The work of O'Brien is restrained and effective in a part that required understatement. Carole Landis ... delivers one of the most accomplished portrayals of her screen career. The other principals, Chester Morris, Ruth Warrick, Barton MacLane, Tom Tully and Wallace Ford are the people they represent, not the performers. It is typical of such excellent work, that we take them for granted because they are flawless.[21]

Chester's consistent off-screen efforts to benefit servicemen and -women had not gone unnoticed. During the year, he and Lillian were honored for their tireless service to wartime causes, including the U.S. military's christening of a B-24 "Liberator" bomber plane as the *Chester and Lili Morris*.

Chester returned to CBS radio for *The Silver Theatre* on March 12, 1944, starring in "Someone Suitable" with K.T. Stevens and the music of Horace Heidt and His Musical Knights. One week later, he again was hosted by Cecil B. DeMille and CBS on *The Lux Radio Theatre*, which continued to broadcast adaptations of feature films from the major studios. Fred MacKaye directed Sanford Barnett's script based on the Daniel Fuchs-Paul Viertel screenplay for Warner Bros.' *The Hard Way* (1943). Joining Chester were Miriam Hopkins and Anne Baxter in film roles played by Ida Lupino and Joan Leslie, respectively.

On April 17, 1944, Chester joined DeMille, Dorothy Lamour and Alan Ladd on the "Coney Island" broadcast of *The Lux Radio Theatre*. Directed by Fred MacKaye, the program was adapted by Sanford Barnett from George Seaton's screenplay for the 1943 20th Century–Fox musical starring Betty Grable and George Montgomery. Following the broadcast, Chester and Ladd mugged and "arm wrestled" for a press photographer. Later in the month, Columbia announced Chester's signing of a contract for three new features.

Oscar ["Budd"] Boetticher, Jr., made his directorial debut shooting "Boston Blackie's

Appointment with Death" at Columbia from May 31 to June 14, 1944. For this series entry, again written by Paul Yawitz, Chester, George E. Stone and Richard Lane were the only regulars reporting to the set. New faces, including Lyle Latell (as Sergeant Matthews), Harrison Greene (as Arthur Manleder) and Joseph Crehan (as "Jumbo" Madigan) replaced Walter Sande, Lloyd Corrigan and Cy Kendall, respectively, and were joined by two lovely young actresses, Janis Carter (as reporter Dorothy Anderson) and Dorothy Malone (in the uncredited role of Eileen, sister of George Daley [Mark Roberts], a hotel manager who becomes fatally involved in the theft of the Blue Star of the Nile diamond).

Yawitz's continuous recycling of the precious-jewel plot began to wear a bit thin with this episode, so Blackie and the Runt's donning of various disguises, appropriating voices intended to fool other characters, and Chester's obvious relish of playing up the humor was increased considerably. His impersonation of "Professor Hunter of Hoover University," involving a gray wig and mustache, spectacles, stooped-over gait and "old geezer" voice (a device he uses in several of the "Blackie" films) elicits the comment, "If you get out of jail, the theater is waiting for you."

In a twist on Farraday's usual condemnation of Blackie as a thief or killer, the Inspector uses his arrest as a ruse to present him with a cop's badge and patrol car, hoping he will draw on his criminal connections to retrieve the purloined diamond. "Whose methods do I use, Inspector, yours or mine?" he inquires.

The plan quickly backfires when Daley is shot down during a fight with Paul Martens (William Wright) and Matt Healy (Robert Williams), his accomplices, and Blackie naturally is arrested for murder. One of the series' most absurdly humorous scenes occurs when Blackie and Runt, having fallen into the hands of the enemy, are tied upside down to a Murphy bed in an apartment closet. After freeing his arms, Runt remarks, "Maybe I should have untied my feet first."

"How could you do that?" asks Blackie earnestly.

Tipped off by the intrepid Dorothy Anderson, Farraday apprehends Blackie, admitting, "Maybe I better hire a detective."

In the back seat of the police car, Blackie, handcuffing the cop to the reporter, informs him, "Sorry, Inspector, but you're interfering with my duties as a police officer." As in all the series films, Chester draws a clear distinction between the broad performance style he uses when Blackie dons a disguise and the straightforward, dry humor that is an essential aspect of the character's personality.

Blackie, tricking Martens and Healy into believing that the diamond is "a hunk of paste," delivers it to Farraday as Runt remains as their hostage. Mathews organizes a police dragnet around the apartment building, and the thieves are rounded up. When the Inspector apologizes, Blackie advises, "If you ever stop misjudging me, you'll make life very dull for both of us." This time, the sleuth cannot resist pursuing the attractive female down the street, but Runt, as ever worried about his "boss," shouts, "Wait for me!" as the film fades out. Columbia, including one reference to the wartime home front (proceeds from the diamond exhibit are intended for the Greater United Nations War Fund) released the film as *One Mysterious Night* on September 19, 1944.

The Film Daily emphasized the film's high points:

> The latest of the Boston Blackie series is rubber-stamp melodrama that succeeds in holding the interest, thanks chiefly to the presence of Chester Morris in the title role....
> The story moves with dispatch under the direction of Oscar Boetticher, Jr. ... Morris plays the leading role jauntily. Of the others Janis Carter catches the eye with her decorative beauty.[22]

One Mysterious Night (1944): Chester Morris, Janis Carter and Richard Lane in the eye-catching poster art for the directorial debut of Oscar ["Budd"] Boetticher, Jr., yet another "Boston Blackie" entry involving the theft of a valuable diamond [original one-sheet poster].

On June 16, 1944, Chester again joined Freeman Gosden and Charles Correll on NBC radio's *The Amos 'n' Andy Show*. He then reported to Paramount for director William Berke's shooting of the Pine-Thomas production *Double Exposure*. Based on a story by Ralph Graves and Winston Miller, the screenplay by Miller and Maxwell Shane begins as a ridiculous comedy about gender roles in the professional workplace and, at midpoint, shifts suddenly into murder mystery mode.

Larry Burke (Chester), editor of the New York–based *Flick* magazine, is ordered by his boss, James R. Turlock (Richard Gaines), to hire Iowa photographer Pat Marvin (Nancy Kelly) after seeing her spectacular photo of an airplane crash. Leaving her boyfriend, Ben Scribner (Phillip Terry), behind, she accepts the job, and Larry, surprised to learn that he's hired a woman, naturally asks her out. At a restaurant, they witness millionaire Sonny

Tucker (Charles Arnt) arguing with his fifth wife, Dolores (Jane Farrar), who ducks into the ladies' room to make her seventh suicide attempt. Following Larry's advice to make the most of opportunities, Pat sneaks in to photograph her lying unconscious on the floor.

At Tucker's apartment the next day, Pat takes his photo and is accosted by the recovering Dolores. When Ben arrives at the New York office, Larry mistakenly believes he is Pat's brother, forcing her to explain the awkward situation to both men. Assigned to produce a "Mystery of the Week" contest in which readers, scrutinizing crime scene photographs, attempt to solve a murder, Pat, assisted by Ben, sneaks back into Tucker's apartment and, dressed in Dolores' clothing, poses as a victim.

Larry, still pursuing Pat, arranges for Ben to be pressed into service as a war photographer in Russia. After Dolores is killed, and the "Mystery of the Week" feature is published, Pat is arrested. Larry tells District Attorney Merkle (Edward Earle) about the phony photo, but Pat is indicted for the murder.

When Tucker reveals a detail about the crime scene not in evidence, Larry mocks up another bogus photo to trick him into making a confession to the D.A. Presumed killed when his U.S. Navy ship was torpedoed, Ben suddenly reappears (with Terry sporting a ludicrous fake beard), accompanied by Natasha, his Russian wife. He punches out Larry, who now has the green light to marry Pat.

The absurd humor of the film's first half (including the characters "breaking the fourth wall" at times) elicited a somewhat over-the-top comic performance from Chester, which is tempered by his more serious approach following Pat's indictment for murder. Nancy Kelly is suitably tough as the 1940s working woman who must deal with the advances of adoring males, including Larry's often unsubtle approach, and she is not afraid to use physical force, if needed, against a fellow female. "Why the whole situation is completely ridiculous," Pat justifiably states to Ben at one point.

Miller and Shane's screenplay features other memorable lines, including Larry's comment to Pat at the nightclub, "Would you like to dance? I doubt there are any suicides going on tonight." Released on December 18, 1944, the film was called "a very amusing opus, marked by good direction, acting and production" by *The Film Daily*.[23]

On June 23, 1944, Chester briefly transformed his most popular character for the NBC radio show *The Adventures of Boston Blackie*, a summer replacement for *Amos 'n' Andy*, on which he was joined by Richard Lane as Inspector Faraday (spelled with one "r") for a total of 13 episodes, the last being broadcast on September 15. Produced by Fred W. Ziv, the series was directed by Don Clark from scripts by Ken Lyons. At the beginning of each 30-minute episode, announcer Harlow Wilcox introduced Chester, describing Blackie as "an enemy to those who make him an enemy, a friend to those who have no friend."

Variety's "Edba" provided a tedious "good" review of "The Canteen Fund," broadcast on July 7, 1944:

> This Fred Ziv package ... patterned after film series, starring Chester Morris in the name role character ... [is] a welcome addition for listeners who go for this brand of melos and whodunits....
> Chester Morris gives a good account as Blackie. Richard Lane gives good support as Farraday. Others are equally good in respective roles.[24]

Chester's nonstop Columbia shooting schedules prevented him from acting in the radio revival the following April, when Richard Kollmar took over the lead role, continuing on the Ziv-syndicated, Mutual, Blue and CBS networks until June 1949.

In early October 1944, Columbia announced acquisition of Richard Wormser's crime story "The Road to Carmichael's," which had been published in *The Saturday Evening Post*. Intended as material for Chester, whom the studio wanted to play U.S. Army Lieutenant Duke Halliday, who doggedly pursues the real culprit after being accused of a robbery in Veracruz, Mexico, the story remained unproduced until RKO bought it in April 1947. Don Siegel, shooting at various times between late December 1948 and the following May, directed Robert Mitchum in the lead role, creating a *film noir* classic released as *The Big Steal* on July 1, 1949.

Hoping to reignite the appeal of the classic Victor McLaglen and Edmund Lowe teaming in such carousing military buddy classics as *What Price Glory* (1926), *The Cock-Eyed World* (1929), *Women of All Nations* (1931), *Hot Pepper* (1933) and the more-recent *Call Out the Marines* (1942), Columbia paired McLaglen with Chester (a decade younger than Lowe, and receiving top billing) in "Men of the Deep," directed by Del Lord from November 15 to December 7, 1944. The original screenplay by Edward T. Lowe received the endorsement of the Salvage Division of the U.S. Army Corps of Engineers, who aided Columbia in producing the film.

Brad Crowder (Chester) places his marine salvage company at the disposal of the U.S. Army, but is refused an expected officer's commission. Crowder's friend, Owen McCarey (McLaglen), a sergeant in the reserves who works as a diver for the company, elects not to attend training with the rest of the employees. While diving, he is pinned between two steel girders, but is rescued by Crowder. The typical competition for the same females, including their childhood "tomboy" pal, Jo Matheson (Jean Rogers), leading to insubordinate brawling, constitutes much of the plot (with similarities to Chester and Richard Dix's relationship in *Devil's Playground*).

Aboard the *August*, they are ordered to work together during a voyage to an island near the Japanese mainland, where McCarey must dive to detonate a sunken enemy ship. Attacked by Japanese planes, the damaged ship slides off an underwater shelf, trapping McCarey, whose air hose becomes wrapped in the craft's propeller. After the doomed diver asks the captain of the *August* to abandon him, U.S. aircraft reach the scene and Crowder again submerges to save his comrade. When he is knocked unconscious by a plummeting propeller, Crowder is then rescued by McCarey, who swims with him to the surface. Crowder is awarded his officer's commission, also predicting accurately that McCarey will be unable to "swear off women for life."

Released as *Rough, Tough and Ready* on March 22, 1945, the highly derivative film, also featuring *Aerial Gunner* veteran Amelita Ward, hit its mark with *The Film Daily*:

> Remember the well-worn yarn about the two buddies constantly at odds over dames? It used to be a common plot of the Victor McLaglen-Edmund Lowe pictures. Here it is again in up-to-date dress. Old though the story is, it still has possibilities for entertainment. The latest version succeeds in capturing the lusty, punchy fast-paced quality that has made the story so long a favorite of film fans.
>
> McLaglen has the same sort of role he had in his teamwork with Lowe, but has Chester Morris as his counterpart.... Morris' femme swiping causes a rupture in his friendship with McLaglen, but at the wind-up all's hunky-dory again when Morris saves his buddy's life in the service.... The acting suffices for a picture of this kind....[25]

Charles Ryweck, in his *Motion Picture Daily* review, noted,

> With a nod in the direction of the Army Engineers Repair Service, Columbia has almost completely bypassed that branch of the service, using it merely to launch into a recital of the doings of that scrap-happy pair, Chester Morris and Victor McLaglen. What results is a lively little film that will appeal chiefly to the masculine mind.... Del Lord has directed briskly, with an eye for action.[26]

Continuing his performances for the troops into another New Year, Chester joined Mischa Auer and Jerry Colonna to appear with the U.S. Army's "Shot from the Sky" show at Long Beach in early January. The Hollywood Victory Committee continued to step-up its efforts, including an expanded schedule of entertainment at military hospitals and a new list of screen stars to perform during transcontinental radio programs on behalf of the annual Infantile Paralysis Foundation drive. A Blue radio network program from the White House featuring Margaret O'Brien and First Lady Eleanor Roosevelt was broadcast on January 18.

Steve Cochran, 27 years old and newly under contract to Samuel Goldwyn, was loaned out to Columbia for *Boston Blackie Booked on Suspicion*, which director Arthur Dreifuss began shooting on January 23, 1945. The darkly attractive, naturalistic actor already was displaying his prodigious talent for playing heavies, having performed in just one previous film, Goldwyn's *Wonder Man* (1945), costarring Danny Kaye and Virginia Mayo, which was released shortly after the "Blackie" episode. (At this time, Kaye and his wife, Sylvia Fine, were living in Chester's former Beverly Hills residence, which he was leasing to them. Actress Ann Miller would subsequently purchase the property.)

Cast as Jack Higgins, the safecracking, escaped convict husband of Constance Gloria Mannard (Lynn Merrick), partner in a book-counterfeiting scheme to defraud businessman Wilfred Kittredge (George M. Carleton), Cochran proves one of the "Blackie" series' most effective villains, capping off his crime caper by throwing a few haymakers, twice tumbling over a sofa, with Chester.

Another Paul Yawitz screenplay, blending humorous situations with the major crime plot, this time eschewing diamonds for a bogus "one of a kind," signed first edition of Charles Dickens' *The Pickwick Papers*, offers Chester several opportunities for impersonations: a reprise of his bent-over old man (as

Rough, Tough and Ready (1945): From left, Victor McLaglen, Chester Morris and Veda Ann Borg in a carousing military "buddy" film intended to reignite the appeal of the classic McLaglen and Edmund Lowe formula in such films as *What Price Glory* (1926) and *The Cock-Eyed World* (1929) [original insert poster].

Boston Blackie Booked on Suspicion (1945): From left, Chester Morris, Lynn Merrick and Steve Cochran in the Columbia series entry involving "Blackie's" attempts to foil a book-counterfeiting scheme [original lobby card].

he doubles the ailing Kittredge, ordered by his doctor to remain in bed for a week); a clever masquerade as a photographer to escape from police headquarters; and another (albeit brief) blackface episode. Supporting Chester, George E. Stone and Richard Lane, Lloyd Corrigan is back as Arthur Manleder, but Sergeant Mathews is now played (in even more obtuse fashion) by Frank Sully, whose one overt mannerism is constantly, happily chewing on a big cigar.

Chester again enjoyed the various bits of comic business, including Blackie's interplay with Manleder and advising Farraday to "lock up" the Runt to prevent him "from roaming the streets." Unlike the earlier series entries, this outing depicts Blackie's sidekick operating independently, continuously returning to Kittredge's bookstore to find "his boss," who, much of the time, is disguised as the bookseller. Captured and tied up by Higgins, Blackie sings the lullaby "Go to Sleep, My Baby" to the fugitive's big-lug stooge, "Diz" (George Lloyd), while burning through the rope with ashes from his stogie. (Though he was a heavy cigarette smoker, and used a pipe in several films, Chester never favored cigars.)

Tracking down Jack and Gloria, Blackie tricks her into writing a confession to the murder of counterfeiter Porter Hadley (George Meader). After she burns it, he fools her a second time, as she stammers out the truth to Farraday. The Inspector confirms Blackie's innocence; and, as they reflect on their long association, the latter remarks, "To be friendly with you for 15 years, I'd have to be nuts!"

Both Chester and Frank Sully suffered minor injuries after falling 20 feet down an incinerator chute specifically built for shenanigans involving Blackie and Mathews. As Sully gripped his feet, Chester slipped, causing them both to tumble. Landing on top of his colleague as they hit bottom, Chester escaped with minimal bruising, but Sully sprained his wrist and wrenched his back. Treated at the studio hospital, Sully was ordered to rest a half day before returning to work.

On January 27, Chester had signed another Columbia contract, agreeing to appear in four more films during 1945 and 1946. Arthur Dreifuss began shooting the next "Blackie" film, "Shadows in the Night" (aka "Surprise in the Night"), immediately after wrapping *Booked on Suspicion*. (*Shadows in the Night* is a "Crime Doctor" film starring Warner Baxter released by Columbia in 1944.) The studio, impressed with the performance of Steve Cochran, retained his services, casting him as psychotic strangler Jimmy Casey, freshly escaped from a sanitarium.

The screenplay for "Surprise in the Night," written by series newcomer Edward Dein, includes more comedy than any other previous film featuring Blackie and the Runt. Dein, who later became a director, had been writing scripts for B films at PRC, RKO Radio and Universal for the past three years.

Dreifuss shot the production from February 15 to March 2, 1945. Chester, George E. Stone, Richard Lane and Frank Sully all were back in their respective roles, but Harry Hayden took over for Lloyd Corrigan as Arthur Manleder. Cochran's Casey is Manleder's unfortunate "homicidal maniac" nephew who initially appears sympathetic when sneaking into Blackie's hotel room, but quickly reveals his true nature as a psychotic strangler. Nina Foch, quite busy at the studio playing female leads in B pictures, including the horror thrillers *Return of the Vampire* (1943), starring Bela Lugosi, and *Cry of the Werewolf* (1944), appears as Sally Brown, a young dance-hall hostess who had been corresponding with Casey during his time at the sanitarium.

The Runt, pleased to see his pal after an extended absence, happily snuggles into his bed right across from that of Blackie. "I missed you like a mother," the little man admits.

Released as *Boston Blackie's Rendezvous* on July 5, 1945, this film is the first in the series to feature murder as its modus operandi, rather than depicting the more serious crime as a circumstance wrought by other illegal activities such as theft, counterfeiting or kidnapping. When the Runt expresses concern that Farraday again will accuse his "boss" of wrongdoing, Blackie, phoning the Inspector, nobly replies, "A girl's life is involved. Nothing else matters."

Lane, delivering Dein's dialogue, makes Farraday more sarcastic than ever. The Inspector, of course, holds Blackie responsible for all the mayhem, now adding maniacal killing to his imagined criminal resume. Ready to arrest the innocent man once more, he explains, "You wake up some morning, and all of a sudden strangling is a lot of fun."

Later, Farraday attempts to question Sally Brown's frightened roommate, Martha (Iris Adrian), who, doubting his identity, refuses access to the apartment. "What do you want me to do," asks the Inspector from the hallway, "put on a uniform and shove myself under the door?" Ever more frustrated with Blackie, he threatens, "I'm going to send you to the chair!"

Chester again enjoyed Blackie's various impersonations and hijinks, including performing magic tricks during a police psychiatrist's attempted examination. The disguises

Boston Blackie's Rendezvous (1945): Chester Morris, Steve Cochran, Nina Foch and Richard Lane in the poster art for the first series entry to feature murder as its modus operandi, rather than depicting the more serious crime as a circumstance wrought by theft, counterfeiting or kidnapping [original one-sheet poster].

and mistaken identities go over-the-top this time, with Sally Brown believing Blackie is the strangler, Farraday detaining him *as* the killer, and the strangler directly telling Sally he is the noble sleuth! The one unnecessarily ridiculous comic scene again involves a blackface routine (both Blackie and Runt, trying to pass themselves off as charwomen). Veteran character actor and songwriter Clarence Muse was cast in the thankless role of a hotel porter who thinks they are actual African American women. (Unlike the brief "sign of the times" gags in two earlier "Blackie" films, this gratuitous material goes on far too long, and may have seemed offensive even outside "black neighborhoods" at the time.) "You look awful," observes Farraday. "What is this: Halloween?"

Variety again prosaically praised a "Blackie" cast:

> In addition to some convincing fast action, film also packs laughs aplenty. George E. Stone is noteworthy as Runt, Blackie's aide. Chester Morris is in good form in the title role, with Steve Cochran doing a convincing job as the killer.... Smart use of lights and shadow heighten tension. Pace and production are smooth.[27]

Chester twice had a great on-screen opponent in Cochran, whose real personality belied the slick, iniquitous characters he often played on-screen and the woman-chasing reputation he achieved off-camera. Like Chester, who always happily sent autographed photos to his fans, Cochran personally answered letters from his admirers, especially young people interested in pursuing the theatrical profession. He briefly had worked as a cowboy before gaining acting experience with the Carmel Shakespeare Festival in his native California, the Federal Theatre Project in Detroit, and on Broadway. After his appearances in the two "Blackie" films, Cochran moved on to a contract at Warner Bros., where he played "Big Ed" Somers, the gangster who back shoots the mother (Margaret Wycherly) of psycho supreme Cody Jarrett (James Cagney) in Raoul Walsh's crime classic *White Heat* (1949) and a host of prime *films noir* during the 1950s.

Columbia publicity portrait of Chester Morris (as Boston Blackie, left) and George E. Stone (as the Runt) used to promote *Boston Blackie's Rendezvous* (1945).

He accepted colorful guest roles in many top television dramas (*The Twilight Zone, Naked City, The Untouchables, Route 66, Burke's Law, Bonanza*) and formed his own production company, Robert Alexander Productions. On June 3, 1965, he embarked upon an ill-fated Pacific voyage aboard his private schooner, ostensibly to scout locations for the proposed film "Captain O'Flynn." Tragically he developed an acute lung infection after sailing from Acapulco with his "all-girl crew." By the time the craft was discovered floating off Port Champerico, Guatemala, Cochran had been dead for 10 days, much to the terror of the young Mexican women, who were suffering from exposure. Rumors of foul play swirled around the incident, but no evidence was discovered.

World War II in Europe officially ended with the German unconditional surrender on May 8, 1945. Chester's domestic participation in the USO tours and selling war bonds had reached a high point during 1943. Following Operation Overlord in June 1944, his friend Edward G. Robinson, who had sold bonds and donated $100,000 to the USO, initiated the Camp Shows in Normandy after becoming the first movie star to entertain U.S. troops stationed there.

On May 20, 1945, Chester was back on the commercial airwaves, guest starring with Ann Sothern and Lee Tracy on the "Boy Meets Girl" broadcast of director-host Harold Lloyd's *The Old Gold Comedy Theatre*. Aired on the Blue radio network, this 30-minute program, employing the former silent film star from October 1944 to June 1945, was the comedy equivalent of the hour-long *Lux Radio Theatre*. Introduced by Lloyd as "that sterling artist," Chester was Mr. Robert Law, previously played by James Cagney in the 1938 Warner Bros. film version.

"Lend-Lease Pix Stars to Re-educate Nazis?" queried a headline in *The Film Daily* on May 25. Speaking in Washington, D.C., the previous day, New York Republican Congressman Joseph Clark Baldwin proposed "the lend-leasing of motion picture personalities to work as administrators in the re-education of peoples who have been under tyranny." He believed these individuals would be able "to do more good in inspiring confidence in the Nazi- and Fascist-turned youth of Europe than all the well-known professional educators." He explained,

> It is my proposal that lend-lease be enlarged to include the lending of leading motion picture personalities who are well known and loved in Europe because of their films to liberated countries. I am thinking in particular of such men as Clark Gable, George Brent, Charles Bickford, Spencer Tracy, Chester Morris and Joe E. Brown, all of whom represent America at its best to the peoples of Europe. The morale value of such a lend-lease arrangement would be enormous.[28]

Twelve years after directing Chester in *Blondie Johnson* and *Tomorrow at Seven*, Ray Enright collaborated with him once again, on the comedy "Hail the Chief," which began shooting at Columbia on August 1, 1945. Two weeks later, Japan surrendered following the U.S. detonation of atomic bombs at Hiroshima and Nagasaki, and the official Japanese Instrument of Surrender was signed aboard the U.S.S. *Missouri* in Tokyo Bay on September 2.

Lester Lee and Larry Marks based their original story for "Hail the Chief," which Columbia purchased for $18,500, on experiences they shared during a cross-country train trip. The studio considered Cary Grant and Lee Bowman for the role of Chicago radio writer Barry Cole before casting Dennis O'Keefe, who eventually was replaced by Chester. Janis Carter, who had worked well with him in *One Mysterious Night*, was cast as his girlfriend, Josie Hart.

Barry Cole wants to sign a $1000-per-week contract with Nu-Youth Products but is unable to write without his former partner, Mitchell Raymond (Willard Parker). Barry and Josie trick Mitch into joining them on a Los Angeles-bound train after sparking an argument between Mitch and his fiancée, Marcia Winthrop (Marguerite Chapman). During the journey, they become involved with various relatives, strangers, military members and a pair of investigators, Hopkins (Frank Sully) and Jensen (Frank Jenks), searching for "escaped lunatic" Eustace Hinkelmuff.

While the two radio men are working on the script "The Green Scorpion," Cole is arrested after Mortimer Henley Kayden (Irving Bacon), the conductor aspiring to be a script writer, suggests that he is Hinkelmuff. The investigators then release Cole and arrest wealthy manufacturer Eustace P. Trumble (Hugh Herbert), who is seeking to sponsor a radio show. In Los Angeles, Trumble also is turned loose after the Hinkelmuff family identifies the actual "lunatic" (Jerome Cowan), who has been masquerading as Nu-Youth president A.J. Gunther. The two couples frantically follow Trumble as he boards the *Chicago Limited* to head back east, with Hinkelmuff, having escaped from the authorities, also insuring the conductor an equally wild time on the return trip.

Having enjoyed working humor into his performances as Boston Blackie, Chester appreciated Columbia giving him the opportunity to develop a fast-paced, full-blown comic characterization, combining agile delivery of Jack Henley and Joseph Hoffman's witty dialogue (including references to the studio's "Crime Doctor" and "Whistler" series) with trademark Stan Laurel–like nonverbal expressions and slapstick actions. He also paraphrases a classic Oliver Hardy line at one point when Cole admits, "That Marsha *makes me sick*." The comic highpoint arrives as Chester masterfully builds the intensity of his performance when Cole indignantly responds to Mitch's accusation of being "framed," culminating with a script being ripped to pieces and tossed into the air, nearly inciting a midnight free-for-all in the sleeping car of the train.

Hugh Herbert contributes his signature goofiness to the gallery of unhinged characters, including Jerome Cowan's captivating "lunatic" and Irving Bacon's delightfully suspicious conductor, interacting within the self-contained environment of the train. All the comic mayhem is situated in the immediate postwar milieu, as military personnel (including Dusty Anderson as a WAC) make brief appearances as the train proceeds to Los Angeles. Columbia released "Hail the Chief" as *One Way to Love* on January 9, 1946.

One Way to Love (1946): From left, Janis Carter, Willard Parker and Chester Morris, who appreciated Columbia giving him the opportunity to a develop a fast-paced, full-blown comic characterization.

On August 13, 1945, Etta, aged 79, passed away at Chester's home in Beverly Hills. She also was interred in the family plot with William, Gordon and Adrian at Hollywood Memorial Cemetery. *Variety* published a brief obituary, mentioning her stage work with Daniel Frohman and David Belasco, on August 18.

A Close Call for Boston Blackie (1946), the 10th film in the popular series, was scripted by Ben Markson from a Paul Yawitz story involving Geraldine ["Gerry"] Peyton (Lynn Merrick), a former flame of Blackie's, who attempts to extort money from her father-in-law by claiming the maternity of a co-conspirator's baby. Lew Landers, back in the director's chair, shot the film at Columbia from October 1–13, 1945.

Chester, George E. Stone, Richard Lane and Frank Sully are all back, as the four series regulars are packed into a speeding police car, its siren blasting away as they head toward the scene of a crime. Blackie, in his usual rascal fashion, mentions "Inspector Farraday and his almost human bloodhound, Sergeant Mathews," who is at the wheel.

The small boy, well-directed by Landers, brings a novel element to the series. When Blackie asks the Runt if he is responsible for the child's presence in their room, the little man replies, "If this was one of my ideas, would it be that *good looking*?"

During a police search for the child, as Mathews rummages through a chest of drawers, Farraday orders, "Get away from there! You don't fold a baby up like a shirt!"

The baby also directly inspires the film's disguises. "Why, sure," the Runt tells himself, "Kids eat the same as human beings," just before he dresses in a nurse's uniform and goes out to buy some milk. An absurd scene ensues, during which George E. Stone appropriates a high-pitched "female" voice and actress Ruth Warren, playing the milkwoman, has her voice overdubbed by a male actor as she speaks from inside the truck.

"I love that outfit," Blackie tells the Runt after he arrives. Later (in convincing makeup) Blackie impersonates Cyrus Peyton to foil Gerry's "motherhood" scheme.

Stone enjoys ample comic screen time, during the Runt's female impersonation and by using dogs to flatten Farraday and Mathews so he and his "boss" can make their usual escape from the law. At one point, Runt tells his girlfriend, Mamie Kirwin (Claire Carleton, as usual a statuesque blonde), "We have 150 years in jail waiting for us, and the chair at the end of that."

Frank Sully, too, has his moments as Mathews obtusely "investigates." Called a "mallet head" by Farraday, he observes (while talking to himself), "How does he do it? I'm going to read a book some time and get as smart as he is." The film concludes with the sergeant also disguising himself as Cyrus Peyton. While Chester again uses his stock "old geezer" voice, Sully approximates a stage English accent. Wrapping up the shenanigans, the baby gets the final close-up.

Prior to the release of *A Close Call for Boston Blackie*, Chester and director D. Ross Lederman completed the shooting of another series entry, produced under the working title "Boston Blackie's Private Ghost," from January 7 to 21, 1946. Three screenwriters new to the series, Richard Wormser, Richard Weil and Malcolm Stuart Boylan, adapted an original story by G.A. Snow focusing on the time-honored device of a stolen diamond necklace but incorporating a phony séance racket operated by Dr. Nejino (Marvin Miller). Featured in the cast is the familiar blend of new female blood, in this instance Jeff Donnell (as Anne Parks Duncan, employer of the Runt's pal Eddie Alexander [Murray Alper]) and Dusty Anderson (as Sandra, Nejino's secretary) with regulars Lane, Stone and Sully. Joseph Crehan makes his second appearance as pawnbroker "Jumbo" Madigan (usually played by Cy Kendall).

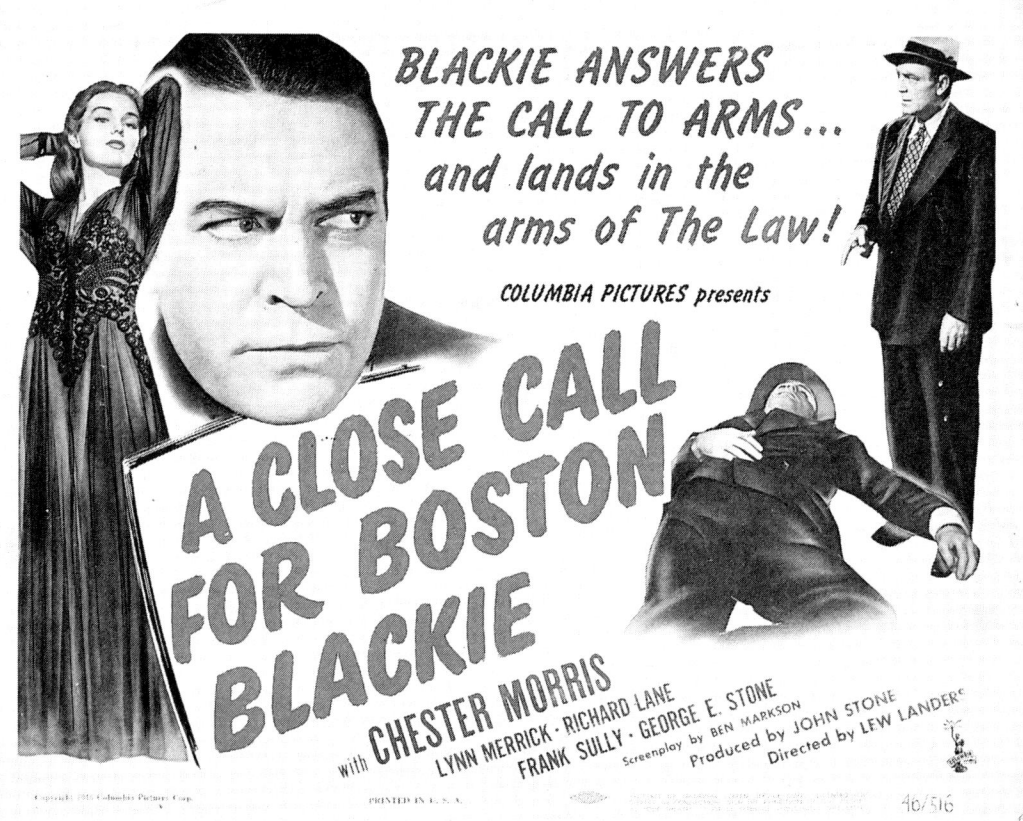

A Close Call for Boston Blackie (1946): Lynn Merrick, Chester Morris and Richard Lane in the 10th film in the popular Columbia series, about a former flame of "Blackie's" who crassly uses a baby as leverage in an extortion scheme [original title lobby card].

Stone enjoys ample screen time courtesy of the fresh writers, further developing the Runt's close personal relationship with Blackie. Resembling a husband, Blackie, entering their apartment, opens the film with the line, "I'm home, Runt. Any calls?"

Frightened during the séance at Nejino's, Runt reminds Blackie, "I'm your pal. You know I love you more than anything in the whole world." Whining his way through much of the film, he is dragged around like a small child by his fatherly friend.

Chester again engages in some "undercover" shtick, as Blackie impersonates a crazed drunk while trying to outwit an "Irish" cop. Farraday and Mathews predictably arrive just after two murders occur in the presence of Blackie, for which he is customarily accused. Outwitting the clueless cops, Blackie hides out *in jail* as the Inspector calls for backup. "I'm going on the principle that two half-wits might make a whole," he explains. As usual, during the final reel, Blackie solves the case to Farraday's satisfaction. "Blackie, with that act of yours," observes the Inspector, "you ought to go on the stage." When the film was released as *The Phantom Thief* on May 2, 1946, *Showmen's Trade Review* was singularly unimpressed:

> These Boston Blackie films seem to fall into the filler class mainly because little effort has been expended to make them anything else. And even in that category, this one is just a standard offering. It is a formula tale about a killing that again forces Blackie to solve the crime just to protect himself.

The Phantom Thief (1946): Dusty Anderson, Chester Morris and Jeff Donnell in the poster art for yet another "Boston Blackie" series entry focusing on purloined diamonds but incorporating the new wrinkle of a phony séance racket [original one-sheet poster].

> There is a certain amount of suspense and excitement to any mystery, and that also holds true for this one.[29]

Chester, who had portrayed many characters on both sides of the law, wrote an article, "Hollywood's Silence on the Crime Wave," published in the *Los Angeles Times* on March 4, 1946. Ten months earlier, Monogram Pictures had released the King Brothers production *Dillinger* (1945), directed by Max Nosseck from a screenplay by Philip Jordan, and starring Lawrence Tierney as the notorious "public enemy." The resulting controversy stirred up by the film prompted Chester to articulate his sociologically based view of the cinema as a potentially noble medium. He explained, in total:

> Although I subscribe to the theory that an actor's mouth has a magnetic attraction for his foot whenever he ventures to speak out on current issues, I feel impelled to have my say on the throttling of Hollywood's throat on the matter of films dealing with the present crime wave.

A picture called "Dillinger" has been responsible for Hollywood's silence on a grave problem which concerns every American. I hold no brief for "Dillinger" and do not wish to take a stand on it, except to point out that it had little or no application to today's crime problem.

But the picture has been used by educators, film opinion groups, parent-teacher associations, women's clubs, religious organizations and other bodies to force Hollywood into an ostrich-like attitude on the growing crime in this country at a time when the screen should be a powerful instrument toward curbing crime.

These groups, I am reasonably certain, had no intention of throttling Hollywood's vigorous voice on important topical matters. Theirs was a protest against the glorification of a gangster era which no longer exists. It was not an objection to serious reporting by the motion picture medium on the causes of present-day crime.

Hollywood, I sincerely submit, wants to hold the mirror up to 1946.

It is, therefore, extremely important that the same groups which decried "Dillinger" now encourage Hollywood to look objectively upon our present crime wave and to report it in motion pictures with accuracy and constructive intent. Our daily newspapers have squarely faced the issue and have sought to show the factors which lead juvenile delinquents, ex-servicemen and the jobless to violate our laws and terrorize whole communities. Radio has attempted to bring the problem to the public through the FBI and police files. The stage has touched upon the subject with honesty.

Hollywood is ready. It remains now for the general public to signify that its objections to "Dillinger" were not intended to silence Hollywood on the tragic story of postwar crime.

The film industry can make a dynamic contribution to the fight against crime by earnest, sincere examination of the economic and social patterns which drive men and women to violation of our laws.[30]

During the previous decade, Chester twice had played undercover federal agents who doggedly hunt down major criminals, including one based on John Dillinger. Published when *film noir* and more violent crime films were becoming increasingly popular (a trend that would not slow down), Chester's comments about the commercial entertainment machine of Hollywood potentially producing non-sensational, serious examinations of criminal activity were honorable but quite quixotic.

On January 13, 1946, Chester joined Edgar Bergen on NBC radio's *The Charlie McCarthy Show*, playing an income tax man investigating the ventriloquist's suspicious activities. On February 25, he performed in "Hair Again for Harrigan" on the *Luck o' the Irish* radio program, and was back with Bergen, this time as an insurance adjuster, on the April 28 broadcast of *The Charlie McCarthy Show*.

In May 1946, Chester and Lillian visited Chicago for a brief vacation. On July 26, Brooks, now age 18, registered for the draft, listing his height as 5'7" (two inches shorter than his diminutive father), weight as 130 pounds, hair color as brown, and eyes as blue.

D. Ross Lederman began shooting the next Boston Blackie entry, tentatively titled "The Clue That Talked" and "Quicker Than the Eye," at Columbia on August 8, 1946. The screenplay, incorporating the *Alias Boston Blackie* premise of staging a benefit show during which an inmate escapes from prison, was tailored by Harry Essex specifically to showcase Chester's talent for magic. Chester even obtained permission from the Pacific Coast Association of Magicians to film the trick of "sawing a woman in half," but the routine does not appear in the finished film (although Blackie is seen with the long saw and wooden box in one scene).

The film opens with Blackie performing a solo Thanksgiving show at the "Women's State Prison," where his use of a cabinet to make a volunteer "disappear" leads to the escape of Dinah Moran (Constance Dowling), who is serving a three-year sentence for her involvement in the theft of $100,000 with her ex-husband, a magician named Lampau (Warren

Ashe), who was acquitted. When a fellow inmate says, "I didn't know Boston Blackie was a magician," Dinah replies, "There isn't a trick he doesn't know."

Inspector Farraday (Richard Lane) naturally believes Blackie complicit in Dinah's escape, although he points out that, having performed the benefit show for five years running, he has no possible interest in such a criminal act. Sergeant Mathews (Frank Sully), forever dumbing down, attempts to inspect the cabinet, but Blackie, eluding him several times, finally escapes police headquarters into a taxi below. Chester's masterful enunciation of the seldom-used word "ventriloquial" is a highlight of the scene, as is Blackie's sarcasm toward Mathews: "You know, you're even going to make a good detective someday."

The majority of *Boston Blackie and the Law*, the title under which the film was released on December 12, 1946, provides Chester with opportunities to flex his magician-ship, and the Runt (George E. Stone, this time sporting the mustache he often wears in non–Blackie films) shares the screen with his "boss" in only a few scenes. "Why can't I go with you?" the little man asks when Blackie prepares to investigate alone.

Blackie, appropriating a "foreign" accent and wearing a turban, mustache and goatee, impersonates Lampau, alias "John Jani," several times, in performance, at his apartment and during a visit to the bank where the magician has stashed the $100,000 in a safe deposit box. While riding in a taxi, he is asked by the cabbie, "United Nations meeting, Sir?" (The U.N. charter had taken effect on October 29, 1945, less than nine months before Columbia began production on "Quicker Than the Eye.")

Jani plans to marry his assistant, Irene (statuesque Trudy Marshall), but, proving a *femme fatale*, she does away with both Dinah and her fiancé. Jailed for the murder of Jani, Blackie and the Runt use a magic routine to escape from the gullible guard, whom they have blindfolded. Tricked by Blackie, who, using ventriloquism, pretends that he has recorded her boastful confession on a phonograph record, Irene is arrested, and the two amateur sleuths again laugh with Farraday into a concluding fadeout.

Charles L. Franke of *Motion Picture Daily* reviewed an advance screening of the film:

> Liberally sprinkling with action, comedy (mostly slapstick) and mysterious doings, this latest edition in Columbia's "Boston Blackie" series rates a place with the better of its predecessors. Chester Morris again renders a neat performance as the roguish sleuth whose abilities prove embarrassing to police inspector Farraday....[31]

With the latest "Blackie" feature in the can, Columbia moved Chester straight on to "Inside Story," former actor-writer Robert Gordon's first directorial assignment, shot at the studio from September 11 to October 2, 1946. Based on an original story by Barry Perowne, Martin Goldsmith's screenplay features Chester as commercially unsuccessful "psychological" novelist Jeffrey Andrews, who, following a lengthy drunken binge, is arrested for the murder of his publisher, Henry Small (William Forrest).

Prevented by alcoholic blackout from recalling the outline for his new novel or the events of the previous evening (during which Small was killed, as proposed in the story, inside a locked room), Andrews sets out to solve both mysteries, which are crucially connected. After suffering a gunshot during a tussle with an overzealous elevator operator (Paul E. Burns), he eventually gathers enough evidence to prompt a confession from Lloyd Harrison (Steven Geray), a mystery writer who stole his novel and murdered both Small and Mike Foster (Sid Tomack), a bartender with whom he had discussed the plot, before trying to throw suspicion on Small's secretary, Evelyn Green (Constance Dowling).

Released as *Blind Spot* on February 6, 1947, the film marked Chester's one venture

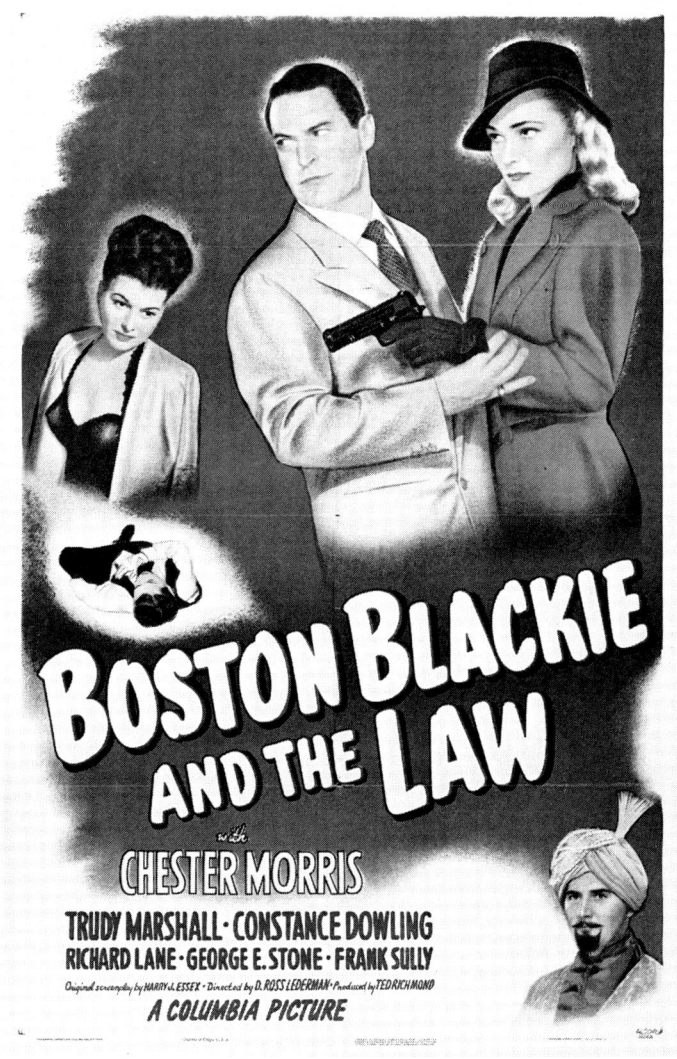

Boston Blackie and the Law (1946): From left, Trudy Marshall, Chester Morris and Constance Dowling in the poster art for the Columbia series entry tailored specifically to showcase Chester's talent as a magician [original one-sheet poster].

into *noir*, featuring his voice-over narration and a challenging characterization ranging from broad, barely coherent inebriation to Bogart-like bitter cynicism after Andrews sobers up. "I don't get drunk very often," he admits. "It's not good for me."

During a lengthy bar scene, Andrews mentions "Sherlock Holmes" and "Humphrey Bogart" prior to a revealing conversation with Evelyn. Shot in a series of close-ups by cinematographer George Meehan, the scene is a high point of Chester's performance, as is a later sequence set in Andrews' dingy basement apartment, where the frustrated writer accuses Evelyn of being guilty of Foster's murder. The *noir* atmosphere also benefits from Meehan's use of subjective camera during the shadowy nighttime scene in which Andrews returns to the murdered Small's office.

Blind Spot (1947): Chester Morris and Constance Dowling in the actor's one venture into *film noir*, featuring his voice-over narration and a challenging characterization ranging from broad, barely coherent inebriation to Bogart-like bitter cynicism.

Constance Dowling's role was a step up from her brief appearance as Dinah Moran in *Boston Blackie and the Law*. Reminiscent of Veronica Lake, she is equally impressive as the cool bleached blonde, bearing the brunt of Harrison's frame-up and Andrews' bad behavior. Born in New York, where she was educated at the New Theatre School, the stunning actress was the older sister of Doris Dowling (*The Lost Weekend* [1945]), who enjoyed a much longer film and television career. Though Constance worked on screen for little more than a decade, she became equally well-known for affairs with director Elia Kazan (who was married) and Italian writer Cesare Pavese (who committed suicide), and her subsequent marriage to writer-producer Ivan Tors. Following a post-film career working as a guide at the "Dolphinarium" research laboratory in St. Thomas, U.S. Virgin Islands, during the 1960s, she died of a heart attack at age 49.

Motion Picture Daily's Irving Kaplan wrote,

> Offering Chester Morris a change of pace from his "Boston Blackie" roles, "Blind Spot" ... is a poor man's "Lost Weekend," complicated by a couple of murders. While there are few subtleties to veil the culprit, the pace of the film is good and the dialogue is above average. Morris turns in a good performance as the creative novelist who is dogged by poverty because he refuses to write for the popular market....[32]

On November 28, 1946, Chester returned to the radio airwaves, joining Hans Conreid and Howard Duff for "The Strange Death of Gordon Fitzroy" on *Suspense*, broadcast by CBS. He also gave a volunteer performance for the Armed Forces Radio Service (AFRS), on *This is the Story*: "Robinson Crusoe, USN," an adaptation of U.S. Navy Radioman George R. Tweed's book recounting his two and one-half years of harrowing experiences from the First Battle of Guam on December 8, 1941, to his rescue on the occupied island's west coast on July 10, 1944.

Chester, who had spent four years performing live, selling bonds and making films to support the U.S. military effort, was pleased to portray a heroic sailor who accomplished a longterm evasion of enemy forces, the only man in a group of five who was not executed (either by gunfire or beheading) after hiding out in the jungles of Guam. His powerful performance provided an excellent example of his facility for radio acting, which required the performer to accomplish all aspects of a characterization, including those achieved nonverbally on film, solely by using the voice. (The book later was adapted for the film *No Man is an Island* [1962], starring Jeffrey Hunter as Tweed.)

In February 1947, Chester signed an agreement, in conjunction with Columbia Pictures Corporation, giving his consent to the Motion Picture Relief Fund, Inc., to use his "autograph, photographic likeness and/or artist's sketch of [his] likeness" for "reproduction on photostamps, gravure, embossed or printed stamps and stamp albums of motion picture celebrities" and for their sale worldwide. The Relief Fund was established to offer assistance and care to those in the motion picture industry with limited or no resources. Class "A" membership in the Screen Actors Guild required compulsory contributions to the charity.

Soon after, the first series of "Hollywood Official Stamps of the Stars and Studios" was issued. Priced at 10 cents for two sheets containing 12 stamps each, the set featured illustrations of Victor McLaglen, Adolphe Menjou, Edgar Kennedy and Groucho Marx, and photographic portraits of Chester, Beverly Simmons, Janet Martin, Claude Rains, "Palomino" (horse), Constance Moore, Frank Sinatra, Kay Kyser, Roy Rogers, Louise Allbritton, Clark Gable, June Vincent, Barbara Britton, Van Johnson, Robert Preston, Dale Evans, Linda Darnell, Ida Lupino, Sylvia Sidney and Phillip Terry.

On February 17, Chester played Gustaf F. Marsh on the "Man Against the Mountain" broadcast of the NBC radio program *The Cavalcade of America*. He again played an insurance adjuster opposite Edgar Bergen on *The Charlie McCarthy Show*, also featuring Anita Gordon, Jack Kruschen, Nelson Eddy and Ray Noble and His Orchestra, aired March 2 on NBC.

Chester proudly welcomed a second son when Lillian gave birth to Kenton Morris on April 20, 1947, at St. John's Hospital in Santa Monica. On May 1, he went back to work, joining Cecil Kellaway, Betty Arnold, Griff Barnett, Francis X. Bushman and composer-musician Meredith Willson in "Mr. Bidderoe's Mission," directed for the Mutual radio network's *Family Theatre*.

On June 4, 1947, *Variety*, reporting on exhibitors' complaints about current Hollywood production, ran the article "Majors' Failure to Develop Stock Stars Leaves 'B' Films Out in the Cold":

> The Bs are taking it on the chin lately at the box office because of a dearth of new bread-and-butter marquee names designed to draw on their own to the scene of the rough-and-tumbles. Failure of the majors to develop new stock star talent ... isn't confined to the region of heavy-budget pix. As with the top bracket films, the studios haven't come across with a single new b.o. power for the Bs since the war began....

> In pre-war days ... the low budgeters which then bulked much higher in the studio's scheme of things, were studded with such names as Edmund Lowe, Victor McLaglen, Chester Morris, Bruce Cabot, Richard Dix and others, all calculated to have their own devotees. These followers were good for dimes and quarters regardless of the pic mazda on marquees....
> Fadeout of some of these names and an exodus of others to greener pastures has left a wide open hole in the roster of steady-drawing names which the majors have failed to plug.... "As soon as a new face shows signs of pulling in the customers," one action peddler said, "the studio ... yanks him into bigger money films."
> Another custom in the trade has the exhibs peeving. That's the business of consigning a star, lock-stock-and-barrel, to a series of pix where the star reprises on the same character. Number of action house operators think that the technique ... of slotting Dix for RKO's Whistler series and Morris on the Columbia chain of Boston Blackie doesn't do the star or the box office too much good.[33]

In their home on Sunday, June 15, Chester, while dancing with Lillian at a Father's Day party held for neighborhood children, slipped and broke his right leg in two places below the knee. The following day, Cedars of Lebanon Hospital reported his condition as "satisfactory." He found the incident, which occurred, not during the performance of a film action scene, but while cutting a rug with his wife, to be quite ridiculous. For some time, his leisure activities were confined to card tricks.[34]

In early September 1947, Rudy Vallee, Ned Bergen and Palm Springs theater maven Earle Strebe organized a "winter strawhat drama company," their version of a summer theater. When they announced that well-known plays would be staged at one of Strebe's local venues, Chester, anxious to get back to work, threw his name in the ring. Other Hollywood notables expressing interest in the November target date were director Vincent Sherman and performers Charles Farrell, Ida Lupino, Paul Lukas, Victor Mature and William Powell.

In October, *Popular Mechanics* magazine published Chester's article "There's Magic Up Your Sleeve," in which he explained the principles of several tricks, including the "Square Circle" and "Center Tear," although he also advised readers "never to give away the secret of any trick that you perform successfully."[35] Chester, whose contribution had been encouraged by the Columbia publicity department, was criticized by some magicians for exposing trade secrets.

Julien J. Proskauer, an amateur prestidigitator and author who served as President of the Society of American Magicians (1935–1936), wrote in the November 1947 issue of *Conjuror's Magazine*, "I state definitely the Chester Morris article is not going to harm magic. It may help it."[36] The following month, *Conjuror's* published Chester's article "Restrained Revealing Helps Magic," in which he argued, "I certainly would not hurt magic in any way, and I want to repeat again that I hope my 'Popular Mechanics' article did plant a seed from which the great magicians of tomorrow will grow."[37]

The International Brotherhood of Magicians and the Society of American Magicians both ruled on the prestidigitators' complaints. As a member of IBM Ring 21 in Hollywood, Chester previously had contributed the article "The Fate of the Fabric" to issue 58 of the magic periodical *The Jinx*. Now, the IBM, in the July 1948 issue of *Linking Ring*, published the "Finding and Judgement of the Ethic and Grievance Committee":

> [B]rother Chester Morris is ... guilty of a violation of his oath as a member ... but in the best interest, both of said member and this Brotherhood, limits the penalty for said violation to a suspension of said brother member from the rights and privileges of membership for a period of six months, effective June 24, 1948.[38]

The Southern California Assembly No. 22, acting for the SAM, judging that his decision "was a hasty, ill-advised and thoughtless act," published its "National Ethics Committee Report on Chester Morris Exposé" in a "Magic-Unity-Might" insert included in *The Sphinx*: "It is the consensus of opinion of our membership that there was no willful disregard of the Society's principles ... that no pecuniary gain was realized by the author; nor has he a record of being a habitual exposer."[39] Chester continued with his amateur and professional magic acts, and shied away from any future "exposure" activities.

Just before the Christmas holiday, Chester announced that he had partnered with English actor-filmmaker Peter Godfrey (who recently had directed Humphrey Bogart in Warner Bros.' *The Two Mrs. Carrolls* [1947]) to develop a magic show that would employ a cast of 15 performers. Tentative plans were made to organize and begin touring with the show after Chester completed the next Columbia "Boston Blackie" assignment.

Chester and George E. Stone made their final joint appearance as Blackie and the Runt in *Trapped by Boston Blackie*, released by Columbia on May 13, 1948. The first film directed by former assistant director Seymour Friedman, it was scripted by Maurice Tombragel from a story by Charles R. Marion and Edward Bock. Having appeared separately in most of the previous series entry, here Blackie (with Chester giving one of his more restrained performances in the role) and the Runt (again sans mustache) primarily work together as a team, and both don a wide variety of disguises during their collective cinematic swansong.

The film opens in domestic fashion, with the sleuthing couple enjoying breakfast together. In their efforts to aid Helen Kenyon (Mary Currier), widow of a deceased friend, in operating her late husband's detective business, they become entangled in the theft of a valuable pearl necklace while attending a costume party disguised as East Indian "mystics." Inspector Farraday (Richard Lane) and Sergeant Matthews (Frank Sully) handle the investigation, resulting in the usual false charges made against the well-intentioned pair.

In the course of events, Blackie and Runt shift from wearing turbans and beards to impersonating an elderly married couple (with Chester doing his "geezer" shtick and George donning drag as "an old hag"). The little man then exchanges his dress for the uniform of a package delivery man and, finally, a taxi driver. To infiltrate the studio of Igor Borio (Edward Norris), the prestigious ballet instructor of Mrs. Claire Carter (Sara Selby), Blackie impersonates a man who "ever since [he] was *that high* ... wanted to dance," and then claims he is an insurance investigator. This content is ironic, considering that Chester recently had broken his right leg while dancing and exhibits a slight limp in the film.

Blackie encounters a bevy of females, Doris Bradley (June Vincent), Joan Howell (Patricia Barry, billed as "Patricia White") and Sandra Doray (Fay Baker), all of whom play a role in the disappearance and discovery of the pearls. Red herrings abound, but the perpetrator proves to be Mason Carter (William Forrest), Claire's penniless husband, who hatched the jewel heist and murdered Joe Kenyon.

Comedy highpoints include Stone's sparring with a large dog after the Runt and Blackie hide in the animal's house to elude Farraday, and Frank Sully's ever-escalating stupidity as Mathews: Phoning the precinct, the Sergeant demands to speak with the Inspector, adding, "and be quick about it!" Following a brief pause, during which he is asked a question by the desk officer, he replies, "Sure, I know *who I am*!"

Variety's "Gilb" focused on the recycled elements in this 13th series installment:

> Lack of originality on the part of the trio of scripters is best revealed by the perennial disguises which, at one point, drape Chester Morris and George E. Stone in beards and Indian turbans, while

Trapped by Boston Blackie (1948): Chester Morris and George E. Stone in the poster art for a series entry in which they don a wide variety of disguises while working together as a cohesive team [original one-sheet poster].

in another scene the pair pose as an elderly couple. This brand of plot technique is pretty much old hat to followers of the "Blackie" melodramas....

Performances are comparable to the thesping found in the average whodunit. Morris is forthright enough as a one-time crook gone straight. Stone is okay as his partner. Both point up their lines for laughs....[40]

On May 18, 1948, just five days after the release of *Trapped by Boston Blackie*, Chester began shooting the final film in the series, "Boston Blackie's Honor," with Seymour Friedman, again working from a screenplay by Maurice Tombragel. After Friedman wrapped the previous picture, George E. Stone had moved on to play "Pablo" in Columbia's *The Untamed Breed* (1948), directed by Charles Lamont from March 25 to April 23, 1948, and then took a hiatus from filmmaking for nearly four years (making only one uncredited appearance, as a film editor, in Irving Reis' *Dancing in the Dark* [1949] at Paramount). Left without his longtime screen partner, Chester teamed with Brooklyn-born character actor Sid Tomack (who had appeared with him in *Blind Spot*) in his sole performance as the Runt.

Blackie and Runt's "domestic" relationship is still intact, but the usual comic hijinks are downplayed in favor of action, namely apprehending the killer of Chinese laundryman Charley Wu, whose niece, Mei Ling (Gloria ["Maylia"] Fong), discovers the body in his Chinatown establishment. Farraday (Richard Lane) naturally detains Blackie, but Mei Ling suspects nightclub owner Bill Craddock (Luis Van Rooten), who also is murdered in the course of events involving hot diamonds, by Pop Gerard (Charles Arnt), who runs the local movie theater.

Chester's final, rough-edged performance as Blackie provides a suitable farewell for the character, whom he was careful to make reasonably distinct from the other roles, notably the rugged Pine-Thomas leading men, he played during the 1941–1948 period. During a scene set at the Cathay Club, as Blackie feigns drunkenness, Chester worked in a humorous reference to magic, slurring the line, "*I'm a prestidigitator*," to which Henry (George Lloyd), the bartender, responds, "I wouldn't know about that. I've always been a Democrat myself."

Tomack, though physically larger than George E. Stone, *sounds* like the Runt moviegoers had come to expect in the long-running series. He and Chester do share a few comic moments, including the duo's masquerade as Chinese actors when they attempt to expose a scam being perpetrated on Chinatown tourists. Wearing a mask and robe, Blackie is described as "a hatchet man running amok" as he and Runt chase down the tour guide who has been fleecing the "yokels."

As "Red, the Bar Girl," Craddock's girlfriend who shills for the tourist racket, Joan Woodbury has few opportunities to make an impression. In his final appearance as the ingenuous Sergeant Mathews, Frank Sully unleashes a zinger after Gerard's diamond-cutting associate, Rolfe (Peter Brocco), is gunned down. Though Farraday requests an ambulance, Mathews, observing the man's actual state, orders, "Get the *meat wagon* for this guy!"

But Tomack gets the last laugh of the 14-film series. Following Blackie's effort to empty all the tea packages in a curio shop to find the diamonds, owner Wong Chung Shee (Philip Ahn) gives him the herbal contents, prompting plans for an evening get-together. "It'll be the biggest tea party in history," announces the little man. "The Boston Blackie Tea Party!"

Several top Asian American character actors fill out the supporting cast. Ahn, though hampered by a less-than-convincing Bob Mieding age makeup, lends his mysterious presence to Wong, whose specialty tea is being used to smuggle the gems. Maylia, born Gloria Suie Chin in Detroit, Michigan, was married to Benson Fong, who appears in the film, in the uncredited role of Ah Hing, sales clerk in Wong's shop. Fong is best known for playing the "Number-Three Son" of Sidney Toler's Charlie Chan in six Monogram series entries. For many years, the couple operated the Ah-Fong Chinese restaurant in Beverly Hills. Longtime Chan "Number-Two Son" Victor Sen Yung also appears, as the ticket taker outside the theater Gerard uses as a criminal front.

Columbia released the film as *Boston Blackie's Chinese Venture* on March 2, 1949. *Showmen's Trade Review* was very positive about the former safecracker's screen valediction:

> Extremely entertaining entry in the Boston Blackie series, with fun from start to finish. Everybody in the family will enjoy this one…. Chester Morris is, as usual, tops in the title role; and Sid Tomack scores as a substitute for George E. Stone as the Runt…. Reputation of the series will be enhanced by this release.[41]

Boston Blackie's Chinese Venture (1949): Chester Morris, Don McGuire, Richard Lane, Maylia and Joan Woodbury in the poster art for Columbia's final entry in the popular crime series [original one-sheet poster].

Chester's magic partnership with Peter Godfrey remained undeveloped, so he rallied by returning to the legitimate theater. Signing on with the Artists' Repertory Theatre in Denver, Colorado, he starred in an August 1948 production of Norman Krasna's melodrama *Small Miracle* at Phipps Auditorium. *Variety* reported,

> With Chester Morris currently starring ... and Gypsy Rose Lee signed to play the lead in "Biography" the next week, interest in the Artists' Repertory Theatre ... has come to life....
> The stock is running with visiting stars and a resident company, and the venture may become a year-round run. Denver has been without winter stock for many years.[42]

During the autumn of 1948, Chester and Lillian enjoyed a relaxing vacation in England. On December 1, they sailed aboard the *Queen Mary* from Southampton, arriving back in New York one week later. Currently, they were living at 609 North Cannon Drive in Beverly

Hills. During this period, one of Chester's neighbors often took care of any plumbing problems. George Oliver recalled,

> My dad was a plumber in Beverly Hills. We lived on Cannon Drive with all the palm trees. We did a lot of work for [Chester].... I used to go with Dad. [Chester] lived four doors down the street from us. I got one of his pictures—nice looking, too. Good actor, one of the best. I can still see him in my eyes, with tears.[43]

Chester's frequent radio forays made him a popular favorite of George Burns and Gracie Allen, who welcomed him to their *Maxwell House Coffee Time* show on February 17, 1949. Broadcast on NBC, "George Collects Alley Cats" also featured regulars Bea Benaderet, Hans Conried, Bill Goodwin, Harry Lubin and His Orchestra, and fellow special guest Robert Young. Chester followed a guest spot on NBC's May 11, 1949, broadcast of *Duffy's Tavern* with three additional visits to Burns and Allen's *Coffee Time* during the month of June, attempting to deal with "Gracie the Magician," "Emily Vanderlip's Boyfriend, Rudy Vallee" and "Robert Young Preparing for [an] England Trip."

9

Boston Blackie Leaves Hollywood

During the summer of 1949, Chester again returned to the stage, trodding the boards for John Kenley, artistic director of the Kenley Players in Barnesville, Pennsylvania. At the Lakewood Park Theatre, he played the lead role in a production of Richard Burke's play *Dressed to Kill*. On July 25, he opened at Guildford, Connecticut's Chapel Playhouse, in Alexander Woollcott and George S. Kaufman's mystery *The Dark Tower*, continuing with the play at the Sea Cliff Summer Theatre in Glen Cove, Long Island.

Assisted by Lillian, he also honed his craft as a professional magician, joining other U.S. performers on a tour of English music halls. Surprised by the stark difference between his earlier experiences in American vaudeville and the more permissive attitudes on the other side of the Atlantic, he explained,

> The acts that we played with—it wasn't the Palladium ... but all the big ones outside of that—was the *obscenity* that they indulge in, in the English music halls. You couldn't present those here ... much worse [than American burlesque]. And the audiences love it, and they think nothing of it. I don't know why the Lord Chamberlain doesn't step in. It's *dreadful*, just *dreadful*. We used to be so embarrassed to be on the stage.
>
> But the audiences were so great.... They are *just wonderful*. I used to call myself the "B Company Danny Kaye." We closed at a theater at Shepherd's Bush there, and we were sailing the next day. When we finished, and the orchestra were playing "Auld Lang Syne," they stood up and applauded and cheered. They presented my wife, who was in the little magic act with me, a bouquet of roses. It was really wonderful.[1]

Chester again attempted to straighten out his pals, George Burns and Gracie Allen, on NBC radio's *The Ammident Show* (retitled to reflect a new sponsor), sharing the airwaves with Bea Benaderet, Hans Conreid, Bill Goodwin, Gale Gordon, Robert Young and Harry Lubin and His Orchestra for "Second Courtship," written by Paul Henning.

Sidney Kingsley's hit stage drama *Detective Story* opened on Broadway at the Hudson Theatre on March 23, 1949, and closed at the Broadhurst Theatre on August 12, 1950, following a total of 581 performances. Produced by the *Arsenic and Old Lace* team of Howard Lindsay and Russel Crouse, the play featured a powerhouse cast, including Ralph Bellamy (in the lead role of Detective McLeod), Edward Binns, Lee Grant, Horace McMahon, Alexander Scourby, Maureen Stapleton, Warren Stevens, Robert Strauss, Michael Strong, Les Tremayne, James Westerfield and Joseph Wiseman.

Simultaneously, the producers sent another company on a national tour of major cities, including Detroit, where the production opened at the Cass Theatre on October 18, 1949, and Chicago, at the Blackstone Theatre beginning November 1. Once again enjoying the energy of live audiences, Chester was thrilled to sign on with Russell and Crouse.

9. Boston Blackie Leaves Hollywood

Boston Blackie's Chinese Venture (1949): **From left, Sid Tomack (in his only performance as the Runt), Maylia and Chester Morris (in his final performance as Boston Blackie).**

As Detective McLeod, whose self-destructive obsession with pursuing criminals likens him to Captain Ahab in Herman Melville's *Moby Dick*, Chester was supported for 14 weeks in Chicago by a fine group of actors, including Studs Terkel (as Joe Feinson, played by Lou Gilbert in the Broadway version). In 1920 at age eight, Terkel had moved with his parents from New York to Chicago, where he excelled as a journalist, broadcaster and actor whose *Detective Story* performance Chester called "wonderful."[2]

In his dressing room at the Blackstone, Chester described the paradox faced by an actor attempting to maintain his status in the Hollywood film industry:

> They used to do a thing at MGM when I was there. For instance, if you had an option coming up, of an increase of maybe $250 a week. And, two months before that option was due, you'd walk on the lot and go to your dressing room, and you might pass executives that you knew very well, and they wouldn't speak to you. They'd just *nod*. And this thing, after a while, would bother you; and you'd say, "Why is this happening?" I was there for two years before I realized what they were doing.
>
> They had a man named [M.E.] Greenwood who was in control of the office, and he'd say, "We're going to take up your option. We like you here, Chet. We'll have you continue for another six months."
>
> And I'd say, "Well, that's fine."
>
> And then he'd say, "But, of course, at the same figure. We can't afford to give you the other $250."

So, you'd start for the door and say, "Thank you very much." And he'd never let you get *out* the door, and call you back, if you were determined to go through with it.

This happened three or four times; and, finally, I said to him. "You know I'm going to go through the door. Why do you do this?"

And he said, "Well, I save *millions of dollars* a year for the studio, because there are so many actors who cannot go through that door, for the thought of security for another six months."[3]

During the first week of performances at the Blackstone, Chester paid a visit to the College Inn at the Hotel Sherman, from where Chicago's NBC affiliate broadcast the radio show *Welcome Travelers*. Delighted to play such a powerful characterization in *Detective Story*, he remained on the road with the company for several months, including dates in St. Paul, Minneapolis, Omaha, Des Moines and St. Louis. After returning to New York, he played in a regional tour, including several shows at Brandt's Theatre in Flatbush, making his bow as Detective McLeod in early 1951.

During this period, when Chester was shifting his focus from Hollywood filmmaking back to performing on the stage, the anti–Communist sentiment resulting in the House Committee on Un-American Activities (HUAC) and the "blacklist" created problems for many of his friends and colleagues, some of whom also gravitated toward the theater when they found it difficult or impossible to work in the film industry. In 1940, the House Committee to Investigate Un-American Activities chaired by congressman Martin Dies, Jr., leaked the names of film industry professionals "identified" by former Communist Party member John L. Leech as fellow communists. These included Chester's close friends Humphrey Bogart, James Cagney and Fredric March (none of whom "ever were a member of the Communist Party"). Targeting of specific individuals sometimes carried overtones of racism and anti–Semitism. Between 1947 and 1960, Chester's blacklisted associates included Edward Dmytryk and Dalton Trumbo (two of the "Hollywood Ten"), Dolores del Rio, Michael Gordon, Larry Parks, Martin Ritt, Edward G. Robinson, Lionel Stander, Studs Terkel and Orson Welles.

Like his friend Boris Karloff, who never stumped in public or ran afoul of HUAC, and gravitated from film to the stage and television, Chester also was a conspicuous volunteer heavily involved in a trailblazing labor union and entertainment activities for the U.S. military during World War II. Karloff, who always retained his British citizenship, eventually moved, first to New York and then back to London, during the HUAC years. He and his widow, Evelyn, admitted to feeling more comfortable in those environments, both geographically distant from Hollywood. Chester enjoyed, not only being back on the stage, but being a New Yorker again.

Prior to U.S. involvement in World War II, Chester's old pal Robert Montgomery had enlisted in London for the American Field Service, driving ambulances in France until the evacuation of Dunkirk, which ended on June 4, 1940. In December 1941, he joined the U.S. Navy and served under PT boat commander Lieutenant (later Vice Admiral) John D. Bulkeley aboard the *U.S.S. Barton* during the D-Day invasion on June 6, 1944. That autumn, he and John Ford were placed on inactive status by the Navy to make MGM's *They Were Expendable* (1945), in which Montgomery portrays Lieutenant John Brickley, naval aviator-turned-screenwriter Frank ["Spig"] Wead's cinematic version of Bulkeley. After Ford was hospitalized during production, Montgomery directed some of the PT boat scenes, before beginning his own filmmaking career with such *noir* fare as *Lady in the Lake* and *Ride the Pink Horse* (both 1947).

In 1946, Montgomery was elected to another term as Screen Actors Guild president.

A staunch Republican, he also testified as a "friendly witness" at the HUAC hearings in 1947. Following the inauguration of President Dwight D. Eisenhower in 1953, he invented the (unpaid) position of "image consultant," advising Ike on how best to impress viewers during national television appearances, and was awarded with his own White House office in 1958.

Like Chester, Montgomery focused primarily on stage and television work during the 1950s. Further explaining his reasons for leaving feature filmmaking behind, Chester recalled his days at MGM:

> They would call an actor in, for instance, to Louis B. Mayer's office, and he would say, "I understand you're driving an old, cheap car around Hollywood."
> And you'd say, "Yes, Mr. Mayer, it's a cheap car, it gets me there."
> He'd say, "Well, an actor of your stature can't afford to be *seen* in a car like that. Go buy a Cadillac." And, of course, this was very flattering.
> So, you couldn't wait, and you'd go out and buy a Cadillac *on time*, and you'd saddle yourself with all of these things. *Your house* had to be in a certain part of town. And then, of course, when option time came up, you were only too happy to grab that extra six months to pay off on these things. They had all the little psychological things that they used to do.[4]

Following the antitrust legislation wrought on May 3, 1948, by the Supreme Court case *United States v. Paramount Pictures, Inc.*, the Hollywood studio system was forced to give way to a new production-company based industry, often managed by actors, in which the old "dream factories" were reduced to positions of land ownership and distribution. Chester explained,

> It's an actors' business. They rent studio space ... and it's the Kirk Douglas productions ... independent producers [making] bigger-budgeted films. Of course, today, the films have to be a *blockbuster* or they're not worth anything.
> I think we used to make the "Blackies" for $125,000 a picture, and they were all presold.... Harry Cohn, who ran Columbia, would say to the exhibitor, "Well ... the Rita Hayworth-Fred Astaire picture: unless you buy 'Blackie,' you don't *get that*." So, the exhibitor was stuck with them. Now, fortunately, the "Blackies" were successful. Kids *loved them* ... on Saturday matinees.[5]

Chester made his official television debut on March 25, 1950, joining host Jerry Lester, singer Kyle MacDonald and trumpeter Dizzy Gillespie on episode 43 of the live DuMont network *Cavalcade of Stars* weekly variety program. Initially hosted by comedian Jack Carter when the show debuted in June 1949, *Cavalcade* again found a new figurehead when Jackie Gleason took over the following year. Proving popular, he moved to CBS in September 1952, where he remained with the program, retitled *The Jackie Gleason Show*, until its close in June 1957.

For this initial small-screen appearance, Chester performed on an empty stage against a black background, giving "a pleasing exhibition of magic."[6] Three weeks later, he made his first guest appearance on *The Ken Murray Show*, sharing the stage with fellow "golden-age" Hollywood greats Ruby Keeler and Gloria Swanson. The weekly variety television program, broadcast live by CBS from 1950 to 1953, was the first to win the Freedom Foundation Award.

Chester's dramatic television debut occurred in the titular role of "The Great Merlini" on *Cameo Theatre*, directed by Curtis Canfield from a Jack Bentkover-George Englund teleplay, and broadcast live by NBC on May 23, 1950. Tailored specifically for Chester, his role as an ace magician called upon to solve a murder committed at a séance was ably supported by the performances of Wyrley Birch and Englund, a multitalented television figure who also produced, directed and was married to Cloris Leachman for more than 25 years (1953–1978).

Chester stumped for U.S. Army and Air Force recruiting on the November 3, 1950, broadcast of the syndicated radio show *Stars on Parade*. On November 18, he made another live television appearance on *The Ken Murray Show*, joining the host and fellow classic Hollywood notables Mary Boland, Anita Louise and The Mills Brothers. One week later, he, Martha Raye and Rudy Vallee helped host Milton Berle headline *The Texaco Star Theatre*, the smash television variety program produced by "Uncle Milty" and broadcast live by NBC for eight seasons (1948–1956). Allen Roth, who began his professional career at age seven in St. Louis, Missouri, served as orchestra leader and musical director for most of the series.

On February 3, 1951, Chester again hobnobbed in real time with the host of *The Ken Murray Show*. Former *Our Gang* child star Darla Hood and Jack Mulhall, his colleague from the early days at Warner Bros., also appeared.

The CBS television anthology series *Danger*, a single-camera program broadcast live from New York, ran for 222 30-minute episodes over five seasons (1950–1955). In a series cast including many of the "usual suspects" from the golden age of the small screen, Chester guest starred in three installments, "The Undertaker Calls" (April 10, 1951), "Death Pulls the Strings" (December 30, 1952) and "Towerman" (November 24, 1953), which paired him with former child star Jackie Cooper.

On August 14, 1951, Chester again gave a volunteer performance to honor U.S. servicemen. The CBS radio show *The Empty Sleeve*, a docudrama about disabled U.S. veterans, featured him in a powerful story about a returning serviceman who had lost his arms and legs in combat.

The *Starlight Theatre* live television anthology series ran on CBS for two seasons, from April 1950 until September 1951. The penultimate 30-minute episode, "Act of God Notwithstanding," aired September 6, 1951, directed by Martin Ritt from a teleplay by Lawrence Hazard, starred Chester as Ed Kennedy, operator of a power plant compromised during a raging blizzard. Struggling against exhaustion to keep the electricity flowing after being trapped in the plant for more than two days, Ed had to rally his crew while worrying about his wife (Olive Deering) undergoing a Caesarean section to deliver their new baby daughter. The excellent supporting cast included Michael Higgins, Joe Mantell, Ray Danton and Doris Roberts.

Chester was the "surprise celebrity guest" on the November 2, 1951, broadcast of *The Frances Langford-Don Ameche Show*, a daytime television variety program that ran on ABC for six months, from September 1951 to March 1952. The hosts previously had been successful on the radio program *The Bickersons* (1946–1951), in which they played a feuding married couple, which aired on NBC for one season before moving to CBS.

In between musical performances, a close-up of Chester's hands, brandishing two .45 automatic pistols, was accompanied by his "gangster voice" as he enacted a "stick up" of the duo. Inquiring about the personality of the guest, the voice asked, "What kind of a guy is he?"

Langford answered, "He's just the nicest guy in the whole world."

"What about his talent?" it continued.

"He's one of the greatest actors on the stage," responded "Nails" Ameche.

"*One* of?" it asked.

"He's *the* greatest," replied "Nails." "He's even better than *Ameche*."

"Go on," it prompted. "What else, Miss Langford."

"Well, he's made about 100 pictures, including the Boston Blackie series," she answered.

"He's a *family* man, ain't he, Ameche?" it queried.

"Yes, he's the best," admitted "Nails." "A loving husband, devoted father. Has three children. His son is a lieutenant in the Air Corps."

The conversation continued with a debate about the guest's age and status as a grandfather before the hosts shouted out, "Chester Morris!" and the camera operator panned from the pistols up to his grinning mug. All three then enacted an "original play by Ameche" titled, "A Great Prison Drama," in which Chester played former mob boss "Rocky Morris," with "Francie" as a gun moll and "Donno" as a "double-crossing thief." Shot primarily in three simple closeups and one wide shot in front of a stage curtain, the seven-minute performance resembled a filmed radio program.

Later in the show, Chester returned to answer Ameche about "what he does to relax from all those mystery stories he acts in." Mentioning the magic kit presented to him by William on his 12th birthday, he called prestidigitation a "disease" affecting him ever since. Referring to Lillian's opinion of his act, he said, "My wife is wonderful. She's beautiful, too. Of course, she stands on the stage, and I can do anything. Nobody watches me at all…. She's terrific."

About their wartime volunteer service, he said, "We did about 400 Camp Shows. Frances, you know what that means," adding, "and we still have a lot to do." He finished the segment by making a bouquet of artificial flowers appear "out of thin air" to present to Langford.

"What an expensive Romeo you must have been," mocked Ameche, looking at the bouquet. "Get a load of those things."

Before leaving the stage, Chester followed up with the first magic trick he ever learned, lengthening a piece of rope, in which he then tied a knot by whipping it up and down. "My, goodness sake, isn't he a sweet guy?" concluded Ameche.

CBS featured Chester as "The Dansker" in the live "Billy Budd" episode of the dramatic anthology series *Schlitz Playhouse of Stars* on January 11, 1952. Adapted from the novel by Herman Melville, the program also included Charles Nolte as the titular character, with solid support from Walter Hampden (Captain Vere), Jeff Morrow (Lieutenant Wyatt), Peter Hobbs (John Claggart), and Walter Burke (Squeak). From its October 1951, debut until summer 1953, the program was broadcast live, after which some episodes were filmed at Revue Studios on the Universal lot for later broadcast. From 1956 until the final episode aired in July 1959, all episodes were produced on film.

Ten days after appearing in "Billy Budd," Chester costarred with Jane Wyatt in the *Lights Out* television episode "The Intruder," directed by Grey Lockwood from a Lucille Fletcher script and broadcast by NBC. Conceived by writer Wyllis Cooper, the *Lights Out* radio program ran from 1934 to 1947, making its transition to television as a series of four live specials in 1946. NBC began the full mystery-horror series in 1949; and, when the final live installment was broadcast in September 1952, the run totaled 160 30-minute television episodes. Chester joined a list of formidable guest stars including Jack LaRue (who narrated 32 episodes), Boston Blackie colleagues Janis Carter and Nina Foch, John Carradine, Henry Daniell, Halliwell Hobbes, Henry Hull, Everett Sloane, Robert Stack, Joseph Wiseman and Donald Woods.

Glenda Farrell, Mary Riva and Chester all appeared on the January 26 *Ken Murray Show* on CBS. Murray greatly enjoyed Chester's appearances, inviting him twice each year.

CBS broadcast the television version of the *Suspense* series (adapted from its 1942–1962 radio program) during six seasons from March 1949 to August 1954. Stories by such writers as Ray Bradbury, John Dickson Carr, Agatha Christie, Sir Arthur Conan Doyle, Charles Dickens, Alexandre Dumas, William Faulker, F. Scott Fitzgerald, W.W. Jacobs, Edgar Allan Poe, Rod Serling, Robert Louis Stevenson and Émile Zola were adapted into a total of 252 half-hour episodes. The outstanding cast included Harry Bellaver, Edward Binns, Joan Blondell, Ward Bond, Richard Boone, Henry Brandon, John Carradine, Sir Cedric Hardwicke, Henry Hull, Boris Karloff, Peter Lorre, Bela Lugosi, Robert Middleton, Thomas Mitchell, Basil Rathbone, Stanley Ridges and dozens of other "golden age" film stars and up-and-coming performers.

On April 8, 1952, Chester starred as Edwards, a diamond smuggler using the store Dolls International as a front, in "Black Panther," directed by Robert Stevens from a Halsted Welles teleplay. When a rare Swiss doll missing an arm is found at a murder scene, Jerry (James Gregory), a young detective, unable to obtain satisfactory answers from Edwards, maintains a watch on the shop. Discovering that "Pops" (Allan Tower), his confederate in crime, has attempted to abscond with the diamond-filled arm, Edwards orders another sidekick to kill him. This murderous act leads, not only Edwards, but also his wife (Olive Deering), who had conspired with Pops, into Jerry's clutches, and the episode concludes with the master criminal being led off in handcuffs.

"Black Panther," like the entire *Suspense* series, was broadcast live and filmed on kinescope. (Though most of the episodes were not preserved, this title is one of 90 that have survived.) Maintaining his high professional standards for performing on stage, Chester always enjoyed an opportunity to act on live television, and this was no exception.

On June 6, 1952, Chester made the first of two appearances on the live television horror and science-fiction series *Tales of Tomorrow*, developed by Theodore Sturgeon and broadcast on ABC from 1951 to 1953. During its two-year run, the program featured scripts and stories by Sturgeon, Mary Shelley, Jules Verne, H.G. Wells, Oscar Wilde and Philip Wylie, and performances by Lon Chaney, Jr., Boris Karloff, Gene Lockhart, Mercedes McCambridge, Robert Middleton, Thomas Mitchell, Rod Steiger and Joanne Woodward. "The Exile," adapted by Edgar Marvin from a story by Alec Coppel, was followed on December 5, 1952, by David E. Durston's script "The Glacier Giant," costarring Chester and Edith Fellows.

Chester acted in his first teleplay written by Rod Serling, "Welcome Home, Lefty," broadcast as an episode of the CBS anthology series *Lux Video Theatre*, on June 23, 1952. Directed by Richard Goode, the 30-minute seriocomedy also featured Don Murray and Robert F. Simon. Making its debut in October 1950, *Lux Video Theatre* was moved from New York to Hollywood in September 1953, where NBC expanded the program to 60 minutes from August 1954 until September 1957, when it took its final bow.

Garry Moore moderated the popular Mark Goodson-Bill Todman game show *I've Got a Secret* for the first 12 years of its original 15-year run (1952–1967). A derivative of the same producers' *What's My Line?* program, it featured panelists who attempt to discover a contestant's "secret," which could be unusual, humorous or embarrassing.

Chester was the contestant on the November 13, 1952, episode, questioned by Bill Cullen, Jayne Meadows, Henry Morgan and Kitty Carlisle. On August 11, 1954, he returned for another round, this time queried by Laraine Day.

On September 8, 1952, Chester played the first of three dramatic roles on the live hour-long television drama hosted by an old friend, *Robert Montgomery Presents*, which ran on

NBC from 1950 to 1957. "The Law-Abiding," a Joel Hammil espionage script directed by Norman Felton, was followed by "The Big Night" (March 23, 1953), an Adrian Spies teleplay starring Chester as Colonel Bobo Nolan, a former U.S. Air Force pilot having difficulty adjusting to civilian life. The third episode, "The Greatest Man in the World" (December 28, 1953), costarred Chester and Edward Binns in another aviation-oriented story, about an "unknown" mechanic who flies solo around the world and the newspaper reporter assigned to uncover his past.

Montgomery also asked Chester to serve as guest host on the December 14, 1953, episode, "No Visible Means," costarring Patricia Breslin, Robert Ellenstein and Robert Middleton. The Jack McClain teleplay about a sweet talker prowling New York speakeasies during the 1920s was also directed by Norman Felton.

The television panel series *20 Questions* debuted on New York's WOR-TV in November 1949 and expanded nationwide on NBC three weeks later. After the show was dropped by NBC in December 1949, it was picked up by ABC, who aired weekly episodes until June 1951. The program experienced far more stability when the DuMont network revived it from July 1951 to May 1954.

On the November 7, 1952, episode, Chester appeared with the host, sportscaster Bill Slater, announcer Frank Waldecker, and the panel of Fred Van Deventer (the show's creator), Florence Rinard (Van Deventer's wife), Bobby McGuire (Van Deventer's son) and Herb Polesie (the producer). The game involved an "answerer" who chose a secret subject about which the other players, the "questioners," made inquiries until one of them chose a correct solution, which allowed him or her to become the "answerer" for the next round. If 20 questions were asked without a solution, then the "answerer" retained the position for another round.

On November 16, Arthur and Kathryn Murray welcomed Chester to *The Arthur Murray Party*, ostensibly a 1950s variety-show version of an "infomercial," which ran for more than a decade, at various lengths (15, 30 or 60 minutes) on different networks (ABC, DuMont, CBS and NBC). Appearing with Chester on this season-three episode were singer Teresa Brewer and the Ray Carter Orchestra.

Chester was the guest in a 15-minute dramatic segment during the January 5, 1953, broadcast of NBC's daytime television program *The Kate Smith Hour*, which had been revamped to feature a sketch starring a major Hollywood performer once each week. John Carradine and Josephine Hull followed his lead later that month.

On January 20, Chester, Haila Stoddard, James Gregory and Vaughn Taylor costarred in Don Swann's theater-in-the-round presentation of Jane Hinton's courtroom drama *The Fourth Degree* at the Sheraton Belvedere Hotel in Baltimore. Adapted from the novel by Eleazor Lipsky, the play, directed by Harald Bromley, was a rushed, rough tryout for a possible Broadway production. *Variety*'s "Burm," who attended several performances, observed,

> This is a murder mystery with a Freudian twist, to the point the zeal for justice in the heart of an altruistic assistant prosecutor up against an ambitious boss who wants convictions and publicity above all else. In the short stretch of rehearsals accomplished for the limited projection via arena presentation here, it doesn't come off. Chester Morris, as the well-meaning assistant district attorney, resorting to actual reading from a script in several scenes, doesn't build a believable characterization, and most of the rest of the parts are stereotyped cop-and-robber guys. Much more secure in the female lead is Haila Stoddard, whose husband, Harald Bromley, directed with aim toward Broadway production. She knows her lines and manages to make her part count up, but it's going to take a major job to whip it all into paydirt.[7]

The tryout did not achieve enough success to make a legitimate production viable for Broadway.

Chester's interest in television game shows continued with the February 3, 1953, broadcast of Mark Goodson and Bill Todman's *The Name's the Same*. Robert Q. Lewis, the original host of the ABC program from 1951 to 1954, welcomed him as the contestant referred to as "Mr. X," to be questioned by panelists Jerry Lester, Joan Alexander and Meredith Willson, each of whom could ask 10 questions in trying to determine his identity.

For the show's "I'd Like to Be" segment, during which the panelists each were allowed four questions to identify the name of a famous person selected by a guest, Chester chose William F. ["Buffalo Bill"] Cody (1846–1917). Willson, who mentioned living down the street from Chester, called him a "splendid actor ... and one of the greatest magicians we have" before asking questions and playing a piccolo, thinking the famous person was Ulysses S. Grant. Lester made no headway whatever, but Alexander zeroed right in on Buffalo Bill. The losers each provided a $25 check for Chester to donate to his "favorite charity."

Impressed with his performance in the "Black Panther" episode of *Suspense*, CBS cast Chester in a second episode of the series, "Point Blank," written by Ben Radin, and costarring his *One Mysterious Night* and *One Way to Love* leading lady, Janis Carter, aired on August 11, 1953. (Unlike "Black Panther," this later series installment did not survive.)

The dramatic anthology series *Kraft Television Theatre* was aired on NBC from 1947 to 1958. Chester made his debut on the show with the May 13, 1953, episode "Final Edition," a suspenseful story in which a newspaper reporter murders his publisher, only to have a colleague discover his crime.

In 1953, Chester acted as the on-screen host for *Captured*, the second series of the true-crime television program *Gang Busters*, which had run on NBC for 36 episodes the previous year. Reworked by the NBC Film Division as a series for "exclusive sponsorship" by local stations in individual cities, the new 29-episode series employed him to narrate the opening and closing scenes, all of which, he told *Variety*'s George Gilbert, "were shot in three-and-one-half days.... Somebody would shout, 'This is Episode Four! Quick, it's the brown coat now.' That more or less typifies my hectic experience."[8] *Gang Busters* did not return to NBC's regular network lineup, although two additional episodes were broadcast during 1955.

Chester costarred in another tryout for a possible Broadway production, Thomas G. Ratcliffe and Louis Macmillan's presentation of Gant Gaither's *The Long Street*, which closed the season for the Sea Cliff Summer Theatre on Long Island, during late August and early September 1953. This seriocomic story of family life focusing on an unfaithful housewife's materialistic obsessions featured Chester in a strong cast including Vincent Gardenia, Wynne Gibson, Phillip Pine, Betsy Von Furstenberg and Joan Wetmore. *Variety*'s "Hank," who attended the September 5 performance, wrote,

> "The Long Street," closing bill at the Sea Cliff Summer Theatre, is possibly the best of the four new plays presented by producers Tom Ratcliffe and Louis Macmillan this season. This is not to say, however, that its success as a Broadway offering is a certainty....
>
> Wynne Gibson does a fine job as Cora Nash, though the part loses credibility by being so one-sidedly mean that one wonders how the family managed to hold together up to the opening curtain. Chester Morris is convincing as Sam Nash, the patient, hard-working husband who wants the boy to make his own decisions. Michael Steele plays the confused youngster to excellent effect, and Betsy Von Furstenberg is good-looking and adequate as a society tramp.[9]

Although the performances were better received than those of *The Fourth Degree*, *The Long Street* also was unable to make the transition to Broadway.

On October 11, 1953, the *Omnibus* episode "The Battler," directed by Paul Nickell from an Arnold Schulman teleplay adapted from an Ernest Hemingway story, featured Chester in the title segment with John Marriott and Dick York. Other segments in this 60-minute installment, codirected by Bob Banner, included "Lola Flores and Her Flamenco Dancers," featuring Spanish music and dance by Lola and Carmen Flores, Paco Aguilera and Faico; "Operation Hurricane," a documentary about the first British atomic bomb detonation in the Pacific; "Preview of King Lear," a rehearsal and discussion of the Shakespeare play with Peter Brook and Virgil Thompson; and "The Automatic Pinspotter," a look at a device used in a bowling alley. Alistair Cooke hosted the program.

The Mark Goodson–Bill Todman mystery television series *The Web* premiered on CBS on July 4, 1950, running for four seasons. On the February 4, 1954, episode "Rock-Bound," Chester guest starred with Howard St. John and Mike Wallace. Four days later, he headlined another CBS drama, "Walk in the Night," written by Verne Jay and Rod Serling, broadcast on *The Philip Morris Playhouse*.

On April 12, 1954, Chester played the first of four guest-starring roles on *Studio One*, the live one-hour CBS program that ran from 1948 to 1958. Directed by Franklin J. Schaffner, "Jack Sparling, Forty-six" cast him, with support from Mary Astor and Lois Smith, as a businessman whose relentless drive for "success" brings on a potential nervous breakdown. He played his second series role, Sam Benson, one month later, in "The Death and Life of Larry Benson," aired on May 31, 1954. Directed by Paul Nickell from a Reginald Rose teleplay, the episode also featured Peg Hillias, Ruth Amos, Lee Remick and Skip Homeier.

10

Unchained

In July 1954, Chester returned to California to make his first feature film in five years, *Unchained*, written, produced and directed by Hall Bartlett. Kenyon Jackson Scudder, warden of the California Institution for Men at Chino, California, published the autobiographical book *Prisoners are People* in 1952. The first minimum security correctional institution built in the United States, "Chino Men's" was founded by Scudder in 1941 as an experimental "prison without walls" to create a sense of self-respect among inmates without requiring guards, uniforms or gun towers to keep them in line. Scudder recently had been named president of the American Prison Association.

Offered $60,000 by a major Hollywood studio to adapt the book as a film tentatively titled "The Chino Story," Scudder, who wanted story approval, instead accepted $5,000 and 15 percent of the profits from Bartlett, a socially conscious filmmaker who, playing down sex and violence, insisted on complete artistic autonomy. Bartlett's previous features as producer included *Navaho* (1952), a drama told in semidocumentary style, and *Crazylegs* (1953), a docudrama about USMC veteran and professional football star Elroy "Crazylegs" Hirsh, whose performance as himself led to his casting as Steve Davitt in *Unchained*. *Variety* reported that "Bartlett's almost idealistic approach toward production was a contributing factor in winning him the rights to the book."[1]

Bartlett obtained financing for the new film prior to securing a distribution deal with Warner Bros. He lived at the Chino facility for three months, observing and interviewing inmates while writing the screenplay, which then went through an approval process with Kenyon and Rebekah Scudder, and the Chino Men's Council, a committee of 17 elected inmates included as characters. Everyone involved in the production, including Richard A. McGee, director of the California Department of Corrections, received a copy of the script before Bartlett and cinematographer Virgil E. Miller filmed on location at Chino. During the shoot, Bartlett encouraged suggestions from the crew, which resulted in a smooth production schedule, wrapping ahead of time.

Like Scudder, Chester also accepted a participation agreement, rather than a flat fee, from Bartlett. In an interview with New York journalist George Gilbert, he explained his long absence from the big screen: "I just didn't have an offer." His interest in *Unchained* resulted from Bartlett's "fresh approach" to prison pictures and his chance of earning a piece of the box-office action.[2]

In his three major prison films, Chester never repeated himself. Reflecting changes in societal values over the course of 25 years, portraying the real-life warden provided him with a complete character evolution, previously having made a moral progression from "slickest crook" John Morgan in *The Big House* to undercover fed Jeff Crane in *Public Hero Number 1*.

Hirsch was joined by three fellow Los Angeles Rams football players: linebacker Don Paul and middle guard Stan West, who played prison control officers, and fullback Paul "Tank" Younger as a Men's Council member. Jazz saxophonist Dexter Gordon, making his screen acting debut, also joined the cast as a member of the group performing for the Council election. (Interestingly, Dexter's parts were overdubbed by musician-composer Georgie Auld, who previously had played with the orchestras of Artie Shaw, Benny Goodman and Bunny Berigan.)

Though Bartlett "witnessed no [violent] encounters" during his three months at the prison, he incorporated four realistic fights, including one for Hirsch and character actor Bill Kennedy, "to add action to the story." He described the completed scene as "one of the most savage encounters ever staged in a prison picture, or any other kind for that matter. Both contestants had no trouble making the fight look good."³

The film opens with Steve Davitt narrating "the story, photographed at Chino, as it happened." Convicted of nearly killing an employee he suspected of robbing him, Davitt has been transferred from San Quentin to the new experimental prison, where he is surprised by the humane, respectful treatment. Warden Scudder explains to the new arrivals that anyone who escapes will not be allowed to return.

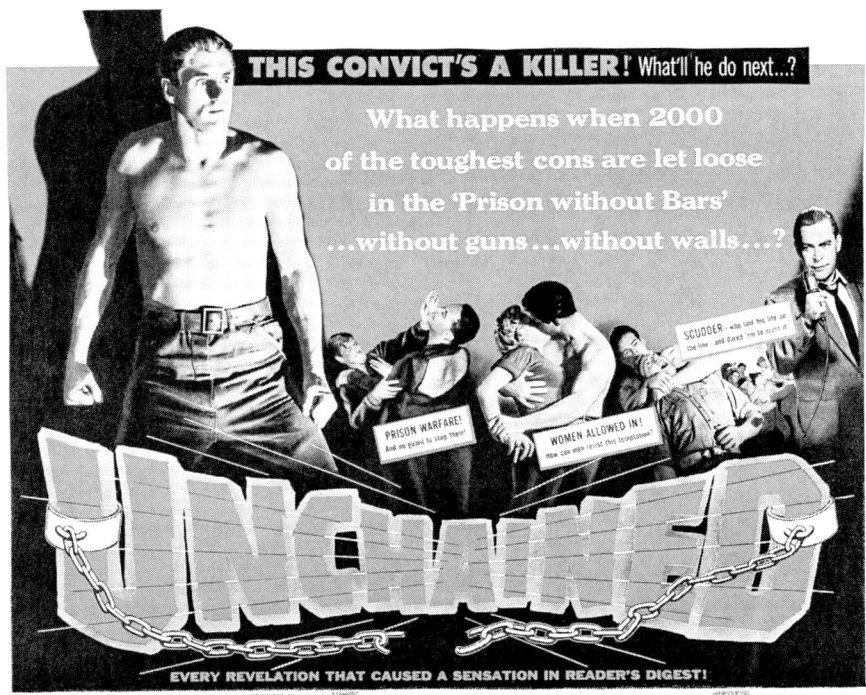

Unchained (1955): Elroy ("Crazylegs") Hirsch and Chester Morris in the actor's first feature film in five years, adapted from Warden Kenyon J. Scudder's autobiographical book *Prisoners Are People*, produced and directed by Hall Bartlett [original half-sheet poster].

Unlike his fellow inmates, Davitt disapproves of visits from his wife, Mary (Barbara Hale), whom he forbids to bring along their young son, Win (Tim Considine). Following a 45-day trial period, Davitt and Joe Ravens (Jerry Paris), moved to the main campus, where they are afforded more responsibility and freedom, make escape plans. After Davitt attacks Sanders (Kennedy), a hardened criminal, for harassing injured pianist Eddie Garrity (Johnny Johnston), Scudder agrees not to enter the incident on his record if he will learn to curb his violent tendencies.

Influenced by Bill Howard (Todd Duncan), a convicted killer whose good behavior has earned him a forthcoming parole, Davitt runs for the Men's Council, hoping the benefits will provide more escape opportunities. Encouraged by Scudder and Sally (Kathryn Grant), the niece of fellow inmate Leonard Haskins (John Qualen), Garrity undergoes surgery to repair his damaged hand, subsequently playing in a jazz band on election night. Elected Council representative, Davitt is attacked by Sanders, who then blames him for starting the fight. Scudder is not convinced of his guilt but has him confined to the "segregation" area until Haskins reveals the truth about the incident.

Having used his solitary time wisely, Davitt tells Howard that he has reconsidered the supposed criminal actions of the employee whom he nearly killed. He also worries that Win will discover that he is a convict, but Howard advises him to tell the truth. Denied parole, Davitt again plans to escape, but Ravens decides to serve the remainder of his sentence. During a boxing match, Howard attempts to stop Davitt from going over the fence but is knocked to the ground. Halfway up, Davitt sees his friend regaining consciousness and climbs back down so they can return to the facility together.

On January 15, 1955, *Unchained* was premiered simultaneously at the local theater in Chino and in the mess hall of the prison, which was festooned like a Hollywood movie palace, where Scudder hosted the event, split into two screenings, one for the 1,500 inmates, and the other for the cast, visiting celebrities and members of the press, who were transported to the location aboard a special "caravan of buses." The visitors' screening was preceded by an extensive tour of the 2,600-acre grounds. Donald Crisp, Joe E. Brown and NBC commentator Shirley Thomas were among the Hollywood notables who signed the prison register.

Hirsch personally promoted the film during a 12-city tour, including special trade screenings in New York and Chicago. Following *Unchained*, he played two more years (and served for nine as general manager) with the Los Angeles Rams, appeared in one more feature film and six television programs, and worked as a sports reporter for L.A. radio station KNX. He was inducted into the Pro Football Hall of Fame in 1967.

The trailblazing Scudder, who "got kicked out of jobs because he wouldn't play ball with the politicians," is played with quiet and evenhanded determination by Chester, who was crafting the role on the Warden's own watch. He deviates from his primary underplaying only during the mess hall scene, when Davitt is attacked by Sanders, and Scudder must talk tough to quell a potential riot. Proving that the food at Chino may be the best of its kind, he then fills a plate for himself and joins a group of inmates at one of the tables. This dramatic high point reflects Bartlett's straightforward writing and directing style, which avoids becoming preachy or overplayed, visualized by the equally unadorned camerawork of Virgil Miller, who also shot *Navaho* and *Crazylegs*. The only moments of sentiment arrive via composer Alex North's inclusion of the "Unchained Melody" in his orchestrations for a few scenes.

As Joe Ravens, prolific actor and director Jerry Paris displays the same honesty he

Unchained (1955): Chester Morris as Kenyon J. Scudder, warden of the California Institution for Men at Chino, California.

later brought to Agent Martin Flaherty during the first season of *The Untouchables* (1959–1960) on CBS television. Though their roles are brief, Barbara Hale, two years prior to her long run as Della Street on the *Perry Mason* series (1957–1966), and John Ford-favorite John Qualen are also memorable.

In the significant role of Davitt's levelheaded friend, vocalist and scholar Todd Duncan, in one of his two screen acting roles, performs a hymn (during which a documentary-style montage depicts various activities at the prison) and the title song, "Unchained Melody" (changed from "Are You Still Mine"), by North and lyricist Hy Zaret, accompanied by a guitarist. Subsequently named "the number one top song of 1955" through voting in several music popularity contests,[4] it also was nominated for the 1956 Academy Award for Best

Original Song (but lost to Sammy Fain and Paul Francis Webster's "Love is a Many-Splendored Thing"). The Kentucky-born Duncan (1903–1998), who costarred with Anne Brown in the original 1935 Broadway production of *Porgy and Bess*, directed by Rouben Mamoulian, was the first African American artist to perform at the New York City Opera. He served as Professor of Voice at Howard University in Washington, D.C., and continued to perform and teach for the rest of his life.

The groundbreaking *Unchained* received a special merit award from *Parents Magazine*, the 1955 Brotherhood Award for "outstanding contribution to the cause of brotherhood," and a special award from the Southern California Motion Picture Council. It also received attention overseas, including at the London Prison Congress and World Prison Congress in Geneva, where it was hailed as "the true story of the greatest advance in prison history."[5] (The "greatest advance" subsequently faced many setbacks to prisoner "rebilitation," including a reduction of the minimum security section to 25-percent of the institution, dilapidated facilities, massive overcrowding, insufficient medical treatment, abuse of inmates, drug proliferation, white supremacist gang activity, riots, escapes and the murder of a guard.)

Following the wrap of *Unchained*, Chester was given the script for Joseph Hayes' play *The Desperate Hours*, a latter-day version of the story in which he had excelled in Columbia's *Blind Alley* 15 years earlier. Robert Montgomery was preparing to direct the Broadway production, to be produced by Hayes and Howard Erskine at the Ethel Barrymore Theatre from February to August 1955. Chester was not cast in the play, which costarred Karl Malden, Nancy Coleman and Paul Newman. (On May 29, 1956, Chester again was mentioned in connection with the play, announced as tentatively cast in "an expanded, festival-type program" for the summer season at the Corning Glass Theatre in Corning, New York.[6])

Independent producer Edward Small had announced that Chester would serve as technical adviser on the mystery thriller *The Mad Magician* (1954), directed by John Brahm and starring Vincent Price as magician-inventor "Gallico the Great," but the film was made for United Artists without his participation. On September 5, 1954, a week before *The Mad Magician* went into production, he returned to the Broadway stage for the first time in more than a quarter-century, replacing Richard Whorf as Johnny Goodwin in Sylvia Regan's comedy *The Fifth Season*, directed by Gregory Ratoff at the Cort Theatre. Originally opening on January 23, 1953, the play also featured Nita Talbot, with John Cassavetes serving as an understudy. Chester's run, also featuring Joseph Buloff, lasted seven weeks, closing at the Cort on October 23, 1954. He promoted the play during a guest visit to WOR radio's *Luncheon at Sardi's* program, which recently had returned to the New York airwaves.

On September 15, "Hobe" reviewed the play in *Variety*:

"The Fifth Season" has become a sort of old grey mare of legit. Back for a brief Broadway run before going on the road, it's a sorry substitute for the hokey but funny and ingratiating comedy that crossed up critics and delighted audiences and backers last season ... as originally played by the hilarious, disarming Menasha Skulnik, the bustling, staccato Richard Whorf and the decorative, skillful Phyllis Hill, it provided bullseye entertainment....

But the recast, badly directed and ill-rehearsed roughhouse that reopened last week is not worthy of Broadway or the road. It is, in fact, shocking and inexcusable.

Without dwelling on the embarrassing details, merely note that Joseph Buloff is woefully lacking in either the comic or endearing qualities that made Skulnik a delight.... His ponderous mugging gets only a fraction of the comedy and not even a suggestion of the sincerity, gentleness and guile that Skulnick had in the role.

Chester Morris overacts acutely as the dynamic, self-indulgent but essentially likable salesman-partner. His drunk scene, like Buloff's, is an ossified orgy, and unfortunately typical.[7]

Regardless of the negative review, the revamped *Fifth Season* was successful enough to spark a road version. Chester joined the tour, also directed by Ratoff, playing dates in Washington, D.C., Philadelphia, Pittsburgh, Chicago and Boston. Sharing the stage with Buloff and Fran Keegan, Chester remained with the production into the spring of 1955.

During 1955, Chester played Lieutenant Commander Philip Francis Queeg in local productions of *The Caine Mutiny Court-Martial* in Bristol, Pennsylvania (with a troupe under the direction of John Kenley) and at the Paper Mill Playhouse in Millburn, New Jersey. Herman Wouk's dramatization of his Pulitzer Prize–winning novel had debuted on Broadway at the Plymouth Theatre on January 20, 1954, running for 415 performances until closing on January 22, 1955. Directed by Charles Laughton, the original production starred Henry Fonda, John Hodiak and Lloyd Nolan as Queeg.

CBS kept Chester busy with television roles, including that of Lieutenant Kiser, supported by Jean Bal and Anthony Eisley, in "Time Bomb," the November 27, 1955, episode of *Appointment with Adventure*, a live series providing viewers with exciting historical dramas set in various parts of the globe. Produced by David Susskind, the episode was written by Anne Howard Bailey and Jean-Charles Tacchella.

He tackled another correctional role, Warden Gary, in his third *Studio One* episode, "Blow Up at Cortland," broadcast by CBS on December 5, 1955. Written by Paul Monash, the hour-long drama, also featuring Philip Coolidge, pitted his prison administrator against Klaus (Neville Brand), the psychopathic leader of a group of rioting inmates.

Before future *Twilight Zone* creator Rod Serling (1924–1975) became one of the most keenly perceptive, original writers of television's golden age, often crafting stories exposing humans' dark tendencies, especially ignorance, paranoia, hatred, racism and violence, he served three rugged, eye-opening years in the U.S. Army. Born on Christmas Day in Syracuse, New York, Rodman Edward Serling entered the Army shortly after his 18th birthday in January 1943 and served as an infantry combat demolition specialist and paratrooper during World War II. Discharged in January 1946 with the rank of Technician 5th Grade (equivalent to a corporal), he had been awarded the Purple Heart and a dozen other significant medals and badges.

Serling began writing while recuperating in an Army hospital during the war. As a civilian, he earned a Bachelor of Arts degree at New York's Antioch College, where he also taught communication studies and wrote and produced radio programs which were broadcast on WJEM in Springfield. His initial professional writing assignments were for WNYC radio in New York and other stations in his home state and Ohio.

In 1950, Serling began writing scripts for advertisements and anthology dramas at WKRC-TV in Cincinnati. For the next five years, in Connecticut and New York, he continued penning scripts for many series, including *The Doctor* (1952), *Suspense* (1953), *Lux Video Theatre* (1952–1953, including the "Welcome Home, Lefty" episode), *Center Stage* (1954), *Kraft Television Theatre* (1953–1955), *The Ford Television Theatre* (1955) and *Climax!* (1955). In 1956, he wrote the original story and script for the television film *Patterns*, directed by Fielder Cook, in which he explored one of his lifelong concerns: that of the constant conflict of ambition vs. ethics within persons of power.

This theme is also featured in the April 9, 1956, episode of *Studio One*, "The Arena," one of six he wrote for the program. Written "especially for Studio One" by Serling and directed by Franklin J. Schaffner, this political drama deals with freshman senator James Norton (Wendell Corey) and his veteran advisor, Jack Feeney (Chester), who attempts to steer him away from an act of vengeance against Harvey Rogers (John Cromwell), the senior senator in his party, who had not supported the reelection of his father, former Senator Frank Norton (Edgar Stehli).

Feeney's knowledge of the U.S. Senate is so vast that "there's a rumor he came [to Washington] with Daniel Webster." Accepting the advisory position to the junior Norton, whose controversial father sat on the Senate for 24 years, he immediately faces an uphill battle in his attempts to keep the inexperienced politician on an impartial course. From the minute he arrives at his Washington office, Norton behaves in a brash manner generally considered unethical in 1956 (but prevalent in a later, more cynical and divisive age).

During a scene expertly played by Chester, who enjoys a brief soliloquy before Corey enters the office, Feeney unintentionally reveals information that Senator Rogers had once been a member of the "subversive" right-wing nativist group the Vindicators. Though Feeney quickly realizes his mistake and begs Norton not to attack Rogers with potentially ruinous remarks about an incident buried in the past, the young senator is anxious to vindicate the reputation of his father at any cost. "Politics isn't a dirty thing, Senator," Feeney points out. "The dirt comes from the men."

Norton is set to cut down Rogers during a subsequent Senate session, but a revelatory visit to the family home finally shows the father's true colors to the son. At the last minute, he withdraws his request to address his colleagues on the chamber floor. Serling's expertly crafted "man in the middle" provided Chester with a well-realized and powerful character; and, demonstrating his preference for live theater, he matched the writing with a fine performance. At certain points during the episode, his costars (Corey and Cromwell) slightly fumbled a line but recovered quickly.

Serling would return to the themes of "The Arena" many times, particularly in his writing of 92 (of 156) *Twilight Zone* episodes (1959–1964), an unprecedented and unmatched achievement that earned him the rank of number one on the "25 Greatest Sci-Fi Legends" published by *TV Guide* magazine on August 1, 2004. (The other 24 names on the list are all fictional series characters.) His prolific career came to a sad end on June 28, 1975, two days after he suffered a third heart attack during a 10-hour open-heart surgical procedure at Strong Memorial Hospital in Rochester, New York. A chain smoker (inhaling three to four packs of cigarettes every day, both off- and on-screen) resulted in the coronary incidents beginning seven weeks earlier. During his lifetime, he won six Emmy Awards (for *Patterns* [1955], *Requiem for a Heavyweight* [1956], *The Comedian* [1958], *The Twilight Zone* [1960–1962] and *It's Mental Work* [1963]), one Peabody Award (for *Requiem for a Heavyweight*), and one Golden Globe Award (for *The Twilight Zone* [1962]).

Chester began acting in *The She-Creature*, his first "horror" film since *The Bat Whispers* made more than a quarter-century earlier, for Golden State Productions in May 1956. Producer Alex Gordon accepted a proposal for the film from Jerry Zigmond, a Los Angeles exhibitor who based the idea for the title character on housewife Ruth Simmons (aka "Virginia Tighe"). In 1952, Simmons, after being placed in a trance by Colorado businessman and amateur hypnotist Morey Bernstein, claimed that she recalled a past life as "Bridey Murphy," a woman supposedly born in Cork, Ireland, in 1798. (Following the publication of Bernstein's book *The Search for Bridey Murphy* in 1956, reporters traveled to Ireland, where they found no evidence for any of Simmons/Tighe's assertions. Examiners did discover details about her childhood, however, proving that her recollections were about a neighbor she had known during her childhood, the facts of which had long been forgotten due to "cryptomnesia," a state from which a person emerges to recall memories he believes is newly realized information.)

Gordon planned to cast Edward Arnold as wealthy businessman "Timothy Chappel," but the 66-year-old actor's sudden death of a cerebral hemorrhage on April 26, 1956, led to Tom Conway accepting the role. To play the mysterious occultist Dr. Carlo Lombardi, Gordon asked Peter Lorre and John Carradine, both of whom turned down the film, considering it beneath their talents. (They would accept lesser projects in ensuing years.)

Gordon later recalled that he met Chester after a performance of *The Dark Tower* at the Sea Cliff Summer Theater. The two men struck up a friendship, and Chester asked him, "Keep me in mind if you ever get any of your things off the ground."[8] Gordon recalled,

> I ... thought to myself, "Well, Chester Morris is more than just an amateur magician, he has appeared at the Magic Castle and other places, he's friendly with Orson Welles and other people who are magicians and so on. He probably could do a very good job as the hypnotist." So, I called Chester and I asked, "Could you come out a week earlier and play the lead for us, the hypnotist in the picture, instead of playing the businessman?" He said ... "It's quite a challenge and I'd like to do it."[9]

Chester had no problem with the part, reporting to the location shoot under the direction of Edward L. Cahn at Paradise Cove, Malibu, during May 1956. Chester narrates in *noir* style as the film opens with Lombardi standing on the seashore, examining large reptilian footprints on the sand. Meanwhile, Chappel and his wife (Freda Inescourt) host a cocktail party at their home. Both Conway and Inescourt had starred in memorable fright films during the previous decade: the former in the Val Lewton classics *Cat People* (1942), *I Walked with a Zombie* (1943) and *The Seventh Victim* (1944) at RKO; and the latter in *Return of the Vampire* at Columbia.

The Chappel's daughter, Dorothy (Cathy Downs), and her fiancé, Dr. Ted Erickson (Lance Fuller), leave the party for a walk on the beach when the family dog runs up to them, leading them across the sand to the beach house owned by the Jeffersons, whom Lombardi had found brutally murdered. They witness the hypnotist exiting the house, and Ted calls for the police. Investigating, Lieutenant Ed James (Ron Randell) discovers seaweed left behind on the floor. Earlier, Lombardi had told Mrs. Chappel that "a creature from out of the pond" would be arriving to live among them.

At the local carnival, Lombardi and his assistant, Andrea (Marla English), perform their act demonstrating reincarnation, during which he places her in a lengthy hypnotic state. Awakened, she is repulsed by Lombardi, from whom she wants to escape, but he declares he will "possess" her for the rest of her life. Questioned by Lieutenant James, Lombardi reveals that he has helped facilitate the "transmigration of a woman's soul" into an earlier form, a prehistoric female living in the ocean.

Chappel wants to capitalize commercially on Lombardi's achievement, but the doctor disagrees. "I've been trained to fight stupidity and ignorance," he tells the businessman, "not get rich on it."

Nonetheless, all the press coverage soon catapults him to national attention. In the tradition of the classic horror genre, *The She-Creature* includes several montages featuring sensationalistic newspaper headlines. The beast's nocturnal rampages are followed by such banners as "SAVAGE PIER MURDER BAFFLES POLICE" and "BEACH KILLER STRIKES AGAIN."

As the mayhem continues, Chester portrays Lombardi with a stolid, passionless detachment. Dr. Erickson refers to his actions as those of "an egomaniac playing God," while Chappel, having attempted to exploit them along the way, calls him "a dirty sideshow fortune teller with delusions of grandeur." Following in the footsteps of traditional horror

The She-Creature (1956): Chester Morris, as Dr. Carlo Lombardi, and the "She-Creature" in a horror thriller inspired by the story of "Bridey Murphy" [original lobby card].

characters like Frankenstein's Monster and the Creature from the Black Lagoon, the She-Creature ultimately destroys its creator.

Alex Gordon also recalled Chester's return flight to New York after completing the shoot:

> Chester Morris was sitting next to Audrey Hepburn. She knew Chester Morris as a stage star, and the conversation got into, "What have you been doing?"
>
> "What have *you* been doing?" Chester said, "Well, Audrey, you'll probably laugh at this, but I just finished doing a nine-day picture for an independent company, *The She-Creature*."
>
> "Oh, *that* must have been a *lot* of fun! I'd love to see that picture!" said Audrey Hepburn!
>
> Chester tried to describe what kind of a slimy seaweed outfit the She-Creature had on, and apparently Audrey Hepburn got a tremendous kick out of his description! Chester was very pleased that a prestige actress like that didn't belittle the thing, and in fact appreciated it for what it was worth![10]

In his September 5, 1956, review, *Variety*'s "Kove" did not share Chester's enthusiasm for the fantastic material:

> A tossed green salad of the Bridey Murphy theme, mixed with a helping of monster-from-the-past, and served up with a dash of Svengali, this pic is aimed at unpretentious billings, in keeping with its

very modest budget, and should serve well in these situations.... [A] disjointed, haphazard.... Lou Rusiff script ... utilizes a fair share of this genre's clichés before the final reel. However, director Edward L. Cahn manages to mix in a good quota of chills, especially for impressionable small fry.

Chester Morris is too able an actor to be entirely submerged in this shoddy material, and manages a capable performance, although he relies much on the baleful glare and the muttered threat for effect.... Tom Conway is properly suave as the money-hungry promoter....

Technical credits are adequate, except that the monster becomes ridiculous when viewed in the strong light of the killings.[11]

On July 17, 1956, Chester reprised his role as Detective McLeod, in a brief guest-starring run of *Detective Story* at the Alley Theatre in Houston. On September 13, he was back in New York, as the guest on the *Tonight!* television program, then hosted by Steve Allen at the Hudson Theatre. The first late-night talk show, it was broadcast on NBC from September 1954 until January 1957. Gene Rayburn, whom Chester would work with many times during his long association with game-show producers Mark Goodson and Bill Todman, was the *Tonight!* announcer, and the band, led by Skitch Henderson, included some jazz heavyweights: guitarist Tony Mottola, drummer Bobby Rosengarden and, on trumpets, Clark Terry and Doc Severinsen, who remained with the program in its various incarnations until 1992.

On October 15, Chester returned to McLeod's investigative persona for more stock dates of *Detective Story*, this time at Milwaukee's Fred Miller Theatre. He then made his second appearance on NBC's *Kraft Television Theater* in "Time Lock," broadcast from New York on November 28. Directed by Harry Herrman, this Arthur Hailey teleplay concerned a young boy (Peter Lazer) who accidentally wanders into a bank vault that is locked by an accountant for 63 hours, and the resulting efforts by police and Dawson (Chester), a safe expert, to rescue him before the oxygen runs out. *Variety*'s "Chan" criticized the author for failing fully to realize the drama afforded by the subject:

> Arthur Hailey, the Toronto ad man-turned-scripter who's been burning up the international television screens ... muffed a beautiful opportunity for a smash suspense vehicle in his "Time Lock...." Herrmann managed to turn Hailey's story ... into a niftily paced melodrama, but considering the opportunities presented by the property in terms of compelling human values, his effort has to be chalked up as a superficial one....
>
> All the melodramatic ingredients were there and exploited, but the performance never struck home and established a sense of reality and impact because the human values were neglected. The viewer couldn't really identify with the characters. In short, it was melodrama instead of drama. Fault lay primarily in the script....
>
> Not much better were the performances. Chester Morris, as the safe expert who finally gets the boy out, was authoritative without any depth; Tom Middleton as the bank manager was somewhat more effective but not wholly convincing. In most cases, the actors had to contend with the superficiality of the script.... With a longer treatment, either as a 90-minute showcase or a motion pic, full advantage could be taken of the real possibilities presented by the premise.[12]

On January 14, 1957, Humphrey Bogart died in his Beverly Hills home following a long and torturous bout with cancer. Of his friend's popularity, Chester later said, "It's the angry young. They're cheering for the heavy today. Everything must be nonconformist. They'd also like to do the things he did. He was a forerunner of James Bond."[13]

Chester was pleased to appear on the March 6 episode of the long-running CBS series *The Red Skelton Hour*. Fifteen years earlier, he and Skelton had contributed to an all-star radio show for the USO. Now, in the television sketch "Clem's Fish Market," Chester played Tony, a mobster menacing Clem Kaddidlehopper, supported by Robert Armstrong (as Lieutenant Flanagan), Veda Ann Borg (as Trixie) and (as mobsters) Leonard Bremen, Frankie Darro and Frank Richards.

On April 12, Chester played Frank Simmons in "Black is for Grief" on the CBS television series *Zane Grey Theater*, hosted by Dick Powell from 1956 to 1961. Directed by Lewis Allen from Aaron Spelling's teleplay, this episode concerns Union soldier Jeff Anderson (Tom Tryon), who returns home after the Civil War to discover that his murdered wife, Barbara (Mala Powers), had not been faithful during his absence. Through a series of flashbacks, told by Mrs. Sarah Simmons (Mary Astor), about her husband, Frank; Tom Roarke (Tom Tully), about his son, Cleve (Skip Homeier); and his mother, Ma Anderson (Beulah Bondi), Jeff learns the bitter truth. Though confined to the early scenes of this well-directed mystery, Chester is convincing as an aging Westerner in love with a much younger married woman.

Zane Grey Theater: "Black Is for Grief" (April 12, 1956), with Chester Morris as Frank Simmons.

Chester returned to CBS on May 2 to play the Warden in "Child of Trouble," a 90-minute live television performance, on the acclaimed program *Playhouse 90*, which also ran from 1956 to 1961. Directed by Paul Nickell from James P. Cavanagh's adaptation of a story by Selma Robinson, the show, also featuring Ricardo Montalban, Lillian Roth, Frank Puglia and 11-year-old Patty McCormack, reunited Chester with former big-screen costars Joan Blondell and Richard Arlen.

On May 22, Chester made another guest appearance on *The Kraft Television Theater*, in "Man of Prey," a Western about rampaging bounty hunters in the 1850s American Southwest. When Mexico offers to pay $500 for every scalp taken from a Native American, rancher Jed Heath (Chester) risks his life to protect them from a band of violent mercenaries (led by Bruce Gordon).

Before the *Kraft* broadcast, Chester was interviewed by journalist Erskine Johnson, who revealed that he was "still trim, youthful looking [and once again] a New Yorker." Johnson added,

> Chester Morris isn't writing a book about Hollywood's dear dead "daze" of free spending and wild temperaments.
> "I don't have a vice to give up and then write about," he laughed. But he could write a book, all right. He's "Mr. I-Was-There" in the Movietown memory league.[14]

With most of his work now centered on the East Coast, Chester and Lillian had permanently relocated to New York. In August 1957, he starred on "Broadway in the Poconos," in Arthur Miller's one-act drama *A View from the Bridge*, at the Pocono Playhouse, a venue of "air-conditioned comfort" located on Route 90 in Mountainhome, 15 miles north of Stroudsburg, Pennsylvania. Originally produced at the Coronet Theatre on Broadway from September 9, 1955, to February 4, 1956, the play featured Chester in the lead role of Eddie Carbone, initiated by Van Heflin, who had portrayed the character for 149 performances.

New York Times theater critic Brooks Atkinson wrote of the Pocono production, "A tense drama of power and reality."[15]

On November 5, 1957, Chester began playing Jack Rance in an off–Broadway production of David Belasco's *The Girl of the Golden West* at New York's Anderson Theatre. Directed by Jerome Kitty, the Theatre Four production ran for eight performances before closing on November 10.

11

Double-Breasted Suits to *Blue Denim*

On February 27, 1958, Chester began playing Major Bartley, U.S. Army, retired, in the original Broadway production of James Leo Herlihy and William Noble's drama *Blue Denim*, directed by Joshua Logan at the Playhouse Theatre. Costarring Warren Berlinger, Carol Lynley, Pat Stanley, June Walker and Burt Brinckerhoff (as Bartley's troubled son), the successful play ran for 166 performances, closing on July 19, 1958.

In May, Chester, discussing his first Broadway run in nearly 30 years, self-deprecatingly admitted,

> Any guy who paints up his face is really kind of ridiculous. Now take me, I never really liked this business. But I grew up in it and that is sort of like being born into a family of acrobats—nobody ever expects you to do anything else. I'm ham enough to love to watch the replays of my old movies on television.[1]

He later revealed how the *Blue Denim* role helped save him from typecasting:

> I think it is [a problem], especially in pictures. I think, in the theater, they give you a little more of a chance to step out of the Boston Blackie formula. Josh Logan, of course, did it with me in *Blue Denim*, and I will be forever grateful. He took me from *Detective Story* and those kinds of things and put me in a character part. I enjoyed doing it. It was fun. No else would have done it but Josh. I was the father of the boy, who couldn't communicate with his son.[2]

Chester signed a new one-year television motion picture contract with the William Morris Agency on May 5, 1958. In exchange for representation in employment limited to made-for-television productions, he agreed to pay the agent the standard "10 percent of all moneys or other considerations received directly or indirectly."[3] On May 27, he was a guest on *Tonight Starring Jack Paar*, the NBC late-night talk show on which he had appeared with original host Steve Allen the previous year. During this visit he was interviewed by Johnny Carson, who was filling in for Paar.

The live dramatic anthology series *Pursuit* aired for only 12 episodes on CBS during the 1958–1959 television season. During its short run, the program employed writers Donald S. Sanford and Rod Serling, composer Bernard Herrmann and a cast including Lew Ayres, Martin Balsam, John Cassavetes, Eduardo Ciannelli, Ralph Meeker, Sal Mineo, Michael Rennie and Rip Torn. For "Tiger on a Bicycle," directed by Paul Nickell on November 12, 1958, Chester shared the screen with Neville Brand, Laraine Day, Dan Duryea and David Ladd.

In January 1959, Chester starred in a production of *A View from the Bridge* produced and directed by Miranda d'Ancona at the Curran Theatre in San Francisco. During the suc-

Blue Denim (June 16, 1958): From left, Chester Morris, June Walker and Burt Brinckerhoff in the original Broadway production of James Leo Herlihy and William Noble's drama, directed by Joshua Logan at the Playhouse Theatre [original playbill].

cessful run of the play, he was contacted by a man in Glendale, California, who informed him that an uncashed MGM studio check, dated 1930 and made out to him for $660, had been discovered in a house recently purchased from Mrs. Halie C. Smith. Chester was not familiar with Smith, nor did he recall exactly what pay the check, now held by the Glendale Police Department, represented.

"I don't remember, but I might have worked awfully hard for that money," he said, admitting that, at the time, he never saw his checks (all of which went to Roland West). The bank on which the check was drawn refused to cash it, informing Chester that current MGM cashier James Hoagy would have to write a new one. The financial officer naturally replied that "it would take a lot of research to determine whether the studio owes Morris anything," noting that a duplicate check may accidentally have been issued. In the meantime, Glendale police told Chester "they would give the check to [him] if he want[ed] it."[4]

Chester continued traveling around the country, playing stage and television roles in a variety of locations. In early March 1959, he was in Marion County, Florida, joining Gary Merrill and Pat Henny to shoot "I, the Hunter," a television program for CBS, in and around the Silver Springs and Lake Weir areas.

Chester and Henny played a pair of murderers tracked down after their victim's body is discovered by a professional hunter (Merrill), whom they disarm. Escaping, the hunter continues to dog the killers, who become lost in a large wooded area, where one perishes in a fall and the other surrenders. CBS had planned to broadcast the 30-minute program as part of an anthology series during the 1959 fall season, but it remained on the shelf until, retitled "The Hunter," it eventually aired on May 6, 1964, as part of a new, short-lived, 12-episode series of *Suspense*.

Chester costarred with Hurd Hatfield, Carol Lawrence, Roddy McDowall and Brad Morrow in "Too Bad About Sheila Troy," a two-part episode of *Oldsmobile Music Theatre* broadcast live by NBC on April 16 and 23, 1959. On June 3, he played Henry Vining in "Whisper of Evil" on the CBS anthology series *The United States Steel Hour*. Initially produced as the radio program *Theatre Guild on the Air* in 1943–1944, the show, broadcast live from New York from 1953 to 1963, was part of a campaign to improve American drama by the much-heralded Theatre Guild. Nina Foch, Chester's costar in *Boston Blackie's Rendezvous*, John Beal and Barbara Dana joined him for the episode.

Oldsmobile Music Theatre: "Too Bad About Sheila Troy" (April 16 and 23, 1959). From left, Chester Morris, Hurd Hatfield, Carol Lawrence and Roddy McDowall.

Chester's association with producers Mark Goodson and Bill Todman continued with the popular game show *To Tell the Truth*, on which he first appeared on September 15, 1959, joining host Bud Collyer and fellow panelists Polly Bergen, Kitty Carlisle and Peter Donald. "One of these men is the former instructor to his highness, Prince Ranier of Monaco," announced Bern Bennett at the opening of the program, on which the panelists attempted to separate the "central character" (who was telling the truth) from the "two imposters." During each program, three groups challenged the panelists, who asked questions, trying to discover the truthful person in each group.

Chester, asking the three men technical questions on maritime and equestrian subjects, picked the wrong one. Carlisle, who broke up everyone with her witty comments, was the only panelist who chose Ranier's actual assistant.

The next guest "to tell the truth" was an Arizona State University student and "world's champion junior cowgirl." Polly Bergen was the only panelist to identify her, while the other three, with Chester being "certain," all picked the wrong woman.

The third "central character" was the Sunday editor of the Memphis, Tennessee, *Commercial Appeal* newspaper. "Your exploits sound like a 'Boston Blackie' film," Chester told guest number one, again asking technical questions and obviously enjoying the game-show atmosphere. He was wrong again, as were the others, except the perceptive Polly Bergen. "I had a lot of fun," Chester admitted. "I'm glad I was *so good*."

On April 25, 1960, Chester played Theodore Swanson in Paul Osborn's adaptation of his stage comedy *Morning's at Seven*, broadcast on National Educational Television's *Play of the Week*. Russell Collins and Dorothy Gish (veterans of the original 1939–1940 Broadway production directed by Joshua Logan), Beulah Bondi (who appears in the 1939 MGM film adaptation of Osborn's *On Borrowed Time*), Ann Harding and Eileen Heckart joined Chester in this story about four aging sisters questioning the path of their lives in a small Midwestern town. Chester later recalled playing the elderly character of Swanson: "Old men, I love to play, because I'm an old man."[5]

During the summer of 1960, CBS gave Chester a chance to appear in his own weekly television series, *Diagnosis: Unknown*, in which he costarred with Patrick O'Neal, Phyllis Newman, Cal Bellini and Martin Huston. As homicide detective Captain Max Ritter, Chester was aided by Dr. Daniel Coffee (O'Neal), head pathologist at a big-city hospital, and his three able assistants. An early small-screen foray into forensic crime investigation, the live series debuted on July 5 with "The Case of the Radiant Wine," directed by Fielder Cook from Arnold Manoff's teleplay based on a novel by Lawrence G. Blochman. In this story involving the suspicious death of a suicidal model, the regular cast was augmented by Tom Bosley, Murray Matheson, Larry Hagman and Patricia Barry. Newman, as Doris Hudson, and Bellini, as Dr. Motital Mookerji, an Indian pathologist on an exchange from Bombay, provided an innovative element, but the story being confined to a few sets made the episode heavy with dialogue and short on action.

Chester also appeared in several promotional advertisements for the series. Produced by Bob Banner Associates in New York, the series was canceled after only nine episodes, the last, "The Red Death," airing on September 20, 1960.

Chester made a second appearance on *To Tell the Truth*, joining guest host Jim Fleming and fellow panelists Polly Bergen, Kitty Carlisle and Tom Poston, on July 21, 1960. The novelty "bubblegum" pop hit "Itsy Bitsy Teenie Weenie Yellow Polkadot Bikini," released the previous month, opened the show, with one of the three young men being Brian Hyland, the 17-year-old singer who recorded the song. Fleming began his remarks by flattering the "vivacious, witty and astonishing panel," asking Chester about playing the detective in *Diagnosis Unknown* and welcoming him to "deduce with us."

Chester made basic queries about recording the song, commenting, "Why don't you record ... something sensible, like we used to have?" The "real Brian Hyland," whom Chester asked about his hairstyling, so he could pass on the information to Kenton, was correctly identified by the panelists, except Kitty Carlisle.

Jobie Arnold, a female racetrack handicapper, was the second guest. During his questions, Chester asked the third challenger, "You're a handicapper. Are you allowed to go out nights?"

"*Certainly*," the young woman answered casually.

"I think you've made an engagement," interjected Fleming before passing the questioning to Polly Bergen.

This time around, Chester, trying to change his decision after already writing it down, was disqualified from the round. "The game is played fair and square, and here is Polly Bergen," said the host.

"I don't understand why we can't cheat *a little*, every now and then," protested Polly. "I mean, the odds are rough enough as it is."

"I don't like you saying I'm not fair and square," Chester told Polly. "*Captain Ritter* is always fair and square." All three honest panelists chose the right woman, leaving Chester the odd man out. The three challengers all received a carton of Camel cigarettes on their way out of the studio.

Clifford Teach, captain of the Niagara Falls sightseeing boat *Maid of the Mist II*, who daringly rescued a young passenger, was the third guest. Poston and Bergen selected the real skipper, while Chester, again asking technical questions, and Carlisle were off the mark. Each of the challengers received his carton of Camels.

Fleming closed with, "As Bud Collyer would always say, 'Remember to *tell the truth*.' Good night."

On November 17, 1960, Chester opened in the original run of *Advise and Consent*, dramatized by Loring Mandel from Allen Drury's bestselling, Pulitzer Prize–winning novel, at the Cort Theatre. Directed by Franklin J. Schaffner, the play featured him as Michigan Senator Bob Munson, the Senate Majority Leader, in an excellent cast including Ed Begley, Henry Jones, Richard Kiley, Kevin McCarthy and Woodrow Parfrey. Munson, unhappy when the President (Judson Laire), without his consultation, nominates the left-leaning Robert Leffingwell to be secretary of state, nevertheless agrees to fight for his confirmation against the conservatives who oppose him. Set primarily in the U.S. Senate chamber, the high drama concludes with the nation led by a new president and secretary of state on the eve of a summit with the Soviet Union. This second new Broadway hit for Chester outlasted his previous effort, closing on May 20, 1961, following its 222nd performance. He remembered a memorable patron who visited him after a performance at the Cort:

> Joan Crawford ... came backstage to see me ... and it was just wonderful. She had her entourage with her, and everything but a bugle played before she came in. And she was in the lamé and the mink, and the tears coming down. I jut *loved* it. And our whole cast peeking around corners to get a glimpse of this.[6]

When interviewed during the successful run of the play, Chester reflected on his recurring role in the Boston Blackie series, which had ended more than a decade earlier. The major difference with each subsequent picture would be the locale, he claimed, doing his best to vary each performance as much as possible. The director would explain, "Oh, this is Blackie in the Orient," and Chester and his colleagues would "close [their] eyes and plunge forward. It wasn't art. It was security."⁷

New York journalist Phyllis Battelle explained,

> A reporter discovers, in the course of interviewing celebrities, that most actors are more attractive behind a spotlight than over a spot of tea.
>
> The reason is, probably, that they are more comfortable in the role of someone else than they are as themselves. Otherwise, they'd never have gone into an insecure business like acting.
>
> The exceptions to this rule, curious as it may sound, are the real veteran actors of Hollywood and Broadway who were pushed into the profession when they were quite young—by economic necessity, perhaps, or by heritage, rather than by choice. They look upon show business as a job to be accomplished, rather than as burning affair of the id, and this objectivity results in normal, natural, non-idiotic behavior.

Advise and Consent (1961): Chester Morris, as Senate Majority Leader Bob Munson, in the original Broadway stage production, dramatized by Loring Mandel from Allen Drury's bestselling, Pulitzer Prize–winning novel.

One such un-actory gentleman is Chester Morris, who became an actor 43 years ago when he was in his teens because his parents were in the theater and "I didn't know what else to do."⁸

As for the political content of *Advise and Consent*, he explained, "It's a strange role for me. I always held politics in the same esteem as I held Hollywood. I couldn't understand a bunch of guys being so palsy-walsy in private, and then ripping one another's reputations apart in public...."

After playing Senator Munson "night after night," he decided, "in view of all I know about politics, I'm going to vote for Caroline [Kennedy, then three years old, and living in the White House] when she runs. That is, if she remains incorruptible."⁹ (More than five decades later, Kennedy would serve as President Barack Obama's Ambassador to Japan, from November 2013 to January 2017.)

Created by Western writer Charles Marquis Warren, the television series *Rawhide* made its CBS debut on January 9, 1959, running for 217 episodes before taking its final first-run bow on December 7, 1965. In the suspenseful episode "Incident on the Road to Yesterday" (November 18, 1960), written by Jan Winters and Winston Miller, Chester plays back-shooting hypocrite and murderer Hugh Clements, manager of the Huntsville stage line, opposite series regulars Eric Fleming (as trail boss Gil Favor) and Clint Eastwood (as Rowdy Yates).

Reformed thief Ralph Bartlett (Frankie Laine), accused of killing Clements' brother-in-law during a robbery, during which $11,000 was taken, seeks to repay all those he had wronged previously. Favor agrees to deliver the actual $250 that Bartlett took to Clements, but the townspeople and Sheriff Ed Stockton (Robert Gist) seek retribution. Determined to see justice done, Rowdy remains in town, where he baits the people by taking bets and claiming that a witness to the crime has been found. Stockton, believing Rowdy drunk, sneaks into his hotel room, but forced to confess his part in the killing, is shot in the back by Clements, who had stolen the money to gain control of the town. Before he dies, however, Stockton guns him down, and Bartlett's innocence is proved.

Directed by B-Western veteran R.G. Springsteen, whose prolific career shifted into television during the late 1950s, "Incident on the Road to Yesterday" cast Chester as the most thoroughly unpleasant character (with no redeeming features) he ever played on television. Following the shoot, he said, "Three days in the saddle after all these years is just too much. I can barely walk. But I'll be back home in New York in a few days and sitting in nothing but overstuffed chairs."[10]

During the 1960 holiday season, Chester joined his *Five Came Back* and *Marines Fly High* costar Lucille Ball and her children, Lucie and Desi Arnaz, Jr., on the December 29 broadcast of *Tonight Starring Jack Paar*. Paar welcomed him back on February 2, 1961, when fashion designer Oleg Cassini also joined the guests.

On February 7, Chester, Glenda Farrell, George Grizzard, Janet Blair, Roland Winters and a young Jane Fonda appeared in "A String of Beads" on NBC's *Story of Love*. Adapted from the W. Somerset Maugham story by Steve Gethers, this one-hour drama was shot in color by director Fielder Cook.

12

From *Naked City* to *Route 66*

Between television appearances, Chester again played Captain Queeg, in a 1961 production of *The Caine Mutiny Court-Martial* at Playhouse-on-the-Mall in Paramus, New Jersey. During the spring, he reported back to the South Bronx to guest star in an episode of the innovative and acclaimed crime-drama television series *Naked City* at Biograph Studios, where he had acted in *Frankie and Johnnie* in 1934. Now in its second season on ABC, *Naked City* (1958–1959 and 1960–1963) was created by the erudite writer Stirling Silliphant, who also was responsible for another contemporary "semi-anthology" series, *Route 66* (1960–1964). Herbert B. Leonard, Silliphant's co-creator on *Route 66*, also served as narrator for the first season of *Naked City*, famous for the line (originating in the 1948 film of the same name) closing each episode, "There are eight million stories in the Naked City. This has been one of them."

The title role in the episode "Make-Believe Man," broadcast on May 17, 1961, afforded Chester an opportunity to create a nuanced, interesting character, a paramount element in the *Naked City* methodology: The episodes invariably placed more emphasis on the roles played by the series' impressive spectrum of guest actors, divided roughly between classic film stars and character actors (Eddie Albert, Lee J. Cobb, Steve Cochran, Richard Conte, Dan Duryea, Betty Field, Henry Hull, Roddy McDowall, Claude Rains, Ruth Roman, Mickey Rooney, Sylvia Sidney) and up-and-coming stage and television performers working in New York (Martin Balsam, Bruce Dern, Robert Duvall, Peter Falk, Peter Fonda, Jack Klugman, George Maharis, Walter Matthau, Lois Nettleton, Susan Oliver, Robert Redford, Frank Sutton).

Sy Salkowitz adapted the teleplay for "Make-Believe Man" from a story he co-wrote with Jerry Devine about Frank Manfred (Chester), a homeless "rummy," who is reported "kidnapped" by his fellow Bowery down-and-outers. Actor-director Lawrence Dobkin (memorable as "Dutch" Schultz in the crime series *The Untouchables* [1959–1963]) opens the episode with the narration, "Frank Manfred stopped living in 1952 and waited for his body to die."

Although NYPD 65th Precinct detectives Lieutenant Mike Parker (Horace McMahon), Adam Flint (Paul Burke) and Frank Arcaro (Harry Bellaver) are skeptical, the deathly ill, alcoholic Manfred has been grabbed from the gutter by Carlos Ruldan (Nehemiah Persoff), vicious supporter of "The Revolution of July 29th," a South American uprising from 20 years earlier. Coached to impersonate a former military leader, Colonel Bryar, Manfred manages to gain support from an old comrade, Don Miguel Cordura (Eduardo Ciannelli), but is repaid by the gun of Ruldan. Aided by his fellow rummies, the resilient Manfred rallies long enough to chase down the murderous rebel; and, in a local warehouse, they break into crates of weapons to engage in a furious shootout. The detectives arrive just as Manfred guns down Ruldan, only to be shot to death in return. The episode fades out as the young son of the doomed Juan Menguado (Jay Novello) weeps on the dead Manfred's chest.

Naked City: "Make-Believe Man" (May 17, 1961). Chester Morris as Frank Manfred, aka "Colonel Bryar," a deathly ill "rummy" grabbed from the gutter by a South American revolutionary to impersonate a former military leader.

Chester's believable, sympathetic characterization provides an artistic balance to the intense style of Nehemiah Persoff, a specialist at portraying psychologically motivated villains. The series regulars (particularly the naturalistic, minimalist Harry Bellaver) and supporting cast, including Italian Americans (Ciannelli, Novello) portraying Latinos (a long-running practice in U.S. film and television casting), is uniformly excellent, driving the story involving the tried-and-true, somewhat fantastic Latin American revolution plot.

More than 57 years after the episode was aired, Nehemiah Persoff recalled,

> Chester Morris: I'd been a fan of his work for many years, so I was very excited to learn that I would be in the same episode of *Naked City* as he.
> When I got on set (on location), he was involved in a very tense scene, so I stayed away. I didn't want to distract him in any way. Somehow our paths never crossed [off camera], and I never got to tell him how much I admired him as an actor. I don't remember so many [other] people with whom I've worked.
> In the 1960s and 1970s, I was doing so many television shows, sometimes two in one week. My mind was constantly occupied with learning new and forgetting old lines.[1]

Persoff's recollection illustrates Chester's approach to acting at this point in his career, 43 years after he first trod the Broadway boards, and 32 since he received an Academy Award nomination for his Hollywood talkie debut. Again a "New York actor," focusing on a variety of stage and television roles, he consistently was collaborating with and observing the work of a new generation of performers. Many of these young thespians were influenced by the "system" (involving emotional experience and subconscious behavior) expounded by Russian actor-director Konstantin Stanislavski and further developed by the New York Group Theatre (1931–1941). The Actors Studio, founded in Hell's Kitchen in 1947, refined the techniques which Group Theatre founder Lee Strasberg called "The Method."

Stella Adler, another founding member of the Group Theatre and creator of the Stella Adler Studio of Acting in 1949, under whom Persoff, a member of the first Actor's Studio "beginner's" class, served as intern, studied with Stanislavski and later agreed with him that relying on Strasberg's paradigm of "emotional memory" to create a characterization was not only limiting but could prove psychologically troubling. She and Stanislavski both believed that actors do not internally possess what is needed to portray a variety of roles, and that extensive research is required to understand the experiences, values and behavior of characters from different cultures.

Adler's basic division of 50-percent internal and 50-percent external factors, and emphasis that an actor must determine his approach based on each specific text, is well-represented by Persoff, a performer adept at a wide array of ethnicities and dialects. As his career progressed, the autodidactic Chester drew both on his private memories and professional experiences of working with other talented actors in a variety of productions (including stage and live television, which often allow one to remain "in character," whereas films are invariably shot out of sequence over an extended time period, with many being confined by genre conventions), and this expanded his versatility. He would maintain this practice while performing until the final day of his life. However, while performing in the touring version of *Advise and Consent*, he did make it clear that he was not a proponent of *the* Method:

> They speak about "method actors." *Every actor* has a method of a kind. The "method" that we are encountering today in the theater is horrible. There is no excuse for it.
>
> I think that an actor should have analyzed his character in rehearsals, and I don't think he has any right to do it in front of an audience. It all should have been done for him, or *by* him, the minute that curtain goes up. I don't have to go into my dressing room and make believe I'm Senator Knox for half an hour before the curtain goes up.
>
> I played Captain Queeg in *The Caine Mutiny* a great many times, and some of these kids in the company used to say, because Queeg is one of the greatest parts, outside of Hamlet, ever written. He's only on stage for 22 minutes in the whole play: six minutes in Act One, and then the big scene in the second act. And these kids used to say, "What do you do? Do you go in there and get in the mood for that second act, when you go to pieces?"
>
> And I said, "Well, if I did *that*, there would be two men in white coats waiting for me." Eight times a week, you couldn't do it. You have to fall back on technique. And I'm in agreement with John Gielgud, who came out in *The New Yorker* ... in that series of articles on actors ... Gielgud came out with a wonderful idea, to me. He said ... "A good actor should be able to play an emotional scene and total his laundry bill at the same time."[2]

The initial season of *Naked City*, premiering on September 30, 1958, included 39 30-minute episodes costarring John McIntire as Lieutenant Muldoon and James Franciscus as Detective Jimmy Halloran. When McIntire left halfway through the season, McMahon took over, but poor ratings led to the show's cancellation. At the request of a sponsor, the Brown and Williamson tobacco company, and some of its crew, the show was reworked as an hour-length procedural drama with greater emphasis on the guest characters. McMahon and Bellaver (who eventually appeared in all but two series episodes) returned, and Burke and Nancy Malone, who plays Flint's girlfriend, actress Libby Kingston, joined the regular cast. Series directors included William Beaudine, John Brahm, Tay Garnett, Arthur Hiller, Irvin Kershner, David Lowell Rich, Stuart Rosenberg and George Sherman. George Duning and Ned Washington composed theme music for the first season, while longtime Frank Sinatra arrangers Billy May and Nelson Riddle handled the work during the second and third seasons.

The television detective series *Checkmate*, created by Eric Ambler and filmed partially on location in San Francisco, ran on CBS for two seasons (1960–1962). Having achieved great popularity playing federal agent Cam Allison in 13 episodes of *The Untouchables* (1960) for the same network, Anthony George was offered the top-billed role of Don Corey in *Checkmate*. In his final *Untouchables* episode "The Frank Nitti Story," Allison, much to the chagrin of leader Eliot Ness (Robert Stack), is killed during a shootout with mobsters, a sudden story shift added by Harry Essex and Lee Blair that freed George to move on to *Checkmate*.

Joining George were Doug McClue as Jed Sills, Corey's partner at the private detective agency Checkmate, Inc., and Sebastian Cabot as British criminologist and professor Carl Hyatt, who serves as their official consultant. The first-season guest casts were another all-star lineup of the era, with Anne Baxter appearing in the debut episode, "Death Runs Wild," followed by the likes of Charles Bickford, Richard Conte, Joseph Cotten, Dan Duryea, Martin Landau, Charles Laughton, Peter Lorre, Lee Marvin, Susan Oliver, H.M. Wynant, and two of Chester's colleagues from the "Boston Blackie" series, Victor Sen Yung and Nina Foch.

In the second season opener, "Portrait of a Man Running," broadcast on October 4, 1961, Chester played career political campaign manager Albert ["Albee"] Dewitt, in support of his friend and *Blind Alley* costar Ralph Bellamy, as flamboyant Governor Tom Barker, currently running for a fourth consecutive term, against a "clean" government candidate, Mervin Everhardt (Wendell Holmes). Working as a "double agent," DeWitt is secretly providing information to shady businessman Frank Castleberry (Oliver McGowan), who lost out on a government contract because of Barker. Now the governor stages an "assassination attempt" on himself and then blames Castleberry, who coerces DeWitt into an attempt to remove his boss from power. As Corey and Sills investigate DeWitt's motivations, the campaigner admits, "I have a great talent for politics, Mr. Corey, but not the face, or the voice, or the smile."

Faced with remaining loyal to Barker or saving his own skin, DeWitt allowed Chester to deliver one of his most emotionally powerful performances. Having enjoyed 25 years of honest, successful campaigning, DeWitt has fallen into five years of political expediency and, finally, the traitorous backstabbing of his friend, whose ethics also have eroded. The episode culminates with the tension-racked DeWitt's breakdown as he threatens to shoot the governor. Playing the scene with the consummate Bellamy helped give Chester the edge he needed to create a thoroughly believable, poignant portrayal. Elliot Silverstein directed the politically astute teleplay by Richard Fielder, featuring a musical score by Morton Stevens.

Shot by Bing Crosby Productions at Desilu Studios, the groundbreaking television medical drama *Ben Casey* made its ABC debut on October 2, 1961. Running for five seasons, the series costarred Vince Edwards as Casey and Sam Jaffe as his mentor, Dr. David Zorba, with Franchot Tone in the recurring role of Dr. Daniel Niles Freeland. The program was another to welcome an impressive roster of guest stars, both current favorites and performers from Hollywood's golden age: Mary Astor, Lew Ayres, Melvyn Douglas, James Dunn, Glenda Farrell, Betty Field, Allen Jenkins, Elsa Lanchester, Maureen O'Sullivan, John Qualen, Cesar Romero, Gloria Swanson and Chester, who plays self-important, seriously ill businessman Walter Tyson in the October 30, 1961, episode "An Expensive Glass of Water."

Directed by Robert Ellis Miller from a teleplay by Gilbert Ralston, the episode focuses on Casey and Zorba's attempts to deal with the stubborn, single-minded Tyson (called "Mister T" by his devoted secretary, Frederica Warren [Neva Patterson]), who is risking death from a brain tumor, even while attempting to run his business from a hospital room. Because he donates $100,000 to the institution on a yearly basis, Tyson believes he has the right to command Casey, who naturally stands for none of it.

"You keep that smart tongue in your head," Tyson orders the young neurosurgeon, "or I'll cut you in half, professionally and every other way, is that clear?"

By the program's end, however, Tyson's recovery from successful surgery performed by Casey, brings him around, physically and somewhat psychologically. Referring to future difficult patients, Tyson informs the doctor, "You're going to get your head bumped a lot," advising, "but don't let them grind you down." Though his business has suffered a huge hit during his hospitalization, he also promises to donate $50,000 to programs favored by Casey when his affairs financially recover.

Tyson provided Chester with another well-shaded character, a tenacious man who experiences a degree of redemption during a nearly fatal experience, from the small-screen medium, again supporting his decision to move from film to television. During the run of the series, Gilbert Ralston shared writing credits with such colleagues as D.C. Fontana, Jack Laird, John Meredyth Lucas, Leo Penn and Alvin Sargent; while Robert Ellis Miller was joined by fellow directors Lucas, Penn, Abner Biberman, Alan Crosland, Jr., Arthur Hiller, Irvin Kershner, Jerry Lewis, Sydney Pollack (who also acted in one episode) and Mark Rydell. Star Vince Edwards also directed seven episodes.

Writer Reginald Rose (*12 Angry Men* [1957]) created the courtroom drama television series *The Defenders*, which ran for four seasons (1961–1965) on NBC. Starring E.G. Marshall and Robert Reed as father-and-son defense attorneys Lawrence and Kenneth Preston, the show's intelligent scripts, by Rose, Ernest Kinoy, Larry Cohen and other top television writers, often depict their efforts to defend controversial clients. The debut episode, a disturbing drama about the "mercy killing" of a newborn baby with Down's Syndrome, guest starring Jack Klugman, Joan Hackett and Gene Hackman, was followed by issues such as PTSD, prison conditions, drug addiction, child custody, mental illness, perjury, police brutality and capital punishment, with performances by Martin Balsam, Edward Binns, Ossie Davis, Robert Duvall, Clu Gulager, Sam Jaffe, Viveca Lindfors, Joanne Linville, Robert Loggia, Frank McHugh, William Shatner, Frank Sutton, and 10-year-old Richard Thomas.

The February 17, 1962, episode "The Empty Chute," written by Max Ehrlich, involves the Prestons' participation in the defense of U.S. Army 109th Airborne Sergeant Jesse Cobb (Michael Strong), charged with murdering a fellow officer during a simulated combat jump. Chester contributes one of his many convincing portrayals of a military officer, as Captain Peters, an army attorney who seeks the assistance of the civilian legal team.

A highlight is Peters' questioning of Mrs. Walsh (Neva Patterson), the murdered officer's widow, followed by the elder Preston's follow-up with the couple's young daughter, Rosemary (Linda Canby). Polly Rowles (in her recurrent series role of Helen Donaldson) and Jerry Stiller (as Sergeant Wysenski) provide able support in this episode, directed by Jack Smight at Filmways Studios in Manhattan.

Repeating his Broadway assignment, Franklin J. Schaffner also directed the national touring production of *Advise and Consent*, with dates spanning late 1961 and early 1962 in 35 cities, including the Hanna Theatre in Cleveland, Wilbur Theatre in Boston, and Orpheum Theatre in Minneapolis. Chester (now playing Senator Orrin Knox) and costar Farley Granger were joined by a supporting cast including Royal Beal, Russell Gaige, House Jameson, Archie Smith, Kay Doubleday and Harry Millard. One of the patrons who attended a road performance was Henry Fonda, who later played Robert Leffingwell in Otto Preminger's film adaptation, released by Columbia on June 6, 1962.[3]

The historic Pabst Theater in Milwaukee heavily advertised its week of dates, beginning Monday, January 15, 1962, tempting theatergoers with the pitch,

> FARLEY GRANGER as Senator Brig Anderson.
> CHESTER MORRIS as Senator Orrin Knox.
> YOU READ ABOUT THEM.
> NOW SEE THEM IN PERSON!
> SEE EVERY EXCITING SUSPENSEFUL MOMENT COME ALIVE ON THE STAGE.
> IT'S A PLAY YOU CAN NEVER-EVER-FORGET!

At a Milwaukee Variety Club annual program meeting during the afternoon of January 15, Chester was crowned "King for a Day," marking the beginning of a drive to raise $50,000 for the epilepsy clinic, then in its fifth year, at Mount Sinai Hospital. Topping off the brow of the 24-hour sovereign were clinic chairman Ben Marcus, first assistant chief barker Lee Rothman and club member Circuit Judge Elmer Roller.

Chester's reign did not extend beyond the play's opening night. While staying in Wisconsin's largest city, he also was targeted by two reactionary local politicians. Having been quoted in *Variety* that "politics is a dirty game," he was attacked in a letter by Republican Secretary of State Robert C. Zimmerman, who expressed "resentment" over the "ill-advised" statement, assiduously defending "the many dedicated, honest, conscientious men and women in Wisconsin politics." Though he did concede that there "may be some corrupt politicians," he emphasized, "by the same token I am sure you will agree that there are some immoral actors, dishonest bankers, hypocritical clergymen and lawyers who pervert the law."[4]

Zimmerman's defensive diatribe, made public immediately after the letter was mailed to Chester, and echoed by Democratic Milwaukee County Executive John Doyne, suggests that the experienced actor (having also played a key role in Rod Serling's perceptive "The Arena" in 1956) was right about a major aspect of politics, after all!

Throughout the tour, Chester received rave notices:

> *Variety*: Morris has the play's standout part and fills it to the hilt. As Senator Orrin Knox from Illinois, he triumphs.
> *Cincinnati Post and Times-Star*: The final act gives him the chance to explode, and a particularly long and difficult Senate speech drew applause from the audience.
> *Columbus Citizen-Journal*: Chester Morris fully lives up to his reputation as an actor's actor.
> *Dayton Daily News*: Chester Morris as an unbuyable senator turns in a fine job.
> *Baltimore Evening Sun*: As the influential and decent senator, he gives an excellent, assured performance.[5]

While performing in the play at Chicago's Blackstone Theatre in late February 1962, Chester sat down with Studs Terkel, with whom he'd appeared in *Detective Story* at the same venue more than 12 years earlier. In discussing switching from the role of Senate Majority Leader Munson to Senator Knox for the touring production, he explained the problem with creating a distinct characterization for local audiences who attended to see Chester Morris, the movie star:

> When I took over the part of Orrin Knox, I tried to characterize it, and I discovered, as the star of the play, or as the costar, even ... people came in to see *Chester Morris*. So, I cut out the characterization, and I went back to playing it as I would have played it *myself*. They came in to *see me*. They didn't come in to see a characterization....
> I'm getting a little old for challenges. Thirty years ago, it was fun. I used to like to do things like *The Case of Sergeant Grischa*, where you shaved your head and played a Russian soldier; but now I wouldn't bother with it.[6]

Just prior to the *Advise and Consent* tour, Chester had tackled the role of Hilary in a production of A.B. Shiffren's *Angel in the Pawnshop* at Chicago's Drury Lane Theatre. He greatly enjoyed the challenge posed by another older character, but began to reconsider his approach for developing stage parts:

> This fellow ... was seventy-five, eighty years old. He was a little old Irish pawnbroker with a bald head and a little mustache. I played the whole thing ... like a sort of male Siobhan McKenna. [The audience] never knew who I was until the middle of the first act—and this taught me a lesson. They do come, I flatter myself ... sometimes, to see Chester Morris. They don't want to see an old man come out there. That [they didn't recognize me] I loved, but it *isn't good for business*.[7]

Discussing his eventual transition from Hollywood leading man to character actor, and the success of *Advise and Consent*, he explained,

> I'm much happier now than I was twenty years ago. I *really am*. I enjoy the theater more. I think, when you get to a certain age, you don't have that awful fear and worry about going to the theater. "Are you going to be *good* tonight?" You're nervous and keyed up.
>
> I sort of take it in stride now. As long as the business is good; and, Lord knows, it's been wonderful on this tour. We've broken records every place.[8]

He elaborated more on the content of the play and the political reaction he had faced in Milwaukee:

> It was ... Walter Kerr's description, in New York—his critique of the play, which was wonderful—he said it was a *gangster* melodrama layed in Washington, which is about what it is. I think it shows the way the maneuverings go on in political circles.
>
> It's so funny that some politicians' eyes are closed to all the things that are going on around them. Lord knows, we have dreadful things happen in the theater, but we don't say they *don't* happen.
>
> You see, I'm a rather peculiar fellow. I could never be a criminal lawyer. I never could go out into a courtroom and *blast* my opponent on the courtroom floor and then go and have lunch with him. If I dislike somebody, I dislike him.
>
> I happened to watch on television a rerun of the Truman-Dewey presidential campaign, and they called each other everything they could lay tongue to—and now, of course, they're the best of friends. And *I can't do that*, and I can't understand that in politics. I either like people or I don't. You can't be two-faced about it.[9]

He also addressed the issue of the Hollywood entertainment industry's obsession with the culture of youth:

> The only thing the older actor must give up is a certain amount of *salary* every week. I had a wonderful father who was in the theater all his life; and he said to me, when I was a kid.... "Beware of the day that you play the girl's father." At that time, I was a leading man. It never meant anything to me. But, as the years passed by, I realized what he meant. Because, in any other profession—a doctor or a lawyer, or a dentist—as they get older, their fees increase. Their stature increases. In our business, it decreases.
>
> I have been very fortunate, I must say, that this business has been very kind to me, and I must appreciate it.... The minute your hair starts to get gray, you play the girl's father; and, accordingly your salary is commensurate with what job you have.[10]

He also saw a major difference in the attitudes of young performers compared to those of his peers in the acting profession two generations earlier:

> Principally, the lack of discipline in the youngsters in the theater today is *intolerable*. It's a *game* with them ... it isn't work. They're ill-equipped and ... it's not their fault, really.... George Burns said, "There's no place to *fail* anymore and ... it's true....
>
> I've played with a lot of kids who have no business in the theater at all. They just have a good-

looking face. Now, in pictures, that's all right, because the audience only sees the good take, and you might have 30 or 40 takes in the scene. And I contend that you're bound to get something that you can show in a theater, in 30 takes....

Of course, the way the kids dress today is *horrible*. We never went to a rehearsal *without a shirt on*."[11]

As for the possibility of young actors performing in road companies, he said,

[E]conomics enters into picture. The young fellow thinks, "Well, I might get a series on TV. I might become a millionaire overnight, and why should I give six or seven months of my time on tour?"

I haven't got that problem. No one is clamoring for me to go out to Hollywood to do a series. I think a fine example of fortitude is Farley Granger, my costar in [*Advise and Consent*], who is certainly a good actor and an extremely handsome fellow, and he's gone out for this training, which I think is wonderful. He's a very charming fellow, and he's willing to learn, *wants* to learn. He'll ask questions about things.... This is rather novel today, because I've played with kids that *know it all* ... and there'll all of 19 or 20 years old.[12]

To provide greater opportunities for aspiring stage actors, Chester, who supported a National Theatre financed by the federal government, accepted a position on the Drama Panel for the Bureau of Education and Cultural Affairs (ECA) of the U.S. Department of State in Washington, D.C. Established in 1961 through passage of the Fulbright-Hays Act, marshaled by Democratic U.S. Senator J. William Fulbright, passed by the 87th Congress and signed into law by President John F. Kennedy, the ECA was developed to "strengthen the ties which unite [the U.S.] with other nations by demonstrating the educational and cultural interests, developments and achievements of the people of the United States and other nations." The agency eventually included academic, cultural, sports and professional programs, as well as public and private partnerships.[13]

Efforts to develop a national theater began during the Great Depression. The Federal Theatre Project (FTP), a New Deal relief program created under President Franklin Roosevelt's Works Progress Administration, had operated from 1935 to 1939, but was criticized for being "too liberal." The non-profit producer American National Theatre and Academy (ANTA), also established in 1935, was promoted as an official, self-sustaining entity to set up venues nationwide. ANTA sponsored touring companies performing abroad following World War II and, by 1955, announced the "Forty Theatre Circuit Plan," intended "to bring the best plays, interpreted by the best actors, at minimum cost" to the largest theatres throughout the U.S.

Unfortunately, the plan was hampered by poor fundraising and objections from theater owners who had no formal representation on the ANTA board, which consisted primarily of their New York City counterparts. The agency was reorganized in the early 1960s, when the ANTA Washington Square Theatre in New York's Greenwich Village was designed as a prototype for the Vivian Beaumont Theater at Lincoln Center in Manhattan, which opened in 1965. That same year, the independent National Endowment for the Arts (NEA), headquartered in Washington, D.C., was created by an act of the U.S. Congress. (The controversial agency would increasingly face defunding and even potential abolishment over the years.)

In the wake of television, the broadcasting of traditional drama and comedy radio shows necessarily had decreased. Busy with stage work, both on Broadway and with touring companies, and a steady stream of television roles, Chester disappeared from the radio airwaves for an extended period. On September 17, 1962, after many years, he reunited with Bing Crosby for the multitalented performer-producer's CBS show with Rosemary Clooney also featuring the music of the Buddy Cole Trio.

Chester made his first of several appearances on the practical-joke comedy series *Candid Camera* (the forerunner to what later became known as "reality television") on November 11, 1962. First broadcast by producer Allen Funt on radio (as *The Candid Microphone*) and released in a series of short films in 1947, the program debuted on ABC television the following year. In 1949, Funt changed the title to *Candid Camera* for its move to NBC.

In October 1960, CBS began broadcasting a Sunday evening version of the show, on which Funt was joined by co-hosts Arthur Godfrey, Durward Kirby and former Miss America Bess Myerson, until the end of its run in 1967. Bob Banner Associates, who had hired Chester for *Diagnosis Unknown*, coproduced the show with Allen Funt Productions. Chester's debut, supporting Funt, Kirby, conductor Sid Ramin and another former Miss America, Marilyn Van Derbur, involved pulling some good-natured shenanigans on unsuspecting victims of the hidden camera. Funt's shooting schedule allowed for enough footage to be filmed for two programs, the second of which was aired the following week.

On December 6, 1962, Chester played movie producer Andrew Hines in "The Contenders," a second season episode of the ABC television anthology series *Alcoa Premiere*. Directed by David Lowell Rich and hosted by Fred Astaire, the drama costarred Edward Asner, Signe Hasso, James Patterson and Suzanne Pleshette (as Carla Hammond, a young Hollywood star whom Hines pursues during an international film award competition).

Chester again worked with director Paul Nickell, on *The Eleventh Hour* episode "Along About Late in the Afternoon," broadcast by NBC on December 26, 1962. The innovative medical drama involving psychiatry, in the style of the popular *Dr. Kildare* series, ran for two seasons (1962–1964) and starred Jack Ging as Dr. Paul Graham. First-year regular Wendell Corey (as Dr. Theodore Bassett) was succeeded by Ralph Bellamy (as Dr. L. Richard Starke) for the second season.

Reminiscent of *Blind Alley*, "Along About Late in the Afternoon" involves Dr. Bassett placing two patients together in the same room: Leo Haynes (Franchot Tone), a city editor who attempted suicide after the failure of his newspaper; and Frankie Morrison (Chester), a former labor organizer and murderer, who blames Haynes for crusading against him.

Chester made a second guest appearance on *Alcoa Premiere*, playing Charles Richardson in the January 13, 1963, episode "The Glass Palace," directed by Lawrence Dobkin from a teleplay by Gilbert Ralston. Host Fred Astaire also introduced fellow cast members Joanna Barnes, Wallace Ford, Anne Francis, Ricardo Montalban and Ed Nelson.

On February 25, Chester, after an absence of two and one-half years, was happy to make a third appearance on *To Tell the Truth* at CBS. He joined guest host Jack Clark and fellow panelists Joan Fontaine, Sam Levenson and Phyllis Newman, with whom he had enjoyed working on *Diagnosis: Unknown*. One of the guests, French makeup artist and beauty consultant André Cartier, was correctly identified only by Fontaine, who asked specific questions about cosmetics. The other panelists, including Chester, who helped raise plenty of audience laughs, all chose one of the imposters.

During the second week of April 1963, Chester made five daily appearances on Mark Goodson and Bill Todman's *The Match Game*, hosted by Gene Rayburn during its original run on NBC (1962–1969) and revamped format on CBS and in first-run syndication (1973–1982). Familiar game-show voice Johnny Olson welcomed team captains Morris and Carol Lawrence to this weekday group of programs, taped in Studio 8H at 30 Rockefeller Plaza in Manhattan. On April 21 and 28, two more *Candid Camera* programs, with Chester revisiting Alan Funt, Durward Kirby and Sid Ramin, with Jack Paar joining for good measure, were aired on CBS.

Two years after his guest appearance on *Naked City*, Herbert B. Leonard and Stirling Silliphant recalled Chester to costar with series regulars Martin Milner and Glenn Corbett in the "Soda Pop and Paper Flags" episode of *Route 66*, broadcast during the show's third season on May 31, 1963. Written by John McGreevey and directed by veteran cinematographer Fred Jackman, Jr., the episode features Chester as Emmett McNeil, a former businessman now riding the rails, who is accused of bringing a "rare type of sleeping sickness" into the small town of Mapleton, Missouri. Alan Alda, who had played a supporting role in an episode of *Naked City* the previous year, here appears in another early career part as Dr. Glazer.

"Soda Pop and Paper Flags" was the ninth episode to feature Corbett (as Lincoln Case), who succeeded George Maharis (as Buz Murdock) in the role of friend and traveling companion to Milner (as Tod Styles), owner and driver of a powder-blue Corvette convertible in which they travel around the nation, seeking temporary work and performing good deeds for troubled people. McGreevey's teleplay shifts between the major plot involving Tod's efforts to aid McNeil, who is persecuted by a group of townspeople, and a rather insignificant subplot about Linc's difficulties with a prospective customer while working as a sales representative for a rubber company where all three men are now employed by Andy Ferguson (Frank Overton). The disjointed structure follows the nature of the 13 previous episodes, produced after Maharis became troubled by a recurrent illness. (He had developed hepatitis toward the end of the previous season, leaving Milner to star solo in four episodes, with Tod speaking via telephone to the hospitalized Buz.) When Corbett was cast, the writers required time to integrate his character into the stories, a move that never caught on with the public, and the show was canceled after the fourth season.

Much of Chester's performance as McNeil is nonverbal, and his understated approach rightly suits a character who is used to the lonely, laconic existence developed during several years on the road, endlessly wandering from one town to the next. After Tod rushes to his defense during a street fight with some local teenagers, McNeil is reluctant to show any gratitude; but, during a subsequent sit down at a diner, he offers his thanks. "You probably would have done the same for me," Tod replies.

"I doubt it," McNeil, truly an honest man, admits. Having recently worked in Texas, from where the disease, carried by ticks, has been spread, he is identified as the "outsider," and the reactionaries are up in arms, ready to drive him out of town. (This Cold War–era element is thematically representative of much of Stirling Silliphant's work.) McNeil is used to being persecuted. As he explains to Tod, he became a patsy for his corrupt banking family, whom he describes as a "bunch of cannibals." At the episode's end, McNeil, cleared of all suspicion, leaves for New Orleans, while Tod and Linc head down the road once more.

Chester appeared in more *Candid Camera* footage, with Alan Funt, Durward Kirby, Sid Ramin and Irish singer Carmel Quinn, to be aired on June 9 and 16, 1963. From July 29 to August 2, he appeared with Canadian-born television actress Gisele MacKenzie on another week of daytime *Match Game* broadcasts, hosted by Gene Rayburn at Rockefeller Center.

On August 21, he joined host Ed McMahon and fellow panelists Milt Kamen and Phyllis Newman for the pilot episode of the Goodson-Todman game show *Missing Links*, during which contestants described events from their careers, leaving out elements to be filled in by the celebrity guests. Shot at the Elysee Theater in New York City, the show initially was broadcast by NBC-TV, beginning with the first official episode, hosted by series regular Dick Clark, on September 9, 1963, and later by ABC-TV, completing its run on December 25, 1964.

Kamen's prowess as a stand-up comic was well to the fore in the pilot episode, during which Chester presented a more serious and thoughtful approach, laced with moments of dry wit, and Newman, with whom Chester had worked on *Diagnosis: Unknown* and *To Tell the Truth*, provided the most correct "missing links" to the problems presented by two contestants. A deep-sea diver and photojournalist each presented six events, but out of 12, only 5 received correct "links" from the "very bright, illustrious panel," three from Newman, and one each from Chester and Kamen. Though Chester's intellectual approach was no more successful than Kamen's *shtick* shenanigans, his tendency to overthink each problem resulted in incorrect responses or a lapsing of the time allotment.

At one point, Chester began to relax, even beginning to dance in his seat to the jaunty theme music. After he delivered an incorrect answer, McMahon's response of "Wrong!" was met with his quick remark, "I thought it was *very good*." One of Kamen's subsequent responses even broke him up completely. The highpoint of absurdity came when McMahon offered a clue to one of the challenges involving a very famous person—the initials "A.L."— to which Chester replied, "Adlai *Levenson*." Though his pondering had him on the right track, his inability to think of an answer as obvious as "Abraham Lincoln" provided the audience with peals of laughter. His one correct solution also brought the most audience applause, to which he responded by throwing kisses to them.

During *Missing Links*, Chester mentioned that he currently was preparing to rehearse the play *The Tender Heel* at the Lyceum Theatre, scheduled to open on November 19, 1963. This production, however, was not produced at the Lyceum, located at 149 West 45th Street, where the play *The Golden Age*, adapted by Richard Johnson from works by William Shakespeare and Thomas Dekker, instead was given a brief run of seven performances from November 14 to 23. However, paired with Signe Hasso, Chester eventually did appear in *The Tender Heel*, produced and directed by Miranda D'Ancona, with whom he earlier had worked on *A View from the Bridge*.

Chester made a second guest appearance on *The Defenders*, in the third-season episode "The Bagman," shot at Manhattan's Filmways Studios and broadcast by CBS on October 19, 1963. Directed by Robert Butler from a Roger H. Lewis teleplay, the episode features regulars E.G. Marshall and Robert Reed, well-supported by Chester (as Judge Philip Benning), Howard Da Silva and Joanna Merlin. The series continued to feature outstanding casts, with this season including contributions from Edward Binns, Ossie Davis, Ludwig Donath, Bramwell Fletcher, Vincent Gardenia, James Gregory, Jack Klugman, Martin Landau, Aline MacMahon, Susan Oliver and Malachi Throne.

Prior to taking a 1963 holiday trip to England with Lillian, Chester completed another five-episode round at *The Match Game* from December 9 to 13, joining host Gene Rayburn and fellow *To Tell the Truth* panelist Kitty Carlisle. While across the pond, Chester acted in "Castles in Spain," his only filmed production made outside the United States. Based in London, Associated Television (ATV) produced 24 episodes of *Espionage*, an anthology series involving spy stories set in various countries and historical periods, broadcast by ITV in the United Kingdom and NBC in the United States during 1963 and 1964. Based on a story by Norman Borisoff, Raymond Bowers' teleplay involves an aging former revolutionary returning to Spain to visit an old American friend. Complications arise when a wounded young man, on the lam from police, hides in his associate's car. Chester played Harry Kemp, supported by Roland Culver, Neil McCallum, Anne Lawson and Alex Scott. The episode was aired in the UK on February 19, 1964.

While staying at White's Hotel at Lancaster Gate, Chester wrote to a British fan who had asked him for a photograph:

Dear Mr. Rintouc,

    Thank you for your nice letter. I'm sorry I have no photos with me, but I will keep your address and send you one when I return to the States next week.

    I wish you a most wonderful New Year!

Gratefully,
Chester Morris[14]

    On January 3, 1964, Chester's second performance for the *Route 66* series was broadcast in "Child of a Night," directed by Allen H. Miner from Stirling Silliphant's teleplay. Cast in the small supporting role of Mr. Hull, Chester appears briefly in this episode focusing on Tod Stiles (Martin Milner) and Lincoln Case (Glenn Corbett) attempting to fulfill the final wish of a dying man (Hershel Bernardi) whom they encounter after his small aircraft crashes in rural Georgia. Chester's *Miracle Man* colleague Sylvia Sidney, Percy Rodrigues, Joanna Pettet and Daniel J. Travanti (in his third television role) costar.

    Hull, a former tavern owner, secretly raised another man's daughter, Nita (Diana Van der Vlis), born out of wedlock to one of his waitresses. Tod and Linc plan to deliver $38,000 bequeathed by the dead pilot to the young woman, but Hull asks, "Do you think it's right to tell her this whole thing is a lie … just because her real father felt guilty and wanted to buy back the years?" Ultimately, Hull decides to tell Nita the truth. Though relegated to two scenes near the end of the episode, Chester gives a nuanced, moving performance.

13

The Last Day of the Play

Chester's "workaholic" lifestyle continued with more major television performances. He enjoyed tackling the colorful role of Walter McGill, an entrenched labor leader of three decades, described as "bull-headed, arrogant" and "a demagogue," in "The Name of the Game," the March 23, 1964, episode of the dramatic series *East Side/West Side*, which ran for one season on the CBS network. Directed by Charles S. Dubin from Mel Goldberg's teleplay, the episode features Chester, Barry Morse, Eugene Roche and Moses Gunn alongside series regulars George C. Scott, Elizabeth Wilson and Cicely Tyson.

Daniel J. Travanti has another role (more substantial than his previous turn in *Route 66*) opposite Chester, as Paul Jerome, the young head of a negotiating committee appointed by McGill to secure a new labor contract guaranteeing a 7-hour day and 35-hour workweek for his union members. Jerome, backed by Congressman Charles Hanson (Linden Chiles), faces an uphill battle in his attempts to persuade the combative McGill to "keep up with the times" and accept a compromise. In the end, he splits with McGill, calling for a committee vote overriding his boss's attempt to gain unanimous support.

Chester first appears, clad in a chef's apron, as McGill emerges from his apartment kitchen while cooking a spaghetti dinner. The blustery, aging union boss decries the "devious" nature of politics to Congressman Hanson before describing his own hardline approach to labor affairs: "What you don't fight for, you don't respect."

In a subsequent scene, the undaunted McGill plays handball with Jerome, continuing to compete though having difficulty catching his breath after his initial opponent leaves the court. Having served for six years in a leadership position of a powerful labor union, Chester developed a personality for McGill differing markedly from the more evenhanded approach he had demonstrated off-screen. His steadfast portrayal is matched by Travanti's more diplomatic characterization, creating an admirable dramatic balance during the one-hour episode.

Just three days later, March 26, 1964, "Knight's Gambit" was broadcast on NBC's *Kraft Suspense Theatre*. Directed by Walter E. Grauman from the Lorenzo Semple, Jr., Halsted Welles and Jonathan Hughes teleplay, the episode features Chester as Blaine Davis, the U.S. Special Envoy in Majorca, Spain, who is under investigation for accepting syndicate bribes while serving in his former position as a district attorney. Roger Smith costars as Anthony Griswold Knight, a rich "international playboy" hired by the U.S. government to go undercover, romancing Davis' secretary, Dorian Smith (Eleanor Parker). Davis, who complains that he is the "Special Envoy to Nowhere," fuels his anger with copious amounts of booze, eventually succumbing to a heart attack. Chester is also supported by Murray Matheson, H.M. Wynant, Vito Scotti and Ted de Corsia.

Chester answered a call from Goodson and Todman for yet another game show appearance, on the April 6, 1964, broadcast of *Get the Message*, a derivative of the producers' other programs, that ran on ABC's daytime schedule for nine months, making its bow on Christmas Day that year. Host Frank Buxton welcomed Chester and Robert Q. Lewis (comprising a male team), and Florence Henderson and Bess Myerson (female team), who used one-word clues to "get the message" to contestants.

Chester returned to the show on May 11 to collaborate with Dick Clark. Television writer Selma Diamond, then in the process of adding actress to her resume, also appeared on the broadcast. That month, Chester played Howard Carol, father of Liza Minnelli's titular character, in Ronald Alexander's stage comedy *Time Out for Ginger* at the Bucks County Playhouse in New Hope, Pennsylvania. The role of Carol had first been played by Melvyn Douglas in the original Broadway production, which ran for 248 performances at the Lyceum Theatre from November 1952 to June 1953. Six years after his *Ginger* performances, Chester would return to New Hope once more, for another revival of *The Caine Mutiny Court-Martial*.

The popular medical drama series *Dr. Kildare*, starring Richard Chamberlain, ran on NBC television for five seasons (1961–1966). Chester guest starred as Tom Monahan in the May 21, 1964, episode "Dolly's Dilemma," written by Ken Kolb and directed by John Newland. His *Blonde Johnson* costar Joan Blondell plays Dolly Marlowe, a widowed friend of Dr. Gillespie (Raymond Massey), whom the administrator attempts to appoint to the Blair General Hospital Board of Trustees. She has a more personal agenda, however, trying to snare Gillespie as her next husband.

Chester made a fourth appearance as a panelist on *To Tell the Truth*, joining Barbara Cook, Sam Levenson and Phyllis Newman for the August 24, 1964, CBS broadcast. One week later, he made his third appearance on *Get the Message*, this time pairing with composer and lyricist Stephen Sondheim to compete against Carol Lawrence and Betty White.

The Goodson and Todman game show that became an American popular culture institution, *The Price is Right*, welcomed Chester to its daytime broadcast on October 5, 1964. The 1956–1963 version hosted by Bill Cullen initially ran on NBC. Following its cancellation, the program was picked up by ABC, where it was upgraded to color for two seasons. Seven years after the original show ended on August 30, 1965, CBS created a new version first aired on September 4, 1972, and hosted by Bob Barker until 2007.

Former "Peter Gunn" Craig Stevens starred as another titular television character in *Mr. Broadway*, a dramatic adventure series that ran on CBS for 13 episodes during the 1964 fall season. Garson Kanin created the character of New York City public relations agent Mike Bell, who, in the November 7, 1964, episode "Don't Mention My Name in Sheboygan," is supported by a fine cast including Chester, Horace McMahon, Joan Bennett, Sandy Dennis, Diana Muldaur and Robert Webber.

Rarely practicing his magic act any longer, Chester had returned to another artistic pastime, painting, for which he was paid on occasion. During 1965, he sold four 14x18 canvases, the first being "Friday Afternoon at the A & P," purchased by Ralph Bellamy. Chester explained, "I'm sort of a male Grandma Moses. Besides the A & P, I go in for kids' playgrounds. There's a good one in my neighborhood on 57th Street."[1]

From 1963 to 1967, NBC broadcast *Bob Hope Presents the Chrysler Theatre*, an hourlong television anthology series encompassing the drama, comedy and musical genres that occasionally included special 90-minute episodes. The series consistently included first-rate stories, directors and performers, including John Cassavetes, who functioned in both capacities, and costarred with Chester in the February 5, 1965, episode "The Fliers," directed by Sydney Pollack from David Rayfiel's teleplay. Also appearing in this tale of military aviators were Carol Lynley, Dabney Coleman, Robert Pine, Alfred Ryder and Tom Simcox.

Chester and Peggy Cass made five guest appearances for a week of daily NBC *Match Game* broadcasts at Rockefeller Center on March 8–12, 1965. At Filmways Studios, Robert Butler directed another Roger H. Lewis teleplay, "A Matter of Law and Disorder," for *The Defenders*, aired by CBS on April 8. E.G. Marshall and Robert Reed were supported by another fine cast, including Chester (in his third series role, as District Attorney Brent), Pat Hingle, Dustin Hoffman and Susan Anspatch. Four days later, he reported to NBC at Rockefeller Center to guest on yet another Goodson-Todman game show, *Call My Bluff*, one of the production team's least successful efforts, which ran for just 16 broadcasts from March to September 1965. Hosted by Bill Leyden, the show again paired Chester with Joan Fontaine.

Chester began acting in another Broadway drama, Frank D. Gilroy's *The Subject Was Roses*, in 1965, replacing Jack Albertson, who won a Tony Award in the lead role of John Cleary. Fellow cast members Irene Dailey and Martin Sheen had opened with Albertson at the Royale Theatre on May 25, 1964, and subsequently moved to the Winthrop Ames Theatre on September 3 and the Helen Hayes Theatre on March 23, 1965. On September 7, 1965, Chester began playing John Cleary opposite Maureen O'Sullivan as his wife, Nettie.

Gilroy won the Pulitzer Prize for his scripting of this postwar domestic drama, and producer Edgar Lansbury won a Tony for his work on the original production, which ran for a total of 832 performances. Chester signed on for the national tour in 1966, costarring at various times with O'Sullivan, Martha Scott and Mercedes McCambridge.

In November, while appearing with O'Sullivan at the Carousel Theater in West Covina, California, where her daughter, Mia Farrow, then married to Frank Sinatra, attended the opening night performance, Chester was interviewed by *Los Angeles Times* staff writer Margaret Harford. Describing himself as a "no-nonsense actor who has always gotten out and played the game," he discussed his stage work, "memorable" film roles, how Boston Blackie "didn't do a thing" for his career, and his participation in several popular television game shows.

In particular, he recalled an incident that occurred one morning while appearing on a popular program hosted by the amiable Allen Ludden. A young contestant, angrily hiding out in her dressing room, admitted to him that she "objected to sitting on the right side of [the] gamesmaster ... because the right side was the wrong side for her."

"Never mind how you look," Chester advised her pragmatically. "Get out there and play the game."

Harford focused on the professional perseverance of "the screen's Boston Blackie":

> He is still working at the acting game, though it is a game of youth, shrewdly sizing up the real actors from the dead fish.
>
> His own durable face retains its square-jawed handsomeness, his voice rings with authority and he is full of zip at 64.

Asked if he ever would "retire," he replied, "Lord, no. I have too many people to support." Reminded that his many performances as Blackie, due to the "Great Resuscitator, TV's Late Show," had assured him some degree of screen immortality, he wittily admitted, "Suddenly I was a big hero with taxi drivers."

Calling him "generous to a fault," Harford also inquired about his relationship with artist Charles Addams:

> [T]he actor once gave the cartoonist ... "an idea" for a picture. It was inspired by a leading bank's "nest egg" publicity plugging safe investments. The cartoon featured a hearse carrying a coffin with a large egg securely tied to a handle.

"Addams gave me the original," Chester admitted proudly, adding that he was not an active collector. "A phony business," he explained. "Too many reproductions hanging around."[2]

Chester made his final round of daytime guest appearances on *The Match Game* at Rockefeller Center during October 18–22, 1965, going out in style with silent-screen great "Miss" Gloria Swanson, with whom he had socialized in Hollywood. Since the dawn of television, she had made frequent guest appearances, both as herself and in occasional dramatic roles, in a variety of popular programs.

On January 4, 1966, Chester rang in the New Year with an appearance on *The Tonight Show Starring Johnny Carson* at Rockefeller Center. His visit to this NBC broadcast ranked him as one of Hollywood's classic actors who accepted an invitation for all three incarnations of the popular late-night talk show, being interviewed by Steve Allen, Jack Paar, Johnny Carson (filling in for Paar) and, substituting for Carson on this occasion, Sammy Davis, Jr., who also welcomed jazz singer Johnny Hartman to the stage.

Aired by ABC in March 1966, *The Soupy Sales Hour* featured the comic actor with Chester, Joan Fontaine, Judy Garland and Ernest Borgnine all playing themselves in a teleplay by Gary Belkin, Bob Klaine, Marc Richards and Steven Vinaver directed by Dwight Hemion, who often specialized in musical television extravaganzas.

When not on the road, Chester enjoyed the five-room apartment he and Lillian shared at 176 East 77th Street in Manhattan, while Kenton was now a student at Northwestern University in Chicago. During 1967 and 1968, fellow New Yorker Pete Arroyo worked as a grocery delivery boy at the D'Agostino Brothers Supermarket between 76th and 77th Streets. In 2018, he recalled,

> Chester Morris lived in the building that was located on the corner of 3rd Avenue and 76th Street. He had his groceries delivered to his apartment, and I got to deliver them a lot of times.
> I remember the first time I saw him. I couldn't believe it. As a kid, my mother used to watch Charlie Chan, Mr. Moto, Boston Blackie, et cetera. I was too shy to tell him, but I wanted to tell him I knew who he was.
> He was a really nice guy. I was very lucky to have met him. Every time I saw him, I was in awe. I also saw his movies and enjoyed them. If I had told him I knew who he was, I could have told him how much I enjoyed his acting. I went into the military in 1969. I didn't know for years that he had passed away.[3]

Following graduation from Northwestern, Kenton began working in the mailroom at WGN TV and Radio, where he eventually was promoted to Executive Program Director. For ten years, he produced the Chicago Flower and Garden Show held at Navy Pier, before pursuing a second career as a commercial pilot.

During the waning days of *Candid Camera* on May 18, 1967, Chester made a final guest appearance on the program. He then turned back to a serious supporting role, as Dr. Michael Wilson, in "A Time to Be Born," the debut episode of *Coronet Blue*, a series inspired by *The Defenders* created by Larry Cohen, starring Frank Converse as a young man suffering from amnesia. Broadcast on May 29, it was the first of only 13 episodes that aired prior to the show's cancellation by CBS. Introduced as "Gigot," the amnesiac, fished from a river, remembers only two words: "Coronet Blue." For the next six weeks, he recovers at Alden General Hospital, where he is aided by Dr. Wilson, naming himself "Michael Alden" (after the physician and institution, respectively) before setting out to discover his past.

Coronet Blue: "A Time to Be Born" (May 27, 1967). Chester Morris, as Dr. Michael Wilson, appears briefly but memorably in one scene.

Chester, who shot his footage at Pathé Studios in New York City, appears only briefly in one scene. "Alden," intent on finding answers to the web of intrigue surrounding his lost identity, ends his medical treatment, against the advice of Wilson, who put him back together "like a jigsaw puzzle." Subsequent episodes included guest appearances by John Beal, Edward Binns, David Carradine, Denholm Elliott, Bramwell Fletcher, Hal Holbrook, Patrick O'Neal, Sally Kellerman, Keye Luke and Joseph Wiseman.

Stuart Whitman played Marshal Jim Crown in 23 episodes of *Cimarron Strip*, an hour-long Western series produced by his own production company and broadcast by CBS during its first-run season from September 7, 1967, to March 7, 1968. For the next-to-last episode, "Without Honor," aired on February 29, 1968, Chester was well cast as George Deeker, the ruthless leader of a murderous gang of robbers who use dynamite in their raids. After stealing a safe from a Wells Fargo office, they enlist a young U.S. Army deserter, Bill Mason (Jon Voight), who happens to be the "secret" son of Major Covington (Andrew Duggan), to blast their way into the mail car of a train, from which they abscond with a payroll strongbox, outside Hays City, Kansas. Crown and Covington join forces to track down Mason and end the exploits of the Deeker Gang.

Using his trademark sideways smile to great effect, Chester gives a fine villainous performance in this episode. When Mason is amused to find the dynamited safe empty, Deeker remarks, "After you've been with me a while, you'll find less to laugh at." Following a violent battle involving firearms and dynamite, Deeker lies dead and Mason, having proved heroic during the conflict, is pardoned, with his father officially listing him as "absent without official leave."

During the summer of 1968, Chester costarred with Barbara Britton in the touring production of Henry Denker's stage comedy *What Did We Do Wrong*? The original Broadway version at the Helen Hayes Theatre ran for only 48 performances, starring Paul Ford as businessman-turned-hippie Walter Davis, the role Chester took over for the tour.

Based on the 1965 children's novel by Walt Morey, the television series *Gentle Ben*, depicting the adventures of Mark Wedloe (Clint Howard) and his pet black bear, was broadcast on CBS for two seasons (1967–1969). Directed by Gerd Oswald from a script by Maurice Tombragel (who wrote the screenplays for *Trapped by Boston Blackie* and *Boston Blackie's Chinese Venture*), the April 27, 1969, episode "Busman's Holiday" guest stars Chester as Ronald Elsmore, a Miami Transit Authority driver who impulsively leaves his route to hide out as a "recluse" near the Wedloe home, where he is aided by Mark and Ben (Bruno the Bear). In a cast including Dennis Weaver and Beth Brickell as Mark's parents, Tom and

Ellen, Chester, in his final small-screen role, contributes a charming comic performance. As Tom prepares to take Elsmore back to the city, the renegade driver acknowledges the bear: "Thank you, too, Ben. You're the warmest blanket I've ever known."

Fourteen years after working with John Kenley on *The Caine Mutiny Court-Martial* in Bristol, Pennsylvania, Chester accepted another part from the Kenley Players artistic director, to head a regional touring production of Robert Anderson's play *You Know I Can't Hear You ...* during the summer of 1969. Centered in Ohio, the company played dates at the Packard Music Hall Theatre in Warren, Veterans Memorial Theatre in Columbus, and Memorial Hall in Dayton.

Chester was ailing by this time but still accepted the role of "Pop" Weaver in Martin Ritt's film *The Great White Hope* (1970), costarring James Earl Jones, Jane Alexander, R.G. Armstrong, Robert Webber and Hal Holbrook. Howard Sackler's Pulitzer Prize–winning play, loosely based on the true story of heavyweight boxing champion John Arthur ["Jack"] Johnson and his first wife, Etta Terry Duryea (who committed suicide in 1912), debuted at the Arena Theatre in Washington, D.C., after receiving two grants from the National Endowment for the Arts, on December 7, 1967. The reception was so positive that it became the first regional production to graduate to Broadway, where, beginning in October 1968, the company gave 546 performances at the Alvin Theatre, closing on January 31, 1970.

When the film rights were purchased by 20th Century–Fox in February 1968, Sackler (who used $225,000 of his studio pay to fund the continuing Broadway production) was hired to adapt the screenplay, and Jones and Alexander (both of whom won Tony Awards) were retained in the lead roles of "Jack Jefferson" and "Eleanor Bachman." On September 8, 1969, they were succeeded in the stage version by Yaphet Kotto and Maria Tucci.

Producer Richard Zanuck budgeted the film at $8 million. Principal photography began in Globe, Arizona, on October 9, 1969, and then moved to Nogales before studio work was done on the 20th Century–Fox lot. On October 24, *Daily Variety* reported that the U.S. State Department had asked Jones to work with a crew from Yugoslav State Television to shoot "a discussion of the status of black Americans" in film and theater productions, to be exhibited in other countries.[4] Although audiences had viewed the play as specifically addressing racism in the United States (the term "Great White Hope" referring to the Caucasian contenders whom Johnson fought), Howard Sackler intended his work to speak to a broader issue. He explained,

> What interested me was not the topicality but the combination of circumstances, the destiny of a man pitted against society. It's a metaphor of struggle between man and the outside world. Some people spoke of the play as if it were a cliché of white liberalism, but I kept to the line straight through, of showing that it wasn't a case of blacks being good and whites being bad. I was appalled at the first reaction.[5]

In mid–December 1969, production moved to Barcelona, Spain, where scenes set in Cuba, Germany and Mexico were filmed. Hampered by pain in his abdomen, Chester soldiered on with the location shooting.

Diagnosed with stomach cancer, Chester realized that his condition would worsen but, back in the States, he joined the cast for another production of *The Caine Mutiny Court-Martial*, at the Bucks County Playhouse in New Hope, Pennsylvania. He called Captain Queeg "a complete paranoiac. He is a strange man, so offbeat. I like that kind of role. Anybody can play nice boys."[6]

On Friday, September 11, 1970, he was scheduled to meet Playhouse producer and artistic director Lee R. Yopp for lunch and had spoken to him and other members of the staff that morning. However, after he failed to arrive at the restaurant on time, Yopp phoned his room at the Holiday Inn.

Repeated calls went unanswered, so Yopp drove to the motel during the noon hour. Like the calls, his raps on the door of room 202 went unheeded. Managing to enter, Yopp discovered Chester's body lying on the floor and phoned the Lambertville Rescue Squad, whose resuscitation attempts were unsuccessful.

Bucks County coroner Samuel B. Willard, who pronounced Chester dead at 1 p.m., concluded that he had died from an overdose of barbiturate sleeping pills. Solebury Township Police Chief Richard J. Mangan reported that the circumstances of his death were "under investigation," but no suicide note was found and the position of his body on the floor also made a verdict of intentional death unlikely. Therefore, an autopsy was not ordered.

Moreover, Chester had continued to exhibit a positive attitude, calmly referring to his condition as a "stomach complaint." His work ethic never wavered, including while playing Queeg in the very demanding dramatic play. Though most performers working at the Bucks County Playhouse lodged at the Lambertville House in neighboring Hunterdon County, New Jersey, he had asked to stay at the Holiday Inn. The Friday night performance was cancelled but the play resumed with his understudy the following evening.

Theodore Britton, son of actress Barbara Britton, Chester's costar in *What Did We Do Wrong?*, also had worked with him during a stage production. In a remembrance for *Variety*, he said,

> There are many actors today who call in sick when they have a cold. There are still some, like Chester Morris, who continue to work until the very end; because to Act is a verb which implies movement, and life, and the refusal to be *in*active. And because that is what an actor does.[7]

Chester's body was transported to the Leaver Funeral Home, located at Route 202 and Quarry Road in Buckingham, and subsequently cremated. His memorial service was held at St. Bartholomew's Episcopal Church at Park Avenue and 50th Street in Manhattan. Lillian continued living at their residence at 176 East 77th Street, while Kenton still resided in Chicago, working as a television director. Chester's ashes subsequently were scattered over a river in Germany.

On October 11, 1970 (exactly one month after Chester's death), *The Great White Hope* premiered at the Baronet Theatre in New York City. On December 23, it opened at Grauman's Chinese Theatre in Hollywood. Both Jones and Alexander received Academy Award and Golden Globe Award nominations for their performances. Jones won the "Most Promising Newcomer—Male" award at the Golden Globes.

The reviews were decidedly mixed. Vincent Canby, who attended the opening, perceptively wrote in *The New York Times*,

> Howard Sackler's "The Great White Hope," which won the Pulitzer Prize, the Drama Critics Prize and the Antoinette Perry Award as the best drama of the 1968–1969 season, never was much of a play. The movie that Martin Ritt has made from it ... is necessarily limited by the nature of the original text. "The Great White Hope" is a polemical, black Passion Play about Jack Jefferson.... The film, like the play, progresses in terms of highly stylized scenes that dramatize Jack Jefferson's initial triumph, his subsequent persecution and his humiliations as if they were Stations of the Cross....
> "The Great White Hope" is one of those liberal, well-meaning, fervently uncontroversial works that pretend to tackle contemporary problems by finding analogies at a safe remove in history. In spite of Muhammad Ali, who was quoted two years ago as saying of the play, "You just change the time, date

and the details and it's about me!," Mr. Sackler's play and screenplay are too smug, too full of stereotypes to be provocative as drama. Similarly, his method is too pretentious.... However ... the film contains a performance that makes the windy, otherwise empty movie seem inhabited, if not by life, at least by art. James Earl Jones ... is marvelous to watch, combining heroic physical presence, technique and (to me) a completely mysterious way of projecting intelligence, so that the character commands attention even when the drama doesn't. There's also an initially charming performance by Jane Alexander ... and good if conventional ones by Lou Gilbert, Hal Holbrook, Robert Webber and the late Chester Morris. Mr. Ritt has staged most of the film in the only way possible, as if all the events were locked inside a huge proscenium arch.[8]

In his *Harvard Crimson* review, Michael Sragow expanded upon some points made by Canby:

If Martin Ritt hasn't transformed the dross of *The Great White Hope* into a good film, at least his jumbling of theatrical convention and film cliché makes it fairly easy to watch.... *The Great White Hope* is severely divided, but many of the tensions the black actors manage to convey are true....

Given the historical context, it may seem nigh impossible to overstate the repressive prejudices of Johnson's time. However, that is precisely what Sackler has done. Most of Johnson's personality has been removed from the playwright's Jack Jefferson, making him more defenseless and unblemished than Johnson's staunchest supporters ever claimed. Sackler's character has none of Johnson's sensual excesses (and only one all-suffering white wife, drearily enacted by Jane Alexander)....

When preceded by the statement, "much of what follows is true," the entire play, and much of the film, strikes me as being terribly obscene. Sackler attempts to voice radical, anti-white-capitalist sentiment, but he seems to have a pretty limited concept of how racism is manifested socially and culturally....

The film does, however, seem somewhat healthier than the play as written.... And this despite the fact that in every plastic sense, Ritt is a perfectly lousy director. Some of the scenes are indistinguishable from those taped on stage for the Ed Sullivan Show. When Ritt wants the audience to know that a crowd is present, he frames a few hundred thousand people cheering. Period. When he wants to emphasize the "frail nobility" and "still small voice" of a group of blacks praying for Johnson before the stadium in Reno, he sticks them in what suddenly seems to be a ghost town, and pans slowly, portentously, to the white-filled stadium. He handles his fight scenes—what there is of them—clumsily.... What Ritt does do besides give the film's supporting acting a derivative panache is make Jefferson a lot more angry than he was on the stage.... Ultimately the film is worth seeing, but only for the events it portrays.[9]

In a later evaluation, Zay Amsbury, understanding the playwright's original intent, noted, "Sackler and Ritt spend their efforts on solid character-based storytelling rather than historicizing and moralizing—and their choices lead to a taught, harrowing and perfectly told story of freedom and love."[10]

In his only feature film shot in color and widescreen, Chester appears as Pop Weaver in the opening scene, prior to the heavyweight championship bout in Reno between Jefferson and "white hope" Franklyn Brady (Larry Pennell). His most significant scene arrives more than halfway into the 103-minute film, after Jefferson, having escaped from the Illinois State Penitentiary, is denied a boxing license in London and brutally pummels his white opponent during a contest in Paris. While viewing fight films with "Cap'n Dan" (R.G. Armstrong) and Fred (George Ebeling), looking for the next "white hope," Weaver is visited by the racist federal agent Dixon (Robert Webber), who earlier had engineered, under the Mann Act, Jefferson's conviction and three-year sentence for "unlawful relations" with Eleanor, and now wants to persuade the champion to throw a fight.

Weaver, who claims, "I'm only a sports promoter, Mr. Dixon," then adds, "There must be another way, Dan."

"Pop ... don't you get on a pedestal," Dan advises, before asking him to speak with Jefferson's manager, "Goldie" (Lou Gilbert), about throwing a fight in exchange for reducing the fugitive's prison sentence to six months. Following a humiliating performance in a Budapest cabaret adaptation of Harriet Beecher Stowe's *Uncle Tom's Cabin*, Jefferson is approached at the train station by Weaver, who tries to persuade him to leave Europe, where World War I is breaking out, and return to the States. In one of many displays of violent anger, Jefferson roughly manhandles Weaver, but a fine testament to Chester's acting prowess and professionalism is the fact that, although in severe abdominal pain, he did not let any of the misery register on his face during the scene.

Jefferson then flees to Juarez, Mexico, where Eleanor asks him to agree to the fixed fight in Havana. Met with more verbal abuse from the angry boxer, Eleanor drowns herself in a well, and Jefferson reluctantly agrees to Dixon's offer of a suspended sentence for taking a dive.

Chester, dapperly attired in a white double-breasted suit and Panama hat, last appears at the Havana bout, where Jefferson, staring into the faces of the white agent and promoters, mightily rallies against his white opponent, "The Kid" (Jim Beattie), but is ultimately defeated. The "polemical, black Passion Play" (as described by Vincent Canby) ends with the physical crucifixion of the protagonist who has been abused socially, politically and legally throughout the film. In many ways, *The Great White Hope* is a painful viewing experience.

Chester's 41-year cinematic career culminates as Pop Weaver, observing the unfortunate fight, exclaims, "Dan!"

Dan responds, "Ah, *shut up*, Pop!"

On May 18, 1971, eight months after his own demise, Chester's sister, Wilhelmina, the last of William and Etta's children, died at age 68 in Buffalo, New York. Chester and Suzanne's daughter, Cynthia Morris Mirasa, who had continued living in Los Angeles, passed away, also aged 68, on April 18, 1998.

Brooks Morris had entered the United States Air Force in 1950. Excelling as a fighter pilot, he was stationed in Europe and Southeast Asia, where he initially served in the Korean War. In Viet Nam, he flew fighter-bombers during two tours of combat duty, and became a respected special weapons and low-altitude bombing tactics expert.

By the time Brooks retired from the USAF in 1974, he had attained the rank of colonel and was awarded the Silver Star, Legion of Merit with oak leaf cluster, Distinguished Flying Cross, Bronze Star, Air Medal with eight oak leaf clusters, and various salad ribbons. His lifelong hobby, fishing, became a second career after he left the military. His love of big-game fishing developed during visits to Japan, the Azores and Florida.

He and his wife, Laura, settled in Dana Point, California, where he and a group of military friends established the Laguna Niguel Billfish Club to secure an invitation to compete in the Hawaiian Invitational Billfish Tournament (HIBT) in the Kona District on the western coast of Hawai'i. The team, during a difficult expedition, first won the tournament in 1985.

In 1986, Brooks, joined by teammate Gil Kraemer aboard the *Ihu Nui*, captained by Freddie Rice, returned to catch the first "grander" (1,062.5-pound) blue marlin in the history of the tournament, capturing the championship two years running. The "Area Rule Doorknob" lure used to land the monster was invented by Brooks, who also designed the "T-Bar Reel Handle," a popular fishing device produced by Tiburon Engineering.

Meanwhile, half-brother Kenton Morris, residing in the Chicago suburb of Batavia, had also taken to the skies. Along with producing the Flower and Garden Show at the Navy Pier until 2006, he worked as a pilot for JetBlue taxi and volunteered for the Angel Flight Network, an organization providing free air transportation for passengers in need of medical treatment, and at Delnor Community Hospital in Geneva, Illinois.

On September 11, 2008, Kenton, who was not scheduled to fly that day, agreed to fill in for a colleague who called him at the last minute to request that he pilot a chartered single-engine aircraft carrying two passengers to Milwaukee. Just as the plane reached Lakeland Airport in Arbor Vitae, Wisconsin, it suddenly crashed, killing all three men. Although Kenton had no immediate survivors, he left behind a fiancée, Lori Bennett, and her daughter, Jillian.

Brooks Morris died at age 82 on May 12, 2011. Honoring his final request, his two sons, Jeff and Gordon, attended the HIBT in Hawaii, where they scattered the ashes of their parents and beloved dog, Jock, off the Kona Coast.

14

Requiem for a Working Actor

The common assumption that Chester Morris' motion-picture career "ended" because of some lack of "star power" on his part is fallacious. Following World War II, when the entire nature of commercial filmmaking began to shift from the studio system to independent production, his attitude changed simultaneously. He had begun his career on Broadway, debuted in films with a star-making, Academy Award–nominated performance, played leads with the top female stars of the day at every studio, headlined many B features, including a long-running popular series, and then starred as home-front he-men in a string of wartime dramas. His experiences tirelessly working in a volunteer capacity for a major labor union and U.S. military troops had affected his worldview substantially.

Chester never was one to "preach" about his social and political views. He was a man who led by example, and an examination of his life clearly shows "where" his head and heart were located. In 1949, he primarily left Hollywood filmmaking behind in favor of returning to the stage, on which he often played major characters with more substance than those offered by the silver screen. His incorporation of modern acting methods became especially useful in interpreting characters of more social, political and moral complexity in several powerful dramatic works: Detective McLeod in Sidney Kingsley's *Detective Story*, Eddie Carbone in Arthur Miller's *A View from the Bridge*, Captain Queeg in Herman Wouk's *The Caine Mutiny Court-Martial* and Senators Munson and Knox in Loring Mandel's *Advise and Consent*.

His move into television also allowed him to explore a greater variety of roles and more often demonstrate his versatility. His array of characters included the Dansker in "Billy Budd," Jack Feeney in "The Arena," Max Ritter in *Diagnosis: Unknown*, Frank Manfred in *Naked City*: "Make-Believe Man," Walter Tyson in *Ben Casey*: "An Expensive Glass of Water," Emmett McNeill in *Route 66*: "Soda Pop and Paper Flags" and Walt McGill in *East Side/West Side*: "The Name of the Game."

Once discussing the possibility of son Brooks becoming an actor, he was humorously dismissive, and none of his three children chose to follow in the family's thespian footsteps. Both sons chose a life of service in the wild blue, although Kenton pursued an initial career behind the cameras in the Chicago television market.

During interviews later in life, Chester often downplayed his Hollywood years, even claiming that Columbia cast him in "thirty-six" Boston Blackie films, misinformation that spread quickly in newspapers of the day. But he also clearly explained the difference between the "responsibilities" borne by a motion picture star and a stage actor:

> Your film actor sells the product—the star. For instance, if they're going to do a picture, the first thing they'll try to do is get Tony Curtis. If they can't get Tony Curtis, they'll get whoever is hot at

the moment: Bill Holden. In order to finance it with the bank, they have to have a name of that stature before the bank will put up any money. And then, of course, if the picture goes out and is a flop, Tony Curtis takes it on the chin, or Bill Holden. And I found out, if you make three bad pictures in a row, you weren't even asked out to dinner by a producer or anybody in Hollywood. It was like being in a leper colony.

And that *doesn't* hold good in the theater. An actor can have eight flops a season, and no one ever blames him for it. The *critics* never blame him. [The Hollywood actor] is the commercial that sells the product.[1]

In 1962, when asked if theatrical "flamboyance" still existed in modern acting, Chester replied,

I think there's more "mixing" today with … as Bogart used to term them, the "private" people, those that weren't connected to the theater. I think there's much more socializing going on, but I do think we still have some great flamboyance in the theater. For instance, Larry Olivier—I say, "Larry," I'm not name dropping, because he's a very dear friend of mine, has been for years—Gielgud, a fellow named Richard Burton. [As to the British actors], I'm speaking of the *classical*, because they can do it as nobody else can. They're *trained* for it.[2]

Explaining the concept of "mixing" on a personal level, he added,

It's not that I want to be snobbish about it, or that I resent the fans, because, God knows, I'm most appreciative. But I always try to go out through the front of the house. On matinee days, if there [is] a crowd of people there, I don't like coming out after a performance and signing. I like to just *go* and let them keep what they've seen.[3]

In 1966, when addressing the possibility of writing his memoirs, he replied in the negative: "Every book ever written by an actor can be bought for 99 cents in front of the book store. Nobody reads those things except actors."[4]

Chester, Brooks and Cynthia Morris, playing mumbley peg, Beverly Hills (1933).

Appendix A
Chester Morris Filmography

Following is a complete listing of theatrical-release films featuring Chester Morris with major credits for each title and running time.

An Amateur Orphan (June 3, 1917)

Credits: *Director*: Van Dyke Brooke; *Producer*: Edwin Thanhouser; *Screenplay*: Agnes Christine Johnston, Van Dyke Brooke; *Cinematographer*: George Webber; *Production Company*: Thanhouser Film Corporation; *Distributor*: Pathé Exchange; *Running Length*: 5 reels.

Cast: Chester Morris (Dick Walton), Gladys Leslie, Isabel Vernon, Thomas A, Curran, Jean Armour, Ray Hallor, Justus D. Barnes, Carey L. Hastings, Grace DeCarlton.

The Beloved Traitor (February 24, 1918)

Credits: *Director*: William Worthington; *Producer*: Samuel Goldwyn; *Screenplay*: Kenneth Macgowan, George Loane Tucker; *Based on the Novel* by Frank L. Packard; *Cinematographer*: George W. Hill; *Editor*: George Loane Tucker; *Production Designer*: Hugo Ballin; *Production Company*: Goldwyn Pictures Corporation; *Distributor*: Goldwyn Distributing Company; *Running Time*: 50 minutes.

Cast: Chester Morris (Dan), Mae Marsh, E.K. Lincoln, Hedda Hopper, George Fawcett, Bradley Barker, James A. Furey, Louis R. Grisel.

Loyal Lives (July 1923)

Credits: *Director*: Charles Giblyn; *Producer*: Whitman Bennett; *Story*: Dorothy Farnum, Charles G. Rich; *Cinematographer*: Edward Paul; *Production Company*: Postman Pictures; *Distributor*: Vitagraph Company of America; *Running Length*: 6 reels.

Cast: Chester Morris (Tom O'Hara), Brandon Tynan, Mary Carr, Faire Binney, William Collier, Jr., Charles MacDonald, Blanche Craig, Tom Blake, Blanche Davenport, Jack Hopkins, Mickey Bennett.

The Road to Yesterday (November 15, 1925)

Credits: *Director and Producer*: Cecil B. DeMille; *Screenplay*: Beulah Marie Dix, Howard Hawks, Jeanie Macpherson; *Based on the Play* by Beulah Marie Dix and Evelyn Greenleaf Sutherland; *Cinematographer*: J. Peverell Marley; *Editor*: Anne Bauchens; *Musical Score*: Rudolph Berliner; *Art Directors*: Anton Grot, Paul Iribe, Mitchell Leisen, Max Parker; *Production Company*: DeMille Pictures Corporation; *Distributor*: Producers Distributing Corporation; *Running Time*: 107 minutes.

Cast: Chester Morris (Party Guest), Joseph Schildkraut, Jetta Goudal, William Boyd, Vera Reynolds, Trixie Friganza, Casson Ferguson, Julia Faye, Clarence Burton, Charles West, Josephine Norman, Wilson Benge, Robert Brower, Frank Coghlan, Walter Long, Sally Rand, Dick Sutherland.

Alibi (April 20, 1929)

Credits: *Director and Producer*: Roland West; *Screenplay*: Roland West, C. Gardner Sullivan; *Based on the Play* by John Griffith Wray, J.C. Nugent and Elaine S. Carrington; *Cinematographer*: Ray June; *Editor*: Hal C. Kern; *Art Director*: William Cameron Menzies; *Production Company*: Feature Productions; *Distributor*: United Artists; *Running Time*: 91 minutes.

Cast: Chester Morris (Chick Williams), Harry

Stubbs, Mae Busch, Eleanor Griffith, Regis Toomey, Purnell Pratt, Irma Harrison, Elmer Ballard, Diana Beaumont, James Bradbury, Jr., Ed Brady, Edgar Caldwell, Kernan Cripps, Virginia Flohri, Al Hill, Edward Jardon, DeWitt Jennings, Pat O'Malley.

Fast Life (September 1, 1929)

Credits: *Director*: John Francis Dillon; *Presenter*: Richard A. Rowland; *Screenplay*: John F. Goodrich; *Based on the Play* by Samuel Shipman and John B. Hymer; *Cinematographer*: Faxon M. Dean; *Editor*: Ralph Holt; *Production Company*: First National Pictures; *Distributor*: Warner Bros.; *Running Time*: 90 minutes.

Cast: Chester Morris (Paul Palmer), Douglas Fairbanks, Jr., Loretta Young, William Holden, Frank Sheridan, Ray Hallor, John St. Polis, Purnell Pratt, Rita Flynn.

Woman Trap (September 28, 1929)

Credits: *Director*: William A. Wellman; *Screenplay*: Bartlett Cormack, Louise Long; *Based on the Play* by Edwin J. Burke; *Cinematographer*: Henry W. Gerrard; *Editor*: Alyson Shaffer; *Musical Score*: Karl Hajos; *Production Company and Distributor*: Paramount Pictures; *Running Time*: 82 minutes.

Cast: Chester Morris (Ray Malone), Hal Skelly, Evelyn Brent, William B. Davidson, Effie Ellsler, Guy Oliver, Leslie Fenton, Charles Giblyn, Joseph L. Mankiewicz, Clarence Wilson, Sailor Vincent, Virginia Bruce, Eddie Kane, Bessie Lyle, Michael Visaroff.

The Show of Shows (December 29, 1929)

Credits: *Director*: John G. Adolfi; *Producers*: Darryl F. Zanuck, Harry M. Warner, Jack L. Warner; *Screenplay*: J. Keirn Brennan, Frank Fay; *Richard III Sequence Based on the Play: Henry VI, Part 3* by William Shakespeare; *Cinematographer*: Barney McGill; *Production Company and Distributor*: Warner Bros.; *Running Time*: 128 minutes.

Cast: Chester Morris (Himself), Frank Fay, William Courtenay, H.B. Warner, Hobart Bosworth, John Barrymore, Harry Akst, Armida, Johnny Arthur, Mary Astor, William Bakewell, Richard Barthelmess, Noah Beery, Sally Blane, Monte Blue, Irene Bordoni, Joseph A. Burke, Marion Byron, Georges Carpentier, Ethlyne Clair, James Clemens, Ruth Clifford, William Collier, Jr., Betty Compson, Chester Conklin, Heinie Conklin, Dolores Costello, Helene Costello, Jack Curtis, Viola Dana, Alice Day, Marceline Day, Sally Eilers, Douglas Fairbanks, Jr., Louise Fazenda, Pauline Garon, Albert Gran, Alexander Gray, Lloyd Hamilton, Julanne Johnston, Sôjin Kamiyama, Lupino Lane, Frances Lee, Lila Lee, Ted Lewis, Winnie Lightner, Beatrice Lillie, Jacqueline Logan, Myrna Loy, Nick Lucas, Tully Marshall, Shirley Mason, Otto Matieson, Philo McCullough, Patsy Ruth Miller, Bull Montana, Lee Moran, Jack Mulhall, Edna Murphy, Carmel Myers, Marian Nixon, Molly O'Day, Sally O'Neil, Gertrude Olmstead, Kalla Pasha, Anders Randolf, Rin Tin Tin, Bert Roach, Sid Silvers, Ann Sothern, Ben Turpin, Ada Mae Vaughn, Alberta Vaughn, Lolita Vendrell, Edward Ward, Alice White, Ted Williams, Lois Wilson, Grant Withers, Loretta Young.

Second Choice (January 4, 1930)

Credits: *Director*: Howard Bretherton; *Screenplay*: Joseph Jackson; *Based on the Story* by Elizabeth Alexander; *Cinematographer*: John Stumar; *Editor*: Robert O. Crandall; *Production Company and Distributor*: Warner Bros.; *Running Time*: 67 minutes

Cast: Chester Morris (Don Warren), Dolores Costello, Jack Mulhall, Edna Murphy, Charlotte Merriam, Ethlyne Clair, James Clemens, Edward Martindel, Henry Stockbridge, Anna Chance, Louise Beavers, Louise Lester.

Playing Around (January 19, 1930)

Credits: *Director*: Mervyn LeRoy; *Screenplay*: Adele Comandini, Humphrey Pearson, Harvey F. Thew; *Based on the Play* by Frances Nordstrom and the Story "Sheba" by Vina Delmar; *Cinematographer*: Sol Polito; *Production Company*: First National Pictures; *Distributor*: Warner Bros.; *Running Time*: 66 minutes.

Cast: Chester Morris (Nickey Solomon), Alice White, William Bakewell, Richard Carlyle, Marion Byron, Maurice Black, Lionel Belmore, Shep Camp, Ann Brody, Nellie V. Nichols, Kernan Cripps, Rollo Dix, Geraldine Dvorak, George ["Gabby"] Hayes, Robert Homans, Brady Kline, Lew Meehan, Jimmy Phillips, Carolynne Snowden.

She Couldn't Say No (February 15, 1930)

Credits: *Director*: Lloyd Bacon; *Screenplay*: Arthur Caesar, Robert Lord, Harvey F. Thew; *Based on the Story* by Benjamin M. Kaye; *Cinematographer*: James Van Trees; *Production Company and Distributor*: Warner Bros.; *Running Time*: 70 minutes.

Cast: Chester Morris (Jerry Casey), Winnie Lightner, Sally Eilers, Johnny Arthur, Tully Marshall, Louise Beavers, Phyllis Haver, Bill Elliott.

The Case of Sergeant Grischa (February 23, 1930)

Credits: *Director*: Herbert Brenon; *Producer*: William LeBaron; *Screenplay*: Elizabeth Meehan; *Based on the Novel* by Arnold Zweig *Cinematographer*: J. Roy Hunt; *Editor*: Marie Halvey; *Art Director*: Max Rée; *Production Company and Distributor*: RKO Radio Pictures; *Running Time*: 91 minutes.

Cast: Chester Morris (Sergeant Grischa Paprotkin), Betty Compson, Alec B. Francis, Gustav Von Seyffertitz, Jean Hersholt, Leyland Hodgson, Paul McAllister, Raymond Whitaker, Bernard Siegel, Frank McCormack, Percy Barbette, Hal Davis.

The Divorcée (April 19, 1930)

Credits: *Director*: Robert Z. Leonard; *Producers*: Robert Z. Leonard, Irving Thalberg; *Screenplay*: Nick Grinde, Zelda Sears, John Meehan; *Based on the Novel: Ex-Wife* by Ursula Parrott; *Cinematographer*: Norbert Brodine; *Editors*: Hugh Wynn, Truman K. Wood; *Art Director*: Cedric Gibbons; *Production Company and Distributor*: Metro-Goldwyn-Mayer; *Running Time*: 84 minutes.

Cast: Chester Morris (Ted), Norma Shearer, Conrad Nagel, Robert Montgomery, Florence Eldridge, Helene Millard, Robert Elliot, Mary Doran, Tyler Brooke, Zelda Sears, George Irving, Judith Wood, Neal Dodd, Charles R. Moore, Lee Phelps, George Reed, Andy Shuford, Carl Stockdale, Jack Trent, Theodore von Eltz.

The Big House (June 14, 1930)

Credits: *Director*: George W. Hill; *Producer*: Irving Thalberg; *Screenplay*: Frances Marion, Joseph Farnham, Martin Flavin; *Based on the Story* by Frances Marion; *Cinematographer*: Harold Wenstrom; *Editor*: Blanche Sewell; *Art Director*: Cedric Gibbons; *Production Companies*: Cosmopolitan, Metro-Goldwyn-Mayer; *Distributor*: Metro-Goldwyn-Mayer; *Running Time*: 87 minutes.

Cast: Chester Morris (John Morgan), Wallace Beery, Lewis Stone, Robert Montgomery, Leila Hyams, George F. Marion, J.C. Nugent, Karl Dane, DeWitt Jennings, Matthew Betz, Claire McDowell, Robert Emmett O'Connor, Tom Kennedy, Tom Wilson, Eddie Foyer, Roscoe Ates, Fletcher Norton, Edgar Dearing, Ethan Laidlaw, Eddie Lambert, George Magrill, Chris-Pin Martin, Louis Natheaux, Charles O'Malley, Herbert Prior, Angelo Rossito, Adolph Seidel, Michael Vavitch, Harry Wilson.

The Bat Whispers (November 13, 1930)

Credits: *Director*: Roland West; *Producer*: Joseph M. Schenck; *Screenplay*: Roland West; *Based on the Play* by Mary Roberts Rinehart and Avery Hopwood; *Cinematographers*: Ray June, Robert H. Planck; *Editors*: James Smith, Hal C. Kern; *Set Designer*: Paul Crawley; *Production Company*: Joseph M. Schenck Productions; *Distributor*: United Artists; *Running Time*: 83 minutes.

Cast: Chester Morris (Detective Anderson/"The Bat"), Chance Ward, Richard Tucker, Wilson Benge, DeWitt Jennings, Sidney D'Albrook, S.E. Jennings, Grayce Hampton, Maude Eburne, Spencer Charters, Una Merkel, William Bakewell, Gustav Von Seyffertitz, Hugh Huntley, Charles Dow Clark, Ben Bard.

Corsair (November 28, 1931)

Credits: *Director and Producer*: Roland West; *Screenplay*: Roland West, Josephine Lovett; *Based on a Novel* by Walton Green; *Cinematographer*: Ray June; *Editor*: Hal C. Kern; *Musical Score*: Alfred Newman; *Settings*: Richard Day; *Production Company*: Art Cinema Corporation; *Distributor*: United Artists; *Running Time*: 75 minutes.

Cast: Chester Morris (John Hawks), Thelma Todd, Fred Kohler, Ned Sparks, Emmett Corrigan, William Austin, Frank McHugh, Frank Rice, Mayo Methot, Gay Seabrook, Addie McPhail, Al Hill, Pat Hartigan, Sidney D'Albrook.

Cock of the Air (January 23, 1932)

Credits: *Director*: Tom Buckingham; *Producer*: Howard Hughes; *Screenplay*: Charles Lederer, Robert E. Sherwood; *Cinematographer*: Lucien N. Andriot; *Editor*: W. Duncan Mansfield; *Musical Score*: Alfred Newman; *Art Director*: Richard Day; *Production Company*: The Caddo Company; *Distributor*: United Artists; *Running Time*: 80 minutes.

Cast: Chester Morris (Lieutenant Roger Craig), Billie Dove, Matt Moore, Walter Catlett, Luis Alberni, Kathryn Sergava, Yola d'Avril, Vivien Oakland, Emile Chautard, Ethel Kenyon, Peggy Watts, Gino Corrado, Mario Dominici, Tenen Holtz, Tom London, Paul McAllister, Lewis Milestone, Larry Steers, Max Wagner.

The Miracle Man (April 1, 1932)

Credits: *Director*: Norman Z. McLeod; *Screenplay*: Samuel Hoffenstein, Waldemar Young; *Based on the Play* by George M. Cohan *and the Novel* by Robert Hobart Davis and Frank L. Packard; *Cinematographer*: David Abel; *Production Company and Distributor*: Paramount Pictures; *Running Time*: 85 minutes.

Cast: Chester Morris (John ["Doc"] Madison), Sylvia Sidney, Robert Coogan, John Wray, Ned Sparks, Hobart Bosworth, Lloyd Hughes, Virginia Bruce, Boris Karloff, Irving Pichel, Frank Darien, Florine McKinney, Veda Buckland, Wong Chung, Davison Clark, Monte Collins, Billy Franey, Harrison Greene, Sherry Hall, Jane Keckley, Lew Kelly, Robert Parrish, Bodil Rosing, Jackie Searl, Jerry Tucker, Florence Wix.

Sinners in the Sun (May 13, 1932)

Credits: *Director*: Alexander Hall; *Screenplay*: Samuel Hoffenstein, Vincent Lawrence, Waldemar Young; *Based on the Story* by Mildred Cram; *Cinematographer*: Ray June; *Musical Score*: Rudolph G. Kopp, John Leipold; *Production Company and Distributor*: Paramount Pictures; *Running Time*: 70 minutes.

Cast: Chester Morris (Jimmie Martin), Carole Lombard, Adrienne Ames, Alison Skipworth, Walter Byron, Reginald Barlow, Zita Moulton, Cary Grant, Luke Cosgrave, Ida Lewis, Russ Clark, Frances Moffett, Pierre de Ramey, Veda Buckland, Rita La Roy, Maude Turner Gordon, Anderson Lawler, Dorothy Dix, Florence Lawrence, Lynn Browning, Dorothy Compton, Mary Cooper, Frank Darien, Lillian Elliott, Muriel Evans, Harriet Matthews, Gale Ronn, Phillips Smalley, Kent Taylor, Ellinor Vanderveer, Gayne Whitman, Gwen Zetter.

Red-Headed Woman (June 25, 1932)

Credits: *Director*: Jack Conway; *Producers*: Albert Lewin, Irving Thalberg; *Screenplay*: Felix E. Feist, F. Scott Fitzgerald, Anita Loos, Bess Meredyth, C. Gardner Sullivan; *Based on a Book* by Katharine Brush; *Cinematographer*: Harold Rosson; *Editor*: Blanche Sewell; *Art Director*: Cedric Gibbons; *Production Company and Distributor*: Metro-Goldwyn-Mayer; *Running Time*: 79 minutes.

Cast: Chester Morris (Bill Legendre, Jr.), Jean Harlow, Lewis Stone, Leila Hyams, Una Merkel, Henry Stephenson, May Robson, Charles Boyer, Harvey Clark, Henry Armetta, Sidney Bracey, Ed Brady, Ralph Byrd, Albert Conti, Leyland Hodgson, James T. Mack, Edmund Mortimer, Wilfrid North, Edgar Norton, William H. O'Brien, Sarah Padden, William Pawley, Lee Phelps, Eddie Phillips.

Breach of Promise (October 23, 1932)

Credits: *Director*: Paul L. Stein; *Producer*: Ben Verschleiser; *Screenplay*: Ben Verschleiser, John F. Goodrich, Anthony Veiller, Art Miller; *Based on the Story* "Obscurity" by Rupert Hughes; *Art Director*: Edward Shulter; *Production Company*: Ben Verschleiser Productions; *Distributor*: Sono Art/World Wide Pictures; *Running Time*: 64 minutes.

Cast: Chester Morris (James Pomeroy), Mae Clarke, Mary Doran, Theodore Von Eltz, Elizabeth Patterson, Charles Middleton, Lucille La Verne, Eddie Borden, Edward LeSaint, Alan Roscoe, Harriet Lorraine, Philo McCullough, Tom McGuire.

Blondie Johnson (February 25, 1933)

Credits: *Directors*: Ray Enright, Lucien Hubbard; *Screenplay and Based on the Story* by Earl Baldwin; *Cinematographer*: Tony Gaudio; *Editor*: George Marks; *Art Director*: Esdras Hartley; *Production Company*: First National Pictures; *Distributor*: Warner Bros; *Running Time*: 67 minutes.

Cast: Chester Morris (Danny Jones), Joan Blondell, Allen Jenkins, Earle Foxe, Claire Dobb, Mae Busch, Joseph Cawthorn, Olin Howland, Sterling Holloway, Toshia Mori, Arthur Vinton, Donald Kirke, Maurice Black, Naomi Childers, Charles Dow Clark, Helena Phillips Evans, Sam Godfrey, Betty Jane Graham, Ben Hall, John Ince, Lloyd Ingraham, Payne B. Johnson, Eddie Kane, Tom Kennedy, Charles Lane, Carl M. Leviness, Walter Long, Sam McDaniel, David Mir, Rolfe Sedan, Tom Wilson.

Infernal Machine (April 8, 1933)

Credits: *Director*: Marcel Varnel; *Screenplay*: Arthur Kober; *Based on a Novel* by Karl Sloboda; *Cinematographer*: George Schneiderman; *Editor*: Ralph Dixon; *Musical Score*: Samuel Kaylin; *Production Company and Distributor*: Fox Film Corporation; *Running Time*: 65 minutes.

Cast: Chester Morris (Robert Holden), Genevieve Tobin, Victor Jory, Elizabeth Patterson, Edward Van Sloan, Josephine Whittell, James Bell, Arthur Hohl, Luis Alberni, Mischa Auer, Stanley Blystone, Leonard Carey, Elise Cavanna, Arthur Hoyt, Robert Littlefield, Louis Mercier, Geneva Mitchell, J. Carrol Naish, Nat

Pendleton, Alexander Pollard, Harry Shutan, Jack Stoney, Dale Van Sickel, Charles C. Wilson, Harry Wilson.

Tomorrow at Seven (June 2, 1933)

Credits: *Director*: Ray Enright; *Producer*: Joseph I. Schnitzer; *Screenplay*: Ralph Spence; *Cinematographer*: Charles Edgar Schoenbaum; *Editor*: Rose Loewinger; *Musical Score*: David Broekman; *Art Director*: Edward C. Jewell; *Production Company*: Jefferson Pictures Corporation; *Distributor*: RKO Radio Pictures; *Running Time*: 62 minutes.

Cast: Chester Morris (Neil Broderick), Vivienne Osborne, Frank McHugh, Allen Jenkins, Henry Stephenson, Grant Mitchell, Charles Middleton, Oscar Apfel, Virginia Howell, Cornelius Keefe, Edward LeSaint, Gus Robinson, Bud Geary.

Hollywood on Parade (mid–September 1933)

Credits: *Director and Producer*: Louis Lewyn; *Production Company*: Louis Lewyn Productions; *Distributor*: Paramount Pictures; *Running Time*: 10 minutes.

Cast: Chester Morris (Himself), Max Baer, Maurice Chevalier, Lew Cody, Joan Crawford, Marie Dressler, Jimmy Durante, Cary Grant, Sid Grauman, Jean Harlow, Mary Pickford, George Raft, Will Rogers, Johnny Weissmuller, Ed Wynn.

Golden Harvest (September 22, 1933)

Credits: *Director*: Ralph Murphy; *Producer*: Charles R. Rogers; *Screenplay*: Casey Robinson; *Based on the Story* by Nina Wilcox Putnam; *Cinematographer*: Milton R. Krasner; *Musical Score*: Harold Lewis; *Production Company and Distributor*: Paramount Pictures; *Running Time*: 72 minutes.

Cast: Chester Morris (Chris Martin), Richard Arlen, Genevieve Tobin, Roscoe Ates, Julie Haydon, Elizabeth Patterson, Berton Churchill, Lawrence Gray, Henry Kolker, Richard Carle, Charles Sellon, Frederick Burton, Jessie Arnold, Irving Bacon, Harry Bowen, Walter Brennan, Edmund Burns, Alphonse Ethier, Joseph W. Girard, Harry Harvey, Edward Hearn, Olin Howard, John Ince, Gladden James, DeWitt Jennings, Lafe McKee, Joe Sawyer, Phillips Smalley, Ellinor Vanderveer, Morgan Wallace, Freeman Wood.

King for a Night (January 9, 1933)

Credits: *Director*: Kurt Neumann; *Producer*: Carl Laemmle, Jr.; *Screenplay*: Jack O'Donnell, Scott Pembroke; *Based on the Story* by William Anthony McGuire; *Cinematographer*: Charles J. Stumar; *Editor*: Philip Cahn; *Musical Score*: David Klatzkin; *Art Director*: Charles D. Hall; *Production Company and Distributor*: Universal Pictures; *Running Time*: 78 minutes.

Cast: Chester Morris (Bud Williams), Helen Twelvetrees, Alice White, John Miljan, Grant Mitchell, Frank Albertson, George Meeker, Warren Hymer, Maxie Rosenbloom, John Sheehan, George E. Stone, Harland Tucker, Harry Galfund, Clarence Wilson, Dorothy Granger, Georgie Billings, Wade Boteler, Ernie Adams, Walter Brennan, Sheila Bromley, Frederick Burton, Wallis Clark, Jane Darwell, Henry Hall, John Indrisano, Lew Kelly, Edgar Kennedy, Walter Miller, Adrian Morris, Frank Sheridan, Larry Steers, Fred ["Snowflake"] Toones.

Let's Talk It Over (June 1, 1934)

Credits: *Director*: Kurt Neumann; *Producer*: B.F. Zeidman; *Screenplay*: John Meehan, Jr.; *Based on the Story* "Loves of a Sailor" by Dore Schary and Lewis R. Foster; *Cinematographer*: Charles J. Stumar; *Musical Score*: Howard Jackson, Hermann Krome; *Production Company and Distributor*: Universal Pictures; *Running Time*: 68 minutes.

Cast: Chester Morris (Mike McGann), Mae Clarke, Frank Craven, John Warburton, Irene Ware, Andy Devine, Russ Brown, Anderson Lawler, Goodee Montgomery, Douglas Fowley, Herbert Corthell, Jane Darwell, Willard Robertson, Frank Reicher, Henry Armetta, Otis Harlan, Dean Benton, George Blackwood, Dorothy Dawes, Mary Dees, Tom Dugan, Earl Eby, Jim Farley, Olaf Hytten, Lois January, Henry Kolker, Charles Lane, Wanda Perry, Phil Tead, Sally Tead.

Gift of Gab (September 1, 1934)

Credits: *Director*: Karl Freund; *Producers*: Rian James, Carl Laemmle, Jr.; *Screenplay*: Rian James, Lou Breslow; *Based on the Story* by Jerry Wald and Philip G. Epstein; *Cinematographers*: George Robinson, Harold Wenstrom; *Editor*: Ray Curtiss; *Musical Score*: Edward Ward; *Art Director*: David S. Garber; *Production Company and Distributor*: Universal Pictures; *Running Time*: 70 minutes.

Cast: Chester Morris (Doyle), Edmund Lowe, Gloria Stuart, Ruth Etting, Phil Baker, Ethel Waters, Paul Lukas, Victor Moore, Alice White, Hugh O'Connell, Roger Pryor, Binnie Barnes, Boris Karloff, Helen Vinson, Bela Lugosi, June

Knight, Andy Devine, Sterling Holloway, Henry Armetta, Douglas Fowley, Marion Byron, Alexander Woollcott, The Downey Sisters, Beale Street Boys, Graham McNamee, Gus Arnheim and His Orchestra, Gene Austin, Tom Hanlon, Edwin Maxwell, Carmen Gould, Billy Barty, Maurice Black, Bob Davis, James Flavin, Jack Harling, John ["Skins"] Miller, Leighton Noble, Dave O'Brien, Dennis O'Keefe, Warner Richmond, Wini Shaw, Sidney Skolsky, Sid Walker, Tammany Young.

Embarrassing Moments (September 1, 1934)

Credits: *Director*: Edward Laemmle; *Producers*: Stanley Bergerman, Carl Laemmle, Jr.; *Screenplay*: Charles Logue, Dickson Morgan, Gladys Unger; *Based on the Story* "The Practical Joker" by William Anthony McGuire; *Cinematographer*: Charles J. Stumar; *Editor*: Daniel Mandell; *Musical Score*: Edward Ward; *Production Company and Distributor*: Universal Pictures; *Running Time*: 61 minutes.

Cast: Chester Morris (Jerry Randolph), Marian Nixon, Walter Woolf King, Alan Mowbray, George E. Stone, John Wray, Henry Armetta, Huntley Gordon, Gay Seabrook, Herman Bing, Virginia Sale, Jane Darwell, Charles C. Wilson, Christian J. Frank, Carl Miller, Lois January, Charles Coleman, John T. Murray.

"The Hollywood Gad-About" (October 5, 1934)

Credits: *Producer*: Louis Lewyn; *Production Companies*: Louis Lewyn Productions, Educational Films Corporation of America; *Distributor*: Fox Film Corporation; *Running Time*: 11 minutes.

Cast: Chester Morris (Himself), Mary Astor, Billy Barty, James Cagney, Eddie Cantor, Gary Cooper, Stuart Erwin, Alice Faye, Wallace Ford, William Gargan, Ann Harding, William S. Hart, May Robson, Shirley Temple, Kenneth Thomson, Alice White, Walter Winchell.

The Gay Bride (December 14, 1934)

Credits: *Director*: Jack Conway; *Producer*: John W. Considine, Jr.; *Screenplay*: Bella Spewack, Sam Spewack; *Based on the Story* by Charles Francis Coe; *Cinematographer*: Ray June; *Editor*: Frank Sullivan; *Musical Score*: Jack Virgil, R.H. Bassett; *Art Director*: Cedric Gibbons; *Production Company and Distributor*: Metro-Goldwyn-Mayer; *Running Time*: 80 minutes.

Cast: Chester Morris (Jimmy ["Office Boy"] Burnham), Carole Lombard, Zasu Pitts, Leo Carrillo, Nat Pendleton, Sam Hardy, Norman Ainsley, Eddie ["Rochester"] Anderson, Irving Bacon, Jack Baxley, Brooks Benedict, Francis X. Bushman, Jr., Jules Cowles, Frank Darien, Max Davidson, Gordon De Main, Clay Drew, Herbert Evans, Lew Harvey, Boothe Howard, Arthur Jarrett, Isabelle Keith, Edward LeSaint, Gene Lockhart, Wilbur Mack, Fred Malatesta, Margaret Mann, Ray Mayer, Francis McDonald, Tom McGuire, Scott Moore, Louis Natheaux, Garry Owen, Lee Phelps, Charles Sullivan, Harry Tenbrook, Fred ["Snowflake"] Toones, Joe Twerp, Wilhelm von Brincken, Bobby Watson.

Society Doctor (January 25, 1935)

Credits: *Director*: George B. Seitz; *Producer*: Lucien Hubbard; *Screenplay*: Michael Fessier, Samuel Marx, Laurence Stallings; *Based on the Play*: The Harbor by Theodore Reeves; *Cinematographer*: Lester White; *Editor*: Ben Lewis; *Musical Score*: Oscar Radin, R.H. Bassett; *Art Director*: Cedric Gibbons; *Production Company and Distributor*: Metro-Goldwyn-Mayer; *Running Time*: 67 minutes.

Cast: Chester Morris (Dr. Morgan), Robert Taylor, Virginia Bruce, Billie Burke, Raymond Walburn, Henry Kolker, Dorothy Peterson, William Henry, Mary Jo Mathews, Robert McWade, Donald Meek, Louise Henry, Johnny Hines, Addison Richards, Bobby Watson, Ernie Alexander, William Bailey, Brooks Benedict, Wade Boteler, Jean Chatburn, Claudia Coleman, Heinie Conklin, Allen Connor, James Flavin, Arthur Hoyt, Perry Ivins, Gladden James, Eulalie Jensen, Isabelle Keith, Inez Palange, Bert Roach, Lee Shumway, Libby Taylor, Richard Tucker, Arthur Vinton.

I've Been Around (March 5, 1935)

Credits: *Director*: Philip Cahn; *Producer*: B.F. Zeidman; *Screenplay*: John Meehan, Jr.; B.F. Zeidman; *Based on the Story* by Gerald Beaumont; *Cinematographer*: John J. Mescall; *Editor*: Ray Curtiss; *Musical Score*: Edward Ward, Arthur Morton; *Art Director*: Harrison Wiley; *Production Company and Distributor*: Universal Pictures; *Running Time*: 63 minutes.

Cast: Chester Morris (Eric Foster), Rochelle Hudson, G.P. Huntley, Phyllis Brooks, Gene Lockhart, Isabel Jewell, Ralph Morgan, William Stack, Henry Armetta, Dorothy Christy, Verna Hillie, Jean Fenwick, Patricia Caron, Carol Wines, Dorothy Grainger, Lorin Raker, C. Daniel Whipple, King Baggot, Frances Morris, Julie Kingdon, William H. O'Brien, Gloria Ann White, Virginia Odeon, Sidney Bracey, Patricia Chapman, Arnold Gray, Paul Power, Jack Mulhall, Betty Blythe.

Princess O'Hara (April 1, 1935)

Credits: *Director*: David Burton; *Producer*: Leonard Spigelgass; *Screenplay*: Harry Clork, Doris Malloy, Nat Ferber, Robert C. Rothafel; *Based on the Story* by David Burton; *Cinematographer*: Norbert Brodine; *Editor*: Albert Akst; *Musical Score*: Arthur Morton; *Art Director*: Albert S. D'Agostino; *Production Company and Distributor*: Universal Pictures; *Running Time*: 79 minutes.

Cast: Chester Morris (Vic Toledo), Jean Parker, Leon Errol, Vince Barnett, Henry Armetta, Verna Hillie, Ralph Remley, Dorothy Gray, Anne Howard, Jimmy Fay, Phillip Trent, Clara Blandick, Pepi Sinoff, Tom Dugan, William Arnold, Eddie Baker, Matthew Betz, Ed Brady, James Burke, A.S. ["Pop"] Byron, Bob Callahan, Patricia Chapman, Russ Clark, Onest Conley, Edith Craig, Floyd Criswell, Anne Darling, Max Davidson, George Davis, J. Gunnis Davis, Edgar Dearing, Clyde Dilson, Florence Dudley, Dick Elliott, Jim Farley, Al Ferguson, Douglas Fowley, Arnold Gray, Raymond Hatton, Ben Hendricks, Jr., Al Hill, George Irving, Bud Jamison, Eddie Kane, Constnace Kent, Ethan Laidlaw, Charles Lane, John Mack, Alphonse Martell, J.N. McBride, Tom McGuire, Harold Miller, Frank Moran, Charles Murphy, Robert Emmett O'Connor, Spec O'Donnell, Pat O'Malley, Lee Phelps, Frank Rice, Henry Roquemore, Celia Ryland, Gertrude Simpson, Edwin Stanley, David Thursby, Maude Truax, Marie Werner, Johnstone White, Lloyd Whitlock, Jay Wilsey, Charles C. Wilson, Tammany Young.

Public Hero Number 1 (May 31, 1935)

Credits: *Director*: J. Walter Ruben; *Producer*: Lucien Hubbard; *Screenplay*: Wells Root; *Story*: Wells Root, J. Walter Ruben; *Cinematographer*: Gregg Toland; *Editor*: Frank Sullivan; *Musical Score*: Edward Ward; *Art Director*: Cedric Gibbons; *Production Company and Distributor*: Metro-Goldwyn-Mayer; *Running Time*: 89 minutes.

Cast: Chester Morris (Jeff Crane), Lionel Barrymore, Jean Arthur, Joseph Calleia, Paul Kelly, Lewis Stone, Paul Hurst, George E. Stone, Sam Baker, Brooks Benedict, Ed Brady, Frank Bruno, Lane Chandler, Cora Sue Collins, Helena Costello, Nell Craig, Frank Darien, James Flavin, Harry Geise, John George, Jonathan Hale, Henry Hall, Lillian Harmer, Eddie Hart, Edward Hearn, Al Hill, Arthur Housman, William Irving, Selmer Jackson, Gladden James, John Kelly, Anderson Lawler, Frank McGlynn, Jr., Larry McGrath, Greta Meyer, Bob Montgomery, Bert Moorhouse, Frank Moran, Philip Morris, James C. Morton, Pat O'Malley, Jack Pennick, Lee Phelps, Russ Powell, Stanley Price, Frank Rice, Bert Roach, Teru Shimada, Landers Stevens, Carl Stockdale, Billy Sullivan, Zeffie Tilbury, Dorothy Vernon, Larry Wheat, Bill Wolfe, William Worthington, Tammany Young.

Pursuit (August 9, 1935)

Credits: *Director*: Edwin L. Marin; *Producers*: Lucien Hubbard, Ned Marin; *Screenplay*: Wells Root, Robert Benchley; *Based on the Story* "Gallant Highway" by Lawrence G. Blochman; *Cinematographers*: Charles G. Clarke, Sidney Wagner; *Editor*: George Boemler; *Musical Score*: William Axt, Herbert Stothart; *Art Director*: Stan Rogers; *Production Company and Distributor*: Metro-Goldwyn-Mayer; *Running Time*: 60 minutes.

Cast: Chester Morris (Mr. "Mitch" Mitchell), Sally Eilers, Scotty Beckett, Henry Travers, C. Henry Gordon, Dorothy Peterson, Granville Bates, Minor Watson, Harold Huber, Dewey Robinson, Erville Alderson, Billy Dooley, Jimmy Dundee, Martin Faust, Sam Flint, Frances Gregg, John Larkin, George Regas, Jim Toney, Frank Yaconelli.

"Pirate Party on Catalina Isle" (November 21, 1935)

Credits: *Director*: Gene Burdette; *Producer*: Louis Lewyn; *Screenplay*: Alexander Van Dorn, Gene Burdette; *Cinematographer*: Ray Rennahan; *Production Company*: Louis Lewyn Productions; *Distributor*: Metro-Goldwyn-Mayer; *Running Time*: 19 minutes.

Cast: Chester Morris (Pirate Captain), Charles ["Buddy"] Rogers, Sterling Young, The Fanchonettes, Robert Armstrong, Vince Barnett, Jack Duffy, Blanche Mehaffey, Bill Casper, Rue Tyler's Banjo Band, Monica Bannister, Bonnie Bannon, Lynn Bari, Virginia Bruce, Betty Burgess, Margaret Carthew, Diane Cook, Lili Damita, Marion Davies, Johnny Downs, Leon Errol, Errol Flynn, Cary Grant, Irene Hervey, Maynard Holmes, Jeanie Lang, Mary Lange, Eddie Peabody, Wanda Perry, Mickey Rooney, Randolph Scott, Sid Silvers, Mary Stewart, Lee Tracy, Rue Tyler, Dick Wessel.

Three Godfathers (March 6, 1936)

Credits: *Director*: Richard Boleslawski; *Producer*: Joseph L. Mankiewicz; *Screenplay*: Edward E. Paramore Jr., Manuel Seff, Joseph L. Mankiewicz, Ainsworth Morgan; *Based on the Book* by Peter B. Kyne; *Cinematographer*: Joseph Ruttenberg; *Editor*: Frank Sullivan; *Musical Score*: William Axt; *Art Director*: Cedric Gibbons; *Production Company and Distributor*: Metro-Goldwyn-Mayer; *Running Time*: 81 minutes.

Cast: Chester Morris (Bob Sangster), Lewis Stone, Walter Brennan, Irene Hervey, Sidney Toler, Dorothy Tree, Roger Imhof, Willard Robertson, Robert Livingston, John Sheehan, Joseph Marievsky, Victor Potel, Helen Brown, Harvey Clark, Virginia Brissac, Jean Kircher, Judith Kircher, Bernard Carr, Richard Cramer, Jesse Graves, Sherry Hall, Tiny Jones, Leonid Kinskey, William McCall, Art Mix, Jeanne Rivello, Rudy Sooter, Gertrude Sutton, Emanuel A. Turner, Minerva Urecal, John Wallace, Joan Wilson.

Moonlight Murder (March 27, 1936)

Credits: *Director*: Edwin L. Marin; *Producers*: Lucien Hubbard, Ned Martin; *Screenplay*: Florence Ryerson, Edgar Allan Woolf; *Based on the Story* by Albert J. Cohen and Robert T. Shannon; *Cinematographer*: Charles G. Clarke; *Editor*: Ben Lewis; *Musical Score*: Herbert Stothart, Edward Ward; *Art Director*: Cedric Gibbons; *Production Company and Distributor*: Metro-Goldwyn-Mayer; *Running Time*: 66 Minutes.

Cast: Chester Morris (Steve Farrell), Madge Evans, Leo Carrillo, Frank McHugh, Benita Hume, Grant Mitchell, Katharine Alexander, J. Carrol Naish, H.B. Warner, Duncan Renaldo, Leonard Ceeley, Robert McWade, Pedro de Cordoba, Charles Trowbridge, Ernie Adams, Ernie Alexander, Jack Baxley, Don Brodie, Ralph Brooks, Claudia Coleman, Billy Dooley, Sarah Edwards, Flora Finch, Rosina Galli, Mahlon Hamilton, Edward Hearn, Louis Hughes, J.P. McGowan, Greta Mayer, Edmund Mortimer, Pat O'Malley, Lee Phelps, Ellinor Vanderveer.

Frankie and Johnnie (May 1, 1936)

Credits: *Directors*: Chester Erskine, John H. Auer; *Producer*: William Saal; *Screenplay*: Lou Goldberg, Moss Hart; *Based on the Story* by Jack Kirkland; *Cinematographer*: Joseph Ruttenberg; *Editor*: William P. Thompson; *Musical Score*: Victor Young; *Art Director*: Sam Corso; *Production Company*: William Saal Production; *Distributor*: Republic Pictures; *Running Time*: 66 Minutes.

Cast: Chester Morris (Johnnie Drew), Helen Morgan, Lilyan Tashman, Florence Reed, Walter Kingsford, William Harrigan, John Larkin, Cora Witherspoon, Jean Brooks, Pedro de Cordoba, Percy Helton, Montagu Love, Robert Middlemass, Sigmund Spaeth.

Counterfeit (May 25, 1936)

Credits: *Director*: Erle C. Kenton; *Producer*: B.P. Schulberg; *Screenplay*: William Rankin, Bruce Manning; *Story*: William Rankin *Cinematographer*: John Stumar; *Editor*: Richard Cahoon; *Musical Score*: Howard Jackson; *Production Company and Distributor*: Columbia Pictures Corporation; *Running Time*: 73 minutes.

Cast: Chester Morris (John Joseph Madden), Margot Grahame, Lloyd Nolan, Marian Marsh, Claude Gillingwater, George McKay, John Gallaudet, Gene Morgan, Pierre Watkin, Marc Lawrence, Stanley Andrews, Beatrice Blinn, Tommy Bond, Wade Boteler, Virginia Brissac, Earle D. Bunn, Harvey Clark, Beatrice Curtis, Harry Depp, Bill Dill, Elspeth Dudgeon, Edward Earle, Pat Flaherty, Gladys Gale, Harold Goodwin, William Gould, James B. ["Pop"] Kenton, Eddie Laughton, Edward LeSaint, George Lloyd, Arthur Loft, James Millican, Frank Moran, Jackie Moran, Jack Mower, Ted Oliver, Edward Peil, Sr., Arthur Rankin, Harry Semels, Kathryn Sheldon, Edwin Stanley, Emmett Vogan, Tammany Young.

Romeo and Juliet (September 3, 1936)

Credits: *Director*: George Cukor; *Producers*: Irving Thalberg; *Adaptation*: Talbot Jennings; *From the Play* by William Shakespeare; *Cinematographer*: William H. Daniels; *Editor*: Margaret Booth; *Musical Score*: Herbert Stothart; *Art Director*: Cedric Gibbons; *Production Company and Distributor*: Metro-Goldwyn-Mayer; *Running Time*: 125 Minutes.

Cast: Chester Morris (extra), Leslie Howard, Norma Shearer, John Barrymore, Edna May Oliver, Basil Rathbone, C. Aubrey Smith, Andy Devine, Conway Tearle, Ralph Forbes, Henry Kolker, Robert Warwick, Virginia Hammond, Reginald Denny, Violet Kemble Cooper, Charles Bancroft, Dean Benton, Carlyle Blackwell, Jr., John Bryan, Lita Chevret, Wallis Clark, Katherine DeMille, Vernon Downing, Harold Entwistle, Fryda Gagne, Fred Graham, Dorothy Granger, Jeanne Hart, Ronald Howard, Phyllis Hurst, Anthony Kemble Cooper, Bella Lewitzky, Anthony

Marsh, Lon McCallister, Maurice Murphy, José Rubio, Frank Whitbeck, Howard Wilson, Ian Wolfe.

They Met in a Taxi (September 9, 1936)

Credits: *Director*: Alfred E. Green; *Producer and Screenplay*: Howard J. Green; *Based on the Story* by Octavus Roy Cohen; *Cinematographer*: James Van Trees; *Editor*: Gene Milford; *Art Director*: Stephen Goosson; *Production Company and Distributor*: Columbia Pictures Corporation; *Running Time*: 70 Minutes.

Cast: Chester Morris (Jimmy Donlin), Fay Wray, Raymond Walburn, Lionel Stander, Henry Mollison, Kenneth Harlan, Sam Ash, Ward Bond, Al Bridge, Mary Lou Dix, James Flavin, Sam Harris, Edward LeSaint, Frank Melton, Martha Merrill, C.L. Sherwood, Rafael Storm.

Devil's Playground (January 24, 1937)

Credits: *Director*: Erle C. Kenton; *Producer*: Edward Chodorov; *Screenplay*: Edward Chodorov, Jerome Chodorov, Liam O'Flaherty, Dalton Trumbo; *Based on the Story* "The Depths Below" by Norman Spinger; *Cinematographer*: Lucien Ballard; *Editor*: Viola Lawrence; *Art Director*: Stephen Goosson; *Production Company and Distributor*: Columbia Pictures Corporation; *Running Time*: 74 Minutes.

Cast: Chester Morris (Robert Mason), Richard Dix, Dolores del Rio, George McKay, John Gallaudet, Pierre Watkin, Ward Bond, Don Rowan, Francis McDonald, Stanley Andrews, William Arnold, Herbert Ashley, Harry Bernard, Sammy Blum, Alma Chester, Harvey Clark, Nick Copeland, Beatrice Curtis, Dorothy Dehn, Ann Doran, Art Dupuis, Eddie Fetherston, Robert Fiske, Bud Geary, Eddie Hart, Edward Hearn, Wesley Hopper, Arthur Stuart Hull, Si Jenks, Arthur Loft, James T. Mack, Frank Marlowe, Tina Menard, Gene Morgan, Miki Morita, Corbet Morris, Garry Owen, Jack Pennick, Buddy Roosevelt, Ernest Shields, Reginald Simpson, Blanca Vischer, Lucille Ward, Lutra Winslow, Bruce Wong, William Worthington.

"Screen Snapshots Series 16, Number 7" (March 23, 1937)

Credits: *Director and Writer*: Ralph Staub; *Producers*: Ralph Staub, Harriet Parsons; *Production Company and Distributor*: Columbia Pictures Corporation; *Running Time*: 10 minutes.

Cast: Chester Morris (Himself), Gene Autry, Mae Clarke, Dolores del Rio, Marlene Dietrich, Patricia Ellis, James Gleason, Betty Grable, Ruby Keeler, Anita Louise, Pat O'Brien, Genevieve Tobin.

I Promise to Pay (April 21, 1937)

Credits: *Director*: D. Ross Lederman; *Producer*: Myles Connolly; *Screenplay*: Mary C. McCall, Lionel Houser; *Cinematographer*: Lucien Ballard; *Editor*: James Sweeney; *Art Director*: Stephen Goosson; *Production Company and Distributor*: Columbia Pictures Corporation; *Running Time*: 68 Minutes.

Cast: Chester Morris (Eddie Lang), Leo Carrillo, Helen Mack, Thomas Mitchell, Thurston Hall, John Gallaudet, Patsy O'Connor, Wallis Clark, James Flavin, Edward Keane, Harry Woods, Henry Brandon, Marc Lawrence, Philip Ahn, Herbert Ashley, Wilson Benge, Harry Bernard, Clark Burroughs, Jack Cheatham, Jack Rube Clifford, Nick Copeland, Jack Daley, Wally Dean, George DeNormand, Estelle Etterre, Frank Fanning, Carl Faulkner, Sam Flint, Bess Flowers, Eddie Foster, Charles K. French, Gladys Gale, William Gould, Chuck Hamilton, John Hamilton, Sam Harris, Ben Hendricks, Jr., Herbert Heywood, Ruth Hilliard, Max Hoffman, Jr., Harry Hollingsworth, Boyd Irwin, Gladden James, Eddie Kane, Robert Emmett Keane, Richard Kipling, Ethan Laidlaw, Eddie Laughton, Edward LeSaint, Tom London, Wilfred Lucas, Stanley Mack, Frank Marlowe, Allen Mathews, Pat McKee, Bruce Mitchell, Corbet Morris, Horace Murphy, Ned Norton, Jimmy O'Gatty, Ted Oliver, Earl Pingree, Lee Prather, Bob Reeves, Francis Sayles, Cy Schindell, Charles Sherlock, Philip Sleeman, Martha Tibbetts, Phillip Trent, Harry Tyler, John Tyrrell, Jerry Uhlick, Leona Valdé, Emmett Vogan, Crawford Weaver.

Flight from Glory (August 20, 1937)

Credits: *Director*: Lew Landers; *Producers*: Robert Sisk, Samuel J. Briskin; *Screenplay*: David Silverstein, John Twist; *Based on the Story* by Robert Hardy Andrews; *Cinematographer*: Nicholas Musuraca; *Editor*: Harry Marker; *Art Director*: Van Nest Polglase; *Production Company and Distributor*: RKO Radio Pictures; *Running Time*: 67 Minutes.

Cast: Chester Morris (Paul Smith), Whitney Bourne, Onslow Stevens, Van Heflin, Richard Lane, Paul Guilfoyle, Solly Ward, Douglas Walton, Walter Miller, Rita La Roy, Pasha Khan.

"Sunday Night at the Trocadero" (October 2, 1937)

Credits: *Director*: George Sidney; *Producer*: Louis Lewyn; *Screenplay*: John W. Kraff; *Production Company*: Louis Lewyn Productions; *Distributor*: Metro-Goldwyn-Mayer; *Running Time*: 21 Minutes.

Cast: Chester Morris (Chester Morris), Reginald Denny, George Hamilton, Louis and Celester, Connie Boswell, Medina & Mimosa, The Brian Sisters, Peter Lind Hayes, Gaylord Carter, International Models, Dick Foran, John Howard, Margot Grahame, Robert Benchley, Sally Blane, Norman Foster, Groucho Marx, Ruth Johnson, Frank Morgan, Bert Wheeler, Eric Blore, June Collyer, Stuart Erwin, Toby Wing, Russell Gleason, Cynthia Lindsay, Glenda Farrell, Frank McHugh, Benny Rubin, Betty Brian, Doris Brian, Gwen Brian, Phyllis Brooks, Steve Carruthers, Marge Champion, Lester Dorr, Jay Eaton, Louis Hightower, Arthur Lake, Alexander Pollard, Ronald R. Rondell, Margaret Vale.

"Screen Snapshots Series 17, Number 5" (January 6, 1938)

Credits: *Director and Writer*: Ralph Staub; *Producers*: Ralph Staub; *Executive Producer*: Harriet Parsons; *Cinematographer*: André Barlatier; *Editor*: Charles Nelson; *Production Company and Distributor*: Columbia Pictures Corporation; *Running Time*: 10 minutes.

Cast: Chester Morris (Himself), Mary Brian, Bette Davis, Nan Grey, Marjorie Gateson, Jack Holt, Rochelle Hudson, George Murphy, Jean Parker, Dick Powell, Ann Sothern, Johnny Weissmuller, Warren William, Robert Young.

Law of the Underworld (May 6, 1938)

Credits: *Director*: Lew Landers; *Producer*: Robert Sisk; *Screenplay*: Bert Granet, Edmund L. Hartmann; *Based on the Story* "The Lost Game" *and the Play* by Samuel Shipman and John B. Hymer; *Cinematographer*: Nicholas Musuraca; *Editor*: Ted Cheesman; *Art Director*: Van Nest Polglase; *Production Company and Distributor*: RKO Radio Pictures; *Running Time*: 61 Minutes.

Cast: Chester Morris (Gene Fillmore), Anne Shirley, Eduardo Ciannelli, Walter Abel, Richard Bond, Lee Patrick, Paul Guilfoyle, Frank M. Thomas, Eddie Acuff, Vinton Hayworth, Jack Carson, Paul Stanton, Joseph E. Bernard, Stanley Blystone, Richard Cramer, Bud Geary, Chuck Hamilton, Cecil Kellaway, Florence Lake, Richard Parker, George Shelley, Wyndham Standing, Larry Steers, Anthony Warde, Bryant Washburn.

Sky Giant (July 22, 1938)

Credits: *Director*: Lew Landers; *Producer*: Robert Sisk; *Screenplay and Based on the Story* by Lionel Houser; *Cinematographer*: Nicholas Musuraca; *Editor*: Harry Marker; *Musical Score*: Roy Webb; *Art Director*: Van Nest Polglase; *Production Company and Distributor*: RKO Radio Pictures; *Running Time*: 80 Minutes.

Cast: Chester Morris (Kenneth ["Ken"] Stockton), Richard Dix, Joan Fontaine, Harry Carey, Paul Guilfoyle, Robert Strange, Max Hoffman, Jr., Vickie Lester, James Bush, Eddie Marr, Hooper Atchley, Harry Campbell, Tom Chatterton, William Corson, Jerry Frank, Jack Gargan, Frances Gifford, Augie Gomez, Harold Goodwin, Harry Hayden, Donald Kerr, George Magrill, Steve Pendleton, Bernice Pilot, Ronald R. Rondell, William Royle.

Smashing the Rackets (August 19, 1938)

Credits: *Director*: Lew Landers; *Producer*: B.P. Fineman; *Screenplay*: Lionel Houser; *Based on the Story* by Forrest Davis; *Cinematographer*: Nicholas Musuraca; *Editor*: Harry Marker; *Musical Score*: Frank Tours; *Art Director*: Van Nest Polglase; *Production Company and Distributor*: RKO Radio Pictures; *Running Time*: 69 Minutes.

Cast: Chester Morris (Jim ["Sock"] Conway), Frances Mercer, Rita Johnson, Bruce Cabot, Edward Pawley, Joe De Stefani, Donald Douglas, Kay Sutton, Ben Welden, Paul Fix, Eddie Acuff, George Irving, Scotty Beckett, Brooks Benedict, Stanley Blystone, Tom Chatterton, Jimmy Conlin, Edith Craig, Mike Donovan, Jimmie Dundee, Al Ferguson, Byron Foulger, Robert Frazer, Bud Geary, George Hackathorne, Kenneth Harlan, Eddie Hart, Howard C. Hickman, Al Hill, Max Hoffman, Jr., Cecil Kellaway, Rita La Roy, Mike Lally, Edward LeSaint, Carl M. Leviness, George Lloyd, Rollo Lloyd, Tom London, Mary MacLaren, George Meeker, Victor Metzetti, Walter Miller, Edmund Mortimer, Horace Murphy, Max Rose, Walter Sande, C. Montague Shaw, Libby Taylor, Frank M. Thomas, Charles Trowbridge, Solly Ward, Pierre Watkin, Leo White, Gayne Whitman.

Pacific Liner (January 6, 1939)

Credits: *Director*: Lew Landers; *Producer*: Robert Sisk; *Screenplay*: John Twist; *Based on the Story* by Anthony Coldeway and Henry Roberts Symonds *Cinematographer*: Nicholas

Musuraca; *Editor*: Harry Marker; *Art Director*: Van Nest Polglase; *Production Company and Distributor*: RKO Radio Pictures; *Running Time*: 76 Minutes.

Cast: Chester Morris (Doctor Craig), Victor McLaglen, Wendy Barrie, Alan Hale, Barry Fitzgerald, Allan Lane, Halliwell Hobbes, Cy Kendall, Paul Guilfoyle, John Wray, Emory Parnell, Adia Kuznetzoff, John Bleifer, Charles Trowbridge, Ted Billings, Eddie Bracken, Tyler Brooke, Donald Douglas, Grace Hayle, Selmer Jackson, Florence Lake, Arthur Loft, Walter Miller, Frank Mills, Miki Morita, Jack Shea, Douglas Walton, Anthony Warde, Ernest Whitman.

Blind Alley (May 11, 1939)

Credits: *Director*: Charles Vidor; *Producers*: Fred Kohlmar, Jack Fier; *Screenplay*: Philip MacDonald, Michael Blankfort, Albert Duffy, Lewis Meltzer; *Based on the Play* by James Warwick; *Cinematographer*: Lucien Ballard; *Editor*: Otto Meyer; *Musical Score*: George Parrish; *Art Director*: Lionel Banks; *Production Company and Distributor*: Columbia Pictures Corporation; *Running Time*: 69 Minutes.

Cast: Chester Morris (Hal Wilson), Ralph Bellamy, Ann Dvorak, Joan Perry, Melville Cooper, Rose Stradner, John Eldredge, Ann Doran, Marc Lawrence, Stanley Brown, Scotty Beckett, Milburn Stone, Marie Blake, Eddie Acuff, James Craig, Dick Curtis, Ralph Dunn, John Hamilton, Grady Sutton.

Five Came Back (June 23, 1939)

Credits: *Director*: John Farrow; *Producer*: Robert Sisk; *Screenplay*: Jerome ["Jerry"] Cady, Dalton Trumbo, Nathanael West; *Based on the Story* by Richard Carroll; *Cinematographer*: Nicholas Musuraca; *Editor*: Harry Marker; *Musical Score*: Roy Webb; *Art Director*: Van Nest Polglase; *Production Company and Distributor*: RKO Radio Pictures; *Running Time*: 75 Minutes.

Cast: Chester Morris (Bill), Lucille Ball, Wendy Barrie, John Carradine, Allen Jenkins, Joseph Calleia, C. Aubrey Smith, Kent Taylor, Patric Knowles, Elisabeth Risdon, Casey Johnson, Dick Hogan, Pedro de Cordoba, Frank Faylen, Bud Geary, Charlie Hall, Robert Homans, Selmer Jackson, Tiny Jones, Frank Mills, Pat O'Malley, Ronald R. Rondell.

"Rhumba Rhythm at the Hollywood La Conga" (September 2, 1939)

Credits: *Director*: Sammy Lee; *Producer*: Louis Lewyn; *Writer*: Stanley Rauh; *Cinematographer*: Paul Vogel; *Editor*: Tom Biggart; *Production Company*: Louis Lewyn Productions; *Distributor*: Metro-Goldwyn-Mayer; *Running Time*: 11 minutes.

Cast: Chester Morris (Himself), Frank Albertson, John Carroll, James Dunn, Bess Flowers, Marsha Hunt, Arthur Lake, June Lang, George Murphy, Lionel Stander, Lana Turner, Arleen Whelan.

Thunder Afloat (September 15, 1939)

Credits: *Director*: George B. Seitz; *Producer*: J. Walter Ruben; *Screenplay*: Wells Root, Harvey S. Haislip; *Based on the Story* by Ralph Wheelwright and Harvey S. Haislip; *Cinematographer*: John F. Seitz; *Editor*: Frank E. Hull; *Musical Score*: David Snell, Edward Ward; *Art Director*: Cedric Gibbons; *Production Company and Distributor*: Metro-Goldwyn-Mayer; *Running Time*: 95 Minutes.

Cast: Chester Morris ("Rocky" Blake), Wallace Beery, Virginia Grey, Douglass Dumbrille, Carl Esmond, Clem Bevans, John Qualen, Regis Toomey, Henry Victor, Addison Richards, Hans Joby, Henry Hunter, Jonathan Hale, Leon Ames, Arthur Belasco, Joseph E. Bernard, Wade Boteler, Al Bridge, Rand Brooks, Don Castle, Jack Chapin, Tom Chatterton, Jack Rube Clifford, Jules Cowles, Hugh De Lacey, Jo De Stefani, Edgar Dearing, Richard Elmore, Frank Faylen, Budd Fine, Allen Fox, Lee Frederick, Eddie Hart, Edward Hearn, Howard C. Hickman, Earle Hodgins, Clarke Jennings, Payne B. Johnson, Charles Jordan, Lew Kelly, Jack Kennedy, Milton Kibbee, Claire McDowell, Larry McGrath, Roger Moore, Philip Morris, Forbes Murray, Frank Orth, Syd Saylor, Harold Schlickenmayer, Ferdinand Schumann-Heink, Hans Schumm, Harry Semels, Lee Shumway, Robert R. Stephenson, Harry Strang, Walter Thiele, Emmett Vogan, Wolfram Von Bock, Hans von Morhart, Doodles Weaver.

The Marines Fly High (March 7, 1940)

Credits: *Directors*: George Nicholls, Jr., Benjamin Stoloff; *Producer*: Lee S. Marcus, Robert Sisk; *Screenplay*: Jerome ["Jerry"] Cady, Lieutenant Commander A.J. Bolton; *Based on the Story* by A.C. Edington; *Cinematographer*: Frank Redman; *Editor*: Frederic Knudtson; *Art Director*: Van Nest Polglase; *Production Company and Distributor*: RKO Radio Pictures; *Running Time*: 68 Minutes.

Cast: Chester Morris (Lieutenant Jim Malone), Richard Dix, Lucille Ball, Steffi Duna, John Eldredge, Paul Harvey, Horace McMahon, Dick

Hogan, Kirby Grant, Ann Shoemaker, Nestor Paiva, Abner Biberman, Selmer Jackson, Ethan Laidlaw, John Sheehan.

Wagons Westward (June 19, 1940)

Credits: *Director*: Lew Landers; *Producer*: Armand Schaefer; *Screenplay*: Joseph Moncure March, Harrison Jacobs; *Cinematographer*: Ernest Miller; *Editors*: Ernest J. Nims, Murray Seldeen; *Musical Score*: William Lava; *Art Director*: John Victor Mackay; *Production Company and Distributor*: Republic Pictures; *Running Time*: 69 Minutes.

Cast: Chester Morris (David Cook/Tom Cook), Anita Louise, Buck Jones, Ona Munson, George ["Gabby"] Hayes, Guinn ["Big Boy"] Williams, Douglas Fowley, John Gallaudet, Virginia Brissac, Trevor Bardette, Selmer Jackson, Charles Stevens, Warren Hull, Wayne Hull, Lynton Brent, Horace B. Carpenter, Lane Chandler, Edmund Cobb, Jimmy Conlin, Tex Cooper, Richard Cramer, Art Dillard, Bert Dillard, Curley Dresden, Joe Garcio, Harrison Greene, Kit Guard, Henry Hall, Chick Hannan, Joe McGuinn, Bill Nestell, Jeanette Noeson, Jack O'Shea, Tex Phelps, Russ Powell, Jason Robards, Sr., Jack Rockwell, Matty Roubert, Tom Smith, Arthur Thalasso, Max Waizmann, Nellie Walker, Bill Wolfe, Silver (horse).

Girl from God's Country (July 30, 1940)

Credits: *Director*: Sidney Salkow; *Producer*: Armand Schaefer; *Screenplay*: Malcolm Stuart Boylan, Robert Lee Johnson, Elizabeth Meehan; *Based on the Story* by Ray Milholland; *Cinematographer*: Jack A. Marta; *Editor*: William Morgan; *Musical Score*: William Lava; *Art Director*: John Victor Mackay; *Production Company and Distributor*: Republic Pictures; *Running Time*: 75 Minutes.

Cast: Chester Morris (Jim Holden [Gary Currier]), Jane Wyatt, Charles Bickford, Mala, Kate Drain Lawson, John Bleifer, Mamo Clark, Ferike Boros, Don Zelaya, Clem Bevans, Edward Gargan, Spencer Charters, Thomas E. Jackson, Victor Potel, Si Jenks, Gene Morgan, Kay Frye, Marvin Davis, Rosina Galli, Ace the Wonder Dog.

Meet Boston Blackie (February 20, 1941)

Credits: *Director*: Robert Florey; *Producers*: Irving Briskin, Ralph Cohn; *Screenplay and Story*: Jay Dratler; *Based on the Character* created by Jack Boyle; *Cinematographer*: Franz Planer; *Editor*: James Sweeney; *Production Company and Distributor*: Columbia Pictures Corporation; *Running Time*: 60 Minutes.

Cast: Chester Morris (Boston Blackie), Rochelle Hudson, Richard Lane, Charles Wagenheim, Constance Worth, Jack O'Malley, George Magrill, James Seay, Harry Anderson, Sam Bernard, James Blaine, Harry Bowen, Stanley Brown, Eddie Fetherston, Budd Fine, Richard Fiske, Byron Foulger, Jack Gardner, John Harmon, Ethan Laidlaw, William Lally, Eddie Laughton, Philo McCullough, George McKay, Edward Mundy, Nestor Paiva, Ralph Peters, Walter Sande, Schlitze, Lee Shumway, Bruce Sidney, Charles Sullivan, John Tyrell, Ed Wolff.

No Hands on the Clock (December 1, 1941)

Credits: *Director*: Frank McDonald; *Producers*: William H. Pine, William C. Thomas; *Screenplay*: Maxwell Shane; *Based on the Novel* by Daniel Mainwaring [Geoffrey Holmes]; *Cinematographer*: Fred Jackman, Jr.; *Editor*: William H. Ziegler; *Musical Score*: Paul Sawtell; *Art Director*: Frank Paul Sylos; *Production Company*: Pine-Thomas Productions; *Distributor*: Paramount Pictures; *Running Time*: 76 Minutes.

Cast: Chester Morris (Humphrey Campbell), Jean Parker, Rose Hobart, Dick Purcell, Astrid Allwyn, Rod Cameron, George Watts, James Kirkwood, Billie Seward, Robert Middlemass, Grant Withers, Lorin Raker, George J. Lewis, Ralph Sanford, Ralph Dunn, Edward Earle, John Gallaudet, Gertrude Hoffman, Eddie Kane, Keye Luke, Jack Norton, Milburn Stone, Pat West.

Confessions of Boston Blackie (January 9, 1942)

Credits: *Director*: Edward Dmytryk; *Producer*: William Berke; *Screenplay*: Paul Yawitz; *Based on the Story* by Paul Yawitz and Jay Dratler *and the Character* created by Jack Boyle; *Cinematographer*: Philip Tannura; *Editor*: Gene Milford; *Musical Director*: Morris W. Stoloff; *Art Director*: Lionel Banks; *Production Company and Distributor*: Columbia Pictures Corporation; *Running Time*: 65 Minutes.

Cast: Chester Morris (Boston Blackie), Harriet Hilliard [Nelson], Richard Lane, George E. Stone, Lloyd Corrigan, Joan Woodbury, Walter Sande, Ralph Theodore, Kenneth MacDonald, Walter Soderling, William ["Billy"] Benedict, Jessie Arnold, Harry A. Bailey, Ralph Brooks, Stanley Brown, Bill Cartledge, Jack Rube Clifford, Herbert Clifton, Dorothy Curtis, Harry

Depp, Mike Donovan, Lorna Dunn, Ralph Dunn, Eddie Fetherston, Budd Fine, Al Hill, Harry Hollingsworth, Eddie Kane, Gwen Kenyon, William Lally, Eddie Laughton, Betty Mack, Jack O'Malley, Benny Petti, Martin Spellman, Brick Sullivan, Julius Tannen, John Tyrrell, Lawrence A. Williams.

"How to Be a Star" (February 1942)

Credits: *Director*: Clay Adams; *Distributor*: RKO Radio Pictures; *Running Time*: 8 minutes.

Cast: Chester Morris (Himself), Anne Baxter, Milton Berle, Joseph Cotten, Leif Erickson, Lum 'n' Abner.

Canal Zone (March 19, 1942)

Credits: *Director*: Lew Landers; *Producers*: Irving Briskin, Colbert Clark; *Screenplay*: Robert Lee Johnson; *Based on the Story* "Heroes Come High" by Blaine Miller and Jean DuPont Miller; *Cinematographer*: Franz Planer; *Editors*: Art Bell, James Sweeney; *Art Director*: Lionel Banks; *Production Company and Distributor*: Columbia Pictures Corporation; *Running Time*: 79 Minutes.

Cast: Chester Morris ("Hardtack" Hamilton), Harriet Hilliard [Nelson], John Hubbard, Larry Parks, Forrest Tucker, Eddie Laughton, Lloyd Bridges, George McKay, Stanley Andrews, John Tyrrell, Stanley Brown, John Shay, Hugh Beaumont, Louis Jean Heydt, James Khan, Arthur O'Connell, Paul Phillips, Betty Roadman.

Alias Boston Blackie (April 2, 1942)

Credits: *Director*: Lew Landers; *Producers*: Wallace MacDonald, Irving Briskin; *Screenplay*: Paul Yawitz; *Based on the Character* created by Jack Boyle; *Cinematographer*: Philip Tannura; *Editor*: Richard Fantl; *Musical Score*: George Parrish; *Art Director*: Lionel Banks; *Production Company and Distributor*: Columbia Pictures Corporation; *Running Time*: 67 Minutes.

Cast: Chester Morris (Boston Blackie), Adele Mara, Richard Lane, George E. Stone, Lloyd Corrigan, Walter Sande, Larry Parks, George McKay, Cy Kendall, Paul Fix, Ben Taggart, Ernie Adams, Lloyd Bridges, Edmund Cobb, Jerome de Nuccio, Harry Depp, Mike Donovan, Lester Dorr, Karen X. Gaylord, Bud Geary, Kit Guard, Dave Harper, Al Herman, George Hickman, Dick Jensen, William Lally, Eddie Laughton, James T. Mack, Teddy Mangean, Sidney Miller, Eileen O'Hearn, Lee Prather, Frank Richards, Suzanne Ridgway, Francis Sayles, Walter Soderling, Cyril Thornton, John Tyrrell, Duke York.

I Live on Danger (June 16, 1942)

Credits: *Director*: Sam White; *Producers*: William H. Pine, William C. Thomas; *Screenplay*: Lewis R. Foster, Richard Murphy, Maxwell Shane; *Based on the Story* by Lewis R. Foster and Alex Gottlieb; *Cinematographer*: Fred Jackman, Jr.; *Editor*: William H. Ziegler; *Musical Score*: Freddie Rich; *Art Director*: Frank Paul Sylos; *Production Company*: Pine-Thomas Productions; *Distributor*: Paramount Pictures; *Running Time*: 73 Minutes.

Cast: Chester Morris (Jeff Morrell), Jean Parker, Elisabeth Risdon, Edward Norris, Dick Purcell, Roger Pryor, Douglas Fowley, Ralph Sanford, Edwin Maxwell, Patsy Nash, Joe Cunningham, Bernadene Hayes, Billy Nelson, Vickie Lester, William Bakewell, Charlotte Henry, Anna Q. Nilsson, William ["Billy"] Benedict, Bill Cartledge, Edward Earle, Eddie Kane, Edward Keane, Herbert Rawlinson, Pat West.

Boston Blackie Goes Hollywood (November 5, 1942)

Credits: *Director*: Michael Gordon; *Producers*: Wallace MacDonald, Irving Briskin; *Screenplay*: Paul Yawitz; *Based on the Character* created by Jack Boyle; *Cinematographer*: Henry Freulich; *Musical Director*: Morris W. Stoloff; *Editor*: Art Seid; *Art Director*: Lionel Banks; *Production Company and Distributor*: Columbia Pictures Corporation; *Running Time*: 68 Minutes.

Cast: Chester Morris (Boston Blackie), William Wright, Constance Worth, Lloyd Corrigan, Richard Lane, George E. Stone, Forrest Tucker, Ernie Alexander, Brandon Beach, Stanley Brown, Ralph Dunn, Jack Gardner, Al Hill, Robert Kellard, Cy Kendall, Eddie Laughton, James C. Morton, Shirley Patterson, Dorothy Phillips, Cyril Ring, Virginia Sale, Walter Sande, Charles Sullivan, Victor Travis, John Tyrrell.

Wrecking Crew (November 7, 1942)

Credits: *Director*: Frank McDonald; *Producers*: William H. Pine, William C. Thomas; *Screenplay*: Maxwell Shane, Richard Murphy; *Based on the Story* by Robert T. Shannon and Mauri Grashin; *Cinematographer*: Fred Jackman, Jr.; *Editor*: William H. Ziegler; *Musical Score*: Freddie Rich; *Art Director*: Frank Paul Sylos; *Production Company*: Pine-Thomas Productions; *Distributor*: Paramount Pictures; *Running Time*: 73 Minutes.

Cast: Chester Morris (Duke Mason), Richard Arlen, Jean Parker, Joe Sawyer, Esther Dale,

Alexander Granach, Evelyn Brent, Billy Nelson, William Hall, Frank Melton, Fred Sherman, Alec Craig, Nigel De Brulier, Byron Foulger, Ralph Dunn, Dick Elliott, Jody Gilbert, Ralph Sanford.

After Midnight with Boston Blackie (March 18, 1943)

Credits: *Director*: Lew Landers; *Producers*: Sam White, Samuel J. Briskin; *Screenplay*: Howard J. Green; *Based on the Story* by Aubrey Wisberg and *the Character* created by Jack Boyle; *Cinematographer*: L. William O'Connell; *Editor*: Richard Fantl; *Musical Director*: Morris W. Stoloff; *Art Director*: Lionel Banks; *Production Company and Distributor*: Columbia Pictures Corporation; *Running Time*: 65 Minutes.

Cast: Chester Morris (Horatio ["Boston Blackie"] Black), Richard Lane, Ann Savage, George E. Stone, Lloyd Corrigan, Walter Baldwin, Don Barclay, Jan Buckingham, Eddy Chandler, Heinie Conklin, Dudley Dickerson, Dick Elliot, Jesse Graves, John Harmon, Al Hill, Robert F. Hill, Robert Homans, Ray Johnson, Eddie Kane, Cy Kendall, Sam McDaniel, George McKay, Joe Palma, Walter Sande, Harry Semels, Cap Somers, Victor Travis, Marguerite Whitten.

Aerial Gunner (March 20, 1943)

Credits: *Director*: William H. Pine; *Producers*: William H. Pine, William C. Thomas; *Screenplay*: Maxwell Shane; *Story Idea*: Jack F. Dailey; *Cinematographer*: Fred Jackman, Jr.; *Editor*: William H. Ziegler; *Musical Score*: Daniele Amfitheatrof; *Art Director*: Frank Paul Sylos; *Production Company*: Pine-Thomas Productions; *Distributor*: Paramount Pictures; *Running Time*: 78 Minutes.

Cast: Chester Morris (Sergeant "Foxy" Pattis), Richard Arlen, Jimmy Lydon, Amelita Ward, Dick Purcell, Keith Richards, William ["Billy"] Benedict, Olive Blakeney, Kirk Alyn, Jeff Corey, Edward Earle, Frank Fenton, Gil Frye, John Hamilton, John James, Charles J. Jordan, William Marshall, Robert Mitchum, Barbara Pepper, Ralph Sanford, Beth Stone, Brick Sullivan, Allen Wood.

High Explosive (March 27, 1943)

Credits: *Director*: Frank McDonald; *Producers*: William H. Pine, William C. Thomas; *Screenplay*: Maxwell Shane, Howard J. Green; *Based on the Story* by Joseph Hoffman; *Cinematographer*: Fred Jackman, Jr.; *Editor*: William H. Ziegler; *Musical Score*: Daniele Amfitheatrof; *Art Director*: Frank Paul Sylos; *Production Company*: Pine-Thomas Productions; *Distributor*: Paramount Pictures; *Running Time*: 60 Minutes.

Cast: Chester Morris (Buzz Mitchell), Jean Parker, Barry Sullivan, Ralph Sanford, Rand Brooks, Dick Purcell, Barbara Lynn, Jack Randall, Vince Barnett.

Tornado (August 1943)

Credits: *Director*: William Berke; *Producers*: William H. Pine, William C. Thomas; *Screenplay*: Maxwell Shane; *Based on the Novel* by John Guedel; *Cinematographer*: Fred Jackman, Jr.; *Editor*; William H. Ziegler; *Musical Score*: Freddie Rich; *Art Director*: Frank Paul Sylos; *Production Company*: Pine-Thomas Productions; *Distributor*: Paramount Pictures; *Running Time*: 83 minutes.

Cast: Chester Morris (Pete Ramsey), Nancy Kelly, William Henry, Gwen Kenyon, Joe Sawyer, Marie McDonald, Morgan Conway, Nestor Paiva, Vince Barnett, Lane Chandler, Wade Crosby, Clyde Dilson, Ralph Dunn, Edward Earle, Frank Reicher, Regis Toomey, Dave Wengren.

The Chance of a Lifetime (October 26, 1943)

Credits: *Director*: William Castle; *Producer*: Wallace MacDonald; *Screenplay*: Paul Yawitz; *Based on Characters* created by Jack Boyle; *Cinematographer*: Ernest Miller; *Editor*: Jerome Thomas; *Musical Director*: Morris W. Stoloff; *Art Directors*: Lionel Banks, Paul Murphy; *Production Company and Distributor*: Columbia Pictures Corporation; *Running Time*: 65 minutes.

Cast: Chester Morris (Horatio ["Boston Blackie"] Black), Erik Rolf, Jeanne Bates, Richard Lane, George E. Stone, Lloyd Corrigan, Richard Alexander, George Anderson, Jessie Arnold, Trevor Bardette, Eddie Bruce, Sally Cairns, Jack Carr, Eddy Chandler, James Conaty, Heinie Conklin, Marie De Becker, Sayre Dearing, Minta Durfee, Maude Eburne, Ben Erway, Douglas Fowley, Jerry Frank, Joel Friedkin, Kit Guard, Bobbie Hale, John Harmon, Arthur Hunnicutt, Cy Kendall, Carl M. Leviness, George Magrill, Sid Melton, Al Murphy, Forbes Murray, Frank O'Connor, Brian O'Hara, Larry Olsen, Dick Rush, Walter Sande, Harry Semels, Ray Teal, John Tyrrell, Pierre Watkin.

Gambler's Choice (April 27, 1944)

Credits: *Director*: Frank McDonald; *Producer*: William H. Pine, William C. Thomas; *Screenplay*: Maxwell Shane, Irving Reis; *Based on the Story* by Howard Emmett Rogers and James Edward Grant; *Cinematographer*: Fred Jackman, Jr.; *Editor*: Howard A. Smith; *Musical Score*: Mort Glickman; *Art Director*: Frank Paul Sylos; *Production Company*: Pine-Thomas Productions; *Distributor*: Paramount Pictures; *Running Time*: 66 minutes.

Cast: Chester Morris (Ross Hadley), Nancy Kelly, Russell Hayden, Lee Patrick, Lloyd Corrigan, Sheldon Leonard, Lyle Talbot, Maxine Lewis, Tom Dugan, Charles Arnt, Billy Nelson, Boots Brown, Bob Burns, Jack Carr, Jimmy Conlin, Clancy Cooper, Joseph Crehan, Dick Curtis, Joe Devlin, Ralph Dunn, Dick Elliott, Jim Farley, Sam Finn, Sam Flint, Byron Foulger, Jack Gardner, Jack Gordon, Eddie Hall, George Humbert, Thomas E. Jackson, Michael Jeffers, Dick Johnstone, Wilbur Mack, Frank Marlowe, Thomas Martin, Pat McKee, Robert Middlemass, Jack Mulhall, Al Murphy, Milton Parsons, William Pawley, Lee Phelps, Bert Roach, Dewey Robinson, Virginia Sale, Cosmo Sardo, Syd Saylor, Ted Stanhope, Milburn Stone, Hal Taggart, Pat West.

Secret Command (July 30, 1944)

Credits: *Director*: A. Edward ["Eddie"] Sutherland; *Producer*: Phil L. Ryan; *Executive Producer*: Pat O'Brien; *Screenplay*: Roy Chanslor; *Based on the Story* "The Saboteurs" by John Hawkins and Ward Hawkins; *Cinematographer*: Franz F. Planer; *Editor*: Viola Lawrence; *Musical Score*: Paul Sawtell; *Art Directors*: Lionel Banks, Edward C. Jewell; *Production Company*: Terneen Productions; *Distributor*: Columbia Pictures Corporation; *Running Time*: 82 minutes.

Cast: Chester Morris (Jeff Gallagher), Pat O'Brien, Carole Landis, Ruth Warrick, Barton MacLane, Tom Tully, Wallace Ford, Howard Freeman, Erik Rolf, Matt McHugh, Frank Sully, Frank Fenton, Charles D. Brown, Carol Nugent, Richard Lyon, Dusty Anderson, Vernon Dent, Mary Gordon, George McKay, Pat Parrish, Cyril Ring, Dewey Robinson, Ray Teal, John Tyrrell, Dorothy Vernon.

One Mysterious Night (October 21, 1944)

Credits: *Director*: Oscar ["Budd"] Boetticher, Jr.; *Producer*: Ted Richmond; *Screenplay*: Paul Yawitz; *Based on the Character* created by Jack Boyle; *Cinematographer*: L. William O'Connell; *Editor*: Al Clark; *Musical Score*: Paul Sawtell; *Art Directors*: Lionel Banks, George Brooks; *Production Company and Distributor*: Columbia Pictures Corporation *Running Time*: 61 minutes.

Cast: Chester Morris (Horatio ["Boston Blackie"] Black), Janis Carter, William Wright, Richard Lane, George E. Stone, Robert B. Williams, Mark Roberts, Ed Allen, James Blaine, Kenneth Brown, Early Cantrell, Joseph Crehan, Lew Davis, Edythe Elliott, Almeda Fowler, Fred Graff, Harrison Greene, Fred Howard, Dick Jensen, Henry Jordan, Edward Keane, Tom Kingston, Lyle Latell, Billy Lenhart, Anee Loos, George Magrill, Cy Malis, Dorothy Malone, George McKay, Pat O'Malley, Constance Purdy, Ben Taggart, John Tyrrell, Minerva Urecal, Robert Walker, Cecil Weston.

Double Exposure (December 18, 1944)

Credits: *Director*: William Berke; *Producers*: William H. Pine, William C. Thomas; *Screenplay*: Winston Miller, Maxwell Shane; *Based on the Story* by Ralph Graves and Winston Miller; *Cinematographer*: Fred Jackman, Jr.; *Editors*: Henry Adams, Howard A. Smith; *Musical Score*: Alexander Laszlo; *Art Director*: Frank Paul Sylos; *Production Company*: Pine-Thomas Productions; *Distributor*: Paramount Pictures; *Running Time*: 63 minutes.

Cast: Chester Morris (Larry Burke), Nancy Kelly, Jane Farrar, Phillip Terry, Richard Gaines, Charles Arnt, Claire Rochelle, Roma Aldrich, Jack Chefe, Charles Delaney, Cyril Delevanti, Edward Earle, Kit Guard, Eddie Hall, Donald Kerr, Al Murphy, Spec O'Donnell, Hugh Prosser, Dewey Robinson.

Rough, Tough, and Ready (March 22, 1945)

Credits: *Director*: Del Lord; *Producer*: Alexis Thurn-Taxis; *Screenplay and Story* ("Men of the Deep"): Edward T. Lowe, Jr.; *Cinematographer*: George Meehan; *Editor*: Richard Fantl; *Musical Score*: Marlin Skiles; *Art Director*: Walter Holscher; *Production Company and Distributor*: Columbia Pictures Corporation; *Running Time*: 66 minutes.

Cast: Chester Morris (Brad Crowder), Victor McLaglen, Jean Rogers, Veda Ann Borg, Amelita Ward, Robert B. Williams, John Tyrrell, Fred Graff, Jessie Arnold, Harry Barris, William Forrest, Tex Harding, Jayne Hazard, Tom Kennedy, Ethan Laidlaw, Nolan Leary, Anne Loos, Alphonse Martell, Bob Meredith, Ida Moore, Jack Overman, Joe Palma, Addison Richards, LeRoy Taylor, Richard Thorne, Loren Tindall, Victor Travis, Dorothy Vernon, Emmett Vogan, Blackie Whiteford.

"Screen Snapshots: Three G.I. Janes in Hollywood" (March 1945)

Credits: *Distributor*: Columbia Pictures Corporation; *Running Time*: 10 minutes.

Cast: Chester Morris (Himself), Joe E. Brown, Ken Carpenter, Jinx Falkenburg, Elsa Lanchester, Charles Laughton, Lum 'n' Abner, Alan Mowbray, Rudy Vallee.

Boston Blackie Booked on Suspicion (May 10, 1945)

Credits: *Director*: Arthur Dreifuss; *Producer*: Michael Kraike; *Screenplay*: Paul Yawitz; *Based on the Story* by Malcolm Stuart Boylan and *the Character* created by Jack Boyle; *Cinematographer*: George Meehan; *Editor*: Richard Fantl; *Art Director*: Perry Smith; *Production Company and Distributor*: Columbia Pictures Corporation; *Running Time*: 66 minutes.

Cast: Chester Morris (Horatio ["Boston Blackie"] Black), Lynn Merrick, Richard Lane, Frank Sully, Steve Cochran, George E. Stone, Lloyd Corrigan, Dudley Dickerson, Bob Alden, Jessie Arnold, Richard Bartell, Lee Bennett, Roy Brent, Eddie Bruce, George M. Carleton, George Ford, Almeda Fowler, Jean Fowler, Jack Frack, Dick Gordon, Dick Jensen, Edward Keane, Colin Kenny, Nolan Leary, George Lloyd, George Meader, Harold Miller, Forbes Murray, Joe Palma, Stanley Price, Jack Rice, Dan Stowell, Victor Travis, Philip Van Zandt, Charles Wagenheim, Cecil Weston, Robert B. Williams, Isabel Withers, Douglas Wood.

Boston Blackie's Rendezvous (July 5, 1945)

Credits: *Director*: Arthur Dreifuss; *Producer*: Alexis Thurn-Taxis; *Screenplay*: Edward Dein; *Based on the Story* by Fred Schiller and *the Character* created by Jack Boyle; *Cinematographer*: George Meehan; *Editor*: Aaron Stell; *Art Director*: Perry Smith; *Production Company and Distributor*: Columbia Pictures Corporation; *Running Time*: 64 minutes.

Cast: Chester Morris (Boston Blackie), Nina Foch, Steve Cochran, Richard Lane, George E. Stone, Frank Sully, Iris Adrian, Richard Alexander, Bing Conley, Lew Davis, Joe Devlin, Eddie Hall, Harry Hayden, Marilyn Johnson, Charles Jordan, Tom Kennedy, Perc Launders, Bob Meredith, Clarence Muse, Joe Palma, Adele Roberts, Wally Rose, Carl Sepulveda, Frank Stevens, Dan Stowell, Charles Sullivan, John Tyrrell, Philip Van Zandt, Robert B. Williams.

One Way to Love (January 9, 1946)

Credits: *Director*: Ray Enright; *Producer*: Burt Kelly; *Screenplay*: Jack Henley, Joseph Hoffman; *Based on the Story* by Lester Lee and Larry Marks; *Cinematographer*: Charles Lawton, Jr.; *Editor*: Richard Fantl; *Musical Score*: Marlin Skiles; *Art Directors*: George Brooks, Stephen Goosson; *Production Company and Distributor*: Columbia Pictures Corporation; *Running Time*: 83 minutes.

Cast: Chester Morris (Barry Cole), Willard Parker, Marguerite Chapman, Janis Carter, Hugh Herbert, Dusty Anderson, Jerome Cowan, Irving Bacon, Roscoe Karns, Frank Sully, Frank Jenks, Lewis L. Russell, Ernie Adams, Joseph Crehan, Kernan Cripps, Hal K. Dawson, Dudley Dickerson, John Elliott, Mary Forbes, Jesse Graves, Al Hill, Sam McDaniel, Larry McGrath, Forbes Murray, Pat O'Malley, Nick Stewart, John Tyrrell, Jasper Weldon, Martin Wilkins, Douglas Wood, Buck Woods.

A Close Call for Boston Blackie (January 24, 1946)

Credits: *Director*: Lew Landers; *Producer*: John Stone; *Screenplay*: Ben Markson, Malcolm Stuart Boylan; *Based on the Story* by Paul Yawitz and *the Character* created by Jack Boyle; *Cinematographer*: Burnett Guffey; *Editor*: Jerome Thoms; *Musical Director*: Mischa Bakaleinikoff; *Art Directors*: Carl Anderson, Jerome Pycha, Jr.; *Production Company and Distributor*: Columbia Pictures Corporation; *Running Time*: 69 minutes.

Cast: Chester Morris (Horatio ["Boston Blackie"] Black/Cyrus Peyton), Lynn Merrick, Richard Lane, Frank Sully, George E. Stone, Kathryn Card, Claire Carleton, Jack Gordon, Russell Hicks, Doris Houck, Charles Lane, George Lloyd, Brian O'Hara, Wanda Perry, Mark Roberts, Erik Rolf, Victor Travis, John Tyrrell, Emmett Vogan, Ruth Warren.

The Phantom Thief (May 2, 1946)

Credits: *Director*: D. Ross Lederman; *Producer*: John Stone; *Screenplay*: Richard Wormser, Richard Weil, Malcolm Stuart Boylan; *Based on the Story* by G.A. Snow and *the Character* created by Jack Boyle; *Cinematographer*: George Meehan; *Editor*: Al Clark; *Musical Director*: Mischa Bakaleinikoff; *Art Director*: Robert Peterson; *Production Company and Distributor*: Columbia Pictures Corporation; *Running Time*: 65 minutes.

Cast: Chester Morris (Horatio ["Boston Blackie"] Black), Jeff Donnell, Richard Lane, Dusty Anderson, George E. Stone, Frank Sully, Marvin Miller, Wilton Graff, Murray Alper, Forbes Murray, Joseph Crehan, John Bagni, Edmund Cobb, Tom Dillon, Eddie Dunn, George Eldredge, Eddie Fetherston, Doris Houck, Charles Jordan, George Magrill, Pat O'Malley, Adele Roberts, Sammy Shack, Brick Sullivan, John Tyrrell, Charles C. Wilson.

Boston Blackie and the Law (December 12, 1946)

Credits: *Director*: D. Ross Lederman; *Producer*: Ted Richmond; *Screenplay*: Harry J. Essex, Malcolm Stuart Boylan; *Based on the Character* created by Jack Boyle; *Cinematographer*: George Meehan; *Editor*: James Sweeney; *Musical Score*: Hans Sommer; *Art Director*: Charles Clague; *Production Company and Distributor*: Columbia Pictures Corporation; *Running Time*: 69 minutes.

Cast: Chester Morris (Horatio ["Boston Blackie"] Black), Trudy Marshall, Constance Dowling, Richard Lane, George E. Stone, Frank Sully, Warren Ashe, Jessie Arnold, Eugene Borden, Kernan Cripps, Lew Davis, Eddie Dunn, Ralph Dunn, Eddie Fetherston, Fred Fox, Fred Graff, Chuck Hamilton, Lew Harvey, Ted Hecht, Selmer Jackson, Edward Keane, Tom Kingston, William Newell, Frank O'Connor, Brian O'Hara, Pat O'Malley, Joe Palma, Wanda Perry, Maudie Prickett, Wally Rose, Robert Ryan, Syd Saylor, Billy Snyder, Eddy Waller.

Blind Spot (February 6, 1947)

Credits: *Director*: Robert Gordon; *Producer*: Ted Richmond; *Screenplay*: Martin Goldsmith; *Based on the Story* "Trapped" by Barry Perowne; *Cinematographer*: George Meehan; *Editor*: Henry Batista; *Musical Score*: Paul Sawtell; *Art Directors*: Ben Hayne, Cary Odell; *Production Company and Distributor*: Columbia Pictures Corporation; *Running Time*: 73 minutes.

Cast: Chester Morris (Jeffrey Andrews), Constance Dowling, Steven Geray, James Bell, William Forrest, Sid Tomack, Paul E. Burns, Harry Strang, Steve Benton, Paul Bryar, Jimmy Gray, Robert Hartford, Charles Jordan, Frank Mayo, Brian O'Hara.

Trapped by Boston Blackie (May 13, 1948)

Credits: *Director*: Seymour Friedman; *Producer*: Rudolph C. Flothow; *Screenplay*: Maurice Tombragel; *Based on the Story* by Charles R. Marion and Edward Bock and *the Character* created by Jack Boyle; *Cinematographer*: Philip Tannura; *Editor*: Dwight Caldwell; *Musical Director*: Mischa Bakaleinikoff; *Art Director*: George Brooks; *Production Company and Distributor*: Columbia Pictures Corporation; *Running Time*: 67 minutes.

Cast: Chester Morris (Boston Blackie), June Vincent, Richard Lane, Patricia Barry, Edward Norris, George E. Stone, Frank Sully, Fay Baker, Abigail Adams, Edward Biby, James Carlisle, Mary Currier, Bryn Davis, Helen Dickson, Franklyn Farnum, Bess Flowers, William Forrest, Dick French, Ray Harper, George Hoagland, Charles Jordan, Harold Miller, Sol Murgi, George Nardelli, Frank O'Connor, Sarah Selby, Bernard Sell, Laura Treadwell, Pierre Watkin, Ben Welden.

Boston Blackie's Chinese Venture (March 2, 1949)

Credits: *Director*: Seymour Friedman; *Producer*: Rudolph C. Flothow; *Screenplay and Story*: Maurice Tombragel; *Based on the Character* created by Jack Boyle *Cinematographer*: Vincent J. Farrar; *Editor*: Richard Fantl; *Musical Director*: Mischa Bakaleinikoff; *Art Director*: Paul Palmentola; *Production Company and Distributor*: Columbia Pictures Corporation; *Running Time*: 59 minutes.

Cast: Chester Morris (Horatio ["Boston Blackie"] Black), Maylia, Richard Lane, Don McGuire, Joan Woodbury, Sid Tomack, Frank Sully, Charles Arnt, Luis Van Rooten, Philip Ahn, George Barrows, Brandon Beach, Paul Bradley, Peter Brocco, Ralph Brooks, Spencer Chan, Noble ["Kid"] Chissell, Aen-Ling Chow, Edgar Dearing, Benson Fong, Harold Fong, Eddie Lee, George Lee, James B. Leong, George Lloyd, Marya Marco, George Nardelli, Ottola Nesmith, Frank O'Connor, Pat O'Malley, Celeste Savoi, Fred F. Sears, Harry Strang, Robert B. Williams, William Yip, Victor Sen Yung.

Unchained (January 19, 1955)

Credits: *Director, Producer and Screenplay*: Hall Bartlett; *Based on the Book: Prisoners are People* by Kenyon J. Scudder; *Cinematographer*: Virgil Miller; *Editor*: Cotton Warburton; *Musical Score*: Alex North; *Production Company*: Hall Bartlett Productions; *Distributor*: Warner Bros; *Running Time*: 75 minutes.

Cast: Chester Morris (Kenyon J. Scudder), Elroy ["Crazylegs"] Hirsch, Barbara Hale, Todd

Duncan, Johnny Johnston, Peggy Knudsen, Jerry Paris, John Qualen, Tim Considine, Sam Flint, Art Gilmore, Dexter Gordon, Sol Gorss, Kathryn Grant, Bill Kennedy, Don Kennedy, Victor Mowrer, Henry Nakamura, Robert Patten, Stafford Repp, Mack Williams.

The She-Creature (August 1956)

Credits: *Director*: Edward L. Cahn; *Producers*: Samuel Z. Arkoff, Israel M. Berman, Alex Gordon; *Screenplay*: Lou Rusoff, Jerry Zigmond; *Based on the Story* by Lou Rusoff; *Cinematographer*: Frederick E. West; *Editor*: Ronald Sinclair; *Musical Score*: Ronald Stein; *Art Director*: Don Ament; *Production Company*: Golden State Productions; *Distributor*: American International Pictures; *Running Time*: 77 minutes.

Cast: Chester Morris (Dr. Carlo Lombardi), Tom Conway, Cathy Downs, Lance Fuller, Ron Randell, Frieda Inescort, Marla English, Frank Jenks, El Brendel, Paul Dubov, William Hudson, Flo Bert, Jeanne Evans, Kenneth MacDonald, Jack Mulhall, Edward Earle, Luana Walters, Paul Blaisdell, Edmund Cobb, Franklyn Farnum, Mari Finley, Bess Flowers, Creighton Hale, Stuart Holmes, Harold Miller, Barry Norton, Felice Richmond, Suzanne Ridgway, Spike (dog).

The Great White Hope (October 16, 1970)

Credits: *Director*: Martin Ritt; *Producer*: Lawrence Turman; *Screenplay and Based on the Play* by Howard Sackler; *Cinematographer*: Burnett Guffey; *Editor*: William Reynolds; *Musical Supervisor*: Lionel Newman; *Production Designer*: John DeCuir; *Art Director*: Jack Martin Smith; *Production Company*: Lawrence Turman; *Distributor*: Twentieth Century–Fox; *Running Time*: 103 minutes.

Cast: Chester Morris (Pop Weaver), James Earl Jones, Jane Alexander, Lou Gilbert, Joel Fluellen, Robert Webber, Marlene Warfield, R.G. Armstrong, Hal Holbrook, Beah Richards, Moses Gunn, Lloyd Gough, George Ebeling, Larry Pennell, Roy Glenn, Bill Walker, Marcel Dalio, Rodolfo Acosta, Virginia Capers, Rockne Tarkington, Oscar Beregi, Jr., Manuel Padilla, Jr., Karl-Otto Alberty, Jim Beattie, Kirk Alyn, Ernest Anderson, Paul Barselou, Donald Buka, Booth Colman, Scatman Crothers, Zara Cully, Basil Dignam, Pitt Herbert, Tom Lawrence, Arthur Malet, Hans Meyer, Frank Noel, Lillian Randolph, Davis Roberts, Scott Lee Scarborough, Chet Stratton, Cal Wilson.

Appendix B
Television Programs

Following is a complete listing of television programs featuring Chester Morris. Major credits for each title are accompanied by the initial broadcast date, Morris' character name, supporting cast, production company/network and running time.

Cavalcade of Stars (March 23, 1950)

Credits: *Production Company*: Drugstore Television Productions; *Network*: DuMont; *Running Time*: 60 minutes.

Cast: Chester Morris (Himself), Dizzy Gillespie, Jerry Lester, Kyle MacDonald.

The Ken Murray Show (April 15, 1950)

Credits: *Network*: CBS; *Running Time*: 30 minutes.

Cast: Chester Morris (Himself), Bonnie Baker, Ruby Keeler, Ken Murray, Gloria Swanson.

Cameo Theatre: "The Great Merlini" (May 23, 1950)

Credits: *Director*: Curtis Canfield; *Producers*: Felix Greenfield, Albert McCleery; *Writers*: Jack Bentkover, Clayton Rawson; *Network*: NBC; *Running Time*: 30 minutes.

Cast: Chester Morris (Merlini), Wyrley Birch, Kirk Brown, George Englund, Cele MacLaughlin, Bram Nossen, William Terry. Alfreda Wallace, Mary K. Wells, Patricia Wheel.

Texaco Star Theatre (November 14, 1950)

Credits: *Musical Conductor*: Allen Roth; *Production Company*: Milton Berle Productions; *Network*: NBC; *Running Time*: 60 minutes.

Cast: Chester Morris (Himself), Milton Berle, Norman Brokenshire, Richard Buckley, Kitty and Fanny, Hal Le Roy, The Magid Triplets, Martha Raye, Hal Sawyer, Sid Stone, Rudy Vallee, Watson Sisters.

The Ken Murray Show (November 18, 1950)

Credits: *Network*: CBS; *Running Time*: 30 minutes.

Cast: Chester Morris (Himself), Milton Berle, Mary Boland, Anita Louise, The Mills Brothers, Ken Murray.

The Ken Murray Show (February 3, 1951)

Credits: *Network*: CBS; *Running Time*: 30 minutes.

Cast: Chester Morris (Himself), Dave Appolon, Darla Hood, Johnny Johnston, Laurette and Clymas, Jack Mulhall, Ken Murray.

Danger: "The Undertaker Calls" (April 10, 1951)

Credits: *Production Company and Network*: CBS; *Running Time*: 30 minutes.

Cast: Chester Morris.

Starlight Theatre: "Act of God Nonwithstanding" (September 6, 1951)

Credits: *Director and Producer*: Martin Ritt; *Writer*: Lawrence Hazard; *Based on the Short Story* by Leonard Lee; *Musical Score*: Fred Feibel; *Production Designer*: Grover Cole; *Network*: CBS; *Running Time*: 30 minutes.

Cast: Chester Morris (Ed Kennedy), Olive Deering, John McGovern, Michael Higgins, Bert Conway, Jock McGraw, Joe Mantell, Ray Danton,

Gorday Clifton, Somar Alberg, Ellen Davey, Doris Roberts.

The Frances Langford-Don Ameche Show (November 2, 1951)

Credits: *Director*: Babette Henry; *Producer*: Edward J. Nugent; *Executive Producer*: Ward Byron; *Writers*: Ray Allen, Michigan Kroll, Art Henley, Jim Allen; *Network*: ABC; *Running Time*: 45 minutes.

Cast: Chester Morris (Himself), Don Ameche, Irene Hayes, Frances Langford, Tony Romano, Richard and Flora Stewart.

Schlitz Playhouse: "Billy Budd" (January 11, 1952)

Credits: *Producer*: William Self; *Based on the Novel* by Herman Melville; *Production Companies*: Meridian Productions, Revue Studios; *Network*: CBS; *Running Time*: 30 minutes.

Cast: Chester Morris (The Dansker), Walter Burke, Walter Hampden, Peter Hobbs, Bernard Kates, Jack Manning, Jeff Morrow, Charles Nolte, Winston Ross, Guy Spaull.

Lights Out: "The Intruder" (January 21, 1952)

Credits: *Director*: Grey Lockwood; *Writer*: Lucille Fletcher; *Production Company and Network*: NBC; *Running Time*: 30 minutes.

Cast: Chester Morris, Jane Wyatt.

The Ken Murray Show (January 26, 1952)

Credits: *Network*: CBS; *Running Time*: 30 minutes.

Cast: Chester Morris (Himself), Glenda Farrell, Mary Raye and Naldi, Ken Murray, Maria Riva.

Suspense: "Black Panther" (April 8, 1952)

Credits: *Director and Producer*: Robert Stevens; *Writer*: Halsted Welles; *Set Designer*: Richard Bernstein; *Production Company and Network*: CBS; *Running Time*: 30 minutes.

Cast: Chester Morris (Edwards), Olive Deering, James Gregory, Allen Tower, Rex Marshall.

Tales of Tomorrow "The Exile" (June 6, 1952)

Credits: *Producers*: George F. Foley, Jr., James Lister; *Writer*: Edgar Marvin; *Based on the Story* by Alec Coppel; *Graphic Art Director*: Arthur Rankin, Jr.; *Set Designer*: James Trittipo; *Production Company*: George F. Foley; *Network*: ABC; *Running Time*: 25 minutes.

Cast: Chester Morris, John Boruff, Robert Herrman, Vera Massey, Luis Van Rooten.

Lux Video Theatre: "Welcome Home, Lefty" (June 23, 1952)

Credits: *Director*: Richard Goode; *Producer*: Cal Kuhl; *Writer*: Rod Serling; *Musical Score*: Wladimir Selinsky; *Art Director*: William Craig Smith; *Production Companies*: J. Walter Thompson Agency; *Network*: CBS; *Running Time*: 30 minutes.

Cast: Chester Morris (Lefty), Jack Dimond, Jay Jackson, Richard McMurray, Don Murray, Jan Sherwood, Robert F. Simon.

Robert Montgomery Presents: "The Law-Abiding" (September 8, 1952)

Credits: *Director*: Norman Felton; *Producer*: Robert Montgomery; *Writer*: Joel Hammil; *Musical Score*: Bob Busby, John Gart; *Production Company*: Neptune Productions; *Network*: NBC; *Running Time*: 60 minutes.

Cast: Chester Morris, Faith Brook, Francis Compton, Kurt Katch, Bruno Wick.

20 Questions (November 7, 1952)

Credits: *Producers*: George Elbes, Gary Stevens; *Production Company*: Fred Van Deventer Productions; *Network*: DuMont; *Running Time*: 30 minutes.

Cast: Chester Morris (Himself), Bobby McGuire, John McPhee, Herbert Polesie, Florence Rinard, Bill Slater, Fred Van Deventer, Frank Waldecker.

I've Got a Secret (November 13, 1952)

Credits: *Production Company*: Mark Goodson-Bill Todman Productions; *Network*: CBS; *Running Time*: 30 minutes.

Cast: Chester Morris (Himself), Kitty Carlisle, Bill Cullen, Jayne Meadows, Garry Moore, Henry Morgan.

The Arthur Murray Party (November 16, 1952)

Credits: *Musicians*: Ray Carter Orchestra; *Network*: DuMont; *Running Time*: 30 minutes.

Cast: Chester Morris (Himself), Teresa Brewer, Nellie Fisher, Bill Lawrence, Jack Miles, Arthur Murray, Kathryn Murray, Jerry Ross, William H. Vaux.

Tales of Tomorrow: "The Glacier Giant" (December 5, 1952)

Credits: *Writer*: David E. Durston; *Production Company*: George F. Foley; *Network*: ABC; *Running Time*: 25 minutes.
Cast: Chester Morris, Edith Fellows.

Danger: "Death Pulls the Strings" (December 30, 1952)

Credits: *Production Company and Network*: CBS; *Running Time*: 30 minutes.
Cast: Chester Morris, Bill Baird.

The Kate Smith Hour (January 5, 1953)

Credits: *Network*: NBC; *Running Time*: 60 minutes.
Cast: Chester Morris, Kate Smith.

The Name's the Same (February 3, 1953)

Credits: *Director*: Herbert Hirshman; *Producers*: Mark Goodson, Bill Todman; *Associate Producer*: Peter Arnell; *Technical Director*: John Broderick; *Production Company*: Mark Goodson-Bill Todman Productions; *Network*: ABC; *Running Time*: 30 minutes.
Cast: Chester Morris (Himself), Joan Alexander, Jerry Lester, Robert Q. Lewis, Meredith Willson.

Robert Montgomery Presents: "The Big Night" (March 23, 1953)

Credits: *Producer*: Robert Montgomery; *Writer*: Adrian Spies; *Musical Score*: Bob Busby, John Gart; *Production Company*: Neptune Productions; *Network*: NBC; *Running Time*: 60 minutes.
Cast: Chester Morris, Robert Montgomery, Katharine Bard, Joan Lorring, Scott McKay.

Kraft Television Theatre: "Final Edition" (May 13, 1953)

Credits: *Production Company*: J. Walter Thompson Agency; *Network*: NBC; *Running Time*: 60 minutes.
Cast: Chester Morris.

Suspense: "Point Blank" (August 11, 1953)

Credits: *Writer*: Ben Radin; *Production Company and Network*: CBS; *Running Time*: 30 minutes.
Cast: Chester Morris, Janis Carter.

Omnibus: "The Battler" (October 11, 1953)

Credits: *Directors*: Bob Banner, Paul Nickell; *Producers*: Paul Feigay, Fred Rickey, Robert Saudek; *Writer*: Arnold Schulman; *Based on the Story* by Ernest Hemingway; *Production Designer*: Henry May; *Production Company*: Ford Foundation; *Network*: CBS; *Running Time*: 55 minutes.
Cast: Chester Morris (The Battler), Paco Aguilera, Peter Brook, Alistair Cooke, Faico, Carmen Flores, Lola Flores, John Marriott, Virgil Thompson, Dick York.

Danger: "Towerman" (November 24, 1953)

Credits: *Production Company and Network*: CBS; *Running Time*: 30 minutes.
Cast: Chester Morris, Jackie Cooper.

Robert Montgomery Presents: "No Visible Means" (December 14, 1953)

Credits: *Director*: Norman Felton; *Producer*: Robert Montgomery; *Writers*: John McClain, Thomas Phipps; *Musical Score*: Bob Busby, John Gart; *Production Company*: Neptune Productions; *Network*: NBC; *Running Time*: 60 minutes.
Cast: Chester Morris (Himself/Host), Robert Montgomery, Patricia Breslin, Robert Ellenstein, Robert Middleton, Claudia Morgan, Robert Wark.

Robert Montgomery Presents: "The Greatest Man in the World" (December 28, 1953)

Credits: *Producer*: Robert Montgomery; *Writers*: Mathilde Ferro, Theodore Ferro; *Musical Score*: Bob Busby, John Gart; *Production Company*: Neptune Productions; *Network*: NBC; *Running Time*: 60 minutes.
Cast: Chester Morris, Robert Montgomery, Philip Abbott, Edward Binns, Ralph Bunker, Les Damon, Jack Hartley, Oliver Thorndike.

Captured [formerly ***Gang Busters***] (1953)

Credits: *Production Company*: NBC Film Division; *Stations*: local; *Number of Episodes*: 29; *Running Time*: 30 minutes.
Cast: Chester Morris (Host/Narrator).

The Web: "Rock-Bound" (February 14, 1954)
   Credits: *Production Company*: Mark Goodson-Bill Todman Production; *Network*: CBS; *Running Time*: 30 minutes.
   Cast: Chester Morris, Howard St. John, Mike Wallace.

The Philip Morris Playhouse: "Walk in the Night" (February 18, 1954)
   Credits: *Writers*: Verne Jay, Rod Serling; *Network*: CBS; *Running Time*: 30 minutes.
   Cast: Chester Morris.

Studio One in Hollywood: "Jack Sparling, Forty-Six" (April 12, 1954)
   Credits: *Director*: Franklin J. Schaffner; *Production Company and Network*: CBS; *Running Time*: 60 minutes.
   Cast: Chester Morris (Jack Sparling), Mary Astor, Betty Furness, Lois Smith.

Studio One in Hollywood: "The Death and Life of Larry Benson" (May 31, 1954)
   Credits: *Director*: Paul Nickell; *Producers*: William Altman, Felix Jackson; *Writer*: Reginald Rose; *Musical Score*: Alfredo Antonini; *Set Designer*: Kim Swados; *Production Company and Network*: CBS; *Running Time*: 60 minutes.
   Cast: Chester Morris (Sam Benson), Peg Hillias, Ruth Amos, Lee Remick, Skip Homeier, Lucie Lancaster, Betty Furness.

I've Got a Secret (August 11, 1954)
   Credits: *Production Company*: Mark Goodson-Bill Todman Productions; *Network*: CBS; *Running Time*: 30 minutes.
   Cast: Chester Morris (Himself), Laraine Day, Garry Moore.

Appointment with Adventure: "Time Bomb" (November 27, 1955)
   Credits: *Producer*: David Susskind; *Writers*: Anne Howard Bailey, Jean-Charles Tacchella; *Production Company*: Talent Associates; *Network*: CBS; *Running Time*: 30 minutes.
   Cast: Chester Morris, Jeanne Bal, Anthony Eisley.

Studio One in Hollywood: "Blow Up at Cortland" (December 5, 1955)
   Credits: *Writer*: Paul Monash; *Production Company and Network*: CBS; *Running Time*: 60 minutes.
   Cast: Chester Morris (Warden Garry), Neville Brand, Philip Coolidge, Betty Furness.

Studio One in Hollywood: "The Arena" (April 9, 1956)
   Credits: *Director*: Franklin J. Schaffner; *Producer*: Felix Jackson; *Writer*: Rod Serling; *Musical Score*: Alfredo Antonini; *Set Designer*: Willard Levitas; *Production Company and Network*: CBS; *Running Time*: 60 minutes.
   Cast: Chester Morris (Jack Feeney), Wendell Corey, John Cromwell, Leora Dana, Edgar Stehli, Peter Turgeon, Frances Sternhagen, Harry Holcombe, Paul Brinson, Betty Furness.

Kraft Television Theatre: "Time Lock" (November 28, 1956)
   Credits: *Director*: Harry Herrmann; *Writer*: Arthur Hailey; *Production Company*: J. Walter Thompson; *Network*: NBC; *Running Time*: 60 minutes.
   Cast: Chester Morris (Dawson), Grace Carney, Peter Lazer, Victor Thorley.

Tonight! (September 13, 1956)
   Credits: *Writers*: Stan Burns, Mike Marmer, Herbert Sargent; *Musicians*: Tony Mottola, Bobby Rosengarden, Doc Severinsen, Clark Terry; *Production Company and Network*: NBC; *Running Time*: 105 minutes.
   Cast: Chester Morris (Himself), Steve Allen, Bobby Dukoff, Skitch Henderson, Gene Rayburn.

The Red Skelton Hour: "Clem's Fish Market" (March 26, 1957)
   Credits: *Director*: Seymour Berns; *Producer*: Cecil Barker; *Writers*: Jesse Goldstein, Dave O'Brien, Sherwood Schwartz, Red Skelton; *Musical Score*: Edgar Nelson Barclift, David Rose; *Art Director*: Edgar Lansbury; *Production Company and Network*: CBS; *Running Time*: 30 minutes.
   Cast: Chester Morris (Tony), Red Skelton, Robert Armstrong, Veda Ann Borg, Leonard Bremen, Frankie Darro, David Rose and His Orchestra, Art Gilmore, Isabel Randolph, Frank Richards.

Zane Grey Theater: "Black Is for Grief" (April 12, 1957)

Credits: *Director*: Lewis Allen; *Producer*: Hal Hudson; *Writer*: Aaron Spelling; *Cinematographer*: Guy Roe; *Editor*: Chandler House; *Art Director*: Bill Ross; *Production Companies*: Four Star Productions, Pamric Productions, Zane Grey Enterprises; *Network*: CBS; *Running Time*: 30 minutes.

Cast: Chester Morris (Frank Simmons), Tom Tully, Tom Tryon, Mala Powers, Skip Homeier, Beulah Bondi, Mary Aston, Richard Anderson, Dick Powell.

Playhouse 90: "Child of Trouble" (May 2, 1957)

Credits: *Director*: Paul Nickell; *Writer*: James P. Cavanagh, Selma Robinson; *Musical Score*: Russell Garcia; *Theme Music*: Sammy Cahn, Alex North; *Production Companies*: Playhouse 90, CBS Television Network; *Network*: CBS; *Running Time*: 90 minutes.

Cast: Chester Morris (Warden), Richard Joy, Patty McCormack, Ricardo Montalban, Joan Blondell, Lillian Roth, Richard Arlen, Frank Puglia.

Kraft Television Theatre: "Man of Prey" (May 22, 1957)

Credits: *Production Company*: J. Walter Thompson; *Network*: NBC; *Running Time*: 60 minutes.

Cast: Chester Morris, Bruce Gordon, Georgann Johnson.

The Jack Paar Tonight Show (May 27, 1958)

Credits: *Production Company and Network*: NBC; *Running Time*: 105 minutes.

Cast: Chester Morris (Himself), Bil Baird, Cora Baird, The Baird Puppets, Johnny Carson, Hugh Downs, Jose Melis, Dmitri Tiomkin, Margaret Truman, Alan Young.

Pursuit: "Tiger on a Bicycle" (November 12, 1958)

Credits: *Director*: Paul Nickell; *Producer*: Norman Felton; *Writer*: Joan Scott; *Based on the Story* by Jonathan Latimer; *Musical Score*: Bernard Herrmann; *Production Company and Network*: CBS; *Running Time*: 60 minutes.

Cast: Chester Morris (Mood), Neville Brand, Laraine Day, Dan Duryea, David Ladd.

Oldsmobile Music Theatre: "Too Bad About Sheila Troy, Part I" (April 16, 1959)

Credits: *Network*: NBC; *Running Time*: 30 minutes.

Cast: Chester Morris, Hurd Hatfield, Bill Hayes, Florence Henderson, Carol Lawrence, Roddy McDowall, Brad Morrow.

Oldsmobile Music Theatre: "Too Bad About Sheila Troy, Part II" (April 23, 1959)

Credits: *Network*: NBC; *Running Time*: 30 minutes.

Cast: Chester Morris, Hurd Hatfield, Bill Hayes, Florence Henderson, Carol Lawrence, Roddy McDowall, Brad Morrow.

The United State Steel Hour: "Whisper of Evil" (June 3, 1959)

Credits: *Production Company*: Theatre Guild; *Network*: CBS; *Running Time*: 60 minutes.

Cast: Chester Morris (Henry Vining), John Beal, Barbara Dana, Nina Foch, Tom Gorman, Jada Rowland, Ruth White.

To Tell the Truth (September 15, 1959)

Credits: *Director*: Paul Alter; *Executive Producer*: Gil Fates; *Associate Producer*: Willie Stein; *Production Company*: Mark Goodson-Bill Todman Productions; *Network*: CBS; *Running Time*: 30 minutes.

Cast: Chester Morris (Himself), Bud Collyer, Bern Bennett, Polly Bergen, Kitty Carlisle, Peter Donald.

Play of the Week: "Morning's at Seven" (April 25, 1960)

Credits: *Director*: Jack Ragotzy; *Writer*: Paul Osborn; *Production Company*: Talent Associates; *Network*: National Educational Television.

Cast: Chester Morris (Swanson), Beulah Bondi, Russell Collins, Frank Conroy, Dorothy Gish, Ann Harding, Eileen Heckart, Hiram Sherman, Ruth White.

Diagnosis: Unknown: "The Case of the Radiant Wine" (July 5, 1960)

Credits: *Director*: Fielder Cook; *Producer*: Leo Davis; *Executive Producer*: Bob Banner; *Associate Producer*: Robert Foshko; *Writer*: Joel Carpenter [Arnold Manoff]; *Based on the Novel* by Lawrence

G. Blochman; *Musical Director*: Irwin Kostal; *Set Designer*: John Ward; *Production Companies*: Bob Banner Associates, Inc., Red Wing Productions, Inc.; *Network*: CBS; *Running Time*: 60 minutes.

Cast: Chester Morris (Captain Max Ritter), Millette Alexander, Patricia Barry, Carl Bellini, Tom Bosley, William Bramley, Larry Hagman, Martin Huston, Murray Matheson, Garry Moore, Phyllis Newman, Patrick O'Neal.

To Tell the Truth (July 21, 1960)

Credits: *Director*: Paul Alter; *Producers*: Mark Goodson, Bill Todman; *Executive Producer*: Gil Fates; *Associate Producer*: Willie Stein; *Production Company*: Mark Goodson-Bill Todman Productions; *Network*: CBS; *Running Time*: 30 minutes.

Cast: Chester Morris (Himself), Jim Fleming, Jobie Arnold, Polly Bergen, Kitty Carlisle, Roger Forster, Brian Hyland, Tom Poston, Clifford Teach.

Diagnosis: Unknown: "Main Course: Murder" (August 2, 1960)

Credits: *Writer*: Theodore Apstein; *Based on Characters* created by Lawrence G. Blochman; *Production Companies*: Bob Banner Associates, Inc., Red Wing Productions, Inc.; *Network*: CBS; *Running Time*: 60 minutes.

Cast: Chester Morris (Captain Max Ritter), Cal Bellini, Jack Carter, Martin Huston, James Monks, Phyllis Newman, Patrick O'Neal, Paul Stewart, Haila Stoddard, Frederic Tozere.

Diagnosis: Unknown: "A Sudden Stillness" (August 9, 1960)

Credits: *Writer*: Alvin Boretz; *Based on Characters* created by Lawrence G. Blochman; *Production Companies*: Bob Banner Associates, Inc., Red Wing Productions, Inc.; *Network*: CBS; *Running Time*: 60 minutes.

Cast: Chester Morris (Captain Max Ritter), Barbara Baxley, Cal Bellini, Don Francks, Martin Huston, Phyllis Newman, Patrick O'Neal, William Raine, Zachary Scott, Gretchen Wyler, Louis Zorich.

Diagnosis: Unknown: "Final Performance" (August 16, 1960)

Credits: *Writer*: Elliot Norman; *Based on Characters* created by Lawrence G. Blochman; *Production Companies*: Bob Banner Associates, Inc., Red Wing Productions, Inc.; *Network*: CBS; *Running Time*: 60 minutes.

Cast: Chester Morris (Captain Max Ritter), Philip Abbott, Cal Bellini, Staats Cotsworth, Bobby Howes, Martin Huston, Phyllis Newman, Patrick O'Neal, Beatrice Straight, Diana Van der Vlis.

Diagnosis: Unknown: "The Case of the Elder" (August 23, 1960)

Credits: *Writer*: Ernest Kinoy; *Based on Characters* created by Lawrence G. Blochman; *Production Companies*: Bob Banner Associates, Inc., Red Wing Productions, Inc.; *Network*: CBS; *Running Time*: 60 minutes.

Cast: Chester Morris (Captain Max Ritter), Victor Beakel, Cal Bellini, Jim Boles, Joan Hotchkis, Martin Huston, Victor Kilian, Judith Lowry, Phyllis Newman, Patrick O'Neal, Addison Powell.

Diagnosis: Unknown: "The Curse of the Gypsy" (August 30, 1960)

Credits: *Writer*: Elliot Norman; *Based on the Story* by Bill S. Ballinger and *Characters* created by Lawrence G. Blochman; *Production Companies*: Bob Banner Associates, Inc., Red Wing Productions, Inc.; *Network*: CBS; *Running Time*: 60 minutes.

Cast: Chester Morris (Captain Max Ritter), Cal Bellini, Martin Huston, Luba Malina, Susan Melvyn, Phyllis Newman, Patrick O'Neal, Gene Patterson, Michael Tolan, Paul Tripp, Jessica Walter.

Diagnosis: Unknown: "Gina, Gina" (September 6, 1960)

Credits: *Based on Characters* created by Lawrence G. Blochman; *Production Companies*: Bob Banner Associates, Inc., Red Wing Productions, Inc.; *Network*: CBS; *Running Time*: 60 minutes.

Cast: Chester Morris (Captain Max Ritter), Cal Bellini, Harold Gary, Joan Hackett, Martin Huston, Johnny Janis, Harry Kadison, Phyllis Newman, Tim O'Connor, Patrick O'Neal, John Rayner, Telly Savalas.

Diagnosis: Unknown: "The Parasite" (September 13, 1960)

Credits: *Writer*: Steve Gethers; *Based on Characters* created by Lawrence G. Blochman; *Production Companies*: Bob Banner Associates, Inc., Red Wing Productions, Inc.; *Network*: CBS; *Running Time*: 60 minutes.

Cast: Chester Morris (Captain Max Ritter), Jeanne Bal, Cal Bellini, Martin Huston, Biff McGuire, Phyllis Newman, Patrick O'Neal, Torin Thatcher, Ruth White.

Diagnosis: Unknown: "The Red Death" (September 20, 1960)

Credits: *Writer*: Elliot Norman; *Based on Characters* created by Lawrence G. Blochman; *Production Companies*: Bob Banner Associates, Inc., Red Wing Productions, Inc.; *Network*: CBS; *Running Time*: 60 minutes.

Cast: Chester Morris (Captain Max Ritter), Cal Bellini, Robert Carroll, Harry Davis, Olive Deering, Martin Huston, Harry Millard, Phyllis Newman, Cynthia O'Neal, Patrick O'Neal.

Rawhide: "Incident on the Road to Yesterday" (November 18, 1960)

Credits: *Director*: R.G. Springsteen; *Producers*: Endre Bohem, Ernest J. Nims, Charles Marquis Warren; *Writers*: Jan Winters, Winston Miller; *Cinematographer*: John M. Nickolaus, Jr.; *Editor*: George A. Gittens; *Musical Theme*: Dmitri Tiomkin; *Art Director*: John B. Goodman; *Production Company and Network*: CBS; *Running Time*: 52 minutes.

Cast: Chester Morris (Hugh Clements), Eric Fleming, Clint Eastwood, Sheb Wooley, Paul Brinegar, James Murdock, Steve Raines, Rocky Shahan, Frankie Laine, Robert Gist, Nan Grey, King Calder, Stephen Joyce, Shirley O'Hara, Charles Tannen, John Erwin, John Cole, George Hickman.

The Jack Paar Tonight Show (December 29, 1960)

Credits: *Production Company and Network*: NBC; *Running Time*: 105 minutes.

Cast: Chester Morris (Himself), Desi Arnaz, Jr., Lucie Arnaz, Lucille Ball, Hugh Downs, Jose Melis, Kay Thompson.

The Jack Paar Tonight Show (February 2, 1961)

Credits: *Production Company and Network*: NBC; *Running Time*: 105 minutes.

Cast: Chester Morris (Himself), Kay Ballard, Joey Carter, Oleg Cassini, Hugh Downs, Bob Elliott, Ray Goulding, Jose Melis, Jack Paar.

A String of Beads (February 7, 1961)

Credits: *Director*: Fielder Cook; *Producer*: Leonard Blair; *Writer*: Steve Gethers; *Based on the Story* by W. Somerset Maugham; *Musical Score*: Wladimir Selinsky; *Network*: NBC; *Running Time*: 60 minutes.

Cast: Chester Morris (Walter Harmon), Jane Fonda, George Grizzard, Louisa Horton, Janet Blair, Dino De Luca, Glenda Farrell, Roland Winters.

Naked City: "Make-Believe Man" (May 17, 1961)

Credits: *Director*: Elliot Silverstein; *Producer*: Herbert B. Leonard; *Writer*: Sy Salkowitz; *Based on the Story* by Sy Salkowitz and Jerry Devine; *Cinematographer*: Jack Priestley; *Editors*: Aaron Nibley, Charles L. Freeman; *Musical Score*: Billy May; *Art Director*: Robert Gundlach; *Production Companies*: Screen Gems, Shelle Productions; *Network*: ABC; *Running Time*: 60 minutes.

Cast: Chester Morris (Frank Manfred), Paul Burke, Horace McMahon, Harry Bellaver, Nehemiah Persoff, Eduardo Ciannelli, Jay Novello, Leonardo Cimino, Victor Junquera, Sam Gray, Epy Baca, Remo Pisani, William Beach, Lester Mack, David Greer.

Checkmate: "Portrait of a Man Running" (October 4, 1961)

Credits: *Director*: Elliot Silverstein; *Producers*: Richard Berg, Jon Kubichan; *Writers*: Eric Ambler, Richard Fielder; *Cinematographer*: Dale Deverman; *Editor*: Richard Belding; *Musical Score*: Morton Stevens; *Art Director*: John J. Lloyd; *Production Company*: Jamco Productions; *Network*: CBS; *Running Time*: 60 minutes.

Cast: Chester Morris (Albert Dewitt), Anthony George, Doug McClure, Sebastian Cabot, Ralph Bellamy, Patricia Huston, Wendell Holmes, Lillian Culver, Frederick DeWilde, Robert Victor, Wright King, Oliver McGowan.

Ben Casey: "An Expensive Glass of Water" (October 30, 1961)

Credits: *Director*: Robert Ellis Miller; *Producers*: James E. Moser, Matthew Rapf; *Writer*: James E. Moser, Gilbert Ralston; *Cinematographer*: Ted Voightlander; *Editor*: Bruce Schoengarth; *Musical Score*: Audrey Granville, David Raksin; *Art Director*: Rolland M. Brooks; *Production Company*: Bing Crosby Productions; *Network*: ABC; *Running Time*: 60 minutes.

Cast: Chester Morris (Walter Tyson), Vince Edwards, Sam Jaffe, Harry Landers, Bettye Ackerman, Jeanne Bates, Neva Patterson, Shirley

Ballard, John Zaremba, George N. Neise, Herb Armstrong, Kenneth Becker, Thom Carney.

***The Defenders*: "The Empty Chute"** (February 17, 1962)

Credits: *Director*: Jack Smight; *Producers*: Herbert Brodkin, Bob Markell; *Writers*: Max Ehrlich, Reginald Rose; *Cinematographer*: Morris Hartzbrand; *Editors*: Sidney Katz, Arline Garson; *Art Director*: Willard Levitas; *Production Companies*: Plautus Productions, Defender Productions; *Network*: CBS; *Running Time*: 60 minutes.

Cast: Chester Morris (Captain Peters), E.G. Marshall, Robert Reed, Michael Strong, Tim O'Connor, Neva Patterson, Polly Rowles, Sidney Armus, Jerry Stiller, Charles White, Dirk Kooiman, Richard Mulligan, Allen Nourse, Linda Canby, Douglas Herrick, Willis Pinkett, Griff Evans, Douglas Reid.

Candid Camera (November 11, 1962)

Credits: *Writer*: Allen Funt; *Production Companies*: Bob Banner Associates, Allen Funt Productions; *Network*: CBS; *Running Time*: 30 minutes.

Cast: Chester Morris (Himself), Allen Funt, Durward Kirby, Sid Ramin, Marilyn Van Derbur.

Candid Camera (November 18, 1962)

Credits: *Production Companies*: Bob Banner Associates, Allen Funt Productions; *Network*: CBS; *Running Time*: 30 minutes.

Cast: Chester Morris (Himself), Allen Funt, Durward Kirby, Sid Ramin, Marilyn Van Derbur.

***Alcoa Premiere*: "The Contenders"** (December 6, 1962)

Credits: *Director*: David Lowell Rich; *Writer*: James Lee; *Musical Theme*: John Williams; *Production Company*: Avasta Productions; *Network*: ABC; *Running Time*: 60 minutes.

Cast: Chester Morris (Andrew Hines), Fred Astaire, Edward Asner, Robert Christopher, David Frankham, Emile Genest, Signe Hasso, James Patterson, Suzanne Pleshette, Robert Roten, Elen Willard.

***The Eleventh Hour*: "Along About Late in the Afternoon"** (December 26, 1962)

Credits: *Director*: Paul Nickell; *Musical Score*: C. King Palmer; *Art Directors*: George W. Davis, Merrill Pye; *Production Companies*: Arena Productions, MGM Television; *Network*: NBC; *Running Time*: 60 minutes.

Cast: Chester Morris (Frankie Morrison), Wendell Corey, Jack Ging, Franchot Tone, Peter Adams, Merritt Bohn, Scott Elliott, George Takei, Vincent Chase, Jon Lormer, Dean Harens, Charles Seel, Nan Leslie, Darrell Howe, Irene Martin, Edith Atwater.

***Alcoa Premiere*: "The Glass Palace"** (January 17, 1963)

Credits: *Director*: Lawrence Dobkin; *Producer*: Richard Berg; *Writer*: Gilbert Ralston; *Musical Theme*: John Williams; *Production Company*: Avasta Productions; *Network*: ABC; *Running Time*: 60 minutes.

Cast: Chester Morris (Charles Richardson), Fred Astaire, Joanna Barnes, Wallace Ford, Anne Francis, Don Hanmer, Ricardo Montalban, Ed Nelson, Paul Newlan.

To Tell the Truth (February 25, 1963)

Credits: *Production Company*: Mark Goodson-Bill Todman Productions; *Network*: CBS; *Running Time*: 30 minutes.

Cast: Chester Morris (Himself), Jack Clark, Joan Fontaine, Sam Levenson, Phyllis Newman.

The Match Game (April 8, 1963)

Credits: *Director*: Mike Gargiulo; *Executive Producers*: Mark Goodson, Bill Todman, Robert Noah; *Production Company*: Mark Goodson-Bill Todman Productions; *Network*: NBC; *Running Time*: 30 minutes.

Cast: Chester Morris (Himself/Team Captain), Gene Rayburn, Carol Lawrence, Johnny Olson.

The Match Game (April 9, 1963)

Credits: *Director*: Mike Gargiulo; *Executive Producers*: Mark Goodson, Bill Todman, Robert Noah; *Production Company*: Mark Goodson-Bill Todman Productions; *Network*: NBC; *Running Time*: 30 minutes.

Cast: Chester Morris (Himself/Team Captain), Gene Rayburn, Carol Lawrence, Johnny Olson.

The Match Game (April 10, 1963)

Credits: *Director*: Mike Gargiulo; *Executive Producers*: Mark Goodson, Bill Todman, Robert Noah; *Production Company*: Mark Goodson-Bill Todman Productions; *Network*: NBC; *Running Time*: 30 minutes.

Cast: Chester Morris (Himself/Team Captain), Gene Rayburn, Carol Lawrence, Johnny Olson.

The Match Game (April 11, 1963)

Credits: *Director*: Mike Gargiulo; *Executive Producers*: Mark Goodson, Bill Todman, Robert Noah; *Production Company*: Mark Goodson-Bill Todman Productions; *Network*: NBC; *Running Time*: 30 minutes.

Cast: Chester Morris (Himself/Team Captain), Gene Rayburn, Carol Lawrence, Johnny Olson.

The Match Game (April 12, 1963)

Credits: *Director*: Mike Gargiulo; *Executive Producers*: Mark Goodson, Bill Todman, Robert Noah; *Production Company*: Mark Goodson-Bill Todman Productions; *Network*: NBC; *Running Time*: 30 minutes.

Cast: Chester Morris (Himself/Team Captain), Gene Rayburn, Carol Lawrence, Johnny Olson.

Candid Camera (April 21, 1963)

Credits: *Directors*: Jules De Benedetto, Lou Tyrrell; *Producers*: Bob Banner, Jules De Benedetto, Allen Funt, Bob Shanks; *Writer*: Allen Funt; *Production Companies*: Bob Banner Associates, Allen Funt Productions; *Network*: CBS; *Running Time*: 30 minutes.

Cast: Chester Morris (Himself), Allen Funt, Durward Kirby, Jack Paar, Sid Ramin.

Candid Camera (April 28, 1963)

Credits: *Directors*: Jules De Benedetto, Lou Tyrrell; *Producers*: Bob Banner, Jules De Benedetto, Allen Funt, Bob Shanks; *Writer*: Allen Funt; *Production Companies*: Bob Banner Associates, Allen Funt Productions; *Network*: CBS; *Running Time*: 30 minutes.

Cast: Chester Morris (Himself), Allen Funt, Durward Kirby, Jack Paar, Sid Ramin.

Route 66: "Soda Pop and Paper Flags" (May 31, 1963)

Credits: *Director*: Fred Jackman, Jr.; *Producers*: Leo Davis, Leonard Katzman, Herbert B. Leonard; *Writer*: John McGreevey; *Cinematographer*: Jack A. Marta; *Editors*: Aaron Nibley, Jack Gleason, Harry Coswick; *Musical Score*: Nelson Riddle; *Art Director*: John T. McCormack; *Production Companies*: Lancer-Edling Production, Screen Gems; *Network*: CBS; *Running Time*: 50 minutes.

Cast: Chester Morris (Emmett McNeill), Martin Milner, Glenn Corbett, Frank Overton, Clifton James, Tom Bosley, Joseph Campanella, Marco St. John, Alan Alda, Tommy Norden, John Bartley Messenger, Bruce Glover.

Candid Camera (June 9, 1963)

Credits: *Directors*: Jules De Benedetto, Lou Tyrrell; *Producers*: Bob Banner, Jules De Benedetto, Allen Funt, Bob Shanks; *Writer*: Allen Funt; *Production Companies*: Bob Banner Associates, Allen Funt Productions; *Network*: CBS; *Running Time*: 30 minutes.

Cast: Chester Morris (Himself), Allen Funt, Durward Kirby, Carmel Quinn, Sid Ramin.

Candid Camera (June 16, 1963)

Credits: *Directors*: Jules De Benedetto, Lou Tyrrell; *Producers*: Bob Banner, Jules De Benedetto, Allen Funt, Bob Shanks; *Writer*: Allen Funt; *Production Companies*: Bob Banner Associates, Allen Funt Productions; *Network*: CBS; *Running Time*: 30 minutes.

Cast: Chester Morris (Himself), Allen Funt, Durward Kirby, Carmel Quinn, Sid Ramin.

The Match Game (July 29, 1963)

Credits: *Director*: Mike Gargiulo; *Executive Producers*: Mark Goodson, Bill Todman, Robert Noah; *Production Company*: Mark Goodson-Bill Todman Productions; *Network*: NBC; *Running Time*: 30 minutes.

Cast: Chester Morris (Himself/Team Captain), Gene Rayburn, Gisele MacKenzie, Johnny Olson.

The Match Game (July 30, 1963)

Credits: *Director*: Mike Gargiulo; *Executive Producers*: Mark Goodson, Bill Todman, Robert Noah; *Production Company*: Mark Goodson-Bill Todman Productions; *Network*: NBC; *Running Time*: 30 minutes.

Cast: Chester Morris (Himself/Team Captain), Gene Rayburn, Gisele MacKenzie, Johnny Olson.

The Match Game (July 31, 1963)

Credits: *Director*: Mike Gargiulo; *Executive Producers*: Mark Goodson, Bill Todman, Robert Noah; *Production Company*: Mark Goodson-Bill Todman Productions; *Network*: NBC; *Running Time*: 30 minutes.

Cast: Chester Morris (Himself/Team Captain), Gene Rayburn, Gisele MacKenzie, Johnny Olson.

The Match Game (August 1, 1963)

Credits: *Director*: Mike Gargiulo; *Executive Producers*: Mark Goodson, Bill Todman, Robert Noah; *Production Company*: Mark Goodson-Bill Todman Productions; *Network*: NBC; *Running Time*: 30 minutes.

Cast: Chester Morris (Himself/Team Captain), Gene Rayburn, Gisele MacKenzie, Johnny Olson.

The Match Game (August 2, 1963)

Credits: *Director*: Mike Gargiulo; *Executive Producers*: Mark Goodson, Bill Todman, Robert Noah; *Production Company*: Mark Goodson-Bill Todman Productions; *Network*: NBC; *Running Time*: 30 minutes.

Cast: Chester Morris (Himself/Team Captain), Gene Rayburn, Gisele MacKenzie, Johnny Olson.

Missing Links [pilot] (August 21, 1963)

Producers: Mark Goodson, Bill Todman; *Production Company*: Mark Goodson-Bill Todman Productions; *Network*: NBC; *Running Time*: 30 minutes.

Cast: Chester Morris (Himself/Panelist), Milt Kamen, Ed McMahon, Phyllis Newman, Johnny Olson.

***The Defenders*: "The Bagman"** (October 19, 1963)

Credits: *Director*: Robert Butler; *Writers*: Roger H. Lewis, Reginald Rose; *Musical Score*: Leonard Rosenman; *Production Companies*: Plautus Productions, Defender Productions; *Network*: CBS; *Running Time*: 60 minutes.

Cast: Chester Morris (Judge Philip Benning), E.G. Marshall, Robert Reed, Howard Da Silva, John Boruff, David Hooks, Walter Klavun, Joanna Merlin, Andreas Voutsinas.

The Match Game (December 9, 1963)

Credits: *Director*: Ira Skutch; *Executive Producers*: Mark Goodson, Bill Todman, Robert Noah; *Production Company*: Mark Goodson-Bill Todman Productions; *Network*: NBC; *Running Time*: 30 minutes.

Cast: Chester Morris (Himself/Team Captain), Gene Rayburn, Kitty Carlisle, Johnny Olson.

The Match Game (December 10, 1963)

Credits: *Director*: Ira Skutch; *Executive Producers*: Mark Goodson, Bill Todman, Robert Noah; *Production Company*: Mark Goodson-Bill Todman Productions; *Network*: NBC; *Running Time*: 30 minutes.

Cast: Chester Morris (Himself/Team Captain), Gene Rayburn, Kitty Carlisle, Johnny Olson.

The Match Game (December 11, 1963)

Credits: *Director*: Ira Skutch; *Executive Producers*: Mark Goodson, Bill Todman, Robert Noah; *Production Company*: Mark Goodson-Bill Todman Productions; *Network*: NBC; *Running Time*: 30 minutes.

Cast: Chester Morris (Himself/Team Captain), Gene Rayburn, Kitty Carlisle, Johnny Olson.

The Match Game (December 12, 1963)

Credits: *Director*: Ira Skutch; *Executive Producers*: Mark Goodson, Bill Todman, Robert Noah; *Production Company*: Mark Goodson-Bill Todman Productions; *Network*: NBC; *Running Time*: 30 minutes.

Cast: Chester Morris (Himself/Team Captain), Gene Rayburn, Kitty Carlisle, Johnny Olson.

The Match Game (December 13, 1963)

Credits: *Director*: Ira Skutch; *Executive Producers*: Mark Goodson, Bill Todman, Robert Noah; *Production Company*: Mark Goodson-Bill Todman Productions; *Network*: NBC; *Running Time*: 30 minutes.

Cast: Chester Morris (Himself/Team Captain), Gene Rayburn, Kitty Carlisle, Johnny Olson.

***Route 66*: "Child of a Night"** (January 3, 1964)

Credits: *Director*: Allen H. Miner; *Producer*: Leo Davis; *Executive Producer*: Herbert B. Leonard; *Writer*: Stirling Silliphant; *Cinematographer*: Jack Marta; *Editors*: Aaron Nibley, Jack Gleason; *Musical Score*: Nelson Riddle; *Art Director*: John T. McCormack; *Production Companies*: Lancer-Edling Productions, Screen Gems; *Network*: CBS; *Running Time*: 60 minutes.

Cast: Chester Morris (Mr. Hull), Martin Milner, Glenn Corbett, Sylvia Sidney, Diana Van der Vlis, Herschel Bernardi, Robert Dryden, Percy Rodrigues, Joanna Pettet, Daniel J. Travanti, Joseph Hanrahan, Grace Carney.

***Espionage*: "Castles in Spain"** (UK: February 19, 1964)

Credits: *Director*: Anton Leader; *Producers*: Herbert Hirschman, George Justin; *Writer*: Raymond Bowers; *Based on the Story* by Norman Borisoff; *Cinematographer*: Ken Hodges; *Editor*:

Lee Doig; *Musical Score*: Benjamin Frankel, Malcolm Arnold (theme); *Production Companies*: Plautus Production, Associated Television; *Network*: NBC; *Running Time*: 60 minutes.

Cast: Chester Morris (Harry Kemp), Roland Culver, Neil McCallum, Anne Lawson, Alex Scott, David Spencer, Carlos Douglas, Anne Padwick, Hyma Beckley, Arthur Goodman, George Holdcroft, Jack Mandeville, Arnold Schulkes.

East Side/West Side: "The Name of the Game" (March 23, 1964)

Credits: *Director*: Charles S. Dubin; *Producer*: David Susskind; *Writer*: Mel Goldberg; *Cinematographer*: Jack Priestley; *Musical Score*: Kenyon Hopkins; *Art Director*: Sy Tomashoff; *Production Companies*: Talent Associates, United Artists Television; *Network*: CBS; *Running Time*: 60 minutes.

Cast: Chester Morris (Walt McGill), George C. Scott, Elizabeth Wilson, Cicely Tyson, Linden Chiles, Henderson Forsythe, John McMartin, Eugene Roche, Daniel J. Travanti, Barbara Mattes, Moses Gunn, Joseph Dolphin, Dan Rubinate, Harry Davis.

Kraft Suspense Theatre: "Knight's Gambit" (March 26, 1964)

Credits: *Director*: Walter Grauman; *Producer*: Robert Blees; *Writer*: Lorenzo Semple, Jr., Halsted Welles, Jonathan Hughes; *Based on the Story* by Robert Blees; *Cinematographer*: Walter Strenge; *Editor*: Carl Pingitore; *Musical Score*: John Williams; *Art Director*: Russell Kimball; *Production Company*: Roncom Films; *Network*: NBC; *Running Time*: 60 minutes.

Cast: Chester Morris (Blaine Davis), Eleanor Parker, Roger Smith, Murray Matheson, H.M. Wynant, Erika Peters, Vito Scotti, Louis Mercier, Ted de Corsia.

Get the Message (April 6, 1964)

Credits: *Executive Producer*: Robert Noah; *Production Company*: Mark Goodson-Bill Todman Productions; *Network*: ABC; *Running Time*: 30 minutes.

Cast: Chester Morris (Himself), Chet Gould, Frank Buxton, Florence Henderson, Robert Q. Lewis, Bess Myerson.

Suspense: "The Hunter" (May 6, 1964)

Credits: *Production Company*: Revue Studios; *Network*: CBS; *Running Time*: 30 minutes.

Cast: Chester Morris, Gary Merrill.

Get the Message (May 11, 1964)

Credits: *Executive Producer*: Robert Noah; *Production Company*: Mark Goodson-Bill Todman Productions; *Network*: ABC; *Running Time*: 30 minutes.

Cast: Chester Morris (Himself), Chet Gould, Frank Buxton, Dick Clark, Selma Diamond.

Dr. Kildare: "Dolly's Dilemma" (May 21, 1964)

Credits: *Director*: John Newland; *Producers*: Norman Felton, David Victor; *Writer*: Ken Kolb; *Editor*: John D. Dunning; *Musical Score*: Jerry Goldsmith (theme), Harry V. Lojewski; *Art Directors*: George W. Davis, Charles K. Hagedon; *Production Companies*: Arena Productions, MGM Television; *Network*: NBC; *Running Time*: 60 minutes.

Cast: Chester Morris (Tom Monahan), Richard Chamberlain, Raymond Massey, Joan Blondell, Alan Hewitt, Steve Bell, Jo Helton, Wilton Graff, Lauren Gilbert.

To Tell the Truth (August 24, 1964)

Credits: *Production Company*: Mark Goodson-Bill Todman Productions; *Network*: CBS; *Running Time*: 30 minutes.

Cast: Chester Morris (Himself), Barbara Cook, Sam Levenson, Phyllis Newman.

Get the Message (August 31, 1964)

Credits: *Executive Producer*: Robert Noah; *Production Company*: Mark Goodson-Bill Todman Productions; *Network*: ABC; *Running Time*: 30 minutes.

Cast: Chester Morris (Himself), Chet Gould, Frank Buxton, Carol Lawrence, Stephen Sondheim, Betty White.

The Price is Right (October 5, 1964)

Credits: *Production Company*: Mark Goodson-Bill Todman Productions; *Network*: NBC; *Running Time*: 30 minutes.

Cast: Chester Morris (Himself), Bill Cullen.

Mr. Broadway: "Don't Mention My Name in Sheboygan" (November 7, 1964)

Credits: *Director*: Alex March; *Producers*: Larry Arrick, Daniel Melnick, David Susskind; *Writers*: Garson Kanin, Robert Russell; *Negative Cutter*: Irving Rathner; *Production Company*: Talent Associates; *Network*: CBS; *Running Time*: 60 minutes.

Cast: Chester Morris (Orin Kelsey), Craig Stevens, Lani Miyazaki, Horace McMahon, Joan Bennett, Sandy Dennis, Diana Muldaur, Robert Webber.

Bob Hope Presents the Chrysler Theatre: "The Fliers" (February 5, 1965)

Credits: *Director*: Sydney Pollack; *Producer*: Richard Berg; *Writer*: David Rayfiel; *Musical Score*: Cyril J. Mockridge; *Production Companies*: Hovue Enterprises, Morpics; *Network*: NBC; *Running Time*: 60 minutes.

Cast: Chester Morris (Major Whitman), John Cassavetes, Carol Lynley, Roxane Berard, Lilyan Chauvin, Dabney Coleman, Albert D'Arno, Maurice McEndree, Robert Pine, Alfred Ryder, Tom Simcox, Anatol Winogradoff.

The Match Game (March 8, 1965)

Credits: *Director*: Ira Skutch; *Executive Producers*: Mark Goodson, Bill Todman, Robert Noah; *Production Company*: Mark Goodson-Bill Todman Productions; *Network*: NBC; *Running Time*: 30 minutes.

Cast: Chester Morris (Himself/Team Captain), Gene Rayburn, Peggy Cass, Johnny Olson.

The Match Game (March 9, 1965)

Credits: *Director*: Ira Skutch; *Executive Producers*: Mark Goodson, Bill Todman, Robert Noah; *Production Company*: Mark Goodson-Bill Todman Productions; *Network*: NBC; *Running Time*: 30 minutes.

Cast: Chester Morris (Himself/Team Captain), Gene Rayburn, Peggy Cass, Johnny Olson.

The Match Game (March 10, 1965)

Credits: *Director*: Ira Skutch; *Executive Producers*: Mark Goodson, Bill Todman, Robert Noah; *Production Company*: Mark Goodson-Bill Todman Productions; *Network*: NBC; *Running Time*: 30 minutes.

Cast: Chester Morris (Himself/Team Captain), Gene Rayburn, Peggy Cass, Johnny Olson.

The Match Game (March 11, 1965)

Credits: *Director*: Ira Skutch; *Executive Producers*: Mark Goodson, Bill Todman, Robert Noah; *Production Company*: Mark Goodson-Bill Todman Productions; *Network*: NBC; *Running Time*: 30 minutes.

Cast: Chester Morris (Himself/Team Captain), Gene Rayburn, Peggy Cass, Johnny Olson.

The Match Game (March 12, 1965)

Credits: *Director*: Ira Skutch; *Executive Producers*: Mark Goodson, Bill Todman, Robert Noah; *Production Company*: Mark Goodson-Bill Todman Productions; *Network*: NBC; *Running Time*: 30 minutes.

Cast: Chester Morris (Himself/Team Captain), Gene Rayburn, Peggy Cass, Johnny Olson.

The Defenders: "A Matter of Law and Disorder" (April 8, 1965)

Credits: *Director*: Robert Butler; *Writers*: Roger H. Lewis, Reginald Rose; *Musical Score*: Leonard Rosenman; *Production Companies*: Plautus Productions, Defender Productions; *Network*: CBS; *Running Time*: 60 minutes.

Cast: Chester Morris (District Attorney Brent), E.G. Marshall, Robert Reed, Pat Hingle, Dustin Hoffman, Susan Anspach, John Barangrey, Mary Fickett, Walter Greaza, Jack Ragotzy, Michael Walker.

Call My Bluff (April 12, 1965)

Credits: *Producer*: Jack Farren; *Production Company*: Mark Goodson-Bill Todman Productions; *Network*: NBC; *Running Time*: 30 minutes.

Cast: Chester Morris (Himself), Joan Fontaine, Bill Leyden, Johnny Olson.

The Match Game (October 18, 1965)

Credits: *Director*: Ira Skutch; *Executive Producers*: Mark Goodson, Bill Todman, Robert Noah; *Production Company*: Mark Goodson-Bill Todman Productions; *Network*: NBC; *Running Time*: 30 minutes.

Cast: Chester Morris (Himself/Team Captain), Gene Rayburn, Gloria Swanson, Johnny Olson.

The Match Game (October 19, 1965)

Credits: *Director*: Ira Skutch; *Executive Producers*: Mark Goodson, Bill Todman, Robert Noah; *Production Company*: Mark Goodson-Bill Todman Productions; *Network*: NBC; *Running Time*: 30 minutes.

Cast: Chester Morris (Himself/Team Captain), Gene Rayburn, Gloria Swanson, Johnny Olson.

The Match Game (October 20, 1965)

Credits: *Director*: Ira Skutch; *Executive Producers*: Mark Goodson, Bill Todman, Robert Noah; *Production Company*: Mark Goodson-Bill Todman Productions; *Network*: NBC; *Running Time*: 30 minutes.

Cast: Chester Morris (Himself/Team Captain), Gene Rayburn, Gloria Swanson, Johnny Olson.

The Match Game (October 21, 1965)

Credits: *Director*: Ira Skutch; *Executive Producers*: Mark Goodson, Bill Todman, Robert Noah; *Production Company*: Mark Goodson-Bill Todman Productions; *Network*: NBC; *Running Time*: 30 minutes.

Cast: Chester Morris (Himself/Team Captain), Gene Rayburn, Gloria Swanson, Johnny Olson.

The Match Game (October 22, 1965)

Credits: *Director*: Ira Skutch; *Executive Producers*: Mark Goodson, Bill Todman, Robert Noah; *Production Company*: Mark Goodson-Bill Todman Productions; *Network*: NBC; *Running Time*: 30 minutes.

Cast: Chester Morris (Himself/Team Captain), Gene Rayburn, Gloria Swanson, Johnny Olson.

The Tonight Show Starring Johnny Carson (January 4, 1966)

Credits: *Writers*: Bob Carmen, Walter Kempley, David Lloyd, Ed Weinberger; *Production Company* and *Network*: NBC; *Running Time*: 105 minutes.

Cast: Chester Morris (Himself), Sammy Davis, Jr., Johnny Hartman, Skitch Henderson, Ed McMahon.

The Soupy Sales Hour (March 1966)

Credits: *Director*: Dwight Hemion; *Producers*: Stan Greeson, James L. Reina, Herbert Sargent; *Writers*: Gary Belkin, Bob Klaine, Marc Richards, Steven Vinaver; *Musical Director*: Peter Matz; *Art Director*: Eugene McAvoy; *Production Company*: Hunton Productions; *Network*: NBC; *Running Time*: 60 minutes.

Cast: Chester Morris (Himself), Ernest Borgnine, Joan Fontaine, Judy Garland, Steve Gaynor, Burt Leigh, Barney Martin, Bob McFadden, Frank Nastasi, Clifford A. Pellow, Soupy Sales, Jeanne Tanzy Williams, Gene Wood.

The Mike Douglas Show (June 23, 1966)

Credits: *Production Company and Network*: Westinghouse Broadcasting Company (syndicated).

Cast: Chester Morris (Himself), Mike Douglas, Soupy Sales, Dan Keefe, Jane Morgan, Jerry Wallace.

Candid Camera (May 18, 1967)

Credits: *Production Companies*: Bob Banner Associates, Allen Funt Productions; *Network*: CBS; *Running Time*: 30 minutes.

Cast: Chester Morris (Himself).

Coronet Blue: "A Time to Be Born" (May 29, 1967)

Credits: *Director*: Paul Bogart; *Producers*: Herbert Brodkin, Edgar Lansbury, Kenneth Utt; *Writers*: Albert Ruben, Larry Cohen; *Story Editor*: Earl Booth; *Cinematographer*: Andrew Laszlo; *Editor*: Sidney Katz; *Musical Score*: Laurence Rosenthal; *Art Director*: John Robert Lloyd; *Assistant Director*: William C. Gerrity, Jr.; *Costume Designer*: Joseph Fretwell, III; *Production Company*: Plautus Productions; *Network*: CBS; *Running Time*: 60 minutes.

Cast: Chester Morris (Dr. Michael Wilson), Frank Converse, Susan Hampshire, Bernice Massi, Robert Burr, Louise Troy, Jon Cypher, Donald Woods, Joe Silver, Marco St. John, James Noble, Jered Barclay, Jose Duval, Peg Murray, Edward McNally, Robert F. Lyons, Jane Holzer.

Cimarron Strip: "Without Honor" (February 29, 1968)

Credits: *Director*: Robert Butler; *Producers*: Douglas Benton, Christopher Knopf, Philip Leacock; *Writers*: Christopher Knopf, Daniel B. Ullman; *Cinematographer*: Harry Stradling, Jr.; *Editor*: Danny B. Landres; *Musical Score*: Maurice Jarre, Morton Stevens; *Art Director*: Gibson Holley; *Production Company*: Stuart Whitman; *Network*: CBS; *Running Time*: 71 minutes.

Cast: Chester Morris (George Deeker), Stuart Whitman, Percy Herbert, Randy Boone, Jill Townsend, Andrew Duggan, Jon Voight, Paul Mantee, Don Pedro Colley, James Davidson, John Neilson, George Sperdakos, Dallas Mitchell.

Gentle Ben: "Busman's Holiday" (April 27, 1969)

Credits: *Director*: Gerd Oswald; *Producer*: Ralph Helfer; *Executive Producer*: Andy White; *Writer*: Maurice Tombragel; *Cinematographer*: Howard Winner; *Editor*: Erwin Dumbrille; *Musical Score*: Harry Sukman; *Art Director*: Jack Collis; *Production Companies*: Ivan Tors Productions; *Network*: CBS; *Running Time*: 30 minutes.

Cast: Chester Morris (Elsmore), Dennis Weaver, Clint Howard, Beth Brickell, Bruno the Bear, Jack Morley.

Appendix C
Radio Programs

Following is a compiled listing of radio programs (local, regional and national) featuring Chester Morris.

Majestic Theatre of the Air: **"Alibi"** (April 21, 1929)

Director: Roland West; *Performers*: Chester Morris, Eleanor Griffith, Roland West; *Running Time*: 60 minutes; *Network*: CBS.

Catherine the Great [U.S. premiere] (February 14, 1934)

Guests: Chester Morris, Lilyan Tashman, Clark Gable, Edmund Lowe, Walter P. Chrysler, Mr. and Mrs. Marshall Field, Lord and Lady Joseph Duveen, British consul general Gerald Campbell; *Station*: WNEW (New York).

Hollywood Radio Previews (June 1934)

Guests: Chester Morris, Douglass Montgomery, Margaret Sullivan, Walter Woolf King; *Stations*: Syndicated.

Shell Chateau (November 9, 1935)

Writer: Howard Emmet Rogers ("Two Men Met at the Vail"); *Host*: Wallace Beery; *Guests*: Chester Morris, Helen Broderick, Lester Crawford; *Vocalists*: Lorraine Bridges, Peggy Gardner, Harriet Hilliard; The Sailor Boy's Octet, Jack Stanton; *Musicians*: Nick Dan, Victor Young and His Orchestra; *Announcer*: Burton Bennett; *Network*: NBC.

Lessons in Hollywood (December 14, 1936)

Host: Jackie Cooper; *Guest*: Chester Morris; *Station*: WOR (New York).

Calling All Cars: **"The History of Dallas Egan"** (February 1, 1938)

Producer and Writer: William N. Robson; *Host*: James E. Davis; *Guest*: Chester Morris; *Narrator*: Charles Frederick Lindsley; *Dispatcher*: Jesse Rosenquist; *Network*: CBS Pacific.

Chester Morris [sketch] (October 12, 1938)

Writer: Jerry Devine; *Station*: WABC-CBS (New York). *Cast*: Chester Morris.

The Kate Smith Hour (October 13, 1938)

Host: Kate Smith; *Guest*: Chester Morris; *Network*: CBS.

The Silver Theatre: **"The Man from Medicine Bow"** (April 9, 1939)

Director and Writer: Paul Franklin; *Host*: Conrad Nagel; *Guests*: Chester Morris, John Brown, Glenda Farrell, Elliott Lewis; *Composer*: Felix Mills; *Announcer*: John Conte; *Narrator*: True Boardman; *Network*: CBS.

Kraft Music Hall (November 9, 1939)

Host: Bing Crosby; *Orchestra Arranger and Conductor*: John Scott Trotter; *Guests*: Chester Morris ("Mysterious Morris the Mad Magician"), Lou Holtz (linguist); *Network*: NBC; *Running Time*: 60 minutes.

The Texaco Star Theatre (February 7, 1940)

Writer: Willard Mack; *Host*: Ken Murray; *Guests*: Chester Morris, Kenny Baker, Margo, Irene Ryan; *Vocalist*: Frances Langford; *Musicians*: David Broekman and His Orchestra;

Composer/Conductor: Lehman Engel; *Announcers*: Jimmy Wallington, Larry Elliott; *Network*: CBS.

Kraft Music Hall (June 12, 1941)

Guests: Chester Morris (Boston Blackie), Bob Burns, Donald Crisp; *Vocalists*: Connie Boswell, Bing Crosby, The Music Maids, Ethel Waters; *Musicians*: John Scott Trotter and His Orchestra; *Announcer*: Ken Carpenter; *Network*: NBC.

Three Thirds of a Nation (May 6, 1942)

Producer: William Robson; *Writer*: Dorothea Lewis; *Narrator*: Conrad Nagel; *Guests*: Chester Morris, Rosemary DeCamp; *Musicians*: Leith Stevens Orchestra; *Presented by* the War Productions Board; *Network*: WJZ-Blue (New York).

USO All Star Show (May 31, 1942)

Guests: Chester Morris, Fanny Brice, Joe E. Brown, Linda Darnell, Deanna Durbin, Judy Garland, John Garfield, Hugh Herbert, Stan Laurel, Oliver Hardy, Mary Martin, Chico Marx, Harpo Marx, the Ritz Brothers, Mickey Rooney, Rosalind Russell, Red Skelton; *Network*: NBC Red.

Armstrong's Theatre of Today (February 6, 1943)

Producer: Ira Avery; *Guests*: Chester Morris, Donna Keath; *Announcer*: George Bryan; *Network*: CBS.

The Lady Esther Screen Guild Theatre: "Stand by for Action" (March 8, 1943)

Adapter: Bill Henry; *Guests*: Chester Morris (Lieutenant Masterman), Brian Donlevy, Charles Laughton; *Musical Conductor*: Wilbur Hatch; *Announcer*: Truman Bradley; *Network*: CBS.

Showtime: "Aerial Gunner" (May 8–9, 1943)

Guests: Chester Morris, William H. Pine, William Thomas, Marjorie Reynolds, Barbara Britton, Johnnie Johnson, Gil Lamb; *Sponsor*: Interstate Theatres; *Network*: KGBS.

The Lux Radio Theatre: "The Great Man's Lady" (June 28, 1943)

Director: Sanford Barnett; *Adapter*: George Wells; *Writers*: Vina Delmar, Seena Owen, W.L. River; *Host*: Cecil B. DeMille; *Guests*: Chester Morris, Charles Calvert, Leo Cleary, Joseph Cotten, Roland Drew, Leone LeDoux, Norman Field, Faye MacKenzie, Ernest Newton, Katherine Siley; Barbara Stanwyck, Katherine Siley, Ernestine Wade; *Vocalist*: Ruby Dandridge; *Musical Director*: Louis Silvers; *Announcer*: John Milton Kennedy; *Network*: CBS.

Coronet Little Show (September 19, 1943)

Guests: Chester Morris, Stuart Erwin; *Network*: CBS.

The Lux Radio Theatre: "Flight for Freedom" (September 20, 1943)

Director: Sanford Barnett; *Adapter*: George Wells; *Writers*: Oliver H.P. Garrett, S.K. Lauren; *Host*: Cecil B. DeMille; *Guests*: Chester Morris, George Brent, Rosalind Russell, Marek Windheim; *Musical Director*: Louis Silvers; *Announcer*: John Milton Kennedy; *Network*: CBS.

The Lux Radio Theatre: "The Navy Comes Through" (November 29, 1943)

Director: Sanford Barnett; *Adapters*: Earl Baldwin, John Twist; *Writers*: Aeneas MacKenzie, Roy Chanslor; *Host*: Cecil B. DeMille; *Guests*: Chester Morris, Arthur Q. Brian, Ed Emerson, Hal Gerard, Robert Harris, Bob Haynes, Edward Marr, Fred MacKaye, Jack Mather, Paul McVey, Tyler McVey, Pat O'Brien; *Musical Director*: Louis Silvers; *Announcer*: John Milton Kennedy; *Network*: CBS.

The Amos 'n' Andy Show (December 3, 1943)

Performers: Freeman Gosden, Charles Correll; *Guest*: Chester Morris; *Announcer*: Harlow Wilcox; *Network*: NBC.

The Silver Theatre: "Someone Suitable" (March 12, 1944)

Guests: Chester Morris, K.T. Stevens; *Musicians*: Horace Heidt and His Musical Knights; *Network*: CBS.

The Lux Radio Theatre: "The Hard Way" (March 19, 1944)

Director: Fred MacKaye; *Writers*: Daniel Fuchs, Paul Viertel; *Adapter*: Sanford Barnett; *Host*: Cecil B. DeMille; *Guests*: Chester Morris, Anne Baxter, Ellen Campbell, Doris Singleton Haynes, Miriam Hopkins, Edward Marr, Charles Seel,

Franchot Tone, Theodore Von Eltz; *Vocalist*: Marion Martin; *Musical Director*: Louis Silvers; *Announcer*: John Milton Kennedy; *Network*: CBS.

***The Lux Radio Theatre*: "Coney Island"** (April 17, 1944)

Director: Fred MacKaye; *Writer*: George Seaton; *Adapter*: Sanford Barnett; *Host*: Cecil B. DeMille; *Guests*: Chester Morris, Bea Benaderet, Boyd Davis, Norman Field, Alan Ladd, Dorothy Lamour, Edward Marr; *Musical Director*: Louis Silvers; *Announcer*: John Milton Kennedy; *Network*: CBS; *Running Time*: 60 minutes.

The Amos 'n' Andy Show (June 16, 1944)

Performers: Freeman Gosden, Charles Correll, Ken Christy, Elinor Harriot; *Guest*: Chester Morris; *Announcer*: Harlow Wilcox; *Network*: NBC.

***Boston Blackie*: "The Jonathan Diamond"** (June 23, 1944)

Producer: Fred W. Ziv; *Performers*: Chester Morris (Boston Blackie), Richard Lane; *Organist*: Charles Cornell; *Announcer*: Harlow Wilcox; *Network*: NBC.

***Boston Blackie*: "50 Hunter Street"** (June 30, 1944)

Producer: Fred W. Ziv; *Performers*: Chester Morris (Boston Blackie), Richard Lane; *Organist*: Charles Cornell; *Announcer*: Harlow Wilcox; *Network*: NBC.

***Boston Blackie*: "The Canteen Fund Mystery"** (July 7, 1944)

Producer: Fred W. Ziv; *Performers*: Chester Morris (Boston Blackie), Richard Lane; *Organist*: Charles Cornell; *Announcer*: Harlow Wilcox; *Network*: NBC.

***Boston Blackie*: "The Star of the Nile"** (July 14, 1944)

Producer: Fred W. Ziv; *Performers*: Chester Morris (Boston Blackie), Richard Lane; *Organist*: Charles Cornell; *Announcer*: Harlow Wilcox; *Network*: NBC.

***Boston Blackie*: "'Black Market' Blackie"** (July 21, 1944)

Producer: Fred W. Ziv; *Performers*: Chester Morris (Boston Blackie), Richard Lane; *Organist*: Charles Cornell; *Announcer*: Harlow Wilcox; *Network*: NBC.

***Boston Blackie*: "The Caretaker of the Devon Estate"** (July 28, 1944)

Producer: Fred W. Ziv; *Performers*: Chester Morris (Boston Blackie), Richard Lane; *Organist*: Charles Cornell; *Announcer*: Harlow Wilcox; *Network*: NBC.

***Boston Blackie*: "Alice Manleder, Dead or Alive"** (August 4, 1944)

Producer: Fred W. Ziv; *Performers*: Chester Morris (Boston Blackie), Richard Lane; *Organist*: Charles Cornell; *Announcer*: Harlow Wilcox; *Network*: NBC.

***Boston Blackie*: "The Missing String of Pearls"** (August 11, 1944)

Producer: Fred W. Ziv; *Performers*: Chester Morris (Boston Blackie), Richard Lane; *Organist*: Charles Cornell; *Announcer*: Harlow Wilcox; *Network*: NBC.

***Boston Blackie*: "The Uninvited Corpse"** (August 18, 1944)

Producer: Fred W. Ziv; *Performers*: Chester Morris (Boston Blackie), Richard Lane; *Organist*: Charles Cornell; *Network*: NBC.

***Boston Blackie*: "The Counterfeit Gas Coupon Ring"** (August 25, 1944)

Producer: Fred W. Ziv; *Performers*: Chester Morris (Boston Blackie), Richard Lane; *Organist*: Charles Cornell; *Network*: NBC.

Boston Blackie (September 1, 1944)

Producer: Fred W. Ziv; *Performers*: Chester Morris (Boston Blackie), Richard Lane; *Organist*: Charles Cornell; *Network*: NBC.

Boston Blackie (September 8, 1944)

Producer: Fred W. Ziv; *Performers*: Chester Morris (Boston Blackie), Richard Lane; *Organist*: Charles Cornell; *Network*: NBC.

Boston Blackie (September 15, 1944)

Producer: Fred W. Ziv; *Performers*: Chester Morris (Boston Blackie), Richard Lane; *Organist*: Charles Cornell; *Network*: NBC.

***Old Gold Comedy Theatre*: "Boy Meets Girl"** (May 20, 1945)

Director and Host: Harold Lloyd; *Guests*: Chester Morris (Mr. Law), Ann Sothern, Lee Tracy; *Musical Director*: Carol Hoff; *Announcer*: Bob Williams; *Network*: Blue.

The Charlie McCarthy Show (January 13, 1946)

Performer: Edgar Bergen; *Guest*: Chester Morris (Tax Man); Network: NBC.

Luck o' the Irish: "Hair Again for Harrigan" (February 25, 1946)

Director and Producer: Gene Burdett; *Guests*: Chester Morris, Bea Benaderet; *Musical Director*: Vern Buck.

The Charlie McCarthy Show (April 28, 1946)

Performer: Edgar Bergen; *Guest*: Chester Morris (Insurance Adjuster), Anita Gordon, Jack Mather; *Musicians*: Ray Noble and His Orchestra; *Announcer*: Ken Carpenter; *Network*: NBC.

Suspense: "The Strange Death of Gordon Fitzroy" (November 28, 1946)

Director and Producer: William Spier; *Writers*: Bruce Cassidy, Robert L. Richards; *Performers*: Chester Morris, Hans Conreid, Howard Duff, William Johnstone, Cathy Lewis, Wally Maher, Lurene Tuttle; *Composer*: Lucien Moraweck; *Conductor*: Lud Gluskin; *Announcer*: Joseph Kearns; *Network*: CBS.

This is the Story: "Robinson Crusoe, USN" (1946)

Based on the Book by George R. Tweed; *Performer*: Chester Morris (George Tweed); *Network*: Armed Forces Radio Service (AFRS).

The Cavalcade of America: "Man Against the Mountain" (February 17, 1947)

Performer: Chester Morris (Gustaf F. Marsh); *Network*: NBC.

The Charlie McCarthy Show (March 2, 1947)

Performer: Edgar Bergen; *Guests*: Chester Morris (Insurance Adjuster), Anita Gordon, Jack Kruschen; *Vocalist*: Nelson Eddy; *Musicians*: Ray Noble and His Orchestra; *Announcer*: Ken Carpenter; *Network*: NBC.

Family Theatre: "Mr. Bidderoe's Mission" (May 1, 1947)

Director: Mel Williamson; *Writer*: Seeleg Lester; *Host*: Jack Haley; *Performers*: Chester Morris, Betty Arnold, Griff Barnett, Bill Bouchey, Francis X. Bushman, Cecil Kellaway, Jack Mather, Anne Morrison, Earle Ross; *Musical Director*: Meredith Willson; *Announcer*: Tony La Franco; *Network*: Mutual.

Maxwell House Coffee Time: "George Collects Alley Cats" (February 17, 1949)

Performers: George Burns and Gracie Allen, Bea Benaderet, Hans Conreid, Bill Goodwin, Gale Gordon, Pamela Mason, Marvin Miller; *Guests*: Chester Morris, James Mason, Robert Young; *Musicians*: Harry Lubin and His Orchestra; *Announcer*: Tobe Reed; *Network*: NBC.

Duffy's Tavern: "Detective Archie Tracks 'Whistling Sam' Roberts" (May 11, 1949)

Director and Producer: John Morris; *Performers*: Charlie Cantor, Ed Gardner, Eddie Green, Florence Halop, Sheldon Leonard, Alan Reed; *Guest*: Chester Morris; *Musicians*: Matty Malneck and His Orchestra; *Network*: NBC.

Maxwell House Coffee Time: "Gracie the Magician" (June 2, 1949)

Performers: George Burns and Gracie Allen, Bea Benaderet, Bob Bentz, Bill Goodwin; *Guest*: Chester Morris (Himself/Magician); *Musicians*: Harry Lubin and His Orchestra; *Announcer*: Tobe Reed; *Network*: NBC.

Maxwell House Coffee Time: "Emily Vanderlip's Boyfriend, Rudy Vallee" (June 16, 1949)

Writers: Keith Fowler, Paul Henning; *Performers*: George Burns and Gracie Allen, Bea Benaderet, Bill Goodwin, Marylee Robb; *Guests*: Chester Morris, Rudy Vallee; *Musicians*: Harry Lubin and His Orchestra; *Announcer*: Tobe Reed; *Network*: NBC.

Maxwell House Coffee Time: "Robert Young Preparing for England Trip" (June 23, 1949)

Writers: Keith Fowler, Paul Henning; *Performers*: George Burns and Gracie Allen, Bea Benaderet, Hans Conreid, Gale Gordon, Marvin Miller; *Guests*: Chester Morris, Robert Young; *Musicians*: Harry Lubin and His Orchestra; *Announcer*: Tobe Reed; *Network*: NBC.

***The Ammident Show*: "Second Courtship"** (September 28, 1949)

Producer: William Burns; *Writer*: Paul Henning; *Performers*: George Burns and Gracie Allen, Bea Benaderet, Hans Conried, Bill Goodwin, Gale Gordon, Hal March, Marvin Miller; *Guests*: Chester Morris, Robert Young; *Musicians*: Harry Lubin and His Orchestra; *Announcer*: Toby Reed; *Network*: NBC.

Welcome Travelers (November 7, 1949)

Master of Ceremonies: Tommy Bartlett; *Performer*: Bob Cunningham; *Guest*: Chester Morris; *Announcer*: Jim Ameche; *Venue*: College Inn, Hotel Sherman, Chicago; *Network*: NBC.

Stars on Parade (November 3, 1950)

Guests: Chester Morris, Helen Christian; *Announcer*: Joe Ripley; *Stations*: U.S. Army and Army Air Force syndication (sponsored by Army and Army Air Force recruiting).

The Empty Sleeve (August 14, 1951)

Guest: Chester Morris; *Network*: CBS.

Luncheon at Sardi's (September 1954)

Guest: Chester Morris; *Station*: WOR (New York).

The Studs Terkel Program (February 27, 1962)

Host: Studs Terkel; *Guest*: Chester Morris; *Station*: WMFT (Chicago).

The Bing Crosby-Rosemary Clooney Show (September 17, 1962)

Producers: Murdo McKenzie, Bill Morrow; *Performers*: Bing Crosby, Rosemary Clooney; *Commercial Spokesman*: Chester Morris; *Musicians*: The Buddy Cole Trio; *Announcer*: Ken Carpenter; *Network*: CBS.

Appendix D
Stage Performances

Following is a listing of stage performances (Broadway, local and touring productions) featuring Chester Morris.

The Copperhead (1918)

Credits: *Producer*: John D. Williams; *Playwright*: Augustus Thomas; *Based on a Story* by Frederick Landis; *Venue*: Shubert Theatre, Broadway, New York; *Number of Performances*: 120; *Dates*: February 19–June 1918.

Cast: Chester Morris (Sam Carter), Evelyn Archer, Lionel Barrymore, Gladys Burgette, Thomas Carrigan, Raymond Hackett, Harry Hadfield, Ethelbert Hales, William Norton, Albert Phillips, Doris Rankin, Grace Reals, Hayden Stevenson, Eugenie Woodward.

Turn to the Right (1918)

Credits: *Producer*: Winchell Smith; *Playwrights*: Winchell Smith, John E. Hazzard; *Performances*: tour.

Cast: Chester Morris.

Thunder (1919)

Credits: *Producer*: John Golden; *Playwright*: Peg Franklin; *Venue*: Criterion Theatre, Broadway, New York; *Number of Performances*: 33; *Dates*: September 22–October 1919.

Cast: Chester Morris (Sam Disbrow), Charles Althoff, Leila Bennett, Marie Day, Wilson Day, Eva Dennison, Sylvia Field, Mart E. Heisey, Horace James, Benjamin Kauser, Marion Kerby, Charles McDonald, Burr McIntosh, Guy Nichols, Sam Reed, Balance Talbot, John Talbot, George Wright, Jr.

The Mountain Man (1921–1922)

Credits: *Directors*: Clare Kummer, Edward Elsner; *Producer*: Charles L. Wagner; *Playwright*: Clare Kummer; *Venue*: Maxine Elliott's Theatre, Broadway, New York; *Number of Performances*: 163; *Dates*: December 12, 1921–April 1922.

Cast: Chester Morris (Carey), Marion Abbott, Sidney Blackmer, Marion Coakley, E.J. DeVarney, Lawrence Eddinger, George Fawcett, Fred Karr, Marjorie Kummer, Lucia Moore, Catherine Dale Owen, Grace Reals, Leonard Rowe.

The Exciters (1922)

Credits: *Director*: Edgar Selwyn; *Producers*: The Selwyns; *Playwright*: Martin Brown; *Venue*: Times Square Theatre, Broadway, New York; *Number of Performances*: 43; *Dates*: September 22–October 1922.

Cast: Chester Morris (Lexington Dalrymple), Marsh Allen, Tallulah Bankhead, Alan Dinehart, Sidney Dudley, Florence Flinn, Echlin Gayer, Roy Gordon, Jerry Hart, Robert Hyman, Frederick Kerr, Wright Kramer, Thais Lawton, Aline MacMahon, Enid Markey, Albert Marsh, Edwin Walter.

Extra (1923)

Credits: *Director*: Walter Wilson; *Producers*: Jack Alicoate, William Collier, Jr.; *Playwright*: Jack Alicoate; *Venue*: Longacre Theatre, Broadway, New York; *Number of Performances*: 21; *Dates*: January 23–February 1923.

Cast: Chester Morris (Wallace King), Frederick Beane, Howard Benton, Marcia Byron, Gertrude Gustin, Clyde Hunnewell, Charles N. Lawrence, William A. Norton, Edward Poland, Hallett Thompson, Robert Thorne, Howard Truesdell.

So This Is London (1923)

Credits: *Producer*: George M. Cohan; *Playwright*: Arthur Goodrich; *Performances*: tour.

Cast: Chester Morris.

All the Horrors of Home (1923–1925)

Credits: *Playwright*: William Morris; *Performances*: vaudeville tour, including dates at the Palace Theatre, New York; Proctor's Theatre, Mount Vernon, New York; and in Los Angeles.

Cast: Chester Morris, William Morris, Etta Hawkins Morris, Wilhelmina Morris, Adrian Morris.

The Home Towners (1926)

Credits: *Producer and Playwright*: George M. Cohan; *Performances*: Chicago, Illinois.

Cast: Chester Morris (Waly Calhoun).

The Home Towners (1926)

Credits: *Director*: John Meehan; *Producer and Playwright*: George M. Cohan; *Venue*: Hudson Theatre, Broadway, New York; *Number of Performances*: 64; *Dates*: August 23–October 1926.

Cast: Chester Morris (Waly Calhoun), Spencer Bentley, Georgia Caine, Walter Calligan, Florence Earle, William Elliott, Peg Entwistle, Doris Freeman, Ben Johnson, Robert McWade, Walter Plummer, William Walcott.

Yellow (1926–1927)

Credits: *Director*: John Meehan; *Producer and Playwright*: George M. Cohan; *Based on a Story* by Frederick Landis; *Venue*: National Theatre, Broadway, New York; *Number of Performances*: 135; *Dates*: September 21, 1926–January 1927.

Cast: Chester Morris (Val Parker), Harry Bannister, Frank Burbeck, Eva Casanova, H. Paul Doucet, Richard Freeman, Joseph Guthrie, Walter Hale, Hale Hamilton, Paul Hanson, Frank Kingdon, Helen Macks, Martin Malloy, Mary Meehan, Daniel Pennell, Jose Rivas, Selena Royle, Spencer Tracy, Shirley Warde, Jane Wheatley, Marjorie Wood.

Crime (1927)

Credits: *Director*: A.H. Van Buren; *Producer*: A.H. Woods; *Playwrights*: Samuel Shipman, John B. Hymer; *Venue*: Eltinge 42nd Street Theatre, Broadway, New York; *Number of Performances*: 186; *Dates*: February 22–August 1927.

Cast: Chester Morris (Rocky Morse), Carol Baldwin, Barbara Barondess, E.F. Bostwick, William Boulias, Neil Bridge, DeLancey Cleveland, Marie Cole, Claude Cooper, Josephine Deffry, Cleve Delland, Katharine Francis, Spurr K. Gould, Walter D. Greene, R.H. Irving, Kay Johnson, Eddie Kelly, Jack La Rue, Michael Markham, Charles P. Mather, Earle Mayne, Douglass Montgomery, John O'Meara, Marvin Oreck, Walter Powers, Irving H. Rapper, James Rennie, Jess Romer, Clifton Self, Phillip M. Sheridan, Sylvia Sidney, Mary Smith, Jack Thomson, John Ward, Gustav Yorke.

Crime (1927–1928)

Credits: *Playwrights*: Samuel Shipman, John B. Hymer; *Performances*: tour, including dates at the Adelphi Theatre, Chicago.

Cast: Chester Morris (Rocky Morse).

Whispering Friends (1928)

Credits: *Director*: Sam Forrest; *Producer and Playwright*: George M. Cohan; *Venue*: Hudson Theatre, Broadway, New York; *Number of Performances*: 112; *Dates*: February 20–May 1928.

Cast: Chester Morris (Al Wheeler), Walter Edwin, Edith Gresham, William Harrigan, Elsie Lawson, Anne Showmaker.

Fast Life (1928)

Credits: *Director*: A.H. Van Buren; *Producer*: A.H. Woods; *Playwrights*: Samuel Shipman, John B. Hymer; *Venue*: Ambassador Theatre, Broadway, New York; *Number of Performances*: 21; *Dates*: September 26–October 1928.

Cast: Chester Morris (Chester Palmer), C. Edwin Brandt, John Burch, Irene Cattell, Goo Chong, Jean Clarendon, Claudette Colbert, Donald Dillaway, Frederick Earle, Frank Graham, Vicent Gulliver, Frank A. Howson, Thomas Irwin, Donald McClelland, Frank B. Miller, Adrian Morris, William Morris, Dorothy Payne, Frank Reyman, Wells Richardson, Muriel Robinson, Anne Tarnoff, Robert Toms, Walter Tyrrell, Crane Wilbur, Mabel Williams, Paul Wilson.

Small Miracle (1948)

Credits: *Playwright*: Norman Krasna; *Venue*: Phipps Auditorium, Denver, Colorado; *Dates*: August 1948.

Cast: Chester Morris, Artists' Repertory Theatre.

Dressed to Kill (1949)

Credits: *Artistic Director*: John Kenley; *Playwright*: Richard Burke; *Venue*: Lakewood Park Theatre, Barnesville, Pennsylvania; *Dates*: Summer 1949.

Cast: Chester Morris; Kenley Players.

The Dark Tower (1949)

Credits: *Playwrights*: Alexander Woolcott, George S. Kaufman; *Performances*: stock dates, at Chapel Playhouse, Guildford, Connecticut (July 1949); Sea Cliff Summer Theatre, Glen Cove, Long Island.

Cast: Chester Morris.

English Music Hall Tour (1949)

Credits: Performances: UK tour, including dates at Shepherd's Bush.

Cast: Chester Morris (Magician), Lillian Morris.

Detective Story (1949–1951)

Credits: *Director and Playwright*: Sidney Kingsley; *Producers*: Howard Lindsay, Russel Crouse; *Performances*: national tour, including dates at the Cass Theatre, Detroit; Blackstone Theatre, Chicago; American Theatre, St. Louis; Auditorium Theatre, St. Paul; Lyceum Theatre, Minneapolis; Omaha and Des Moines; regional tour, including dates at Brandt's Theatre, Flatbush, New York.

Cast: Chester Morris (Detective McLeod), Leonard Yorr, Marian Winters, Arthur Hanson, Donnell O'Brien, Barbara Winchester, Studs Terkel, Bill Terry, John Quigg, Paul Lipson, Frank Daly, Walter Starkey, Willis Pinkett, Steve Gravers, Allan Rich, Ludmilla Toretzka, Raoul de Leon, Kirk Brown, Elinor Randel, Tommy MacDonald, Gordon Peters, Marcia Walter, Marian Greene, Stapleton Kent, Jerry Fritz, Pitt Herbert, William Phelps, Lydia Clarke, James Bender, Leo Bayard, Patricia Canty, Philip Abbott, Charles Ross, Ruth Bryant.

The Fourth Degree (1953)

Credits: *Director*: Harald Bromley; *Producer*: Don Swann; *Playwright*: Jane Hinton; *Based on the Novel* by Eleazor Lipsky; *Venue*: Sheraton Belvedere Hotel, Baltimore; *Dates*: January 1953.

Cast: Chester Morris (Esau Frost), Rudy Bond, James Byrd, Angus Cairns, Ken Calfee, James Gregory, Jesse Jacobs, George Jansson, Thomas Mallory, Donald McClelland, John O'Shaughnessy, Sidney Plotkin, Martin Rudy, Penny Santon, Josephine Shyers, Elaine Swann, Haila Stoddard, Vaughn Taylor, Warren Lee Terry, O. Tolbert-Hewitt, Hal Winter.

The Long Street (1953)

Credits: *Director*: Ernestine Perrie; *Producers*: Thomas G. Ratcliffe, Louis Macmillan; *Playwright*: Grant Gaither; *Venue*: Sea Cliff Theatre, Long Island; *Dates*: August-September 1953.

Cast: Chester Morris (Sam Nash), Bruce Adams, Vincent Gardenia, Wynne Gibson, Phillip Pine, Betsy Von Furstenberg, Michael Steele, Joan Wetmore, Barbara Winchester.

The Fifth Season (1954)

Credits: *Director*: Gregory Ratoff; *Producer*: George Kondolf; *Associate Producer*: Sherman S. Krellberg; *Playwright*: Sylvia Regan; *Venue*: Cort Theatre, Broadway, New York; *Number of Performances*: 654 (January 23, 1953–1954); *Dates*: September 5–October 23, 1954.

Cast: Chester Morris (Johnny Goodwin) [replacement for Richard Whorf], Joseph Buloff, Carolyn Block, Allen Collins, John Griggs, Phyllis Hill, Patricia Jenkins, Dick Kallman, Fran Keegan, John Kullers, David Kurlan, Dorian Leigh, Lucille Patton, Donna Pearson, Augusta Roeland, Norman Rose, Andy Sanders, Sandu Scott, Menasha Skulnick, Nita Talbot, Teddy Tavenner, Midge Ware, Lois Wheeler.

The Fifth Season (1954–1955)

Credits: *Director*: Gregory Ratoff; *Producers*: George Kondolf, Sherman S. Krellberg; *Playwright*: Sylvia Regan; *Performances*: national tour, including dates at the Nixon Theatre, Pittsburgh; Plymouth Theatre, Boston; Erlanger Theatre, Chicago; and in Washington, D.C., and Philadelphia.

Cast: Chester Morris (Johnny Goodwin), Rita Bernard, Ann Buckles, Joseph Buloff, Allen Collins, Marilyn Garion, John Griggs, June Henry, Patricia Jenkins, Fran Keegan, Augusta Roeland, Andy Sanders, Shirley Talbott, Melissa Weston, Max Wilner.

The Caine Mutiny Court-Martial (1955)

Credits: *Director*: William Cottrell; *Playwright and Novel*: Herman Wouk; *Venue*: Paper Mill Playhouse, Millburn, New Jersey.

Cast: Chester Morris (Lieutenant Commander Philip Francis Queeg).

The Caine Mutiny Court-Martial (1955)

Credits: *Artistic Director*: John Kenley; *Playwright and Novel*: Herman Wouk; *Performances*: Bristol, Pennsylvania.

Cast: Chester Morris (Lieutenant Commander Philip Francis Queeg), Kenley Players.

Detective Story (1956)
Credits: *Playwright*: Sidney Kingsley; *Performances*: stock dates, at the Alley Theatre, Houston (July 1956), and Fred Miller Theatre, Milwaukee (October 1956).
Cast: Chester Morris (Detective McLeod).

A View from the Bridge (1957)
Credits: *Playwright*: Arthur Miller; *Venue*: Pocono Playhouse, Mountainhome, Pennsylvania; *Dates*: August 1957.
Cast: Chester Morris (Eddie Carbone).

The Girl of the Golden West (1957)
Credits: *Director*: Jerome Kitty; *Playwright*: David Belasco; *Venue*: Anderson Theatre, New York; *Number of Performances*: 8; *Dates*: November 5–10, 1957.
Cast: Chester Morris (Jack Rance), Robert Baines, Alan Becker, Peter Cookson, Ted Curtis, William DuFrene, Josip Elic, Logan English, Jack Hollander, Cavada Humphrey, Moultrie Patten, John Peters, Eugene Piciano, Gerald Price, Rod Rogers, Wallace Rooney, Reuben Singer, Ben Stone, Scott Ware, Nancy Wickwire.

Blue Denim (1958)
Credits: *Director*: Joshua Logan; *Producers*: Barbara Wolferman, James Hammerstein; *Playwrights*: James Leo Herlihy, William Noble; *Venue*: Playhouse Theatre, Broadway, New York; *Number of Performances*: 166; *Dates*: February 27–July 19, 1958.
Cast: Chester Morris (Major Bartley), Warren Berlinger, Burt Brinckerhoff, Carol Lynley, Pat Stanley, June Walker.

A View from the Bridge (1959)
Credits: *Director and Producer*: Miranda d'Ancona; *Playwright*: Arthur Miller; *Venue*: Curran Theatre, San Francisco; *Dates*: January 1959.
Cast: Chester Morris (Eddie Carbone).

Advise and Consent (1960–1961)
Credits: *Director*: Franklin J. Schaffner; *Producers*: Robert Fryer, Lawrence Carr; *Playwright*: Loring Mandel; *Based on the Novel* by Allen Drury; *Venue*: Cort Theatre, Broadway, New York; *Number of Performances*: 212; *Dates*: November 17, 1960–May 20, 1961.
Cast: Chester Morris (Senator Bob Munson), Ed Begley, Henry Jones, Richard Kiley, Kevin McCarthy, Staats Cotsworth, Barnard Hughes, Sally Kemp, Judson Laire, Woodrow Parfrey, Tom Shirley, Joan Wetmore, Conrad Bain, John Boyd, Wilson Brooks, Dan Charles, Richard Dickens, David Elliot, William Farmer, Peggy Fenn, Joan Hotchkis, Al Kavanagh, Clarence Kavanaugh, Leslie Litomy, Ed Moroney, Kayton Nesbitt, Vince O'Brien, Hack Rightor, Michael Ryan, Garrison P. Sherwood, James P. Truax, Wynn Wright.

The Caine Mutiny Court-Martial (1961)
Credits: *Producer*: Robert Ludlum; *Playwright and Novel*: Herman Wouk; *Venue*: Playhouse-on-the-Mall in Paramus, New Jersey.
Cast: Chester Morris (Lieutenant Commander Philip Francis Queeg), Robert Ludlum.

Angel in the Pawnshop (1961)
Credits: *Playwright*: A.B. Shiffren; *Venue*: Drury Lane Theatre, Chicago.
Cast: Chester Morris (Hilary).

Advise and Consent (1961–1962)
Credits: *Director*: Franklin J. Schaffner; *Producers*: Robert Fryer, Lawrence Carr; *Playwright*: Loring Mandel; *Based on the Novel* by Allen Drury; *Performances*: national tour of 35 cities, including dates at the Hanna Theatre, Cleveland; Wilbur Theatre, Boston; Auditorium Theatre, Rochester; Pabst Theater, Milwaukee; Orpheum Theatre, Minneapolis; and Blackstone Theatre, Chicago.
Cast: Chester Morris (Senator Orrin Knox), Farley Granger, Royal Beal, Russell Gaige, House Jameson, Atwood Levensaler, Betty Rollin, Archie Smith, Kay Doubleday, Grant Code, Harry Millard.

The Tender Heel (1963)
Credits: *Director and Producer*: Miranda d'Ancona.
Cast: Chester Morris, Signe Hasso.

Time Out for Ginger (1964)
Credits: *Playwright*: Ronald Alexander; *Venue*: Bucks County Playhouse, New Hope, Pennsylvania.
Cast: Chester Morris (Howard Carol), Liza Minnelli.

The Subject Was Roses (1965–1966)
Credits: *Director*: Ulu Grosbard; *Producer*:

Edgar Lansbury; *Playwright*: Frank D. Gilroy; *Venues*: Helen Hayes Theatre, Henry Miller's Theatre, Belasco Theatre, Broadway, New York; *Number of Performances*: 832 (1964–1966); *Dates*: September 7, 1965–May 21, 1966.

Cast: Chester Morris (John Cleary) [replacement for Jack Albertson], Irene Dailey, Maureen O'Sullivan, Martin Sheen.

The Subject Was Roses (1966)

Credits: *Playwright*: Frank D. Gilroy; *Performances*: national tour, including dates at the Mineola Theatre, Long Island; North Shore Music Theatre, Beverly, Massachusetts; Cape Playhouse, Dennis, Massachusetts; Paper Mill Playhouse, Millburn, New Jersey; Carousel Theatre, West Covina, California.

Cast: Chester Morris (John Cleary), Martha Scott, Mercedes McCambridge, Maureen O'Sullivan, Walter McGinn.

What Did We Do Wrong? (1968)

Credits: *Playwright*: Henry Denker; *Performances*: tour, including dates (July 15–20, 1968) at the John Drew Theater, Easthampton, Long Island.

Cast: Chester Morris (Walter Davis), Barbara Britton.

You Know I Can't Hear You ... (1969)

Credits: *Artistic Director*: John Kenley; *Playwright*: Robert Anderson; *Performances*: regional tour, including dates at Packard Music Hall Theatre, Warren, Ohio; Veterans Memorial Theatre, Columbus, Ohio; Memorial Hall, Dayton, Ohio.

Cast: Chester Morris, Kenley Players.

The Caine Mutiny Court-Martial (1970)

Credits: *Producer*: Lee R. Yopp; *Playwright and Novel*: Herman Wouk; *Venue*: Bucks County Playhouse, New Hope, Pennsylvania; *Dates*: September 1970.

Cast: Chester Morris (Lieutenant Commander Philip Francis Queeg).

Appendix E
Films Announced for Chester Morris but Produced with Another Actor

Following is a listing of film projects initially announced as featuring Chester Morris but eventually produced with another actor in his intended role. The actor who plays the role in the finished film is included in each entry.

He also was considered for other lead roles, which are mentioned in the text. The titles listed below are those for which he had been chosen but replaced prior to production.

The Front Page (United Artists, 1931)

Chester Morris was announced for the role of Hildy Johnson (played by Pat O'Brien).

The Bitter Tea of General Yen (Paramount, 1933)

Chester Morris was announced for the role of General Yen (played by Nils Asther).

The Warrior's Husband (Fox, 1933)

Chester Morris was announced for the role of Theseus (played by David Manners).

The Invisible Man (Universal, 1933)

Chester Morris was announced for the role of Dr. Kemp (played by William Harrigan).

Come On, Marines! (Paramount, 1934)

Chester Morris was announced as costarring with Richard Arlen (Roscoe Karns was cast).

Romance in the Rain (Universal, 1934)

Chester was announced for the role of Charlie Denton (played by Roger Pryor).

Strange Wives (Universal, 1934)

Chester Morris was announced for the role of Jimmy King (played by Roger Pryor).

The Glass Key (Paramount, 1935)

Chester Morris was announced for the role of Ed Beaumont (played by George Raft).

King Solomon of Broadway (Universal, 1935)

Chester Morris was announced for the role of Solomon McGuire (played by Edmund Lowe).

Speed (MGM, 1936)

Chester Morris was announced for the role of Terry Martin (played by James Stewart).

Fixer Dugan (RKO Radio, 1939)

Chester Morris was announced for the role of Charlie ["The Fixer"] Dugan (played by Lee Tracy).

The Girl and the Gambler (RKO Radio, 1939)

Chester Morris was announced for the role of Johnny Powell (played by Tim Holt).

Men Against the Sky (RKO Radio, 1940)

Chester Morris was announced for the role of Martin Ames (played by Kent Taylor).

Alaska Highway (Paramount, 1943)

Chester Morris was announced for a starring role. (The cast includes Richard Arlen and Ralph Sanford.)

Dark Mountain (Paramount, 1944)

Chester Morris was announced for the role of Don Bradley (played by Robert Lowery).

The Big Steal (RKO Radio, 1949)

Chester Morris was announced by Columbia for the role of Duke Halliday (played by Robert Mitchum when the film was produced by RKO).

Chapter Notes

Introduction

1. "No Book—Says Chester Morris," *Spokane Daily Chronicle*, 8 November 1966.
2. DeWitt Bodeen, "Chester Morris," *Films in Review*, Volume 31, National Review of Motion Pictures, 1980, p. 395.

Chapter 1

1. Chester Morris, interview with Studs Terkel, WFMT radio, Chicago, 27 February 1962.
2. "Women Caught in a Raid," *The New York Times*, 12 May 1907.
3. Adrian O'Hara [Morris], "I Know Chester Morris," *Talking Picture Magazine*, December 1929, p. 11.
4. Chester Morris, interview with Studs Terkel.
5. Chester Morris, interview with Studs Terkel.
6. Adrian O'Hara [Morris], p. 11.
7. *The New Movie Magazine*, June 1931, p. 57.
8. Adrian O'Hara [Morris], p. 11.
9. Adrian O'Hara [Morris], p. 11.
10. Alma Whitaker, "Bad Roles Leave No Mark," *Los Angeles Times*, 23 February 1930.
11. *The New York Times*, 19 February 1918.
12. Chester Morris, interview with Studs Terkel.
13. Chester Morris, interview with Studs Terkel.
14. Chester Morris, interview with Studs Terkel.
15. DeWitt Bodeen, p. 396.
16. *The New York Times*, 10 October 1926.
17. Adrian O'Hara [Morris], p. 11.

Chapter 2

1. *Picture Play*, August 1929, p. 106.
2. Chester Morris, interview with Studs Terkel.
3. *Picture Play*, February 1930, p. 111.
4. *Talking Screen*, August 1930, p. 88.
5. *Motion Picture*, March 1929, p. 124.
6. *Screenland*, July 1929, pp. 99–100.
7. *The Film Daily*, 13 March 1929, p. 6.
8. Adrian O'Hara [Morris], p. 11
9. *Variety*, 10 April 1929, p. 23.
10. *The Film Daily*, 12 April 1929, p. 8.
11. *The Film Daily*, 14 June 1929, p. 12.
12. *The Film Daily*, 12 May 1929, p. 4.
13. "You'll See Lots of Chester Morris After His Fine Work in 'Alibi,'" *The Evening Independent*, St. Petersburg, Florida, 9 May 1929.
14. *Motion Picture*, June 1929, p. 63.
15. Chester Morris, interview with Studs Terkel.
16. *Silver Screen*, June 1929, pp. 30–31.
17. *Screenland*, July 1929, p. 26.
18. *Screenland*, July 1929, p. 27.
19. *Screenland*, July 1929, p. 99.
20. *Screenland*, July 1929, p. 100.
21. *Photoplay*, July 1929, p. 63.
22. *The Film Daily*, 16 August 1929, p. 1.
23. *The Film Daily*, 16 August 1929, p. 1.
24. *Photoplay*, November 1929, p. 117.
25. *Picture Play*, December 1929, p. 119.
26. *Picture Play*, February 1930, p. 110.
27. *Variety*, 21 August 1929, p. 18.
28. *Photoplay*, December 1929, p. 111.
29. *Picture Play*, October 1929, p. 96.
30. *Screenland*, November 1929, p. 52.
31. Adrian O'Hara [Morris], p. 11
32. *The New York Times*, 4 January 1930.
33. *Hollywood Filmograph*, 22 February 1930, p. 20.
34. *The Film Daily*, 12 January 1930, p. 12.
35. *Variety*, 15 January 1930, p. 37.
36. *Picture Play*, February 1930, p. 110.
37. *The New Movie Magazine*, March 1930, p. 84.
38. *Talking Screen*, March 1930, p. 56.
39. *Hollywood Filmograph*, 1 March 1930, p. 21.
40. *Variety*, 19 February 1930, p. 33.
41. *The Film Daily*, 18 November 1929, p. 13.
42. Herbert Brenon, "Great Opportunities Offered for Strong Dramatic Talking Pictures," *Hollywood Daily Screen World*, 31 December 1929.
43. *Screenland*, March 1930, p. 58.
44. Herbert Brenon.
45. *Motion Picture*, April 1930, p. 6.
46. *Photoplay*, February 1930, p. 54.
47. *The Film Daily*, 2 March 1930, p. 10.
48. *Variety*, 12 March 1930, p. 21.
49. *The Film Daily*, 12/31 December 1929, p. 1.
50. *Photoplay*, June 1930, p. 57.
51. *The Film Daily*, 20 April 1930, p. 10.
52. *Broadway and Hollywood "Movies,"* July 1930, p. 23.

Chapter 3

1. *Photoplay*, June 1930, p. 164.
2. *Picture Play*, October 1930, pp. 66–67.
3. *Photoplay*, March 1931, p. 94.
4. *Variety*, 16 July 30.
5. *Motion Picture*, February 1931, p. 59.
6. *Silver Screen*, February 1931, p. 38.
7. *The Film Daily*, 31 December 1930, p. 2.
8. *The New York Times*, 16 January 1931.
9. *Picture Play*, February 1931, p. 100.
10. *Picture Play*, April 1931, p. 26.
11. *Motion Picture*, January 1932, p. 64.
12. *Variety*, 24 November 1931, p. 21.
13. *The Film Daily*, 22 November 1931, p. 10.
14. *Motion Picture*, June 1931, p. 67.
15. *Motion Picture*, May 1932, p. 90.
16. Colonel Jason Joy, American Motion Picture Pilots (AMPP), letter to Howard Hughes, Caddo Company, Inc., November 1931.
17. *Cock of the Air* pressbook, United Artists Corporation, 1932, ps. 3, 6.
18. *The New York Times*, 25 January 1932.
19. *Silver Screen*, October 1931, pp. 66–67.
20. *Variety*, 13 October 1931, p. 21.
21. *Los Angeles Times*, 10 January 1932.
22. *The New Movie Magazine*, June 1932, p. 62.
23. *Motion Picture Herald*, 16 April 1932, p. 55.
24. *Silver Screen*, June 1932, p. 46.
25. *Los Angeles Times*, 1 February 1931.
26. *Modern Screen*, June 1932, p. 19.
27. *Motion Picture*, April 1932, p. 6.
28. *Los Angeles Times*, 3 April 1932.
29. Erskine Johnson, "Hollywood Today," *Ironwood Daily Globe*, Michigan, 23 May 1957.
30. *Picture Play*, February 1933, p. 20.
31. *Screenland*, September 1932, p. 60.
32. *The Film Daily*, 23 November 1932, p. 4.
33. *Hollywood Filmograph*, 17 September 1932, p. 3.
34. *Broadway and Hollywood "Movies,"* August 1932, p. 41.
35. Herbert Wilcox, *Daily Mail*, October 1932.
36. *Motion Picture Herald*, 22 October 1932, p. 11.
37. *The Film Daily*, 1 March 1933, p. 6.
38. *Motion Picture*, October 1932, p. 85.
39. *Motion Picture*, April 1934, p. 41.
40. *The Film Daily*, 8 April 1933, p. 7.
41. *Variety*, 11 April 1933, p. 17.
42. *The Hollywood Reporter*, 13 January 1933, p. 1.
43. *Modern Screen*, August 1933, p. 19.
44. *Modern Screen*, May 1934, p. 41.
45. *Modern Screen*, May 1934, p. 114.
46. *Hollywood*, May 1937, p. 39.
47. *Motion Picture Herald*, 5 August 1933, p. 16.
48. *Broadway and Hollywood "Movies,"* November 1933, p. 21.
49. *Motion Picture Herald*, 23 September 1933, p. 33.
50. *Motion Picture*, December 1933, p. 58.

Chapter 4

1. "Screen Actors Guild Here Reorganized," *Los Angeles Examiner*, 5 October 1933.
2. *Photoplay*, April 1936, p. 35.
3. *The Hollywood Reporter*, 1 June 1933, p. 4; *Motion Picture Herald*, 10 June 1933, p. 46.
4. *Universal Weekly*, 10 June 33, p. 12.
5. *The Hollywood Reporter*, 19 June 1933, p. 6.
6. *Universal Weekly*, 10 June 33, p. 12.
7. *Variety*, 27 June 1933, p. 6.
8. *Universal Weekly*, 18 November 1933, pp. 12–13.
9. *The New York Times*, 11 December 1933.
10. *Hollywood*, 1 January 1934, p. 8.
11. *Motion Picture*, January 1934, p. 58.
12. *The Film Daily*, 9 December 1933, p. 18.
13. *Motion Picture Daily*, 24 October 1933, p. 2.
14. *Motion Picture Daily*, 22 November 1933, p. 12.
15. *Motion Picture Daily*, 20 February 1934, p. 7.
16. *Los Angeles Times*, 26 November 1933.
17. Valerie Yaros, Screen Actors Guild Timeline, Los Angeles, California, 2018.
18. *The Hollywood Reporter*, 9 January 1934, p. 6.
19. *The Hollywood Reporter*, 10 January 1934, p. 3.
20. *The Hollywood Reporter*, 18 January 1934, p. 1.
21. *The Hollywood Reporter*, 24 June 1934, p. 1.
22. *Universal Weekly*, 27 January 1934, p. 8.
23. *Hollywood*, January 1934, p. 43.
24. *Hollywood*, January 1934, p. 54.
25. *The Modern Screen*, September 1934, ps. 61, 94.
26. *The Modern Screen*, September 1934, pp. 94–95.
27. *The Modern Screen*, September 1934, p. 95.
28. *The Film Daily*, 8 February 1934, p. 11.
29. *Motion Picture Herald*, 3 March 1934, p. 16.
30. *The Modern Screen*, May 1934, p. 35.
31. *Broadway and Hollywood "Movies,"* July 1934, p. 15.
32. *Hollywood*, June 1934, p. 19.
33. *The Film Daily*, February-June 1934.
34. *Motion Picture Daily*, 19 May 1936, p. 8.
35. *Broadway and Hollywood "Movies,"* July 1934, pp. 48–49.
36. *Film Bulletin*, 25 March 1936, p. 9.
37. *Universal Weekly*, 12 May 1934, p. 14.
38. *The Film Daily*, 5 September 1934, p. 8.
39. *The Film Daily*, 26 May 1934, p. 4.
40. *The Hollywood Reporter*, 12 May 1934, p. 12.
41. *Hollywood*, August 1934, ps. 37, 63.
42. *Variety*, 10 April 1934, p. 19.
43. *Photoplay*, August 1934, p. 50.
44. *Hollywood Reporter*, 19 May 1934, p. 3.
45. Ann Harding, "The Frolic vs. Apathy," *The Screen Player*, 15 June 1934; Larry Beilenson, "For the Record," *Screen Guild Magazine*, June 1937.
46. *Motion Picture Daily*, 10 September 1934, p. 2.
47. *The Hollywood Reporter*, 1 September 1934.
48. *Los Angeles Times*, 11 September 1934.

49. *Variety*, 18 September 1934, p. 54.
50. *The New Movie Magazine*, February 1935.
51. *Silver Screen*, February 1935, p. 10.
52. *Screenland*, September 1934, p. 75.
53. *Motion Picture Daily*, 28 December 1934, p. 7.
54. *The Film Daily*, 5 March 1935, p. 11.
55. *Modern Screen*, June 1936, p. 78.
56. *The Film Daily*, 3 February 1935, p. 22.
57. *Motion Picture Daily*, 4 January 1935, p. 16.
58. *Variety*, 5 February 1935, p. 31.
59. *Motion Picture Daily*, 18 March 1935, p. 14.
60. *Variety*, 17 April 1935, p. 15.
61. *The Film Daily*, 20 February 1935, p. 2.

Chapter 5

1. *Los Angeles Times*, 25 April 1935.
2. *Screenland*, March 1935, p. 84.
3. *Silver Screen*, June 1935, p. 75.
4. *Motion Picture Herald*, 15 June 1935, p. 103.
5. *Motion Picture Herald*, 15 June 1935, p. 103.
6. *Hollywood*, August 1935, p. 18.
7. *The Hollywood Reporter*, 16 May 1935.
8. *Variety*, 25 May 1935.
9. *Motion Picture Daily*, 26 June 1935, p. 4.
10. Chester Morris, interview with Studs Terkel.
11. *Motion Picture Daily*, 31 July 1935, p. 14.
12. *Screenland*, September 1935, ps. 19, 80.
13. *Variety*, 4 September 1935, p. 3.
14. *Modern Screen*, October 1935, p. 64.
15. *Motion Picture Daily*, 23 January 1936, p. 8.
16. *Motion Picture*, May 1936, p. 8.
17. *Silver Screen*, May 1936, p. 59.
18. *Motion Picture Daily*, 13 February 1936, pp. 10–11.
19. *Variety*, 11 March 1936, p. 15.
20. Andy Edmonds, *Hot Toddy: The True Story of Hollywood's Most Sensational Murder* (Thorndike, Maine: Thorndike Press, 1989), p. 8.
21. Erskine Johnson.
22. *Motion Picture*, May 1936, p. 87.
23. *Motion Picture Daily*, 17 March 1936, p. 6.
24. Valerie Yaros.
25. American Film Institute Catalog of Feature Films, www.afi.catalog.com/Catalog.
26. *Modern Screen*, June 1936, p. 78.
27. *Motion Picture Daily*, 4 June 1936, p. 12.
28. *Photoplay*, May 1936, p. 33.
29. *The Motion Picture and the Family*, 15 May 1936, p. 3.
30. *Variety*, 10 June 1936, p. 4.
31. *Photoplay*, May 1936, p. 27.
32. *Motion Picture Daily*, 31 July 1936, p. 10.
33. *Motion Picture Herald*, 8 August 1936, p. 39.
34. *Screen Guild Magazine*, August 1936, p. 3.
35. *Screen Guild Magazine*, August 1936, p. 17.
36. *Silver Screen*, December 1936.
37. *Film Bulletin*, 27 February 1937, p. 9.
38. *Motion Picture Daily*, 16 September 1936, p. 11.
39. *Photoplay*, October 1936, p. 110.
40. *Photoplay*, October 1936, p. 110.
41. *Los Angeles Times*, 8 November 1936.
42. *Los Angeles Times*, 15 November 1936.
43. *Modern Screen*, January 1937, p. 129.
44. *Motion Picture Herald*, 21 November 1936, p. 44.
45. *Photoplay*, February 1937, p. 92.
46. *The Film Daily*, 18 February 1937, p. 8.
47. *The New York Times*, 26 April 1937.
48. *Film Bulletin*, 27 February 1937, p. 2.
49. *Screenland*, December 1936, p. 54.
50. *Screenland*, December 1936, p. 55.
51. *Screenland*, December 1936, ps. 55, 76.
52. *Screenland*, December 1936, p. 76.
53. *Movie Classic*, January 1937, p. 58.
54. *Photoplay*, August 1937, p. 66.

Chapter 6

1. Valerie Yaros.
2. Valerie Yaros.
3. *Motion Picture Daily*, 10 August 1937, p. 4.
4. *Variety*, 11 August 1937, p. 19.
5. *Variety*, 18 August 1937, p. 46.
6. *Motion Picture*, August 1937, p. 30.
7. *Picture Play*, December 1937, p. 66.
8. *Motion Picture Herald*, 2 April 1938, p. 10.
9. *Hollywood*, January 1941, p. 65.
10. *Motion Picture Daily*, 17 March 1938, p. 3.
11. *Variety*, 20 October 1938, p. 45.
12. *Variety*, 25 October 1939, p. 6.
13. Miss Cellania, "The Story Behind 'Frankie and Johnny,'" http://mentalfloss.com.
14. *Variety*, 27 April 1938, p. 4.
15. *St. Petersburg Times*, Florida, 4 June 1938.
16. *Motion Picture Herald*, 9 July 1938, p. 25.
17. *The New York Times*, 9 August 1938.
18. *Los Angeles Times*, 18 January 1939.
19. *Variety*, 19 October 1938, p. 40.
20. *Boxoffice*, 10 December 1938, p. 24-A.
21. *Variety*, 24 August 1938, p. 21.
22. *Los Angeles Times*, 18 January 1939.
23. *Photoplay*, July 1939, p. 63.
24. *Motion Picture Herald*, 29 April 1939, 54.
25. Bert Harlen, "Criminal's Mind is Taken Apart," *Hollywood Spectator*, 29 April 1939, p. 11.
26. Chester Morris, interview with Studs Terkel.
27. *Motion Picture*, April 1939, pp. 36–37.
28. *Motion Picture*, May 1939, p. 13.
29. Cindy De la Hoz, *Lucy at the Movies: The Complete Films of Lucille Ball* (Philadelphia: Running Press Book Publishers, 2007), p. 189.
30. *Motion Picture Daily*, 12 June 1939.
31. *The Film Daily*, 19 September 1939, p. 7.
32. *Silver Screen*, September 1939, p. 80.
33. "Chester Morris Wed Lillian Kenton Barker," International News Photo, L.A. Bureau, 18 November 1940.
34. *Variety*, 4 October 1939, p. 16.
35. *Variety*, 4 October 1939, p. 16.
36. Nikara Choudri, *The Complete Guide to Divorce Law* (New York: Kensington Publishing Corporation, 2004), p. 8.

37. "Divorce Decree Given Wife of Chester Morris," *The Telegraph-Herald*, Dubuque, Iowa, 12 November 1939.
38. *Photoplay*, February 1940, p. 82.
39. "Chester Morris Will Visit Bing Crosby Thursday Night," *The Lima News*, Ohio, 9 November 1939.
40. *Motion Picture*, March 1940, p. 85; *Motion Picture Herald*, 18 November 1939, p. 62.
41. *The Film Daily*, 8 March 1940, p. 9.
42. *The New York Times*, 5 March 1940.
43. "At the Riverside—Chester Morris," *Milwaukee Journal*, 28 January 1940.
44. *Motion Picture*, August 1940, p. 79.
45. *The Film Daily*, 24 June 1940, p. 4.
46. *Motion Picture Daily*, 23 July 1940, p. 6.
47. *The Film Daily*, 23 July 1940, p. 6.

Chapter 7

1. "Chester Morris Wed Lillian Kenton Barker."
2. *Modern Screen*, March 1941, p. 70.
3. *Boxoffice*, 30 November 1940, p. 30.
4. *The Film Daily*, 27 February 1941, p. 7.
5. *The Film Daily*, 8 December 1941, p. 5.
6. *Motion Picture Herald*, 13 December 1941, p. 406.
7. *Variety*, 10 December 1941, p. 18.
8. *Showmen's Trade Review*, 13 June 1942, p. 12.
9. *The New York Times*, 22 August 1942.
10. Will H. Hayes, Motion Picture Producers and Distributors of America (MPPDA), telegram to President Franklin Delano Roosevelt, 8 December 1941.
11. Schaefer, George, Motion Picture Committee Co-operating for National Defense (MPCCND), telegram to President Franklin Delano Roosevelt, 8 December 1941.
12. *The Evening Independent*, St. Petersburg, Florida, 22 April 1942.
13. *Motion Picture Herald*, 4 April 42, p. 585.
14. *Variety*, 25 February 1942, p. 46.
15. "Chester Morris Meets Old Chum in Army," *Milwaukee Sentinel*, 9 August 1942.
16. *Variety*, 1 April 1942, p. 17.
17. *Variety*, 8 April 1942, p. 17.
18. *Showmen's Trade Review*, 2 May 1942, p. 25.
19. *Showmen's Trade Review*, 7 November 1942, p. 12.
20. *Film Bulletin*, 16 November 1942, p. 6.
21. *Variety*, 6 May 1942, p. 32.
22. *The Hollywood Reporter*, 21 November 1942, p. 186.
23. *Variety*, 12 August 1942, p. 4.
24. *Showmen's Trade Review*, 27 March 1943, p. 12.

Chapter 8

1. *Photoplay*, September 1942, p. 88.
2. *Motion Picture Herald*, 12 September 1942.
3. *Motion Picture Herald*, 26 September 1942, p. 24.
4. *Showmen's Trade Review*, 26 September 1942, p. 8.
5. *Variety*, 7 July 1943, p. 2.
6. *Variety*, 18 November 1942.
7. *Variety*, 27 January 1943, p. 43.
8. *Variety*, 3 February 1943, p. 4.
9. *Motion Picture Daily*, 22 March 1943, p. 2.
10. *Film Bulletin*, 5 April 1943, p. 7.
11. *The Film Daily*, 19 April 1943, p. 6.
12. *Variety*, 31 March 1943, p. 7.
13. *Variety*, 11 August 1943, p. 10.
14. *Los Angeles Times*, 17 July 1943.
15. *Variety*, 22 December 1943, p. 12.
16. *Variety*, 25 August 1943, p. 2.
17. *Photoplay*, November 1943, pp. 106–107.
18. *Motion Picture Daily*, 18 November 1943; *Motion Picture Herald*, 27 November 1943, p. 48.
19. *Showmen's Trade Review*, 29 April 1944, ps. 13, 30.
20. *The Hollywood Reporter*, 5 July 1944.
21. *Showmen's Trade Review*, 3 June 1944, p. 16.
22. *The Film Daily*, 31 October 1944, p. 6.
23. *The Film Daily*, 18 December 1944, p. 9.
24. *Variety*, 12 July 1944.
25. *The Film Daily*, 2 April 1945, p. 8.
26. *Motion Picture Daily*, 2 April 1945, p. 14.
27. *Variety*, 22 August 1945, p. 20.
28. *The Film Daily*, 25 May 1945, p. 1.
29. *Showmen's Trade Review*, 13 July 1946, p. 24.
30. *Los Angeles Times*, 4 March 1946.
31. *Motion Picture Daily*, 18 November 1946, p. 23.
32. *Motion Picture Daily*, 24 January 1947, p. 6.
33. *Variety*, 4 June 1947, p. 7.
34. *The New York Times*, 17 June 1947; *St. Petersburg Times*, 21 June 1947; *Variety*, 7/23/47, p. 18.
35. Chester Morris, "There's Magic Up Your Sleeve," *Popular Mechanics*, October 1947.
36. Julien J. Proskauer, *Conjuror's Magazine*, November 1947.
37. Chester Morris, "Restrained Revealing Helps Magic," *Conjuror's Magazine*, December 1947.
38. *The Linking Ring*, International Brotherhood of Magicians, July 1948.
39. Genii: The Conjuror's Magazine, https://geniimagazine.com.
40. *Variety*, 28 April 1948, p. 8.
41. *Showmen's Trade Review*, 8 January 1949, p. 22.
42. *Variety*, 4 April 1948, p. 50.
43. Turner Classic Movies. www.tcm.com.

Chapter 9

1. Chester Morris, interview with Studs Terkel.
2. Chester Morris, interview with Studs Terkel.
3. Chester Morris, interview with Studs Terkel.
4. Chester Morris, interview with Studs Terkel.
5. Chester Morris, interview with Studs Terkel.
6. *Variety*, 29 March 1950, p. 37.
7. *Variety*, 28 January 1953, p. 56.
8. *Variety*, 11 August 1954, p. 22.
9. *Variety*, 9 September 1953, p. 70.

Chapter 10

1. *Variety*, 20 October 1954, p. 3.
2. *Variety*, 11 August 1954, p. 4.
3. *Unchained* pressbook, Warner Bros. Pictures, 1955.
4. *The Hollywood Reporter*, January 1955.
5. *The Hollywood Reporter*, May 1955.
6. *Variety*, 30 May 1956, p. 57.
7. *Variety*, 15 September 1954, p. 58.
8. Tom Weaver, *Science Fiction Confidential: Interviews with 23 Monster Stars and Filmmakers* (Jefferson, North Carolina: McFarland and Company, Publishers, 2010), p. 127.
9. Tom Weaver, p. 127.
10. Tom Weaver, p. 127.
11. *Variety*, 5 September 1956, p. 6.
12. *Variety*, 5 December 1956, p. 36.
13. David Hanna, *Bogart* (New York: Nordon Publications, Inc., 1976), p. 182.
14. Erskine Johnson.
15. "A View from the Bridge," *Pocono Playhouse Daily Record*, Stroudsburg, Pennsylvania, 17 August 1957.

Chapter 11

1. "3 Well-Known Actors Here for Filming of Show in TV Series," *Ocala Star Banner*, Marion County, Florida, 3 March 1959.
2. Chester Morris, interview with Studs Terkel.
3. "Television Motion Picture Agency Contract (Artists' Manager Contract)," William Morris Agency, Inc., and Chester Morris, Beverly Hills, California, 5 March 1956.
4. "Will Try to Cash Check 20 Years Old," *Kokomo Tribune*, 1 January 1959.
5. Chester Morris, interview with Studs Terkel.
6. Chester Morris, interview with Studs Terkel.
7. Phyllis Battelle, "Chester Morris Likes Acting but Worries About Security," *Anderson Daily Bulletin*, Indiana, 29 August 1961.
8. Phyllis Battelle.
9. Phyllis Battelle.
10. "Vernon Scott Story on Chester Morris," United Press International, 6 June 1960.

Chapter 12

1. Nehemiah Persoff, letter to Scott Allen Nollen, 13 November 2018.
2. Chester Morris, interview with Studs Terkel.
3. James Bawden and Ronald G. Miller, *You Ain't Heard Nothin' Yet: Interviews with Stars from Hollywood's Golden Era* (Lexington, Kentucky: The University Press of Kentucky, 2017).
4. "Zimmerman Raps Actor's Slap at Politics," *Milwaukee Sentinel*, 20 January 1962.
5. *Advise and Consent* souvenir program, touring company, 1961.
6. Chester Morris, interview with Studs Terkel.
7. Chester Morris, interview with Studs Terkel.
8. Chester Morris, interview with Studs Terkel.
9. Chester Morris, interview with Studs Terkel.
10. Chester Morris, interview with Studs Terkel.
11. Chester Morris, interview with Studs Terkel.
12. Chester Morris, interview with Studs Terkel.
13. United States Senate, https://www.senate.gov.
14. Chester Morris, letter to Mr. Rintouc, London, England, 30 December 1963.

Chapter 13

1. *Los Angeles Times*, 4 November 1966.
2. *Los Angeles Times*, 4 November 1966.
3. Pete Arroyo, messages to Scott Allen Nollen, 10–12 November 2018.
4. *Daily Variety*, 24 October 1969, p. 8.
5. *The New York Times*, 1982.
6. *The New York Times*, 12 September 1970.
7. DeWitt Bodeen, p. 403.
8. *The New York Times*, 12 October 1970.
9. Michael Sragow, "Ersatz Athos The Great White Hope Opening Dec. 21 at the Music Hall," *The Harvard Crimson*, 17 December 1970.
10. Zay Amsbury, "Classic Hollywood Spotlight: 'The Great White Hope,'" www.hollywood.com.

Chapter 14

1. Chester Morris, interview with Studs Terkel.
2. Chester Morris, interview with Studs Terkel.
3. Chester Morris, interview with Studs Terkel.
4. *Los Angeles Times*, 4 November 1966.

Sources and Bibliography

Interviews

Karloff, Evelyn. Discussion with Scott Allen Nollen, June 1991.

Morris, Chester. Interview with Studs Terkel, WFMT radio, Chicago, 27 February 1962.

Correspondence

Arroyo, Pete. Messages to Scott Allen Nollen, 10–12 November 2018.

Hays, Will H., Motion Picture Producers and Distributors of America (MPPDA). Telegram to President Franklin Delano Roosevelt, 8 December 1941.

Joy, Colonel Jason, American Motion Picture Pilots (AMPP). Letter to Howard Hughes, Caddo Company, Inc., November 1931.

Morris, Chester. Letter to Mr. Rintouc, London, England, 30 December 1963.

Persoff, Nehemiah. Letter to Scott Allen Nollen, 13 November 2018.

Schaefer, George, Motion Picture Committee Co-operating for National Defense (MPCCND). Telegram to President Franklin Delano Roosevelt, 8 December 1941.

Official Documents

Beverly Hills (1937) City and Telephone Directory. Beverly Hills, California, 1937.

Consent agreement between Chester Morris and Columbia Pictures Corporation, regarding the Motion Picture Relief Fund, Inc. Los Angeles, California, 28 February 1947.

"Fifteenth Census of the United States: 1930—Population Schedule." Block No. 208, Assembly District 55, Los Angeles, Los Angeles County, California, 1930.

"Fourteenth Census of the United States: 1920—Population." City Ward No. 5, Mount Vernon, Westchester County, New York, 19 January 1920.

"List of In-Bound Passengers (United States Citizens and Nationals)." Treasury Department, United States Customs Service, New York, New York, 8 December 1948.

Morris, Cynthia Suzanne. Los Angeles County Birth Records, Los Angeles County, California: Vital Records, 16 October 1930.

Morris, John Brooks. U.S. Draft Card. National Archives and Records Administration, St. Louis, Missouri: Records of the Selective Service System, 147, Box 1265.

"Sixteenth Census of the United States: 1940—Population Schedule." West Hollywood, Los Angeles County, California, 13 and 15 April 1940.

"Television Motion Picture Agency Contract (Artists' Manager Contract)," William Morris Agency, Inc., and Chester Morris. Beverly Hills, California, 5 March 1956.

"Thirteenth Census of the United States: 1910—Population." City Ward 5, Mount Vernon, Westchester County, New York, 15 April 1910.

Yaros, Valerie. Screen Actors Guild Timeline. Los Angeles, California, 2018.

Original Photograph Tags

"Advise and Consent," Orpheum Theatre, Minneapolis, Minnesota, January 1962.

"Advise and Consent," Sunday Screen, 12 November 1961.

"Chester Morris," Cass Theatre, Detroit, Michigan, 18 October 1949.

"Chester Morris Wed Lillian Kenton Barker," International News Photo, L.A. Bureau, 18 November 1940.

"The Contenders," ABC Television, 19 November 1962.

"Divorces Film Actor, Chester Morris," International News Photo, L.A. Bureau, 10 November 1939.

"Ex-Star Again a Member of the Film Colony," Associated Press Photo, 15 February 1937.

"Film Star Weds Society Matron," ACME Newspictures, Inc., 2 December 1940.

"Mary Brian and Chester Morris," Modern Screen Photograph, December 1940.

"Prison Premiere," Warner Bros. Pictures, Inc., New York, 1955.

"Stars and Director After Broadway Opening," Associated Press Photo, 17 November 1960.
"'Studio One' Stars," CBS Television Photo Division, 5 April 1954.
"Time Out for Ginger," Bucks County Playhouse, New Hope, Pennsylvania, 31 May 1964.
"Vernon Scott Story on Chester Morris," United Press International, 6 June 1960.

Studio, Distributor and Theater Materials

Advise and Consent play program. Auditorium Theatre, Rochester, 1961.
Advise and Consent play program. Hanna Theatre, Cleveland, 1961.
Advise and Consent play program. National Theatre, Washington, D.C., 1960.
Advise and Consent play program. On Stage, Wilbur Theatre, Boston, 1961.
Advise and Consent play program. The Playgoer, Shubert Theatre, New York, 1960.
Advise and Consent play program. The Playgoer, Walnut Theatre, New York, 1960.
Advise and Consent Playbill. Playbill, Incorporated, Cort Theatre, New York, 1961.
Advise and Consent souvenir program. Touring company, 1961.
Blue Denim play program. Locust Street Theatre, New York, 1958.
Blue Denim play program. The Playgoer, Shubert Theatre, New York, 1958.
Blue Denim Playbill. Playbill, Incorporated, The Playhouse Theatre, New York, 1958.
Cock of the Air pressbook. United Artists Corporation, 1932.
Detective Story play program. Chicago Stagebill, Blackstone Theatre, Chicago, 1949.
The Fifth Season play program. On Stage, Plymouth Theatre, Boston, 1955.
The Fifth Season play program. The Playboard, Erlanger Theater, Chicago, 1954.
The Fifth Season Playbill. Playbill, Incorporated, Cort Theatre, New York, 1954.
Girl from God's Country pressbook. Republic Pictures Corporation, 1940.
The Mountain Man play program. Magazine Theatre Program, Maxine Elliott's Theatre, New York, 1921.
No Hands on the Clock pressbook. Paramount Pictures Corporation, 1941.
The Subject Was Roses play program. Mineola Theatre, Long Island, New York, 1966.
The Subject Was Roses Playbill. Playbill, Incorporated, Belasco Theatre, New York, 1966.
The Subject Was Roses Playbill. Playbill, Incorporated, Helen Hayes Theatre, New York, 1966.
Unchained pressbook. Warner Bros. Pictures, 1955.
Whispering Friends play program. New York Magazine Program, Hudson Theatre, New York, 1928.

Periodical Articles

"Actors Become Magicians," *Los Angeles Times*, 17 July 1943.
"Adrian M. Morris," *The New York Times*, 1 December 1941.
"Aging Prison in Disrepair, Costly, Deadly," *The Sun*, San Bernardino, California, 23 July 2006.
Ahmed, Azam, "Kenton Morris, 1947–2008," *Chicago Tribune*, 14 September 2008.
"At the Riverside—Chester Morris," *Milwaukee Journal*, 28 January 1940.
Battelle, Phyllis, "Chester Morris Likes Acting but Worries About Security," *Anderson Daily Bulletin*, Indiana, 29 August 1961.
Beilenson, Larry, "For the Record," *Screen Guild Magazine*, June 1937.
Bledsoe, Steve, "Brooks Morris: The Passing of a Legend," *Western Outdoor News*, 19 July 2011.
Bodeen, DeWitt, "Chester Morris," *Films in Review*, Volume 31, National Review of Motion Pictures, 1980.
Boxoffice, 1938–1945.
Brenon, Herbert, "Great Opportunities Offered for Strong Dramatic Talking Pictures," *Hollywood Daily Screen World*, 31 December 1929.
Broadway and Hollywood "Movies," 1930–1934.
Canby, Vincent, "'Great White Hope' Brought to Screen," *The New York Times*, 12 October 1970.
"Career of Screen Sin Concluded," *Los Angeles Times*, 10 January 1932.
"Chatter in Hollywood," *The Milwaukee Sentinel*, 25 February 1936.
"Chester Morris and Wife Part," *Los Angeles Times*, 18 January 1939.
"Chester Morris Back on Screen," *The Pittsburgh Press*, 1 October 1969.
"Chester Morris Breaks Leg," *The New York Times*, 17 June 1947.
"Chester Morris Dies," *Pittsburgh Post-Gazette*, 12 September 1970.
"Chester Morris Dies in New Hope of Drug Overdose," *The Daily Intelligencer*, Doylestown, Pennsylvania, 12 September 1970.
"Chester Morris Enough of a Ham to Watch Replays of His Movies," *Ocala Star Banner*, Marion County, Florida, 14 Mat 1958.
"Chester Morris Fund Planned," *Los Angeles Times*, 7 November 1939.
"Chester Morris Gets Around Divorce Delay by Wife," *Warsaw Union*, Indiana, 26 November 1940.
"Chester Morris is Dead at 69; Created Role of Boston Blackie," *The New York Times*, 12 September 1970.
"Chester Morris Meets Old Chum in Army," *Milwaukee Sentinel*, 9 August 1942.
"Chester Morris' Stage Hit is Return to First Love," *St. Petersburg Times*, Florida, 17 May 1958.
"Chester Morris Variety Club's 'King,'" *Milwaukee Sentinel*, 16 January 1962.

"Chester Morris Wed on Coast," *The New York Times*, 2 December 1940.
"Chester Morris Weds Socialite," *St. Petersburg Times*, Florida, 13 December 1940.
"Chester Morris' Wife Gets Divorce," *The San Antonio Light*, 12 November 1939.
"Chester Morris Will Visit Bing Crosby Thursday Night," *The Lima News*, Ohio, 9 November 1939.
The Circleville Herald, Ohio, 10 July 1931.
"'The Copperhead,' New Thomas Play," *The New York Times*, 19 February 1918.
"Deaths Reported Jan. 27, Manhattan and Bronx," *The New York Times*, 28 January 1902.
"Divorce Decree Given Wife of Chester Morris," *The Telegraph-Herald*, Dubuque, Iowa, 12 November 1939.
"Even Stars Themselves Admit That They're Not Entitled to Private Life," *Los Angeles Times*, 26 November 1933.
The Evening Independent, St. Petersburg, Florida, 22 April 1942.
"Everything That Spells Box Office," *The Hollywood Reporter*, 1 September 1934.
Film Bulletin, 1934–1945.
The Film Daily, 1929–1947.
Francis, Bob, "Speaking of Legit," *Billboard*, 21 August 1954.
"A Gallant Fighter," *The New York Times*, 11 December 1933.
Gebhardt, Myrtle, "Hollywood Protects Itself Against Kidnappers: Precautions Taken in the Movie Colony," *Los Angeles Times*, 3 April 1932.
Genii: Pacific Coast Magic News, Volume 2, Number 5, January 1938.
Hall Mordaunt, "Chester Morris and Billie Dove in a Wild War Romance with Some Rowdy Humor—New French Picture," *The New York Times*, 25 January 1932.
Hall, Mordaunt, "The Screen: An Old Mystery Drama," *The New York Times*, 16 January 1931.
Harding, Ann, "The Frolic vs. Apathy," *The Screen Player*, 15 June 1934.
Harford, Margaret. "Chester Morris—an Actor Who Plays Hard at Work," *Los Angeles Times*, 4 November 1966.
Harlen, Bert, "Criminal's Mind is Taken Apart," *Hollywood Spectator*, 29 April 1939.
Harrison's Reports, 1942–1945.
Hollywood, 1934–1942.
Hollywood Filmograph, 1929–1934.
Hollywood Low Down, 1935–1938.
The Hollywood Reporter, 1933–1934.
"'I Promise to Pay,' With Chester Morris and Leo Carrillo, Opens at the Central," *The New York Times*, 26 April 1937.
Johnson, Erskine, "Hollywood Today," *Ironwood Daily Globe*, Michigan, 23 May 1957.
"Kenton Morris," *The Beacon-News*, Aurora, Illinois, 14 September 2008.
"Kenton Morris," *Chicago Tribune*, 14 September 2008.

Kester, Marshall, "Barbecue Pit Launches Series of Parties," *Los Angeles Times*, 6 June 1937.
Kester, Marshall, "Film Notables Gather at Tenth Wedding Anniversary," *Los Angeles Times*, 8 November 1936.
Lawson, Carol, "Howard Sackler, 52, Playwright Who Won Pulitzer Prize, Dead," *The New York Times*, 15 October 1982.
The Linking Ring, International Brotherhood of Magicians, July 1948.
Los Angeles Times, 5 June 1953.
Mayer, Mary, "Newest Morris Seeks 'It,'" *Los Angeles Times*, 1 February 1931.
Merrick, Mollie, "Stars and Wives Ride in Circus Parade Incognito," *Los Angeles Times*, 11 September 1934.
Mintz, Howard, "Prison on the Brink: Correctional Facilities Like Chino are Overcrowded and Dangerous," *Mercury News*, San Jose, California, 11 September 2009.
The Modern Screen, 1930–1942.
Morris, Chester, "Hollywood's Silence on the Crime Wave," *Los Angeles Times*, 4 March 1946.
Morris, Chester, "Restrained Revealing Helps Magic," *Conjuror's Magazine*, December 1947.
Morris, Chester, "There's Magic Up Your Sleeve," *Popular Mechanics*, October 1947.
"Most Film Folk Home for Holiday," *The New York Times*, 25 December 1933.
Motion Picture, 1929–1941.
The Motion Picture and the Family, 1936–1938.
Motion Picture Daily, 1931–1947.
Motion Picture Herald, 1931–1956.
Movie Classic, 1931–1937.
Murray, Feg, "Seein' Stars," 5 February 1939.
The New Movie Magazine, 1930–1935.
New York, 15 July 1968.
The New York Times, 4 January 1930; 29 September 1954.
"No Book—Says Chester Morris," *Spokane Daily Chronicle*, 8 November 1966.
Nugent, Frank S., "The Screen," *The New York Times*, 5 March 1940.
O'Hara, Adrian [Adrian Morris], "I Know Chester Morris," *Talking Picture Magazine*, December 1929.
Paramount International News, 1932–1934.
Photoplay, 1929–1943.
Picture Play, 1929–1938.
Pittsburgh Post-Gazette, 5 November 1954.
Poff, Tip, "That Certain Party," *Los Angeles Times*, 15 November 1936.
Proskauer, Julien J., *Conjuror's Magazine*, November 1947.
"Ruben's Direction, Story Stand Out; Swell Acting Cast," *The Hollywood Reporter*, 16 May 1935.
St. Petersburg Times, Florida, 4 June 1938; 21 June 1947.
Scott, John, "Belasco Books 'First Legion'; drama by Lipscomb Slated," *Los Angeles Times*, 25 April 1935.

"Screen Actors Guild Here Reorganized," *Los Angeles Examiner,* 5 October 1933.
Screen Guild Magazine, August 1936; October 1936.
Screenland, 1929–1946.
Showmen's Trade Review, 1942–1945.
Silver Screen, 1931–1940.
"'Smashing the Rackets,' Featuring Chester Morris and Bruce Cabot, Opens at the Rialto," *The New York Times,* 9 August 1938.
Sragow, Michael, "Ersatz Athos The Great White Hope Opening Dec. 21 at the Music Hall," *The Harvard Crimson,* 17 December 1970.
"The Story of Chester Morris," *The New York Times,* 10 October 1926.
Talking Screen, 1930.
"3 Well-Known Actors Here for Filming of Show in TV Series," *Ocala Star Banner,* Marion County, Florida, 3 March 1959.
"Today's Television Picture," *The Milwaukee Journal,* 16 April 1959.
Universal Weekly, 1932–1936.
Variety, 1929–1956.
"Veteran Actor Chester Morris Is Found Dead," *The Times-News,* 12 September 1970.
"A View from the Bridge," *Pocono Playhouse Daily Record,* Stroudsburg, Pennsylvania, 17 August 1957.
Whitaker, Alma, "Bad Roles Leave No Mark," *Los Angeles Times,* 23 February 1930.
"Who's Who on the Screen," *The New York Times,* 3 July 1932.
Wilcox, Herbert, *Daily Mail,* October 1932.
"Will Try to Cash Check 20 Years Old," *Kokomo Tribune,* 1 January 1959.
"William Morris, 75, Veteran Actor, Dies," *The New York Times,* 12 January 1936.
"Women Caught in a Raid," *The New York Times,* 12 May 1907.
"You'll See Lots of Chester Morris After His Fine Work in 'Alibi,'" *The Evening Independent,* St. Petersburg, Florida, 9 May 1929.
"Zimmerman Raps Actor's Slap at Politics," *Milwaukee Sentinel,* 20 January 1962.

Books

Alicoate, Jack, ed. *The 1931 Film Daily Yearbook of Motion Pictures.* New York: The Film Daily, 1931.
Ball, Lucille. *Love, Lucy.* New York: Berkley, 1997.
Bawden, James, and Ronald G. Miller. *You Ain't Heard Nothin' Yet: Interviews with Stars from Hollywood's Golden Era.* Lexington, Kentucky: The University Press of Kentucky, 2017.
Bernds, Edward. *Mr. Bernds Goes to Hollywood: My Early Life and Career in Sound Recording at Columbia with Frank Capra and Others.* Lanham, Maryland: Scarecrow Press, 1999.
Choudri, Nikara. *The Complete Guide to Divorce Law.* New York: Kensington Publishing Corporation, 2004.
De la Hoz, Cindy. *Lucy at the Movies: The Complete Films of Lucille Ball.* Philadelphia: Running Press Book Publishers, 2007.
Edmonds, Andy. *Hot Toddy: The True Story of Hollywood's Most Sensational Murder.* Thorndike, Maine: Thorndike Press, 1989.
Hanna, David. *Bogart.* New York: Nordon Publications, Inc., 1976.
Nollen, Scott Allen. *Boris Karloff: A Gentleman's Life.* Baltimore: Midnight Marquee Press, 2005.
Nollen, Scott Allen. *Three Bad Men: John Ford, John Wayne, Ward Bond.* Jefferson, North Carolina: McFarland, 2013.
Nollen, Scott Allen. *Warners Wiseguys: All 112 Films That Robinson, Cagney and Bogart Made for the Studio.* Jefferson, North Carolina: McFarland, 2007.
A Study Guide for Sidney Kingsley's "Detective Story." Farmington Hills, Michigan: Gale Cengage, 2017.
Weaver, Tom. *Science Fiction Confidential: Interviews with 23 Monster Stars and Filmmakers.* Jefferson, North Carolina: McFarland, 2010.

Websites

American Film Institute. AFI Catalog of Feature Films. www.afi.catalog.com/Catalog.
Amsbury, Zay, "Classic Hollywood Spotlight: 'The Great White Hope.'" www.hollywood.com.
"Brooks Morris, Col., USAF (Ret.), Legion of Merit, w/cluster, Silver Star, DFC, Bronze Star, 8 Air Medals," Freedom Committee of Orange County, 2014. https://fc-oc.org/speakers/brooks-morris/.
The Digital Deli Too: Preserving the Golden Age of Radio for a Digital Future. www.digitaldeliftp.com.
Genii: The Conjuror's Magazine. https://genii magazine.com.
Hastings, Larry, "Momentary Fascinations: A Eulogy for Chester Morris." www.http://momentary fascinations.com/eulogies/a.eulogy.for.chester. morris.html.
Internet Broadway Database. https://www.ibdb.com.
Internet Movie Database. https://www.imdb.com.
Internet Off-Broadway Database. http://www.lortel. org/Archives.
Magicpedia. https://geniimagazine.com/wiki/index. php?title=Chester_Morris.
"Mayors and Postmasters of Mt. Vernon New York." http://politicalgraveyard.com.
Miss Cellania, "The Story Behind 'Frankie and Johnny.'" http://mentalfloss.com/article/78308/ story-behind-frankie-and-johnny.
Old Time Radio Downloads. https://www.oldtime radiodownloads.com.
Radio Gold Index. www.radiogoldindex.com.
She Blogged by Night. http://sheblogggedbynight. com/2014/the-big-house-1930-triple-feature-from-warner-archive/.
Turner Classic Movies. http://www.tcm.com.
United States Senate. https://www.senate.gov/ reference/reference_item/advise_and_consent. htm.

Index

Numbers in *bold italics* indicate pages with illustrations

Abbott, Bud 118, 163, 179
Abbott, George 86
Abel, Walter 127–128, 130, 147, 276
Academy of Motion Picture Arts and Sciences [AMPAS] 3, 4, 19, 21, 34, 37, 59, 61, 66, 69, 112, 116, 188, 227–228, 244, 261, 265
Across the Pacific (1942 film) 173
"Act of God Nonwithstanding" (television episode) 218, 285
Action (1921 film) 106
Actors Studio 244
Acuff, Eddie 130, 133, 276–277
Adams, Maude 7
Addams, Charles 258
Adelphi Theatre (Chicago) 16, 304
Adler, Buddy 141, 148, 150
Adler, Jay 141
Adler, Stella 5, 244–245
Adolfi, John G. 24, 268
Adrian, Iris 195, 282
The Adventures of Boston Blackie [aka *Boston Blackie*] (radio show) 191, 300
The Adventures of Robin Hood (1938 film) 61
Advise and Consent (1962 film) 247
Advise and Consent (play) 240–*241*, 245, 247, 249–250, 265, 306
Aerial Gunner (1943 film) 173–176, *174*, *175*, 180–181
After Midnight with Boston Blackie (1943 film) 176–178, *177*, 280
The Age for Love (1931 film) 47
Age of Indiscretion (1935 film) 94

Aguilar, Magdelino 180
Aguilera, Paco 223
Ahn, Philip 211, 275, 283
Alaska Highway (1943 film) 178, 309
Albee, Edward 13
Albert, Eddie 243
Albertson, Frank 72, 271, 277
Albertson, Jack 257, 307
Albuquerque (1948 film) 162
Alcoa Premiere (television series) 251, 292
Alda, Alan 252, 293
Alderson, Erville 103, 273
Alexander, Elizabeth 26, 268
Alexander, Jane 260–262, 284
Alexander, Joan 222, 287
Alexander, Katherine 16, 274
Alexander, Ronald 256, 306
Alias Boston Blackie (1942 film) 162, 164–166, *165*, 203, 279
Alibi (1929 film) 3, 17–23, *19*, 25–26, 29, 31, 40, 45–47, 54, 61, 74, 102, 267–268
Alicoate, Jack 31
All Quiet on the Western Front (1930 film) 22, 37, 147
All Quiet on the Western Front (novel) 37
All the Horrors of Home (play) 12–14, 304
Allbritton, Louise 207
Allen, David 188
Allen, Elizabeth 75, 111
Allen, Gracie 125, 213–214, 301–302
Allen, Lewis 234, 289
Allen, Steve 233, 236, 258, 288
Allen Funt Productions 251, 292–293, 297
Alley Theatre (Houston) 233, 306
Allwyn, Astrid 157, 278

"Along About Late in the Afternoon" (television episode) 251, 292
Alper, Murray 200, 283
Alter, Louis 157
An Amateur Orphan (1917 film) 10, 267
The Ambulance Chaser (play) 52
Ameche, Don 218–219, 286
American Expeditionary Forces [AEF] 10
American Federation of Labor [AFL] 145
American National Theatre and Academy [ANTA] 250
American Prison Association 224
Ames, Adrienne 54, 270
Ames, Robert 14, 52
The Ammident Show (radio show) 214, 302
Amos, Ruth 223, 288
The Amos and Andy Show (radio show) 185, 190–191, 299, 300
Amy, George 65
Anderson, Dusty 199, 200, 202, 281–283
Anderson, Eddie "Rochester" 89, 272
Anderson, Maxwell 34
Anderson, Robert 260, 307
Anderson Theatre (New York City) 235, 306
Andes, Keith 142
Andrews, Dana 185
Andrews, Robert Hardy 125, 275
Andrews, Stanley 163, 274–275, 279
Andriot, Lucien 49, 269
Angel, Heather 87
Angel Flight Network 264

Index

Angel in the Pawnshop (play) 249, 306
Angels with Dirty Faces (1938 film) 75, 94, 185–186
Anspatch, Susan 257, 296
Anthony Adverse (1936 film) 61
Anthony in Wonderland (play) 10
Apfel, Oscar 63, 271
Appointment with Adventure (television series) 229, 288
Archer, Evelyn 11, 303
Archibald, Jean 16
"The Arena" (television episode) 229–230, 248, 265, 288
Arena Theatre (Washington, DC) 260
Arizona (1931 film) 52
Arlen, Richard 53, 58, 67–68, 88, 104, 155, 167–169, **168**, 173–175, **174**, 178–181, 234, 271, 280, 289, 309
Arliss, George 23, 37, 84
Armed Forces Radio Service [AFRS] 207, 301
Armendariz, Pedro 110
Armetta, Henry 83, 86, 91, 95, 270–273
Armstrong, Louis 94, 105, 177
Armstrong, R. G. 260, 262, 284
Armstrong, Robert 105, 112, 233–234, 273, 288
Armstrong's Theatre of Today (radio show) 179, 299
Arnaz, Desi Jr. 242, 291
Arnaz, Lucie 242, 291
Arnold, Betty 207, 301
Arnold, Edward 102, 112, 116, 124, 144–145, 147, 231
Arnt, Charles 185, 191, 211, 281, 283
Arsenic and Old Lace (play) 214
Arthur, Jean 3, 40, 97, 99–101, **99**, **100**, 119, 124, 273
The Arthur Murray Party (television show) 221, 286
Ashe, Warren 203–204, 283
Asner, Edward 251, 292
Associated Actors and Artistes of America [AAAA] 147
Astaire, Fred 217, 251, 292
Asther, Nils 52, 57, 308
Astor, Mary 52, 76, 78, 86, 223, 234, 246, 268, 272, 288
Astor Theatre (Broadway) 50, 78
Ates, Roscoe 52, 67–68, 78, 269–271
Atkinson, Roy 22
Atwill, Lionel 73
Auer, John H. 80, 274
Auer, Mischa 193, 270

Auld, Georgie 225
Austin, Gene 86, 272
"Avalon" (song) 105
Ayres, Lew 44, 236, 246

Babes in Toyland (1934 film) 160
Baby Cyclone (play) 16
Bacon, Irving 198–199, 271–272, 282
Bacon, Lloyd 28, 268
Baer, Max 66, 271
"The Bagman" (television episode) 253, 294
Bahr, Hermann 8
Bailey, Anne Howard 229, 288
Bainter, Fay 69
Baker, Fay 209, 283
Baker, Frances "Frankie" 130–131
Baker, Kenny 147, 298
Baker, Phil 86, 271
Bakewell, William 26, 28, 148, 268–269, 279
Bal, Jean 229
Baldwin, Earl 59–61, 270, 299
Baldwin, Joseph Clark 198
Baldwin, Walter 176, 280
Bale, Christian 44
Ball, Lucille 141, 144, 146–147, 242, 277, 291
Ballard, Lucien 117, 120, 139, 275, 277
Balsam, Martin 236, 243, 247
Bancroft, George 54
Bankhead, Tallulah 11, 80, 303
Banky, Vilma 18
Banner, Bob 223, 239, 287, 289, 293
Bari, Lynn 94, 105, 273
Barker, Bob 256
Barker, Michael 152
Barlow, Reginald 59, 66
Barnes, Binnie 86–**87**, 176, 271
Barnes, Joanna 251
Barnett, Griff 207, 301
Barnett, Sanford 182–183, 185, 188, 299–300
Barnett, Vince 95, 105, 273, 280
Barrett, Lawrence 7
Barrie, Wendy 112, 136, 141–142, 144, 277
Barry, Gene 142
Barry, Patricia 209, 239, 283, 290
Barrymore, John 11, 23, 25–26, 29, 44, 71, 111, 268, 274
Barrymore, Lionel 11, 52, 55, 84, 97, 99–102, 153, 273, 303
Barthelmess, Richard 25, 54, 104, 268
Bartholomae, Philip 8
Bartlett, Hall 224–226, 283

Basie, William "Count" 179
The Bat (1926 film) 44
The Bat (1920 play) 41–42
The Bat Whispers (1930 film) 40–45, **42**, **43**, 230, 269
Bates, Jeanne 183, 280, 291
Batman (1989 film) 44
Batman Begins (2005 film) 44
"The Battler" (television episode) 223
Baxter, Anne 188, 246, 279, 299
Baxter, Warner 21, 44, 59, 66, 94, 102, 104, 136, 150, 195
Beal, John 238, 259, 289
Beal, Royal 247, 306
Beale Street Boys 86–87, 272
Beattie, Jim 263, 284
Beaudine, William 245
Beaumont, Gerald 90, 272
Beckett, Scotty 103–**104**, 122, 133, 273, 276–277
Beery, Noah 26, 268
Beery, Wallace 35–**38**, 41, 80, 94, 99, 106, 142–144, **143**, 269, 277, 298
Beethoven, Ludwig van 8
Begley, Ed 240, 306
Behind Office Doors (1931 film) 52
Belasco, David 7–8, 16, 31, 200, 235, 306
Belasco Theatre 8, 307
Belkin, Gary 258, 297
Bell, Art 164, 279
Bell, James 62, 270, 283
Bellamy, Ralph 63, 66, 69, 80, 86, 94, 102, 119, 124, 139–**140**, 152, 179, 214, 246, 251, 256, 277, 291
Bellaver, Harry 220, 243–245
Bellini, Cal 239, 290–291
The Beloved Traitor (1918 film) 10–**11**, 35, 267
Ben Casey (television series) 246–247, 265, 291–292
Ben Verschleiser Productions 57–58, 270
Benaderet, Bea 213–214, 300–302
Benchley, Robert 185, 273, 276
Bendix, William 185
Benedict, Howard 144
Benedict, William "Billy" 158, 181, 278–280
Bennett, Bern 239, 289
Bennett, Joan 52, 54, 102, 256, 296
Bennett, Whitman 12, 267
Benny, Jack 80, 124
Bentkover, Jack 217, 285
Bergen, Edgar 166, 203, 207, 301
Bergen, Ned 208

Index

Bergen, Polly 239–240, 289–290
Bergerman, Stanley 82–83, 87, 272
Berigan, Bunny 225
Berke, William 181, 187, 190, 278, 280–281
Berkeley, Busby 65
Berlinger, Warren 236, 306
Berman, Pandro S. 116
Bernardi, Hershel 254, 294
Bernstein, Morey 230
Bevan, Billy 71
Biberman, Abner 247, 278
The Bickersons (radio show) 218
Bickford, Charles 52, 54, 63, 106, 108, 150–151, 198, 246, 278
The Big House (1930 film) 11, 35–39, *36*, *38*, 44–45, 50–51, 54, 56, 61, 77, 99, 101, 106, 133, 142, 224, 269
The Big Steal (1949 film) 192, 309
The Big Trail (1930 film) 41
Billy Budd (novel) 219, 287
"Billy Budd" (television episode) 219, 265, 287
Billy the Kid (1930 film) 41
Bing Crosby Productions 246, 291
The Bing Crosby-Rosemary Clooney Show (television show) 250, 302
Binns, Edward 214, 220–221, 247, 253, 259, 287
Bioff, William Morris "Willie" 125, 145
Biograph Studios 78–*79*, 243
Biograph Theater (Chicago) 101
Birch, Wyrley 217, 285
Birth of the Blues (1941 film) 159
The Bitter Tea of General Yen (1932 film) 57, 308
Black, Frank 127
The Black Cat (1934 film) 73, 86
"Black Is for Grief" (television show) ***234***, 289
"Black Panther" (television episode) 220, 222, 286
The Black Room (1935 film) 148–149
Blackie's Redemption (1919 film) 153
Blackmer, Sidney 11, 303
Blackstone Theatre (Chicago) 214–216, 248, 305–306
Blackwell, Carlyle 9
Blair, Aubrey 124
Blair, Janet 242, 291
Blair, Lee 246
Blandick, Clara 95, 273
Blankfort, Michael 138–139, 277

Bleifer, John 150, 277–278
Blind Alley (1939 film) 138–141, ***140***, 228, 246, 251, 277
Blind Alley (play) 138–141, 277
Blind Spot (1947 film) 204–***206***, 211, 283
The Blindness of Virtue (play) 8
Blochman, Lawrence G. 103–104, 239, 273, 289–291
Blondell, Joan 3, 59–61, ***60***, 124, 220, 234, 256, 270, 289, 295
Blondie Johnson (1933 film) 59–61, ***60***, 270
"Blow Up at Cortland" (television episode) 229, 288
Blue Denim (play) 236–***237***, 306
Blun, Gustav 8
Boardman, True 141, 298
Bob Banner Associates 251, 290–293, 297
Bob Hope Presents the Chrysler Theatre (television series) 256, 296
Bock, Edward 209, 283
The Body Snatcher (1945 film) 138
Boetticher, Oscar, Jr. "Budd" 188–190, 281
Bogart, Humphrey 61, 94, 124, 138–139, 147, 152, 179, 186, 205–206, 209, 216, 233, 266
Boland, Mary 218, 285
Boles, John 54
Boleslawski, Richard 106, 108, 119, 274
Bonanza (television series) 197
Bond, Richard 128–130, ***129***, 276
Bond, Ward 94, 110, 116–117, 220, 275
Bondi, Beulah 142, 234, 239, 289
The Boogie Man Will Get You (1942 film) 162
Boone, Richard 220
Booth, Edwin 7
Booth, John Wilkes 117
Booth Theatre (Broadway) 138
Borg, Veda Ann ***193***, 234, 281, 288
Borgnine, Ernest 258, 297
Borisoff, Norman 253, 294
Borland, Barlowe 16
Borzage, Frank 158
Bosley, Tom 239, 290, 293
Boston Blackie (literary character) 1, 3, 126, 152–155, 183, 188, 199, 203, 206, 208–209, 215, 219, 236, 239–240, 257–258, 265
Boston Blackie (1923 film) 153
Boston Blackie and the Law

(1948 film) 203–206, ***205***, 283
Boston Blackie Booked on Suspicion (1945 film) 193–195, ***194***, 282
Boston Blackie Goes Hollywood (1942 film) 169–171, ***170***, 279
Boston Blackie's Chinese Venture (1949 film) 211–***212***, ***215***, 259, 283
Boston Blackie's Little Pal (1918 film) 153
Boston Blackie's Rendezvous (1945 film) 195–197, ***196***, ***197***, 282
Boswell, Connie 155, 176
Bosworth, Hobart 39, 50–51, 268, 270
Bow, Clara 55
Bowers, Raymond 253, 294
Bowman, Lee 141, 163, 176, 198
Boy Meets Girl (1938 film) 198
"Boy Meets Girl" (radio show) 198, 300
Boyd, William 14, 17, 267
Boyd, William "Stage" 40
Boyer, Charles 38, 55–56, 270
Boylan, Malcolm Stuart 200, 278, 282–283
Boyle, Jack 152–154, 170, 278–283
Brabin, Charles 52
Brackett, Charles 128
Bradbury, Ray 220
Brady, William A. 8, 16
Brahm, John 228, 245
Branch, William E. 76
Brand, Neville 229, 236, 288–289
Brand, Phoebe 125
Brandon, Henry 119–120, 220, 275
Brandt's Theatre (Flatbush) 216, 305
Brant, Gerald C. 180
Breach of Promise (1932 film) 57–***58***, 63, 270
Breen, Joseph I. 80, 113
Bremen, Leonard 234, 288
Brennan, Walter 73, 106–***109***, 271, 274
Brenon, Herbert 28–32, 57, 269
Brent, Evelyn 24–***25***, 40, 52, 167, 268, 280
Brent, George 136, 183, 198, 299
Brentwood Service Players, Inc. 176
Breslin, Patricia 221, 287
Bretherton, Howard 26, 268
Brewer, Teresa 221, 286
Brian, Mary 63, 102, 138, 276
Brice, Fanny 80, 160, 299
Brickell, Beth 259–260, 297

Bride of Frankenstein (1935 film) 44, 73, 90
The Bridge of San Luis Rey (1929 film) 21
Bridges, Lloyd 162, 164, 279
Brinckerhoff, Burt 236–*237*, 306
Briskin, Samuel J. 125, 275, 280
Britt, Allen "Albert" 130
Britton, Barbara 180, 207, 259, 261, 299, 307
Britton, Theodore 261
The Broadway Melody (1929 film) 21
Brocco, Peter 211, 283
Broderick, Helen 106, 298
Brody, Ann 27, 268
Broekman, David 147, 271, 298
Bromfield, Louis 173
Bromley, Harald 221, 305
"Broncho Billy and the Baby" (short story) 106
Brook, Clive 54, 57, 63
Brook, Peter 223, 287
Brooke, Van Dyke 10, 267
Brooks, Phyllis **91**, 176, 272, 276
Brooks, Rand 172, 277, 280
Brothers (1930 film) 40
Brothers (play) 24
Brown, Anne 228
Brown, Charles D. 187, 281
Brown, Helen 108, 274
Brown, Joe E. 102, 135, 169, 171, 198, 226, 282, 299
Brown, Johnny Mack 41, 102
Brown, Martin 11, 303
Brown, Melville H. 52
Brown, Rowland 138
Brown, Russ 84, 271
Browne, George 148
Browning, Tod 44
Bruce, Virginia 50, 92–*93*, 105, 268, 270, 272–273
Bryan, George 179, 299
Buck, Frank 122
Buck Privates (1941 film) 163
Buckingham, Jan 176, 280
Buckingham, Thomas 47, 269
Bucks County Playhouse (Pennsylvania) 256, 260–261, 306–307
Bulkeley, John D. 216
Buloff, Joseph 228–229, 305
Burdette, Gene 104, 273
Bureau of Education and Cultural Affairs [ECA] 250
Bureau of Missing Persons (1933 film) 70
Burgess, Betty 105, 273
Burke, Billie 92–*93*, 176, 272
Burke, Edwin J. 24, 268
Burke, Paul 243, 245, *291*
Burke, Richard 214, 304

Burke, Walter 219, 286
Burke's Law (television series) 197
Burnet, Dana 86
Burns, Bob 155, 281, 299
Burns, George 125, 213–214, 249, 301–302
Burns, Paul E. 204, 283
Burns, William J. 47
Burns International Detective Agency 47
Burr, Raymond 158
Burton, David 53, 94–96, 273
Burton, Frederick 72, 271
Burton, Richard 266
Burton, Tim 44
Busch, Mae 17–18, 61, 268, 270
Bush, Katherine 55
Bushman, Francis X. 9, 207, 301
Bushman, Francis X. Jr. 89, 272
"Busman's Holiday" (television episode) 259–260, 297
Butler, Robert 253, 257, 294, 296–297
Butterworth, Charles 167, 169
By Candlelight (1933 film) 90
Byron, Walter 54, 270

Cabanne, Christy 96
Cabin in the Sky (Broadway show) 155
Cabot, Bruce 52, 133–134, 208, 276
Cabot, Sebastian 246, 291
Cady, Jerome "Jerry" 141–142, 147, 277
Cagney, Frances 97, 119, 152
Cagney, James 24, 57, 59–60, 63, 69–70, 75–76, 78, 86, 93–94, 97, 102–103, 109, 112–113, 116, 118–119, 124–125, 128, 138, 147, 152, 178–179, 186, 197–198, 216, 272
Cagney, Jeanne 179
Cahn, Edward L. 231, 233, 284
Cahn, Philip 73, 90, 271–272
Cahoon, Richard 113, 274
The Caine Mutiny Court-Martial (play) 229, 243, 245, 256, 260, 265, 305–307
California Shipbuilding Corporation "Calship" 187
Call My Bluff (television game show) 257, 296
Call Out the Marines (1942 film) 192
Call the Doctor (play) 16
Calleia, Joseph 97, 99–102, **100**, 140–142, 273, 277
Calling All Cars (radio show) 128, 304
Calm Yourself (1935 film) 94

Cameo Theatre (television show) 217, 285
Cameron, Rod 157, 278
Campbell, Gerald 78, 298
Campbell, Muriel 138
Canal Zone (1942 film) 162–164, **163**, 170, 279
Canby, Linda 247, 292
Candid Camera (television series) 251–252, 258, 292–293, 297
The Candid Microphone (radio show) 251
Canfield, Curtis 217, 285
Cantor, Eddie 54, 69, 75, 86, 102–103, 272
Cantor, Lew 69
Capra, Frank 39, 57, 95, 112, 116, 123, 128
Captured (television series) 222, 287
Carewe, Arthur Edmund 44
Carewe, Edwin 57
Carey, Harry Jr. 110
Carey, Harry Sr. 54, 57, 94, 106, 109–110, 131, 276
Carleton, Claire 200, 282
Carleton, George M. 193, 282
Carlisle, Kitty 220, 239–240, 253, 286, 289–290, 294
Carlisle, Mary 78
Carlyle, Richard 26, 268
Carnovsky, Morris 125
Carol, Sue 18
Carousel Theater (West Covina) 257, 307
Carr, John Dickson 220
Carr, Mary 12, 267
Carradine, David 259
Carradine, John 44, 141–142, 219–221, 231, 277
Carrigan, Thomas 153, 303
Carrillo, Leo 88, 111–112, 120–121, 146, 272, 274–275
Carrington, Elaine Stern 17, 267
Carrington, Helen 14
Carroll, Nancy 54, 94, 128
Carroll, Richard 141–142, 277
Carson, Jack 128, 276
Carson, Johnny 236, 258, 289, 297
Carter, Jack 217, 290
Carter, Janis 189–**190**, 198–**199**, 209, 219, 222, 281–282, 287
Carter, O. C. 180
Carter, Ray 221, 286
The Case of Sergeant Grischa (1930 film) 28–32, **30**, **32**, 44, 47, 248, 269
Casella, Alberto 34
Cass, Peggy 257, 296
Cass Theatre (Detroit) 214, 305

Cassavetes, John 228, 236, 256, 296
Cassini, Oleg 242, 291
Castle, William 41, 183, 280
"Castles in Spain" (television episode) 253, 294-295
The Cat and the Canary (1927 film) 44
The Cat and the Canary (1922 play) 44
Cat People (1942 film) 4
Catherine the Great (1934 film) 78, 298
"Catherine the Great" (radio show) 78, 298
The Cavalcade of America (radio show) 207, 301
Cavalcade of Stars (television show) 217, 285
Cavallero, Carmen 179
Cavanagh, Paul 103
Cavanaugh, James P. 234, 289
Cavane, Alice 145
Cawthorn, Joseph 124, 270
Center Stage (television series) 229
Chains (play) 16
Chamberlain, Richard 256, 295
The Chance of a Lifetime (1943 film) 183-**184**, 280
Chandler, Janet 53
Chaney, Lon Jr. 94, 138, 220
Chaney, Lon Sr. 17, 35, 44, 51
Chanslor, Roy 185, 187, 281, 299
Chaplin, Charles 50, 54, 105
Chapman, Marguerite 198, 282
Charlie Chan at the Opera (1936 film) 111
The Charlie McCarthy Show (radio show) 203, 207, 301
Charters, Spencer 41-**42**, 269, 278
Chatterton, Ruth 44-45
Cheating Cheaters (play) 8
Checkmate (television series) 245-246, 291
Chevalier, Maurice 66, 271
Chicago Flower and Garden Show 258, 264
Chicago Theatre 130
"Child of a Night" (television episode) 254, 294
"Child of Trouble" (television episode) 234, 289
Chiles, Linden 255, 295
Chodorov, Jerome 117, 275
Chopin, Frédéric 8
Christie, Agatha 220
A Christmas Carol (1938 film) 104
Chrysler, Walter P. 78, 298
Churchill, Berton 52, 63, 67, 271

Churchill, Winston 179
Ciannelli, Eduardo 128, 130, 176, 236, 243-244, 276, 291
Cimarron Strip (television series) 259, 297
The Circular Staircase (novel) 41
The Cisco Kid and the Lady (1939 film) 94
Claire, Ina 25
Clare, Phyllis 52
Clark, Charles Dow 41-**42**, 269-270
Clark, Dick 252, 256, 295
Clark, Don 191
Clark, Fred 142
Clark, Jack 251
Clark, Wallis 119, 271, 274-275
Clark, Willis Henry 130
Clarke, Mae 57-**58**, 84-86, **85**, 270-271, 275
Clayworth, June 82
Climax! (television series) 229
Cline, Charles 41
Clive, Colin 58-59, 71
Clooney, Rosemary 250, 302
Clork, Harry 94, 273
A Close Call for Boston Blackie (1946 film) 200-202, **201**, 282
Coast Guard (1939 film) 94
Cobb, Lee J. 243
Coburn, Charles 141
Cochran, Steve 193-197, **194**, **196**, 282
The Cock-Eyed World (1929 film) 192-193
Cock of the Air (1932 film) 47-49, **48**, 269
Codd, Jack 76
Cody, Lew 66, 271
Cody, William F. "Buffalo Bill" 222
Coe, Charles Francis 88, 272
Cohan, George M. 3, 11, 14-16, 18, 50, 270, 303-304
Cohen, Emanuel 66
Cohen, Larry 247, 258, 297
Cohn, Harry 39, 117, 119, 123, 125, 217
Colbert, Claudette 16, 31, 41, 102, 104, 304
Coldeway, Anthony 136, 276
Cole, Buddy 251, 302
Coleman, Dabney 257, 296
Coleman, Nancy 228
Collier, Buster 50
Collier, William Jr. 12, 267-268, 303
Collier, William Sr. 26, 52, 55
Collins, Frank J. 59
Collins, Russell 239, 289
Collyer, Bud 239-240, 289
Collyer, June 63, 75, 276

Colman, Ronald 4, 22, 34, 44, 94, 123, 148
Colonna, Jerry 193
Columbia Pictures 39-40, 52, 57, 94-95, 113, 115-121, 123, 125-126, 138-140, 152-155, 157-159, 162-166, 169-171, 176-178, 183-184, 187-212, 217, 222, 231, 247, 265, 274-283, 309
Comandini, Adele 27, 268
Come On, Marines! (1934 film) 53, 308
"The Comedian" (1958 television episode) 230
Compson, Betty 25, 28-29, **32**, 40, 51, 268-269
Conan Doyle, Arthur 153, 220
The Concert (play) 8
Coney Island (1943 film) 188
"Coney Island" (radio show) 188
Confessions of Boston Blackie (1942) 157-**159**, 162, 278-279
Connelly, Walter 119
Conreid, Hans 207
Considine, John W. 88, 272
Considine, Tim 226, 284
Conte, Richard 243, 246
"The Contenders" (television episode) 251, 292
Converse, Frank 258-259, 297
The Convict's Code (1930 film) 39
Conway, Jack 54-56, 88, 270, 272
Conway, Morgan 181, 280
Conway, Tom 231, 233, 284
Coogan, Jackie 50
Coogan, Robert 50-51, 270
Cook, Barbara 256, 295
Cook, Donald 24
Cook, Fielder 229, 239, 242, 289, 291
Cooke, Alistair 223, 287
Coolidge, Philip 229, 288
Cooper, Gary 25, 44, 50, 54, 58, 86, 272
Cooper, Jackie 123, 167, 218, 287, 298
Cooper, Violet Kemble 111, 274
Cooper, Wyllis 219
Coppel, Alec 220, 286
The Copperhead (play) 10-11, 303
Corbett, Glenn 252, 254, 293-294
Corey, Wendell 229-230, 288, 292
Cormack, Bartlett 24, 268
Coronet Blue (television series) 258-**259**, 297

Coronet Little Show (radio show) 183, 299
Coronet Theatre (Broadway) 234
Correll, Charles 185, 190, 299–300
Corrigan, Emmett 7, 45, 269
Corrigan, Lloyd 119, 158, 164, 169–170, 183, 185, 187, 189, 194–195, 278–282
Cort Theatre (Broadway) 228, 240, 305–306
Cortez, Ricardo 52, 86, 88
Cory, Ray 188
Costello, Dolores 3, 18, 23, 25–26, 40, 268
Costello, Lou 118, 163, 179
Cotten, Joseph 182, 246, 299
Counsellor-at-Law (1933 film) 71
Counterfeit (1936 film) 113–**114**, 120, 133, 274
Courtenay, William 44, 268
Cowan, Jerome 198–199, 282
Cram, Mildred 53, 270
Craven, Frank 84–85, 271
Crawford, Broderick 138
Crawford, Joan 44, 54, 66, 97, 102, 124–125, 138, 147, 240, 271
Crawford, Lester 106, 298
Crawley, Paul Roe 41–42, 269
Crazylegs (1953 film) 224, 226
Crees, James 28
Crehan, Joseph 189, 200, 281–283
Crespo, José 38
Crime (play) 16–17, 73, 80, 128, 304
The Criminal Code (play) 35
Crisp, Donald 155, 226, 299
Criterion Theatre (Broadway) 10–11, 303
Cromwell, John 119, 229–230, 288
Crooked Alley (1923 film) 153
Crosby, Bing 124, 146, 155, 159, 177, 250, 298–299, 302
Crosland, Alan 102–103
Crosland, Alan Jr. 247
Cross, Milton 127
Crouse, Russell 214, 305
Cry of the Werewolf (1944 film) 195
Cugat, Xavier 179
Cukor, George 104, 111, 274
Cullen, Bill 220, 256, 286, 295
Culver, Roland 253, 295
Cunningham, Joe 160, 279
Curran Theatre (San Francisco) 236, 306
Currier, Mary 209, 283
Curtis, Alan 166

Curtis, Tony 265–266
Curtis-Wright Flying Service 49
Curtiz, Michael 73, 75

Dailey, Irene 257, 307
Dailey, Jack F. 174, 280
"Daisy Bell (Bicycle Built for Two)" (song) 26
Dale, Esther 167, 279
Damita, Lili 52, 105, 179, 273
Dana, Barbara 238, 289
The Dancer (play) 8
Dancing in the Dark (1949 film) 211
D'Ancona, Miranda 236, 253, 306
Dandridge, Ruby 182, 299
Danger (television series) 218, 285, 287
Danger Street (1947 film) 162
Daniell, Henry 219
Daniels, Victor "Chief Thunder Cloud" 102
Danton, Ray 218, 285
The Dark Knight (2008 film) 44
The Dark Knight Rises (2012 film) 44
Dark Mountain (1944 film) 187, 309
The Dark Past (1948 film) 139
The Dark Tower (play) 214, 231, 304–305
Darnell, Linda 169, 171, 207, 299
Darro, Frankie 70, 234, 388
Da Silva, Howard 253, 294
Davies, Marion 102, 105, 273
Davis, Bette 70, 73, 93, 102, 276
Davis, Forrest 133, 276
Davis, James E. 128
Davis, Ossie 247, 253
Davis, Owen 8
Davis, Robert Hobart 50, 270
Davis, Sammy Jr. 258, 297
Dawson, Hal K. 69, 282
Day, Laraine 176, 220, 236, 288–289
Day, Richard 49, 269
Death Takes a Holiday [*La Morte in vacanza*] (play) 34
Death Takes a Holiday (1934 film) 34
DeCamp, Rosemary 169, 299
De Cordoba, Pedro 111, 274, 277
De Corsia, Ted 255, 295
Deering, Olive 218, 220, 285–286, 291
The Defenders (television series) 247, 253, 257–258, 292, 294, 296
De Gaulle, Charles 179
De Grasse, Sam 153

Dein, Edward 195, 282
Dekker, Thomas 253
Del Rio, Dolores 102, 116, 216, 275
DeMille, Beatrice 7
DeMille, Cecil B. 7, 14, 182–183, 185, 188, 267, 299–300
DeMille, Henry C. 7
DeMille, William C. 7, 53
DeMille Pictures Corporation 14, 267
Dennis, Sandy 256, 296
Denny, Reginald 111, 274, 276
Depp, Johnny 102
DeRahm, Whitney 125
Dern, Bruce 243
De Sano, Marcel 55
Desilu Studios 246
The Desperate Hours (1955 film) 139
The Desperate Hours (play) 139, 228
DeSylva, Buddy 105
Detective Story (play) 214–216, 233, 236, 248, 265, 305–306
Detour (1945 film) 176
The Devil Commands (1941 film) 157
Devil's Playground (1937 film) 116–118, **117**, 132, 192, 275
The Devil's Squadron (1936 film) 113
Devine, Andy 84–85, 271–272, 274
Devine, Jerry 136, 243, 291, 298
Dewey, Thomas 133–134, 249
Diagnosis: Unknown (television series) 239–240, 251, 253, 265, 289–291
Dickens, Charles 193, 220
Dickerson, Dudley 176, 280, 282
Dies, Martin Jr. 216
Diessl, Gustav 38
Dietrich, Marlene 78, 104, 171, 275
Digges, Dudley 71, 86
Dillaway, Donald 16, 304
Dillinger (1945 film) 202–203
Dillinger, John 99, 101–102, 202–203
Dillingham, Charles 16
Dillon, John Francis 23, 268
Dinehart, Alan 11, 303
Dirigible (1931 film) 39
Disraeli (1929 film) 37
Ditrichstein, Leo 8
The Divorcée (1930 film) 31–35, **33**, 38, 50, 56, 77, 91, 269
Dix, Richard 116–118, **117**, 124, 131–133, **132**, 136, 144, 146–147, 192, 208, 275–277

Dmytryk, Edward 157, 159, 216, 278
Dobkin, Lawrence 243, 251, 292
The Doctor (television series) 229
Dr. Kildare (television series) 251, 256, 295
Dr. Socrates (1935 film) 93
Dodsworth (play) 69
"Dolly's Dilemma" (television episode) 256, 295
"Dolores" (song) 157
Donald, Peter 239, 289
Donath, Ludwig 253
Donlevy, Brian 179, 299
Donnell, Jeff 200, **202**, 283
Donnie Brasco (1997 film) 102
"Don't Mention My Name in Sheboygan" (television episode) 256, 295
Don't Tell (play) 16
Dooley, Bill 130
Dorn, Philip 176
Dorsey, Tommy 157
Double Exposure (1944 film) 190–191
Doubleday, Kay 247, 306
Douglas, Kirk 217
Douglas, Melvyn 44, 71, 147, 246, 256
Dove, Billie 47–49, **48**, 52, 269
Dowling, Constance 203–206, **205**, **206**, 283
Dowling, Doris 206
Dowling, Joseph J. 51
Downey Sisters 86–87, 272
Downs, Cathy 231, 284
Downs, Johnny 105, 273
Doyne, John 248
Dracula (1931 film) 44, 73
Drake, Dona 159
Dratler, Jay 153, 157, 278
The Dream Maker (play) 16
Dreifuss, Arthur 193, 195, 282
Dressed to Kill (play) 214, 304
Dressler, Marie 66
Drew, Ellen 159, 184
Drury, Allen 240–241, 306
Drury Lane Theatre (Chicago) 249, 306
Dubin, Charles S. 255, 295
Duff, Howard 207, 301
Duffy, Albert 138–139, 277
Duffy, Jack 105, 273
Duffy's Tavern (radio show) 213, 301
Duggan, Andrew 259, 297
Dumas, Alexandre 220
Duna, Steffi 146, 277
Dunbar, Helen 9
Duncan, Todd 226–228, 283–284
Duning, George 245

Dunlap, Scott R. 178
Dunn, J. Allan 106
Dunn, James 75, 246, 277
Dunne, Irene 14, 124
Durante, Jimmy 66, 86
Durbin, Deanna 167, 169, 185, 299
Durkin, Gertrude 141
Durston, David E. 220, 287
Duryea, Dan 236, 243, 246, 289
Duryea, Etta Terry 260
Duvall, Robert 243, 247
Dvorak, Ann 66, 93, 135, 139–**140**, 277

Earhart, Amelia 183
Earle, Edward 191, 274, 278–281, 284
East Side/West Side (television series) 255, 295
Eastwood, Clint 241–242, 291
Ebeling, George 262, 284
Eburne, Maude 41–44, **42**, 269, 280
Eddy, Nelson 207, 301
Edison Manufacturing Company 9
Edwards, Vince 246–247, 291
Edwin, Walter 8, 303
Ehrlich, Max 247, 292
Eilers, Sally 28, 102–**104**, 268–269, 273
Eisenhower, Dwight D. 217
Eisley, Anthony 229, 288
Ekberg, Anita 142
Eldredge, John 146–147, 277
Eldridge, Florence 32, 34, 125, 128, 269
The Eleventh Hour (television series) 251, 292
Ellenstein, Robert 221, 287
Elliott, Denholm 259
Ellison, James 141, 176
Ellsler, Effie 23, 268
Eltinge 42nd Street Theatre (Broadway) 16, 304
Embarrassing Moments (1934 film) 73, 82–**83**, 85, 87, 96, 272
Emery, Gilbert 16
Empire Theatre (Broadway) 16
"The Empty Chute" (television episode) 247, 292
The Empty Sleeve (radio show) 218, 302
English, Marla 231, 274
Englund, George 217, 285
Enright, Ray 59, 63–64, 198, 270–271, 281
Entwistle, Peg 14, 274
Errol, Leon 86, 94–95, 102, 105, 273
Erskine, Chester 78–81, 130, 274

Erskine, Howard 228
Erwin, Stuart 75, 183, 272, 276, 299
Espionage (television series) 253, 294–295
Essex, Harry 203, 246, 283
Ethel Barrymore Theatre (Broadway) 228
Etting, Ruth 86–87, 271
Evans, Dale 207
Evans, Madge 94, 111–**112**, 274
Every Day's a Holiday (1937 film) 94
The Exciters (play) 11, 303
"An Expensive Glass of Water" (television episode) 246–247, 265, 291–292
Extra (play) 11, 303
Ex-Wife (novel) 31, 33, 269
The Face Behind the Mask (1941 film) 158
The Face in the Fog (1922 film) 153
Fain, Sammy 228
Fairbanks, Douglas Jr. 23, 25–26, 125, 268
Fairbanks, Douglas Sr. 44, 50
Falk, Peter 243
The Family Cupboard (play) 8
Family Theatre (radio show) 207, 301
Famous Players-Lasky Corporation 51
Fantl, Richard 166, 279–283
Farnham, Joe 35, 269
Farrar, Jane 191, 281
Farrell, Charles 18, 158, 208
Farrell, Glenda 70, 124, 141, 219, 242, 246, 276, 286, 291, 298
Farrow, John 141–142, 173, 277
Farrow, Mia 257
Fast Life (1929 film) 23–24, 268
Fast Life (play) 16–17, 73, 268, 304
Faulkner, William 220
Fawcett, George 10, 267, 303
Fay, Frank 26, 268
Faye, Alice 86, 94, 272
Federal Bureau of Investigation [FBI] 47, 98
Federal Kidnapping Act ["Little Lindbergh Law"] 103
Federal Theatre Project [FTP] 197
Fejös, Pál 38
Fellows, Edith 220, 287
Felton, Norman 221, 286–287, 289, 295
Fenton, Leslie 24, 135, 268
Ferber, Nat 94, 273
Ferréol (play) 7
Ferris, Walter 34
Field, Betty 243, 246

Field, Marshall 78, 298
Field, Sid 183
Fielder, Richard 246
Fields, W. C. 94
The Fifth Season (play) 228–229, 305
Fifty Fathoms Deep (1931 film) 116
The Fighting Marines (1935 serial) 94
Filmways Studios 247, 253, 257
Fine, Sylvia 193
Fisk, Edwin M. 10
Fitzgerald, Barry 137, 277
Fitzgerald, F. Scott 55, 220, 270
Five Came Back (1939 film) 141–142, 242, 277
Fix, Paul 133, 166, 276, 279
Flaherty, Pat 82–83, 274
Flavin, Martin 35, 269
Flegenheimer, Arthur "Dutch Schultz" 133, 243
Fleming, Eric 241–242, 291
Fleming, Jim 239–240, 290
Fletcher, Bramwell 253, 259
Fletcher, Lucille 219, 286
"The Fliers" (television episode) 256–257, 296
Flight for Freedom (1943 film) 183
"Flight for Freedom" (radio show) 183, 299
Flight from Glory (1937) 125–127, *126*, 153, 275
Flores, Carmen 223, 287
Flores, Lola 223, 287
Flynn, Errol 61, 105, 273
Foch, Nina 195–*196*, 219, 238, 246, 282, 289
Fonda, Henry 104, 185, 229, 247
Fonda, Jane 242, 291
Fonda, Peter 243
Fong, Benson 211, 283
Fong, Gloria "Maylia" 211–*212*, *215*, 283
Fontaine, Joan 131–*132*, 251, 257–258, 276, 292, 296–297
Fontana, D. C. 247
Footlight Parade (1933 film) 59
Foran, Dick 163, 276
Forbes, Harry 96
Forbes, Ralph 111, 274
Ford, John 54, 106, 110, 112, 117, 120, 136, 138, 155, 216, 227
Ford, Paul 259
Ford, Wallace 86, 138, 188, 251, 272, 280, 292
The Ford Television Theatre (television series) 229
Forrest, Frank 127
Forrest, Sam 16, 304
Forrest, William 204, 209, 281, 283

Foster, Lewis R. 160, 271, 279
Foster, Norman 52, 276
Four Walls (play) 86
The Fourth Degree (play) 221–223, 305
Fowley, Douglas 148, 160, 183, 271–273, 278–280
The Frances Langford-Don Ameche Show (television show) 218–219, 286
Francis, Alec B. 28, 269
Francis, Anne 251, 292
Francis, Kay 102, 136, 185
Franciscus, James 245
Frankenstein (1910 film) 9
Frankenstein (1931 film) 44, 51, 73, 147
Frankie and Johnnie (1936 film) 76, 78–82, *79*, 130–131, 243, 274
"Frankie and Johnny" (song) 55, 130–131
"Frankie Killed Allen" (song) 130
Franklin, Paul 141, 298
Franklin, Peg 11, 303
Fred Miller Theatre (Milwaukee) 233, 306
Freed, Ralph 181
Freud, Sigmund 29, 139, 221
Freund, Karl 73, 86, 101, 271
Friderici, Blanche 52
Friedman, Seymour 209–210, 283
Friganza, Trixie 14, 267
Frohman, Bert 125
Frohman, Charles 16
Frohman, Daniel 200
Fuchs, Daniel 188, 299
Fulbright, J. William 250
Fulbright-Hays Act 250
Fuller, Lance 231, 284
Fulton, John P. 86
Fulton Theatre (Broadway) 44
Funny Lady (1975 film) 162
Funt, Allen 251–252, 292–293, 297

"G" Men (1935 film) 97
Gable, Clark 57–58, 75, 78, 80, 86, 88, 91, 102, 119, 124, 135, 178, 198, 207, 298
Gaboriau, Émile 9
Gahagan, Helen 16
Gaige, Russell 247, 306
Gaines, Richard 190, 281
Gaither, Gant 222, 305
Gallaudet, John 114, 117, 155, 157, 274–275, 278
Gambler's Choice (1944 film) 184–187, *186*
Gandhi, Mahatma 116
The Gang Buster (1931 film) 40

Gang Busters (television series) 222, 287
Garbo, Greta 31, 44, 54, 124–125
Gardenia, Vincent 222, 253, 305
Gardiner, Reginald 166–167
Garfield, John 169, 299
Garland, Judy 167, 169, 258, 297, 299
Garnett, Tay 245
Garr, Eddie 145
Garrett, Oliver H. P. 183, 299
Gaudio, Tony 61, 270
Gay, Alden 63
The Gay Bride (1934 film) 88–*90*, 272
Gaynor, Janet 158
Genii (magazine) 78, 128
Gentle Ben (novel) 259
Gentle Ben (television series) 259–260, 297
George, Anthony 245–246, 291
George, Gladys 186
Geray, Steven 204, 283
Get the Message (television game show) 256, 295
Gethers, Steve 242, 290
The Ghost of Frankenstein (1942 film) 118
Gibbons, Cedric 21, 39, 269–270, 272–274, 277
Giblyn, Charles 12, 267–268
Gibson, Hoot 94, 106
Gibson, Wynne 40, 54, 222, 305
Gielgud, John 245
Gifford, Max 145–146
Gift of Gab (1934 film) 86–*87*, 271–272
Gilbert, John 22
Gilbert, Lou 215
Gillespie, Dizzy 217, 285
Gillette, William 16
Gillingwater, Claude 113, 274
Gilroy, Frank D. 257, 307
Ging, Jack 251, 292
Giraud, Henri 179
The Girl and the Gambler (1939 film) 146
Girl from God's Country (1940 film) *150*–151, 278
The Girl of the Golden West (play) 235, 306
Gish, Dorothy 239, 289
Gish, Lillian 80
Gist, Robert 242, 291
The Glass Key (1935 film) 53, 308
"The Glass Palace" (television episode) 251, 292
Gleason, Jackie 217
Gleason, James 22, 102, 119, 275
Gleason, Lucile 22, 75, 102, 112, 124, 145, 147
Glenn, Raymond 153

Godfrey, Arthur 251
Godfrey, Peter 209, 212
"The Gold-Diggers' Song (We're in the Money)" (song) 105
Goldbeck, Willis 52
Goldberg, Lou 80, 274
Goldberg, Mel 255, 295
Golden, John 11, 303
The Golden Age (play) 253
Golden Globe Awards 230, 261
Golden Harvest (1933 film) 66–**68**, 73, 271
Golden State Productions 230, 284
The Golden West (1932 film) 52–53, 65
Goldsmith, Martin 204, 283
Goldwyn, Samuel 10, 34, 76, 193, 267
Goldwyn Pictures Corporation 10, 35, 267
Gone with the Wind (1939 film) 94
Goode, Richard 220, 286
Goodman, Benny 225
Goodman, Jules Eckert 16
Goodrich, Arthur 11, 303
Goodrich, John F. 23, 57, 268, 270
Goodson, Mark 222–223, 233, 239, 251, 256, 286–290, 292–297
Goodwin, Bill 213–214, 301–302
Goodwin, Harold 39, 274, 276
Goodwins, Leslie 144
Gorcey, Leo 174
Gordon, Alex 230–232, 284
Gordon, Anita 207, 301–302
Gordon, Bruce 234, 289
Gordon, C. Henry 52, 273
Gordon, Dexter 225, 284
Gordon, Gale 214, 301
Gordon, Mack 66
Gordon, Max 69
Gordon, Michael 169, 216, 279
Gordon, Robert 204, 283
Gosden, Freeman 185, 190, 299–300
Gottshalk, Ferdinand 65
Goudal, Jetta 14, 267
Gould, Thomas C. 145, 152
Grable, Betty 188
Grahame, Margot 113–**114**, 123, 274, 276
Granach, Alexander 167, 280
Granet, Bert 128, 276
Granger, Farley 247–248, 250, 306
Grant, Cary 54, 66, 86, 104–105, 124, 141, 176, 198, 270–271, 273
Grant, James Edward 185, 281
Grant, Kathryn 226, 284
Grant, Lawrence 62

Grant, Lee 214
Grant, Ulysses S. 222
Grapewin, Charley 103
Grauer, Ben 127
Grauman, Sid 66, 271
Grauman, Walter E. 255, 295
Grauman's Chinese Theatre 18, 261
Graves, Ralph 39, 190, 281
The Great Divide (play) 10
The Great Man's Lady (1942 film) 181–182
"The Great Man's Lady" (radio show) 181–182, 299
"The Great Merlini" (television episode) 217–218, 285
The Great White Hope (1970 film) 4, 260–263, 284
Green, Alfred E. 59, 115–116, 275
Green, Harry 52
Green, Howard J. 116, 171, 176, 275, 280
Green, Jackie 145
Green, Mitzi 167
Greene, Harrison 189, 270, 278, 281
Greenwood, M. E. 215
Gregory, James 220–221, 253, 286, 305
Gresham, Edith 16, 304
Grey, John 128
Grey, Virginia **143**–144, 277
Gribbon, Eddie 41
Griffith, D. W. 16–17, 78
Griffith, Eleanor 17–20, **19**, 268, 298
Grinde, Nick 31, 269
Grizzard, George 242, 291
Der große Krieg der weißen Männer [*The Great War of the White Men*] (novel cycle) 29
Guilfoyle, Paul 126, 130, 132, 137, 275–277
Gulager, Clu 247
Gulf Coast Air Training Center 180
Gunn, Moses 255, 284, 295
Guy-Blanché, Alice 9

Hackett, Joan 247, 290
Hackett, Raymond 11, 303
Hackman, Gene 247
Hagman, Larry 239, 290
Hailey, Arthur 233, 288
Haislip, Harvey S. 143, 277
Hal Roach Studios 138, 160
Hale, Alan 137, 277
Hale, Barbara 226–227, 283
Haley, Jack 80, 301
Hall, Alexander 53–54, 270
Hall, Charles D. 73, 271
Hall, James 50

Hallor, Ray 23, 267–268
Halton, Charles 69
Hamilton, Cosmo 8
Hamilton, Hale 14, 304
Hamilton, John 139, 275, 277, 280
Hamilton, Neil 21, 50, 63
Hammil, Joel 221, 28
Hampden, Walter 219, 286
Hampton, Grayce 41, **43**, 269
Hanna Theatre (Cleveland) 247
Hard to Handle (1933 film) 59
The Hard Way (1943 film) 188
"The Hard Way" (radio show) 188, 299–300
Hardie, Russell 88
Harding, Ann 54, 69, 75, 78, 86, 102–103, 239, 272, 289
Hardwicke, Cedric 178, 220
Hardy, Oliver 4, 17, 105, 169, 171, 199, 299
Hardy, Sam 88, **90**, 272
Harford, Margaret 257–258
Hargrave, Roy 138, 141
Harlow, Jean 3, 47, 54–57, **56**, 66, 88, 104, 124–125, 270–271
Harmon, John 183, 278, 280
Harrigan, William 16, 71, **79**, 81, 274, 304, 308
Hart, Moss 80, 274
Hart, William S. 86, 153, 272
Hartman, Johnny 258, 297
Hartmann, Edmund L. 128, 276
Harvey, Paul 124, 277
Hasso, Signe 231, 253, 292, 306
Hatfield, Hurd **238**, 289
Hatton, Raymond 94–95, 106, 273
Hauptmann, Bruno 103
Hawaiian Invitational Billfish Tournament [HIBT] 263
Hawkins, Anna Gutherza 7
Hawkins, John 187, 281
Hawkins, Ward 187, 281
Hawkins, William Delos 7
Hawks, Howard 267
Hayden, Harry 195, 276, 282
Hayden, Russell 181, 281
Haydon, Julie 67, 271
Hayes, George "Gabby" 94, 147–149, 268, 278
Hayes, Joseph 139, 228
Hays, Will 162
Hayward, Louis 148
Hayworth, Rita 166, 217
Hazard, Lawrence 218, 285
Hazzard, John E. 11, 303
He Comes Up Smiling (play) 8
"He Done Me Wrong [The Death of Bill Bailey]" (song) 131
Healy, Ted 112

The Heart of the Night Wind (1914 film) 8
Heckart, Eileen 239, 289
Heflin, Van 125–*126*, 234, 275
Heggie, O. P. 44, 52
Heidt, Horace 188, 299
Helen Hayes Theatre (Broadway) 257, 259, 307
Hell's Angels (1930 film) 47, 49
Hell's Heroes (1929 film) 106–108, 110
Hemingway, Ernest 223, 287
Hemion, Dwight 258, 297
Henderson, Florence 256, 289, 295
Henderson, Skitch 233, 288, 297
Henley, Jack 199, 282
Henning, Paul 214, 301–302
Henny, Pat 238
Henry, Charlotte 160, 279
Henry, Louise 103, 272
Henry, William 92, 181–*182*, 272, 280
Henry Miller's Theatre (Broadway) 16, 307
Henry VI, Part 3 (play) 26, 268
Hepburn, Audrey 232
Herbert, Hugh 147, 167, 169, 198–199, 282, 299
Herlihy, James Leo 236–237, 306
Heroes for Sale (1933 film) 61
Herrman, Harry 233, 288
Herrmann, Bernard 236, 289
Hersholt, Jean 28, 75, 147, 269
Hervey, Irene 105, 107, 176, 273–274
Higgins, Michael 218, 285
High Explosive (1943 film) 171–*172*, 280
High Sierra (1941 film) 61
Hill, George W. 10–11, 35–39, 267, 269
Hill, Phyllis 228
Hill, Robert F. 176
Hiller, Arthur 245, 247
Hilliard, Harriet 106, 158–*159*, 162–164, *163*, 278–279, 298
Hillias, Peg 223, 288
Hillie, Verna 95, 272–273
Hillstreet Theatre (Los Angeles) 14
Hillyer, Lambert 153
Hines, Johnny 92, 272
Hingle, Pat 257, 296
Hinton, Jane 221, 305
Hirai, Juro "Joe Evergreen" 29
Hirsch, Elroy "Crazylegs" 224–226, *225*, 283
"The History of Dallas Egan" (radio episode) 128, 298
Hitchcock, Alfred 138

Hitler, Adolf 29, 144
Hobbes, Halliwell 52, 136, 219, 277
Hobbs, Peter 219, 286
Hoch, Winton C. 110
Hodges, Joy 141
Hodiak, John 229
Hoffe, Monckton 10
Hoffman, Dustin 257, 296
Hoffman, Joseph 171, 199, 280, 282
Hogan, Dick 141, 277
Hohl, Arthur 62, 270
Holbrook, Hal 259–260, 262, 284
Holden, William 139
Holiday Inn (1942 film) 177
Hollander, Frederick 161
Holloway, Sterling 59, 86, 270, 272
"The Hollywood Gad-About" (1934 short film) 86, 272
Hollywood on Parade (short-film series) 66, 271
Hollywood Playhouse (Los Angeles) 52
Hollywood Radio Previews (radio show) 86, 298
Hollywood Victory Committee 169, 171, 173, 185, 183
Holmes, Wendell 246, 291
Holt, Jack 96, 116
Holt, Tim 146
Holtz, Lou 146, 298
The Home Towners (play) 14, 304
Homeier, Skip 223, 234, 288–289
Honor of the Range (1934 film) 148
Hood, Darla 218, 285
Hopkins, Miriam 75, 94, 102, 188, 299
Hopper, Hedda 10, 59, 63, 66, 124, 267
Hopwood, Avery 8, 41–42, 269
Horn, Camilla 17
Horton, Edward Everett 23, 103, 119
Hot Pepper (1933 film) 192
Houdini, Harry 9, 144
House Committee on Un-American Activities [HUAC] 216–217
House of Dracula (1945 film) 118
House of Frankenstein (1944 film) 118
Houser, Lionel 119, 133, 275–276
How Green Was My Valley (1941 film) 155
Howard, Bronson 7

Howard, Clint 259, 297
Howard, David 53
Howard, Leslie 45, 57, 93, 111, 274
Howard, Sidney 69
Hubbard, John 162–164, 279
Hubbard, Lucien 86, 92, 270, 272–274
Huber, Harold 94, 103, 273
Hudson, Rochelle 91, 94, 124, 153, 272, 276, 278
Hudson Theatre (Broadway) 14–16, 214, 233, 304
Hughes, Howard 47–49, 52, 131–132, 269
Hughes, Jonathan 255, 295
Hughes, Lloyd 50, 270
Hughes, Rupert 8, 57, 270
Hull, Henry 145, 219–220, 243
Hull, Josephine 221
Hume, Benita 111, 274
Hundley, John 78
Hunnicutt, Arthur 183, 280
Hunt, J. Roy 52, 269
"The Hunter" (television episode) 238, 295
Hunter, Jeffrey 207
Huntley, G. P. *91*, 272
Huntley, Hugh 41, 269
Hurlbut, William J. 8
Hussey, Ruth 176
Huston, John 173
Huston, Martin 239, 290–291
Huston, Walter 69
Hutchinson, Josephine 104
Huth, Harold 58
Hyams, Leila 36, 40, 50, 55–56, 269–270
Hyland, Brian 239–240, 290
Hymer, John B. 16, 73, 128, 268, 276, 304
Hymer, Warren 1, 16, 73, 94, 271

I Am a Fugitive from a Chain Gang (1932 film) 60–61, 116
I Live on Danger (1942 film) 160–162, *161*, 279
I Promise to Pay (1937 film) 1, 119–*121*, 133, 275
I Walked with a Zombie (1943 film) 231
If I Were King (1938 film) 94
Il trovatore (opera) 111
I'll Love You Always (1935 film) 94
"I'm Afraid of You" (song) 181
In Old Arizona (1929 film) 21
"Incident on the Road to Yesterday" (television episode) 241–242, 291
Inescourt, Freda 231
The Infernal Machine (1933 film) *62*, 270–271

The Informer (1935 film) 112, 117
International Brotherhood of Magicians [IBM] 169, 208
The Invisible Man (novel) 70–71
The Invisible Man (1933 film) 44, 70–71, 73, 308
The Iron Mask (1929 film) 138
Is Matrimony a Failure? (play) 8
Island of Lost Souls (1933 film) 113
It Ain't Hay (1943 film) 118
It Happened One Night (1934 film) 116
"It's Mental Work" (television episode) 230
I've Been Around (1935 film) 90–*91*, 96, 272–273
I've Got a Secret (television game show) 220, 286, 288

Jack in the Pulpit (play) 14, 150
"Jack Sparling, Forty-six" (television episode) 223, 288
The Jackie Gleason Show (television show) 217
Jackman, Floyd 160
Jackman, Fred Jr. 160, 179, 252, 278–281, 293
Jackman, Fred Sr. 160
Jackson, Joseph 26, 268
Jackson, Thomas E. 75, 278, 281
Jacobs, Harrison 148, 278
Jacobs, W. W. 220
Jaffe, Sam 246, 291
James, Rian 86, 271
Jay, Verne 223, 288
Jenkins, Allen 60, 63, 124, 141–142, 246, 270–271, 277
Jenks, Frank 198, 282, 284
Jennings, DeWitt 37, 268–269, 271
Jennings, Talbot 111, 274
Jet Pilot (1957 film) 48
Jewell, Edward 63, 271, 281
Jewell, Isabell *91*, 272
Joby, Hans 29, 277
Johnny Presents Ginny Simms (radio show) 180–181
Johnson, Casey 142, 277
Johnson, Erskine 111, 234
Johnson, John Arthur "Jack" 260, 262
Johnson, Johnnie 180, 299
Johnson, Kay 16, 304
Johnson, Richard 253
Johnson, Rita 94, 133, 276
Johnson, Robert Lee 151, 163, 278–279
Johnson, Van 207
Johnston, Johnny 226, 284–285
Jolson, Al 23, 27–28, 80, 94, 105, 167, 178

Jolson's 59th Street Theatre (Broadway) 39
Jones, Allan 176
Jones, Buck 147–150, *149*, 178, 278
Jones, Henry 240, 306
Jones, James Earl 260–262, 284
Jordan, Dorothy 52
Jordan, Philip 202
Jory, Victor 62, 270
Journey's End (1930 film) 59
June, Ray 21, 41–42, 54, 267, 269–270, 272

Kamen, Milt 252–253, 294
Kamiyama, Sôjin 26, 268
Kandel, Judith 69
Kane, Bob 44
Kane, Joseph 67
Kanin, Garson 256, 295
The Karate Kid (1992 film) 162
Karloff, Boris 4, 44, 50–51, 67, 69–70, 73, 75–76, 86–88, *87*, 102–104, 111, 124, 147–149, 157, 162, 216, 220, 270–271
Karloff, Evelyn 216
Karns, Roscoe 39, 52, 282, 308
The Kate Smith Hour (radio show) 136, 298
The Kate Smith Hour (television show) 221, 287
Kaufman, George S. 214, 304
Kaye, Danny 193, 214
Kaye, Sammy 179
Kazan, Elia 206
Keane, Edward 160, 275, 279, 281–283
Keath, Donna 179, 299
Keaton, Buster 44, 50, 54
Keaton, Michael 44
Keegan, Fran 229, 305
Keeler, Ruby 217, 275, 285
Keep 'Em Flying (1941 film) 163
Keith, Ian 44
Keith, Isabelle 89, 272
Kellaway, Cecil 207, 276, 301
Kellerman, Sally 259
Kelly, Nancy 181–*182*, *186*–187, 190–191, 280–281
Kelly, Paul 16, 100, 273
The Ken Murray Show (television show) 217–219, 285–286
Kendall, Cy 136, 166, 176, 183, 189, 200, 277, 279–280
Kendall, Henry 58
Kenley, John 214, 229, 260, 304–305, 307
Kenley Players 214, 229, 260, 304–305, 307
Kennedy, Bill 225–226, 284
Kennedy, Caroline 241
Kennedy, Edgar 207, 271
Kennedy, John F. [JFK] 250

Kennedy, Tom 40, 269–270, 281–282
Kenton, Edwin C. 145
Kenton, Erle C. 113–114, 116–118, 274–275
Kenyon, Doris 9
Kenyon, Gwen 181, 279–280
Kern, Hal C. 21, 267, 269
Kerr, Frederick 11, 303
Kershner, Irvin 245, 247
Keystone Cops 9, 113, 116, 119
Kiley, Richard 240, 306
King, Claude 75, 78, 112, 124
King, Katie 8
King, Walter Woolf 83, 86, 272, 298
King for a Night (1933 film) 1, 70–75, *72*, 89, 96, 111, 271
King Lear (Shakespeare play) 223
King Solomon of Broadway (1935 film) 102, 308
Kingsford, Walter *79*, 81, 131, 274
Kingsley, Sidney 214, 265, 305–306
Kinnell, Murray 124
Kinoy, Ernest 247, 290
Kirby, Durward 251–252, 292–293
Kircher, Jean 108–*109*, 274
Kircher, Judith 108–*109*, 274
Kirkland, Jack 80, 130, 274
Kirkwood, James 157, 278
Klaine, Bob 258, 297
Klugman, Jack 243, 247, 253
"Knight's Gambit" (television episode) 255, 295
Knowles, Patric 141–142, 277
Knox, Frank 166
Kober, Arthur 62, 270
Kohler, Fred 46, 106, 269
Kolb, Ken 256, 295
Kolker, Henry 52, 92, 271–272, 274
Kollmar, Richard 192
Kotto, Yaphet 260
Kraft Music Hall (radio show) 146, 155, 298–299
Kraft Suspense Theatre (television series) 255, 295
Kraft Television Theatre (television series) 222, 229, 233–234, 287–289
Krasna, Norman 212, 304
Kruger, Otto 176
Kruschen, Jack 207, 301
Kummer, Clare 11, 303
Der Kurier des Zaren [*The Czar's Courier*] (1936 film) 116
Kurosawa, Akira 26
Kusnick, Harry 188

Kyne, Peter B. 106, 110, 274
Kyser, Kay 207

Lachman, Harry 75, 119
Ladd, Alan 188, 300
Ladd, David 236, 289
The Lady Esther Screen Guild Theatre (radio show) 179, 299
Lady for a Day (1933 film) 95
Lady in the Lake (1947 film) 216
Lady Killer (1933 film) 59
Laemmle, Carl Jr. 70–71, 82, 90, 271–272
Laemmle, Carl Sr. 73–74, 82
Laemmle, Edward 82–83, 272
Laine, Frankie 242, 291
Laird, Jack 247
Laire, Judson 240, 306
Lake, Veronica 185, 206
Lamb, Gil 180
Lamont, Charles 210
Lamour, Dorothy 188, 300
The Land of Joy (musical revue) 8
Landau, Martin 246, 253
Landers, Lew 125, 127–131, 133, 136, 146–147, 149, 162–164, 176, 200, 275–276, 278–280, 282
Landi, Elissa 63, 103, 123
Landis, Carole 171, 187–188, 281
Landis, Cullen 39
Landis, Frederick 11, 303–304
Lane, Allan "Rocky" 137, 277
Lane, Richard 126–127, 153–155, ***154***, 158, 164–165, 169–170, 183, 189–191, ***190***, 194–***196***, 200–201, 204, 209, 211–***212***, 275, 278–284, 300
Lane, Toni 145
Lang, Walter 40, 63, 119
Langford, Frances 147, 218–219, 286, 298
Lansbury, Edgar 257, 288, 297, 307
Larkin, John 104, 273–274
La Roy, Rita 54, 126, 133, 270, 276
Larric, Jack 8
LaRue, Jack 16, 219
Las Vegas Army Gunnery School 180
Las Vegas Nights (1941 film) 157
Lasky, Jesse L. 63
The Last Parade (1931 film) 113
Latimer, Jonathan 142
Laughing Boy (1934 film) 74
Laughton, Charles 179
Laurel, Stan 4, 17, 105, 169, 171, 199, 299

Lauren, S. K. 183, 299
Law of the Underworld (1938 film) 128–130, ***129***, 133, 276
Lawrence, Carol ***238***, 251, 256, 289, 292–293, 295
Lawrence, Marc 119–120, 139, 274–275, 277
Lawrence, Viola 188, 275
Lawson, Anne 253, 295
Lawson, Elsie 16, 304
Lawson, Kate Drain 151, 278
Lawyer Man (1932 film) 61
Lazer, Peter 233, 288
Leachman, Cloris 218
Leal, Bonifacio Salinas 180
Le Baron, William 16, 269
Lederer, Francis 124–125
Lederman, D. Ross 119–120, 200, 203, 275, 282–283
Lee, Dixie 54
Lee, Gypsy Rose 212
Lee, Lester 198, 282, 285
Leech, John L. 216
Lehman, Gladys 34
Leiber, Fritz 9
Leigh, Janet 47–48
Leighton, Bert 131
Leisen, Mitchell 34, 287
Leni, Paul 44
Leonard, Herbert B. 243, 252, 291, 293–294
Leonard, Robert Z. 31, 59, 269
Leonard, Sheldon 185, 281, 301
Leonardo Da Vinci 44
LeRoy, Mervyn 26, 268
LeSaint, Edward J. 106, 270–272, 274–276
Leslie, Joan 188
Lessons in Hollywood (radio show) 123, 298
Lester, Jerry 217, 222, 285, 287
Let's Talk It Over (1934 film) 73, 84–***85***, 87, 96, 271
Levant, Oscar 179
Level, Maurice 52
Levenson, Sam 251, 256, 292, 295
Levine, Nat 94
Lewis, Dorothea 169, 299
Lewis, Jerry 247
Lewis, Robert Q. 222, 256, 287, 295
Lewis, Roger H. 253, 257, 294, 296
Lewis, Sinclair 302
Lewton, Val 231
Lewyn, Louis 66, 105, 271–273, 276–277
Leyden, Bill 257, 196
The Life of Emile Zola (1937 film) 61
Lightner, Winnie 28, 40, 268–269

Lights Out (television series) 219, 286
Lincoln, Abraham 11, 253
Lincoln, E. K. 10, 267
Lincoln Center (Manhattan) 250
Lindbergh, Charles 54, 103
Linden, Eric 52
Lindfors, Viveca 247
Lindsay, Howard 214, 305
Linville, Joanne 247
Lipsky, Eleazor 305
Little Caesar (1931 film) 59, 61, 152, 158
The Little Giant (1933 film) 59, 70
Little Miss Brown (play) 8
Livingston, Robert 107, 274
Lloyd, Frank 47
Lloyd, George 194, 211, 274, 276, 282–283
Lloyd, Harold 50, 198, 300
Lloyd, Victor 79–80
Locke, Edward 8
Lockhart, Gene 89
Lockwood, Grey 219, 286
Loesser, Frank 157, 181
Logan, Joshua 236–237, 239, 306
Loggia, Robert 247
Logue, Charles 82, 272
Lombard, Carole 3, ***53***–54, 66, 88–***90***, 104, 119, 178, 270, 272
Lombardo, Guy 179
London Prison Congress 228
Long, Johnny 179
Long, Louise 24, 268
Long, Walter 14, 61, 153, 267, 270
The Long Street (play) 222–223, 305
Longacre Theatre (Broadway) 11, 303
Loos, Anita 55
Lord, Del 192, 281
Lorre, Peter 94, 158, 162, 220, 231, 246
Lost Horizon (1937 film) 123, 150
The Lost Patrol (1934 film) 138
The Lost Weekend (1945 film) 206
Louise, Anita 52, 141, 147–150, ***149***, 178, 218, 275, 278, 285
Lovett, Josephine 45, 269
Lowe, Edmund 25, 44, 78, 80, 86–87, 94, 103, 124, 192–193, 208, 271, 298, 308
Lowe, Edward T. 192, 281
Lowery, Robert 187, 309
Loy, Myrna 14, 23, 26, 63, 75, 101, 268
Loyal Lives (1923 film) 12, 267

Lubin, Harry 213–214, 301–302
Lucas, John Meredyth 247
Luciano, Charles "Lucky" 133
Luck o' the Irish (radio show) 203, 301
Ludden, Allen 257
Lugosi, Bela 44, 73, 86–88, **87**, 175, 220, 271
Lukas, Paul 57, 71, 73, 86–**87**, 94, 208, 271
Luke, Keye 94, 156, 259, 278
Luncheon at Sardi's (radio show) 228, 302
Lupino, Ida 188, 207–208
The Lux Radio Theatre (radio show) 182–183, 185, 188, 198, 299–300
Lux Video Theatre (television series) 220, 229, 286
Lyceum Theatre (Broadway) 10, 253, 256, 305
Lydon, Jimmy 175, 179, 181, 280
Lynley, Carol 236, 257, 296, 306
Lynn, Barbara 172, 280
Lynn, Ralph 58
Lyon, Richard 187, 281
Lyons, Ken 191
Lytell, Bert 40, 153

MacArthur, Douglas 164
MacBeth (Shakespeare play) 108
MacDonald, J. Farrell 52
MacDonald, Jeanette 55, 102, 124, 171
MacDonald, Kenneth 157–**159**, 278, 284
MacDonald, Kyle 217, 285
MacDonald, Philip 138–139, 277
Macgowan, Kenneth 10, 267
Mack, Helen 102, 119–120, 275
Mack, Willard 147, 298
MacKaye, Fred 188, 299–300
MacKenzie, Aeneas 185, 299
MacKenzie, Gisele 252, 293–294
MacLane, Barton 187–188, 281
MacLaughlin, Thomas M. 92
MacMahon, Aline 11, 253, 303
Macmillan, Louis 222, 305
MacMurray, Fred 183, 185
Mad Love (1935 film) 101
The Mad Magician (1954 film) 228
Madison, Noel 103, 112
Madsen, Michael 102
The Magic Key of RCA (radio show) 127
Maharis, George 243, 252
Majestic Theatre of the Air (radio show) 20, 298

"Make-Believe Man" (television episode) 5, 243–**244**, 265, 291
Mala 150, 278
Malden, Karl 228
Malloy, Doris 94, 273
Malmgreen, Russell 188
Malone, Dorothy 189
Malone, Nancy 245, 281
Mamoulian, Rouben 59, 228
"The Man from Medicine Bow" (radio episode) 141, 298
The Man in the Iron Mask (1939 film) 148
"Man of Prey" (television episode) 234, 289
Mandel, Loring 240–241, 265, 272, 306
Manhandled (1949 film) 162
Manhattan Melodrama (1934 film) 75, 101, 185–186
Manhattan Theatre 8
Mankiewicz, Joseph L. 40, 106, 108, 268, 274
Manners, David 63, 308
Manning, Bruce 113–114, 274
Mannix, Eddie 125
Manoff, Arnold 239
Mantell, Joe 218, 285
Mara, Adele 164–**165**, 279
March, Fredric 4, 34, 44, 57–58, 66, 69, 86, 102, 112, 119, 124–125, 128, 139, 216
March, Joseph Moncure 148, 278
Marcin, Max 8
Margo 147, 298
Marievsky, Joseph 107, 274
Marin, Edwin L. 103–104, 111–112, 119, 273–274
The Marines Fly High (1940 film) 146–147, 242, 277–278
Marion, Charles R. 209, 283
Marion, Frances 35–37, 269
Mark Goodson-Bill Todman Productions 286–290, 292–297
The Mark of Zorro (1920 film) 44
Marked Men (1919 film) 106
Markson, Ben 200, 282
Marriott, John 223, 287
Marsh, Mae 10, 267
Marsh, Marian 113–**114**, 274
Marshall, E. G. 247, 253, 257, 292, 294, 296
Marshall, Trudy 204–**205**, 283
Marshall, Tully 28, 268–269
Martin, Janet 207
Martin, Mary 159, 169, 299
Marvin, Edgar 220, 286
Marvin, Lee 246
Marx, Chico 171, 299
Marx, Groucho 69, 75, 207, 276

Marx, Harpo 167, 169, 171, 185, 299
Mascot Pictures 80, 94
The Mascotte of the Three Star (novel) 106
Massey, Ilona 167
Massey, Raymond 44, 256, 295
The Match Game (television game show) 251–253, 257–258, 292–294, 296–297
Matheson, Murray 239, 255, 290, 295
"A Matter of Law and Disorder" (television episode) 257, 296
Matthau, Walter 243
Mature, Victor 208
Maude, Beatrice 69
Maugham, W. Somerset 242, 291
Maxwell, Edwin 160, 272, 279
Maxwell House Coffee Time (radio show) 213, 301
May, Billy 245
May Blossom (play) 7
Mayer, Louis B. 59, 125, 217
Mayfair Theatre (Broadway) 74
Mayflower Photoplay Company 51
Maynard, Ken 148
Mayo, Virginia 193
The Mayor of Hell (1933 film) 59, 70
McAllister, Paul 29
McCall, Mary 119, 275
McCallum, Neil 253, 295
McCambridge, Mercedes 220, 257, 307
McCarthy, Kevin 240, 306
McClain, Jack 221, 287
McClure, Doug 246, 291
McCormack, Patty 234, 289
McCrea, Joel 94
McDaniel, Hattie 176
McDaniel, Sam 176
McDonald, Francis 40, 117, 272, 275
McDonald, Frank 155, 157, 167, 169, 171, 178, 185, 278–280
McDowall, Claire 40, 269, 277
McDowall, Roddy **238**, 243, 289
McGee, Richard A. 224
McGowan, Oliver 246, 291
McGreevey, John 252, 293
McGuire, Bobby 221, 286
McGuire, Don **212**, 283
McGuire, William Anthony 72, 82, 271–272
McHugh, Frank 46, 63, 111–112, 118, 124, 171, 247, 269, 271, 274, 276
McIntire, John 245

McKay, George 113–114, 264–265, 274–275, 278–281
McKenna, Siobhan 249
McLaglen, Victor 25, 64, 112, 136–*137*, 192–*193*, 207–208, 277, 281
McLeod, Norman Z. 51, 270
McMahon, Ed 252–253, 294, 297
McMahon, Horace 147, 214, 243, 245, 256, 277, 291, 296
McWade, Robert 92, 111, 272, 274, 304
Me and My Gal (1932 film) 52
Meader, George 194, 282
Meadows, Jayne 220, 286
Meehan, Elizabeth 29, 151
Meehan, John Jr. 31, 33
Meeker, George 71, 271, 276
Meeker, Ralph 236
Meet Boston Blackie (1941 film) 153–155, *154*, 157, 159, 278
Mehaffey, Blanche 105, 273
Meighan, Thomas 51
Melville, Herman 211, 219, 286
Men Against the Sky (1940 film) 144, 308
Men and Women (play) 7
Men in White (1934 film) 91, 93
Menjou, Adolphe 66, 69, 207
Menzies, William Cameron 21, 267
Mercer, Frances *134*, 276
Meredith, Burgess 94, 138
Merkel, Una 41–*42*, 56, 89, 269–270
Merlin, Joanna 253, 294
Merrick, Lynn 193–*194*, 200–*201*, 282
Merrill, Gary 238, 295
Merrill, Martha 115, 275
Mescall, John J. 90–91, 272
Messner, Johnny 136
Metaxa, Georges 41
Metro-Goldwyn-Mayer Pictures [MGM] 14, 21, 31–40, 52, 54–57, 60, 74–75, 77, 86, 88–94, 97–113, 115, 118, 125, 142–144, 171, 176, 179, 215–217, 237, 239, 269–270, 272–274, 276–277, 292, 295, 308
Metro Pictures 9, 153
Michael, Gertrude 103
Michel Strogoff (1936 film) 116
Michel Strogoff [*Michael Strogoff: Courier of the Czar*] (novel) 116
Middlemass, Robert 185, 278, 281
Middleton, Charles 57–*58*, 63, 270
Middleton, Robert 220–221, 274, 287

Milestone, Lewis 21, 37, 47–48, 128, 138, 269
Miljan, John 71, 271
Millard, Harry 247, 291, 306
Miller, Ann 167, 171, 193
Miller, Art 57, 270
Miller, Arthur 234, 265, 306
Miller, Blaine 163, 279
Miller, Charles 63
Miller, Ernest 148, 278, 280
Miller, Jean DuPont 163, 279
Miller, Marvin 200
Miller, Robert Ellis 246–247, 291
Miller, Virgil E. 224, 226, 283
Miller, Walter 126, 271, 275–277
Miller, Winston 190–191, 241, 281, 291
Mills, Felix 141, 298
The Mills Brothers 218, 285
Milner, Martin 252, 254, 293–294
Mineo, Sal 236
Miner, Allen H. 254, 294
Miner, C. Worthington 138
Minnelli, Liza 256, 306
The Miracle Man (novel) 50
The Miracle Man (play) 50–51
The Miracle Man (1920 film) 51
The Miracle Man (1932 film) 50–*51*, 66, 254, 270
Missing Links (television game show) 252–253, 294
Missing Millions (1922 film) 153
Mr. Broadway (television series) 256, 295–296
Mr. Moto's Gamble (1938 film) 94
Mitchell, Grant 16, 63–*64*, 71–74, 111, 271, 274
Mitchell, Thomas 119–120, 220, 275
Mitchum, Robert 174, 192, 309
Moby Dick (novel) 215
Moffat, Graham 16
Mollison, Henry 115, 275
Monash, Paul 229, 288
Monogram Pictures 39, 178, 202, 211
Monsieur Lecoq (1915 film) 9
Montalban, Ricardo 234, 251, 289, 292
Montez, Maria 184
Montgomery, Douglass 16, 86–*87*, 298, 304
Montgomery, George 188
Montgomery, Robert 18, 21, 31–32, 34–38, 44–45, 58, 65–66, 69, 75–78, 86, 88, 94, 97, 102–103, 105–106, 111–112, 118–119, 124–125, 128, 138, 147, 216–217, 220–221, 228, 269, 286–287

Moody, William Vaughn 10
Moonlight Murder (1936 film) 111–112, 151, 274
Moore, Colleen 55
Moore, Constance 207
Moore, Garry 220, 286, 288, 290
Moore, Matt 49, 269
Moore, Victor 86, 271
Moorehead, Natalie 22
Moreno, Antonio 78
Morey, Walt 259
Morgan, Frank 69, 75, 119, 122, 125, 147, 152–153, 276
Morgan, Gene *114*, 274–275, 278
Morgan, Helen 76, 78–81, *79*, 130, 274
Morgan, Henry 220, 286
Morgan, J. R. 180
Morgan, Ralph 63, 78, 91, 112, 124, 138, 144, 147, 272
Morison, Patricia 159
Morita, Miki 136, 275, 277
Morley, Karen 52, 86
Morning's at Seven (play) 239
Morning's at Seven (television show) 239, 289
Morris, Adrian 5, 7–10, *12*–14, *13*, 16, 18–19, 25, 39, 47, 52, 70–72, 93–94, 119, 122, 160, 200, 271, 304
Morris, Chester: Academy Award nomination 3, *19*, 21, 265; amateur filmmaking projects 2, 45, 121–123, *135*, 137–138; artistic abilities 10, 25, 45, 256; athletic and leisure activities 47, 97, 103, 135, 208; awards and honors 44, 188, 248, 250; birth 7; Broadway roles 10–11, 14–16, *15*, 228–229, 236–*237*, 240–*241*, 257, 303–307; childhood 8–10, 25; death 4, 261; divorce 5, 138, 145–147, 152; early film roles 10–14, *11*; early radio performances 20, 78, 86; early stage roles 10–16, *13*, *15*; early television roles 217–220; education 9–10; fears and phobias 63, 65, 131; Hollywood contracts 23, 40, 46, 65, 70–71, 75–77, 102–103, 111, 115, 148, 155, 167, 181, 184, 188, 195, 207, 224; home cooking 21, 123, 125; illnesses and injuries 76, 114–115, 208, 260–261; labor activism 4, 59, 62–63, 66, 69, 75–76, 78, 86, 97, 102–104, 112, 116, 124–125, 138, 144–145, 147, 265; marriages 5, 16, 44, 89, 105, 118–119, 123,

135, 137–138, 145–146, 152–*153*, 178, 188, 207–208, 212–214, 253, 258; musical abilities 8, 75, 133; performance of magic 2, 9, 50, *78*, 97, 125, 128, 135–136, 141, *144*–148; 162, 167, 182–183, 204, 208–209, 211–212, 214, 217, 256; personal appearance tours 4, 86, 130, 135–137, 145, 147, 214, 305; political and social views 61, 128, 202–203, 241, 248–250, 265; U.S. military volunteer activities 3–4, 10, 162, 166–167, 169, 171, 173, 178–181, 185, 188, 193, 197, 207, 218, 265
Morris, Cynthia Suzanne 44, 65, 75, 88, 114, 123, *135*, 145–146, 263, **266**
Morris, Etta Hawkins 5, 7–10, *12*–15, *13*, 65, 119, 200, 263, 304
Morris, Gordon 5, 7, 10, 14, 150, 160, 200
Morris, Henry 7
Morris, John Brooks 16, 22, 44, 54, 65–66, 75, 88, 112–115, 122–123, 125, 128, *135*, 145–146, 203, 263–***266***
Morris, Kenton 207, 240, 258, 261, 263–265
Morris, Lillian Kenton 5, 145, 152–*153*, 167, 178, 188, 203, 207–208, 212, 214, 219, 234, 253, 258, 261, 305
Morris, Lloyd 7
Morris, Maria 7
Morris, Suzanne Reddeman Kilborn 5, 15–18, 20–22, 29, 34, 41, 44–45, 65, 67, 75, 77–79, 83, 89, 94, 97, 102, 107, 114, 118–119, 122–124, 135–138, 145–146, 152, 263
Morris, Wilhelmina 5, 7, *12*–14, *13*, 52, 263, 304
Morris, William 5, 7–16, *12*, *13*, 39–40, 52–53, 65, 69, 150, 160, 219, 263, 304
Morrow, Brad 238, 289
Morrow, Jeff 219, 286
Morse, Barry 255
Morton, Michael 8
Mostel, Zero 179
Motion Picture Committee Co-operating for National Defense [MPCCND] 162
Motion Picture Producers and Distributors of America [MPPDA] 48, 162
Motion Picture Relief Fund, Inc. 207
Mottola, Tony 233, 288

Moulin Rouge (1934 film) 78
The Mountain Man (play) 11, 303
The Mouthpiece (1932 film) 59
The Mouthpiece (play) 59
Mowbray, Alan 124, 272, 282
Much Ado About Nothing (Shakespeare play) 8
Muir, Esther 146
Muir, Jean 103, 116, 145
Muldaur, Diana 256, 296
Mulhall, Jack 26, 78, 218, 268, 273, 281, 284–285
Mulhauser, James 82
The Mummy (1932 film) 73
Muni, Paul 44, 60, 71, 78, 86, 93–94, 124
Munson, Ona 147–148, 150, 278
Murders in the Rue Morgue (1932 film) 73
Murphy, Edna 52, 268
Murphy, George 94, 166, 276–277
Murphy, Ralph 67, 271
Murphy, Richard 160, 167, 279
Murray, Arthur 221, 286
Murray, Don 220, 286
Murray, Kathryn 221, 286
Murray, Ken 147, 217–219, 285–286, 295
Murray, Mae *11*, 65
Muse, Clarence 39, 196, 283
Musuraca, Nicholas 131, 136, 142, 275–277
Mutual (radio network) 192, 207, 301
Mutual Corporation 9
Myerson, Bess 251, 256, 295

Nagel, Conrad 32, 52, 54, 63, 169, 269, 298–299
Naish, J. Carrol 111, 270, 274
Naked City (television series) 5, 197, 243–245, *244*, 252, 265, 291
"The Name of the Game" (television episode) 255, 295
The Name's the Same (television game show) 222, 287
Napolitano, Dominick "Sonny Black" 102
National Educational Television 239, 289
National Endowment for the Arts 250, 260
National Labor Relations Act (Wagner Act) 104
National Recovery Administration 69
National Theatre (Broadway) 8, 14, 304
Natwick, Mildred 110

Navaho (1952 film) 224, 226
The Navy Comes Through (1942 film) 185
"The Navy Comes Through" (radio show) 185, 299
Neill, Roy William 116
Nelson, Billy 167, 279–281
Nelson, Ed 251, 292
Nelson, George "Baby Face" 99
Nelson, Ozzie 158
Nettleton, Lois 243
Neumann, Kurt 70, 72–73, 84, 271
Neville, Edgar 38
New York Dramatic Workshop 5
New York Group Theatre 244
New York School of Fine and Applied Arts 10
Newland, John 256, 295
Newman, Paul 228
Newman, Phyllis 239, 251–252, 256, 290–292, 294–295
Niblo, Fred 59
Nicholls, George Jr. 116, 146, 277
Nichols, Dudley 112, 117
Nichols, Nellie V. 27, 268
Nickell, Paul 223, 234, 236, 251, 287–289, 292
Nightstick (play) 17
Nixon, Marian 83, 268, 272
No Hands on the Clock (1941) 2, 155–157, *156*, 169, 278
No Man Is an Island (1962 film) 207
Noble, Ray 207, 301
Noble, William 236–237, 306
Nolan, Christopher 44
Nolan, Lloyd 113–***114***, 229, 274
Nolan, Warren 20
Nolte, Charles 219
Nora Bayes Theatre (Broadway) 16
Nordstrom, Frances 27, 268
Norris, Edward 160, 209, 279, 283
North, Alex 226–227, 283, 289
North of the Rockies (1942 film) 164
Northwestern University 258
Norton, Edgar 9, 63, 270
Norton, Fletcher 37, 269
Nosseck, Max 202
Novarro, Ramon 44, 74, 77, 80
Novello, Jay 244, 291
Nugent, Carol 187, 281
Nugent, Edward 22, 75, 286
Nugent, Elliott 17, 125
Nugent, Frank S. 110, 146
Nugent, J. C. 17, 267, 269

Index

Oakie, Jack 40, 44, 179
Obama, Barack 241
Oberon, Merle 103
O'Brien, George 53
O'Brien, Margaret 193
O'Brien, Pat 70, 78, 94, 185, 187–188
The Ocean Waif (1916 film) 9
O'Connor, Donald 185
O'Connor, Patsy 119–*121*, 275
O'Connor, Robert Emmett 37, 269, 273
O'Connor, Una 44
O'Donnell, Jack 72, 271
Of Mice and Men (1939 film) 138
Of Mice and Men (novel) 138
Office of War Information 3
O'Flaherty, Liam 117, 275
Ogle, Charles 8–9
O'Keefe, Dennis 198, 272
Oland, Warner 111
The Old Dark House (1932 film) 44, 147
The Old Gold Comedy Theatre (radio show) 198, 300
Oldsmobile Music Theatre (television series) *238*, 289
Oliver, Edna May 111, 124, 274
Oliver, Susan 243, 246, 253
Olson, Johnny 251, 292–294, 296–297
O'Malley, Pat 18, 20, 268
Omnibus (television series) 223, 287
On Borrowed Time (play) 239
On with the Dance (play) 8
One Frightened Night (1935 film) 94
One More River (1934 film) 90
One Mysterious Night (1944 film) 189–*190*, 222
One Way to Love (1946 film) 198–*199*
O'Neal, Patrick 239, 259, 290–291
O'Neil, Sally 26, 268
Ongley, Byron 8
Orpheum Theatre (Los Angeles) 13–14
Orpheum Theatre (Minneapolis) 145, 247, 306
Ortiz, Eulogio 180
Osborn, Paul 239, 289
Osborne, Hubert 10
Osborne, Vivienne 63–*64*, 271
O'Sullivan, Maureen 52, 246, 257, 307
Oswald, Gerd 269, 297
Ottiano, Rafaela 52
The Outlaw (1943 film) 48
Overton, Frank 252, 293
Owen, Catherine Dale 52, 303

Paar, Jack 236, 242, 251, 258, 289, 291, 293
Pabst Theater (Milwaukee) 247, 306
Pacific Coast Association of Magicians 128, 182, 203
Pacific Liner (1939 film) 136–*137*, 276–277
Pacino, Al 102
Packard, Frank L. 10, 50, 267, 270
Padilla, Benecio Lopez 180
Pagan Lady (1931) 52
Page, Anita 18, 52
Page, Dorothy 102
Pagel, Raoul 67
Paisano Productions 158
Paiva, Nestor 153, 181, 278, 280
Palace Theatre (Broadway) 12–13, 304
Paramore, Edward E. Jr. 106–107, 274
Paramount Pictures 15–16, 24, 31, 34, 40–41, 50–51, 53–54, 60, 66–67, 80, 94, 113, 125, 131, 153, 155, 157, 159–160, 162, 167, 169, 172–174, 177–181, 184–185, 187, 190, 211, 217, 268, 270–271, 278–281, 308–309
Paramount-Publix (theater chain) 62
Pardon My Sarong (1942 film) 118
Parfrey, Woodrow 240, 306
Paris, Jerry 226–227, 284
Parker, Eleanor 255, 295
Parker, Jean 94–96, *95*, 155–157, *156*, 160–162, *161*, 167–169, *168*, 171–*172*, 178, 273, 276, 278–280
Parker, Willard 198–*199*, 282
Parks, Larry 162–164, 216, 279
Parrott, Katherine Ursula 31, 33, 269
Pathé Exchange 10, 267
Pathé Studios 259
Patrick, Lee 128–130, 185, 276, 281
Patterns (1956 television movie) 229–230
Patterson, Elizabeth 57, 62–63, 67, 270–271
Patterson, James 251, 292
Patterson, Neva 246–247, 291–292
Paul, Don 225
Paul, Val 67
Pawley, Edward 103, 133–134, 276
Pembroke, Scott 72, 271
Pendleton, Nat 88, *90*, 270–272
Penn, Leo 247

Pennell, Larry 262, 284
Pennies from Heaven (1936 film) 177
Perowne, Barry 204, 283
Perry Mason (television series) 158, 227
Persoff, Nehemiah 5, 243–245, 291
Peterson, Dorothy 92, 103, 272–273
The Petrified Forest (1936 film) 94
Pettet, Joanna 254, 294
The Phantom Thief (1946 film) 200–*202*, 282–283
The Philip Morris Playhouse (television series) 223, 288
Pichel, Irving 51, 270
Pickford, Mary 11, 35, 54, 66, 78–80, *79*, 271
The Pickwick Papers (novel) 193
Picture Corporation of America 155
Picture Snatcher (1933 film) 59
Pidgeon, Walter 94, 119
Pine, Howard 162
Pine, Phillip 222, 305
Pine, Robert 257, 296
Pine, William H. 155–157, 160–162, 167–176, 178–182, 184, 186–188, 190, 211, 278–281, 299
Pine-Thomas Productions 155–157, 160–162, 167–176, 178–182, 184, 186–188, 190, 211, 278–281
"Pirate Party on Catalina Isle" (1935 short film) 105–106, 273
Pistone, Joseph D. 102
Pitts, Zasu 89–*90*, 272
Planck, Robert H. 41–42, 269
Planer, Franz 164, 278–279, 281
Play, Genius, Play! (play) 69
Play of the Week (television series) 239, 289
Playhouse 90 (television series) 234
Playhouse Theatre (Broadway) 236–*237*, 306
Playing Around (1930 film) 26–28, *27*, 268
Pleshette, Suzanne 251, 292
Plymouth Theatre (Broadway) 229, 305
Poe, Edgar Allan 220
"Point Blank" (television episode) 222, 287
Polesie, Herb 221, 286
Polglase, Van Nest 141, 275–277
Pollack, Sydney 247, 257, 296
Poppy (1936 film) 94

The Poppy Girl's Husband (1919 film) 153
Porgy and Bess (Broadway show) 228
"Portrait of a Man Running" (television episode) 246, 291
Postman Pictures 12, 267
Poston, Tom 239–240, 290
Powdersmoke Range (1935 film) 94
Powell, David 153
Powell, Dick 63, 75, 86, 124, 185, 234, 276, 289
Powell, William 44, 75, 104, 124, 208
Power, Tyrone 94
Power, Tyrone Sr. 50
Powers, Mala 234, 289
Pratt, Purnell 20, 52, 63, 268
Preston, Robert 184
Price, Vincent 228
The Price Is Right (television game show) 256, 295
Princess O'Hara (1935 film) 94–96, **95**, 118, 273
Princess Theatre (Broadway) 8, 14
The Prisoner of Shark Island (1936 film) 117, 136
The Prisoner of Zenda (1937 film) 148
The Prisoner of Zenda (1922 film) 148
Prisoners Are People (book) 224–225, 283
Pro Football Hall of Fame 226
Producers Distributing Corporation 14, 267
Producers Releasing Corporation (PRC) 195
Production Code Administration 33, 48, 54, 56, 80, 83, 89–90, 113, 129, 139
Proskauer, Julien J. 208
Prud'Homme, Cameron 142
Pryor, Alice 130–131
Pryor, Roger 82, 86–**87**, 271, 279, 308
The Public Enemy (1931 film) 24
Public Hero Number 1 (1935 film) 97–102, **99**, **100**, 113, 224, 273
The Public Menace (1935 film) 113
Puglia, Frank 234
Purcell, Dick 179
Pursuit (1935 film) 103–**104**, 133, 176, 273
Pursuit (television series) 236, 289
Putnam, Nina Wilcox 67

Qualen, John 226–227, 277, 284

Radin, Ben 222, 287
Raft, George 66, 94, 135, 185, 271, 308
Rains, Claude 71, 207, 243
Raker, Lorin 155, 272, 276
Ralston, Gilbert 246–247, 251, 291–292
Ralston, Jobyna 67
Ramin, Sid 251–252, 292–293
Rand, Sally 14, 267
Randell, Ron 231, 284
Rankin, Doris 11, 303
Rankin, William 113–114, 274
Rapper, Irving 16, 304
Rathbone, Basil 25, 94, 111, 159, 166, 220, 274
Rathbone, Ouida 166
Ratoff, Gregory 228, 305
The Raven (1935 film) 88
Rayburn, Gene 233, 251–253, 288, 292–294, 296–297
Rawhide (television series) 241–241, 291
Raye, Martha 124, 167, 171, 185, 218, 285
Rebecca (1940 film) 138
Red Dust (1932 film) 57
Red-Headed Woman (1933 film) 54–57, **56**, 63, 270
The Red Skelton Hour (television series) 233, 288
Redford, Robert 243
Rée, Max 29, 269
Reed, Florence 81–82, 274
Reed, Robert 247, 263, 257, 292, 294, 296
Reed, Tom 107
Regan, Phil 159
Regan, Sylvia 228, 305
Reis, Irving 186, 211, 280
Remarque, Erich Maria 37
Remick, Lee 223, 288
Remley, Ralph 94–**95**, 273
Renaldo, Duncan 111, 274
Rennahan, Ray 105, 273
Rennie, Michael 236
Republic Pictures 79, 130–131, 138, 147, 151, 274, 278
Requiem for a Heavyweight (1956 television movie) 230
The Return of Boston Blackie (1927 film) 153
The Return of the Cisco Kid (1939 film) 94
The Return of the Vampire (1943 film) 195, 231
Revel, Harry 66
Revier, Harry J. 39
Reynolds, Marjorie 180, 299
Reynolds, Vera 14, 267

Rich, David Lowell 245, 251, 292
Richards, Addison 92, 272, 277, 281
Richards, Frank 234, 288
Richards, Marc 258, 297
Riddle, Nelson 245, 293–294
Ride the Pink Horse (1947 film) 216
Ridges, Stanley 220
Rin Tin Tin 23, 268
Rinehart, Mary Roberts 41–42
Ringling Brothers-Barnum and Baily Circus 88
Ritt, Martin 216, 218, 260–262, 284–285
The Ritz Brothers 169, 299
Riva, Mary 219, 286
River, W. L. 182, 299
RKO Radio Pictures 28–29, 52, 54, 57, 63–64, 80, 82, 94, 110, 116, 125–134, 136–137, 141–142, 144, 146–147, 153, 183, 185, 192, 195, 208, 231, 269, 271, 275–277, 279, 308–309
Roach, Hal 119, 125, 138
The Road to Yesterday (1925 film) 14, 267
The Roadhouse Murder (1932 film) 52
The Roaring Twenties (1939 film) 186
Robards, Jason Sr. 22, 278
Robert Montgomery Presents (television series) 200–221
Roberts, Doris 218, 286
Roberts, Mark 189, 281–282
Robinson, Bill 124
Robinson, Casey 67, 271
Robinson, Dewey 103, 273, 281
Robinson, Edward G. 4, 59, 61, 66, 70, 86, 104, 112–113, 140, 147–148, 152, 158, 197, 216
Robinson, Gus 63, 271
Robinson, Selma 234, 289
"Robinson Crusoe, USN" (radio show) 207, 301
Robson, May 56, 84, 86, 95, 116, 270, 272
Roche, Eugene 255, 295
"Rock-Bound" (television episode) 223, 288
Rodrigues, Percy 254, 294
Rogers, Charles "Buddy" 18, 57, 105, 273
Rogers, Charles R. 67, 271
Rogers, Howard Emmett 106, 185, 281, 298
Rogers, Jean 192, 281
Rogers, Roy 94, 178, 207
Rogers, Will 84, 271
Rolf, Eric 183, 280–282
Roman, Ruth 243

336 Index

Romance in the Rain (1934 film) 87, 308
Romeo and Juliet (1916 film) 9
Romeo and Juliet (1936 film) 111, 274
Romeo and Juliet (Shakespeare play) 9, 34, 111, 274
Romero, Cesar 94, 246
Rooney, Mickey 105, 167, 169, 171, 243, 273, 299
Roosevelt, Eleanor 179, 193
Roosevelt, Franklin D. [FDR] 3, 61, 69, 162, 178–179, 250
Root, Wells 99, 103–104, 143, 273, 277
Rose, Reginald 223, 247, 288, 292, 294, 296
Rose, Vincent 105
Rose of Washington Square (1939 film) 94
Rosenberg, Stuart 245
Rosenblatt, Sol 78
Rosenbloom, Max "Slapsie Maxie" 73, 171, 271
Rosengarden, Bobby 233, 288
Rosson, Harold 56, 270
Roth, Allen 218, 285
Roth, Lillian 54–55, 234, 289
Rothafel, Robert C. 94, 273
Rothman, Lee 248
Rough, Tough and Ready (1945 film) 192–**193**, 281
Route 66 (television series) 197, 243, 252, 254–255, 265, 293–294
Rowles, Polly 247
Royale Theatre (Broadway) 257
Royle, Selena 14, 304
Ruben, J. Walter 52, 97, 101, 142, 273
Ruggles, Charles 135, 159
Ruggles, Wesley 104
Runyon, Damon 94–96
Russell, Jane 47
Russell, Rosalind 119, 167, 169, 171, 183, 299
Russell, William 153
Rutherford, Ann 167, 171
Ruttenberg, Joseph 81, 106, 108, 110, 274
Ryan, Phil L. 187, 281
Ryan, Robert 142
Rydell, Mark 247
Ryder, Alfred 257, 296

Saal, William 76, 78, 80, 274
Sackler, Howard 260–261, 284
Sadie Love (play) 8
Saenger Theatre (New Orleans) 160
St. James Theatre (Broadway) 69
St. John, Howard 223, 288
Sales, Soupy 258, 297
Salkow, Sidney 150–151, 278
Salkowitz, Sy 243, 291
Sande, Walter **154**, 158, 164, 169, 183, 189, 276–280
Sanders, George 61
Sandrich, Mark 177
Sanford, Donald S. 236
Sanford, Ralph 157, 160, 178, 181, 278–280, 309
Sardou, Victorien 7
Sargent, Alvin 247
Savage, Ann 176, 280
Sawyer, Joseph 167, 181, 271, 279–280
Scarface (1932 film) 48
The Scarlet Man (play) 16
Schaefer, Armand 148, 151, 278
Schaefer, George 162
Schaffner, Franklin J. 223, 229, 240, 247, 288, 306
Schayer, Richard 67
Schenck, Joseph M. 17, 33, 125, 269
Schertzinger, Victor 52
Schildkraut, Joseph 14, 31, 44, 267
Schildkraut, Rudolph 28
Schlitz Playhouse of Stars (television series) 219, 286
Schnitzer, Joseph I. 28
Schoenbaum, Charles 63, 271
Schorr, William 53
Schulberg, Bud P. 59, 66, 113–114, 274
Schulman, Arnold 223, 289
Scott, Alex 254, 295
Scott, George C. 255, 295
Scott, Hazel 179
Scott, Martha 257, 307
Scott, Randolph 94, 104–105, 124, 273
Scotti, Vito 255, 295
Scourby, Alexander 214
Screen Actors Guild [SAG] 4–5, 63, 66, 69, 75–76, 78, 86, 97, 102–105, 112, 116, 118, 124–125, 128, 138, 144, 147, 207, 216
The Screen Guild Theatre (radio show) 140
Scudder, Kenyon Jackson 224–228, 283
Scudder, Rebekah 224
Sea Cliff Summer Theatre 214, 222, 231, 305
The Search for Bridey Murphy (book) 230
Seaton, George 188, 300
Sebastian, Dorothy 40
Second Choice (1930 film) 26, 28, 268

Secret Command (1944 film) 187–188, 281
Secret of the Blue Room (1933 film) 73
Secrets of a Secretary (1931 film) 41
Secrets of an Actress (1938 film) 136
Seeger, Miriam 52
Seff, Manuel 106–107, 274
Seitz, George B. 91–92 142–**143**, 272, 277
Seitz, John F. 144, 277
Selby, Sara 209, 283
Sellon, Charles 52, 271
Selwyn, Edgar 52, 303
Selwyn Theatre (Broadway) 17
Selznick, David O. 12–13, 52, 59, 104, 119
Selznick, Myron 119
Semple, Lorenzo Jr. 255, 295
Sen Yung, Victor 211, 283
Sennett, Mack 113, 119
Serling, Rod 220, 223, 229–230, 236, 248, 286, 288
Seven Samurai (1954 film) 26
7th Heaven (1927 film) 158
The Seventh Victim (1944 film) 231
Severinsen, Doc 233, 288
Seward, Billie 155, 278
Sewell, Blanche 56, 269–270
Shadows in the Night (1944 film) 195
Shakespeare, William 8–9, 26–27, 34, 108, 111, 197, 223, 253, 268, 274
Shane, Maxwell 157, 160, 167, 169, 171, 181, 186, 190, 278–281
Shannon, Peggy 55
Shannon, Robert T. 167, 274, 279
Shatner, William 247
Shaw, Artie 225
She Couldn't Say No (1930 film) 28, 268
The She-Creature (1956 film) 230–233, **232**, 284
She Done Him Wrong (1933 film) 131
She Had to Say Yes (1933 film) 65
She Married a Cop (1939 film) 138
Shearer, Douglas 37
Shearer, Norma 3, 25, 31–34, **33**, 37, 40, 44, 50, 77, 111, 269, 274
Sheehan, Winfield 59
Sheen, Martin 257, 307
The Sheik (1921 film) 40
Shell Chateau (radio show) 106, 298

Shelley, Mary 9, 220
Shepherd, Sheldon 152
Sheridan, Ann 171
Sheridan, Frank 23, 73, 268, 271
Sherlock Holmes (literary character) 47, 153, 171, 205
Sherlock Holmes (play) 16
Sherman, Fred 167, 280
Sherman, George 245
Sherman, Vincent 208
Sherriff, R. C. 71
Shiffren, A. B. 249, 306
Shilkret, Nathaniel 127
Shipley, Eva Virginia 52
Shipman, Samuel 16, 128, 268, 276, 304
Shirley, Anne 128–130, **129**, 276
Shore, Dinah 185
"Shot from the Sky" (U.S. Army show) 193
Show Boat (1936 film) 81
The Show of Shows (1929 film) 25–26, 268
"Show Time at the Roxy" (USO show) 178
Showtime (radio show) 180, 299
Shubert, Lee 13
Shubert Theatre (Broadway) 11, 69, 303
"The Sidewalks of New York" (song) 186
Sidney, Sylvia 3, 16, 50–**51**, 66, 94, 181, 207, 243, 254, 270, 294, 304
Siegel, Don 192
The Silk Lined Burglar (1919 film) 153
Silliphant, Stirling 243, 252, 254, 294
The Silver Theatre (radio show) 141, 188, 298–299
Silvers, Sid 105, 268, 273
Silverstein, David 125, 275
Silverstein, Elliott 246, 291
Simcox, Tom 257
Simmons, Beverly 207
Simmons, Ruth 230
Simms, Ginny 180–181
Simon, Robert F. 220, 286
Simpson, Ivan 75
Sinatra, Frank 157, 207, 245, 257
Singleton, Penny 141
Sinners in the Sun (1932 film) **53**–54, 56, 91, 104, 270
Sir Harry Lauder (vaudeville revue) 39
Sisk, Robert 127, 136, 141–142, 146, 147, 275–277
6,000 Enemies (1939 film) 94
Skelly, Hal 24–25, 268
Skelton, Red 169, 233, 288, 299
Skipworth, Alison 54, 270

Sky Giant (1938 film) 2, 131–133, **132**, 136–137, 276
Skyscraper Souls (1932 film) 52
Slater, Bill 221, 286
A Sleepless Night (play) 8
Sloane, Everett 219
Sloane, Paul H. 86
Sloboda, Karl 62, 270
Small Miracle (play) 212, 304
Smashing the Rackets (1938 film) 133–135, **134**, 276
Smight, Jack 247, 292
Smith, Archie 247, 306
Smith, C. Aubrey 111, 141–142, 274, 277
Smith, Kate 136, 221, 287, 298
Smith, Lois 223, 288
Smith, Roger 255, 295
Smith, Winchell 11, 303
Snow, G. A. 200, 282
Snowden, Carolynne 28, 268
So This Is London (play) 11, 303
Society of American Magicians 50, 144, 167, 208–209
"Soda Pop and Paper Flags" (television episode) 252, 265, 293
Solax Film Company 9
The Soldier and the Lady (1937 film) 116
Solow, Eugene 138
The Son of the Sheik (1926) 40–41
Sondheim, Stephen 256, 295
Sothern, Ann 94, 141, 198, 268, 276, 300
The Soupy Sales Hour (television movie) 258, 297
Southern California Motion Picture Council 228
Spaeth, Sigmund 131, 274
Sparks, Ned 50–51, 269–270
Speed (1936 film) 112, 308
Spelling, Aaron 234, 289
Spence, Ralph 63, 271
Spewack, Bella 88, 272
Spewack, Samuel 88, 272
The Sphinx: An Independent Magazine for Magicians (magazine) **144**, 209
Spigelglass, Leonard 94, 96, 273
Spivak, Charlie 179
Springsteen, R. G. 242, 291
Stack, Robert 219, 245
Stallings, Laurence 110, 272
Stand by for Action (1942 film) 179
"Stand by for Action" (radio show) 179, 299
Stander, Lionel 115–116, 124, 216, 275, 277

Stanislavski, Konstantin 244
Stanley, Forrest 153
Stanley, Pat 236, 306
Stanwyck, Barbara 57, 94, 142, 181, 299
Stapleton, Maureen 214
"Star Dust" (comic strip) 47
A Star Is Born (1976 film) 162
Starlight Theatre (television series) 218, 285
Starrett, Charles 52
Stars on Parade (radio show) 218, 302
State-Lake Theatre (Chicago) 130
Steele, Michael 222, 305
Stehli, Edgar 230, 288
Steiger, Rod 142, 220
Stein, Paul L. 57, 270
Steinbeck, John 138
Steiner, Max 112
Stenseth, Martinus 180
Stephenson, Henry 55, 63–**64**, 119, 270–271
Stevens, Charles 149, 278
Stevens, Craig 256, 296
Stevens, K. T. 188, 299
Stevens, Leith 169, 299
Stevens, Morton 246, 291, 297
Stevens, Onslow 53, 125–127, 275
Stevens, Robert 220, 286
Stevens, Warren 214
Stevenson, Coke R. 180
Stevenson, Robert Louis 220
Stewart, James 112, 308
Stiller, Jerry 247, 292
Stoddard, Haila 221, 290, 305
Stoloff, Benjamin 146–147, 277
Stone, George E. 73, 94, 100, 153, 155, 157–159, 164–166, 169–171, 176–177, 183–184, 189–190, 194–**197**, 200–202, 204–205, 209–211, **210**, 271–273, 278–283
Stone, Lewis 37, 55–56, 63, 84, 99, 106–110, **109**, 119, 148, 269–270, 273–274
Stone, Milburn 139, 157, 277–278
Storm, Rafael 115, 275
Storm Over the Andes (1935 film) 96, 102
The Story of Louis Pasteur (1936 film) 61
The Story of Love (television series) 242
Stowe, Harriet Beecher 263
Straight Is the Way (1934 film) 86
The Strand Magazine 153
Strand Theatre (Manhattan) 136

"The Strange Death of Gordon Fitzroy" (radio episode) 207, 301
Strange Wives (1934 film) 4, 308
Strasberg, Lee 244
Strauss, Robert 214
Strebe, Earle 208
Der Streit um den Sergeanten Grischa [*The Case of Sergeant Grischa*] (novel) 29–30, 32, 269
"A String of Beads" (television episode) 242
Stroheim, Erich von 17, 75
Strong, Michael 214, 247, 292
Stuart, Gloria 73, 86–87, 271
Stubbs, Harry **19**, 21, 266–267
Studio One (television series) 223, 229–230, 288
Stumar, Charles J. 73, 96, 271–272
Stumar, John 113–114, 268, 274
Sturgeon, Theodore 220
The Subject Was Roses (play) 257, 307
Submarine (1928 film) 116
Sullivan, Barry 171–**172**, 280
Sullivan, Ed 262
Sullivan, Frank 101, 272–274
Sullivan, Margaret 86, 298
Sully, Frank 194–195, 198, 200, 204, 209, 211, 281–283
Sunderland, Nan 16, 69
Suspense (radio show) 207, 301
Suspense (television series) 220, 222, 229, 238, 286–287, 295
Susskind, David 229, 288, 295
Sutherland, A. Edward "Eddie" 40, 187–188, 281
Sutton, Frank 243, 247
Swann, Don 221, 305
Swann, Russ 141
Swanson, Gloria 119, 217, 246, 258, 285, 296–297
Swarthout, Gladys 179
Sweeney, James 119–120, 164, 275, 278–279, 283
Symonds, Henry Robert 136

Tachella, Jean-Charles 229, 288
Talbot, Lyle 97
Talbot, Nita 228, 305
Tales of Tomorrow (television series) 220, 286–287
Tannura, Philip 166, 278–279, 283
Tashman, Lilyan 78, 80–81, 130, 274, 298
Taurog, Norman 66
Taylor, Eloise 39
Taylor, Kent 141, 144, 270, 277, 308
Taylor, Libby 133, 272, 276

Taylor, Robert 92–93, 130, 179, 272
Taylor, Vaughn 221, 305
Teach, Clifford 240, 290
Teal, Ray 183, 280–281
The Tender Heel (play) 253, 306
Terkel, Studs 215–216, 248, 302, 305
Terneen Productions 187, 281
Terry, Clark 233, 288
Terry, Phillip 190–191, 207, 281
The Texaco Star Theatre (radio show) 147, 298–299
The Texaco Star Theatre (television show) 218, 285
Thalberg, Irving 35, 37, 54, 77, 111, 118, 269–270, 274
Thanhouser Film Corporation 9–10, 267
Theatre Guild 238, 289
Theatre Guild on the Air (radio show) 238
Their Own Desire (1929 film) 34
"There Goes My Dream" (song) 181
There Goes the Groom (1937 film) 94
Thesiger, Ernest 44
They Met in a Taxi (1936 film) **115**–116, 275
They Were Expendable (1945 film) 216
Thirteen Women (1932 film) 14
This Is the Story (radio series) 207, 301
Thomas, Augustus 11, 303
Thomas, Richard 247
Thomas, Shirley 226
Thomas, William C. 155–157, 160–162, 167–169, 171, 173, 175, 178–182, 184, 186–188, 190, 211, 278–281, 299
Thompson, Virgil 223, 287
Thompson, William P. 81, 274
Thomson, Kenneth 63, 78, 86, 97, 102–103, 112, 116, 124–125, 145, 147, 272
Thorpe, Richard 82
The Three Godfathers (1916 film) 106
Three Godfathers (1936 film) 101, 106–112, 107, 109, 274
3 Godfathers (1948 film) 106, 110
Three Godfathers (novel) 106–110, 274
Three on a Match (1932 film) 61
Three Thirds of a Nation (radio show) 169, 299
Throne, Malachi 253
Through the Dark (1924 film) 153
Thunder (play) 11, 303

Thunder Afloat (1939 film) 142–144, **143**, 277
Tibbett, Lawrence 147
Tierney, Gene 173
Tierney, Lawrence 202
"Tiger on a Bicycle" (television episode) 236, 289
Tiger Shark (1932 film) 61
"Time Bomb" (television episode) 229, 288
"Time Lock" (television episode) 233, 288
Time Out for Ginger (play) 256, 306
"A Time to Be Born" (television episode) 258–**259**, 297
To Tell the Truth (television game show) 239–240, 251, 253, 256, 289–290, 292, 295
Tobin, Genevieve **62**, 67–**68**, 75, 102, 270–271, 275
Todd, Thelma 45–46, 63, 76, 110–111, 269
Todman, Bill 222–223, 233, 239, 251, 256, 286–290, 292–297
Toland, Gregg 101, 273
Toler, Sidney 107, 211, 274
Tomack, Sid 204, 211, **215**, 283
Tombragel, Maurice 209–210, 259, 283, 297
Tomlin, Pinky 103
Tomorrow at Seven (1933 film) 63–**64**, 72, 111, 198, 271
Tone, Franchot 86, 97, 124–125, 128, 142, 185, 246, 251, 292, 300
Tonight! (television talk show) 233, 288
The Tonight Show Starring Johnny Carson (television talk show) 258, 297
Tonight Starring Jack Paar [*The Jack Paar Tonight Show*] (television talk show) 236, 242, 289, 291
"Too Bad About Sheila Troy" (television episode) **238**, 289
Toomey, Regis 18, 20, 53, 63, 187, 268, 277, 280
Toones, Fred "Snowflake" 73, 89, 271–272
Torn, Rip 236
Tornado (1943 film) 181–**182**, 280
Tors, Ivan 206, 297
Tower, Allan 220, 286
"Towerman" (television episode) 218, 287
Tracy, Lee 105, 124, 198, 273, 300, 308
Tracy, Spencer 14, 16, 52, 54, 66, 69, 73, 75, 198, 304

Trans-World Air Line School of Aeronautics 131
Trapped by Boston Blackie (1948 film) 209-***210***, 259
Travanti, Daniel J. 254-255, 294-295
Travers, Henry 71, 103-104, 273
Trem Carr Pictures 39
Tremayne, Les 214
The Triangle (play) 8
Trivers, Barry 82
Trotter, John Scott 146, 155, 298-299
Truman, Harry S. 249
Trumbo, Dalton 117, 141-142, 216, 275, 277
Tryon, Glen 50
Tryon, Tom 234, 289
Tucci, Maria 260
Tucker, Forrest 162, 169-170, 279
Tucker, George Loane 10, 51, 267
Tucker, Harland 71, 271
Tucker, Richard 40, 78, 102, 116, 269, 272
Tucker, Sophie 80
Tully, Tom 187-188, 234, 281, 289
Turn to the Right (play) 11, 303
Turpin, Ben 25, 78, 268
Tweed, George R. 207, 301
12 Angry Men (1957 film) 247
Twelvetrees, Helen 22, 54, 71, 74, 271
20th Century-Fox Pictures 94, 111, 125, 173, 188, 260
20 Questions (television show) 221, 286
20,000 Years in Sing Sing (1932 film) 73
The Twilight Zone (television series) 197, 229-230
Twist, John 125, 136, 275-276, 299
The Two Mrs. Carrolls (1947 film) 209
Tyson, Cicely 255, 295

Ulmer, Edgar G. 73, 86, 176
Unchained (1955 film) 224-228, ***225***, ***227***, 283-284
"Unchained Melody" (song) 226-227
Uncle Tom's Cabin (novel) 263
Under the Pampas Moon (1935 film) 150
"The Undertaker Calls" (television episode) 218, 285
Unger, Gladys 82, 272
Union Pacific (1939 film) 94
United Artists 17-18, 20, 23, 34, 41-42, 46-47, 49, 52, 60, 80, 228, 267, 269, 295, 308
United Service Organizations [USO] 3, 162, 166-167, 169, 178-179, 197, 233, 299
U.S. Army 166-167, 173-174, 178-180, 192, 218, 229, 302
U.S. Army Air Corps [U.S. Air Force] 166, 218, 263, 302
U.S. Navy 143, 166-167, 179, 207, 216
U.S. Office of Air Force History 166
The United States Steel Hour (television series) 238, 289
Universal Pictures 8, 22, 31, 44, 51, 67, 70-76, 79, 81-88, 90-91, 94-96, 101-103, 106, 113, 115, 118, 125, 147-148, 163, 171, 185, 195, 219, 271-273, 308
The Untamed Breed (1948 film) 210
The Untouchables (television series) 197, 227, 243, 245

Vail, Lester 52
Valentino, Rudolph 40-41, 49
Vallee, Rudy 166, 208, 213, 218, 282, 285, 301
Van Buren, A. H. 16, 304
Van der Vlis, Diana 254, 290, 294
Van Derbur, Marilyn 251, 292
Van Deventer, Fred 221, 286
Van Dyke, W. S. 74
Van Rooten, Luis 211, 283, 286
Van Sloan, Edward 62, 270
Varnel, Marcel 62, 270
Veidt, Conrad 44
Veiller, Anthony 57, 270
Velez, Lupe 74
Verdi, Guiseppe 111
Verne, Jules 116, 220, 223
Vernon, Margaret 14
Verschleiser, Ben 57, 270
The Very Minute (play) 8
Victor Film Company 8
Vidor, Charles 138, 277
Vidor, King 41
Viertel, Paul 188, 219
A View from the Bridge (play) 234, 236, 253, 265, 306
Vinaver, Steven 258, 297
Vincent, June 207, 209, 283
The Vinegar Tree (play) 53
Vinton, Arthur 59, 270, 272
Vitagraph Company of America 12, 267
Vivian Beaumont Theater (Lincoln Center) 250
Voight, Jon 259, 297
Von Eltz, Theodore 57, 269-270, 300
Von Furstenberg, Betsy 222, 305
Von Seyffertitz, Gustav 28, 41, ***43***, 52, 269
Von Sternberg, Josef 78
Von Stroheim, Erich 17, 75

Wagenheim, Charles 153, 155, 158, 278, 282
Wagner, Charles L. 11, 303
Wagons Westward (1940 film) 147-150, ***149***, 178, 278
Wake Island (1942 film) 173
Walbrook, Anton 116
Walburn, Raymond 92, 116, 272, 275
Waldecker, Frank 221, 286
"Walk in the Night" (television episode) 223, 288
Walker, Joseph 39
Walker, June 236-***237***, 306
Walker, Stuart 87
Walker, Walter 89
The Walking Dead (1936 film) 75
Wall Street Cowboy (1939 film) 94
Wallace, Mike 223, 288
Wallis, Hal 125
Walsh, Raoul 41, 52, 197
Walthall, Henry B. 52
Walton, Douglas 126, 275, 277
Wanger, Walter 104
Warburton, John 84-85, 271
Ward, Amelita "Lita" ***174***-175, 181, 192, 280-281
Ward, Solly 126-127, 275
Ware, Irene 85, 271
Waring, Fred 179
Warner, H. B. 23, 26, 268, 274
Warner, Jack L. 59
Warner Bros.-First National Pictures 12, 21, 23-28, 47, 59-61, 65, 70, 73, 75, 88, 93, 97, 103, 116, 118, 125, 134, 136, 138, 141, 158, 173, 186, 188, 197-198, 209, 218, 224, 268-270, 283
Warren, Charles Marquis 241, 291
Warrick, Ruth 187-188, 281
The Warrior's Husband (1933 film) 63, 308
Warwick, James 138-140, 277
Washington, Ned 245
The Washington Masquerade (1932 film) 52, 55
Washington Square Theatre (Greenwich Village) 250
Waters, Ethel 86-87, 155, 271, 299
Watts, George 155, 157, 278
The Way to Love (1933 film) 66

Wayne, John 41, 52, 110, 148
Wead, Frank "Spig" 216
Weaver, Dennis 259, 297
Weaver, Marjorie 94
The Web (television series) 223, 288
Webber, Robert 256, 260, 262, 284, 296
Weber, Lois 35
Webster, Daniel 230
Webster, Paul Francis 228
Weil, Richard 200
Weissmuller, Johnny 66, 271, 276
"Welcome Home, Lefty" (television episode) 229, 286
Welcome Travelers (radio show) 216
Welden, Ben 133, 276, 283
Welles, Halsted 220, 255, 286, 295
Welles, Orson 216, 231
Wellman, William A. 24–25, 268
Wells, George 182–183, 299
Wells, H. G. 70–71, 220
Wenstrom, Harold **36**, 39, 269, 271
Wessel, Dick 105, 272
West, Edna 14
West, Mae 94, 131
West, Nathaneal 141–142
West, Roland 5, 16–18, 20–23, 34, **40**–47, 49, 65, 70, 76–78, 90, 110–111, 237, 267, 269, 298
West, Stan 225
West Point of the Air (1935 film) 94
Westchester Players 10
Westerfield, James 214
Westley, Helen 78
Weston, Doris 127
Wetmore, Joan 222, 305–306
Wexler, Irving "Waxey Gordon" 133
Weyerhauser, George 102
WGN TV and Radio (Chicago) 258
Whale, James 44, 47, 51, 70–71, 73, 81, 90
Wharton, Edith 82
What Did We Do Wrong? (play) 259, 261, 307
What Price Glory (1926 film) 192–193
What's My Line? (television game show) 220
Wheeler, Bert 86, 135–136, 276
Wheelwright, Ralph 143, 277
"Whisper of Evil" (television episode) 238, 289
Whispering Friends (play) **15**–16, 304

White, Alice 26–28, 54, 71, 84, 86–**87**, 268, 271–272
White, Betty 256, 295
White, Lester 92, 272
White, Sam 160, 279–280
White Heat (1949 film) 197
Whiting, Jack 80
Whitman, Ernest 136, 277
Whitman, Stuart 259, 297
Whitten, Marguerite 176, 280
Who Done It? (1942 film) 118
The Whole Town's Talking (1935 film) 148
Whorf, Richard 176, 228, 305
The Widow from Chicago (1930 film) 59
Wilbur, Crane 16, 304
Wilbur Theatre (Boston) 247, 306
Wilcox, Harlow 191, 299–300
Wilcox, Herbert 58
Wild Boys of the Road (1933 film) 61, 70
Wilde, Oscar 220
Wiley, G. Harrison 96, 272
Willard, John 44
Willard, Samuel B. 261
William, Warren 52, 58–59, 75, 102–103, 276
William Morris Agency 236
Williams, Guinn "Big Boy" 138, 148–**149**, 278
Williams, John D. 11, 303
Williams, Robert B. 189, 281–283
Willson, Meredith 169, 207, 222, 287, 301
Wilshire Ebell Theater (Los Angeles) 182
Wilson, Elizabeth 255, 295
Wilson, Lois 52, 75, 268
Wilson, Teddy 179
Winchell, Walter 86, 272
Windsor Theatre (Broadway) 140
Wing, Ward 38
Winter Garden Theatre (Broadway) 25
Winters, Jan 241, 291
Winters, Roland 242, 291
Winthrop Ames Theatre (Broadway) 257
Wisberg, Aubrey 176, 280
Wise, Robert 138
Wiseman, Joseph 214, 219, 259
Withers, Grant 156, 268, 278
"Without Honor" (television episode) 259, 297
The Woman Between (1931 film) 52
The Woman I Love (1937 film) 94

Woman Trap (1929 film) 24–**25**, 268
Women of All Nations (1931 film) 192
Wonder Man (1945 film) 193
Wong, Anna May 25, 75
"Won't You Come Home, Bill Bailey?" (song) 131
Wood, Marjorie 14, 304
Woodbury, Joan 158, 211–**212**, 278, 283
Woods, A. H. 16–17, 304
Woods, Donald 112, 124, 219, 297
Woodward, Joanne 220
Woollcott, Alexander 214, 272, 304
Woolsey, Robert 86
World Prison Congress 228
World Wide Pictures 57, 60, 270
Worlock, Frederic 69
Wormser, Richard 191, 200, 282
Worth, Constance 153, 278–279
Worthington, William 10, 267, 273, 275
Wouk, Herman 229, 265, 305–307
Wray, Fay 39, 92, 115–116, 275
Wray, John 44, 50–51, 270, 277
Wray, John Griffith 17, 267
Wrecking Crew (1942 film) 167–169, **168**, 179, 279–280
Wright, Robert 188
Wright, William 170, 189, 279, 281
The Writing on the Wall (play) 8
Wyatt, Jane 123, **150**–151, 219, 278, 286
Wycherly, Margaret 197
Wyler, William 71, 106
Wylie, Philip 220
Wynant, H. M. 246, 255, 295
Wynn, Ed 66, 271
Wynn, Nan 179

Yawitz, Paul 157, 164, 169, 183, 188–189, 193, 200, 278–280, 299
Yellow (play) 14–15, 18, 304
Yopp, Lee R. 261, 307
York, Dick 223, 287
You and Me (1938 film) 94
You Know I Can't Hear You... (play) 260, 307
Young, Loretta 3, 23, 25, 65, 178, 268
Young, Robert 94, 104, 119, 124, 178, 213–214, 276, 301–302
Young, Roland 112
Young, Victor 81, 106, 274, 298

The Young Mrs. Winthrop (play) 7
Younger, Paul "Tank" 225

Zane Grey Theater (television series) *234*, 289
Zanuck, Darryl F. 23, 25, 119, 268
Zanuck, Richard 260
Zaret, Hy 227
Ziedman, B. F. 90
Ziegfeld Follies 80
Ziegler, William H. 179, 278–280
Zigmond, Jerry 230
Zimmerman, Robert C. 248
Ziv, Fred W. 191, 300
Zola, Émile 220
Zukor, Adolph 125
Zweig, Arnold 29–32, 269